# FEDERAL TRADE COMMISSION PRIVACY LAW AND POLICY

The Federal Trade Commission, a US agency created in 1914 to police the problem of "bigness," has evolved into the most important regulator of information privacy – and thus innovation policy – in the world. Its policies profoundly affect business practices and serve to regulate most of the consumer economy. In short, it now regulates our techno- logical future. Despite its stature, however, the Agency is often poorly understood by observers and even those who practice before it. This volume by Chris Jay Hoofnagle – an internationally recognized scholar with more than fifteen years of experience interacting with the FTC – is designed to redress this confusion by explaining how the FTC arrived at its current position of power. It will be essential reading for lawyers, legal academics, political scientists, historians, and anyone who is interested in understanding the FTC's privacy activities and how they fit in the context of the Agency's broader consumer protection mission.

Chris Jay Hoofnagle is adjunct full professor at the University of California, Berkeley, School of Information, and faculty director of the Berkeley Center for Law & Technology at the School of Law. He teaches about the regulation of technology, focusing on computer crime law, cybersecurity, internet law, privacy law, and consumer protection law. Licensed to practice in California and Washington, DC, Hoofnagle is of counsel to Gunderson Dettmer LLP, a firm focused solely on advising global venture capital and emerging technology companies. He is an elected member of the American Law Institute.

# Federal Trade Commission Privacy Law and Policy

## CHRIS JAY HOOFNAGLE

University of California, Berkeley

CAMBRIDGE
UNIVERSITY PRESS

# CAMBRIDGE
## UNIVERSITY PRESS

32 Avenue of the Americas, New York, NY 10013-2473, USA

Cambridge University Press is part of the University of Cambridge.

It furthers the University's mission by disseminating knowledge in the pursuit of education, learning, and research at the highest international levels of excellence.

www.cambridge.org
Information on this title: www.cambridge.org/9781107565630

© Chris Jay Hoofnagle 2016

First published 2016
Reprinted 2016

Printed in the United States of America by Sheridan Books, Inc.

A catalog record for this publication is available from the British Library.

Library of Congress Cataloging in Publication Data
Hoofnagle, Chris Jay, author.
Federal Trade Commission privacy law and policy / Chris Jay Hoofnagle.
New York : Cambridge University Press, 2016. | Includes bibliographical references and index.
LCCN 2015048481 | ISBN 9781107126787 (hardback)
LCSH: Privacy, Right of – United States. | Data protection – Law and legislation – United States. | Consumer protection – Law and legislation – United States. | United States. Federal Trade Commission.
LCC KF1262 .H66 2016 | DDC 342.7308/58–dc23
LC record available at http://lccn.loc.gov/2015048481

ISBN 978-1-107-12678-7 Hardback
ISBN 978-1-107-56563-0 Paperback

*For my parents*

The spectacle presents itself as a vast inaccessible reality that can never be questioned. Its sole message is: "What appears is good; what is good appears."

*Guy Debord*

# Contents

# Figures

# Text boxes

# Introduction

At the Pennsylvania Avenue entrance to the Federal Trade Commission (FTC) headquarters in Washington, DC, one encounters a statue of a powerful man wrestling an enormous, elegant horse. The beast has a sinister look. Its ears turned back, it is about to bite the man. The man's exaggerated brawn is not enough to bridle the menace, as the horse's positioning is dominant. While titled Man Controlling Trade, the work suggests that trade is an irrational evil that will escape man's control.

Just around the corner, on Constitution Avenue, stands an accompanying work. But in this work, the man appears sinister, a vengeful punisher of the horse. He has a powerful hold upon a more sympathetic animal. The man has bridled the horse.

In crafting these two works, Michael Lantz (1908–1988) captured the ambivalence many have about the regulation of trade. Businesses are a driver of wonderful innovations and conveniences, and an engine of American power. But at the same time, without some control, business can run wild, serving only itself.

The statuaries also serve as a metaphor for supporters and critics of the FTC, now a 100-year-old institution. Some see it as a misguided, even harmful, burden to business, while others view any discipline it can muster against business as a good.

This book will explain these tensions through the lens of the FTC as a primary regulator of information privacy. Its activities, often in the form of public settlement agreements with companies, form the most important regulation of information privacy in the United States. Given the political economy of online regulation, Congress is unlikely to take action on online privacy. For the immediate future, the FTC will be the most important institution shaping the course of the information economy.

## THE FTC AND PRIVACY

The FTC (also "Agency" or "Commission") has a colorful 100-year-long history. It is a complex agency. Practice before the Agency has suffered because of a lack of familiarity with its broad powers and with its diverse responsibilities in commerce.

For instance, the FTC is responsible for over seventy laws, concerning fraud in college scholarships, false labeling of "dolphin-free" tuna, health warnings on cigarettes, the labeling of furs and wool products, and even the sanctioning of boxing matches. Thus, privacy is just a small part of the Agency's efforts, but other areas of concentration inform how the FTC handles privacy matters. For the purposes of this book, privacy is defined broadly as the FTC's consumer protection activities relating to regulation of data about people. Thus, for this work, privacy includes both informational interests (how data are collected, used, and secured) and access to self-interests (how businesses contact or gain the attention of consumers).

Businesses and governments can use information to increase efficiencies, build new products and services, and enhance security. But privacy advocates have valid concerns about these practices, as privacy rights are about allocations of power, and these allocations are often "zero sum." A business or government right to use data about someone can come at a personal or societal cost. Often, uses of information for security simply shift risk, sometimes making the risk systemic (consider business adoption of the Social Security number to decrease business and credit risk and the concomitant rise of identity theft) rather than reducing it. The FTC's task is to chart a path acknowledging these competing values and risks. The need for an expert agency to elucidate these values and risks is more important today than ever. The FTC approach assumes that once options are elucidated, competition will help consumers come to a privacy outcome that is consistent with their preferences.

The FTC was founded during a time of widespread public concern about monopoly and trusts. The nation was primarily agrarian, and most people probably felt the

FIGURE I.1. Michael Lantz's *Man Controlling Trade*: the Pennsylvania Avenue version. Photo credit: Rachel Lincoln.

FIGURE I.2. Michael Lantz's *Man Controlling Trade*: the Constitution Avenue version. Photo credit: Rachel Lincoln.

effects of industrialization without understanding them. New businesses and opportunities arose much too quickly for existing law to police abuses or to serve as a check on massive concentration of industries.

A hundred years later, our society is facing serious economic change and uncertainty as a result of the information industry. Today the FTC is as relevant as it was in 1915 as an arbiter of fairness and a check on "bigness" and efficiency. For this reason, more academics have started writing about the FTC. In particular, Professors Daniel J. Solove and Woodrow Hartzog have written an important article explaining the FTC as creating a law of privacy through a common law approach.[1] This book agrees with and builds on the Solove and Hartzog observations through an extensive history of the FTC, an analysis of it as an agency, and a survey of all of its privacy activities.

This book argues that the FTC is among the best alternatives for regulation of privacy. It has matured into a careful, bipartisan, strategic, and incrementalist policy actor. It has shaped the marketing of internet services by establishing early in its enforcement actions that companies needed a justification to claim that their services were more private or secure. It also brought cases to establish the proposition that clear disclosures and affirmative consent are necessary when technologies monitored people in an invasive way or inside the home. The FTC is well informed by economics, while not allowing economic theory to supplant the reality of consumer experiences. Despite its moderate approach, the FTC is pilloried by

---

[1] Daniel J. Solove & Woodrow Hartzog, *The FTC and the New Common Law of Privacy*, 144 COLUM. L. REV. 583 (2014).

organized business interests. This book gives context to the FTC's actions and explains the flaws of attacks on the FTC. Now more than ever, the FTC needs a defense, because attacks on it are calculated to blunt the inventiveness and efficacy of consumer protection law.

## THE FTC AS AN AGENCY

This book explores several threads about the FTC itself as an administrative agency. First, the FTC was a radical innovation; it was unlike anything else when it was created. As Professor Gerald Berk argues, the Agency was a product of "creative syncretism." Berk explains: "those who built regulated competition were successful precisely because they reached across historical, institutional, and cultural boundaries to find resources, which they creatively recombined in experiments in business regulation, public administration, accounting and trade associations."[2] The result was an entity with many different tools that could be emphasized, deemphasized, or arranged differently to address new problems in the economy. Indeed, in the privacy field, the FTC's many tools and jurisdictional breadth are used to fashion different approaches and different compromises to privacy problems.

Second, the Commission has extraordinary powers. For a small agency, it has a tremendous effect on business. The FTC's powers, its structure, and the Agency's broad range of activities throughout its history are little understood. This book elucidates the FTC's privacy activities by situating it in its broader context and in the context of the history of consumer protection. It will broaden the understanding of privacy scholars and lawyers unfamiliar with the Agency's role in other areas of consumer protection.

Third, much FTC scholarship attempts to hang a public choice garb on the Agency. But the FTC is a public choice anomaly. Congress granted it a broad but vague mandate and then empowered it greatly over the last century. Yet, throughout its history, it has taken up the challenge of regulating new problems, such as cigarettes, "green" marketing, and, today, information privacy. It is an innovative agency that has avoided reification. The FTC has not fallen victim to capture, and, in fact, it seems to deliberately target the biggest actors in relevant markets. The FTC has also been much less swayed by partisan changes than its sister agencies. While it is true that its privacy activities changed focus under Republican Party leadership, the FTC is not a tool to discipline party loyalty among industries, nor do its privacy activities cease under Republican leadership. In recent years, competition for jobs at the Agency has been fierce, with partner-level lawyers applying for work. The Agency's leaders – both staff and commissioners – often act selflessly, for far less money than can be earned in the private sector. They also take on matters that cause enmity in industry and foreclose future opportunities for private-sector work. Public

---

[2]   GERALD BERK, LOUIS D. BRANDEIS AND THE MAKING OF REGULATED COMPETITION, 1900–1932 (2009).

choice theory narratives of self-interest do not fit the Agency well, but we shall see that they fit better when public choice scholars run the Agency.

Fourth, Congress did not place traditional common law elements in the Federal Trade Commission Act. Yet, the specter of the common law still haunts the Agency. Today, commission critics emphasize the need for the FTC to prove that a practice "harmed" consumers, but this requirement does not exist anywhere in Title 15. More broadly, this book makes it clear that effective policing of information wrongs requires deviation from nineteenth-century limits on cases. It may even be the case that modern information problems cannot even be policed by an enforcement agency, and that, instead, supervisory oversight is needed.

OUTLINE OF THIS BOOK

Part I of this book explores the history, procedure, and basic powers of the FTC. Chapter 1 recounts the history of the FTC's founding and its consumer protection mission. The FTC was a product of intensely felt anxiety concerning changes in the economy, and its first mandate was to prevent "unfair competition." The FTC faced major challenges in its early years: World War I, courts that tried to cabin the Commission's powers of policing common law wrongs, and mediocre leaders who made it difficult for the Agency to be effective. Still, the Agency strived to be innovative and relevant. For instance, the Agency's first matters involved technology and false advertising as a form of unfair competition.

With a historical lens in place, Chapters 2 and 3 present modern controversies surrounding the FTC's role. Chapter 2 guides the reader through several tests of the Commission – from industry attempts to clip the wings of the Agency to highlights of its interventions. This history helps situate the modern FTC and gives context for how and why the Agency acts. It also shows that the FTC transcended many of its early challenges, finding acceptance by the courts, empowerment by Congress, and support from both Republican and Democratic executives. Chapter 3 recounts the FTC's turn to electronic commerce and privacy. The FTC brought its first internet case in 1994, long before most Americans were online. It began privacy saber rattling in 1995, and shortly thereafter, it brought matters involving children's privacy.

Chapters 4 and 5 are primarily descriptive, focusing the broad-ranging powers and jurisdiction of the Commission. Chapter 4 explains that the FTC can investigate and sue almost any entity. Its investigatory powers are important to understand, as the Agency tends to probe dozens of industry players before choosing investigation and enforcement actions that will promote its policy goals. Its organizational structure shields the Agency from the winds of political change and, as a practical matter, gives staff attorneys great autonomy and discretion in matter selection.

Chapter 5 focuses on the FTC's unfair and deceptive trade practices authority, known as "Section 5." The FTC's authorities are broad and largely undefined. Thus, this portion of the book discusses how political efforts to define or rein in Section 5 have generally been resisted, as the Agency has needed great flexibility to deal with new forms of noxious business practices. It also shows that much of Section 5's precedent is driven by advertising cases, which have dynamics that may not be appropriate for regulation of privacy.

Part II (Chapters 6–11) of this book dives deeply into the FTC's authorities in the context of specific privacy issues: online privacy, children's privacy, information security, anti-marketing and malware, financial privacy, and international privacy efforts. Each of these chapters presents a description of the doctrine of FTC law, but then continues to discuss and critique these doctrines normatively.

The discussion of online privacy in Chapter 6 traces how third-party information sharing and concerns about online advertising have shaped much of the privacy debate. This has skewed our understanding of privacy problems, with the public at times focusing on relatively innocuous uses of data and away from more fundamental issues such as the power of dominant social networking and search platforms, and the problem of automated decision systems that are fed by surveillance networks deployed for advertising purposes.

Chapter 7 discusses the FTC's efforts to protect children online. Because there is a broad social agreement that protecting children is important, the FTC's efforts in children's privacy are particularly strong. At the same time, Congress' emphasis on parental consent to collecting personal information about children is a burdensome requirement that drives services to avoid embracing child-oriented status and the resulting obligations. Perhaps counterintuitively, children's privacy would be better protected with weaker statutory protections for it.

Chapter 8 canvasses the FTC's many information security matters. Here again, a broad social agreement about the importance of security has given the FTC political support for bringing enterprising cases against insecurity. Security is a public good and a victim of a tragedy of the commons. Viewed in that light, the Agency's attention should be focused on structural problems that lead to identity theft and other products of insecurity.

Chapter 9 presents the "anti-marketing" laws. These are statutes and regulations that specify how technologies can be used to contact the consumer. They do little to establish information privacy rights. Yet, they demonstrate how technologically specific regulations paired with enforcement can shape consumers' privacy expectations and reduce interruptions in their lives. Anti-marketing laws complicate the narrative that regulation should be "technology-neutral" and, at the same time, they sometimes mask problematic information uses, so long as those uses do not involve contacting the consumer.

Chapter 10 turns to financial privacy, an area where the FTC now shares jurisdiction and responsibilities with the Consumer Financial Protection Bureau. Perhaps half of all Americans do not qualify for the best credit terms, meaning that many have to use financial services offered by those operating at the margins of legitimacy. The FTC's role is thus critical, as it has jurisdiction over the most fly-by-night actors in the field. More generally, the Agency's activities in financial consumer protection are important because the relevant laws also protect interests in equity, inclusion, and fairness. Approaches learned from financial privacy matters may be helpful in resolving tensions arising from "big data" and algorithmic decision-making systems.

Chapter 11 provides an overview of how the FTC addresses international consumer protection problems. With the advent of spam and internet telephony, fraudsters can target Americans from afar. Congress granted the FTC strong new powers to address this problem in 2006. This chapter also summarizes European data protection law and explains how the FTC has acted as a champion of the American approach to privacy while, at the same time, moving the United States to a more European approach.

Finally, Part III (Chapter 12) assesses the FTC and suggests a path for it to intensify its pro-privacy posture. The FTC has impressive jurisdictional and enforcement powers, but its internal organization has blunted its privacy efforts. Specifically, the FTC must make its Bureau of Economics part of the pro-privacy team and update its methods for assessing consumer detriment and remedies for the internet age. The FTC must also stand up to its critics who try to impose nineteenth-century common law requirements on the Agency's cases. These critics are part of an ideological movement intent on disassembling the administrative state. While supported by the business community, these critics are more radical than their sponsors understand, and they are casting a pall on the FTC's activities.

As a society, we are always subject to changes that new technologies bring us. But today we stand at a precipice that is not well understood by the public or policymakers. Current debates about privacy almost always focus on whether there is "harm" from activities such as behavioral advertising (marketing that is targeted based on one's past behavior). This narrative does not capture the aspirations of technology entrepreneurs. At its core, Silicon Valley has dreams of perfect control and efficiency.

The mechanisms that are being trained on one's internet clicks and decisions in order to pitch advertising today could be used for very different purposes in the future. These include technologies designed to manipulate others, to selectively make disclosures to them, and to make decisions about consumers in ways they cannot comprehend or even perceive. Someday soon, the amount of time you wait on hold to speak with a customer service representative will be keyed to your overall value to the company, whether you are likely to cancel your account, and so on. The prices you see on the Web may be set by your propensity to comparison-shop, or by your perceived desperation to get a product. Because these decisions are part of a technological system, we may not recognize the values that these systems propagate. We may also fail to understand that as a society we can choose the values that these systems propagate.

Consumers will need more than just the common law to address these kinds of inequities, if indeed we are even able to understand the problem and its provenance. Consumers will need institutions too. This final part of the book suggests interventions that the FTC could take to protect the digital citizen.

# Acknowledgments

The author owes many thanks to the individuals who assisted in locating historical resources and in providing feedback. They are: Drew Kloss, Shruti Chopra, Emmie Tran, I-Wei Wang, Ellen Gilmore, Dean Rowan, Michael Levy, Edna Lewis, Megan E. Gray, Marci Hoffman, Ramona Martinez, Misa Eiritz, Anna Slomovic, Jack Cunningham, Daniel J. Solove, Aaron Perzanowski, Lydia Parnes, Katherine Armstrong, Laura Berger, Thomas Brown, Frederik Zuiderveen Borgesius, Jeffrey Rabkin, Ryan Calo, Jan Whittington, Lauren Willis, FTC staff who requested not to be identified, the FTC's FOIA team, the FTC's librarians, the librarians at the University of California Northern and Southern Regional Library Facilities, the students in my spring 2015 privacy course with Deirdre Mulligan, and Matthew Gallaway. My parents, Doctors Jay Houston Hoofnagle and Cheryl Winchell, read every page of the manuscript in an attempt to reform unfortunate lawyerly constructions. Several colleagues, including David Medine, Woodrow Hartzog, Danielle Citron, William Cuddihy, Gautam Hans, Paul Schwartz, David Vladeck, and James Rule, read the entire work and gave formal comment. Priscilla Regan led a workshop on the book's final chapter at the 8th Annual Privacy Law Scholars Conference, where it received comment from Manas Mohapatra, Jon Mills, Viola Schmid, William McGeveran, Gautam Hans, Omer Tene, Paul Ohm, Joseph Hall, Lee Bygrave, Ashkan Soltani, Aaron Burstein, Timothy Edgar, Christopher Yoo, and Isis Miranda. A portion of the book was the topic of a faculty workshop at the University of California, School of Law, in 2015, where my colleagues Pamela Samuelson, Holly Doremus, Jonathan Simon, Mark Gergen, Katerina Linos, Anne Joseph O'Connell, Richard Buxbaum, Aaron C. Smyth, and David Schraub provided helpful feedback.

The author also owes thanks to the University of California. Fiat Lux!

The photographs of the Federal Trade Commission building and of the *Man Controlling Trade* statuary are by Rachel Dawn Lincoln, http://lincoln.photography/.

It is difficult to create a visual metaphor for privacy, yet, the cover image, known as "12 Men in a Row Looking into Binoculars," features many elements of modern privacy problems. The modern internet is similar to a one-way mirror. The user, often in physical seclusion, is being silently watched by many different kinds of people – small and large businesses, governments, law enforcement, and perhaps even some scam artists. It is practically impossible to understand exactly why they are watching. Perhaps most of us know that we are being watched, but few can block their gaze.

# PART I

# The history, powers, and procedure of the Federal Trade Commission

# 1

# History of the Federal Trade Commission

## INTRODUCTION

How did a small, independent antitrust agency come to be among the most important forces in consumer protection and privacy law? This chapter explains the founding of the Federal Trade Commission (FTC, "Agency," or "Commission"), how it quickly pivoted to handle false advertising issues, and how its role and powers grew even while it was subject to periodic, withering criticism. Several themes emerge: First, the FTC has cycles where it is criticized for inactivity, but when it takes an activist posture, Congress sometimes punishes it. Second, until recently, the FTC has been plagued by mediocre appointments. Its reputation has improved greatly as a result of better appointments. Third, compromises in the passage of the FTC's organic act (the Federal Trade Commission Act, or "FTC Act") caused broad disagreements about the purpose of the Agency. Today, we see this as conflicts between those who want the FTC to help businesses comply with laws versus those who want it to strongly enforce laws. Fourth, the FTC was a revolutionary concept at its time, breaking away from the strictures imposed by the common law. Modern agency critics have never quite accepted the rationale for departing from the common law and seek to reimpose common law elements to cabin the Commission's activities. Finally, the FTC's genesis in antitrust and false advertising matters profoundly shapes how it handles all consumer protection issues, including privacy. Familiarity with FTC precedents in policing false advertising provides context for how the Agency addresses privacy.

The FTC was created in 1914 to address the problem of monopoly and of trusts – large, powerful business conglomerates. These organizations posed economic and social problems that became a major social concern.[1] The FTC did not formally have a consumer protection mission until the passage of the Wheeler–Lea Amendments in 1938. However, the FTC's first reported matters concerned false

---

[1] For an early-twentieth-century summary of the trust problem, see JEREMIAH WHIPPLE JENKS, JR., THE TRUST PROBLEM (1903).

advertising.[2] The FTC's early foray into advertising regulation came at the request of the advertising industry itself.[3] These were matters where a deception, sometimes made directly to a consumer, harmed competition.

The 1938 amendments dramatically increased the power and jurisdiction of the FTC, as did the rise of the administrative state, subsequent amendments to the FTC Act, and judicial deference to the Agency.

The Agency's roots in the trust problem and the characteristics of the powers it needed to address it shed light upon the FTC's modern consumer protection mission. Similarly, the special dynamics of advertising regulation embedded in the FTC Act help inform its current efforts to police privacy.

## THE PROBLEMS OF MONOPOLY AND TRUST

Business became "big" after the Civil War. A wave of consolidation and growth among companies triggered a public debate concerning "bigness." Through gentlemen's agreements, issuance of stock, and pooling arrangements, companies could fix prices and outputs, effectively stopping competition and raising prices for the consumer.[4] Concerns were so intense that the period saw a break with dominant ideologies. The nineteenth century was the last period of a laissez-faire business environment. But the perceived unfairness and fears raised by consolidation caused even price controls to be considered as a remedy for heavily concentrated industries. The Progressive Era reflected an unparalleled antibusiness sentiment,[5] and perhaps never in history has it been as intense as at the turn of the century.

This antibusiness sentiment was driven by a substantial number of mergers that gave control over key industries to small groups of businesses. Where companies did not merge, other arrangements could have the same effect of combination.[6] Conglomerates controlled most or almost all of the relevant industries that produced

---

[2]  See FTC v. Yagle et al., 1 F.T.C. 13 (1916); FTC v. Muenzen, 1 F.T.C. 30 (1917). "In 1925, for example, the percentage of cases directed primarily to the protection of customers against deceptive trade practices constituted 70 percent of the whole number of complaints issued, as against the average of 59 percent for the preceding decade." Myron W. Watkins, The Federal Trade Commission: A Critical Survey, 40(4) Q. J. ECON. 561 (1926). The emphasis on false advertising only increased, according to Watkins. By 1932, 91 percent of cases concerned false advertising. Myron W. Watkins, An Appraisal of the Work of the Federal Trade Commission, 32(2) COLUMBIA L. REV. 272 (1932).

[3]  Commission minutes show an informal conference between all five commissioners and representatives of four advertising self-regulatory groups in November 1915. This attention to deceptive advertising came in part from requests from advertiser self-regulatory groups such as the Associated Advertising Clubs of the World and the Vigilance Committee, which urged the Agency to consider false advertising as a form of unfair competition. Jack Crespin, A History of the Development of the Consumer Protection Activities of the Federal Trade Commission 112 (1975)(Ph.D. dissertation, New York University). See also Daniel Pope, Advertising as a Consumer Issue: An Historical View, 47(1) J. SOC. ISSUES 41 (1991).

[4]  FRANCIS W. HIRST, MONOPOLIES, TRUSTS AND KARTELLS (1905).

[5]  RICHARD HOFSTADTER, THE PARANOID STYLE IN AMERICAN POLITICS AND OTHER ESSAYS (1964).

[6]  See Louis D. Brandeis, How the Combiners Combine, 58 HARPER'S WEEKLY, November 13, 1913.

household necessities. Goods used in production were also the products of highly concentrated trusts, such as the United States Steel Corporation and the International Paper Company. Concerns about industrialization and a changing economy, with shifting norms for personal lives, triggered a popular antitrust movement.

By 1888, both the Republican and Democratic parties included measures to address trusts in their party platforms. States began to regulate trusts through railroad commissions, and by 1890 Congress enacted the Sherman Act to address the trusts. In enacting it, Congress prohibited "every contract, combination in the form of trust or otherwise, or conspiracy, in restraint of trade or commerce among the several States, or with foreign nations."[7] Congress took a broad approach, similar to the strategy it applied almost twenty-five years later in creating the FTC. Nevertheless, mergers continued and even accelerated. United States Steel became the first billion-dollar corporation, and by 1900, this single company produced most steel in the nation. Increased concentration was attributed to the Sherman Act's provisions (which were so broad that they invited judges to evaluate the reasonableness of restraints of trade), to inadequate prosecutorial resources, to a prosecutorial concentration on the biggest trusts, and to the powerful economic factors that caused firms to merge.[8]

---

THE PROGRESSIVE PARTY PLATFORM OF 1912

We believe that true popular government, justice and prosperity go hand in hand, and so believing, it is our purpose to secure that large measure of general prosperity, which is the fruit of legitimate and honest business, fostered by equal justice and by sound progressive laws.

We demand that the test of true prosperity shall be the benefits conferred thereby on all the citizens not confined to individuals or classes and that the test of corporate efficiency shall be the ability better to serve the public; that those who profit by control of business affairs shall justify that profit and that control by sharing with the public the fruits thereof.

We therefore demand a strong National regulation of inter-State corporations. The corporation is an essential part of modern business. The concentration of modern business, in some degree, is both inevitable and necessary for National and international business efficiency. But the existing concentration of vast wealth under a corporate system, unguarded and uncontrolled by the

---

[7] Sherman Antitrust Act, 26 Stat. 208 (1890).
[8] See generally GERALD C. HENDERSON, THE FEDERAL TRADE COMMISSION: A STUDY IN ADMINISTRATIVE LAW AND PROCEDURE (1924); Huston Thompson, *Highlights in the Evolution of the Federal Trade Commission*, 8 GEO. WASH. L. REV. 257 (1939). For an exhaustive overview of antitrust challenges of the time, see JOSEPH E. DAVIES, TRUST LAWS AND UNFAIR COMPETITION (1916).

Nation, has placed in the hands of a few men enormous, secret, irresponsible power over the daily life of the citizen – a power insufferable in a free government and certain of abuse.

This power has been abused, in monopoly of National resources, in stock watering, in unfair competition and unfair privileges, and finally in sinister influences on the public agencies of State and Nation. We do not fear commercial power, but we insist that it shall be exercised openly, under publicity, supervision and regulation of the most efficient sort, which will preserve its good while eradicating and preventing its evils.

To that end we urge the establishment of a strong Federal administrative commission of high standing, which shall maintain permanent active supervision over industrial corporations engaged in inter-State commerce, or such of them as are of public importance, doing for them what the Government now does for the National banks, and what is now done for the railroads by the Inter-State Commerce Commission.

Such a commission must enforce the complete publicity of those corporation transactions which are of public interest; must attack unfair competition, false capitalization and special privilege, and by continuous trained watchfulness guard and keep open equally to all the highways of American commerce.

Thus the business man will have certain knowledge of the law, and will be able to conduct his business easily in conformity therewith; the investor will find security for his capital; dividends will be rendered more certain, and the savings of the people will be drawn naturally and safely into the channels of trade.

Under such a system of constructive regulation, legitimate business, freed from confusion, uncertainty and fruitless litigation, will develop normally in response to the energy and enterprise of the American business man.[9]

The Supreme Court's 1911 decision in *Standard Oil* v. *United States* was a watershed moment for the creation of the FTC. In *Standard Oil*, the Court applied a "rule of reason" to Sherman Act cases, in effect holding that the government could not prevent all activities in restraint of trade. Instead, courts would evaluate the context and fairness of contracts. Unreasonable restraints of trade violated the Sherman Act, and judges would ultimately decide what was reasonable and what was not. Presumably, conservative judges would find trusts acceptable, leading to a general unraveling of antitrust policy.

A rule of reason for antitrust meant the death of the Sherman Act to some, and for different reasons, both businesses and individuals clamored for intervention.[10] Businesses were concerned that the economic theories of the Supreme Court and

---

[9] Platform of the Progressive Party, August 7, 1912.
[10] Dow Votaw, *Antitrust in 1914: The Climate of Opinion*, 24 ABA ANTITRUST SEC. 14 (1964).

inferior tribunals could result in no or unpredictable enforcement. Additionally, prosecution of the Sherman Act, if left to the attorney general, could become too political, and thus it needed to be cared for by an independent agency.

Others thought the prevention of unlimited economic power animated the Sherman Act, and whether this power resulted in unreasonable restraints of trade was beside the point. Economic power itself had to be checked. Thus a rule of reason that parsed out efficient versus inefficient arrangements did not serve the political end of ensuring liberty against market power. For instance, declaring "the trusts have won," William Jennings Bryan devoted seven pages of critique and analysis of the decision in his weekly progressive newspaper, *The Commoner*, eleven days after the decision was released.[11]

---

### THE DEMOCRATIC PARTY PLATFORM OF 1912

A private monopoly is indefensible and intolerable. We therefore favor the vigorous enforcement of the criminal as well as the civil law against trusts and trust officials, and demand the enactment of such additional legislation as may be necessary to make it impossible for a private monopoly to exist in the United States.

We favor the declaration by law of the conditions upon which corporations shall be permitted to engage in interstate trade, including, among others, the prevention of holding companies, of interlocking directors, of stock watering, of discrimination in price, and the control by any one corporation of so large a proportion of any industry as to make it a menace to competitive conditions.

We condemn the action of the Republican administration in compromising with the Standard Oil Company and the tobacco trust and its failure to invoke the criminal provisions of the antitrust law against the officers of those corporations after the court had declared that from the undisputed facts in the record they had violated the criminal provisions of the law.

We regret that the Sherman antitrust law has received a judicial construction depriving it of much of its efficiency and we favor the enactment of legislation which will restore to the statute the strength of which it has been deprived by such interpretation.[12]

---

The concern about economic power occupied a central role in political debates, with critics of "bigness" arguing that concentration was an affront not only to household economics but also to political freedom itself.[13] The word "tyranny"

---

[11] Williams Jennings Bryan, *The Trusts Have Won*, 11(20) THE COMMONER, May 26, 1911.

[12] Democratic Party Platform of 1912, June 25, 1912.

[13] Rudolph J. Peritz, *The "Rule of Reason" in Antitrust Law: Property Logic in Restraint of Competition*, 40 HASTINGS L. J. 285 (1988–1989); RICHARD HOFSTADTER, THE PARANOID STYLE IN AMERICAN POLITICS AND OTHER ESSAYS (1964).

was invoked to describe the problem not of government power but of economic concentration.[14] Far from its agrarian roots, the country had evolved to a nation of employees, as then antitrust advocate (and sometimes lawyer to trusts)[15] Louis D. Brandeis put it. Brandeis published an eleven-part series of editorials in *Harper's Weekly* castigating the trusts for their "curse of bigness" and calling them "inefficient oligarchs." The spirit of these skeptics of bigness is reflected today in advocates calling for the FTC to police the powers gained from aggregation of personal information.

---

### THE REPUBLICAN PARTY PLATFORM OF 1912

The Republican party is opposed to special privilege and to monopoly. It placed upon the statute-book the interstate commerce act of 1887, and the important amendments thereto, and the antitrust act of 1890, and it has consistently and successfully enforced the provisions of these laws. It will take no backward step to permit the reestablishment in any degree of conditions which were intolerable.

Experience makes it plain that the business of the country may be carried on without fear or without disturbance and at the same time without resort to practices which are abhorrent to the common sense of justice. The Republican party favors the enactment of legislation supplementary to the existing antitrust act which will define as criminal offences those specific acts that uniformly mark attempts to restrain and to monopolize trade, to the end that those who honestly intend to obey the law may have a guide for their action and those who aim to violate the law may the more surely be punished. The same certainty should be given to the law prohibiting combinations and monopolies that characterize other provisions of commercial law; in order that no part of the field of business opportunity may be restricted by monopoly or combination, that business success honorably achieved may not be converted into crime, and that the right of every man to acquire commodities, and particularly the necessaries of life, in an open market uninfluenced by the manipulation of trust or combination, may be preserved.

Federal Trade Commission

In the enforcement and administration of Federal Laws governing interstate commerce and enterprises impressed with a public use engaged therein, there

---

[14] At this same time, Americans were awakening to the idea that the power of private actors created problems for personal privacy. *See* David J. Seipp, *The Right to Privacy in American History* (July 1978) (Ph.D. dissertation, Harvard University).

[15] THE WASHINGTON POST, BRANDEIS THE REFORMER, July 26, 1912 (attacking Brandeis for trust-busting activities while representing the Western Shoe Trust).

is much that may be committed to a Federal trade commission, thus placing in the hands of an administrative board many of the functions now necessarily exercised by the courts. This will promote promptness in the administration of the law and avoid delays and technicalities incident to court procedure.[16]

## DYNAMICS OF SOLVING THE TRUST PROBLEM

To address the trust problem, Congress chose to endow an agency with a number of different attributes. Later in 1938, when Congress explicitly gave the FTC a consumer protection mission, these attributes shaped how the Agency dealt with consumer problems. The attributes are well suited for the FTC's modern role in policing privacy.

### The need for expertise

In 1903, Congress created the Bureau of Corporations to help document and understand the trust problem. Empowered to investigate and make recommendations about the regulation of almost all industries, it served an information forcing and investigatory role against the trusts.[17] As a component of the then Department of Commerce and Labor, the Bureau of Corporations was partisan and subject to control of the ruling executive. The Bureau of Corporations reported on several industries and the Agency's investigative activity helped focus the antitrust enforcement of the attorney general.

### The need for certainty

After the 1911 *Standard Oil* decision, a number a factors militated toward the creation of some entity more powerful than the Bureau of Corporations. Supporters of greater antitrust enforcement felt that the Bureau's investigation and publicity functions were inadequate. The business community felt that the Sherman Act was too broad and that it provoked too much uncertainty.[18] Business leaders also thought that it was unfair to be sued by the attorney general for violation of its terms, given its breadth. The business community wanted to avoid the chill of the Sherman Act by having options to obtain advice and even clearance and immunity from prosecution when that advice was followed.[19] There was also a great concern that

---

[16] Republican Party Platform of 1912, June 18, 1912.

[17] Act Establishing the Department of Commerce and Labor, Pub. L. No. 57–87, § 6, 32 Stat. 825 (1903).

[18] Danny A. Bring, The Origins of the Federal Trade Commission Act: A Public Choice Approach (1993) (Ph.D. dissertation, George Mason University).

[19] Woodrow Wilson, Address to a Joint Session of Congress on Trusts and Monopolies, January 20, 1914 ("The business of the country awaits also, has long awaited and has suffered because it could not obtain, further and more explicit legislative definition of the policy and meaning of the existing

judges would apply their own economic ideas about trusts in Sherman Act cases, and that an expert body should make these decisions.

## The need for flexibility

The legislative process revealed the many limitations of laws that banned specific business wrongdoing. The kinds of unfair behavior were too numerous to enumerate, and legislative prohibitions of them invited businesses to engage in practices that fell though minor loopholes.[20] To address the trust problem, Congress eventually took both the specific prohibition (in the Clayton Act) and the broad prohibition approach in the FTC Act.

## The need for quick, preventative action

The Sherman Act approach tended to focus prosecution on industries that had already consolidated. There was a need for an agency to focus on incipient concentration and on smaller trusts. Joseph Davies, who then directed the Bureau of Corporations, recommended to President Wilson that the FTC have a quasi-judicial role. Under Davies' proposal, which was largely adopted, the FTC could make findings and formal recommendations to companies to take effect in sixty days, thereby aiding the courts and providing a quick remedy.[21]

## The need for compromise

The trust problem invoked strongly held beliefs that went to the core of individuals' political identity. A product of compromise, the FTC Act's vagueness allowed different political actors to ascribe different and conflicting purposes for the Agency. The FTC Act's legislative process gave the Agency two functions:

antitrust law. Nothing hampers business like uncertainty. Nothing daunts or discourages it like the necessity to take chances, to run the risk of falling under the condemnation of the law before it can make sure just what the law is. Surely we are sufficiently familiar with the actual processes and methods of monopoly and of the many hurtful restraints of trade to make definition possible, at any rate up to the limits of what experience has disclosed. These practices, being now abundantly disclosed, can be explicitly and item by item forbidden by statute in such terms as will practically eliminate uncertainty, the law itself and the penalty being made equally plain [...] And the business men of the country desire something more than that the menace of legal process in these matters be made explicit and intelligible. They desire the advice, the definite guidance and information which can be supplied by an administrative body, an interstate trade commission.")

[20]   Eugene R. Baker & Daniel J. Baum, Section 5 *of the Federal Trade Commission Act: A Continuing Process of Redefinition*, 7 VILL. L. REV. 517 (1962).

[21]   Joseph E. Davies, Memorandum of Recommendations as to the Trust Legislation by Joseph E. Davies, Commissioner of Corporations, *in* ARTHUR S. LINK, THE PAPERS OF WOODROW WILSON, Vol. 29, pp. 78–85 (1979).

prosecution and information gathering. The investigative powers were part of a package promoted by the House, where members envisioned a commission that would be information forcing and advisory, while the Senate, more influenced by agrarian states, steered the legislation toward prosecution.

*FTC Timeline: 1887–1915*

| Year | Month | Event | Relevance |
|------|-------|-------|-----------|
| 1887 | 2 | Interstate Commerce Act | First independent regulatory agency, became a model for the FTC |
| 1890 | 7 | Sherman Antitrust Act | Every contract…in restraint of trade…is declared illegal |
| 1902 | 2 | Industrial Commission Report | Recommends government agency to register corporations |
| 1903 | 2 | Bureau of Corporations | Investigational agency subsumed by FTC |
| 1906 | 6 | Pure Food and Drug Act | Capstone of a 25-year effort to address safety of food and drugs |
| 1911 | 5 | *Standard Oil* decision | Established "rule of reason" |
| 1914 | 9 | Federal Trade Commission Act (FTC Act) | 63rd Cong. 2nd Sess. Chap. 311, Public Law No. 63-203, 38 Stat. 717 |
| 1914 | 10 | Clayton Act | Accompanying the FTC Act, which followed the general-prohibition approach, the Clayton Act banned specific business activities |
| 1915 | 3 | First meeting of the FTC | George Rublee served as temporary chair until Joseph E. Davies was installed formally as Chairman of the new agency |
| 1915 | 4 | Commissioner Harris secures promise of furniture | Much of the Agency's early attention focused on simple logistical matters, such as getting furniture |

## A CHILD OF QUARRELING PARENTS

All three political parties announced policies on antitrust reform in anticipation of the 1912 election, but there was much disagreement about the specifics of how to address the trust problem. Progressive candidate Theodore Roosevelt, having developed a reputation as a trust buster, favored the strongest intervention: federal licensure of large corporations. The Republicans supported the creation of a "Federal Trade Commission," complete with enforcement power.

FIGURE 1.1. Edward W. Kemble, "Having a Bully Time," *Harper's Weekly*, March 30, 1912

President Wilson initially favored a weak commission that would give advice to business and, in so doing, reduce uncertainty in the business community. Wilson supported parallel legislation – the Clayton Act – that, unlike the eventually enacted FTC Act, was characterized by specific prohibitions on business behavior. As the Clayton Act was considered by and weakened by Congress, Wilson's antitrust strategy changed. Wilson relied heavily on the advice of Louis D. Brandeis, a devoted public servant, who in turn had delegated finding a solution to the trust problem to George Rublee. Rublee spent his life engaged in public service. He was a full-time lobbyist for the passage of the FTC Act and was later appointed commissioner.

Like Wilson, Brandeis' original idea was to regulate businesses with specific, Clayton Act-like prohibitions. But Rublee convinced Brandeis (and then Wilson) that a bill banning specific practices would be inefficacious and perverse, creating incentives for companies to engage in the very evils sought to be prohibited.[22] In an editorial attributed to Rublee, *Harper's Weekly* criticized the Clayton Act proposal and endorsed the Rublee approach: "unfair or oppressive competition would be declared to be unlawful without further definition. This would be the general rule for the Commission to administer."[23] Brandeis embraced Rublee's argument and helped convince Wilson to create a much stronger trade commission with an indeterminate charge that could evolve as business practices shifted.

Writing as a Supreme Court Justice eight years later, Brandeis explained:

> Instead of undertaking to define what practices should be deemed unfair, as had been done in earlier legislation [the Clayton Act], the [Federal Trade Commission] act left the determination to the Commission ... In leaving to the Commission the determination of the question whether the method of competition pursued in a particular case was unfair, Congress followed the precedent which it had set a quarter of a century earlier, when by the Act to Regulate Commerce it conferred upon the Interstate Commerce Commission power to determine whether a preference or advantage given to a shipper or locality fell within the prohibition of an undue or unreasonable preference or advantage.[24]

To this day, controversies surrounding the FTC can be traced to the Agency's parentage.[25] Brandeis and advocates of small business were ardently against "bigness,"[26] and they desired an agency that would allow competition on more equal grounds among small and larger businesses.[27] This may also have been driven by aesthetic objections to the kinds of consumption that big firms encourage. Such objections continue today: consider how some today look down on the customers of Wal-Mart and similar stores.

Some think that while Brandeis' legal thought was exceptional, his economic thinking was underdeveloped. In many respects, bigness creates efficiencies and

[22] George Rublee, Memorandum Concerning Section 5 of the Bill to Create a Federal Trade Commission, n.d., in Wilson Papers, Lib. Cong., Reel 60, Series 2.

[23] HARPER'S WEEKLY, THE TRUST PROBLEM 4, June 13, 1914.

[24] *FTC v. Gratz*, 253 US 421, 436–437 (1920).

[25] An excellent overview of these tensions appears in Marc Winerman & William Kovacic, *Outpost Years for a Start-up Agency: The FTC from 1921–1925*, 77(1) ANTITRUST L. J. 145 (2010).

[26] Elizabeth K. Maclean, *Joseph E. Davies: The Wisconsin Idea and the Origins of the Federal Trade Commission*, 6(3) J. GILDED AGE PROGRESSIVE ERA (2007).

[27] Louis D. Brandeis, *A Curse of Bigness*, 58 HARPER'S WEEKLY 18–21, December 20, 1913.

lowers prices for the consumer. Still, there are political reasons to be skeptical or fearful of large business. Large businesses can be too big to fail or too big to regulate, or both. Thus Brandeis' objections are partly based upon other principles than just efficiency.

GEORGE RUBLEE, A FATHER OF THE FTC

(Photo by Harris and Ewing)
GEORGE RUBLEE.

FIGURE 1.2. Commissioner George Rublee

Legislation always has many parents, but George Rublee made special efforts to instill progressive politics into federal antitrust law. Rublee was a kind of political itinerant. Not formally affiliated with any party, Rublee's legal training, conviction, and wealth made it possible for him to lead an interesting career with contributions to public policy in several fields. Rublee was a speechwriter for President Theodore Roosevelt, a progressive party activist, and internationalist, ending his career with an effort to find havens for German Jews in 1938.[28]

Despite Rublee's affiliation with the Roosevelt campaign, Louis D. Brandeis tapped Rublee to assist in the Wilson administration's antitrust plan. While Brandeis had muckraked for radical reform of big business, favoring prohibitions on a wide range of business practices, Rublee set upon the problem and determined that Brandeis' approach would fail. In a meeting with President Wilson in May 1914, Rublee convinced both Brandeis and Wilson that a general law banning unfair competition paired with a strong agency was the most efficacious approach. This view carried the day, in part because of Rublee's tireless lobbying for the FTC Act. Rublee later served as a commissioner (and technically was the Agency's first Chairman), but his tenure was marred by what he saw as inept fellow commissioners, by budget constraints at the new Agency, and by his inability to gain formal confirmation to the Agency.[29]

As commissioner, Rublee had many "modern" leadership instincts. He attempted to hire top economists, to steer the Agency away from becoming an advice-giving body, and to focus on big matters instead of petty frauds.

Rublee married Juliet Barrett, who earned her own place in American history as Suffragist, birth control advocate, and contemporary of Margaret Sanger. Her papers are maintained by Smith College.[30] Rublee was the son of Horace Rublee, a Republican Party leader, journalist, and ambassador to Switzerland.

---

Brandeis also reflected the moralism of lawyers, who have a respect for law even where its application may be inefficient. We will see that many conflicts at the Commission come from attachment to the letter of the law where society may benefit from a looser interpretation or no enforcement at all.

Ambiguity concerning the purpose of the FTC also comes from President Wilson's leadership. Although Wilson's intervention in favor of a strong FTC was critical to its success, Wilson himself was skeptical of expert bureaucrats. Wilson's public pronouncements on the issue of regulating business were also ambiguous. Both before the campaign for the FTC Act and after, Wilson described the FTC as a

---

[28] *See generally* Marc Eric McClure, Earnest endeavors: The Life and Public Work of George Rublee (2003).

[29] For an alternative take, see Elizabeth K. Maclean, *Joseph E. Davies: The Wisconsin Idea and the Origins of the Federal Trade Commission*, 6(3) J. Gilded Age Progressive Era (2007)(Arguing that Rublee's vision was in conflict with Davies, thus causing turmoil on the Commission that hampered its early effectiveness).

[30] Juliet Barrett Rublee Papers, 1917–1955.

pro-business, advice-giving agency.[31] In modern debates, FTC critics latch on to this rhetoric for the proposition that the FTC should enforce less vigorously and help advise businesses.

These conflicts were never resolved and perhaps led to the relatively easy enactment of the FTC Act. As George C. Davis explained, "every group saw in the FTC the potential solution to its own special problems and complaints. Reformers envisioned a powerful harness upon business activity and a deterrent to misbehavior; businessmen saw a friendly and helpful liaison with an otherwise unsympathetic government; political economists rejoiced at the embodiment of their aspirations for efficiency and expertise in public administration."[32] But the many faces of the FTC resurfaced as conflicts in the early commission, as Wilson's first appointments held different assumptions about the Agency's role. And these conflicts continue today, largely in the same form, with pro-business forces desiring an advisory body and consumer advocates favoring more enforcement.

## THE EARLY COMMISSION

President Wilson signed H.R. 15613, creating the FTC on September 26, 1914.[33] The FTC's first meeting was held Tuesday, March 16, 1915 (perhaps to avoid Monday's Ides of March).

The FTC superseded the then eleven-year-old Bureau of Corporations, and inherited much of its staff and its director, Joseph Davies, as the first Chairman of the FTC.

The new Agency's powers included the ability to prevent "persons, partnerships, or corporations, except banks, and common carriers … from using unfair methods of competition in commerce." This astonishingly broad power was tempered by limits on the Agency's enforcement tools. But Congress and the courts stripped away these limits over time, making the Agency more and more powerful, and raising deeper questions about the due process issues implicated by the FTC Act.

At its inception, the FTC could issue cease and desist orders, but for these to be enforceable, the Agency had to go to federal court to obtain an injunction against the business. Like the Bureau of Corporations, it could conduct investigations and publish reports. To this day, its power to issue civil penalties is constrained in part because of due process concern that the FTC could both define prohibited conduct and fine companies for it (see Chapter 4).

---

[31] In 1916, President Wilson told a group of businessmen, "It is hard to describe the functions of that commission; all I can say is that it has transformed the government of the United States from being an antagonist of business into being a friend of business." E. Pendleton Herring, *Politics, Personalities, and the Federal Trade Commission, I*, 28(6) AMER. POL. SCI. REV. 1016 (1934).

[32] George C. Davis, The Federal Trade Commission: Promise and Practice in Regulating Business, 1900–1929 (1969) (Ph.D. dissertation, University of Illinois).

[33] 63rd Cong. 2nd Sess. Chap. 311, Public Law No. 63–203, 38 Stat. 717.

**JOSEPH E. DAVIES.**
(Photo by Harris & Ewing)

FIGURE 1.3. Chairman Joseph Davies

Several challenges confronted the early commission: The initial appointees failed to develop a coherent policy for the Agency,[34] and this shortcoming was aggravated by the onset of World War I and churn in membership of the Commission. The early commission struggled with the issue of whether it should merely be an advice-giving body for businesses. The courts weakened the Agency by limiting it to the enforcement of wrong already illegal under the common law. When the FTC investigated industries aggressively, factions would organize against it and cause "blowback," that is, a counterattack on the Agency by Congress. The FTC's quasi-judicial role invited criticism and fear of government abuse. And finally, the early commission lacked basic resources to function efficaciously. Despite all of these challenges, the

---

[34] Nelson B. Gaskill, The Regulation of Competition: A Study of Futility as Exemplified by the Federal Trade Commission and National Industrial Recovery Act with Proposals for Its Remedy (1936).

Commission accomplished a great deal of good work, and critiques of the Agency frequently discount or simply ignore this work.[35]

## Early leadership

External factors of a hostile Congress and World War I made it difficult for the early commission to thrive. But it had internal problems as well. For the FTC to function properly, it needs a special kind of leader – one who conveys a sense of fair-minded balance.[36] Throughout its history, however, weak appointments have plagued the FTC.

President Wilson's initial commission appointments, which he described as having "common sense,"[37] were thought by others to be inept. This presents a puzzle: Why did Wilson support a strong commission but then appoint leadership incapable of realizing the potential of the Agency? One of the founding commissioners, George Rublee, thought his colleagues agreeable but too cautious and unqualified for the job: "It really had no chance to do its job with that kind of membership. It was hopeless, really. I didn't then quite know that it was hopeless, but I was discouraged."[38] Marc Eric McClure suggested that an economic downturn caused Wilson to give the first Chairman a charge to just consult with business and act in a conciliatory manner.[39]

If the Chairmanship were entrusted to Rublee, it might have had a very different early history. During his term, Rublee attempted to focus the Commission on large matters instead of small frauds and to increase the economic sophistication of the Agency by hiring the best economists, and he wanted to avoid advice-giving to business. These are the very strategies employed in the decades that have seen increased efficacy of the Agency.

---

[35] For an overview of this work, consult the Agency's annual reports. An early commissioner discusses some FTC successes in Huston Thompson, *Highlights in the Evolution of the Federal Trade Commission*, 8 GEO. WASH. L. REV. 257 (1939). A summary of 110 general investigations completed by the FTC is published in *Investigations by the Federal Trade Commission 1915–1939*, 8 GEO. WASH. L. REV. 708 (1939).

[36] E. Pendleton Herring, *The Federal Trade Commissioners*, 8 GEO. WASH. L. REV. 339 (1939). The Chamber of Commerce, perhaps the Commission's oldest enemy, gave the Agency only three years before complaining that "Conditions [have] lead to impressions that the Commission is no longer a responsible body approaching its duties with a serious purpose to promote the public interest alone, but that it seeks aggrandizement for itself and its members and that it lacks the impartiality essential to any public agency which is to speak with authority and to promote the common cause of the nation, rather than to create discord, confusion, and disorganization." Rush C. Butler et al., *The Case of the Federal Trade Commission: Originally designed for impartial investigation the Commission is charged with bias and abuse*, 6(10) THE NATION'S BUSINESS 9, October 1918.

[37] SAN FRANCISCO CHRON., NO THEORISTS ON THE TRADE COMMISSION, December 19, 1914, p. 14.

[38] Marc Eric McClure, EARNEST ENDEAVORS: THE LIFE AND PUBLIC WORK OF GEORGE RUBLEE 112 (2003) (McClure characterizes three of the five initial commissioners as inept).

[39] *Id.*

The early commission suffered another blow in its leadership because of President Calvin Coolidge, who appointed William Ewart Humphrey, perhaps the Agency's most infamous leader. An outspoken proponent of big business, Humphrey, and a coalition of two other Republican appointees changed the Agency's rules, limiting the kinds of matters the Agency could bring, making more proceedings informal, and reducing the publicity given to commission actions.[40]

Starting under Humphrey, the Commission entered into voluntary compliance agreements with companies. These agreements were informal, not legally enforceable, and, most importantly, not publicized. In periods where the Commission leadership wishes it to be an information-providing agency, there is greater reliance on these informal mechanisms.[41] Following these changes, companies and advertisers could engage in unfair practices, be caught, promise to change their practices, and escape the entire matter with no publicity whatsoever. When minority-party members of the FTC attempted to bring publicity to agency actions through dissenting opinions, Humphrey threatened them with criminal sanctions.[42] The combination of changes brought on by Humphrey caused the Agency's constituencies to flip, with progressives becoming sharp critics of the FTC and the business community evincing support of it.[43]

While well liked and loyal to friends, Humphrey's personality made the Commission less effective.[44] As Thomas K. McCraw put it, "Despite Humphrey's clowning, incompetence, and violent partisanship, President Hoover appointed him to a second six-year term …"[45]

Later, as part of a strategy to clear the decks of federal agencies of officials who might oppose New Deal initiatives, President Franklin Delano Roosevelt attempted to remove Humphrey from office.[46] Roosevelt lost the legal fight. The Supreme Court held that Humphrey could only have been removed for "inefficiency, neglect of duty, or malfeasance in office."[47]

---

[40] E. Pendleton Herring, *Politics, Personalities, and the Federal Trade Commission, II*, 29(1) AMER. POL. SCI. REV. 21 (1935).

[41] Informal mechanisms may ease overloaded dockets and be a rational approach to limited resources. At times, critics have argued that informal mechanisms are unfair to businesses, because businesses may agree to them in order to avoid litigation with the government. *See* Thomas L. Bohen, An Analysis of the Formal and Informal Enforcement Procedures of the Federal Trade Commission as Devices for Restraining Unfair Methods of Competition and Unfair and Deceptive Business Practices (1971) (Ph.D. dissertation, University of Minnesota).

[42] Jack Crespin, A History of the Development of the Consumer Protection Activities of the Federal Trade Commission (1975)(Ph.D. dissertation, New York University).

[43] George C. Davis, *The Transformation of the Federal Trade Commission, 1914–1929*, 49(3) MISS. VALLEY HIST. REV. (December 1962).

[44] *See* Marc Winerman & William E. Kovacic, *The William Humphrey and Abram Myers Years: The FTC from 1925–1929*, 77(3) ANTITRUST L. J. 701 (2011).

[45] THOMAS K. McCRAW, PROPHETS OF REGULATION 151–152 (Belknap Press 1984).

[46] This episode is described in WILLIAM E. LEUCHTENBURG, THE SUPREME COURT REBORN: THE CONSTITUTIONAL REVOLUTION IN THE AGE OF ROOSEVELT 52–81 (1995).

[47] *Humphrey's Executor v. US.*, 295 US 602 (1935)(Humphrey died before the case resolved.).

Gerald C. Henderson's 1924 study of the Agency's law and procedure – written even before Humphrey's appointment – concludes by first discussing the importance of personality in commissioners. Henderson politely suggested that any body formed to be both prosecutor and judge faces the challenge of having its leadership perceived as fair-minded and impartial.[48] Professor Milton Handler, who played a major role in drafting the 1938 amendments to the FTC Act and the Food and Drug Administration amendments, attributed the FTC's poor reputation "in large measure to the disappointing exercise of the power of selection by our Presidents. The commissioners have failed to establish a tradition of fair dealing inspiring public confidence."[49]

## Early (and enduring) challenges

### The FTC as advice-giving body

The early FTC had deep conflicts concerning giving advice to businesses about compliance with the antitrust laws,[50] and this tension continues to exist in the modern commission. Throughout its history, some commission leaders have wanted the Agency to be primarily an advice-giving body, as it was in its early years. The theme echoes back to the Bureau of Corporations, and is supported in particular by statements made by President Wilson before and after passage of the FTC Act.

Yet, there are many legal and policy problems with the FTC as advice-giving body. It obviously is concerned that advice it gives in one matter could estop an enforcement action in another. Then again, even if the FTC were to give advice, it would not foreclose action by the federal or state attorneys general. Furthermore, advice is not mentioned in the FTC Act, and Congress could simply have kept the Bureau of Corporations if it wanted an advice-giving function. The 1920 Republican Party Platform proposed that the FTC Act be amended to create an advice-giving role, but Congress never heeded this recommendation.[51]

---

[48] Gerald C. Henderson, The Federal Trade Commission: A Study in Administrative Law and Procedure 327–328 (1924).

[49] Milton Handler, *Introduction: The Fiftieth Anniversary of the Federal Trade Commission*, 64(3) Colum. L. Rev. 385, 387 (1964).

[50] George C. Davis, The Federal Trade Commission: Promise and Practice in Regulating Business, 1900–1929 (1969) (Ph.D. dissertation, University of Illinois).

[51] "We approve in general the existing Federal Legislation against monopoly and combinations in restraint of trade, but since the known certainty of a law is the safety of all, we advocate such amendment as will provide American business men with better means of determining in advance whether a proposed combination is or is not unlawful. The Federal Trade Commission, under a Democratic Administration, has not accomplished the purpose for which it was created. This commission properly organized and its duties efficiently administered should afford protection to the public and legitimate business interests. There should be no persecution of honest business; but to the extent that circumstances warrant we pledge ourselves to strengthen the law against unfair practices." Republican Party Platform of 1920, June 8, 1920. One of the earliest critiques of the

Policy considerations also militate against advice giving. Advice creates hazard, as some commissioners leave the FTC before finishing their entire term to lucrative law firm partnerships that concentrate on lobbying the FTC or sometimes directly to companies that are frequent targets of FTC investigation.

Nevertheless, on its fourth day of operation in March 1915, representatives of the coal industry appeared before the assembled commissioners to request an informal meeting. Following the coal industry, Commission minutes document a parade of different industries briefing the Agency, describing their plans for merger, and sometimes explicitly requesting immunity from prosecution. Rublee, reflecting upon the creation of the Commission, said, "It appeared to be the common belief of business men that the chief function of the Commission was to give advice in regard to the legality under the Sherman Act of proposed combinations or contracts." Rublee opposed such advice, noting the absence of statutory support for it, and the problem that the advice would not bind other government enforcement and policy efforts.[52]

### Challenges to Agency power and the FTC as common law enforcer

Companies were quick to challenge the FTC Act as unconstitutionally vague and as an improper delegation of power – arguments that resurfaced in modern challenges concerning the Agency's ability to police information security. In an early challenge to the FTC's power, Sears, Roebuck & Company argued that the term "unfair methods of competition" was too indefinite to be enforceable, and that absent a specific definition, it should only pertain to practices that were illegal under the common law on September 26, 1914, the day the Act passed. But the Seventh Circuit rejected this argument, reasoning in part that other key provisions of the law are similarly vague and that Congress' intent was clear. The appellate court held: "On the face of this statute the legislative intent is apparent. The commissioners are not required to aver and prove that any competitor has been damaged or that any purchaser has been deceived. The commissioners, representing the government as parens patriae, are to exercise their common sense, as informed by their knowledge of the general idea of unfair trade at common law, and stop all those trade practices that have a capacity or a tendency to injure competitors directly or through deception of purchasers, quite irrespective of whether the specific practices in question have yet been denounced in common-law cases."[53]

Yet, the common law continued to haunt the Agency. As Thomas Blaisdell explained in his 1932 analysis of the Commission, the courts were much more likely to uphold agency orders when it used legal theories consistent with common law

---

FTC focused on the use of public resources for prosecution, rather than for advising companies. Rush C. Butler et al., *The Case of the Federal Trade Commission: Originally designed for impartial investigation the Commission is charged with bias and abuse*, 6(10) THE NATION'S BUSINESS 9, October 1918.

[52] George Rublee, *The Original Plan and Early History of the Federal Trade Commission*, 11(4) PROCEEDINGS OF THE ACADEMY OF POLITICAL SCIENCE IN THE CITY OF NEW YORK 114, 119 (January 1926).

[53] *Sears, Roebuck & Co. v. FTC*, 258 F. 307, 311 (7th Cir. 1919)

prohibitions. Faced with what appears to be an unbounded statutory mandate, courts found comfort in reverting to the common law strictures to interpret the Agency's powers. Today, critics who try to cabin the power of the Commission argue that the FTC should only act when there are violations of common law elements. They argue that the FTC should only act where there is "harm" (usually implying economic damage) and to prove a specific intent to defraud, but neither is required by Section 5.

There are a number of reasons to reject appeals to cabin the FTC to common law strictures. For instance, if Congress intended the FTC to have a prophylactic function, how could it address new business models and technologies relying upon a body of law frozen in 1914? Why create an agency when other policy levers, such as funding private suits or the Department of Justice, could serve to enforce the common law?

On a higher level, appeals to the "common law" are a form of question begging. The common law does not speak with a single, coherent voice. How would the FTC address thin or conflicting common law precedent?

Turning to privacy, we will see that the common law in practice protects only a narrow range of business activities. If the FTC were to limit itself to common law causes of action, its most important privacy activities would cease.

---

UNFAIR METHODS OF COMPETITION IN THE 1920S

A sample of "condemned" business practices the Agency identified in its 1920 annual report include the following:[54]

- Adulteration of commodities, misrepresenting them as pure or selling them under such names and circumstances that the purchaser would be misled into believing them to be pure.
- Procuring the business or trade secrets of competitors by espionage, by bribing their employees, or by similar means.
- Procuring breach of competitors' contracts for the sale of products by misrepresentation or by other means.
- Inducing employees of competitors to violate their contracts or enticing away employees of competitors in such numbers or under such circumstances as to hamper or embarrass them in business.
- Making false or disparaging statements respecting competitors' products, their business, financial credit, etc.

---

[54] FTC, Annual Report 1920, September 16, 1920; *see also* Gilbert Holland Montague, *Unfair Methods of Competition*, 25(1) Yale Law J. 20 (1915); FTC, Memorandum on Unfair Competition at the Common Law (1916).

- Making vague and indefinite threats of patent infringement suits against the trade generally.
- False claims to patents or misrepresenting the scope of patents.
- Intimidation for the purpose of accomplishing enforced dealing by falsely charging disloyalty to the Government.
- Tampering with and misadjusting the machines sold by competitors for the purpose of discrediting them with purchaser.
- Unauthorized appropriation of the results of a competitor's ingenuity, labor and expense, thereby avoiding costs otherwise necessarily involved in production.
- Preventing competitors from procuring advertising space in newspapers or other periodicals by misrepresenting their standings or other misrepresentation calculated to prejudice advertising hated to prejudice advertising mediums against them.
- Harassing competitors by fake requests for estimates on bills of goods, for catalogues, etc.
- Sales of goods at cost, coupled with statements misleading the public into the belief that they are sold at a profit.
- Any and all schemes for compelling wholesalers and retailers to maintain resale prices on products fixed by the manufacturer.
- Combinations of competitors to enhance prices, maintain prices, bring about substantial uniformity in prices, or to divide territory or business.

## The blowback problem

In 1919, the FTC completed an extensive investigation of the meatpacking industry.[55] The six-volume tome caused the attorney general to file criminal suit against meatpackers. But the report also called for nationalization of some businesses.[56] The sting of the report and the call for nationalization caused blowback – Senator Watson of Indiana accused FTC investigators of criminal anarchy and sedition.[57] Eleven employees identified by Watson quickly departed from or were booted from the Commission, despite being cleared by an agency investigation. Even the *New York Times* joined in, characterizing the FTC as carrying on the "propaganda of a

---

[55] FTC, Report on the Meat-Packing Industry (June 24, 1919).

[56] Paul A. Pautler, *A Brief History of the FTC's Bureau of Economics: Reports, Mergers, and Information Regulation*, 46 Rev. Ind. Org. 59 (2015).

[57] Thomas C. Blaisdell, Jr. The Federal Trade Commission: An Experiment in the Control of Business (1967), *citing* George T. Odell, *The Federal Trade Commission Yields to Pressure*, 112(2897) The Nation 36–37, January 12, 1921. ("The persecution that these men were subjected to during the past year it is only necessary to indicate by saying that the espionage of Mr. A. Mitchell Palmer's band of 'Red Raiders' went so far as to examine every bit of trash which was taken from the homes of these four men.")

class struggle," and urging Congress to cure it of its "Bolshevist and propagandist tendencies."[58] Senator Sherman, speaking on the floor, named several FTC commissioners (Murdock, Davies, and Colver) as do-nothing political climbers.[59] At one point, commissioner Colver testified before Congress that agency employees had been victims of "frame up" arrests organized by the meatpackers![60]

The meatpackers were rewarded by gaining exemption from the FTC's Section 5 jurisdiction, and placed under oversight of the friendlier Department of Agriculture. This is the first of several episodes where aggressive FTC action was met with congressional punishment.[61] The infamous KidVid episode (covered in Chapter 2) involved the Commission's proposed rule to regulate advertising to children on television. It too resulted in blowback, causing Congress to shut down the Agency twice. Today, business lobbyists try to threaten the FTC with similar blowback if it oversteps on privacy.

### Prosecutor, judge, jury, and appellate court

As originally conceived, the FTC was to have a quasi-judicial role. The FTC would identify violations of the FTC Act, and bring adjudicative actions before an administrative law judge based upon its pleadings. The Commission itself approves of and hears appeals of the administrative law judge's determinations. Thus, when pursuing administrative proceedings, the Agency has elements of an inquisitorial court: it is actively involved both in refereeing the dispute and in investigating it (Chapter 4 will discuss the FTC's power to bring suit in federal court). Although commission decisions can be further appealed to the Circuit Courts, the Agency itself is prosecutor, judge, jury, and appellate court.

We will see that the FTC's quasi-judicial role attracts strong critique concerning separation of powers and due process. The 1955 Hoover Commission Report recommended transferring the FTC's judicial functions to a centralized administrative

---

[58]  THE N.Y. TIMES, THE TRADE COMMISSION, September 3, 1918 at 10. For a detailed description of the Chamber of Commerce's crusade against the Commission, *see* George C. Davis, The Federal Trade Commission: Promise and Practice in Regulating Business, 1900–1929 (1969) (Ph.D. dissertation, University of Illinois).

[59]  56 CONG. REC. 10002–10003 (September 5, 1918) ("instead of being a fair-minded instrumentality of Government, as the Interstate Commerce Commission has been, to settle questions between shippers and carriers, the Federal Trade Commission has been just the reverse of it … This commission has been merely an addled egg, perfectly rotten, in the nest for the incubation of still more addled candidates. That is its history. There is not one of its members that is not a radical, a bolshevist in this country, a firebrand, an economic incendiary; and all or the most of them were in private life business failures of the most pronounced type. They have succeeded in no profession. They have built up no business. They have accomplished nothing but ceaseless agitation.").

[60]  N.Y. TIMES, ACCUSES PACKERS OF FRAMING ARRESTS, CAUSED SEIZURE OF TRADE COMMISSION AGENT, COLVER TELLS SENATORS, January 10, 1920, at 9.

[61]  Judge Richard Posner explained: "if the Commission takes on the really big-money problems of consumer protection, the political process is unlikely to defer to its resolution of them. The Commission's role turns out to be a gadfly, spurring legislative action; a catalyst." Richard A. Posner, *The Federal Trade Commission: A Retrospective*, 72(3) ANTITRUST L. J. 761 (2005).

court.[62] One prolific critic, commissioner Lowell Mason, known as the "Great Dissenter," repeatedly sounded the alarm that FTC's quasi-judicial role and procedure foreshadowed a government tyranny. Mason even described a straw man he created to embody the growing lack of respect for business rights brought on by the New Deal and the growing administrative state: "X-53." X-53 was the FTC staff person who would trample rights to satisfy the Agency's ends: "When you find yourself dealing with defendants as though they were people, your staff should see to it that decisions reached in such moments of weakness are channeled back to you for reconsideration."[63]

These concerns conflict somewhat with one purpose of the FTC Act – to provide remedies and proceedings quickly, and outside federal court. How to balance a quick remedy with procedural fairness has been a prime consideration of the Agency. Agency leaders address it by adopting more court-like procedures, which add delay, and thus invite critique from Congress, which accuses the Agency of being too slow.

---

### THE FEDERAL TECHNOLOGY COMMISSION?

*Technology* is an ancient concept. The Greeks differentiated *epistêmê*, the idea of knowledge, from *technê*, which meant craft or arts or applied knowledge. The Oxford English Dictionary defines technology as the "branch of knowledge dealing with the mechanical arts and applied sciences; ... The application of such knowledge for practical purposes, esp. in industry, manufacturing, etc.; the sphere of activity concerned with this; the mechanical arts and applied sciences collectively."

Despite technology's antiquity and its connection to industrial and mechanical activities, today some commentators have labeled the FTC as the Federal *Technology* Commission.[64] These commentators suggest that the FTC does something today qualitatively different from the past. But this is not the case. The FTC has always regulated technology – the technology of the day. The FTC has always been a technology commission.

---

[62] Commission on Organization of the Executive Branch of the Government, Legal Services and Procedure (March 1955). The problem and merits of this proposal are discussed in greater detail in Task Force on Legal Services and Procedure, Report on Legal Services and Procedure (March 1955).

[63] LOWELL MASON, THE LANGUAGE OF DISSENT (1959). In this book, the author also articulated Mason's Law: "that bureaucracy will arrogate to itself all power available under a statute in spite of the limitations against tyranny in the Constitution. This it will do, quietly and unobtrusively, through decisions at the lowest rung of the quasi-judicial ladder where the issue seldom meets the eye of the public."

[64] Brian Fung, *The FTC Was Built 100 Years Ago to Fight Monopolists. Now, It's Washington's Most Powerful Technology Cop*, Wash. Post, September 25, 2014.

The 1910s and 1920s were exciting times for technology, just as revolutionary and life changing as today. The period saw the popularization of the automobile (an invention that actually connects people), a technology that had immense social and economic implications. The first news programs on the radio started in the 1920s, and by this decade, most towns had movie theaters. The rotary-dial telephone was commercialized during this period, and the first intercontinental phone calls were made.

Meanwhile at the Commission, the Agency lacked a formal consumer protection mission. Nonetheless, the Agency tackled matters concerning technology in many fields. The first matter reported in the first volume of the FTC reporter involved technology – the passing off of chemically treated cotton as silk.[65] More generally, the nineteenth-century advent of modern marketing was a product of technological innovation.[66]

Among the FTC's first Trade Practice Conferences included proceedings on chemical and biological products, on direct selling and cooperative marketing techniques, on electrical power, on fertilizers, on insecticides, on motion pictures and even on the rebuilt typewriter industry. Many of these were the raw commodities necessary to build a mass consumer society. Today we take them as a given, and do not appreciate their novelty and importance.

Saying that the FTC has suddenly become a technology regulator is a useful rhetorical device. It casts the FTC as a vengeful Zeus, punishing a titan for bringing something new to the masses. But it is ahistorical. It treats technology as something that exists today, forgetting the innovation and social implications of technology from decades past.

## Resources

The Commission struggled at its inception, and reading the Agency's minutes, one sees that it spent substantial time on administrative tasks such as procuring furniture. Of course, anyone who has run an organization knows that such petty concerns can be frequent and that in government, unlike the private sector, decision-making is complicated by the lack of a chief executive officer who can make such decisions by fiat. The early FTC had a budget of less than $200,000 – the equivalent of $4 million in today's dollars. Its initial appropriation was so low that it sent a commissioner to the President to ask for old furniture from the White House. Resources continue to be an issue for the FTC – the entire agency today has a budget of over $300 million (smaller than the Consumer Financial Protection

---

[65] *FTC* v. *Yagle* et al., 1 FTC 13 (1916).

[66] Rebecca Tushnet and Eric Goldman, Advertising & Marketing Law: Cases and Materials 3 (2012) (explaining the contributions of the printing press, the rise of mass manufacturing, and the railroads in developing modern marketing).

Bureau, and dwarfed by the Food and Drug Administration, with its $4 billion budget). Just under 60 employees are charged today with protecting privacy.

*FTC Timeline: 1918–1937*

| Year | Month | Event | Relevance |
|------|-------|-------|-----------|
| 1918 | | FTC Meatpacking Report | Critical report calling for nationalization of industry invites accusations of sedition from meatpacking state Senators |
| 1919 | | Trade Practice Conference Concept Introduced | Self-regulatory predecessor to trade practice regulations |
| 1920 | 6 | FTC v. *Gratz* | Court appeared to limit FTC to enforcing common law |
| 1924 | | Henderson's "Federal Trade Commission" published | The first systemic review of the Agency |
| 1931 | 5 | FTC v. *Raladam* | FTC must prove injury to competition to proceed in cases |
| 1933 | 5 | Securities Act of 1933 | Originally overseen by FTC, but transferred to the Securities and Exchange Commission in 1934 |
| 1933 | 6 | National Industrial Recovery Act | Allowed industry agreements on price, production, but held to be unconstitutional in 1935 |
| 1936 | 6 | Robinson–Patman Act | This populist, pro-small business measure banning price discrimination has largely backfired |
| 1937 | 1 | Brownlow Report | Finds that independent agencies were haphazard, irresponsible, ungovernable, headless "fourth branch" of government |

## The early commission's waxing and waning powers

Throughout its history, the FTC's power has been shaped by Congress and the courts, and the general trend has been to increase the Agency's power over time. At its inception, at least on paper, the Agency's powers seemed unbounded, and so courts looked to the common law and to the Sherman Act for guidance in interpreting Congress' intent.[67] This occurred in 1920, when the Supreme Court declared that the courts, not the Commission, would determine the scope of unfair methods of competition.[68] In the case, the FTC sued a company for tying the purchase of steel ties to jute bags. The Warren, Jones & Gratz company was alleged

---

[67] *See generally* CARL MCFARLAND, JUDICIAL CONTROL OF THE FEDERAL TRADE COMMISSION AND THE INTERSTATE COMMERCE COMMISSION 1920–1930 (1933).

[68] *FTC v. Gratz*, 253 US 421 (1920).

to have only sold steel ties used for bundling cotton to jobbers who would also purchase jute bagging from the company. The Court held, "The words 'unfair method of competition' are not defined by the statute, and their exact meaning is in dispute. It is for the courts, not the Commission, ultimately to determine as matter of law what they include. They are clearly inapplicable to practices never heretofore regarded as opposed to good morals because characterized by deception, bad faith, fraud, or oppression, or as against public policy because of their dangerous tendency unduly to hinder competition or create monopoly. The act was certainly not intended to fetter free and fair competition as commonly understood and practiced by honorable opponents in trade." This decision appeared to limit the FTC to policing practices that were already illegal at common law – not acts currently practiced in trade.

Just two years later, the Court backpedaled. In *FTC* v. *Beech-Nut Packing Co.*, the Court found it within the FTC's jurisdiction to pursue a matter against a company that did not appear to meet all the necessary elements of a Sherman Act claim. Rather than write an express contract that fixed prices, the company published suggested price lists, and simply would not distribute its product to sellers that undercut the suggested price. After quoting *Gratz*, the Court explained, if Beech-Nut's activities were "against public policy because of 'its dangerous tendency unduly to hinder competition or to create monopoly,' it was within the power of the Commission to make an order forbidding its continuation."[69]

Louis Brandeis, who played an important role in forming the FTC and then rejected the opportunity to serve as commissioner, was later appointed to the Supreme Court. Writing for the Court in the 1922 Winsted Hosiery Co. case, Brandeis upheld the Agency's authority to police false advertising in matters where competitive injury occurred. Winsted Hosiery was charged with attaching various versions of the word "wool" in its marketing of mostly cotton underwear. Tradesmen were well aware of this kind of deception, but, nevertheless, the Court held that the public interest was served by suppressing it, both because the labels deceived the public, and because competitors might follow suit and falsely advertise their goods in order to compete with Winsted Hosiery.[70] This was the first case where the Court recognized that "Section 5 of the act makes the Commission's findings conclusive as to the facts, if supported by evidence." The FTC's pursuit of false advertising was also the beginning of what we recognize today as the FTC's consumer protection mission.[71]

Less than ten years later, the Court slightly narrowed the Agency's authority. In *FTC* v. *Raladam Co.*, the Agency alleged that the company's advertisements for "Marmola," a weight loss supplement made of laxatives and desiccated thyroid

---

[69] *FTC* v. *Beech-Nut Packing Co.*, 257 US 441 (1922).
[70] *FTC* v. *Winsted Hosiery Co.*, 258 US 483 (1922).
[71] Marc Winerman & William Kovacic, *Outpost Years for a Start-Up Agency: The FTC from 1921–1925*, 77(1) ANTITRUST L. J. 145 (2010).

glands, were false.[72] The Supreme Court ruled that the Agency did not have the authority to interfere with the marketing of the "cure" on behalf of consumers alone. The FTC had not proven that the "advertisements substantially injured or tended thus to injure the business of any competitor or of competitors generally, whether legitimate or not."[73] This raises an obvious problem: if an entire industry is engaging in a fraudulent or dangerous practice, or otherwise lacks incentives to expose a fraud through counteradvertising, should the FTC be restrained from intervening?

The back-and-forth on the Agency's powers continued. In the 1934 case *FTC v. R. F. Keppel & Bro., Inc.*,[74] the Agency sought to prevent a candy company from marketing its product to children with lottery-like inducements. In the scheme, the purchaser did not know the price of the candy until it was opened, whereupon the candy could be free (because it included a penny that the purchaser kept) or some higher specified price. The Agency argued that this practice was against public policy, as it encouraged children to engage in a form of gambling. The candy company argued that the practice was not monopolistic; that any competitor could engage in like practices; and thus that competition had not been harmed. The Court rejected this argument, noting that the FTC's power to address unfair methods of competition was not limited to addressing practices illegal at common law, under the Sherman Act, or to behavior subject to previous litigation before the courts. The FTC had the power to define a new body of illegal acts independent of these established categories.

The Supreme Court further held that a practice could be unfair even if competitors were free to adopt it but chose not to do so. The Court reasoned that "a trader may not, by pursuing a dishonest practice, force his competitors to choose between its adoption or the loss of their trade. A method of competition which casts upon one's competitors the burden of the loss of business unless they will descend to a practice which they are under a powerful moral compulsion not to adopt, even though it is not criminal, was thought to involve the kind of unfairness at which the statute was aimed."[75]

The Court specified that findings of the FTC should be given weight in determining whether a practice is an unfair method of competition. Finally, the Court employed language similar to the Brandeis dissent in the *Gratz* decision – language that supported the congressional intent of creating an agency that could evaluate and correct new commercial practices as they evolve: "We hold that the Commission correctly concluded that the practice was an unfair method of competition within the meaning of the statute. It is unnecessary to attempt a comprehensive definition of the unfair methods which are banned, even if it were possible to do so ... New or

---

[72] *In the Matter of Raladam Co.*, 12 F.T.C. 363 (1929).
[73] 283 US 643 (1931).
[74] 291 US 304 (1934).
[75] *Id.* at 311.

different practices must be considered as they arise in the light of the circumstances in which they are employed."[76]

Since *Keppel*, the courts have deferred to the Commission's determination of what is unlawful in both the competition[77] and consumer protection areas.[78]

## CONCLUSION

Reviewing the history of the FTC's early years shows that many issues surrounding regulation of trade are still contested. Just as the early FTC struggled with challenges to its authority and claims that it should only police practices illegal at common law, today commission critics insist that it only act when common law elements are satisfied. Just as the early FTC struggled with resources, today it is vested with policing a broad swath of commerce for not just privacy violations, but many other kinds of consumer protection issues.

In some ways, the modern FTC has transcended its early challenges. For instance, mediocre appointments plagued the Agency until the 1960s. The modern commission has well-qualified commissioners and expert staff. The FTC's attributes – its expertise, its ability to provide certainty, its ability to be flexible, its ability to act to prevent problems, and its role as a forum for compromise – were forged by Congress to fight problems of trust and monopoly. These are remarkably well suited attributes for resolving modern privacy tussles.

The next chapters discuss Congress' formal grant of jurisdiction to address consumer protection issues, the second and third "waves" of consumerism, and the FTC's embrace of e-commerce cases.

---

[76] *Id.* at 313.
[77] "Congress advisedly left the concept [of unfair methods of competition] flexible to be defined with particularity by the myriad of cases from the field of business. It is also clear that the Federal Trade Commission Act was designed to supplement and bolster the Sherman Act and the Clayton Act to stop in their incipiency acts and practices which, when full blown, would violate those Acts as well as to condemn as 'unfair method of competition' existing violations of them." *FTC* v. *Motion Picture Adver. Serv. Co.*, 344 US 392 (1953)(internal citations omitted).
[78] "Congress amended the Act in 1938 to extend the Commission's jurisdiction to include 'unfair or deceptive acts or practices in commerce'—a significant amendment showing Congress' concern for consumers as well as for competitors ... This statutory scheme necessarily gives the Commission an influential role in interpreting § 5 and in applying it to the facts of particular cases arising out of unprecedented situations. Moreover, as an administrative agency which deals continually with cases in the area, the Commission is often in a better position than are courts to determine when a practice is 'deceptive' within the meaning of the Act. This Court has frequently stated that the Commission's judgment is to be given great weight by reviewing courts. This admonition is especially true with respect to allegedly deceptive advertising since the finding of a § 5 violation in this field rests so heavily on inference and pragmatic judgment. Nevertheless, while informed judicial determination is dependent upon enlightenment gained from administrative experience, in the last analysis the words 'deceptive practices' set forth a legal standard and they must get their final meaning from judicial construction." *FTC* v. *Colgate-Palmolive Co.*, 380 US 374 (1965)(internal citations omitted).

# 2

# The FTC and the rise of consumerism

Consumer protection historians recognize three waves of consumer rights activism.[1] The first, at the turn of the century, led to the passage of a first-of-its-kind pure food and drug law in 1906, its strengthening in 1912, and to the creation of the FTC in 1914. The second wave started in the 1930s and led to the main topic of this chapter: the formal adoption of consumer protection authority for the FTC and how the Agency implemented it.

While the FTC's powers were strengthened in the 1930s, historical forces beyond the Agency's control rose again. The Agency did not again gain footing until the 1960s, when the third wave of consumer protection – now labeled "consumerism" – came into force. This era saw some of the strongest presidential support of the consumer movement, some of the Agency's most qualified commissioners, and an earnest commitment to make the FTC more effective from both political parties. It also saw the FTC change from case-by-case enforcement to the creation of rules, which could have structural effects on the market.

Ambition in promulgating these rules, however, began to invoke the ire of the business community, and the Reagan administration used the FTC as an example of government out of control. This is interesting because KidVid, the controversial proposal to regulate advertising to children, was the capstone of a Republican-initiated campaign, reflecting a bipartisan and incremental approach to an intractable industry. KidVid offers lessons for privacy policy today, as information security cases were initiated by Republican commission leadership, yet have become controversial when policed by a Democratic Party-led FTC. More broadly, KidVid events offer lessons for us today in considering how the Agency should police privacy (by rule or by enforcing cases), and the extent to which it should take an activist posture.

---

[1] For an overview of the three major waves of consumerism, *see* JAMES BISHOP & HENRY W. HUBBARD, LET THE SELLER BEWARE (1969).

## THE SECOND WAVE OF CONSUMER PROTECTION

Recession-era realities in the 1930s focused consumers on product quality and reliability. There was much more widespread skepticism of advertising, both in its claims and in its value as an economic and social force. With the advent of the New Deal, there was also more trust in correcting problems with social programs.

In the mid-1930s, Congress again visited landmark consumer protection legislation. Congress reacted to growing public concern regarding the manufacturing process and the presence of dangerous products in commerce. Americans were disconnected from the production of these products, and enhanced guarantees of their integrity and safety were needed to establish consumer trust.

The continued presence of "patent" medicines, a target of the turn-of-the-century food and drug laws, in the marketplace further heightened concern about product safety. (The word "patent" is confusing here. Most sellers of such products usually rested on trade secrecy, not patents, in part because the "medicine" being sold was often just alcohol.[2]) Books concerning product safety, such as Kallet and Schlink's 100,000,000 *Guinea Pigs*, became very popular.[3] That book argued that a "hundred million Americans act as unwitting test animals in a gigantic experiment with poisons, conducted by the food, drug, and cosmetic manufacturers." Kallet and Schlink highlighted dozens of examples of this experimentation, including a product to remove freckles that contained mercury, fruits and vegetables coated in arsenic and lead, and hair removal crèmes that contained rat poison. The marketing documented by the authors were equally troubling; they included recommendations that Lysol, the household cleaner, be used as a vaginal douche and that the mouthwash Listerine could be used to prevent tuberculosis.

---

### 100,000,000 GUINEA PIGS

Imagine living in a country where one's main protection against dangerous products comes through labeling. From 1906 until passage of stronger regulation for foods, drugs and cosmetics, the government could do very little about dangerous products that were popularly marketed to the public. Arthur Kallet and Frederick J. Schlink shocked the public with the publication of their best-selling 1,000,000 *Guinea Pigs* in 1933. It illuminated the extent of dangerous products sold, the marketing of those products, and the weakness of federal regulation.[4] The book, which underwent over a dozen printings and was widely

---

[2]  *See, for example,* Inger L. Stole, *Consumer Protection in the Historical Perspective: The Five-Year Battle over Federal Regulation of Advertising, 1933–1938,* 3(4) MASS COMMUN. SOC. 351–372 (2000).

[3]  ARTHUR KALLET & F.J. SCHLINK, 100,000,000 GUINEA PIGS, DANGERS IN EVERYDAY FOODS, DRUGS, AND COSMETICS (1933).

[4]  *Id.*

read, led directly to the passage of stronger laws in 1938. Throughout the book's anecdotes, a common theme emerged: individuals could become very affluent by experimenting on the public. When individuals were harmed, the government and victims could do little to remedy the problem because the law primarily was concerned with giving consumers notice of ingredients. If an experiment failed, the entrepreneur could simply move on to some other product. Kallet and Schlink saw the law as a license to kill. Consider these examples:

- Kopp's Baby Friend, marketed as a soothing agent for babies, secretly contained morphine, and it led to the deaths of nine infants. The government's remedy at the time was limited to prosecuting mislabeling. Thus, after a $25 fine, Kopp's reappeared on the market, albeit with a disclosure of morphine as an ingredient.
- Entrepreneurs were free to create "cures" that were crude and dangerous experiments on the consumer. For instance, William J. A. Bailey marketed Radithor, water irradiated with radium, to affluent people. When a prominent patient died, Bailey told the *New York Times* that "I have drunk more radium water than any man alive and I never have suffered any ill effects."
- Pebeco Toothpaste contained potassium chlorate (a poisonous, combustible chemical originally used to ignite bullets), so much that, "[i]n 1910, a German army officer committed suicide by eating the contents of a tube of Pebeco."
- Some hair removal products contained the highly toxic thallium acetate, and others promoted hair removal treatment with x-rays.
- The "Hoxsey" anticancer treatment, a mixture of herbs promoted by layman Harry Hoxsey, allegedly contained arsenic (the exact ingredients are still unknown). Banned in the United States in 1956, one can still obtain the Hoxsey treatment, in Tijuana. To this day, its advocates see a conspiracy among doctors and the government to suppress it.

Philip Hilts notes that the lack of a regulatory regime created a market for lemons (a situation where the bad drives out the good) in medicines. He attributes advances in modern pharmaceutical science to the emergence of rules requiring safety and efficacy for drugs.[5]

Nevertheless, Kallet and Schlink's basic point that individuals with no scientific training could mix together chemicals and market it as a nostrum still is a problem today in the form of nutritional supplements. While such

---

[5] PHILIP J. HILTS, PROTECTING AMERICA'S HEALTH: THE FDA, BUSINESS, AND ONE HUNDRED YEARS OF REGULATION (2003).

supplements are marketed similarly to drugs, they are not preapproved by the Food and Drug Administration (FDA), nor are they subject to rigorous safety or efficacy testing. The self-regulatory group for pet food products subjects dog food to six months of testing on live animals; no such requirement exists in the self-regulatory regime for human nutritional supplements.

Anyone is free to order vitamins or other chemicals online (vitamins are chemicals; "vitamin C" is a kinder name for ascorbic acid, and most of it is sourced in China) and mix them into new products for public consumption. They may not make false health claims, nor may they mislabel the concoction. The firm is entrusted with verifying safety, and it can go to market with no FDA review.[6]

Frederick J. Schlink founded Consumers Research but following a labor dispute, a rift formed, and Arthur Kallet went on to form the very successful Consumers Union.[7]

---

The consumer movement operated in a social backdrop with negative attitudes toward advertising. Popular and even economic assumptions concerning advertising's role in the economy were entirely different than today. As Professor Inger Stole explains in ADVERTISING ON TRIAL,[8] the progenitor to Consumers Union, Consumers Research, along with the Columbia University academic and member of President Franklin Roosevelt's "brain trust," Rexford Tugwell, proposed aggressive regulation of advertising in the early 1930s. Tugwell, then serving as Undersecretary of the Department of Agriculture, favored legislation that prohibited all advertising representations that left a false impression.

Regulators of the era also held more skeptical views about advertising. For example, the Commission released a report in 1945 that examined whether advertising was uneconomical. The report broke down the cost of advertising against net sales in dozens of industries, with the record held by "drugs and medicines," where advertising soaked up over $0.13 of every dollar in net sales. The Commission wrote, "advertising may be so used in some of its forms as to result in sales at relatively high consumer cost and also may be the means of bolstering and perpetuating the strong position of large concerns at the expense of small, less financially strong competitors."[9] It is unimaginable today that the FTC would describe advertising in this way, or that it would even consider advertising as a tax on consumers that favors big business. The economics

---

[6]  A. Cohen, *Hazards of Hindsight – Monitoring the Safety of Nutritional Supplements*, 370 N. ENGL. J. MED. 1277–1280, April 3, 2014.

[7]  *See generally* NORMAN I. SILBER, TEST AND PROTEST: THE INFLUENCE OF CONSUMERS UNION (1983).

[8]  INGER L. STOLE, ADVERTISING ON TRIAL: CONSUMER ACTIVISM AND CORPORATE PUBLIC RELATIONS IN THE 1930S (2006).

[9]  FTC, ANNUAL REPORT OF THE FEDERAL TRADE COMMISSION FOR THE FISCAL YEAR ENDING JUNE 30, 1945 (1945).

and benefits of advertising are much better understood, and these kinds of concerns are assumed to order themselves properly in the marketplace.

*FTC Timeline: 1938–1959*

| Year | Mo | Event | Relevance |
|---|---|---|---|
| 1938 | 3 | Wheeler–Lea Amendments to the FTCA | Unfair or deceptive acts or practices in commerce are hereby declared unlawful |
| 1940 | 10 | Wool Products Labeling Act | Banned misrepresentations of wool content |
| 1943 | 5 | Commission files complaint concerning Carter's Little Liver Pills | Case becomes an albatross for the Agency and example of its lethargy |
| 1949 | | Commissioner salary raised from $10,000 to $15,000 | The once flush commissioners salary was statutorily set – and undisturbed – for over three decades |
| 1949 | 3 | Hoover Commission Report | Recommended empowering the FTC Chair, raising salaries, need for delegation |
| 1950 | 3 | FTC Act penalties clarified and strengthened | Congress specified that separate violations were separate offenses, with each day of continuing violation a separate offense |
| 1951 | 8 | Fur Products Labeling Act | Addressed mislabeling of furs, rampant after advances in dyeing and processing of animals |
| 1952 | 7 | Fair Trade Amendments to FTC Act | Exempted banks and common carriers from §5 |
| 1954 | | Howrey reorganization | Added layers of review to staff decisions and considered a failure by Landis |
| 1954 | 8 | Flammable Fabrics Act | Motivated by horror stories of highly flammable clothing and related injuries |
| 1958 | 9 | Packers and Stockyards Act Amended | Amendments gave FTC jurisdiction over meat, poultry, and margarine sales |
| 1958 | 9 | Textile Fiber Products Act | Proscribed mislabeling of fiber content |
| 1959 | 12 | Final hearing denied in Carter's Little Liver Pills case | FTC action took 16 years to remove "liver" from Carter's Little Liver Pills |
| 1959 | 12 | Conference on public deception | FTC's first consumer conference, held by Chairman Kintner |

The old adage of "you have to spend money to make money" applies to advertising. Studies show that advertising can temper swings in product demand, spark competition, and expand the market for a product, thus lowering production and distribution costs. But hostility toward advertising in the 1930s and 1940s was intense enough to cause an industry-wide reaction. In the 1940s, advertisers started a concentrated campaign to elevate the status of advertising in the mind of the public. Advertisers even created teaching aids for consumer education classes in school to teach "buymanship," and as a bulwark against "penny-pinching," "product-rating," and "extremist pressure groups advocating restrictive government legislation, to crusaders sponsoring consumer cooperative enterprise, or to leftist economic zealots."[10]

## PASSAGE OF THE 1938 WHEELER–LEA AMENDMENTS TO THE FTC ACT

It was in the atmosphere of this intense, antibusiness sentiment that Congress took up a number of bills to increase consumer protection regulation. But the 1937 sulfanilamide disaster was a seminal event in passage of legislation. One hundred people died after taking a liquid version of sulfanilamide, a compound then commonly used as an antibacterial.[11] An investigation found that the Postal Office had charged the creator with fraud. Pre-market animal testing of the liquid version of the extract would have prevented the disaster. After the discovery that it was poisonous, the search for the distributed product in an effort to prevent further deaths elucidated the many gaps in the tracking of dangerous products in the marketplace. The sulfanilamide disaster came on the heels of death and blindness caused by diet pills containing dinitrophenol.

### The Wheeler–Lea Amendment debate

As is the case today with privacy, much of the debate concerns what regulator will be entrusted to protect the public. In the privacy realm, different agencies today are competing to claim ownership over consumer privacy, with the Federal Communications Commission, Consumer Financial Protection Bureau, FTC, and other agencies all at the table. Similarly, in debating the 1938 Amendments to the FTC Act, the FDA and the FTC competed to own the regulation of advertising issue.

In the 1930s, advertisers favored giving power to police marketing to the FTC. Advertisers (and others) saw the FTC as less effective than the FDA. The FTC was considered more pro-business, and, despite its nature as an independent agency, the

---

[10] Harold E. Green, *How Advertisers Are Helping Consumers in Their Buying*, PRINTERS' INK, February 15, 1946.

[11] Kirstin Downey, *Health Scare Leads to New Powers for the FTC*, in THE INSIDER'S GUIDE TO THE HISTORY OF THE FEDERAL TRADE COMMISSION (Kirstin Downey & Lesette Heath eds., 2015).

FTC was seen as easier to influence than the FDA.[12] A significant amount of the floor debate implied that the FTC was too weak for the task of regulating food, drugs, and cosmetic advertising. The abuses of the patent medicine industry and that industry's continued perseverance despite the existence of the FTC and FDA were evidence that the laws needed strengthening. Indeed, several members of Congress, describing nostrums varying from innocuous wastes of money to deforming poisons, wanted broader, criminal penalties for false advertising.

But in addition to business contests over regulatory strength, there were serious concerns about the plight of the consumer. Senator Wheeler was motivated by a number of concerns in proposing amendments to the FTC Act. Wheeler wanted to reverse the *Raladam*[13] limitation on the FTC, thus allowing the Agency to police deception of the public without explicit evidence of harm to competitors. Removing this limitation served another goal – to quicken the pace of FTC actions, which historically have been critiqued as too slow and involving too much government expense. To temper concerns about government power, Congressmen emphasized that the FTC Act's purpose was preventative, cooperative, and not penal.[14] Wheeler's argument is one of the most enduring and most powerful reasons why one should be skeptical of giving the FTC civil penalty authority – with its broad jurisdiction and mandate, a grant of penalty authority could allow the Agency to trample on due process rights.

Others were concerned that the existing cease and desist order process was too weak to deal with wily advertisers, who could subtly change their advertising, or just ignore it until enforced by a court. Representative John Coffee gave the example of Welch Grape Juice, which continued to advertise itself as a weight loss remedy (indeed, its company advised consumers to drink grape juice, which is more caloric than Coca-Cola, before meals and bedtime to lose weight) months after agreeing to discontinue such representations.[15]

### Substance of the Wheeler–Lea Amendments

The Wheeler–Lea Amendments significantly broadened the scope of FTC power by allowing the Agency to prevent "unfair or deceptive acts or practices" in addition to "unfair methods of competition."[16] Congress did not define "unfair or deceptive acts or practices," thus empowering the Agency to determine the bounds of commercial

---

[12]   Inger L. Stole, ADVERTISING ON TRIAL: CONSUMER ACTIVISM AND CORPORATE PUBLIC RELATIONS IN THE 1930S (2006); David F. Cavers, *The Food, Drug, and Cosmetic Act of 1938: Its Legislative History and Its Substantive Provisions*, 6(1) L. CONTEMP. PROBS. 2 (1939); N. ENG. J. MED., WHEELER–LEA ACT 846 (May 19, 1938).

[13]   283 US 643 (1931).

[14]   Amendments to the Federal Trade Commission Act, To Accompany S. 1077, Sen. Rep. No. 221, 75th Cong. 1st Sess.

[15]   Speech of the Honorable John M. Coffee, 83 CONG. REC. APPENDIX 1002–1007 (January 18, 1938).

[16]   Federal Trade Commission Act, Pub. L. No. 75–447, §3, 52 Stat. 111 (1938).

decency. A statutory maximum fine of $5,000 was set for violations of the Agency's final orders.[17] Commission orders, which previously had no force until the Agency petitioned a court, would now become final (if not appealed) 60 days after they were issued. The Agency was further empowered to address the dissemination of materially misleading advertisements of foods, drugs, devices, and cosmetics.[18] The FDA was given authority over the labeling of these products.[19]

As with the original FTC Act, Congress chose a broad, vaguely defined mandate to address consumer protection. The benefit of this open-ended mandate was great flexibility to address new problems. For instance, during the first thirty years of the FTC, the Agency focused on print advertising. With the rise of radio advertising, the Agency was able to pivot and investigate false claims on the airwaves,[20] without having to await enactment of a new law. Similarly, in the late 1940s with the spread of television into Americans' households, the FTC pivoted again to focus on television broadcast advertising, with broadcasters submitting sampled programming that was reviewed by the Agency.[21] With innovations in advertising, such as the mock-up (a demonstration of a product's features or functions), the FTC again crafted its advertising review to carefully examine the kinds of misimpressions that can be left by demonstrations.[22] (This meant that some FTC employees went to work and watched television as part of their duties to screen demonstrations, resulting in some predictable problems.) The flexible approach adopted in Section 5 enabled the Agency to take up privacy in the 1990s without an internet privacy statute.

---

[17] *Id.*

[18] *Id.* at §4.

[19] In 1971, the FDA and FTC developed a memorandum of understanding in which the FDA is responsible for the advertising for prescription drugs, and labeling of food, drugs, and cosmetics. The FTC is responsible for the advertising of foods, cosmetics, and medical devices.

[20] "The Commission, on May 16, 1934, requested all networks, transcription companies, and individual broadcasting stations to file with it duplicate copies of their advertising continuities. To this request all of the 10 networks, all of the 596 broadcasting stations, and practically all of the transcription companies which make commercial continuities have responded. This cooperation has been most gratifying. The Commission has already received approximately 180,000 continuities, of which it has made preliminary detailed examination of almost 150,000. Of the latter number, more than 125,000 were found unobjectionable and filed without further action, while about 21,000 were distributed among members of the special board of investigation for further checking. There remained approximately 33,000 continuities to be examined. In all cases where false and misleading advertising is found, the Commission is applying substantially the same procedure as is followed in cases of false and misleading advertising in newspapers and periodicals." FTC, ANNUAL REPORT ON THE FEDERAL TRADE COMMISSION FOR THE FISCAL YEAR ENDED JUNE 30, 1934 (1934).

[21] By the 1950s, the FTC was reviewing thousands of television transcripts and investigating over 1,000 a year. Peter Braton Turk, The Federal Trade Commission Hearings on Modern Advertising Practices: A Continuing Inquiry into Television Advertising (1977)(Ph.D. dissertation, University of Wisconsin, Madison).

[22] *FTC v. Colgate-Palmolive Co.*, 380 US 374 (1965)("the undisclosed use of plexiglass in the present commercials was a material deceptive practice, independent and separate from the other misrepresentation found").

ON MAN CONTROLLING TRADE

Almost two hundred and fifty artists submitted models in a competition for public sculptures to accompany the Federal Trade Commission. The Works Progress Administration artist Michael Lantz (1908–1988) won the "Apex Competition," named so because the statuaries would be placed at the apex of Federal Triangle. Lantz, surviving on a $94/month job, won $46,500 for the competition (about $750,000 in today's dollars), sparking media attention and even an offer to marry from a California woman.

Lantz' two statues depict a powerful man restraining an enormous horse, and stand alongside the FTC building. Titled *Man Controlling Trade*, the works have received varying interpretations by observers of the Commission:

"The horse, representing big business, with its dynamic energy suggests that it could easily go on a rampage and leave a path of destruction behind it, oblivious to its own actions. The muscular man stripped to the waist standing beside the horse and gripping its reins symbolizes the federal government, which through intelligence and restraint forces the horse to submit its power to a useful purpose. This 1937 monument is an insightful interpretation of what George Rublee and the Progressive Party sought in an antitrust program. Had the New Freedom platform as originally proposed by Louis Brandeis succeeded, there would be no such monument – there would be no such horse."[23]

"Had [Lantz] accepted Congressman Emanuel Celler's animal symbolism, he perhaps would have depicted the FTC restraining a goat labeled the consumer. But he apparently took his inspiration from what Congress intended in 1914 rather than what the FTC has become."[24]

"The FTC has become the horse and consumers the man ... So powerful and harmful an agency must be constrained. Consumers simply cannot afford otherwise."[25]

"It is said that the artist intended to portray the application of reins upon the wild practices of industry. It is equally symbolic, however, of business as a dumb animal being subjected to the arbitrary will of its master."[26]

## *Post-Wheeler–Lea and the Robinson–Patman Act*

Post-Wheeler–Lea, the Supreme Court fully recognized the broad mandate given to the FTC by Congress. The FTC brought a new matter against Raladam for its

---

[23] Marc Eric McClure, EARNEST ENDEAVORS: THE LIFE AND PUBLIC WORK OF GEORGE RUBLEE (2003).

[24] LOUIS M. KOHLMEIER, JR., THE REGULATORS: WATCHDOG AGENCIES AND THE PUBLIC INTEREST (1969).

[25] Timothy J. Muris, *What can be done? in* THE FEDERAL TRADE COMMISSION SINCE 1970: ECONOMIC REGULATION AND BUREAUCRATIC BEHAVIOR (1981).

[26] Willis W. Hagen, *The State of the Collective Liver of the Federal Trade Commissioners*, 47(3) MARQUETTE L. REV. 342 (1963).

marketing of Marmola in 1935, and by the time the Court took up the case in 1942 it upheld the Commission's order.[27] The Supreme Court refused to review a 10th Circuit decision rejecting a due process and delegation challenge to the amendments.[28]

The Agency's antitrust mission was also expanded during this era. In 1936, Congress enacted the Robinson–Patman Act, which prohibited some forms of price discrimination.[29] The Act was intended to be a pro-small business measure, passed to remedy the problem that large, chain stores could demand special discounts from suppliers.[30] An FTC Bureau of Economics report found that chain store discounts were not being passed on to consumers, and thus small businesses were being squeezed, yet consumers were not benefiting from the advantages brought about by larger, chain stores. Many view Robinson–Patman as an uneconomical intervention, one that was perversely applied against small businesses in many matters, for instance, when they attempt to organize collectively to compete with larger chains. Much of the policy and economic critique of the FTC is based upon its responsibilities under Robinson–Patman, and this critique reflects a larger ideological disagreement with the act's assumptions. One only need look at Wal-Mart to see that large chain stores today can create unimagined efficiency by making demands to cut costs of suppliers, and pass these savings onto consumers.

In the following decades, the FTC busied itself with many activities that were not strategic or efficient uses of its resources. The Agency maintained a Bureau of Industry Guidance and issued thousands of advisory opinions to businesses, an activity shunned by the modern commission. Organized around functional lines (with an entire bureau devoted to policing textile and fur representations), matters seemed to delve into the irrelevant. Among other things, the Agency released rules on the leather content of men's waist belts.[31]

---

[27] *FTC v. Raladam*, 316 US 149 (1942). See also Conference Report Agreed To by Senate, 83 CONG. REC. 4430–4436 (March 14, 1938). ("[The FTC has] been unsuccessful because the unscrupulous vendors of nostrums were secure in the knowledge that no penalty was risked for any number of publications of false advertisements occurring up to the time an [cease and desist] order became effective ... When that effective date arrives these scoundrels change to some other misrepresentation, or change their commodities in some trifling manner and start all over again – safely insulated against all risk.")

[28] *Ostler Candy Co v. FTC*, 106 F.2d 962 (10th Cir. 1939), *cert. denied, Glade Candy Co. v. FTC*, 309 US 675 (1940).

[29] "That it shall be unlawful for any person engaged in commerce, in the course of such commerce, either directly or indirectly, to discriminate in price between different purchasers of commodities of like grade and quality ... where the effect of such discrimination may be substantially to lessen competition or tend to create a monopoly in any line of commerce, or to injure, destroy, or prevent competition with any person", 74 Cong. Ch. 592, June 19, 1936, 49 Stat. 1526 §2.

[30] Kirstin Downey, *Robinson–Patman Act Devised to Save Main Street Shops, in* THE INSIDER'S GUIDE TO THE HISTORY OF THE FEDERAL TRADE COMMISSION (Kirstin Downey & Lesette Heath eds., 2015).

[31] FTC, THE FEDERAL TRADE COMMISSION DURING THE ADMINISTRATION OF PRESIDENT LYNDON B. JOHNSON, NOVEMBER 1963–JANUARY 1969 (1969). Styled as a history, this is an FTC-written report on the Agency's activities. Its appendix contains the complete text of FTC News Summaries from 1963 to 1969.

## THE RISE OF CONSUMERISM

The third wave of consumer protection was recognized as an "ism": consumerism. As a political movement, consumerism was skeptical of markets and favored expanded consumer rights for individuals.[32] Consumerism was reflected in public policy, with Congress passing a growing number of consumer rights bills, and with increases in media attention to consumer issues.[33]

While the Commission of the 1960s was considered ineffectual and focused on trivia, it began to advance in sophistication and power in that decade. The 1961 appointment of commissioner Philip Elman was a turning point. While at the Department of Justice, Elman earned fame for his proposal of the "with all deliberate speed" standard for racial integration of the public schools in *Brown v. Board of Education*. Elman had a strategic mind and strong desire to elevate the reputation of the Agency. Elman proposed a number of advances that increased commission productivity and moved the Agency toward structural, rather than case-by-case, intervention. Mary Gardiner Jones, the first female commissioner, was also appointed during this period. commissioner Jones too was concerned about policy leadership. She interacted with the academic community and was one of the more aggressive critics of advertising. Her speeches sometimes included references to critical theorists, including Herbert Marcuse. In 1971, rumors circulated that she might be the first female nominee to the Supreme Court.

---

PRESIDENT KENNEDY: CONSUMER BILL OF RIGHTS, MARCH 15, 1962

To the Congress of the United States:

> Consumers, by definition, include us all. They are the largest economic group in the economy, affecting and affected by almost every public and private economic decision. Two-thirds of all spending in the economy is by consumers. But they are the only important group in the economy who are not effectively organized, whose views are often not heard . . .

> The march of technology – affecting, for example, the foods we eat, the medicines we take, and the many appliances we use in our homes – has increased the difficulties of the consumer along with his opportunities; and it has outmoded many of the old laws and regulations and made new legislation necessary. The typical supermarket before World War II stocked about 1,500 separate food items – an impressive figure by any standard. But today it carries over 6,000. Ninety percent of the prescriptions written today are for drugs that

---

[32] David A. Aaker & George S. Day, *A Guide to Consumerism, in* CONSUMERISM: SEARCH FOR THE CONSUMER INTEREST (Aaker & Day, eds., 2nd edn, 1974).

[33] MARK V. NADEL, THE POLITICS OF CONSUMER PROTECTION (1971).

were unknown twenty years ago. Many of the new products used every day in the home are highly complex. The housewife is called upon to be an amateur electrician, mechanic, chemist, toxicologist, dietitian, and mathematician – but she is rarely furnished the information she needs to perform these tasks proficiently.

Marketing is increasingly impersonal. Consumer choice is influenced by mass advertising utilizing highly developed arts of persuasion. The consumer typically cannot know whether drug preparations meet minimum standards of safety, quality, and efficacy. He usually does not know how much he pays for consumer credit; whether one prepared food has more nutritional value than another; whether the performance of a product will in fact meet his needs; or whether the "large economy size" is really a bargain.

Nearly all of the programs offered by this Administration – e.g., the expansion of world trade, the improvement of medical care, the reduction of passenger taxes, the strengthening of mass transit, the development of conservation and recreation areas and low-cost power – are of direct or inherent importance to consumers. Additional legislative and administrative action is required, however, if the Federal Government is to meet its responsibility to consumers in the exercise of their rights. These rights include:

(1) The right to safety: to be protected against the marketing of goods which are hazardous to health or life.

(2) The right to be informed: to be protected against fraudulent, deceitful, or grossly misleading information, advertising, labeling, or other practices, and to be given the facts he needs to make an informed choice.

(3) The right to choose: to be assured, wherever possible, access to a variety of products and services at competitive prices; and in those industries in which competition is not workable and Government regulation is substituted, an assurance of satisfactory quality and service at fair prices.

(4) The right to be heard: to be assured that consumer interests will receive full and sympathetic consideration in the formulation of Government policy, and fair and expeditious treatment in its administrative tribunals.

To promote the fuller realization of these consumer rights, it is necessary that existing Government programs be strengthened, that Government organization be improved, and, in certain areas, that new legislation be enacted.[34]

---

[34]  108 Cong. Rec. 4263 (1962).

### Innovation in consumer interventions

In 1962, influenced by Elman, the Commission amended its procedure to create binding trade regulation rules, in an attempt to reach a broader array of business activity with limited agency resources. One of the first trade regulation rules concerned cigarette advertising, and it includes an extensive discussion of the Agency's authority written by commissioner Elman.[35] Elman wanted the cigarette industry to be the first to challenge the Agency's authority to propose rules. The Agency's exegesis on its authority and the dangers of smoking take up fifty pages in the Federal Register.

Commissioner Elman's leadership resulted in some of the Agency's most important legal theories. One example was Elman's argument that mock-ups could deceive. In 1961, the Commission held that a demonstration of the quality of a razor was misleading. The television demonstration showed the razor shaving sandpaper, but in reality it could not do this, and so the advertiser simulated sandpaper by showing the razor scrape sand off a piece of Plexiglas. While controversial at the time, the Supreme Court upheld Elman's deception theory.[36] In 1963, David Ogilvy wrote that the FTC's activity against mock-ups had sensitized the American consumer to fakery, and thus advertisers had to be even more ingenious in creating believable demonstrations.[37]

---

#### THE SURGEON GENERAL'S REPORT OF 1964 AND THE CIGARETTE RULE

The FTC often experiences blowback when it does its job well. Consider the FTC's dutiful attempt to quickly require warning labels on cigarettes following the seminal 1964 surgeon general's report. The commissioners gathered on a Saturday morning to read the long-anticipated report (it was released on the weekend to avoid affecting the stock market). As told by then commissioner Philip Elman to Professor Norman I. Silber,[38] Chairman Paul Rand Dixon was deeply affected by the report:

> Dixon read the report, read the conclusions, and he put down his cigarette and said, 'That's my last cigarette.' He stopped smoking cigarettes right then and there. He started talking about his boys and how worried he was

---

[35] Trade Regulation Rules: Unfair or Deceptive Advertising and Labeling of Cigarettes, In Relation to the Health Hazards of Smoking, 29 C.F.R. 8324 (July 2, 1964). The FTC approach was upheld in *National Petroleum Refiners Ass'n v. Federal Trade Commission* 482 F.2d 672 (1973). The *National Petroleum* case led to the adoption of the Magnuson–Moss Warranty Act, discussed below.

[36] *FTC v. Colgate-Palmolive Co.*, 380 US 374 (1965).

[37] David Ogilvy, Confessions of an Advertising Man 161 (1963).

[38] Norman I. Silber, With All Deliberate Speed: The Life of Philip Elman (2004).

that his boys were smoking cigarettes. That report had an enormous effect on Dixon personally.

Elman, working with then lawyer Richard Posner (now Judge Posner), within a week developed and persuaded the other commissioners to release a notice of proposed rule-making that specified an option of two different strong warnings for cigarettes:

"CAUTION: cigarette smoking is dangerous to your health and may cause death from cancer and other diseases"

"CAUTION – CIGARETTE SMOKING IS A HEALTH HAZARD. The Surgeon General's Advisory Committee has found that 'cigarette smoking contributes to mortality from specific diseases and to the overall death rate' "

The FTC stood up to formidable political opposition, with the President, Congress, powerful law firms, advertisers, and broadcasters all against the proposed warning, and yet managed to approve the cigarette rule in just 5 months.

But in the end, Congress intervened, mandating the rather milquetoast: "Cigarette smoking may be hazardous to your health." It also barred the FTC from specifying stronger warnings on packs or advertising of them, and pre-empted the states from similar measures.

The former *Wall Street Journal* reporter Louis M. Kohlmeier recounted, "After Congress slapped down the FTC, a grateful tobacco industry demonstrated its thanks with cash ... at least $10,490 [most of which was] divided among members of the House Commerce Committee."[39]

Consider that in retrospect that the FTC was not only right about cigarettes causing cancer and death, but might also have headed off lawsuits by smokers who claimed they did not know smoking was harmful. If the FTC's bold, accurate warning had been embraced by Congress, the FTC could have protected the cigarette industry from itself.

The 1960s FTC developed other innovative approaches to consumer problems. In August 1965, the Watts riots left dozens dead and caused tens of millions in property damage. The perceived unfairness of urban retailers contributed to rioters attacking businesses in their own neighborhoods. Attention to the consumer protection problems of the urban poor became a class and racial justice issue.[40]

In response to the riots, the FTC established a program to better understand and bring more enforcement against consumer problems facing the poor in Washington,

---

[39] Louis M. Kohlmeier, Jr., The Regulators: Watchdog Agencies and the Public Interest (1969).

[40] *See generally,* Mary Gardiner Jones, *The Federal Trade Commission in 1968: Times of Turmoil and Response,* 7 J. Pub. Pol'y Mktg. 1 (1988); Frederick D. Sturdivant, The Ghetto Marketplace (1969); Eric Schnapper, *Consumer Legislation and the Poor,* 76(4) Yale L. J. 745 (1967).

DC.[41] The Commission's investigation uncovered many basic problems. For instance, the Agency had to be innovative to even document consumer complaints, because the Agency found that the poor were unlikely to make a complaint to the government. Just getting in touch with consumers was difficult. The FTC partnered with community organizations and even examined local court records to find businesses that sued consumers and garnished wages. It was thought that these retailers might be engaging in the most aggressive practices toward consumers.

*FTC Timeline: 1960–1979*

| Year | Month | Event | Relevance |
|------|-------|-------|-----------|
| 1960 | 12 | Landis Report | Recommended centralizing more power in the Chair, reform of ex parte communications |
| 1962 |   | Auerbach Report | Among other things, recommended a focus on national advertising |
| 1962 | 5 | FTC announces policy to create trade regulation rules, advisory opinions | Industry-wide rules were an attempt to reach more business activity with limited agency resources |
| 1962 | 3 | President Kennedy Consumer Bill of Rights | Four rights articulated, legislation proposed, signaling rebirth of consumer movement |
| 1964 | 1 | President's Committee on Consumer Interests formed | Outgrown of Consumer Bill of Rights |
| 1964 | 1 | Esther Peterson named Special Presidential Assistant for Consumer Affairs | First in a series of chiefs for consumer protection |
| 1965 | 5 | Ralph Nader writes *Unsafe at Any Speed* | Sells hundreds of thousands of copies, directing attention toward design of cars instead of driver error |
| 1965 | 7 | Federal Cigarette Labeling and Advertising Act | Requiring health warnings on labels and advertising; watered-down FTC's warning label |
| 1965 |   | FTC begins District of Columbia Consumer Program | Report detailed problems with credit marketing and practices to the poor |
| 1966 |   | Amendments to Rule 23 on class actions | Created the modern class action, where individuals must opt out of the suit |

*(Continued)*

---

[41]  FTC, Report on District of Columbia Consumer Protection Program (June 1968).

(Continued).

| Year | Month | Event | Relevance |
|------|-------|-------|-----------|
| 1966 | 7 | FTC proposes model state mini-FTC acts | Subsequently enacted state unfair and deceptive practices acts are often broader than the FTC Act |
| 1966 | 11 | Fair Packaging and Labeling Act | Directed FTC to develop rules for labeling consumer commodities |
| 1967 | 12 | Flammable Fabrics Act Amendments | Expanded act, transferred to CPSC in 1972 |
| 1968 | 3 | Kerner Report on race riots released | Listed "discriminatory consumer and credit practices" as one of twelve deeply held grievances driving race riots |
| 1968 | 5 | Consumer Credit Protection Act | Known as the Truth in Lending Act |
| 1968 | 6 | FTC Promotes Uniform State Unfair Trade Practice Act | A formal proposal for mini-FTC acts for the states |
| 1968 | 9 | *Pfizer* v. *FTC* Decided by 6th Circuit | Appeals court upholds FTC's remedy requiring compulsory licensing of tetracycline |
| 1969 | 1 | Nader Report | This vitriolic attack on the FTC's Chairman, Paul Rand Dixon, led to study and reform |
| 1969 | 9 | ABA Report | A more sober, but strong attack, following the Nader Report, triggers substantial reform |
| 1970 | 7 | Newspaper Preservation Act of 1970 | Exempted newspapers from some antitrust prohibitions |
| 1970 | 7 | Weinberger Reorganization Plan | Staff slashed, power centralized, focus turns to structural cases, modern Consumer Protection/Competition Bureau structure created |
| 1970 | 10 | Fair Credit Reporting Act | First federal information privacy law; FTC prohibited from rule-making under it |
| 1971 | 1 | Ash Council Report | Recommended abolition of commissioners in favor of a single agency leader, separate antitrust and consumer protection agencies |
| 1972 | | Advertising Substantiation Program begins | Required advertisers to have proof of factual product claims |

*(Continued)*

(Continued).

| Year | Month | Event | Relevance |
|------|-------|-------|-----------|
| 1972 | 3 | FTC v. Sperry & Hutchinson | Power of FTC to proscribe activities as unfair or deceptive to protect consumers upheld |
| 1973 | 6 | *National Petroleum v. FTC* | DC Circuit upholds FTC's authority to promulgate trade regulation rules which have the effect of law |
| 1973 | 11 | Cooling-off period rule | Gave consumers a three-day window to cancel door-to-door sales, 16 CFR 429 |
| 1973 | 11 | Trans-Alaska Pipeline Act | Gave FTC injunction power, power to appear in court directly, upped fines from $5,000 to $10,000 |
| 1975 | 1 | Magnuson–Moss Warranty–Federal Trade Commission Improvements Act | Substantial increase in agency power: it could sue directly under the FTC Act, seek consumer redress, seek civil penalties, establish trade regulation rules |
| 1975 | 12 | Energy Policy Conservation Act | Required commission to develop energy labels for appliances |
| 1976 | 8 | *Spiegel v. FTC* | FTC's unfairness power may be applied against acts legal under a state's law |
| 1976 | 9 | Hart–Scott–Rodino Antitrust Improvements Act of 1976 | Established premerger notification requirements |
| 1977 | 8 | *Warner–Lambert Co. v. FTC* | DC Circuit affirms order requiring corrective advertising concerning Listerine |
| 1977 | 9 | Fair Debt Collection Practices Act | Proscribes certain kinds of debt collection activities |

In order to engage poor consumers, the Agency had to meet with them at their places of employment, in the evenings, and on the weekends.[42] The FTC found that the most cited complaints among the poor were bait-and-switch selling and deceptive marketing claims. A study by the Bureau of Economics found that the average goods purchased at wholesale for $100 cost $255 in low-income stores versus $159 in general market stores. However, much of the difference in price was related to other economic factors, such as less efficient selling methods and higher credit losses.[43]

---

[42] Susan Wagner, The Federal Trade Commission 194–196 (1971).
[43] FTC, Economic Report on Installment Credit and Retail Sales Practices of District of Columbia Retailers (1968).

Still, the report suggested an absence of effective price competition and that "ghetto" retailers were competing by making "easy credit" easier.[44] The focus on lowering transaction costs to obtain credit obscured the higher prices being charged.

The "holder in due course doctrine" also emerged in the 1960s as a major consumer problem. This doctrine allows a third party to purchase debt, but immunizes the new debt holder from claims against the seller of the merchandise. Under the doctrine, individuals inexperienced in credit sales found themselves defrauded by a seller, yet bound to pay a third party that argued it was not responsible for the seller's misbehavior. In 1976, the FTC promulgated the "holder rule" to preserve buyers' claims against anyone who holds a consumer credit contract or purchase money loan.[45]

### The Nader and American Bar Association reports

Despite Elman's advances, the Commission was regarded as ineffectual, with critics referring to it as the "little old lady of Pennsylvania Avenue."[46] Intense scrutiny was focused on the Agency's shortcomings in January 1969 when consumer advocate Ralph Nader released a biting report on the FTC. At the time, Nader was a well-known automobile safety activist. His 1965 book, *Unsafe at Any Speed*, focused on design choices in automobile manufacturing and argued that cars were dangerous by design.[47] After publication of the book, General Motors led a campaign to discredit Nader and invaded his privacy so egregiously that Nader won a suit against the company.[48] Nader's work was a major factor in creation of the National Highway Traffic Safety Administration, and after these successes in the automobile industry, Nader focused on other consumer protection issues.

The Nader report on the FTC roundly critiqued the Agency, identifying it as pathologically fixated on small, trivial matters, and painting Chairman Paul Rand Dixon's hand-selected leadership as his cronies.[49] A group of students

---

[44] FTC, News Release: Advertising and Unfair Practices (Docket 8714), December 14, 1968. (Respondent "promises people 'easy credit' and induces them to sign credit contracts ... while at the same time charging prices which are greatly in excess of that other retailers charge, knowing that such customers are unaware of this fact.")

[45] The rule requires the following statement in consumer credit contracts: "ANY HOLDER OF THIS CONSUMER CREDIT CONTRACT IS SUBJECT TO ALL CLAIMS AND DEFENSES WHICH THE DEBTOR COULD ASSERT AGAINST THE SELLER OF GOODS OR SERVICES OBTAINED WITH THE PROCEEDS HEREOF ..." FTC, Trade Regulation Rule Concerning the Preservation of Consumers' Claims and Defenses (The Holder Rule), 16 C.F.R. §433.

[46] The first use of this phrase appears to come from commissioner Lowell Mason, in a speech at the annual New York State Bar Association Antitrust Law Symposium in 1964. Lowell B. Mason, *A Funny Thing Happened on the Way to the Federal Trade Commission*, 1964 N.Y. State Bar Association Antitrust Law Symposium 1 (1964).

[47] Ralph Nader, Unsafe at Any Speed (1965).

[48] *Nader v. Gen. Motors Corp.*, 25 N.Y.2d 560, 255 N.E.2d 765 (1970).

[49] The report was read into the Congressional Record; *see* The Consumer and The Federal Trade Commission, 115 Cong. Rec. 1539 (January 22, 1969). Years earlier, the Administrative Conference had made recommendations that the FTC focus on more structural, national cases. *See* Carl A. Auerbach,

from elite law schools wrote the data-heavy report in a single summer – President Taft's great-grandson was one of the authors (he went on to advise later FTC Chairman Caspar Weinberger). In a strident tone and often employing language one normally does not find in a Washington report,[50] the students argued that the Agency had misplaced priorities: while consumer complaints had dramatically risen, the Commission had diminished its enforcement caseload; instead of bringing hard-hitting enforcement actions and naming wrongdoers, the Commission had shifted to "assurances of voluntary compliance" that kept the names of violating companies secret; and the Agency took too long to resolve matters and did not invoke enough civil penalties. According to the report, the average investigation from inception to complaint took over two years, and in the preceding four years, the Agency had only imposed $400,000 in civil penalties (about $2.5 million in today's dollars). The students found one high-level agency attorney asleep under a copy of the *Washington Post*, roused him, and determined that his work entailed "very little." The report personally attacked Kennedy-appointed Chairman Dixon, and compared his tenure to the notorious Coolidge-appointed Chairman, William Humphrey (see Chapter 1). The report portrayed Dixon personally as an indolent crony who had packed the Agency with second-rate attorneys from his home state, Tennessee. Dixon was seen at the center of a circus, satisfying political favors largely by appointing his fellow Southerners to high-level staff positions, and requiring staff to make contributions to the Democratic Party. The report called for his resignation.

---

### THE TENNESSEE GANG

In 1967, with regional offices in large population centers such as Boston, New York City, Houston, and Atlanta, why would the FTC create a new office in Oak Ridge, Tennessee (population 28,000)?

The Nader Report in 1969 critiqued the FTC's cronyism, particularly with political forces from Tennessee. The Yale and Harvard students on the Nader team highlighted that applicants from the "mediocre" University of Tennessee were being hired at greater rates than law students from elite eastern universities. Commissioner Philip Elman saw too much political cronyism that

---

ADMINISTRATIVE CONFERENCE OF THE UNITED STATES, REPORT ON THE INTERNAL ORGANIZATION AND PROCEDURE OF THE FEDERAL TRADE COMMISSION (1962).

[50] "Traditionally, the most serious threats to the American public, the most dangerous economic crises, have occurred when changing business practices bypass market pressure and subvert the legitimate operating principles of free enterprise, sometimes becoming in themselves reified symbols of worship. In such a case the resultant system can resemble in practice the monolithic structure of a communist economic system – the economy allied with the state in an impregnable combination."

rewarded Southerners: "There was a Tennessee gang in the Commission, a Texas gang, a North Carolina gang ..."[51]

The Oak Ridge office was a political favor from then Chairman Paul Rand Dixon to the leader of the House committee that made appropriations for the FTC, also a Tennessean. The favor allowed a local county judge to double his salary and stay close to home. The Nader students called the office over a dozen times, but could not get anyone to answer.

An award-winning investigative journalist for the *Wall Street Journal*, Jerry Landauer, wrote: "The so-called Tennessee gang dominates the FTC today no less than in the heyday of Tennessee Democrat Kenneth McKellar, chairman of the Senate Appropriations subcommittee who constantly pestered President Franklin Roosevelt for jobs. FDR obligingly let the Senator install friends at the FTC, presumably because the damage would be minimal. After Estes Kefauver succeeded Mr. McKellar in the Senate, Tennessee's hold hardened; the big favor Tennessean Kefauver wrangled from President Kennedy was Tennessean Dixon's appointment as FTC Chairman."

The Oak Ridge office was closed by 1976.

Dixon responded formally to the report, framing it as a smear campaign against the small agency.[52] Dixon argued that the Agency had a positive view of businesspeople, while the Nader students viewed business with suspicion. In fairness to Dixon, one should note that the Nader report did not cite a single success of the Agency or of Dixon, despite that under his leadership, many bold initiatives were pursued.[53] Dixon concluded by recounting some of the great successes of the FTC during his era, including the cigarette rule (see box on the rule) and the Agency's contribution to the Truth in Lending Act. But others were unmentioned by Dixon, such as the pursuit of both manufacturer and advertising agency in matters,[54] and pursuit of matters where the Agency required affirmative disclosures from fraudulent advertisers.[55] Then

---

[51] NORMAN I. SILBER, WITH ALL DELIBERATE SPEED, THE LIFE OF PHILIP ELMAN (2004).

[52] Statement of Chairman Paul Rand Dixon, 115 CONG. REC. 1568 (January 22, 1969).

[53] For a spirited defense of Dixon's tenure, *see* BERNICE ROTHMAN HASIN, CONSUMERS, COMMISSIONS, AND CONGRESS: LAW, THEORY, AND THE FEDERAL TRADE COMMISSION, 1968–1985 40 (1987). Hasin argued that "[u]pon reexamination, then, Dixon, far from incompetent, was keenly attuned to the political climate and expert at walking the fine line of the Agency's responsibilities"; *see also* Mary Gardiner Jones, *The Federal Trade Commission in 1968: Times of Turmoil and Response*, 7 J. PUB. POL'Y MKTG. 1 (1988).

[54] *Doherty, Clifford, Steers & Shenfield, Inc.* v. *FTC*, 392 F.2d 921 (6th Cir. 1968)(affirming order "precluding pharmaceutical company from representing that its throat lozenge would kill or have any effect upon germs contributing to an existing throat infection"); *Carter Products, Inc.* v. *FTC*, 323 F.2d 523 (5th Cir. 1963)(FTC did not abuse its authority in ordering an advertising agency to desist from practices where the advertising agency participated in the deception).

[55] Affirmative disclosure has its roots in the 1940s, but victories in this space continued with the notable case against vitamin "Geritol," where the company made misleading claims concerning fatigue and vitamin deficiency. *J. B. Williams Co.* v. *FTC*, 381 F.2d 884 (6th Cir. 1967). *See also* William L. Wilkie,

Commissioner Philip Elman, a critic of Dixon, greatly aided the Nader researchers. Many of the Nader report's themes proved consonant with Elman's critique of Dixon as a crony. Elman described two of the other commissioners as do-nothing drunks, and one as a buffoon who liked being a commissioner because it allowed him to travel. As Elman saw it, the Commission had a very pro-small business posture, leading to uneconomical application of policy.[56]

President Nixon then requested an evaluation of the FTC by the more temperate American Bar Association. Led by Miles W. Kirkpatrick and with Robert Pitofsky as counsel (both later FTC Chairmen), it made findings similar to the Nader group.[57] The ABA critiqued the FTC's lack of planning and noted that it was focused on trivial matters. For instance, the Agency investigated wool manufacturers for stating that a product was 90 percent wool when it was really 93 or 89 percent. The ABA report recommended reform of ex parte contacts between businesses and commissioners, along with a devolution of power to staff so that commissioners would appear to be acting less as judge and jury over matters. The ABA recommended that field offices have full power to operate proceedings in the deceptive advertising field.

### Posner's separate statement

The ABA report was accompanied by a particularly harsh "separate statement" written by then Professor, now Judge Richard Posner. Posner, a former FTC attorney-advisor to commissioner Elman, dismissed much of the Agency's consumer protection activities as pointless and misdirected.[58] To Posner, the FTC as a venture was unsound and its flaws were a product of its structure, rather than of poor implementation. Posner's critique, discussed in Chapter 12 again in depth, forms the basis for most conservative critique of the FTC, including modern objections to the Agency's policing of privacy.

On the competition side, Posner argued that the FTC was inferior to the Department of Justice's Antitrust Division;[59] that structurally the FTC would not

---

*Affirmative Disclosure at the FTC: Objectives for the Remedy and Outcomes of Past Orders*, 4 J. Pub. Pol'y Mktg. 91 (1985).

[56] Norman I. Silber, With All Deliberate Speed, The Life of Philip Elman (2004).

[57] American Bar Association, Report of the ABA Commission to Study the Federal Trade Commission (September 15, 1969). *See also*, Thomas L. Bohen, An Analysis of the Formal and Informal Enforcement Procedures of the Federal Trade Commission As Devices for Restraining Unfair Methods of Competition and Unfair and Deceptive Business Practices (1971)(Ph.D. dissertation, University of Minnesota)("the Commission has not allocated its resources in terms of the formal and informal enforcement procedures into all of the important industries in the economy; into the most concentrated industries in the economy; nor into the most serious forms of economic abuse.")

[58] He later wrote a more substantiated version of the statement as a law review article, and then as a monograph. Richard A. Posner, *The Federal Trade Commission*, 37(1) U. Chi. L. Rev. 47 (1969); Richard A. Posner, Regulation of Advertising by the FTC (1973).

[59] This echoes a 1952 critique. *See* William Simon, *The Case Against the Federal Trade Commission*, 19(2) U. Chi. L. Rev. 297 (1952).

attract great talent, because federal judgeships are more remunerative than the Agency's administrative judges; and that 99.5 percent of the Agency's antitrust matters were misguided.

Turning to consumer fraud issues, Posner questioned the very need for government enforcement against deceptive practices. Consumers could rely upon their own skepticism in many situations, and in others competition would give sellers an incentive to treat customers fairly. Many commission actions were at the behest of competitors, who could have sued on their own without government assistance.[60] He questioned interventions to benefit the poor, because he could not think of a theory that would cause more fraud to be present in sales to the poor.[61] Posner concluded that 90 percent of the Agency's consumer activity was of questionable value, if not harm, to the economy: "Besides wasting a good deal of money in tilting at windmills, the Commission inflicted additional social costs of unknown magnitude by impeding the free marketing of cheap substitute products, including foreign products of all kinds, fiber substitutes for animal furs, costume jewelry, and inexpensive scents; by proscribing truthful designations; by harassing discount sellers; by obstructing a fair market test for products of debatable efficacy; and, most of all perhaps, simply by imposing on sellers the costs of furnishing additional information and on buyers the costs of absorbing that information ..."[62] Posner did allow that some advertising would not be policed by the market, for instance, where "the fraud embraces all close substitutes of a product, and there is consequently no incentive for competing sellers to furnish correct information or to bring suit, this has not been the emphasis of the FTC."[63] Posner's views later softened, but the core of his critique is echoed today by many.

In response to these multiple attacks from different viewpoints, a consensus emerged that the FTC was in need of reform. Commissioners Elman, Mary Gardiner Jones, and James M. Nicholson together opposed Chairman Dixon and demanded reform. The Agency formed a review group to examine the backlog of matters and ended hundreds of them, clearing the decks for the arrival of Dixon's successor, Caspar Weinberger (later, the Secretary of Defense under President Reagan). Upon dismissing hundreds of backlogged matters, a commissioner declared, "We have cleaned out the Augean stables."[64]

---

[60] Posner's critique would be better targeted at Congress, as it was widely understood that the FTC would be a forum for complaints about competitors. *See* Edward Mott Woolley, *What the Federal Trade Commission Will Do for You*, COLLIER'S WEEKLY, November 18, 1916; JOHN B. DAISH, THE FEDERAL TRADE COMMISSION LAW AND RELATED ACTS (1914).

[61] Just a year earlier, the FTC's report on the District of Columbia gave a plausible explanation: sellers in poor neighborhoods were competing on low-down payment credit offers instead of price. A year later, Albert Hirschman explained the poor marketplace as constituting "lazy" monopolies that served consumers unable to exit to higher-performing competitors. ALBERT O. HIRSCHMAN, EXIT, VOICE, AND LOYALTY 59–60 (1970).

[62] Richard A. Posner, *The Federal Trade Commission*, 37(1) U. CHI. L. REV. 47, 77–78 (1969).

[63] *Id.* at 69.

[64] *FTC Drops 70% of its Cases to Untie Hands*, 40 ADVERTISING AGE 1, 26, December 8, 1969.

---

## DOES THE FTC EFFECTIVELY REGULATE ADVERTISING?

Perhaps the better question is: *Can* the FTC (or anyone else) comprehensively regulate advertising? Writing for a fiftieth-anniversary symposium analyzing the FTC in 1964, Professor Ira M. Millstein observed:

> "it is not possible to say that the advertising 'industry' has or has not been brought to heel, or ever could be. It is impossible to prove empirically that advertising, as a result of the efforts of the Commission and others, is more or less truthful, 'better' or 'worse' than it was, for there is no one advertising industry capable of statistical evaluation. Rather advertising is an activity comprehending every company that has ever attempted to substitute for its personal salesmen some written, spoken, or visual message . . ."[65]

Consider the conclusion of the famous 1981 study by University of Chicago Professor Sam Peltzman:

> "The 'toothless tiger' image of FTC advertising regulation is wrong. Visible and sometimes very substantial effects of the regulation show up in the product market, the advertising market, and, especially, the capital markets . . . [the large loss in capital value in firms attacked by the FTC] seems even larger than the entire advertising capital of the brand, not just the part which may be due to false advertising. That finding would surely appear to imply more durable product-market effects and, perhaps, more conservative advertising scripts than we find."[66]

---

### THE 1970S: ACTION AND REACTION

In Chairman Weinberger's very short tenure, he was given wide latitude to shake up the Agency. Under his plan, Weinberger, along with FTC executive director Basil J. Mezines, centralized the control of staff and their activities in part by requiring staff attorneys to obtain permission from higher-ups to open investigations. They shifted focus from the retrospective, "mailbag" approach, where attorneys reacted to complaints that were filed by consumers, to more planned, forward-looking, structural matters. They also slashed staff. Through eliminating positions, by ostracization of staff to Kansas City, transfers to other government departments, and outright firings, Weinberger, nicknamed "Cap the Knife," eliminated half of the top-level staff and a third of the attorneys in the Bureaus of Competition and Consumer Protection, including top-level attorneys. On the policy front, Weinberger strongly advocated for both more funding and more authority for the Commission.

---

[65] Ira M. Millstein, *The Federal Trade Commission and False Advertising*, 64 COL. L. REV. 439, 440 (1964).
[66] Sam Peltzman, *The Effects of FTC Advertising Regulation*, 24(3) J. L. ECON. 403 (December 1981).

## Forces empowering the FTC

On the heels of the Weinberger reforms, the 1970s saw another dramatic expansion of commission power, on par with the 1938 Wheeler–Lea Amendments. Greater power came from the courts, Congress, activist groups, and the Agency itself. By the end of the decade, however, the FTC experienced a wave of reaction that limited its powers.

### The courts

In 1972, the Supreme Court decided *FTC v. Sperry & Hutchinson Co.*, a decision that affirmed the FTC's broad authority to define and prevent unfair practices.[67] In that case, the FTC alleged that Sperry & Hutchinson was unfairly restraining the market for "trading stamps." Trading stamps were the frequent-flier miles of the era – very popular, paper coupons distributed by merchants to consumers in order to build loyalty.[68] After the consumer collected enough stamps, they could be redeemed for various products. But unlike frequent-flier miles, trading stamps could be exchanged with other consumers. Exchanges arose to enable consumers to trade them (stamps were linked to specific merchants, and an incomplete set of stamps was worthless, thus causing consumers to trade them in order to assemble a complete set for redemption). Sperry attempted to stop this trade by contractually prohibiting consumers' distribution of the stamps to others, and the FTC thought this illegal and in violation of Section 5. Sperry argued that the FTC's actions were ultra vires, as its conduct did not violate the antitrust laws nor was immoral, and the 5th Circuit agreed.[69]

The Supreme Court reversed, affirming the Agency's power to proscribe unfair competitive practice beyond the letter of the antitrust laws, and the Agency's power to proscribe practices that harm consumers, even if there is not a corresponding harm to competition. The Court opined that the Commission "does not arrogate excessive power to itself . . . [if it] considers public values beyond simply those enshrined in the letter or encompassed in the spirit of the antitrust laws." The Court appended a footnote quoting the unfairness standard that the FTC articulated in the cigarette rule: "(1) whether the practice, without necessarily having been previously considered unlawful, offends public policy as it has been established by statutes, the common law, or otherwise – whether, in other words, it is within at least the penumbra of some common-law, statutory, or other established concept of unfairness; (2) whether it is immoral, unethical, oppressive, or unscrupulous; (3) whether it causes substantial injury to consumers (or competitors or other businessmen)."[70]

---

[67]  405 U.S. 233 (1972).

[68]  For a discussion of trading stamps, *see* Carolyn Shaw Bell, *Liberty and Property, and No Stamps*, 40(2) J. Bus. 194 (1967); E. Beem & L. Isaacson, *Schizophrenia in Trading Stamp Analysis*, 41(3) J. Bus. 340 (1968).

[69]  *FTC v. Sperry & Hutchinson*, 432 F. 2d 146 (5th Cir. 1970).

[70]  405 US 233 at Fn. 5, *citing* Statement of Basis and Purpose of Trade Regulation Rule 408, Unfair or Deceptive Advertising and Labeling of Cigarettes in Relation to the Health Hazards of Smoking, 29 Fed. Reg. 8355 (1964). The fact that this apparent endorsement appeared in a footnote instead of the

## Congress

In the 1970s, Congress had a more consumerist tone. It emphatically encouraged the Commission to become more consumer oriented, made advertising to children a priority, and passed landmark consumer protection laws.

TRANS-ALASKA PIPELINE AUTHORIZATION ACT. Congress greatly expanded the power of the FTC in 1973, through little-debated amendments to the FTC Act passed as part of the Trans-Alaska Pipeline Authorization Act.[71] The 1973 amendments increased FTC civil penalties from $5,000 to $10,000, empowered the FTC to appear in court on its own behalf after consulting with the Department of Justice (previously it could do so only in food, drug, and cosmetic cases), and empowered the Agency to demand documents from banks and common carriers if they had evidence relevant to an investigation of another entity (this latter evidentiary power is important because the FTC is statutorily barred from applying Section 5 to banks and common carriers, but at the same time it needs documents from these entities in the course of investigations of other entities).

MAGNUSON–MOSS WARRANTY ACT. In 1975, the FTC's jurisdiction was expanded through the passage of the Magnuson–Moss Warranty Act.[72] Title II of the Act contained "Federal Trade Commission Improvements," including an amendment that expanded the Agency's jurisdiction from activities "in commerce" to those that were "in or affecting commerce."[73] This amendment clarified that the Agency could address local practices that had interstate effects.

Title II codified a framework for the Agency to draft "interpretive rules and general statements of policy" defining specific practices as unfair or deceptive.[74] This was a legislative recognition of the holding in *National Petroleum* v. *FTC*, where the DC Circuit read into the FTC Act the power to create trade regulation rules that have the effect of law.[75]

But in formalizing this power, Congress added procedures that had the effect of slowing down the FTC drastically. In addition to the requirements of the Administrative Procedures Act, Magnuson–Moss required the Agency to be more specific in detailing the reasons for proposing a rule; required it to provide more opportunities for public participation in the rule-making, including informal hearings; required it to engage in more regulatory analysis, including economic analysis

---

body of the decision has led critics to claim that the Court's endorsement of the unfairness standard was lukewarm.

[71] Pub. L. No. 93–153, 87 Stat. 591, §408–409.

[72] Pub. L. 93–637, 88 Stat. 2183 (1975).

[73] *Id.* at §201.

[74] *Id.* at §202.

[75] *Nat'l Petroleum Refiners Ass'n* v. *FTC*, 482 F.2d 672 (D.C. Cir. 1973).

and considerations of the rule's effects on small business; and required it to engage in more fact-finding and justification, including stating the prevalence of an unwanted practice and the basis for considering it deceptive and/ or unfair. Prior to the rule's enforcement, interested parties can challenge it substantively or procedurally for violating these requirements. Nevertheless, the Agency quickly began rule-making, initiating seventeen proceedings in the next year.[76]

Burdensome procedures is one of the main reasons why the FTC has not sought to promulgate rules for privacy – the thought is that by the time the procedures are satisfied, any privacy rule would be out of date. The modern commission is so committed to the idea that Magnuson–Moss rule-making is too burdensome that discussion of a privacy rule is a nonstarter. There is much evidence that the Commission is correct in this judgment. In fact, some even believe that the FTC lacks rule-making authority because of the Agency's refusal to consider promulgation of a privacy rule.

HART–SCOTT–RODINO ACT. Finally, Congress further empowered the Commission with the 1976 Hart–Scott–Rodino Act. It imposed a statutory premerger notification requirement and a waiting period before covered mergers could be consummated. That law greatly expanded the Agency's ability to fashion effective relief to maintain competition in merger challenges.

### Activist groups

Following the Nader Report, liberal consumer groups took up a litigation strategy to reform the Commission. Students Opposing Unfair Practices (SOUP), Action on Safety and Health, and Students against Volvo Exaggerations (SAVE) all attempted to intervene in Commission matters, in order to suggest new remedies and to strengthen them. Their petitions caused much consternation and were denied, but the commissioners were influenced by their arguments.[77] In fact, Robert Pitofsky wrote in 1977 that "[t]he major innovations in ad regulation in the last ten years or so – ad substantiation, required disclosure of various categories of information, and corrective advertising – grew out of proposals contained in submissions by petitioning or intervening consumer advocates."[78] In addition to consumer advocates, citizens who participated in rule-makings tended to be more pro-regulation than the general public.[79]

---

[76]  FTC, ANNUAL REPORT OF THE FEDERAL TRADE COMMISSION 1976 (1976).

[77]  *See, for example*, FTC, Oral History Interview: Mary Gardiner Jones (2003).

[78]  Robert Pitofsky, *Beyond Nader: Consumer Protection and the Regulation of Advertising*, 90 HARV. L. REV. 661 (February 1977).

[79]  PRICILLA LA BARBERA, CONSUMERS AND THE FEDERAL TRADE COMMISSION: AN EMPIRICAL INVESTIGATION (1977).

## The Commission

As the 1970s proceeded, the Agency took an increasingly consumerist posture.[80] Chairman Miles Kirkpatrick, who succeeded Caspar Weinberger, focused on more aggressive advertising matters. Under Chairman Kirkpatrick, the FTC opened avenues of inquiry that would never be the topic of FTC discussion today. For instance, the FTC looked into the "planned obsolescence" of products,[81] and one official saber rattled against movie theaters that showed commercials.[82]

Kirkpatrick led the Agency's still-in-effect advertising substantiation program, which requires advertisers and advertising agencies to develop a reasonable basis for claims before they are made to consumers.[83] Substantiation caused a large reallocation of duties in advertising law – in effect, the Commission switched the burden of proof of facts from the government to the private sector where companies make express or implied claims that make objective assertions about the item or service advertised.

Other commissioners agitated to pursue larger, more structural matters. commissioner Mayo J. Thompson publicly released memos criticizing staff for bringing matters without demonstrated harm to consumers. He called for an investigation of branded prescription drugs, on the theory that they resulted in economic waste of over $200 million a year. He also urged the regional offices of the FTC to be more aggressive and even proposed a computer-based monitoring system to detect price fixing.[84]

The commissioner of the 1970s were some of the best qualified ever. There were also signals of a renewed commitment to economic justifications of policies and of enforcement of advertising rules. On the policy front, the FTC worked to eliminate state occupational licensure laws that were serving as a barrier to entry, laws that prevented certain industries and professions from price advertising, and state laws that restricted pharmacists from filling prescriptions with generics. The Agency also began a program where marketing professors were embedded in the Bureau of Consumer Protection. This led to greater sophistication in the interpretation of advertising, and, perhaps, the first agency use of copy testing (the evaluation of consumer interpretation of advertising by survey and lab experiments) in a matter.[85]

In an article published in the *Harvard Law Review*, Robert Pitofsky, who was the Director of the Bureau of Consumer Protection in the early 1970s, offered a lucid

---

[80] Kirk Victor, *Michael Pertschuk's Turbulent Years as FTC Chairman, in* THE INSIDER'S GUIDE TO THE HISTORY OF THE FEDERAL TRADE COMMISSION (Kirstin Downey & Lesette Heath eds., 2015).

[81] FTC, ANNUAL REPORT OF THE FEDERAL TRADE COMMISSION 1970 (1970).

[82] N.Y. TIMES, TRADE COMMISSION AIDE PRODS MOVIE THEATERS ON COMMERCIALS, November 6, 1977.

[83] The first substantiation case came in 1963, but limited the duty to health and safety claims. See *Kirchner v. FTC*, 337 F.2d 751 (9th Cir. 1964).

[84] The memos are reprinted in 7 ANTITRUST L. ECON. REV. 49 (1974–1975).

[85] William L. Wilkie, *My Memorable Experiences as a Marketing Academic at the Federal Trade Commission*, 33(2) J. PUB. POL'Y MKTG. 194 (2014).

explanation of the market failures that justified FTC action. Although the article's title, "Beyond Nader," suggested a rebuff to the moralism of Ralph Nader, the article spoke most directly to the 1969 ABA Report's "Separate Statement," the scathing critique of the FTC by Richard Posner.[86] Pitofsky explained the many reasons why Posner's critique failed to describe the reality of the consumer marketplace. For instance, competitors often lack incentives to sue others for false advertising, and almost never engage in counteradvertising. Also, companies had to be induced to provide critical information to consumers in several contexts. Most importantly, Pitofsky sketched a much more strategic and tempered approach to the regulation of advertising. Generally speaking, the period reflected a more nuanced under- standing of advertising, as reflected by the work of Phillip Nelson, George Alexander, and Howard Beales.[87] Later, Posner recognized these changes, partially softening his 1969 critique.[88]

---

### ON ADVERTISING ANXIETY

Americans have very different attitudes toward advertising. Some see it as promoting a richer lifestyle through providing information about the remark- able choices available to consumers.

But advertising also causes anxiety across the political spectrum. There is continuing concern that modern innovations in advertising have somehow tipped the balance of power between the firm and the person, resulting in advertisers being able to trigger irresistible impulses in the consumer. In previous eras, motivation research (studying the "why" of consumer behavior) and subliminal advertising (messages flashed to the consumer so quickly that they are not consciously perceived) were the claimed innovations. Today, it is highly tailored ads based upon tracking of past behavior.

Advertisers stoke these anxieties by making dramatic claims about these innovations – they are, after all, advertisers selling advertising. In hindsight we know claims about motivation research were inflated and that the subliminal claims were a hoax. In general, when advertisers focus on the methods of selling and describe a power to sell anything to anyone, it triggers anxiety about autonomy, and thus calls for rules of the advertising road.

---

[86]  Robert Pitofsky, *Beyond Nader: Consumer Protection and the Regulation of Advertising*, 90 HARV. L. REV. 661 (1977).

[87]  J. Howard Beales III, Richard Craswell, & Steven C. Salop, *The Efficient Regulation of Consumer Information*, 24(3) J. L. ECON. 491 (1981); Phillip Nelson, *Advertising as Information*, 82(4) J. POL. ECON. 729 (1974); GEORGE J. ALEXANDER, HONESTY AND COMPETITION: FALSE-ADVERTISING LAW AND POLICY UNDER FTC ADMINISTRATION (1967).

[88]  Richard A. Posner, *The Federal Trade Commission: A Retrospective*, 72(3) ANTITRUST L. J. 761 (2005).

Some think that advertising is wasteful in that it adds expense to products; that it promotes materialism and superficial values; that it creates "false needs;" that the worst products are advertised most loudly; that it focuses on brand loyalty instead of upon comparative characteristics; that it relies upon emotional rather than reasoned appeals; that it increases barriers to entry; that it promotes monopoly; that it corrupts the independence of media; that it corrupts the young; that it is too repetitive, loud, or interruptive; and that it is tasteless or aesthetically objectionable.[89] Some of these critiques are at times correct. But the more difficult question surrounds what can be done about these problems and the collective harm to the economy that might result. Some interventions have perverse outcomes.

Adding to the complexity is that in most consumers' minds, aesthetic concerns, the values promoted in advertising, and annoyance with ubiquity of advertising probably drive most objections with advertising. How should regulators, if at all, police social dimensions of advertising? Subject to the limits imposed by obscenity laws and prohibitions on advertising illegal activity, we have to live with offensive advertising in most situations.

Students of the Commission must understand that the FTC Act does not concern itself with general, ideological objections to advertising. Sometimes activist groups take up the FTC Act to air objections to advertising generally, but they must find some hook in deception or unfairness to establish a legal basis for intervention.

Congress increasingly intervened in the Agency's activities as the FTC promulgated more trade regulation rules, and as the country turned more conservative in the late 1970s. This took the form of direct meddling with the Agency's rules through restricting appropriations to the Agency and eventually in shutting down the Agency in response to rule-making activity in children's

---

[89] A pair of works by Professor Inger Stole, ADVERTISING ON TRIAL: CONSUMER ACTIVISM AND CORPORATE PUBLIC RELATIONS IN THE 1930S (2006) and ADVERTISING AT WAR (2012), describe an era where there was seemingly much more skepticism of advertising's value, but in modern times it is clear that advertising is much more fully embraced as a useful economic tool and as part of the fabric of American life. *See also* LUCY BLACK CREIGHTON, PRETENDERS TO THE THRONE (1976). For modern responses to consumerist advertising critiques, see William L. Wilkie & Elizabeth S. Moore, *A Larger View of Marketing: Marketing's Contributions to Society,* and Y. Hugh Furuhashi & E. Jerome McCarthy, *Social Issues of Marketing in the American Economy,* both of which appear in MARKETING AND THE COMMON GOOD (Patrick E. Murphy & John F. Sherry, Jr., eds., 2014). For a spirited and brief response to these critiques, see David Ogilvy's essay *Should Advertising Be Abolished?,* in CONFESSIONS OF AN ADVERTISING MAN (1963); LOWELL MASON, THE LANGUAGE OF DISSENT 166–168 (1959); Stephen H. Greyser, *Advertising: Attacks and Counters, in* CONSUMERISM: SEARCH FOR THE CONSUMER INTEREST (Aaker & Day, eds., 2nd edn, 1974).

advertising.[90] The Agency had always experienced some Congressional meddling, but at some point in the 1970s, it misread changing political signals and
became too aggressive for the politics of the era. Although several commission
proceedings contributed to a reaction against the FTC (including the used-car
rule and the funeral rule), the children's advertising proceeding symbolized a
regulatory agency out of control.

### THE KIDVID CONTROVERSY

The KidVid controversy refers to the late 1970s attempt of the Commission to
regulate children's advertising. KidVid was a catalyzing force in the 1980 shutdowns
of the FTC, and it still has a powerful psychological effect on the Agency. When
KidVid is mentioned, it often is as a kind of threat that Congress will neuter the
Agency if it takes the wrong action.

Throughout the 1970s, public interest groups and Congress urged some kind of
policy intervention to address television advertising to children. Televisions were
proliferating, and the Saturday morning cartoon-watching "marathon" was very
popular. During this period, children were shown dozens of ads, almost all of
which were for foods with added sugar.[91] Others directly advertised vitamins to
children, raising concerns about poisoning and whether children could judge the
need for vitamins. Liberal and conservative thinkers were concerned, and the FTC
began to take action on the issue in the early 1970s, under Republican leadership.
A 1970 staff report characterized children's advertising as more aggressive than adult
advertising, as employing more special effects, and faulted it for masking "product
placement" (the intentional presence of a product in the program) in even the
tamest shows.[92] Staff recommended that the commissioners devote two hours of
their time to the "unfortunate" task of watching Saturday morning cartoons to get the
feel of the situation.

In 1972, the Agency held five weeks of hearings, featuring ninety witnesses to learn
about television advertising and advertising's power in the medium.[93] During this
time, the FTC's scrutiny of television as a medium increased, with the Agency

---

[90] In addition to appropriations bills passed, Congress during this period held many hearings and
considered various measures that would have deeply affected the Commission's power. These are
detailed in Charles Louis Mitchell, Federal Trade Commission Policy Making and Congress 1970–
1983 (1984) (Ph.D. dissertation, University of Tennessee).

[91] A University of Texas undergraduate who focused her thesis on children's advertising monitored a
Saturday morning's worth of food commercials in 1978. In the first half-hour, Alpha Bits (two times),
Dairy Queen, Lifesavers, Reese's, Burger King (two times), Snickers, and Foot Loops were advertised.
Andrea E. Eisenkraft, Nutrition Advertising and Children: The Decisions and Events Leading Up to
the 1978 Federal Trade Commission Proposal (1978) (B.A. thesis, University of Texas).

[92] FTC, STAFF MEMORANDUM ON TELEVISION ADVERTISING TO CHILDREN, November 23, 1970.

[93] Peter Braton Turk, The Federal Trade Commission Hearings on Modern Advertising Practices: A
Continuing Inquiry into Television Advertising (1977)(Ph.D. dissertation, University of Wisconsin,
Madison).

recommending to the FCC at one point that controversial advertisements should be subject to the fairness doctrine, thus requiring networks to carry countercommercials.[94]

In a move that still reflects FTC style, the Agency tried to get the industry to self-regulate before enforcing cases or proposing a rule. Concerned that "people on both sides of the issue appeared to be talking at each other rather than with each other,"[95] in 1973, Nixon-appointed FTC Chairman Lewis A. Engman convened advertising groups, consumer advocates, and FTC staff to develop a voluntary code that could be enforced by the Agency.[96] Engman also created a Children's Television Advertising Project (CTAP) at the FTC to encourage development of a voluntary code.[97]

In a matter concerning the advertising of Wonder Bread, Engman argued that advertising to children was unfair under Section 5, and that, "In my opinion, advertising directed to or seen by children which is calculated to, or in effect does, exploit their known anxieties or capitalize upon their propensity to confuse reality and fantasy is unfair within the meaning of Section 5 ..."[98]

Engman left the Commission in 1975 to run for a US Senate seat in Michigan on a "too much regulation in Washington" platform. At the same time, he expressed disappointment that he had not made more progress on the children's advertising issue. He lost the election.

By 1978, the FTC felt that self-regulatory and enforcement actions were ineffective in addressing the children's advertising controversy. The Commission thus invited comment on a new trade regulation rule-making, which proved to be a disaster for the Agency.

Petitions filed with the FTC had urged it to investigate whether televised advertising of products to "children who are too young to understand the selling purpose of, or otherwise comprehend or evaluate, commercials may be unfair and deceptive within the meaning of Section 5 ..."[99] The FTC sought to address several harms, the most prominent of which was tooth decay.[100] It also invoked the risk of

---

[94] *Id*; Advertising Age, FTC Tells FCC It Supports 'Counter' Ads, January 10, 1972.

[95] *Interview of Lewis A. Engman*, 43 Antitrust L. J. 443 1973–1974.

[96] Association Management Magazine, The Aggressive New Chairman at FTC (November 1973).

[97] Gerald J. Thain, Television Advertising to Children & the Federal Trade Commission: A Review of the History & Some Personal Observations, University of Illinois Advertising Working Paper No. 9, July 1981.

[98] *In re ITT Continental Baking Co.*, 83 F.T.C. 865, 942 (1973–1974).

[99] Children's Advertising, Proposed Trade Regulation Rulemaking and Public Hearing, 43 Fed. Reg. 17,967 (April 27, 1978).

[100] This seems esoteric, given the modern obesity problem, but Tracy Westen explains: "We knew that by the age of two, half the children in this country had gum disease and one decayed tooth; by the age of eighteen, the average child had fourteen decayed teeth; yet half of all fifteen year-olds never saw a dentist. Pediatricians told us tooth decay was the number one childhood illness at that time." Tracy Westen, *Government Regulation of Food Marketing to Children: The Federal Trade Commission and the Kid-Vid Controversy*, 39 Loy. L. A. L. Rev. 79 (2006).

obesity, but the prevalence of that condition accelerated after the 1970s – childhood obesity more than doubled among children and quadrupled among adolescents between 1980 and 2012. Some believed that advertising of sugary cereal did not grow the economy but rather just shifted investments in food away from healthier, less-advertised alternatives and, in the process, created unwarranted public health costs.

The FTC quoted advertising executives discussing how they could manipulate children and, in so doing, their parents. For instance, quoting *Advertising Age*'s coverage of a conference devoted to kids' advertising, the FTC relayed one execu-tive's comment: "When you sell a woman on a product and she goes into the store and finds your brand isn't in stock she'll probably forget about it. But when you sell a kid on your product, if he can't get it he will throw himself on the floor, stamp his feet, and cry. You can't get a reaction like that out of an adult."[101] Even in advertising textbooks, one can find insensitive and even offensive advice about selling to children. In the 1975 textbook *Advertising Management*, the authors quote a memo from a San Francisco advertising firm that advised: "With children, the problem is to reach the head through the emotions ... Girls are less effective in communicating with both girls and boys ... [A]nimation is ... credible. Animation tends to be trusted even by most of the more critical children."[102]

Yet, the FTC's proposals for addressing the problem caused a major controversy because of their breadth.[103] The Agency asked for comment on "the advisability and manner of implementation of a rule" with the following elements: first, a ban on all television advertising "for any product which is directed to, or seen by, audiences composed of a significant proportion of children who are too young to understand the selling purpose of or otherwise comprehend or evaluate the advertising." The FTC thought that children under the age of eight years could not comprehend advertising. Second, a ban on television advertising for "sugared food products directed to, or seen by, audiences composed of a significant proportion of older children ..." Third, whether there should be counteradvertising for older children that included "nutritional and/or health disclosures funded by advertisers."[104]

Critiques rained down on the FTC. Bernice Hasin called this proposal "[c]ompli-cated and confusing, to say nothing of ill conceived and unworkable ..."[105] The

[101] FTC, Federal Trade Commission Staff Report on Television Advertising to Children 17, quoting *Reach Kids on Adult TV Shows: Wilk; It's Cheaper on Kids' Shows: Halock*, 36 Advertising Age 40–41, July 19, 1965 (quoting Jerry Ringlein of Oscar Mayer & Co.); for an overview of psychological research on children's understanding of ads, *see* Dale Kunkel & Donald Roberts, *Young Minds and Marketplace Values: Issues in Children's Television Advertising*, 47(1) J. Soc. Issues 57 (1991).

[102] This advice is attributed to Hoefer, Dietrick, and Brown *in* David A. Aaker & John G. Myers, Advertising Management 43–44 (1975).

[103] Teresa Moran Schwartz & Alice Saker Hrdy, *FTC Rulemaking: Three Bold Initiatives & Their Legal Impact*, 90th Anniversary Symposium of the Federal Trade Commission (2004).

[104] Children's Advertising, Proposed Trade Regulation, Rulemaking, & Public Hearing, 43(82) Fed. Reg. 17967 (April 27, 1978).

[105] Bernice Rothman Hasin, Consumers, Commissions, & Congress: Law, Theory, & the Federal Trade Commission, 1968–1985 (1987).

proposal would require some definition of "children's television," with an important division between programming for those under eight and those under twelve. Compliance could have been very tricky, and spread to programming other than (then popular) after-school and Saturday morning cartoons. This is because many adults watch children's shows,[106] perhaps in role as caretaker.

Critics also pointed to a logical disconnect in the FTC's reasoning: children cannot buy anything, and so advertising to them is filtered through the parent as decision-maker.[107] Thus, there is no deception or unfairness to the actual consumer – the parent. But, all parents can recognize the trick in this reasoning. One point of advertising is to trigger cues. The cues manifest themselves in desires that children do not even understand – they recognize a product from a television show while in a store, but often do not even understand what the product is. Demands for the unknown product create conflict and sometimes compromise from parents.[108]

On a more abstract level, opponents of the rule saw a battle over values. Supporters of the rule were concerned about the values that advertising taught kids. Others saw it as an attack on conservative power structures.

Advertisers went full tilt against the FTC, and even obtained an order disqualifying Chairman Michael Pertschuk from the proceeding based on bias.[109] The *Washington Post* labeled the Agency a "national nanny" and sneered that "the proposal, in reality, is designed to protect children from the weakness of their parents (who cannot say no to sugary treats) – and the parents from the wailing insistence of their children. That, traditionally, is one of the roles of a governess – if you can afford one."[110]

The *Washington Post*'s criticism is often invoked as evidence that "the left" agreed that the FTC had gone too far. But there is another way to look at this: the institutional editorial board was concerned about its parent company eventually becoming a regulated entity under children's advertising rules. It had an interest in attacking the proceeding. Throughout the century, publishers have opposed consumer protection in situations where it threatens advertising dollars (see box titled "Publishers' hair shirt on consumer protection" in Chapter 3). The *Post* developed a liberal reputation for its courageous service in exposing the Watergate affair. Characterizing it as "the left" signals a narrow understanding of the range of political thought of this newspaper, however, as it has often followed the establishment line.

---

[106] J. Howard Beales, III, Advertising to Kids & the FTC: A Regulatory Retrospective That Advises the Present (2004).

[107] Susan Bartlett Foote & Robert H. Mnookin, *The "Kid Vid" Crusade*, 61 THE PUBLIC INTEREST 90 (Fall 1980).

[108] Molly Pauker, *The Case for FTC Regulation of Television Advertising Directed Toward Children*, 46 BROOK. L. REV. 513 (1979).

[109] *Ass'n of Nat. Advertisers, Inc. v. FTC.*, 627 F.2d 1151 (D.C. Cir. 1979)(the disqualification was reversed on appeal).

[110] THE WASHINGTON POST, THE FTC AS NATIONAL NANNY (March 1, 1978).

Current histories of KidVid rarely, if at all, discuss the bipartisan nature of the genesis of KidVid. Concern about children's health spans the left and right, to this day in the form of the Agency's working group on children's advertising and nutrition. Today, we better understand sugar's role in the problem of obesity and diabetes, and that the problem of childhood obesity is practically irreversible and causes misery. If these regulations caused cereals to be more expensive, perhaps healthier alternatives would take their place, with attendant cost savings in public health.[111]

Existing histories also elide how KidVid was an appealing front in the business community's struggle with the FTC. KidVid occurred against a backdrop of other regulations, including the FTC's funeral rule and used-car rule. These other rule-makings angered many politically powerful small business leaders. Yet, the public was unlikely to rally in favor of funeral directors and used-car salesmen. KidVid offered FTC opponents a topic that fit a "nanny state" narrative about the federal government, one that the news media embraced and helped fan, because the news media was concerned about losing advertising revenue. A broad range of FTC opponents could march under the banner of KidVid and, in so doing, slow down the FTC's other rules that many consumers may have supported.

The FTC was ahead of its time on KidVid, in being concerned about the risks to children's health from pervasive availability of junk food masquerading as a healthy breakfast. The fundamental problem was not that it was an unmeritorious or partisan idea to improve children's health, but that solutions to the problem are complex and could result in deeply perverse results. Limiting advertising of these products would likely not ameliorate the problem, as children love sugar and will learn one way or the other about it.[112] We learned from the regulation of tobacco that deep structural changes (e.g., bans on indoor smoking) had to be put in place to reduce smoking. Even with restrictions on advertising and the increasing inconvenience and expense of tobacco, about seventeen percent of Americans still smoke. Turning back to sugar, our society still faces expensive and complex structural challenges, such as how to provide more healthful alternatives to sugar-frosted sugar cereals.

---

[111]  In recent years, there have been increasingly strenuous calls for control over advertising to children as a result of obesity and diabetes rates: "We believe that the accumulation of evidence on this topic [advertising to children] is now compelling enough to warrant regulatory action by the government to protect the interests of children, and therefore offer a recommendation that restrictions be placed on advertising to children too young to recognize advertising's persuasive intent." AMERICAN PSYCHOLOGICAL ASSOCIATION, REPORT OF THE APA TASK FORCE ON ADVERTISING AND CHILDREN, February 20, 2004; *see also* SUSAN LINN, CONSUMING KIDS: THE HOSTILE TAKEOVER OF CHILDHOOD (2004); THE LANCET, SELLING TO – AND SELLING OUT – CHILDREN, September 28, 2002. *See also*, Paul M. Schwartz & Daniel J. Solove, *The PII Problem: Privacy and a New Concept of Personally Identifiable Information*, 86 N.Y.U. L. Q. REV. 1814 (2011).

[112]  There is also the question of what advertising would replace marketing for highly sugared food. A look back report at KidVid determined that much of the modern advertising to children focused on sedentary entertainment. DEBRA J. HOLT, PAULINE M. IPPOLITO, DEBRA M. DESROCHERS, CHRISTOPHER R. KELLEY, FTC, CHILDREN'S EXPOSURE TO TV ADVERTISING IN 1977 AND 2004 INFORMATION FOR THE OBESITY DEBATE (2007).

## THE KIDVID REACTION

Forces opposed to KidVid and the Agency's other activities made strong appeals to Congress, which reacted with the Federal Trade Commission Improvement Act of 1980.[113] Much of the FTC's powers were left unchanged, yet the substance and procedure of the act's passage did much political and psychological damage to the Agency. The act included the ability of Congress to exercise a legislative veto of FTC action, a feature President Carter thought unconstitutional, but Carter nevertheless signed the bill to keep the Agency going.[114] The indeterminacy surrounding passage of the bill caused the FTC to close its doors on May 1, 1980, probably the first time an agency has been shut down over a policy matter.[115] Still in need of permanent operating funds, it asked employees to come to work at the next shutdown a month later, but apparently the staff did not work on matters that day.[116]

The 1980 act limited the Agency's use of administrative subpoenas, reflecting concerns that the Agency could demand too much information before a complaint had been filed. It created detailed procedures for the protection of information furnished to the Agency in response to a leak that showed that smoking bans in public places would harm cigarette sales.[117]

The 1980 act placed procedural limitations on the Agency's rule-making authority, requiring the Commission to announce in advance to the public and to Congressional committees when it intends to propose new rules.[118] It also required regular congressional oversight of the Agency.[119] Congress flatly prohibited the Agency from initiating rule-makings to determine that children's advertising was unfair or deceptive.[120] Congress also punished the Agency by prohibiting the Commission from using its funds for 3 years "for the purpose of initiating any new rulemaking proceeding ... which prohibits or otherwise regulates any commercial advertising ..."[121]

The FTC is still reeling from the 1980 act. The worst fears of business interests were awakened by the Agency's interpretation of its unfairness power. Former FTC Chairman and staffer to Senator Magnuson, Michael Pertschuk, attributed the backlash against the Agency to a number of factors.[122] Among them, business interests had become much more disciplined in organizing against federal

---

[113] Pub. L. No. 96–252, 94 Stat. 374 (1980).
[114] N.Y. Times, F.T.C. Funds Bill Is Signed, May 29, 1980 at D3.
[115] J. Howard Beales, III, Advertising to Kids and the FTC: A Regulatory Retrospective That Advises the Present (2004).
[116] Jeffrey Mills, *FTC Again Is Marking Time*, Washington Post, June 3, 1980.
[117] Pub. L. No. 96–252, 94 Stat. 374 (1980).
[118] *Id.* at §8.
[119] *Id.* at §22.
[120] *Id.* at §11.
[121] *Id.*
[122] Michael Pertschuk, Revolt against Regulation: The Rise and Pause of the Consumer Movement (1982).

regulation and regulators. Organizations such as the Business Roundtable were formed, and once-sleepy groups such as the Chamber of Commerce were reinvigorated. Chairman Pertschuk angered the business community by taking up an old Brandeisian notion: that antitrust policy should factor in the social dangers of bigness.[123] Pertschuk overestimated the political capital he possessed in an era where the consumer movement peaked and then quickly went into decline and where Americans – and even Carter administration officials – were becoming more skeptical of government regulation.

Adding to these problems, apparently, the FTC did not use its economists to study its overall consumer protection mission. Funds were finally budgeted in 1978 for economic analysis of consumer protection policy.[124] The FTC had issued a number of trade regulation rules that affected a variety of small business interests, which in turned complained loudly to Congress. These rules dug into the profits of small businesses such as funeral homes, which, prior to the funeral practices rule, did not have to disclose a price list.

## CONCLUSION

The FTC formally entered the consumer protection sphere in the 1930s, and had massive gains in power and sophistication as a result of changes brought on by the courts, Congress, and commissioners themselves in the 1970s. But by the end of the 1970s, the commissioners' ambition got ahead of existing political support. The FTC was active on a number of fronts where consumers probably supported more intervention, such as the regulation of used-car sales and of funeral parlor practices. Business frustration with those interventions probably did not have popular appeal with consumers. But KidVid implicated the news media and the myriad businesses that advertised to children. KidVid thus became the banner under which a wide range of businesses, in partnership with news media that were dependent on advertising dollars, could vent their anti-FTC frustration. The KidVid reaction resulted in the Agency being shut down twice and threatened its very existence. KidVid still has a psychological effect on the modern commission. KidVid is routinely invoked by commission critics who oppose the Agency's privacy efforts. KidVid also offers a cautionary lesson, as regulation of online advertising too has broad effects on businesses, advertisers, and the news media itself. These factions could unite and develop an anti-FTC narrative and political campaign if they feel threatened by the Agency's privacy actions.

---

[123] AMERICAN ENTERPRISE INSTITUTE, A CONVERSATION WITH MICHAEL PERTSCHUK (1979). ("The issue is fundamental Jeffersonian democracy. It is an essential distrust of substantial concentrations of power.")

[124] Paul A. Pautler, *A Brief History of the FTC's Bureau of Economics: Reports, Mergers, and Information Regulation*, 46 REV. IND. ORG. 59 (2015); William C. MacLeod & Robert A. Rogowsky, *Consumer Protection at the FTC during the Reagan Administration*, in REGULATION AND THE REAGAN ERA: POLITICS, BUREAUCRACY AND THE PUBLIC INTEREST (Roger E. Meiners & Bruce Yandle, eds., 1989).

# 3

## The modern FTC

After a decade of empowerment of the FTC, the pendulum swung in the other direction. President Reagan appointed James Miller as Chairman to slow down or reverse the course of the Agency. Miller strengthened the FTC in some respects, but his appointment was met with fear and resistance among agency staff, who believed that the Commission would be neutered or worse under Miller's leadership. Miller indeed slowed down agency activity greatly, and used his post to promote public choice theory views of the Commission and regulation more generally. Modern FTC critics share some intellectual affinity with the Miller regime – Part III of this book will revisit that theme.

The FTC's doldrums were short-lived. President George H. W. Bush appointed a relative outsider, Janet Steiger, to lead the Agency in 1989. Chairwoman Steiger did much to heal the Agency and to put it on a path to policing electronic commerce and privacy. Also during this period, the weaknesses of common law legal theories for policing information privacy wrongs became clear. Congress enacted a bevy of privacy laws concerning direct marketing and the resale of information related to cable viewership and video rentals, while the FTC started investigating the state of privacy online.

From a historical perspective, the FTC has been remarkably well led in the past two decades. Commissioners have been well qualified, and the Agency as a whole has been wise in its case selection. While periodically the focus of Capitol Hill criticism, Congress continued to empower the Agency in the 2000s by increasing its budget and by granting additional investigative authorities. Since the 1990s, typically one or two commissioners have developed expertise in privacy and championed a role for the FTC as privacy enforcer. The FTC even changed its structure in 2006 in order to formalize its privacy role, and started hiring technologists to advise the lawyers about technology. Its main setback has been the creation by Congress of the Consumer Financial Protection Bureau – this action sent the message that the FTC was simply not up to the task of policing financial consumer protection.

The FTC has clearly emerged as the country's top privacy cop. Still, the nature of what kind of privacy policy the FTC is to pursue remains a matter of controversy.

When led by Republicans, the FTC has taken a "harms-based" approach to selecting cases. When led by Democrats, the FTC adopts a more expansive set of principles worth protecting, focusing on consumer expectations, human rights, and dignity. When led by Republicans it opposes federal legislation, and it endorses legislation when led by Democrats.

## THE REAGAN YEARS

The Reagan revolution brought great change to the FTC, most notably in President Reagan's choice to head the Agency, James C. Miller III. Miller was appointed to address the excesses of the 1970s commission. He was lead author of a transition report calling for an end to all agency matters based on "social theories."[1] Former FTC attorney Pamela Stuart recounts his arrival: "On his first day at the FTC, he assembled the top-level staff, arranged for musical accompaniment, and entered the room behind a procession of the new bureau directors and attorney advisers wearing a pair of pink plastic stick-on horns. With as much ceremonial flourish as he could muster, Miller removed his headgear and said, 'I'm taking my horns off.' The reaction of the assembled staff was stunned silence. Not one of them laughed."[2] The fear of his agenda caused FTC staff not to be able to recognize this attempt at humor. Over time, Miller proved to be a personable and likable individual.

Miller's tenure was nonetheless controversial. FTC watchers have characterized the Miller- (and successor Daniel Oliver-) led agency variously as a "travesty,"[3] as having leadership tasked with "dismantling the Agency,"[4] as being a do-nothing agency,[5] as having abandoned structural antitrust matters as well as promulgation and enforcement of rules,[6] as incompetently led,[7] as suffering from "the slows,"[8] as

---

[1]   Federal Trade Commission Transition Team, Report submitted to the Reagan administration (1981).

[2]   PAMELA B. STUART, THE FEDERAL TRADE COMMISSION (1991).

[3]   Louis W. Stern, *The Federal Trade Commission: Going, Going, . . .*, in MARKETING AND ADVERTISING REGULATION: THE FEDERAL TRADE COMMISSION IN THE 1990S (Patrick E. Murphy & William L. Wilkie, eds., 1990).

[4]   *Id.*

[5]   NORMAN I. SILBER, WITH ALL DELIBERATE SPEED, THE LIFE OF PHILIP ELMAN 349 (2004). Stuart commented, "Consumer protection enforcement declined during the Miller years. Consent orders (out-of-court settlements), a key measure of case-by-case enforcement, declined from a total of 57 in 1977 to 16 in 1983. In the antitrust arena, FTC consent orders declined from a total of 19 in 1977 to 13 in 1983, and administrative complaints dropped from 9 tiled in 1977 to 1 complaint tiled in 1983. Total antitrust enforcement actions declined from 42 in 1977 to 25 in 1983." PAMELA B. STUART, THE FEDERAL TRADE COMMISSION (1991).

[6]   William J. Baer, *At the Turning Point: The Commission in 1978*, in MARKETING AND ADVERTISING REGULATION: THE FEDERAL TRADE COMMISSION IN THE 1990S (Patrick E. Murphy & William L. Wilkie, eds., 1990).

[7]   Thomas H. Stanton, *Comments on the Commission in 1978*, in MARKETING AND ADVERTISING REGULATION: THE FEDERAL TRADE COMMISSION IN THE 1990S (Patrick E. Murphy & William L. Wilkie, eds., 1990).

[8]   FTC Review (1977–1984) A Report Prepared by a Member of the Federal Trade Commission Together with Comments from Other Members of the Commission for the use of the Subcommittee on

"search[ing] for ways to narrow the commission's authority,"[9] as typifying "a pattern of placing implacable critics of the new social regulation in charge of the very agencies responsible for implementing it,"[10] and as having "a poisonous mixture of messianic and bizarre economic theory with a truncated capacity for reacting to injustice."[11]

Claiming that he was realigning the mission of the FTC to a Wilsonian ideal, the Miller FTC set policy that curbed the Agency's power and reduced the Agency's activity.

But Miller's conceptions about the Agency's inception are ahistorical.[12] To support the idea that the Reagan administration was Wilsonian, Miller had to cite his own scholarship,[13] where he relied primarily on Wilson's campaign speeches concerning regulation of business.[14] But Wilson's 1912 campaign speeches clearly did not reflect deep thought about the regulation of business. Kolko, giving the example of Wilson's "I am for big business, and I am against the trusts," argued that such campaign rhetoric was just that – not a doctrine but rather a kind of triangulation that drew upon progressive views but without specifics of policy meaning.[15] Others, seeking a more activist FTC, including Brandeis, used these same passages to justify regulation against big business.[16]

James C. Lang nicely described the confusion surrounding Wilson's antitrust policy, which may explain Miller's misconceptions: "Because of his lack of

Oversight and Investigations of the Committee on Energy and Commerce, 98th Cong. 2d Sess., Committee Print 98-CC (September 1984).

9 Stanley E. Cohen, *Consumer Safety Net Starting to Unravel*, 53(28) ADVERTISING AGE (March 8, 1982).
10 RICHARD A. HARRIS & SIDNEY M. MILKIS, THE POLITICS OF REGULATORY CHANGE: A TALE OF TWO AGENCIES (1989).
11 FTC Review (1977–1984) A Report Prepared by a Member of the Federal Trade Commission Together with Comments from Other Members of the Commission for the use of the Subcommittee on Oversight and Investigations of the Committee on Energy and Commerce, 98th Cong. 2d Sess., Committee Print 98-CC (September 1984).
12 William R. Childs, *Measures of the Presidents: Hoover to Bush*, 21(2) *Presidential Studies Quarterly* 385–387 (Spring 1991)(*reviewing* JAMES C. MILLER, THE ECONOMIST AS REFORMER: REVAMPING THE FTC, 1981–1985 (1991)). ("While Miller correctly identifies some of the FTC's problems, he undermines his analyses with historical misconceptions, omissions, and inaccuracies ... The original laws were written by and for businessmen as an attempt to rationalize business competition, but Miller's brief account here selectively and incorrectly focuses on Woodrow Wilson's influence ...")
13 JAMES C. MILLER III, THE ECONOMIST AS REFORMER: REVAMPING THE FTC, 1981–1985 (1991) at Fn. 1, *citing* James C. Miller III et al., *Industrial Policy: Reindustrialization through Competition or Coordinated Action?*, 2 YALE J. REG. 1 (1984).
14 Miller et al., at 8–9.
15 GABRIEL KOLKO, THE TRIUMPH OF CONSERVATISM: A REINTERPRETATION OF AMERICAN HISTORY 1900–1916 209–210, 255 (1963).
16 *See, for example*, Louis D. Brandeis, *The Inefficiency of the Oligarchs*, 58 HARPER'S WEEKLY 18–21 (January 17, 1914), where Brandeis quotes from Wilson's New Freedom: "No country can afford to have its prosperity originated by a small controlling class. The treasury of America does not lie in the brains of the small body of men now in control of the great enterprises ... It depends upon the inventions of unknown men, upon the originations of unknown men, upon the ambitions of unknown men. Every country is renewed out of the ranks of the unknown, not out of the ranks of the already famous and powerful in control."

knowledge of the trust problem's complexity ... Wilson's early posture on the issue appeared essentially Jeffersonian with emphasis upon minimal government involvement."[17] Miller grabbed onto the Jeffersonian patina of Wilson's rhetoric, and failed to account for Wilson's own change in attitudes and Congress' ultimate actions. As Chapter 1 recounted, by the time the FTC Act was enacted in 1914, Wilson's views had shifted and were more in line with those of Brandeis. Congress both considered but failed to pass a weak (investigatory-only) and a superagency bill, one characterized by supervisory control. Instead, Congress created a strong commission with prosecutorial powers – after Wilson intervened to support it. In a work attributed to Judge Learned Hand, *The New Republic* editorialized, "The Trade Commission act represents a totally different approach, a spirit strangely contradictory to the campaign theories of the President ... A Democratic Congress has actually delegated the broadest kind of personal discretion to a commission of 'experts,' a commission, mind you, which combines executive, legislative, and judicial functions. Could there be anything more portentous to those who believe in the adequacy of the Logos, as it comes to us from the Fathers; could there be a more impious attack upon the triune separation of powers? The act achieves a very happy but a most amazing delegation of legislative function."[18] In this passage, Hand explained, in a major publication of the day, the radical, actual nature of the FTC. This is a different portrait than depicted by President Wilson's rhetoric.

---

### A SHAPE-SHIFTING AGENCY

Professor Gerald Berk describes the FTC as a product of "creative syncretism." Berk explains that "institutions are better thought of as a bundle of resources ... that can be accessed for problem solving through decomposition and recombination, than they are as order-making machines."[19]

Consistent with Berk's description, Professor J. Howard Beales described the Commission as using the functions of different branches of governments. Until the 1970s, the FTC was a quasi-judicial body, with much of its resources devoted to administrative cases. The Commission then entered a legislative period, where it asserted rule-making power and quickly generated many rules. Following the Reagan revolution, the FTC shifted its resources away from judicial and legislative functions, to focusing upon its role as prosecutor.[20]

---

[17] James C. Lang, *The Legislative History of the Federal Trade Commission Act*, 13(6) Washburn L. J. 23 (1974). (Lang wrote that the FTC Act was an abandonment of the New Freedom campaign concepts "in favor of bold progressive economic legislation.")

[18] The New Republic, An Unseen Reversal, January. 9, 1915 at 7–8. (George Rublee, architect of the FTC Act, kept Judge Hand in the loop on the act's progress.)

[19] Gerald Berk, Louis D. Brandeis and the Making of Regulated Competition, 1900-1932 (2009).

[20] J. Howard Beales, III, *The FTC in the 1980s*, in Marketing and Advertising Regulation: The Federal Trade Commission in the 1990s (Patrick E. Murphy and William L. Wilkie, eds., 1990).

Despite the critiques, Miller did much to refocus and strengthen the Agency, both substantively and procedurally.[21] After the KidVid episode, the FTC needed a leader willing to administer bitter medicine to the Agency, and satisfy the business community. While Miller reduced enforcement activity, he should be credited with focusing the FTC on more important advertising matters. Miller's FTC focused on "post-experience goods." These are goods that consumers may not be able to evaluate at all, or only after a very long time, such as a claim that consumption of a fruit drink reduces the risk of heart attack.[22]

Part of the Miller controversy surrounds the different approaches that economists and lawyers have toward consumer protection. Economists are more likely to focus on consumer welfare, often ignoring the motives and sometimes-unseemly deeds of marketplace actors. Lawyers are more likely to have a moralistic respect for the law – indeed an ethical duty to uphold it – even if compliance with it has perverse effects or is simply inefficient. Among Miller's contributions to the Agency was a healthier respect for the economists' worldview. But also Miller installed "Chicago school" economists in the Bureau of Economics, who had a different view toward the FTC than lawyers.

---

### CONSUMERISM AND ITS CRITIQUES

Consumerism is characterized by a strong mistrust (and sometime ignorance) of macroeconomics, a desire to include social costs and benefits in the valuation of products (instead of just price), and alacrity to take action to identify and remedy problems in the marketplace. Many modern consumer movements, such as the environmental, and the anti-GMO and organic food movements share characteristics of consumerism.

Some common critiques of consumerism include that it fails to identify the biggest problems facing buyers in the economy; that it rarely will engage in cost–benefit analysis to determine whether interventions are economical; that consumer advocates can readily find examples of bad or dangerous products, but these are just anecdotal and do not support a broad condemnation of the marketplace; that expertise is a mask for consumerists' own taste, which is anti-populist and anti-consumption; and, finally, that consumer advocates have never articulated a theoretical explanation for why the economy would produce unsafe products or services that consumers do not really want.[23]

---

[21] Emily Rock, *Commerce and the Public Interest: James C. Miller at the Federal Trade Commission*, in STEERING THE ELEPHANT (Robert Rector & Michael Sanera, eds., 1987).

[22] Ross D. Petty, *FTC Advertising Regulation: Survivor or Casualty of the Reagan Revolution?*, 30(1) AMER. BUS. LAW J. 1 (1992); Phillip Nelson, *Advertising as Information*, 82(4) J. POL. ECON. 729 (1974).

[23] For a full articulation of these arguments, *see* Ralph K. Winter, *The Consumer Advocate versus the Consumer*, in CONSUMERISM: SEARCH FOR THE CONSUMER INTEREST (Aaker and Day, eds., 2nd edn, 1974).

Miller used the FTC as a forum to discuss government regulation as a policy matter from the public choice theory perspective. Public choice theory seeks to apply economic principles to government and regulation. Thus, just as individuals act in self-interest in the marketplace, public choice theory holds that politicians act selfishly when governing. Similarly, industries use government regulation to promote their own interests. Consistent with this idea, Miller held a two-day conference in 1982 that broadly presented regulation as an effort by business to raise barriers to entry and prices.[24] On the surface, this event would appear to be a misallocation of agency resources, because almost all the purported examples of business interest groups imposing costs on competitors through regulation came from industries that were outside the jurisdiction of the FTC. In a roundtable discussion following paper presentations, then First Circuit Court of Appeals Judge Stephen Breyer quipped that Hannah Arendt's[25] theories of political action were more consistent with his experiences than the special-interest group theories discussed at the conference.[26]

The Miller FTC also relied more heavily on federal court actions against defendants instead of adjudicatory matters before an administrative law judge. Going directly to federal court can have advantages, especially in garden-variety fraud cases. First, it can result in a more expeditious outcome for the FTC when pursuing obvious fraudsters because the court can provide injunctive relief. Second, pursuing cases in federal court reduces legitimacy problems that flow from the Agency's role as both prosecutor and judge in administrative proceedings. Miller introduced other innovations as well that are used to this day. For instance, the Miller-era FTC used the Agency's 13(b) authority to obtain preliminary injunctions and equitable relief in consumer protection cases.[27] By using asset freezes, the Miller-era FTC took the financial incentive out of an approach that some unscrupulous defendants took, where they would bet on making money and hence an adequate return on an illegal scheme during the time it took for the FTC to discover it and build a case.

Nevertheless, much of Miller's deregulatory zeal was unsuccessful. In 1980, the Commission adopted a statement detailing the contours of its unfairness authority (see Chapter 5). Following this effort, Miller tried to limit the FTC's deception powers by issuing a similar statement on deception (see Chapter 5). But he could not convince Congress to endorse his approach. Miller's underlying problem related to business support of deregulation. As much as businesses may complain about the FTC, they also want it to function well and police outliers in their own industries. The public as well as businesses depend on and are a product of government investment,[28]

---

[24]  FTC, The Political Economy of Regulation: Private Interests in the Regulatory Process (1984).

[25]  Hannah Arendt was famous for describing the phenomenon of the "banality of evil" and is sometimes confused with Heinz Arndt, an economist who was deeply skeptical of privacy as a value.

[26]  FTC, The Political Economy of Regulation: Private Interests in the Regulatory Process (1984).

[27]  15 U.S.C. § 53(b).

[28]  Mariana Mazzucato, The Entrepreneurial State: Debunking Public vs. Private Sector Myths (2013); Paulina Borsook, Cyberselfish: A Critical Romp through the Terribly Libertarian Culture of High Tech (2001).

infrastructure, education, and the rule of law provided in markets with functioning governments. Simply put, some public choice theory and most libertarian notions of the state's regulatory role are more radical than the business community's needs for a healthy environment.

In fact, the business community broadly supports regulation of advertising – the bane of the Reagan-era FTC. The strongest regulation of advertising came at the behest of the advertising industry itself. For example, the *Printers' Ink* model statute, a law proposed in the 1910s by advertisers and widely adopted among states, imposed criminal penalties and strict liability for false advertising (see Chapter 5).[29] In more modern times, *Advertising Age* has editorialized that it wanted a strong FTC and that weakening it could result in a jungle marketplace.[30] A March 1982 editorial in *Advertising Age* credited the FTC of the 1970s with eliminating poisonous "flim-flam" and for producing higher ethical standards industry-wide. It pointed out that the Reagan-era cost–benefit analysis approach would be a license for small-dollar retailers to loot, with a corresponding unjustified emphasis on large-ticket sellers.[31] A public choice scholar, attuned to rent-seeking, might respond that these are all examples of self-interest and anticompetitive uses of regulation. Others might see a broader benefit to these interventions, even if they contain some elements of self-interest.

Thus while, on the surface, businesses fund libertarian and ideological movements opposed to government intervention, this is strategic behavior rather than a reflection of strongly held business community beliefs. Sometimes it is even unclear whether business leaders even understand their libertarian bedmates. For instance, some libertarians see all regulation, even industry self-regulation, as a product of special-interest group conspiracy. Yet, businesses broadly support self-regulation.

Ultimately, slowing down the FTC is ineffective because a large, democratic demand exists for consumer protection. Ironically, Miller, the public choice scholar so fond of labeling government action as perverse, created incentives for action by private litigants and state attorneys general. The reduction in FTC pressure on business during the Miller years led to greater attention by other government agencies and by private individuals.

## THE MODERN FTC AND ITS EMERGENCE AS PRIVACY REGULATOR

In 1989, President George Herbert Walker Bush appointed Janet Dempsey Steiger to chair the FTC. She previously had served as Chairwoman of the Postal Rate Commission. Steiger was the first woman appointed to chair the Agency and was neither a lawyer nor an economist. Steiger led a dramatic increase in consumer protection matters, obtained reauthorization for the Agency, and established the Agency's

---

[29] Blake Clark, The Advertising Smoke Screen (1943).
[30] Daniel Pope, *Advertising as a Consumer Issue*, 47(1) J. Soc. Issues 41 (1991).
[31] Stanley E. Cohen, *Consumer Safety Net Starting to Unravel*, 53(28) Advertising Age (March 8, 1982).

international consumer protection program. Steiger lived up to her strong reputation for bipartisanship and good government-style leadership. As California began to regulate claims that products were good for the environment, Steiger brought stakeholders to the table, resulting in the first green marketing guides. In 2014, Steiger was posthumously awarded the award for lifetime FTC achievement, named for Chairman Miles W. Kirkpatrick. The American Bar Association runs a fellowship in her name.

*FTC Timeline:* 1980–2006

| Year | Month | Event | Relevance |
|------|-------|-------|-----------|
| 1980 | 5 | FTC closes | Battle over appropriations leaves the Agency in the lurch |
| 1980 | 5 | Federal Trade Commission Improvements Act of 1980 | Legislative reaction to activist FTC banned rule-making on advertising for two years |
| 1980 | 6 | FTC stops cases for two days | FTC asks employees to come to work but not pursue cases until operating funds are restored |
| 1980 | 10 | Used Oil Recycling Act | Banned FTC from requiring used oil to be labeled as recycled |
| 1982 | 5 | Congress exercises legislative veto | Blocking used-car rule, which would have required dealers to disclose defects |
| 1989 | 4 | ABA 1989 study on the FTC | The "Kirkpatrick II" report made no structural recommendations and is relatively modest |
| 1994 | 9 | *FTC v. Corzine*, FTC's first internet case | The respondent offered a credit repair system on America Online |
| 1995 | 4 | First FTC workshop on internet consumer protection | The FTC held three events in 1995 to examine consumer protection online |
| 1997 | 7 | Kidscom.com letter | FTC sets forth principles for online collection of information |
| 1999 | 4 | FTC brings pretexting case | Case notable because it involved a company deceiving a third party in order to obtain consumer data |
| 2003 | 10 | FTC enforcement of Do Not Call begins | The anti-telemarketing registry proved to be one of the most popular consumer protection efforts ever |
| 2006 | 1 | Passage of US SAFE WEB Act of 2006 | Established rules for information sharing with foreign law enforcement agencies |
| 2006 | | Division of Privacy and Identity Protection established | Drawing from the Agency's financial practices group, DPIP has jurisdiction over most privacy matters |

In the 1980s and 1990s, Congress enacted many of the most important federal privacy laws. Still, there were many gaps in protections, resulting in the problem that companies with the same information could either be strongly regulated, or not regulated at all, based on their business model. Consumer plaintiffs tried several theories to remedy sale of personal data, including traditional tort theories. Plaintiffs tried actions for intentional invasion of privacy, public disclosure of private facts, and appropriation, but these suits generally have failed to address modern information privacy problems. Consumers could not prove that an ordinary person would suffer shame or humiliation from the data transfer for direct marketing purposes, and any individual's data are simply worth too little to support an appropriation claim.[32] These early cases signaled tort law as a dead end for plaintiffs attempting to police business use of data.[33] Similarly, contract law did not provide a remedy despite the similarity between privacy policies and traditional legal agreements. This failure is because few users, if any, read the policy or rely on it, and because of the principle that general statements of policy are not contracts.[34]

In this atmosphere, the FTC was poised to fill the legal gaps between sectoral privacy statutes, tort, and privacy promises. Chairwoman Steiger's leadership healed the Agency from its Reagan-era trauma, and she performed so well that when President Clinton was elected, he kept her in the Chair (typically, party changes come with new chairpersons, with the former leader becoming an ordinary commissioner for the remainder of the seven-year appointment). Two years later, Clinton appointed perhaps the most qualified person possible to run the Agency – Robert Pitofsky. Pitofsky was a former Director of the Bureau of Consumer Protection and a commissioner from 1978 to 1981.

As Chairman, Pitofsky launched the FTC's privacy program, brought enforcement sweeps, held workshops, founded the Agency's consumer response center, and expanded the Agency's outreach and education mission. Pitofsky had played a key role in the 1969 American Bar Association report on the FTC and was keenly aware of the Agency's missteps in the 1970s. Much of the privacy activity was centered in the Agency's Division of Financial Practices, a natural fit for such cases, because of its responsibility for administering the Fair Credit Reporting Act.

Pitofsky believed that the Agency's unfairness power, which was used to justify actions such as the KidVid rule-making, was politically dangerous and he was reluctant to employ it. Commission complaints from this era are thus somewhat

---

[32] *Dwyer* v. *American Express*, 652 N.E.2d 1351 (Ill. App. 1995); *Shibley* v. *Time, Inc.* 341 N.E.2d 337 (Ohio Ct. App. 1975). *See generally* Andrew Jay McClurg, *A Thousand Words Are Worth a Picture: A Privacy Tort Response to Consumer Data Profiling*, 98(1) NORTHWESTERN UNIV. L. REV. 63 (2003).

[33] Neil M. Richards & Daniel J. Solove, *Prosser's Privacy Law: A Mixed Legacy*, 98 CAL. L. REV. 1887 (2010); Robert Gellman, *Does Privacy Law Work?*, *in* TECHNOLOGY AND PRIVACY: THE NEW LANDSCAPE (Philip E. Agre & Marc Rotenberg, eds., 1997).

[34] *In re JetBlue Airways Corp. Privacy Litig.*, 379 F. Supp. 2d 299 (E.D.N.Y. 2005); *Dyer* v. *Nw. Airlines*, 334 F. Supp. 2d 1196 (D.N.D. 2004). *But see In re Pharmatrak, Inc.*, 329 F.3d 9 (1st Cir. 2003)(health website did not consent to personally identifiable monitoring).

confusing, in that they sometimes employ the language of unfairness yet rest on the Agency's other principal power – the policing of deception. Pitofsky's FTC brought the first internet case in 1994.[35] Jodie Z. Bernstein served as Director of Consumer Protection. During this period, the Commission made its foray into online privacy; this is treated in greater detail in Chapter 6.

---

### PUBLISHERS' HAIR SHIRT ON CONSUMER PROTECTION

Journalists lead great careers by exposing consumer rip-offs and corporate wrongdoings. American consumer movements always feature muckraking, popular reporting, and editorials elucidating abuses of industries. But at the same time, news media industries often are of two minds on consumer protection, and sometimes seem to act to protect advertisers over consumers.

- In a seminal exposé of the patent medicine industry, Mark Sullivan and Samuel Hopkins Adams argued that no news media organization would report on the hazards of patent medicines.[36] Adams estimated the patent medicine industry to be worth $60,000,000 ($1.5 trillion in today's dollars). Much of this money went to newspapers that advertised patent medicines. Adams uncovered numerous contracts between patent medicine sellers and newspapers that made two crucial conditions on receipt of lucrative advertising dollars: that patent medicines not be regulated by state law, and that the publication not report on "any matter otherwise detrimental" to the patent medicine vendor.
- The legendary journalist George Seldes made his career by publishing information about regulatory fines against companies. He had a virtual monopoly on such coverage because it was ignored by other publications.[37]
- With the rise of the 1930s consumer movement, advertisers and publishers aggressively campaigned to promote advertising as a social good.[38] When the FTC Act amendments were considered by the Senate, the National Editorial Association opposed the bill because of the grant of authority the FTC would receive to regulate advertising.

---

[35] *FTC v. Corzine*, CIV-S-94–1446 (E.D. Cal. 1994).

[36] Mark Sullivan, *The Patent Medicine Conspiracy against the Freedom of the Press*, COLLIER'S, November 4, 1905. Sullivan's essay was reprinted along with the work of Samuel Hopkins Adams by the American Medical Association. See SAMUEL HOPKINS ADAMS, THE GREAT AMERICAN FRAUD: ARTICLES ON THE NOSTRUM EVIL AND QUACKS (1907).

[37] TELL THE TRUTH AND RUN: GEORGE SELDES AND THE AMERICAN PRESS (New Day Films 1996). BLAKE CLARK, THE ADVERTISING SMOKE SCREEN 20 (1943)(noting that FTC actions are essentially "free" news that can be reprinted at will by newspapers but are rarely published).

[38] INGER L. STOLE, ADVERTISING ON TRIAL: CONSUMER ACTIVISM AND CORPORATE PUBLIC RELATIONS IN THE 1930S (2006).

- William Randolph Hearst waged an early battle with the FTC over the Agency's investigation and case concerning *Good Housekeeping* magazine's seal. Writing in the New Republic, Frank Jellinek observed that the major newspapers published pieces objecting to the FTC's investigation but did not cover the substance of the allegations at all. The FTC's investigation revealed some stains on the seal, including allegations of payola where the magazine conditioned issuance of the seal on purchase of advertising. Instead of covering Hearst's wrongdoing, magazine officials and trade group representatives whipped up an investigation into whether consumer groups were communist.[39]
- Newspapers attempted to systemically weaken the National Telemarketing Do Not Call Registry,[40] because newspaper subscriptions used to be driven by telemarketing.[41] In recent years, media organizations have been strong opponents of internet privacy rules, because of that industry's dependence on ad revenue models following the decline of subscription sales. Some publishers extensively use advertising networks. If journalists from these publishers write critically about the online advertising industry, they face retorts of hypocrisy – the journalist's salary is being subsidized in part by revenue from the privacy invasions reported on.

A press aide to President Johnson warned officials to never argue with a man who buys ink by the barrel.[42] Yet, the FTC seems to be doing exactly this with respect to news outlets that promote dubious weight loss remedies, such as açaí berries. The Agency released a guide in 2014 explaining how news organizations can spot fraudulent ads and separately noted that it has the power to police news media organizations.

In addition to Chairmen who have focused on privacy, since the 1990s, individual commissioners have been interested in this topic. Starting in the Clinton years, commissioners Christine A. Varney and Mozelle W. Thompson led efforts to involve the FTC in privacy. Commissioner Orson Swindle became an expert in

[39] Frank Jellinek, *Dies, Hearst and the Consumer*, 102(1) NEW REPUBLIC 10 (January. 1, 1940).
[40] The Newspaper Association of America opposed creation of a do-not-call registry, asked that newspapers be exempt from it if created, asked that newspapers be exempt from caller ID transmission requirements, and asked that opt-out retention rules be weakened. Comments of the Newspaper Association of America, In the Matter of Rules and Regulations Implementing the Telephone Consumer Protection Act of 1991, CG Docket No. 02-278, December 9, 2002.
[41] Janet Whitman, *Newspapers Press to Keep Subscribers*, THE WALL STREET JOURNAL, February 4, 2004. ("Gannett Co., the largest newspaper publisher in the US generates 37.8% of its subscribers through telemarketing, compared to 39.1% for the newspaper industry overall. . .")
[42] Alan L. Otten, *Politics and People: Final Rules*, THE WALL STREET JOURNAL, September 28, 1978.

this area, but as a critic who opposed some of the Agency's early efforts, including a case that in retrospect appears to have been well justified.[43]

The Pitofsky era ended with the election of President George W. Bush, who appointed Timothy J. Muris. Muris had held several leadership positions at the Agency, including as Director of the Bureau of Competition and the Bureau of Consumer Protection under Chairman Miller. Muris also worked in the Agency's Office of Policy Planning in the 1970s.

While Pitofsky was an advocate for privacy legislation, Muris was not. Still, Muris led several key advances in privacy while Chairman from 2001 to 2004. He was the main proponent of what is perhaps the most popular consumer protection measure ever – the National Do Not Call Registry (DNCR). The idea of a no-call list had been developed by staff but shelved internally. Muris championed its cause, over-came industry objections, outmaneuvered powerful opponents in Congress, and beat a First Amendment challenge to the DNCR. President George W. Bush, not known for his regulatory zeal, had a Rose Garden reception for the signing of the bill.

Muris also appointed the first economist to lead the Bureau of Consumer Protection, George Washington University Professor J. Howard Beales III, lead author of the influential *Efficient Regulation of Consumer Information*.[44] Together Muris and Beales began to use the unfairness power in privacy matters, and the Agency's first unfairness matters in data security sprang from their leadership. The pair also declared that the FTC would pursue a "harms-based" approach to privacy, a strategically wise move that grounded many of the FTC's early privacy matters in uncontroversial areas. It also had the effect of reducing the scope of privacy by denying recognition of norms, human rights, and consumer expectations as justify-ing privacy rights. Muris also established the Criminal Liaison Unit (discussed in Chapter 4) to better link the FTC with law enforcement agencies and to promote referral of fraud schemes for criminal prosecution.

During Muris' tenure, commissioners Pamela Jones Harbour and William E. Kovacic focused on consumer privacy. Harbour championed the idea that information privacy concerns should be considered in antitrust matters, and thus tried to expand privacy into the realm of the Agency's Bureau of Competition. Kovacic, an eminent antitrust expert and law professor, remains one of the Agency's most qualified commissioners. He was honored with a Liber Amicorum in 2012.[45]

After stepping down as Chairman to return to academia, Muris was succeeded by Deborah Platt Majoras. Under Chairwoman Majoras, the information security

---

[43] Swindle objected to the Touch Tone matter, in which private investigators tricked banks into revealing private account details of consumers. *In the Matter of Touch Tone Information, Inc.* File No. 982 3619 (1999).

[44] J. Howard Beales III, Richard Craswell, & Steven C. Salop, *The Efficient Regulation of Consumer Information*, 24(3) *J. L. Econ.* 491 (1981).

[45] William E. Kovacic: An Antitrust Tribute: Liber Amicorum (Nicholas Charbit, Elisa Ramundo, Anna Chehtova, Abigail Slater, eds., 2012).

cases came to fruition. In addition, Congress enacted the "Undertaking Spam, Spyware, And Fraud Enforcement with Enforcers beyond Borders Act of 2006" (US SAFE WEB Act, discussed in Chapter 11), yet another law expanding the powers of the Agency.[46] With these amendments to the FTC Act, the Agency was formally empowered to obtain information on consumer protection targets from businesses (such as internet domain registrars) without the target learning of the investigation. It immunized a wide range of companies when they voluntarily provide information concerning FTC Act violations. It also explicitly permitted international cooperation in the investigation of consumer protection violations.

While Majoras' legacy has been characterized as "undistinguished,"[47] this is uncharitable. Majoras – and other Chairwomen – have had understated styles and lack the boorishness of some Chairmen. While her predecessor was busy promoting the phrase "miracle of instant credit" during the credit bubble, Majoras had the foresight to see problems in the mortgage market of the 2000s. *FTC:WATCH* credits her with holding "a prescient workshop on the advent of nontraditional housing loans that had such problematic terms that they soon earned the moniker 'toxic' loans." Reflecting on her tenure, Majoras wished that she had pushed even harder on risky lending.[48]

When the housing market crashed in 2008, the FTC's actions and inactions in the 2000s made it an unlikely venue for new consumer protection rules. In the Dodd–Frank Act, Congress decided to start from scratch and created a new consumer protection agency, the Consumer Financial Protection Bureau (CFPB). This action gave the FTC a black eye. The FTC lost some of its legal authorities in the CFPB's creation, but on a larger level, the need for a new agency spoke to the feeling that the FTC was not up to the task of policing the financial marketplace.

In addition to shepherding the SAFE WEB Act, under Majoras' leadership the Agency consolidated its different international offices and created the Division of Privacy and Identity Protection (DPIP). Commissioner Julie Brill became the FTC's privacy champion in Majoras' tenure.

In 2009, President Obama appointed Jonathan D. Leibowitz, a longtime Congressional staff attorney who served in a number of important roles on Capitol Hill. Just prior to his appointment, Chairman Leibowitz led the Motion Picture Association of America's government relations efforts. Leibowitz appointed long-time public interest litigator and Georgetown University Law Professor David Vladeck to head the Agency's Bureau of Consumer Protection. The appointment of Vladeck, a storied litigator, signaled a commitment to increased FTC enforcement activity. The pair hired a number of top experts for short-term stints at the FTC who increased the Agency's privacy sophistication: a chief technologist (Princeton

---

[46] Pub. L. No. 109–455.

[47] Thomas O. McGarity, Freedom to Harm: The Lasting Legacy of the Laissez-Faire Revival (2013).

[48] Kirstin Downey, *FTC at 100: The Agency in recent times to infinity and beyond!*, 869 Ftc: Watch, March 13, 2015.

Professor Edward Felten), senior advisers (then Colorado Law Professor Paul Ohm and Columbia Law Professor Tim Wu), and staff technologists (including Ashkan Soltani and Christopher Soghoian). In 2012, the FTC created a "Mobile Technology Unit" housed in the Division of Financial Practices to focus on privacy and security of mobile applications.

Leibowitz also led the charge to increase the statutory powers of the Commission. He asked Congress to reduce the barriers to rule-making imposed by the Magnuson–Moss amendments, to give it direct civil penalty authority (discussed in Chapter 4), and to establish aiding and abetting liability for violations of Section 5. Currently, the FTC can only use aiding and abetting theories where authorized by specific statute, such as the telemarketing fraud law. Despite Leibowitz' efforts, Congress did not grant these additional authorities.

In 2013, President Obama appointed Edith Ramirez to the chairmanship. Ramirez was a longtime litigator, and a partner at Quinn Emanuel Urquhart & Sullivan, LLP, in Los Angeles before joining the FTC as commissioner in 2010. Highly qualified, but understated, Ramirez served on *Harvard Law Review* with President Obama and clerked on the Ninth Circuit Court of Appeals. During her nomination, she discussed her longtime service to poor consumers in the Los Angeles area, and highlighted the potential of the FTC to protect the poor.

Ramirez appointed the Harvard University computer scientist Latanya Sweeney as Chief Technologist, who served for a year at the Agency. Sweeney is well known for research into de-identification of anonymous data sets, thus signaling an agency interest in how to evaluate business claims that consumer data sets are anonymous. Ramirez then appointed Ashkan Soltani to the chief technologist position. Ramirez also hired Professor Andrea Matwyshyn as a Senior Policy Advisor on privacy and data security issues. Matwyshyn's expertise in innovation policy signals the Commission's concern surrounding how technology regulation can affect development of internet services.

In recognition of the efficacy of having in-house technologists, and because of the high demand for these experts' time, in 2015, Ramirez converted the Mobile Technology Unit into the Office of Technology Research and Investigation (OTRI). Located within the Bureau of Consumer Protection, OTRI's purpose is to expand on the Commission's efforts to provide technical expertise on its matters.

The FTC's newest privacy-focused commissioner is Terrell McSweeny, who indicated an interest in privacy matters upon entering office in 2014.

## CONCLUSION

Consumer protection, if effective, cures the ills it seeks to address. As the years pass, consumers and policy-makers forget the circumstances leading to consumer law. Divorced from context, consumer law appears irrational and stringent. That is why studying the history of consumer protection is important. It helps us understand what led to the creation of agencies such as the FTC and to understand the debates over legal approaches.[49] These history chapters provided context for the creation of the FTC and explained how it faced challenges to its authority and approaches from Congress, industries, and consumers unhappy with the Agency's performance. A recurring theme is whether the FTC should simply police wrongs that were illegal under the common law. This theme will emerge again, as an argument that the FTC should only police "harms," in the following chapters that focus on specific subject matters of FTC privacy activity.

---

[49] The history of the FTC is rich, and reading it enriches one's understanding of the Agency. Some of the best historical work on the Agency is written by former FTC staff attorney Marc Winerman and former Chairman and general counsel, Professor William E. Kovacic.

# 4

## Organizational and procedural basics

### INTRODUCTION

The Federal Trade Commission is one of the most powerful regulatory agencies in the country, but it is also small and depends on close working relationships among staff. The FTC is recognized as one of the best agencies to work for, and, in recent years, openings at the Agency have attracted hundreds of applications, from even partner-level attorneys. This chapter gives an overview of the FTC's organization, its consumer protection powers, and investigative procedures. This chapter is primarily descriptive and intended to introduce the reader to a high-level portrait of the FTC's structure, jurisdiction, and powers. In Chapter 12, we return to these elements, invoking them to evaluate changes the FTC could make in order to optimize its privacy activities.

The FTC is a staff-driven agency. In practice, most matters are identified by staff and brought before the Commission. The commissioners' power is expressed mainly through up/down votes on requests to bring matters or accept settlements, or through public dissents and other commentary warning the staff to switch direction or focus.

Many advocates and others wishing to influence the FTC focus on commissioners, but the staff is in a way more powerful and more enduring. In particular, advocates tend to ignore the FTC's Bureau of Economics. The economists play a key role in evaluation of matters, and, in privacy, the economists' role steers the Agency away from monetary remedies in its cases. Engagement with the Bureau of Economics is key to changing the Agency's posture on privacy, and this theme will be taken up again in Chapter 12.

The FTC conceives of itself as a law enforcement agency. It thus shares some characteristics of such agencies. For instance, it has a strong internal culture to meet in person, one purpose of which is to avoid creating records that might attract Congressional attention or be obtained through Freedom of Information Act requests. FTC employees take secrecy of agency investigations seriously. Starting with the 1914 act[1] and persisting to this day, FTC employees can be charged with a

---

[1]   63rd Cong. 2nd Sess. Chap. 311 §10.

misdemeanor and fined for making "public any information obtained by the commission without its authority, unless directed by a court."[2]

As federal law enforcement is increasingly occupied with antiterrorism efforts, the FTC has had to pursue matters that in the past would have been charged as criminal frauds by the Department of Justice. Where the FTC thinks criminal enforcement of a consumer protection order is appropriate, it refers the matter to its Criminal Liaison Unit (CLU). Established in 2003 under Chairman Muris, the CLU identifies law enforcement agencies potentially interested in parallel enforcement. This means that lawyers should consider whether an FTC investigation may lead to criminal charges, and should advise clients concerning their right against self-incrimination in the FTC proceeding.[3] More broadly, the FTC can share investigatory information with any government agency with which it has an information-sharing agreement, and even with city-level consumer protection authorities.

## ORGANIZATION

The FTC is one of the nation's oldest independent agencies. Over the years it has been reorganized several times. Today it is divided into three bureaus (the Bureau of Consumer Protection, Bureau of Competition, and Bureau of Economics) and eight regional offices. The regional offices are increasingly involved in bringing privacy cases.[4]

### The Commissioners

Five commissioners, appointed by the President and confirmed by the Senate, lead the FTC. They serve staggered, seven-year terms. The Agency can still function without a full complement of commissioners,[5] but an evenly divided vote results in no action. Commissioners can only be removed for cause.[6]

No more than three commissioners can hail from the same party. While this rule was intended to promote a nonpartisan commission, from its founding appointments by President Wilson, Presidents have nominated Commissioners from third parties and candidates with only a weak commitment to the opposite party's values.

---

[2]   15 U.S.C. §50.

[3]   FTC: WATCH recently reported that the CLU has led to 770 indictments and that in fiscal year 2014, CLU-inspired convictions resulted in an average sentence of over forty months. Neil Averitt, *Viewing Consumer Abuses as Crimes*, 878 FTC: WATCH (July 30, 2015); see also Barry J. Cutler, *The Criminalization of Consumer Protection – A Brave New World for Defense Counsel*, 22(1) ANTITRUST 61 (Fall 2007).

[4]   The Northwest Regional Office, based in Seattle, has filed high-impact cases against a software company and a rent-to-own chain for using software to spy on customers.

[5]   *LaPeyre v. FTC*, 366 F.2d 117 (5th Cir. 1966).

[6]   See *Humphrey's Executor v. US* 295 US 602 (1935) (inefficiency, neglect of duty, or malfeasance in office are grounds for dismissal).

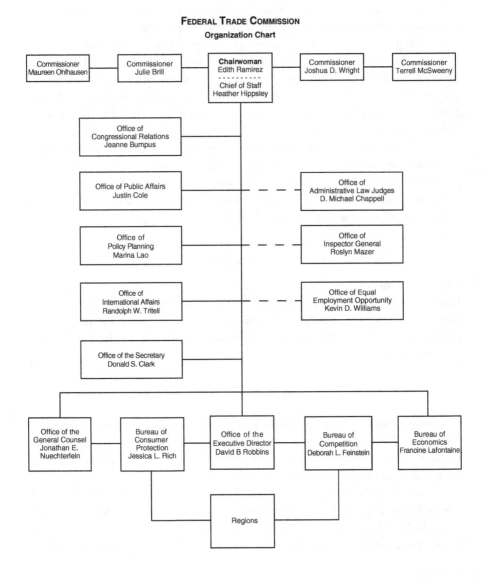

FEDERAL TRADE COMMISSION
Organization Chart

Three Progressive Party members (beginning with FTC Act author George Rublee) and five independents have served as commissioners.

Historically, Democratic appointees have served as commissioner longer than Republican appointees (mean term 2,160 days versus 1,812); however, the difference in the average term is not statistically significant. Overall, there is wide variation in length of term, with some serving less than a year, and sixteen that served more than eight years. Two commissioners – the legendary Paul Rand Dixon and Garland S. Ferguson – served for over twenty years.

---

### THE EFFECTIVE COMMISSIONER

It is unclear what the "right stuff" is for being a commissioner. Highly qualified candidates are sometimes duds but those without economic or legal training can shine (e.g., Chairman Steiger, or the secondary school-educated commissioner Hurley). While political patronage is often bemoaned, all commissioners are political to some extent, and strongly connected ones are often very effective (e.g., Chairman Muris). Political party is also not a reliable indicator. While consumer protection is traditionally a Democratic Party hobbyhorse, Republican Chairmen are some of the Agency's most beloved and bold leaders (e.g., Chairmen Kirkpatrick, Weinberger, and Muris). Conflicts of interest also do not explain laggard commissioners; some who represented industry join the Agency and pursue its interests with vigor.

President Wilson is said to have wanted commission membership to have three lawyers and two business leaders, and that the membership be geographically diverse.[7] But lawyers have predominated, and it is common to have an all-lawyer commission.

In a 1997 article, William E. Kovacic examined leadership of the Commission broadly and proposed a model for makeup of the Agency's membership: all candidates should have significant accomplishments in areas relevant to FTC practice, one of the five commissioners should be an economist, one member should have significant business experience, and at least one should have significant consumer protection or antitrust policy-making experience.[8]

---

A generous $10,000 salary was specified for commissioners in 1914; in today's dollars, about $230,000. This same salary stayed in effect for decades and began to become a drag upon recruitment of quality leaders. Today, commissioners' salaries are keyed to the federal judiciary and are about $170,000.

### Disqualification of Commissioners

Because commissioners sometimes advocate for new legislation and policies, they can appear to be biased against entire industries or specific companies that

---

[7] Pendleton Herring, *The Federal Trade Commissioners*, 8 GEO. WASH. L. REV. 339 (1939); James M. Graham, APPOINTMENTS TO THE REGULATORY AGENCIES THE FEDERAL COMMUNICATIONS COMMISSION AND THE FEDERAL TRADE COMMISSION, 1949–1974 (1976).

[8] William E. Kovacic, THE QUALITY OF APPOINTMENTS AND THE CAPABILITY OF THE FEDERAL TRADE COMMISSION, 49 ADMIN. L. REV. 915 (1997).

attract the Agency's attention. These public activities create tension with the commission's quasi-judicial role.

Over the years, some litigants have attempted to disqualify commissioners. But disqualification requires overcoming a very high hurdle.[9] For instance, consider the failure to disqualify Reagan-era Chairman Miller from a case concerning General Motors, a major former client of Miller's consulting firm. Miller cast the deciding, favorable vote for General Motors in a case concerning car defects. He had previously recused himself from GM matters for two years. The District Court for the District of Columbia reviewed Miller's decision on an "abuse of discretion" standard, and let the vote stand. A high degree of trust is vested in commissioners themselves to decide when to recuse when there is an apparent conflict.[10] Ownership of stock probably causes most commissioner recusals.

### Ex parte contacts and lobbying

The FTC, as with many other agencies, lacks the same kinds of lobbying disclosure rules applied to Congress. As a result, it is a venue for intense yet opaque lobbying, often by former staff and commissioners since the Agency was founded.[11] Academics have produced policy work to affect the commission, sometimes without disclosing that it is client funded,[12] and that it is not formal academic work.[13]

---

9   "... a commissioner should be disqualified only when there has been a clear and convincing showing that the Agency member has an unalterably closed mind on matters critical to the disposition of the proceeding. The 'clear and convincing' test is necessary to rebut the presumption of administrative regularity." *Ass'n of Nat. Advertisers, Inc. v. FTC*, 627 F.2d 1151, 1170 (D.C. Cir. 1979).

10   *Ctr. for Auto Safety v. FTC*, 586 F. Supp. 1245 (D.D.C. 1984).

11   Professor William E. Leuchtenburg related that the FTC has been assaulted by, "interest groups speaking through Congressmen. One commissioner recalled, 'Senators who would not think of seeking to influence a court in the decision of a case pending before it have no compunction about stalking the halls of the Commission and offering ex parte arguments and representations concerning cases pending before it.' " WILLIAM E. LEUCHTENBURG, THE SUPREME COURT REBORN: THE CONSTITUTIONAL REVOLUTION IN THE AGE OF ROOSEVELT 77 (1995).

12   See Willard F. Mueller, *Advertising, Monopoly, and the FTC's Breakfast-Cereal Case: An "Attack on Advertising?,"* 6 ANTITRUST L. ECON. REV. 59 1972 (discussing University of Chicago's Yale Brozen). Rules concerning disclosure of consulting work vary from school to school, and lawyers and business school professors may be obligated not to disclose such sponsorship, to protect client confidentiality. Nonetheless, there is some surprise when these relationships become public. *See, for example*, Robert Weisman, *Academics' 'PR' work raises eyebrows Ethicists questioning efforts for Greenberg Maurice R. "Hank" Greenberg, resigned in 2005*, THE BOSTON GLOBE, April 5, 2005 (discussing University of Chicago's Richard Epstein); Glenn Simpson, *Consumer-Privacy Issue Turns a Retired Professor into a Hot Item*, THE WALL ST. J., June 25, 2001 (discussing Columbia University's Alan F. Westin: "[Westin] is on the payrolls of many of the large financial services, technology and marketing companies that have resisted new privacy rules and legislation").

13   Writing in 1932, Blaisdell summarized thousands of pages of reports concerning methods of "making" public opinion that would be recognized today as modern public relations strategies. These included: "Newspapers and magazines had been supplied with articles, news releases, and 'boiler plate' favorable to the ideas of those in charge of the corporations in the industry. Speakers with the 'right attitude' had

The Commission has an open-door policy for companies under investigation. Most commissioners will meet once with a company under investigation, sometimes even after a complaint has been filed. These meetings give the Commission the opportunity to hear the other side of the story and to express how committed it is to litigation.

Private practitioners who have clients in the FTC's crosshairs regularly do rounds at the Agency to maintain goodwill with commission leadership and staff before and even during investigations. This gives potential respondents the opportunity to convince commissioners that they should not be sued.[14] Staff is present for these visits and are on hand to rebut arguments that respondents make after the meeting.

---

### THE COMMISSION AS SCAPEGOAT

"It is easy to make a scapegoat of federal regulatory agencies, which stand in a vulnerable position somewhere between the White House and Congress. Shouldn't we, rather, ask ourselves why the Agency has been denied sufficient funds to do a real job, why Congress has pre-empted the field in the few instances when the FTC stepped forward boldly, why the White House has undercut its operation with the appointment of mediocre political hacks, why the people of the United States have failed to rise up and demand adequate consumer protection or protection against economic concentration?"[15]

---

Many critics have framed ex parte contacts between those investigated by the FTC and its leadership as a problem.[16] Some argue that the promise of lucrative careers pitches commissioners and staff toward industry-friendly positions. Consider Posner's argument as a young academic: "[A commissioners] will receive no bonus upon entry (or reentry) into private practice for the vigorous championing

---

been made available to meetings of the Rotary Clubs ... Articles by college professors, also in the employ of publicity committees, had been distributed without indicating the relationship of the professor to the industry. Outlines had been prepared to assist instructors giving course in public utility economics. Textbooks had been written ... influence brought to bear to have 'prejudiced' textbooks dropped, well-known college administrators employed to organize conferences ... All this had been done for the purpose of cultivating good-will towards the industry." THOMAS L. BLAISDELL, THE FEDERAL TRADE COMMISSION: AN EXPERIMENT IN THE CONTROL OF BUSINESS 261 (1932). The reports on industry good-will can be found in Utility Corporations, Letter from the Chairman of the Federal Trade Commission in Response to Senate Resolution No. 83, Senate Doc. 92, 70th Congress 1st Sess. March 15, 1928.

[14] In what appears to be standard practice, LabMD officials were invited to visit commissioners before the filing of a formal complaint against the company. *See* MICHAEL J. DAUGHERTY, THE DEVIL INSIDE THE BELTWAY (2013).

[15] Susan Wagner, THE FEDERAL TRADE COMMISSION (1971).

[16] Report on Regulatory Agencies to the President-Elect (December 21, 1960) ("The Landis Report").

of the consumer interest. The gratitude of consumers – indulging the improbable assumption that such a thing exists – cannot be translated into a larger practice. On the other hand, the enmity of the organized economic interests, the trade associations and trade unions, that a zealous pursuit of consumer interests would engender may do him some later harm, while making his tenure with the Commission more tense and demanding than would otherwise be the case . . ."[7] Posner's assessment is puzzling given that the Commission has taken bold investigatory steps since its inception, including the meatpacking effort (see Chapter 1). During his own tenure at the FTC, Posner worked on the cigarette rule, an example of strong intervention against a very powerful, very American industry. More fundamentally, the Commission's historic role is unlike that of the Department of Justice. The FTC is supposed to be in touch with the business community. From a historical viewpoint, regular commission interaction with the business community is a core function of the Agency.

Despite its interactions with industries, the Commission has been relatively free of scandal. Yet, two incidents are of note, both involving President Eisenhower's FTC Chairman, Edward F. Howrey. First, the Vicuña Coat Affair concerned President Eisenhower's Chief of Staff, L. Sherman Adams, who accepted a free vicuña coat from a company under FTC investigation. Vicuña is a soft and expensive wool. Today a vicuña coat costs as much as $50,000. Adams met with Howrey to discuss the matter under investigation, and arranged a meeting between Howrey and the company's president. After the renowned journalist Jack Anderson brought these relationships to light, Adams left the administration. It does not appear that Adams' intervention altered the FTC's course, as the initial examiner and the Commission brought a complaint against the company.

Second, as Chair, Howrey postured the FTC as an advice-giving body, did not seek additional appropriations for the FTC, and used his position to hire Republican allies for patronage purposes. Howrey also hired a management-consulting firm that had access to confidential agency files, yet at the same time the firm was performing services for a company with a matter before the Commission. The reorganization recommended by the consulting firm was a failure and criticized in later reviews of the Agency. During his period as Chairman, Howrey had a number of client conflicts with the Agency, but Howrey seemed to continue with these relationships. The worst example was his formation of an anti-antitrust lobbying practice while he was still Chairman.[18]

---

[17]  Richard Posner, *The Federal Trade Commission*, 37 U. CHI. L. REV. 47, 86 (1969).

[18]  Subsequently Congress enacted 18 U.S.C. §203 to create criminal penalties for such behavior. The Hoover Commission's 1955 report commented unfavorably on outside legal practice by government attorneys. COMMISSION ON THE ORGANIZATION OF THE EXECUTIVE BRANCH OF GOVERNMENT, LEGAL SERVICES AND PROCEDURE (March 1955).

## The revolving door

Title 18 sets forth the general rules for former government employees who advise private-sector clients.[19] Former senior employees have a general one-year "cooling-off" period from representing clients before the Commission. In some situations they may participate in an advisory role "behind the scenes." Other rules supplement the general cooling-off period, and these rules are *matter based* rather than *client based*.

Under eighteen U.S.C §207, there is a permanent ban on "switching sides," that is representing a client on a matter that the employee participated in "personally and substantially." For instance, an employee who worked on Facebook's 2009 privacy policy changes could never represent the company on that matter before the Commission, nor advise the company on how to comply on the consent order.

A two-year cooling-off period is imposed in any matter before the Commission over which the employee had some official responsibility for during the employee's last year at the Agency. However, this appears to be a narrow exception to the permanent ban rule. Any involvement in a matter, such as approving or recommending a course of action, is personal and substantial participation. It triggers the permanent ban for that matter. Former employees who wish to advise clients or appear before the Commission in matters that were pending during their employment must inform the Secretary and obtain clearance from the general counsel's office.[20]

## The Chairmen and Chairwomen

Following the 1949 Hoover Commission Report, a reorganization of the FTC centralized power in the Chairman.[21] Under the Reorganization Plan of 1950, the President of the United States selects the Chairman or Chairwoman (through a new appointment or selection of an existing commissioner). The Chairman selects and supervises personnel, distributes business among the staff, and controls agency funds. Prior to the 1950 plan, the Chairman was appointed by vote among the commissioners.

Because the Chairman has so much power, in effect, the commissioners only have a veto right over major agency decisions. A critical point is that the Chairman selects bureau directors and other key staff leadership. This means that the Chairman broadly sets the Agency's agenda, sets it tone, and can supervise its case selection.

---

[19] 18 U.S.C. §203.
[20] Clearance is governed by 16 C.F.R. §4.1.
[21] The Commission on Organization of the Executive Branch of the Government: The Independent Regulatory Commissions (March 1949) ("The Hoover Commission Report").

## THE THREE BUREAUS

The FTC has three bureaus: the Bureau of Consumer Protection, the Bureau of Competition, and the Bureau of Economics.

### Bureau of Consumer Protection

The Bureau of Consumer Protection (BCP) is tasked with stopping unfair, deceptive, and fraudulent business practices through the collection of complaints, through suits against companies, through the development of trade regulation and other rules, and through consumer education. The BCP has eight divisions: the divisions of Privacy and Identity Protection (DPIP, forty-eight employees), Advertising Practices (DAP, forty-eight employees), Consumer & Business Education, Enforcement (DENF, forty-five employees), Marketing Practices (DMP, forty-two employees), Consumer Response and Operations, Litigation Technology and Analysis, and Financial Practices (DFP, forty-six employees). The Office of the Director of Consumer Protection has thirty-one employees. Responsibility for policing privacy laws can mostly be found in DPIP, but other divisions have authority over issues related to privacy: Advertising Practices (children's advertising, word-of-mouth marketing), Marketing Practices (telemarketing and spam, other high-tech frauds), and Financial Practices (Fair Debt Collection Practices Act). DENF oversees all of the privacy orders.

Established in 2006 and with a staff of approximately fifty, the DPIP is tasked with consumer privacy, identity theft, and information security, and thus almost all privacy activities are centered at the DPIP, with the exceptions noted above, and the placement of a few staff attorneys in the San Francisco Regional Office tasked to privacy (presumably to be close to the technology industry in Silicon Valley). DPIP is responsible for enforcement of the Children's Online Privacy Protection Act, data security, and general enforcement of privacy policies and practices under Section 5. DPIP was first led by Joel Winston, and now by Maneesha Mithal.

Passage of the landmark Dodd–Frank Act and the creation of the Consumer Financial Protection Bureau (CFPB) have made federal responsibility for privacy laws more complex. The FTC had long enforced Section 5 against non-bank entities. But the CFPB was created in part to police such companies. The agencies now share concurrent enforcement authority, and the CFPB received additional rule-making and supervisory authority. A memorandum of understanding between the agencies details the procedure for handling enforcement matters.[22] This is detailed in Chapter 10.

---

[22] Interagency Cooperation Agreement and MOU: Memorandum of Understanding between the Consumer Financial Protection Bureau and the Federal Trade Commission to Ensure Effective Cooperation to Protect Consumers, Prevent Duplication of Efforts, Provide Consistency, and Ensure a Vibrant Marketplace for Consumer Financial Products and Services (January 2012).

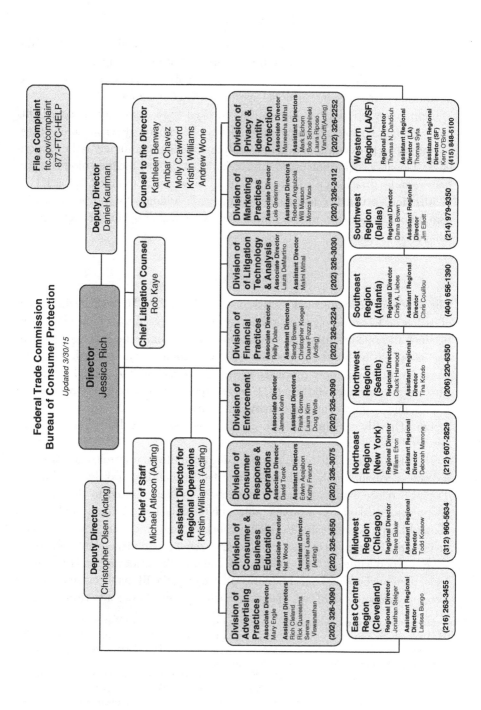

Federal Trade Commission
Bureau of Consumer Protection

Updated 3/30/15

**File a Complaint**
ftc.gov/complaint
877-FTC-HELP

**Director**
Jessica Rich

**Deputy Director**
Christopher Olsen (Acting)

**Deputy Director**
Daniel Kaufman

**Counsel to the Director**
Kathleen Benway
Ambar Chavez
Molly Crawford
Kristin Williams
Andrew Wone

**Chief of Staff**
Michael Atleson (Acting)

**Chief Litigation Counsel**
Rob Kaye

**Assistant Director for Regional Operations**
Kristin Williams (Acting)

**Division of Advertising Practices**
Associate Director
Mary Engle
Assistant Directors
Rich Cleland
Rick Quaresima
Serena
Viswanathan
(202) 326-3090

**Division of Consumer & Business Education**
Associate Director
Nat Wood
Assistant Director
Jennifer Leach
(Acting)
(202) 326-3650

**Division of Consumer Response & Operations**
Associate Director
David Torok
Assistant Directors
Edwin Acajabon
Kathy French
(202) 326-3075

**Division of Enforcement**
Associate Director
James Kohm
Assistant Directors
Frank Gorman
Laura Kim
Doug Wolfe
(202) 326-3090

**Division of Financial Practices**
Associate Director
Reilly Dolan
Assistant Directors
Sandy Brown
Christopher Koegel
Duane Pozza
(Acting)
(202) 326-3224

**Division of Litigation Technology & Analysis**
Associate Director
Laura DeMartino
Assistant Director
Malini Mithal
(202) 326-3030

**Division of Marketing Practices**
Associate Director
Lois Greisman
Assistant Directors
Roberto Anguizola
Will Maxson
Monica Vaca
(202) 326-2412

**Division of Privacy & Identity Protection**
Associate Director
Maneesha Mithal
Assistant Directors
Mark Eichorn
Bob Schoshinski
Laura Riposo
VanDruff(Acting)
(202) 326-2252

**East Central Region (Cleveland)**
Regional Director
Jonathan Steiger
Assistant Regional Director
Larissa Bungo
(216) 263-3455

**Midwest Region (Chicago)**
Regional Director
Steve Baker
Assistant Regional Director
Todd Kossow
(312) 960-5634

**Northeast Region (New York)**
Regional Director
William Efron
Assistant Regional Director
Deborah Marrone
(212) 607-2829

**Northwest Region (Seattle)**
Regional Director
Chuck Harwood
Assistant Regional Director
Tina Kondo
(206) 220-6350

**Southeast Region (Atlanta)**
Regional Director
Cindy A. Liebes
Assistant Regional Director
Chris Couillou
(404) 656-1390

**Southwest Region (Dallas)**
Regional Director
Dama Brown
Assistant Regional Director
Jim Elliott
(214) 979-9350

**Western Region (LA/SF)**
Regional Director
Thomas N. Dahdouh
Assistant Regional Director (LA)
Thomas Syta
Assistant Regional Director (SF)
Kerry O'Brien
(415) 848-5100

## Bureau of Competition

The Bureau of Competition enforces the antitrust provisions of the FTC Act and the Clayton Act, in collaboration with the Department of Justice. The bureau investigates violations of these laws, consults with policy-makers on competition issues, and attempts to harmonize international approaches to competition.

Information privacy has rarely been invoked as a competition issue. This approach may change because of the tendency of companies to create all-inclusive platforms that track consumers ubiquitously and mediate consumers' online experiences. Google's acquisition of DoubleClick in 2007 created the then most comprehensive online tracking platform, and privacy concerns were raised in the FTC's deliberation of whether to permit the merger.[23] Additionally, privacy concerns surrounding first-degree price discrimination (see Chapter 6) could be reframed as competition matters.

## Bureau of Economics

The Bureau of Economics (BE) is tasked with helping the FTC evaluate the impact of its actions by providing analysis for competition and consumer protection investigations and rule-makings, and by analyzing the economic impact of government regulations on businesses and consumers. With commission approval, it has the power to use compulsory processes to engage in general and special economic surveys, investigations, and reports. Congress required the BE to perform some of its most interesting recent privacy activities, such as a study of accuracy in consumer reports. The BE is often led by an academic economist on leave from a faculty position.[24]

The BE is divided into three areas focusing on antitrust, research, and consumer protection. About eighty Ph.D.-level-educated economists work for the bureau. Twenty-two economists and eight research analysts are tasked to the over 300 attorneys focused on the consumer protection mission. The economists help design compulsory processes, evaluate evidence collected from processes, provide opinions on penalties to be levied in cases, conduct analyses of cases independent of the BCP, serve as expert witnesses, support litigation, and provide perspective on larger policy issues presented by enforcement. In this last category, the BE has been an important force in eliminating state laws that restrict certain types of price advertising.[25]

---

[23] Maureen K. Ohlhausen & Alexander P. Okuliar, *Competition, Consumer Protection, and The Right [Approach] to Privacy*, ___ Antitrust L. J. ___ (2015); Pamela Jones Harbour & Tara Isa Koslov, *Section 2 in a Web 2.0 World*, 76(3) ANTITRUST L. J. 769 (2010); Peter Swire, *Protecting Consumers: Privacy Matters in Antitrust Analysis* (October 19, 2007).

[24] FTC OFFICE OF THE INSPECTOR GENERAL, EVALUATION OF THE FEDERAL TRADE COMMISSION'S BUREAU OF ECONOMICS OIG EVALUATION REPORT NO. 15-03 (June 30, 2015).

[25] For a general discussion of these contributions, *see* Janis K. Pappalardo, *Contributions by Federal Trade Commission Economists to Consumer Protection: Research, Policy, and Law Enforcement*, 33(2) J. PUB. POL'Y MKTG. 244 (2014).

The BE has a disciplining effect on the Agency's instinct to intervene to protect consumers. As former Chairman Kovacic and David Hyman explained, the BE "is a voice for the value of competition, for the inclusion of market-oriented strategies in the mix of regulatory tools, and for awareness of costs of specific regulatory choices ... BE has helped instill within the FTC a culture that encourages ex post evaluation to measure the policy results of specific initiatives."[26] According to the duo, the BE plays a major policy coordination role because of a culture of insularity among the other bureaus.

In recommending remedies to the commissioners, the BE weighs options that could make the consumer whole, by putting the consumer in the position she occupied before the illegal transaction. BE also considers how a deception shapes demand for a product, thereby inducing individuals to buy who would not make a purchase absent an illegal practice, or whether customers paid more for a product because of a deception. The BE considers whether remedies will deter future unfair or deceptive practices.

In its evaluative activities, the BE's lodestar is consumer welfare, and its economists claim that they have no other social agenda in their activities. The BE's approach "has traditionally focused on fostering 'informed consumer choice' in well-functioning markets."[27]

The special dynamics of personal information transactions makes it difficult for the BE to justify monetary remedies in privacy cases. Consider a fraud where consumers are promised an 18-karat gold trinket but delivered a 10-karat one. The FTC can easily calculate the injury to the consumer based on the price differential between the two products. A market exists that clearly differentiates between these products and assigns a higher price to the 18-karat object. Turning to privacy cases, the calculation is not as simple. Many services provided to a consumer lack a price tag because they are "free." The deception might be unrelated to price, but rather to a subtle feature, such as the degree of publicity given to some fact about the user.

Furthermore, individual privacy preferences vary. Some consumers may have never considered privacy attributes in their service selection or may not care about privacy a great deal. Unlike something as salient as the purity of a gold object, specific information uses may not enter into the consumer's awareness when selecting a service. Without a functioning market for privacy that features prices, the BE struggles to assign value to information privacy wrongs. These uncertainties may explain why there are so few privacy actions with any kind of monetary relief.

---

[26] David A. Hyman & William E. Kovacic, *Why Who Does What Matters: Governmental Design, Agency Performance, the CFPB and PPACA*, 82 GEO. WASH. L. REV. 1446 (2014).

[27] Paul A. Pautler, *A Brief History of the FTC's Bureau of Economics: Reports, Mergers, and Information Regulation*, 46 REV. IND. ORG. 59 (2015).

Other dynamics cause the BE to be skeptical of information privacy cases.[28] The economists systematically dismiss survey research in this field, because decisions about privacy can implicate complex short- and long-term trade-offs that are not well presented in surveys. Sometimes economists will argue that consumer behavior belies stated preferences for privacy. One oft-stated rationale is that if consumers really cared about privacy, they would read privacy notices.

---

### AGENCY OPERATING COST AND RECOVERY OF MONETARY RELIEF

The FTC proclaimed in 2014 that "Over the past 3 years ... the FTC returned over $196 million to victims of deceptive or unfair practices and forwarded $117 million to the US Treasury." But during this period, operating the Agency cost taxpayers over $900 million.

Actually collecting on the FTC's many judgments and settlements is a major challenge. In 2012, the Commission created a unit focused on collections within the Bureau of Consumer Protection. Still, over the past ten years, only about 25 percent of judgments and settlements result in full payment.

There are many reasons for non-collection of judgments and settlements. First, many companies resist paying. As a result, the FTC has to engage in significant investigation and garnishments in order to fully collect. For instance, to complete almost $16 million of collections against Hi-Tech Pharmaceuticals, the FTC had to subpoena sixty-four different entities and obtain thirty-five garnishments. Second, especially with true scam artists, there is little money left from the fraud. Third, some respondents attempt to evade penalties by filing bankruptcy, but in those cases, the FTC has intervened to make the judgment non-dischargeable. Finally, some respondents hide assets. In suspended judgment cases, the FTC uses an "avalanche" clause in order to reimpose the full amount of a penalty if the respondent hides assets. In other cases, it has used coercive detention. For instance, Kevin Trudeau was ordered to jail based on his unwillingness to reveal to a receiver the location of hidden assets.

---

There is some tension between the legal, more moralistic culture of the BCP and the BE.[29] BCP lawyers are likely to view a misrepresentation as an inherent wrong, while the BE is more likely to want harm to be present in addition to a deceptive

---

[28] Peter P. Swire, *Efficient Confidentiality for Privacy, Security, and Confidential Business Information*, BROOKINGS-WHARTON PAPERS ON FINANCIAL SERVICES (2003). ("my experience from government service that graduate training in economics is an important predictor that someone will not 'get' the issue of privacy protection.")

[29] Joshua L. Wiener, *Federal Trade Commission: Time of Transition*, 33(2) J. PUB. POL'Y MKTG. 217 (2014). ("Prior to working at the FTC, I naively thought in terms of FTC versus business. I quickly learned that a more adversarial contest was lawyers versus economists.")

practice before taking action. Kenneth Clarkson and former Chairman Timothy Muris explain: "The economists' role is controversial. Many attorneys, sometimes even those the top of the bureau, are dissatisfied with the economists' substantive positions, with their right to comment, and what they perceive as the undue delay that the economists cause."[30] Professor Patrick Murphy characterized the BE as having a "more conservative mindset" than the lawyers in the BCP, and that the two bureaus seemed to be in an ongoing battle.[31]

The BE has a more independent, academic culture than the BCP as well – the economists are free to express their opinions, and even press them in situations where they are in disagreement with the Agency's actions.[32] This internal questioning can cause attorneys to think that the economists are not fully participating in the consumer protection mission, and instead frustrating it by trying to engage in academic discourse about situations attorneys see as law enforcement matters. Attorneys know that the Agency's hand is weakened in litigation when it is apparent that a matter is controversial within the FTC. Attorneys also see economists as serving in an expert witness role, a service function that should be deferential to the strategic decisions of the litigators.

Economistic reasoning sometimes flummoxes lawyers. Economists are more likely to take a long view of a challenge, allowing the marketplace to work out the problem even where the law prohibits certain practices or gives the Agency tools to redress the problem.

An example of economistic reasoning comes from John Calfee, a longtime expert with the American Enterprise Institute and former BE advisor. Calfee thought that most advertising regulation was perverse. To press the point, he used cigarette advertising as a model. He argued that when tobacco companies touted their products as healthy or as healthier than alternatives, the claims actually undermined tobacco companies. Claims such as "Not a single case of throat irritation due to smoking Camels" are the bête noire of lawyer/regulators. Tobacco companies engaged in vigorous counteradvertising on health effects of smoking, and, although the claims were false, in Calfee's view they taught consumers that all smoking was unhealthful. In fact, no amount of regulation could tell consumers about smoking's danger than the very ads produced by tobacco companies. According to Calfee, FTC regulation then caused tobacco companies to stop mentioning health completely, and the industry's advertising became less information-rich. In short, Calfee argued that regulation caused smoking to be portrayed in a kinder light.[33]

---

[30] Kenneth W. Clarkson & Timothy J. Muris, *Commission Performance, Incentives, and Behavior, in* THE FEDERAL TRADE COMMISSION SINCE 1970: ECONOMIC REGULATION AND BUREAUCRATIC BEHAVIOR (Kenneth W. Clarkson & Timothy J. Muris, eds., 1981).

[31] Patrick E. Murphy, *Reflections on the Federal Trade Commission*, 33(2) J. PUB. POL'Y MKTG 225 (2014).

[32] Joshua D. Wright, *Statement of Commissioner Joshua D. Wright on the FTC's Bureau of Economics, Independence, and Agency Performance*, August 6, 2015.

[33] JOHN H. CALFEE, FEAR OF PERSUASION (1997); Posner too expressed qualified support for this reasoning. *See* ABA, REPORT OF THE ABA COMMISSION TO STUDY THE FEDERAL TRADE COMMISSION (September 15, 1969) (Separate Statement of Richard Posner).

Attorneys are likely to dismiss such reasoning as crazy talk.[34] Inherently, Calfee argued that regulators should ignore a form of false advertising. This would put the FTC in an impossible situation where it failed to honor its statutory mandate.

The BCP/BE tension is unfortunate, because the BE is poised to contribute substantially to consumer protection matters. A recent example of labor-intensive, high-quality BE work comes from the economists Beth A. Freeborn, Loren Smith, and Peter Vander Nat, who carried out a valuable and complex study of the accuracy of consumer reporting agency files. The report found that 13 percent of consumers had material errors in their files, meaning that tens of millions of Americans could be getting credit on worse terms because of inaccurate files.[35]

### OVERSIGHT

Six committees in Congress exercise power over the Commission: the Commerce, Appropriations, and Judiciary committees in the House and Senate. As the FTC touches many industries, it can attract the attention and displeasure of additional committees.

Other federal agencies, such as the Federal Communications Commission (FCC), have a natural constituency. For instance, telecommunications providers have a vested interest in the basic health of the FCC and vice versa. The FTC has no natural industry or consumer constituency,[36] which leads to structural weaknesses for the Agency. On the other hand, its broad mandate reduces the risk of capture by a specific industry.

---

#### BLOWBACK AND CREATING A CONSTITUENCY

"Congress gets upset only when an agency does something, does what it's supposed to do. Congress doesn't, or rarely does, get upset when an agency does nothing ..."[37]

A fully engaged pursuit of information privacy efforts will make many enemies in Congress and in the business community. E. Pendleton Herring noted in 1934 that "Making political enemies was soon found to be an incident in the routine of administration. The discharging of official duties meant

---

[34] Neil Postman, CRAZY TALK, STUPID TALK (1976).
[35] FTC, Section 319 of the Fair and Accurate Credit Transactions Act of 2003: Third Interim Federal Trade Commission Report to Congress Concerning the Accuracy of Information in Credit Reports (December 2008).
[36] A narrow exception to this may be the fees received by the FTC from companies for filing premerger review under the Hart–Scott–Rodino Antitrust Improvements Act.
[37] NORMAN I. SILBER, WITH ALL DELIBERATE SPEED, THE LIFE OF PHILIP ELMAN (2004) (quoting Commissioner Philip Elman).

interfering with business, and often 'big business.' "[38] The FTC learned in the meatpacking, insurance, and children's advertising efforts that some industries strike back, weakening the Agency.

Mark V. Nadel observed in 1971 that "Given the new public concern with consumer protection the agencies (FTC and FDA) were surprisingly reticent in mobilizing that concern to their benefit. They failed to seize constituency-building opportunities . . ."[39] A lack of constituency is a challenge for the FTC. Unlike many other government agencies, the FTC lacks an industry that is heavily interested in its thriving.[40] Writing in the context of the KidVid controversy, William Baer observed that the FTC "simply took on much more than its political base could support." In this, Baer identified a pathology that has plagued the Commission since 1919: at the behest of Congress, the FTC investigates a problem and it finds awful practices and campaigns against them. Meanwhile other members of Congress hear from constituents stung by the Commission's activities, and, instead of addressing the wrongs found by the Agency they attack the FTC. The meatpackers, insurance industry, and funeral industry all responded to Congressionally requested investigations by attempting to decapitate the FTC.

In the privacy space, the US–EU Safe Harbor creates strong incentives for industry to be invested in the FTC. Companies that join the Safe Harbor are allowed to handle Europeans' personal information without risking enforcement actions from all the European Union nations. Instead, the FTC handles enforcement of wrongdoing at the urging of EU member nations. If for some reason the FTC could not enforce Safe Harbor (because of an appropriations shutdown or adverse court decision), European Union nations could demand a right to directly enforce their laws against American companies. Thus, although they may not realize it, services that control or process data internationally have a very strong stake in a functioning FTC.

To address the pendulum swinging and problems of blowback, Thomas H. Stanton recommended (1) that the FTC focus on case-by-case enforcement, because the alternative of rule-making has the effect of policing the most responsible while bad actors just ignore the rules; (2) that FTC leadership

---

[38] E. Pendleton Herring, *Politics, Personalities, and the Federal Trade Commission*, I, 28(6) AMERICAN POLITICAL SCIENCE REVIEW 1016 (1934).

[39] THE POLITICS OF CONSUMER PROTECTION 81–82 (1971).

[40] William J. Baer, *At the Turning Point: The Commission in 1978, in* MARKETING AND ADVERTISING REGULATION: THE FEDERAL TRADE COMMISSION IN THE 1990S (Patrick E. Murphy & William L. Wilkie, eds., 1990). (". . . unlike such regulatory agencies as the Federal Communications Commission, the Interstate Commerce Commission, or the Food and Drug Administration, the Federal Trade Commission lacks a single industry with a strong, vested interest in its continued vitality. Thus, any significant agency law enforcement activity is likely to receive little support and to generate much controversy and criticism.")

should court responsible industry by participating in business workshops and explain that the Agency is concerned primarily with policing the minority of business wrongdoers; (3) that the FTC use its fact-finding powers to bring publicity to bad actors without using enforcing sticks.[41]

## POWERS OF THE COMMISSION

The FTC has extraordinary powers. It can bring cases against individual companies, partnerships, individuals,[42] the professions,[43] trade associations,[44] successors to dissolved corporations,[45] and, in some situations, nonprofits[46] and even government agencies.[47] The FTC has the power to bring administrative complaints and actions in federal court (for purposes of this book, most FTC investigations, actions, and administrative proceedings are referred to as "matters," but federal lawsuits are specified as "cases").

The Commission lacks statutory "aiding and abetting" authority, except where granted by statute (e.g., in telemarketing and spam enforcement matters).[48] However, at least two courts have imposed liability for aiding and abetting frauds.[49] In 2009, the Agency requested the power to sue those who "knowingly or recklessly . . . provide . . . substantial assistance to another" in Section 5 cases, but Congress did not grant this power. Despite this limitation, in some matters, the FTC has articulated a "means and instrumentalities" theory to address contributory liability.[50]

Congress set a low bar for the Commission to bring an administrative proceeding. It can issue a complaint whenever it has "reason to believe that any such person, partnership, or corporation has been or is using any unfair method of competition or

---

[41] Thomas H. Stanton, *Comments on the Commission in 1978, in* Marketing and Advertising Regulation: The Federal Trade Commission in the 1990s (Patrick E. Murphy & William L. Wilkie, eds., 1990).

[42] An individual can be liable under the FTC Act if he participated directly in the deceptive acts or had the authority to control them, and had knowledge of the misrepresentations, was recklessly indifferent to the truth or falsity of the misrepresentation, or was aware of a high probability of fraud along with an intentional avoidance of the truth. *See POM Wonderful, LLC v. FTC*, 777 F.3d 478 (D.C. Cir. 2015); *FTC v. Amy Travel Serv., Inc.*, 875 F.2d 564 (7th Cir.), *cert. denied*, 493 US 954 (1989). In practice, individuals are named when the defendant is a closely held or private corporation. The FTC can also obtain money from individuals who benefited from frauds yet were not party to the fraud (so-called "relief defendants"). See *FTC v. AmeriDebt, Inc.*, 343 F. Supp. 2d 451 (D. Md. 2004).

[43] *Am. Med. Ass'n v. FTC*, 638 F.2d 443 (2d Cir. 1980), *aff'd*, 455 US 676 (1982).

[44] *Nat'l Harness Mfrs.' Ass'n v. FTC*, 268 F. 705 (6th Cir. 1920).

[45] *P.F. Collier & Son Corp. v. FTC*, 427 F.2d 261 (6th Cir. 1970), *cert. denied*, 91 S.Ct. 188 (1970).

[46] *See, for example, Community Blood Bank v. FTC*, 405 F.2d 1011 (8th Cir. 1969); *California Dental Ass'n v. FTC*, 526 US 756 (1999) (Commission's jurisdiction "extends to an association that . . . provides substantial economic benefit to its for-profit members").

[47] The FTC can sue government agencies under the Fair Credit Reporting Act.

[48] *S.E.C. v. Apuzzo*, 689 F.3d 204 (2d Cir. 2012).

[49] *Waltham Watch Co. v. FTC*, 318 F.2d 28 (7th Cir. 1963); *Deer v. FTC*, 152 F.2d 65 (2d Cir. 1945).

[50] *In the Matter of DesignerWare, LLC*, 155 F.T.C. 421 (2013).

unfair or deceptive act or practice in or affecting commerce," and "if it shall appear to the Commission that a proceeding by it in respect thereof would be to the interest of the public . . ."[51]

Because one of the FTC's purposes is to prevent violations of the Federal Trade Commission Act (FTC Act), the Agency can bring cases even where there is no intent to deceive or harm the public. It can bring cases where the public has not yet been injured (e.g., the matter against Microsoft for falsely claiming that its identity authentication technology was more secure than others).[52] It can sue to prevent practices even where they are commonplace in the market.[53] It can even selectively enforce the law against a single company where competitors engage in the same practices.[54]

---

CONTROLLING THE POWER OF THE FTC

A 1981 study of the Agency edited by Kenneth Clarkson and Timothy Muris (then FTC BCP director and future Chairman) concluded that the FTC was largely uncontrolled by other branches of government. Clarkson argued that Congress had only a limited ability to oversee it, and that oversight and ad hoc monitoring rarely influenced the Agency.[55] The executive branch has several levers to rein in the Commission, including choice in appointment, scrutiny focused on major efforts of the Agency, and trimming of the FTC's budget by the Office of Management and Budget.[56] However, since President Franklin Roosevelt's failed attempt to remove a commissioner, the executive has largely not intervened in FTC activities. In fact, it appears that no president visited the FTC, despite its location just blocks from the White House, between 1937 and 2015.

---

[51] 15 U.S.C. §45(b).

[52] *Spiegel, Inc.* v. *FTC.*, 494 F.2d 59 (7th Cir. 1974), *cert. denied*, 419 US 896 (1974); *Bear Mill Mfg. Co.* v. *FTC*, 98 F.2d 67 (2d Cir. 1938). ("We think that the Commission is authorized to guard the public against such dangers. Indeed, it exists to promote fair rules of trade and in so doing to curb practices that involve a likelihood of injury to the public, even if in a particular case the acts complained of are, as here, innocent in purpose and may thus far have done little harm.")

[53] *FTC* v. *Standard Educ. Soc.*, 86 F.2d 692, 695 (2d Cir. 1936) *modified on other grounds*, 302 US 112 (1937); *FTC* v. *Winsted Hosiery Co.*, 258 US 483 (1922).

[54] *Johnson Products Co.* v. *FTC*, 549 F.2d 35 (7th Cir. 1977); *Ger-Ro-Mar, Inc.* v. *FTC*, 518 F.2d 33 (2d Cir. 1975).

[55] Kenneth W. Clarkson, *Legislative Constraints*, in THE FEDERAL TRADE COMMISSION SINCE 1970: ECONOMIC REGULATION AND BUREAUCRATIC BEHAVIOR (Kenneth W. Clarkson & Timothy J. Muris, eds., 1981).

[56] Kenneth W. Clarkson, *Executive Constraints*, in THE FEDERAL TRADE COMMISSION SINCE 1970: ECONOMIC REGULATION AND BUREAUCRATIC BEHAVIOR (Kenneth W. Clarkson & Timothy J. Muris, eds., 1981).

The FTC has several autonomy-preserving features (commissioner tenure, for-cause removal, multimember composition, litigation and adjudication authority) that make it more independent from the executive than other agencies. Muris argued that, since the 1930s, the courts have deferred to the FTC on policy matters, especially when it uses Section 5 as the basis for action: "The courts place almost no restraint upon what commercial practices the FTC can proscribe . . ."[57]

On the other hand, Charles Mitchell, in his study of interactions between Congress and the FTC from 1970 to 1983,[58] found that Congress substantially influenced the Agency but only with sustained effort: "In many different matters, Congress was able to change an FTC policy only after years of effort." Mitchell continues, between 1970 and 1977 Congress passed several laws, transforming it from "a lethargic commission into an aggressive antitrust and consumer agency." Mitchell emphasizes the appropriations committees as primary sources of oversight and interference.

With all these powers, the FTC is entrusted with great discretion in matter selection and priority setting. Furthermore, the Agency does not appear to have any formal factors for matter selection. A 2014 Inspector General Report noted the use of five different rationales among the BCP divisions. These included consumer harm; whether related matters were being litigated; the volume of sales made by a respondent; whether the respondent was a repeat offender; and whether the behavior was egregious.[59]

Despite having these wide-ranging powers, the FTC's primary tactic in privacy is an information-forcing one, namely the workshop. The FTC has held dozens of workshops that are open to the public where companies, trade associations, advocates, and academics help build a record about privacy problems, new business models, and public policy approaches. Many industry lawyers and businesses are eager to participate in these events, and it is common for panels to have ten or more speakers for a single session.

---

[57] Timothy J. Muris, *Judicial Constraints*, in THE FEDERAL TRADE COMMISSION SINCE 1970: ECONOMIC REGULATION AND BUREAUCRATIC BEHAVIOR (Kenneth W. Clarkson & Timothy J. Muris, eds., 1981).

[58] Charles Louis Mitchell, Federal Trade Commission Policy Making and Congress 1970–1983 (1984) (Ph.D. dissertation, University of Tennessee).

[59] FTC Office of Inspector General, Evaluation of the Federal Trade Commission's Bureau of Consumer Protection Resources, OIG Evaluation Report No. 14-003, October 2, 2014.

## Trade regulation rules

The 1975 Magnuson–Moss Warranty Act[60] formalized the FTC's power to promulgate rules that "define with specificity acts or practices which are unfair or deceptive acts or practices in or affecting commerce."[61] The FTC can enforce trade regulation rules and obtain civil penalties for their violation (when the rule provides for such penalties). Existing trade regulation rules appear in title 16 of the Code of Federal Regulations under subchapter D. Trade regulation rules have fallen out of favor following the reaction to the KidVid proceeding, the funeral rule, and the used car rule (see Chapter 2).

The rule-making structure created by Congress in the Magnuson–Moss act is considered a failure by the Commission and is unlikely to be used for privacy matters. Magnuson–Moss proceedings take many years, because the procedural requirements are more demanding than standard Administrative Procedures Act rule-making. Pamela B. Stuart summarizes one such proceeding concerning mobile homes: "More than 400 motions and other pleadings were filed. Three sets of hearings were held at which the staff, industry, and consumer lawyers examined expert and lay witnesses concerning warranty practices in the industry . . ." Eleven years and 260,000 pages of records later, the Commission voted unanimously to terminate the rule-making.[62]

---

### SO MANY RULES

Starting in the 1960s, the FTC read its organic statute as conveying the power to create trade regulation rules. Many of the rules from the 1960s have been repealed, but when they were in effect, violators could be subject to significant fines. Some, such as the cigarette rule, which required health hazard labels on tobacco products, were forward-looking and important interventions in the marketplace. Others were not so seminal. In 1995, the FTC repealed a quarter of the existing trade regulation rules, including the following:

The quick-freeze spray rule: The FTC promulgated this rule to require warning labels on cans of refrigerant used to frost cocktail glasses at bars. Apparently bartenders used dichlorofluoromethane (better known as Freon or R 21) for frosting glasses. People were critically injured or killed from inhaling the product, and so the FTC mandated a label warning: "inhalation of the concentrated vapors of this product is harmful and may cause death."[63]

---

[60] Pub. L. 93–637, 88 Stat. 2183 (1975).
[61] 15 U.S.C.A. §57a(a)(1)(B). In 1973, the D.C. Circuit held that the Agency had power to create rules based on the FTC Act. *See Nat'l Petroleum Refiners Ass'n v. FTC*, 482 F.2d 672 (D.C. Cir. 1973).
[62] Pamela B. Stuart, THE FEDERAL TRADE COMMISSION (1991).
[63] 16 CFR Part 417.

The spray was eventually phased out along with other R 21-based products because of their effect on the ozone layer.

The sleeping bag and tablecloth rules: These products were advertised with "cut sizes," meaning the dimensions of the product before they were finished. The rules required sleeping bags[64] and tablecloths to be advertised with their finished size.[65]

Fiberglass curtain and draperies rule: Required warnings that fiberglass window dressings could cause skin irritation when handled.[66]

The binocular rule: Specified terms for the marketing of binoculars and field glasses. This came about because manufactures made field glasses disguised as real binoculars (devices with a mirror or prism).[67]

The extension ladder rule: Required ladders to be advertised with their maximum working length rather than their overall length.[68]

A 1979 assessment of agency rule-making found that the average one created a record of over 40,000 pages.[69] It is popularly believed that if a general, online privacy rule-making were to be started, it simply would be stale by its implementation date. Just consider what a rule promulgated in 2007 to address Facebook and Google would apply today – these services change so quickly that it is difficult to imagine that a rule could capture their problematic activities. As a result, the privacy rules that do exist (such as the children's privacy rule discussed in Chapter 7) were one-off proceedings where Congress directed the Agency to act under the faster-moving Administrative Procedures Act instead of Magnuson–Moss.

## Investigations

The FTC's investigatory power is very broad[70] and is akin to an inquisitorial body. On its own initiative, it can investigate a broad range of businesses without any indication of a predicate offense having occurred.[71] Though several kinds of businesses have been exempted from Section 5 authority (including common carriers and banks), under the 1973 Amendments, the FTC may use compulsory processes to

[64] 16 CFR Part 400.
[65] 16 CFR Part 404.
[66] 16 CFR Part 413.
[67] 16 CFR Part 402.
[68] 16 CFR Part 418.
[69] Administrative Conference of the United States, Hybrid Rulemaking Procedures of the Federal Trade Commission, Recommendation Number 79–1 (1979).
[70] John Maynard Harlan & Lewis M. McCandless, The Federal Trade Commission: Its Nature and Powers (1916). ("The investigative power of the Trade Commission is comprehensive.")
[71] 15 U.S.C. §46(a); FTC v. *Carter*, 464 F. Supp. 633 (D.D.C. 1979) *aff'd*, 636 F.2d 781 (D.C. Cir. 1980); *but see* FTC v. Am. *Tobacco Co.*, 264 US 298 (1924).

obtain information from these exempt entities in investigating other businesses.[72] The FTC can also obtain income tax returns from the Internal Revenue Service.[73] It receives Suspicious Activity Reports (SARs) from the Department of the Treasury's Financial Crimes Enforcement Network (FinCEN), a central repository of suspect transactions.

The FTC's Operating Manual, available online, describes an intricate system of "initial phase" and "full investigations." However, the Operating Manual was released in 2003, and soon became out of date. Today, the FTC's consumer protection investigations operate very differently for several institutional and privacy case-specific reasons. First, the work overhead and personal reputational investment involved in obtaining approval for compulsory processes can be considerable. Thus, FTC attorneys rely on internet "investigations" where the target's website is visited, the privacy policy is copied, and the like. At times, the Agency heavily relies on "voluntary" requests for information as well. Second, the Agency's culture prevents the memorialization of information that might harm the Agency's law enforcement efforts. It encourages in-person meetings and oral communications. The FTC automatically deletes internal e-mail after 45 days, unless the Agency employee moves it to a folder or when the message is being preserved because of litigation.[74] Third, statistical reporting can tarnish the Agency's reputation, especially if those statistics show many investigations opened and later closed (or never closed), or the length of time investigations take. This too militates in favor of informal processes.

Investigations can be initiated in any number of ways – from consumer complaints made to the Consumer Sentinel system, from businesses exposing the practices of competitors, from members of Congress who often forward consumer complaints on to the FTC, or just from the observations of staff attorneys as they interact with companies. It is rumored that most privacy cases were actuated by complaints from competitors. Some investigations are the result of trade and popular press news articles that attract the attention of an FTC employee. There is no formal complaint procedure for consumers and competitors – they can simply send a signed statement to the Commission detailing wrongdoing.[75]

In the privacy field, there is every indication that FTC attorneys are following a structural case model, where they study an industry or range of practices to make strategic policy change. This means that case-by-case enforcement is being used to achieve the kinds of ends normally met through a rule. Because so many companies have privacy problems, and because there are so many different kinds of privacy issues, FTC attorneys operate in a target-rich environment. They enjoy a

[72] 15 U.S.C. §46(l). The FTC can even obtain records prepared by businesses confidentially for the Census Bureau. *See St. Regis Paper Co.* v. *US*, 368 US 208 (1961).

[73] Exec. Order No. 10544, Inspection of Income Tax Returns by Federal Trade Commission, 19 Fed. Reg. 4289 (July 12, 1954).

[74] *FTC* v. *Lights of Am. Inc.*, No. SACV 10–1333 JVS, 2012 WL 695008 (C.D. Cal. January 20, 2012).

[75] 16 C.F.R. §2.2.

great deal of autonomy in selecting targets, and planning what amounts to policy change in the field.

---

### STRUCTURAL VERSUS CASE-BY-CASE APPROACHES

Thomas C. Blaisdell's 1932 analysis of the Agency concluded that it "has been little more than a body for the regulation of the trade practices of 'small business.' This is contrary to the expectation and plan of its founders, who conceived a body to protect both small business and the consumer ..."[76] Similarly, the National Industrial Conference Board published three reports on the early commission, concluding that the Agency directed its attention against insignificant companies, and characterized the Agency's trade conference procedures as a form of tokenism.[77]

In modern times, pursuit of trivial matters is signified by the "mailbag approach," where the FTC merely reacts to whatever complaints are submitted by consumers. This is opposed to structural approaches, where the FTC plans a litigation strategy against a certain practice, and takes high-impact cases or engages in rule-making. Both approaches have advantages and disadvantages. The case-by-case approach is incremental and conducive to a kind of consensus-making, but it can be abused through the pursuit of marginal, poorly resourced actors. It can act as a ratchet for more and more requirements. The case-by-case approach presents a kind of prisoner dilemma problem, where individual companies have incentives to sign a broad consent agreement to save their own skin. In the process, the company effectively binds all other companies to the promises in the consent agreement.

Industry-wide approaches may be more comprehensive, with more input from stakeholders. At the same time, industry-wide rules can be stultifying, and critics see such regulation as "transcendent and dangerous."[78]

Consider Professor Stephen Calkins' defense of mailbag cases: "These cases raise few of the subtle issues associated with traditional advertising cases; they do not challenge actions by major advertising agencies; and they are rarely defended by the traditional advertising bar ... However, no one suggests that this kind of fraud is declining, and it is an odd notion to say that the FTC should avoid these cases because the wrongdoing is so obvious."[79]

---

[76] THE FEDERAL TRADE COMMISSION: AN EXPERIMENT IN THE CONTROL OF BUSINESS 261 (1932).

[77] National Industrial Conference Board., Watkins, M. W., United States., & National Industrial Conference Board (1940). Public regulation of competitive practices in business enterprise. New York City: National Industrial Conference Board, Inc.

[78] BERNICE ROTHMAN HASIN, CONSUMERS, COMMISSIONS, AND CONGRESS: LAW, THEORY, AND THE FEDERAL TRADE COMMISSION, 1968–1985 (1987).

[79] Stephen Calkins, *Kirkpatrick II: Counsel Responds, in* MARKETING AND ADVERTISING REGULATION: THE FEDERAL TRADE COMMISSION IN THE 1990S (Patrick E. Murphy & William L. Wilkie, eds., 1990).

When opening an investigation, FTC lawyers check an internal "Matter Management System" to see whether others at the Agency are examining the same defendant. Consumer Sentinel is checked for relevant consumer complaints. The Consumer Sentinel database appears to be primarily used to bolster existing investigations by finding victims rather than as a source for new investigations. The investigation is assigned a "seven-digit" FTC matter number. The first two digits refer to the fiscal year that the Agency started the investigation. The next number corresponds to the kind of investigation, with 1 for competition, 2 consumer protection, 3 advisory opinions, and 4 special investigations. The last four digits are the case number, which are issued sequentially. Thus, case 142-0010 would indicate the tenth investigation initiated in fiscal year 2014, and that it was a consumer protection effort.

## Litigation holds

When future litigation is probable, the FTC must issue a litigation hold.[80] This requires the Agency to retain all records concerning the matter. The issuance of a voluntary or compulsory process, or initiation of a full-phase investigation itself does not necessarily require a hold to be established. This reflects the FTC's broad power to investigate and the fact that most investigations do not result in litigation.

Litigation holds are very burdensome, as many different employees from various offices within the Commission might review or comment on a case. The Agency tries to delay triggering litigation holds and to reduce records subject to the holds by relying on in-person meetings, and by avoiding e-mail and voice mail.

## Voluntary process: access letters

Some agency investigations start with the issuance of a voluntary "access letter" by a staff attorney. These are information requests that carry no legal force. A company may ignore the access letter, but this is fraught with peril,[81] especially in privacy matters. A nonresponse, excessive delay, or a combative response signals to the staff attorney that something is amiss.

The access letter may be exceedingly broad and specify an unreasonable date for compliance. But consider it from the perspective of the FTC staff attorney – the request is sent "in the dark." The attorney is not trying to engage in a fishing expedition but, at the same time, the attorney has no insight into the company's inner workings, accounting systems, and general practices. The staff attorney

See also Richard A. Posner, *The Federal Trade Commission*, 37(1) U. Chi. L. Rev. 47, 81 (1969). ("Strange as it may seem, the FTC's frequently decried proclivity for going after small chiselers rests, one imagines accidentally, on sound economic foundations. In general the problem of consumer deception is created by the fly-by-night operator and the con man, not by the reputable firm.")

[80]  *FTC v. Lights of Am. Inc.*, No. SACV 10–1333 JVS, 2012 WL 695008 (C.D. Cal. January 20, 2012).

[81]  Marcy J. K. Tiffany, *Consumer Protection: The Nuts and Bolts of an FTC Investigation*, 60 Antitrust L. J. 139 (1991).

probably knows it is overbroad, and hopes it will trigger a phone call from the investigative target to discover the information sought. On such a call, one can come to a compromise on the scope and timeline of the request, establish goodwill, and, importantly, obtain an extension for compliance. One may be able to learn the basis and potential legal theories of the FTC's inquiry – did the staff attorney come across a privacy policy that raised questions? Did the attorney find consumer complaints that possibly could be resolved? Did a company representative say something at a conference that raised eyebrows? Or is more serious wrongdoing suspected? The key to client advocacy at this stage is to find a way to satisfy the FTC's curiosity and head off pursuit of the investigation.

Historically, the use of voluntary process may have indicated that the investigation was in its earliest stages, but in the privacy realm, since so much information can be gathered through examining public documents such as the privacy policy, news articles, and the like, or through technological testing, a privacy case can be evaluated without using voluntary or compulsory process at all. FTC attorneys engage in undercover investigation by making test accounts on websites and other services, and the attorneys even engage in "test shopping" (for instance, buying information from investigatory targets). As early as the 1990s, the FTC developed consumer aliases (complete with credit card accounts) to make purchases from websites in the course of an investigation. These test activities always occur before voluntary or compulsory processes have been sent.

There are institutional reasons for a company to take a voluntary access letter seriously. Recall that the FTC has been around for 100 years. It has more patience and bureaucratic resources than most companies. Little has been by the FTC invested at the access letter stage – another staff attorney and the associate director of the relevant division would have reviewed it, but it has not received commission or even bureau-level approval.

Key to these initial investigations is that if the staff and associate director (a division director) are satisfied with the company's response, they can end the inquiry. And there are indications that many, perhaps most, inquiries are ended early and informally.

FTC attorneys, especially in the privacy area, are not interested in "gotcha" actions. They know that each matter attracts significant scrutiny and public debate, and thus they are willing to close matters when companies can clarify negative news coverage, as FTC attorneys certainly know that the media can get facts wrong. Companies that address concerns raised by privacy advocates, or even cure security lapses by responsibly and quickly addressing them can find their investigation closed. Consider the closing letter issued by the FTC concerning Verizon, a DSL provider that issued modems that by default used an outdated security system, leaving its customers vulnerable to hacking.[82] The FTC closed the matter, observing

---

[82] Letter from Maneesha Mithal, Associate Director, Division of Privacy and Identity Protection, FTC, to Dana Rosenfeld, Partner, Kelley Drye, November 12, 2014.

that Verizon had made substantial efforts to cure the oversight, including pulling modems with the old standard from its distribution centers and instructing its customers how to upgrade their current modems.

On the whole, as Chapters 6–11 demonstrate, the matters that the FTC chooses to take are the egregious ones. These cases typically have bad company policy followed by a reluctance to remedy it or make consumers whole. This is evidence that combative or uncivil responses to inquiries from FTC staff can harm the client.

## Compulsory processes: civil investigative demands, subpoenas, access orders, and reports

### Civil investigative demands

Civil investigative demands (CIDs) are the principal method for investigating unfair and deceptive trade practices cases under commission rules.[83] The basis for the issuance may be that the FTC lawyer is dissatisfied with the voluntary process, that the recipient requests it,[84] or that information needs to be obtained from third parties (banks, telecommunications companies, domain registrars), or a CID may be issued in cases where the investigative target is uncooperative. CIDs and other compulsory process tools are not self-enforcing; to enforce them, the FTC must obtain an order from a federal district court.

The CID is a flexible tool that blends the documentary demand power of the subpoena with requirements that an investigative target or third party produce reports, produce tangible things, appear to give testimony, or otherwise answer questions the Commission poses. FTC attorneys often have a "meet and confer" with an investigative target's attorney to specify the scope of a CID after it is sent.

On paper at least, a CID requires bureau-level approval and a commission vote. In practice, however, bureau approval and only a single commissioner's approval are necessary. The Commission has passed "omnibus resolutions" to cover many kinds of deceptive practices.[85] Thus, in a telemarketing fraud case, the CID would be directed to the commissioner responsible for CIDs (the Compulsory Process Commissioner), who could approve it by relying upon the consent of the other commissioners under the existing omnibus resolution for telemarketing cases. At the compulsory process stage, the Agency's incentives shift, because the effort in convincing the BCP director and the commissioner requires time, and the Agency's credibility is placed at stake.

---

[83] 16 C.F.R. §2.7.

[84] Third-party record holders often request a formal process before sharing information about a customer. However, under 2006 amendments to the FTC Act, many companies have statutory immunity for voluntarily sharing information with the FTC. See 15 U.S.C. §57b-2b.

[85] Reorganization Plan No. 4 of 1961 empowered the Commission to delegate certain functions to an individual commissioner, to a subset of commissioners, and to Agency staff. These delegations are announced in the Federal Register and are described in the C.F.R. 63 Stat. 203 (1961).

Information obtained from a CID can be shared with other government agencies, even international ones. Under the US SAFE WEB Act (discussed in Chapter 11), foreign law enforcement agencies can request that the FTC issue domestic CIDs.

Many ordinary law enforcement access orders contain a "gag provision," to stop service providers and others from notifying the subject of the investigation about the order. In order for the FTC to delay notice or to bind a third party to confidentiality, it must obtain this authority from a judge.[86] Thus, the FTC obtains voluntary commitments from services providers (such as domain registrars, e-mail services, and the like) to refrain from notifying the subscriber of the CID. This is done to preserve ex parte options, such as asset freezes, as some companies hide assets upon learning of an investigation.

CIDs can implicate privacy laws and can be narrowed by respondents and third parties. Consider a CID that seeks complaints that a respondent company has concerning some practice. If those complaints were received as e-mails, they would be considered the content of a communication, subject to the protections of the Electronic Communications Privacy Act.[87] A respondent may attempt to narrow such a request by arguing that a warrant is required for access to e-mail content. Similarly, the Right to Financial Privacy Act is a limited brake on the scope of CIDs – requests to "financial institutions" concerning consumer customers (not business customers) may trigger notice requirements to the account holder.[88] Finally, the Cable Communications Policy Act of 1984, perhaps the nation's strongest privacy law, arguably bars the Commission from obtaining cable subscriber records.[89]

### Section 6(b) reports

The Commission has a broad power to compel companies to file annual or special reports, in writing and under oath. Section 6(b) reports generally are used to learn more about an industry. These are not often used, because each report takes many years to complete. The most recent FTC publication based on a 6(b) report request in the data privacy space was a wide-ranging investigation into the practices of the data brokerage industry. It only concerned nine companies (to avoid Office of Management and Budget preclearance, which is triggered by a request to ten or more organizations) and yet took three years to complete.

---

[86]   15 U.S.C. §57b-2a (c).

[87]   18 U.S.C. §2701 *et seq.*

[88]   12 U.S.C. §3401 *et seq.* The FTC is not required to give notice to individuals if the financial institution itself (e.g., a payday lender) is the investigative target.

[89]   47 U.S.C. §551.

## Other compulsory processes: subpoenas, access orders, investigational hearings, depositions

The FTC can use other forms of compulsory process, including subpoenas, access orders (allowing physical access to an investigational target's files), investigational hearings, and depositions.[90] Investigative targets may file a petition to limit or to quash compulsory process. However, the Commission itself evaluates such petitions.[91] The Commission determination can be appealed to the federal courts.

## Actions in federal court or adjudicative proceeding

The Commission has the option of pursuing actions either in federal court as cases or in adjudicative proceedings as matters before an administrative law judge. Perhaps the most important factor in choosing between the two comes from the relief sought – the FTC can obtain stronger forms of relief in federal district court.

---

### THE SLOWS

Since its inception, the FTC has been described as being too slow in resolving investigations. Henderson's 1924 report argued that remedies for dishonest advertising must be immediate, but recounted a case that took almost four years from issuance of the complaint to preliminary injunction.[92] The Hoover Commission Report in 1949 concluded that the Agency needed to delegate more responsibility to staff and to cut "unnecessary red tape."[93] The 1960 Landis transition report for President Kennedy observed, "The Federal Trade Commission as of June 30, 1959, had 309 cease and desist orders pending, of which 118 had been pending for more than one year and 30 for more than 3 years."[94] Landis attributed the problem to the early history of the Agency. He argued that the Supreme Court's narrow interpretation of the Agency's power caused it to engage in too much fact-finding to support its cases.[95] Senator Warren Magnuson and Jean Carper, in their 1968 book on consumer

---

[90] 16 C.F.R. §2.7.
[91] 16 C.F.R. §2.10.
[92] Gerald C. Henderson, The Federal Trade Commission: A Study in Administrative Law and Procedure 232–233 (1924).
[93] The Commission on Organization of the Executive Branch of the Government: The Independent Regulatory Commissions (March 1949)("The Hoover Commission Report.")
[94] Report on Regulatory Agencies to the President-Elect (December 21, 1960) ("The Landis Report.").
[95] "If the advertiser of a drug states that 'four out of five doctors' recommend it, to prove the falsity of such an allegation much massing of evidence ensues."

protection, noted that Holland Furnace, a company notorious for "tear down and scare tactics," operated for thirty-five years after the FTC first investigated it.[96] (In defense of the FTC, the defendant in the case was intractable and the Agency was eventually successful in charging its leadership with criminal contempt.[97]) The Agency waged a sixteen-year saga against Carter's Little Liver Pills, a nineteenth-century patent medicine that the FTC claimed was deceptive because it mentioned "liver." The pills are still sold today as "Carter's Little Pills."

The FTC has always occupied a difficult position between Congress, which orders it to speed up, and the realities of adjudicating cases against companies. If the FTC accelerates, it likely comes at a cost to the due process of companies. The enactment of the Administrative Procedure Act and the legitimate interests of defendants militate in favor of adopting more court-like procedures.

Since the 1980s, the FTC has shifted toward bringing litigation in federal court. This approach can enable the Agency to relatively quickly obtain enforceable remedies, such as temporary restraining orders, and preliminary injunctions. The Agency can even obtain secret, ex parte asset freezes in consumer fraud cases in order to stop companies from hiding its gains. Federal court actions give the FTC legitimacy, because the Agency is not acting as judge over its own proceedings.[98] In the privacy arena, just more than half of the Agency's enforcement efforts are brought in federal court.

Matters are also brought in administrative proceedings, which require the FTC to win the proceeding, and then go to federal court if civil penalties are sought. Generally speaking, civil penalties are not available in most administrative actions but various other forms of monetary relief can be obtained. Administrative orders are not finalized until public comment is sought.

Still, there are several strengths of administrative proceedings. First, there is the matter of judicial deference. Under the FTC Act, findings of the Commission as to facts, if supported by evidence, are conclusive.[99] On review of commission orders,

---

[96] THE DARK SIDE OF THE MARKETPLACE: THE PLIGHT OF THE AMERICAN CONSUMER 22–23 (1968). A "tear down and scare" scam occurs where a serviceperson takes apart some appliance and then refuses to reassemble it, asserting that it is too dangerous to operate. The authors wrote that the Holland Furnace salespeople were "'merciless.' In New England, branch salesmen from one office sold an elderly infirm woman nine new furnaces in six years, for a total take of $18,000."

[97] *In re Holland Furnace Co.*, 341 F.2d 548 (7th Cir. 1965) *aff'd sub nom. Cheff v. Schnackenberg*, 384 US 373 (1966) (only the president of the company was held criminally liable – the directors were just grossly negligent).

[98] As early as 1955, there have been recommendations to allocate the Commission's adjudicatory role to a separate court. COMMISSION ON THE ORGANIZATION OF THE EXECUTIVE BRANCH OF GOVERNMENT, LEGAL SERVICES AND PROCEDURE (March 1955).

[99] 15 U.S.C. §45(c).

courts afford great deference not only to these facts, but also to the Commission's judgment as to what is deceptive or unfair.[100] Second, administrative proceedings also allow the FTC to settle a matter without obtaining approval from a federal judge. Third, reviews of administrative decisions go to the Commission itself, which acts as a court of review. Fourth, an administrative proceeding may allow the Commission to target and "fence in" a larger scope of the respondent's practices than a federal court action.

In an administrative proceeding, the FTC lawyer (the "complaint counsel") presents the matter before an administrative law judge (ALJ), who ultimately renders a decision with findings of fact and conclusions of law. The ALJ may recommend a cease and desist order or dismissal. Either party can appeal the result to the full commission, which in turn carries on a de novo (no new evidence may be considered, but the Commission may weigh evidence differently than the ALJ), appellate-like procedure. The Commission's final order is directly appealable to a circuit court of appeal where the respondent resides or carries on business or where the challenged practice occurred.[101] If not appealed, a cease and desist order becomes final in sixty days, at which point the FTC can request the DOJ to bring suit to enforce it and to obtain civil penalties if the order is violated.

The vast majority of privacy matters are settled before administrative proceedings or a federal case begins in earnest. The bureau director can give staff consent authority to negotiate a settlement with an investigatory target. Under this procedure, a consent agreement is negotiated, and, once accepted by the Commission, a complaint is released detailing the alleged wrongdoing along with a press release and guidance to industry. The agreement is not finalized until a notice-and-comment process is completed. The FTC politely acknowledges public comment, but such comment almost never alters the settlement agreement.[102]

Investigatory targets prefer settling matters for all the reasons that criminal defendants plea-bargain. A settlement gets the matter over quickly. It avoids an extended bout of publicity during the administrative process, a problem to which publicly traded companies in particular are sensitive. It allows the company to put the problem behind it. Frequently, the matter concerns a practice that does not go to the "core" of the business' activities, and so settling is preferable over battling the Agency.

In many matters where respondents do not settle, it is not because of great legal principles, but rather a conflict between personalities. Periodically, the FTC targets an incorrigible or litigious respondent, and these respondents create terrible

---

[100] *Resort Car Rental System, Inc.* v. *FTC*, 518 F.2d 962 (9th Cir. 1975), *cert. denied*, 423 US 827 (1975).

[101] 15 U.S.C. §45(c). The detailed rules for adjudicative proceedings are found in 16 C.F.R. §3.

[102] This procedure is detailed at 16 C.F.R. §2.31. There is no public comment on cases brought in federal court.

precedents for other companies in tension with the Commission. In fact, repeatedly, cases with bad or even horrible facts for respondents are litigated.[103]

---

### THE PERSONAL CRUSADES AGAINST THE FTC

Joe Sugarman is a beloved advertiser. He was a leader in mail-order and direct marketing in the 1970s and 1980s, and wrote ads for microelectronics and "BluBlocker" sunglasses. They were text-heavy ads, imbued with dreamy optimism of gadgets improving life. They are a delight to read, and Sugarman's style is widely copied. (One read: "This is the story of an incredible product. So incredible that we know of no future consumer product that will have such a far reaching technological impact on society.") The closest contemporary example of Sugarmanesque marketing is the SkyMall catalog.

In 1979, the FTC's Chicago Regional Office investigated Sugarman's JS&A Group, Inc., for potential violations of the mail-order rule. Sugarman felt greatly mistreated by the FTC investigation and went on the offensive. He took out ads lambasting the FTC in the *Washington Post, Wall Street Journal,* and *New York Times.*

Sugarman hired a graphic artist to write a thirty-four-page comic book about the FTC's abuses and JS&A's plight. Titled *The Monster That Eats Business,* it depicted the FTC as a giant, hairy monster that pursued JS&A without mercy. Sugarman aired many grievances, ones that might sound familiar: the FTC had a vendetta against Sugarman, JS&A was a good business with many happy customers, there was no harm from JS&A's rule violation, JS&A is more responsive to consumers than the FTC, there are worse companies out there than JS&A, the FTC abuses its investigative authority, and so on.

The comic book concluded with an appeal to the reader to send examples of FTC misbehavior to JS&A so that Sugarman could investigate them in an effort to reform the FTC.

Those frustrated with the FTC pinned their hopes to Sugarman's cause. Sugarman was able to trigger Congressional oversight of the FTC, and, in 1981, the Subcommittee on Oversight and Investigations of the House Committee on Energy and Commerce looked into the JS&A case. Sugarman also challenged the FTC in court, litigating his case to the 7th Circuit, but it upheld the Agency's authority to issue the mail-order rule, to issue fines under it, and to

---

[103] A recent example of this is the POM Wonderful case, where a company relied on thin scientific evidence to repeatedly make disease-treating claims about its juice (see Chapter 5). It lost on appeal to the D.C. Circuit in a 3–0 decision.

impose an injunction against JS&A's activities.[104] Sugarman ultimately agreed to pay a $115,000 civil penalty.[105]

In 1989, the FTC had a second go at Sugarman, charging that he engaged in false advertising by creating a fake news show to promote "BluBlocker" sunglasses.[106] "Consumer Challenge TV" was an infomercial created by Sugarman to provide a review of BluBlocker glasses. It included this hilarious interlude: "We interrupt this program for a special announcement. This program is unable to handle the number of calls requesting the sunglasses featured in this program. If you are interested in obtaining the BluBlocker sunglasses, you may call the manufacturer directly at the number shown here." Sugarman settled the case.

Sugarman personalized his conflict with the FTC, and some argued that this distracted him from his business. Business strategy aside, personal crusades are unlikely to work on the legal front too. As much as businesses are frustrated with the FTC, their appeals do not resonate because consumers are frustrated by scams and security breaches. Federal judges are not impressed with personal campaigns either, and are likely to turn the screws on the respondent.

---

Under fifteen U.S.C §45(b), one may intervene in administrative proceedings "upon good cause shown."[107] In the 1970s, student consumer groups attempted to intervene in FTC false advertising matters, but to date consumer privacy groups have not attempted to intervene in matters. Intervention, public interest funding for participation in rule-makings, and public comment on settlement agreements all were supposed to heighten engagement with the FTC. But all of these mechanisms have been short-circuited by modern FTC procedures in privacy cases, because these cases almost always settle before public participation could be meaningful.

The FTC Act does not create a private right of action for individuals.[108] But other statutes enforced or administered by the FTC, such as the Fair Credit Reporting Act and Fair Debt Collection Practices Act, do. Additionally, state unfair and deceptive trade protection acts often offer a private right of action.

## Civil penalties

In most privacy matters, the FTC cannot levy civil penalties. Under Section 13(b) of the FTC Act, the FTC can sue directly to obtain injunctive relief, including

---

[104] *United States v. JS & A Grp., Inc.*, 716 F.2d 451 (7th Cir. 1983).

[105] FTC, FTC 1985 ANNUAL REPORT 18 (1985).

[106] 111 F.T.C. 522 (1989).

[107] Barry B. Boyer, *Funding Public Participation in Agency Proceedings: The Federal Trade Commission Experience*, 70 GEORGETOWN L. REV. 51 (1981).

[108] *Carlson v. Coca-Cola Co.*, 483 F.2d 279 (9th Cir. 1973).

monetary relief. Civil penalties are only triggered in certain situations and where certain procedures have been followed. In all cases where the FTC seeks civil penalties, it must first give the Department of Justice forty-five days to bring suit. If the DOJ does not take action, the FTC can bright suit in its own name to seek civil penalties in circumstances where:

- The respondent violates a final order of the Commission, and suit is brought to impose a civil penalty.[109]
- The respondent knowingly violates a rule that provides for civil penalties (such as the mail-order rule).[110]
- The Commission can obtain rescission or reformation of contracts, the refund of money or return of property, the payment of damages, and public notification respecting the rule violation or the unfair or deceptive act or practice if the Agency obtains a final order in an administrative proceeding, and then brings a separate proceeding in federal district court proving that "the act or practice to which the cease and desist order relates is one which a reasonable man would have known under the circumstances was dishonest or fraudulent."[111]
- A person fails to comply with compulsory process or lies in a response to the Agency.[112]
- A statute, such as the Fair Credit Reporting Act, grants the Agency power to levy penalties.
- A person engages in an unfair or deceptive trade practice identified as such by a final cease and desist order (not including consent orders) pertaining to another company, and the person has actual knowledge of the order.[113] This is known as "nonrespondent" liability. In such situations, the FTC sends the company a synopsis of relevant decisions and conduct to establish actual knowledge. Nonrespondent liability is rarely used because it requires the Commission to have a fully adjudicated matter with an order that is directly relevant to the nonrespondent's practices. The FTC has found it more convenient to use its Section 13(b) authority (discussed below).

In privacy matters, this structure has five practical effects: First, because there is no information privacy rule, most matters result in settlement without civil penalties or any other form of monetary relief such as disgorgement or restitution. The FTC

---

[109] 15 U.S.C. § 45(l).

[110] 15 U.S.C. § 45(m)(1)(A).

[111] 15 U.S.C. 57b(a)(2). *See FTC v. Figgie Int'l, Inc.*, 994 F.2d 595 (9th Cir. 1993) *FTC v. AMREP Corp.*, 705 F. Supp. 119 (S.D.N.Y. 1988); *FTC v. Turner*, 1982 WL 1947 (M.D. Fla. December 29, 1982).

[112] 15 U.S.C. § 50.

[113] 15 U.S.C. § 45(m)(1)(B). *See* David O. Bickart, *Civil Penalties under Section 5(m) of the Federal Trade Commission Act*, 44 U. CHI. L. REV. 761 (1977); *FTC v. Sears, Roebuck & Co.*, No. 81-A-503, 1983 WL 1889 (D. Colo. October 18, 1983). The Commission obtains a final order in an administrative proceeding, and then brings a separate proceeding in federal district court proving that "the act or practice to which the cease and desist order relates is one which a reasonable man would have known under the circumstances was dishonest or fraudulent."

corrects companies through consent decrees with extended periods of oversight, typically twenty-years and through extracting a series of promises from the company to have reasonable privacy and security programs. Sometimes these promises are "fencing in" – restrictions that extend far beyond the actual conduct at issue in the matter,[114] or conduct prohibited by the FTC Act.

Second, where the FTC can impose civil penalties, they have the potential to become annihilative, depending on the statute. Civil penalties under the FTC Act are set by the Federal Civil Penalties Inflation Adjustment Act of 1990 and currently are a maximum of $16,000 per violation.[115] Each violation is subject to a statutory fine, and in continuing violations the FTC can impose the fine on a per-day basis. Early cases concerning direct marketing suggest that each consumer contact can be a separate violation.[116] Following this logic, information-intensive companies with records on millions of individuals could amass million- or even billion-dollar fines that would destroy even the largest technology company.

In practice, however, most companies are able to negotiate downward from the $16,000 FTC Act per-violation standard. Several courts have approved a five-factor test for evaluating the reasonableness of FTC penalties: "(1) the good or bad faith of the defendants; (2) the injury to the public; (3) the defendant's ability to pay; (4) the desire to eliminate the benefits derived by a violation; and (5) the necessity of vindicating the authority of the FTC."[117] In weighing these factors, the BE has a significant voice in setting the Commission's goals for fines, and this voice has a downward effect on fines.

Third, despite the risk of annihilative penalty awards, the FTC has never imposed particularly large penalties. One of the largest to date concerned Google tracking users in a deceptive way. The resulting $22.5 million civil penalty represented a tiny percentage of the company's revenue.

More broadly, it is probably more pragmatic from a policy standpoint for the FTC to obtain broad fencing in relief than enormous fines. Such fines would lead to significant internal and external pushback. Big fines would create resistance from the Bureau of Economics, and would cause the targeted firm to resist settlement. Moreover, fines would have to be gigantic today – in the nine- to ten-figure range – to even matter to some large, successful information-intensive firms.

Fourth, because FTC actions signal the Agency's interpretation of the FTC Act, privacy practitioners carefully observe FTC matters in order to advise their own clients. Firms concentrating in FTC practice regularly send client alerts within hours of a new FTC decision.

Finally, although the Commission obtains broad consent orders, complete with fencing in relief, many of the provisions may be difficult for the Agency to supervise

---

[114] *Telebrands Corp.* v. *FTC*, 457 F.3d 354 (4th Cir. 2006).

[115] 16 C.F.R. §1.98.

[116] *United States* v. *Reader's Digest Ass'n, Inc.*, 662 F.2d 955 (3d Cir. 1981) (holding that each mail piece from a mass mailing is a separate violation of the FTC Act).

[117] *United States* v. *Reader's Digest Ass'n, Inc.*, 662 F.2d 955, 967 (3d Cir. 1981).

and enforce. This is because courts interpret consent orders to be similar to contracts. Courts require the FTC to prove by clear and convincing evidence in a contempt action that the respondent has violated an express and unequivocal command.[118] It is difficult to clearly and unequivocally command a company to respect consumer privacy and to secure data.

Consider the promise of Google to create a "comprehensive privacy program that is reasonably designed to address privacy risks related to the development and management of new and existing products and services for consumers." The command mandated by the order could be complied with "substantially" and still be inadequate to protect privacy in a meaningful way. While it would be simple for the FTC to obtain a contempt order if the respondent did not comply at all, a weak or partial embrace of the duty may be practically difficult to police. In effect, in contempt cases, the FTC has to re-litigate the underlying merits of its matter if the various commands in an order are subject to any interpretation. Thus, the FTC has incentives to craft orders with increasing complexity, that have conditions where noncompliance can be detected, and with duties that are amenable to the proof standard required in contempt actions.

### Injunctive relief

Under Chairman Miller, the FTC interpreted its authority under the 1973 amendments to the FTC Act to allow broad use of preliminary and permanent injunctions as well as temporary restraining orders in consumer protection matters. The FTC has used this authority to obtain civil penalty-like monetary redress, such as asset freezes, disgorgement, redress, and restitution, as well as the appointment of receivers, access to premises of businesses to inspect documents, and rescission of contracts.

Section 13(b) of the act empowers the Agency to obtain injunctive relief whenever it has "reason to believe" that a proper investigative target is violating "any provision of law enforced by" the Agency.[119] The FTC Act specifies a low standard for obtaining this relief. It need not prove irreparable harm or a likelihood of success on the merits. Instead, the court "weigh[s] the equities and consider[s] the Commission's likelihood of ultimate success," requires notice to the defendant, and requires that the FTC show that the injunctive relief is in the public interest.

Separately from Section 13(b), the FTC can obtain contempt sanctions when there is a violation of a federal court order.

---

[118] In the case against Kevin Trudeau, the Seventh Circuit stated the test as follows: "(1) the Order sets forth an unambiguous command; (2) [Trudeau] violated that command; (3) [Trudeau's] violation was significant, meaning it did not substantially comply with the Order; and (4) [Trudeau] failed to take steps to reasonable [*sic*] and diligently comply with the Order." *FTC v. Trudeau*, 579 F.3d 754 (7th Cir. 2009).

[119] 15 U.S.C. §53(b).

### *Other remedies in deception and unfairness matters: affirmative disclosure and corrective advertising*

The FTC has pursued remedies in its advertising matters that could be applied in privacy disputes. For instance, in 1942 the Commission brought its first "affirmative disclosure" case, requiring a company that made veneered products to label them as such. The case was notable because the company made no disclosure at all – the Commission thought its veneered products to be so realistic that the company should disclose their real content.[120] In the 1960s and 1970s, the FTC brought more affirmative disclosure cases.[121]

In the famous Listerine case, a product notorious for being advertised with deceptive claims such as its purported ability to prevent tuberculosis, the FTC ordered corrective advertising.[122] In such cases, the company, if it chooses to advertise, must include a corrective statement to repair the false belief propagated by earlier advertising.[123]

In Listerine's case, it was ultimately ordered to warn the consumer, "Listerine will not help prevent colds or sore throats or lessen their severity." Another prominent corrective advertising case concerned a back pain reliever. The FTC required the following statement: "Although Doan's is an effective pain reliever, there is no evidence that Doan's is more effective than other pain relievers for back pain."[124] The FTC has also pursued quack cancer remedies, with the following required statement: "Competent and reliable scientific evidence does not demonstrate that any of the ingredients in BioShark, 7 Herb Formula, GDU or BioMixx, are effective when used for prevention, treatment or cure of cancer."[125] Courts have upheld corrective advertising requirements in First Amendment challenges, evaluating the requirements on an intermediate scrutiny basis.

### CONCLUSION

The FTC has extraordinarily broad jurisdiction and an impressive set of legal tools to address unfair and deceptive practices. Concerns about due process problems have prevented the Commission from obtaining a general civil penalty power. Still, Congress has empowered the Agency repeatedly over the decades such that it can still do much with the tools it has.

This chapter explained that privacy cases have several different dynamics that allow the FTC to investigate without using legal process, and to test a targeted firm's

---

[120] *Haskelite Mfg. Corp. v. FTC*, 127 F.2d 765 (7th Cir. 1942).
[121] *See, for example, J. B. Williams Co. v. FTC*, 381 F.2d 884 (6th Cir. 1967).
[122] *Warner Lambert Co. v. FTC*, 562 F.2d 749 (D.C. Cir. 1977), *cert. denied*, 435 US 950 (1978).
[123] David A. Anderson & Jonathan Winer, *Corrective Advertising: The FTC's New Formula for Effective Relief*, 50 TEX. L. REV. 312 (1971).
[124] *In the Matter of Novartis Corp., et al.*, 127 F.T.C. 580, 726 (1999), *aff'd* 223 F.3d 783 (D.C. Cir. 2000).
[125] In the Matter of Daniel Chapter One, A Corp., & James Feijo, 2010 WL 387917 (January 25, 2010).

systems from the comfort of the Agency's offices. Despite these investigative efficiencies, there is evidence that privacy specialists are looking for landmark cases –
those that set a policy precedent or those that reflect particularly bad facts. In almost
all actions, the respondent settles the case.

The FTC could create a privacy rule, but a strong consensus holds that it would
be too difficult and it would take too long to do so. Thus, FTC lawyers have pursed
a policy-making enforcement agenda. For the foreseeable future, FTC privacy law
will be a series of complaints and settlement agreements that lawyers must decode
when counseling clients.[126]

---

[126] For an overview of the Agency's structure, the challenges it faces, and a self-assessment of the
Commission, *see* William E. Kovacic, FTC, The Federal Trade Commission at 100: Into Our 2nd
Century, The Continuing Pursuit of Better Practices (January 2009).

# 5

## Unfair and deceptive practices

In enacting the Wheeler–Lea Amendments to the Federal Trade Commission Act in 1938, Congress dramatically expanded the power of the Federal Trade Commission. Congress broadened the FTC's organic power from the prevention of "unfair methods of competition in commerce" to include prevention of "unfair or deceptive acts or practices in commerce."[1] Theories of unfairness and deception now form the basis of FTC privacy law.

This chapter traces the contours of this broad prohibition, focusing on the case-by-case development of the doctrine and policy statements. It is analyzed separately here from the subject-matter chapters in Part II because the FTC's authorities to police unfair and deceptive trade practices are broader than many realize in privacy cases. This chapter makes clear that the FTC could go further in policing privacy practices based on precedent in advertising and other cases. Furthermore, the development of the substantiation doctrine (discussed below) could have profound effects on the market for privacy-protective services when competition on privacy begins in earnest.

Cynics say that the commission does not use an objective or standardized definition of unfairness and deception. There is some truth to that, in part because, by statute and by custom, courts defer to the Commission's judgment concerning what is deceptive and unfair.[2] As we saw in Chapter 1, Congress affirmatively made a

---

[1] Pub. L. No. 75–447, 38 Stat. 717 (1938). Codified at 15 U.S.C §45(a)(2), "Section 5" of the FTC Act today reads: "The Commission is hereby empowered and directed to prevent persons, partnerships, or corporations, except banks, savings and loan institutions . . . Federal credit unions . . . common carriers subject to the Acts to regulate commerce, air carriers and foreign air carriers . . . and persons, partnerships, or corporations insofar as they are subject to the Packers and Stockyards Act . . . from using unfair methods of competition in or affecting commerce and unfair or deceptive acts or practices in or affecting commerce."

[2] 15 U.S.C. §45 (2013) ("The findings of the Commission as to the facts, if supported by evidence, shall be conclusive"); FTC v. Colgate-Palmolive Co., 380 US 374, 385 (1965)("This statutory scheme necessarily gives the Commission an influential role in interpreting Section 5 and in applying it to the facts of particular cases arising out of unprecedented situations. Moreover, as an administrative agency which deals continually with cases in the area, the Commission is often in a better position than are courts to determine when a practice is 'deceptive' within the meaning of the Act. This Court has frequently

policy decision to choose vague language in 1914 and again in 1938 because business practices and technology were constantly evolving, causing new problems that Congress could not quickly act to remedy. Section 5 does not have a static meaning, and lawyers will always have to grapple with its application in new business contexts. As two FTC attorneys put it in 1962, "[Section 5] cannot be defined in terms of constants. More broadly, it is a recognition of an ever-evolving commercial dexterity and the personal impact of economic power as important dimensions of trade. Its underlying proposition is that a free competitive society must have some means of preventing that very freedom to compete from destroying our economic system."[3]

It is also clear that Congress chose to free the FTC from the restraints imposed by the common law in fraud matters. Yet, imposing common law requirements tends to be the first kind of reform proposed by critics of the FTC. At the same time, agency officials have resisted articulating any bounds on the FTC Act, in order to prevent any undermining of the Agency's matters.

---

### HOW THE COMMON LAW ADDRESSED DECEPTION

Under the common law, civil actions could be brought for deception involving false statements between the buyer and seller; however, successful suit required a showing of injury. The victim would recover the difference in value between the product as sold and as stated. Thus, recovery was limited, and the individual would not have strong incentives to bring suit.

The common law treated difficult-to-detect frauds as public wrongs, in recognition that such frauds presented a collective action problem. For instance, falsifying a weight or scale in order to cheat the buyer would be a common law fraud, remediable by criminal punishment, because no one individual is likely to detect the fraud, but many are likely to be affected by it.

Public prosecutions could be brought where private transactions deceived the public at large. While this principle seems directly applicable to advertising, a different common law requirement – intent to deceive – complicated matters. As buyers were increasingly divorced from dealing directly with creators of products, it became easier to introduce deception into a transaction, and more difficult to prove a specific intent to defraud. Advertising itself creates a problem because it is possible to create misrepresentations without an in-person interaction. As we will see, modern deception problems involve implicit

---

stated that the Commission's judgment is to be given great weight by reviewing courts. This admonition is especially true with respect to allegedly deceptive advertising since the finding of a Section 5 violation in this field rests so heavily on inference and pragmatic judgment") (internal citations omitted).

[3] Eugene R. Baker & Daniel J. Baum, Section 5 *of the Federal Trade Commission Act: A Continuing Process of Redefinition*, 7 VILL. L. REV. 517 (1962).

misrepresentations,[4] and these may have been accidental or intentional. Sometimes advertisers subjectively believe false claims about their own products.[5]

Common law fraud could also result in the revocation of a corporate charter, and this is a remedy that modern progressives sometimes invoke as a cure to corporate power. But public policy easing barriers to formation of corporations makes this a weak remedy – fraudsters can quickly incorporate in another state.

While, on their face, the common law fraud remedies appear to address modern consumer protection, in practice they failed. Proving intent to deceive was a substantial barrier to success in suit. Prosecutors have limited resources and preferred to use them against crimes that caused physical harm or large-scale financial harm. The common law required that the buyer was an actual recipient of the misrepresentation and relied upon it. The problem of proving damages also was a barrier to suit.

Some characterize the FTC as rudderless in Section 5 matter selection, but one must remember that the Agency has been led by dozens of commissioners with different priorities, with different resources, and operating in different political landscapes. Critics can invoke 100 years of cases and matters to argue that the Commission is irregular or not strategic in case selection. However, the modern FTC is careful in its selection and attempts to build upon its precedent. Lawyers can also read the FTC's many tea leaves: commissioners and top-level staff often comment publicly on enforcement priorities. Enforcement actions are often accompanied by news releases, blog posts, and guidance to business. Moreover, the Commission and the courts have tried to give meaning to Section 5 through case-by-case development. The FTC also released two policy statements in the 1980s: the FTC Policy Statement on Deception (1984) and the FTC Policy Statement on Unfairness (1980).

The political context of these two documents is important. The Unfairness Statement was created in response to the FTC's zeal in applying unfairness in novel ways. It attempts to give businesses more certainty about the application of unfairness. It is a consensus document signed by all five commissioners. Congress codified its elements in 1994. However, the Deception Statement was controversial, both at the Commission and in Congress. Congress never acted to codify it despite the requests of then Chairman James Miller.

---

[4]  Guang-Xin Xie & David M. Boush, *How Susceptible Are Consumers to Deceptive Advertising Claims? A Retrospective Look at the Experimental Research Literature,* 11 The Marketing Rev. 293 (2011). ("Many alleged deceptive claims nowadays are implicitly manipulative rather than outright false.")

[5]  Lowell Mason, THE LANGUAGE OF DISSENT 162 (1959)("many of those who get into trouble over false and misleading claims for their good do so from sheer industrial conceit. They truly think their merchandise is not only good, it's the best . . .").

### THE PRINTERS' INK STATUTE

In 1911, Harry D. Nims was hired by *Printers' Ink* magazine to write a model law to address the problem of deceptive advertising.[6] It read:

> Any person, firm, corporation or association who, with intent to sell or in any wise dispose of merchandise, securities, service, or anything offered by such person, firm, corporation or association, directly or indirectly, to the public for sale or distribution, or with intent to increase the consumption thereof, or to induce the public in any manner to enter into any obligation relating thereto, or to acquire title thereto, or an interest therein, makes, publishes, disseminates, circulates, or places before the public, or causes, directly or indirectly, to be made, published, disseminated, circulated, or placed before the public, in this State, in a newspaper or other publication, or in the form of a book, notice, hand-bill, poster, bill, circular, pamphlet, or letter, or in any other way, an advertisement of any sort regarding merchandise, securities, service, or anything so offered to the public, which advertisement contains any assertion, representation or statement of fact which is untrue, deceptive or misleading, shall be guilty of a misdemeanor.

As envisioned by *Printers' Ink*, the model statute would patch holes in existing state legislation. Then editor John Irving Romer argued that it was in the best interest of honest advertisers to adopt a stringent law punishing false advertising, and that the Advertising Clubs of America (then a federation of over 100 local advertising clubs, now known as the American Advertising Federation) should prepare cases for prosecution by local authorities.[7] Romer opposed a new federal law, given that the recently amended mail-fraud statute encompassed many types of fraud. As Romer and Nims saw it, the main problem was prosecutorial resources and the feeling among advertisers that it was not their responsibility to police unethical advertising when they encountered it.

The statute has several interesting elements: it is a criminal statute, it has strict liability (the mens rea for the law goes to intent to publicize a product for sale, not for an intent to deceive[8]), and it focuses on advertisers, not publications.

[6]   John Irving Romer, *Legal Repression of Dishonest Advertising*, 77(8) PRINTERS' INK 66, 68 (November 23, 1911).

[7]   The Progressive Era saw a proliferation of business ethics groups, several of which were focused upon truth in advertising in an attempt to raise the public perception of advertising and to professionalize its practice. Gabriel Abend explains that some of these groups evangelized business ethics as being good for business. THE MORAL BACKGROUND: AN INQUIRY INTO THE HISTORY OF BUSINESS ETHICS (2013).

[8]   *Many States Still Lack Protection of "Printers Ink" Model Statute: National Vigilance Committee to Work for Its Adoption in States Where It Is Not Now a Law*, 121(4) PRINTERS' INK 101 (October 26, 1922). ("The Statute, as the reader will see, contains no qualifying phrase, such as 'knowingly,' 'with fraudulent intent,' or 'calculated to mislead.' The inclusion of any such phrase most effectually takes

> The Printers' Ink Statute is at core a self-regulatory model, because it assumes that enforcement would only occur when an industry group made a referral to a prosecutor.

The Deception Statement is indeed a policy statement because it voluntarily constrains the bounds of the FTC's powers. It was considered for only a matter of weeks by the commissioners before being advanced for vote. The vote (3–2) was held on Republican-appointment commissioner David Clanton's last day in office.[9] Two commissioners, Republican-appointed Patricia Bailey and Democratic-appointed Michael Pertschuk, filed dissenting statements, and later wrote a law review article detailing their view of the statement's inadequacies.[10]

At any time, the Commission could abandon the Deception Statement formally. While the FTC internally vets matters using the statement's factors, in the next chapter, it will become clear that the Deception Statement's limitations do not cabin the Agency's privacy enforcement activities. In the deception field, practically any statement about privacy is considered material, and in unfairness matters, the Agency has been willing to aggregate small harms into "substantial" injuries, because information-intensive firms often have millions of users.

## DECEPTION STATEMENT

The 1983 FTC Policy Statement on Deception[11] articulates a "single definitive statement of the Commission's view of its authority." It sets forth three key elements of a deception case: There must be (1) a representation, omission, or practice that is likely to mislead a consumer; (2) the interpretation of that act or practice is considered from the perspective of a reasonable consumer; and (3) the representation must be material.

### A representation, omission, or practice that is likely to mislead

The 1983 letter articulates the definition of misrepresentation and misleading omissions:

A misrepresentation is an express or implied statement contrary to fact. A misleading omission occurs when qualifying information necessary to prevent a

---

the teeth out of the law and renders it inoperative. Many attempts have been made to ring changes on the word 'knowingly' by opponents of the Model Statute . . .")

[9] In case of a voting tie, the Commission takes no action; thus, presumably, if commissioner Clanton had left office, the Deception Statement would have failed on a 2–2 vote.

[10] For a short summary of these conflicts, *see* Thomas C. Kinnear & Ann R. Root, *The FTC and Deceptive Advertising in the 1980s: Are Consumers Being Adequately Protected?*, 7 J. PUB. POL'Y MKTG 40 (1988).

[11] Letter from James C. Miller III, FTC Chairman, to John D. Dingell, Chairman, House Comm. on Energy and Commerce 5–6 (October 14, 1984). The Policy Statement is appended to *Cliffdale Associates, Inc.*, 103 F.T.C. 110, 174 (1984).

practice, claim, representation, or reasonable expectation or belief from being misleading is not disclosed. Not all omissions are deceptive, even if providing the information would benefit consumers ...”

### The entire consumer experience

The FTC will evaluate the “entire advertisement, transaction or course of dealing” to determine whether there is a misleading practice.[12] While one can imagine what a “course of dealing” is like in the offline world, the term is more ambiguous online. One could argue that all web pages on a site are part of the course of dealing, or just those that the consumer visits. Only a very small number of consumers click on the privacy policy or terms of service on websites, yet the FTC considers disclosures on such pages as material. This problem will only become more complex as consumers adopt “internet of things” products – devices that can connect to each other or to the internet, sometimes in surprising ways.

### The problem of implied claims and omissions

Express claims are easiest for consumers and the Commission to identify and evaluate as misleading. Implied claims and omissions are both more problematic and more difficult to evaluate. In such implied representation and omission cases, the Commission will consider a number of factors, including other representations made, the order and context in which they are made, the nature of the claim, and the nature of the transactions. The Commission can even use surveys, although it is not required to do so, or other extrinsic evidence, including consumer testimony, to determine how individuals interpret an implied claim or omission.[13]

### Intent to deceive

The FTC need not establish intent to deceive,[14] nor must it establish actual deception.[15] Congress’ passage of the FTC Act in 1914 and consumer protection

---

[12] When analyzing a misleading advertisement, the FTC can limit its analysis to that single ad.

[13] For a comprehensive overview of social science research on consumer deception, *see* DAVID M. BOUSH, MARIAN FRIESTAD & PETER WRIGHT, DECEPTION IN THE MARKETPLACE: THE PSYCHOLOGY OF DECEPTIVE PERSUASION AND CONSUMER SELF-PROTECTION (2009). For a thoughtful overview of the intersection between legal definitions of deception and behavioral research into why consumers are deceived, *see* JEF I. RICHARDS, DECEPTIVE ADVERTISING: BEHAVIORAL STUDY OF A LEGAL CONCEPT (1990).

[14] *See, for example*, FTC v. *Freecom Commc’ns, Inc.*, 401 F.3d 1192 (10th Cir. 2005); *United States* v. *Johnson*, 541 F.2d 710, 712 (8th Cir.1976), *cert. denied*, 429 US 1093, 97 S.Ct. 1106 (1977); FTC v. *Balme*, 23 F.2d 615 (2d Cir. 1928); *Indiana Quartered Oak Co.* v. *FTC*, 26 F.2d 340, 342 (2d Cir. 1928) (“It was not necessary for the Commission to establish intent to deceive the purchasing public; for the test of unfair competition was whether the natural and probable result of the use by the petitioner of such woods was deceptive to the ordinary purchaser, and made him purchase that which he did not intend to buy”); FTC v. *Algoma Lumber Co.*, 291 US 67 (1934) (even innocently made misrepresentations can be addressed by the FTC Act).

[15] *Trans World Accounts, Inc.* v. *FTC*, 594 F.2d 212, 214 (9th Cir. 1979), (“Proof of actual deception is unnecessary to establish a violation of Section 5. Misrepresentations are condemned if they possess a tendency to deceive.”)

amendments in 1938 were partly motivated by the need to free consumer protection from some common law requirements, such as the requirement to show specific intent and detrimental reliance. Advertisements and practices are judged by their likelihood to mislead, instead of the intent of the ad's author or the creator of the business practice.

### The perspective of the consumer acting reasonably under the circumstances

The second prong focuses on the perspective of the consumer: "The test is whether the consumer's interpretation or reaction is reasonable." This part of the Deception Statement is the most controversial, because it is most powerful in restricting the Agency's authority.

The Deception Statement does not create a reasonable person standard. Instead, it attempts to ground the Commission's analysis in reasonable interpretations of a practice. A too-literal or esoteric interpretation of a representation might mistake humor or hyperbole as a genuine claim. Similarly, a "lawyer's read" of representations may be inconsistent with how ordinary people understand claims. The Deception Statement sets forth some guidelines for taking a reasonable perspective. The FTC weighs the clarity of the representation, whether there is conspicuous information that qualifies the representation, and whether omitted information is important.

This section of the Deception Standard has attracted criticism for several reasons. By statute and judicial interpretation, the FTC Act is not cabined by a "reasonable person standard." Indeed, before the 1983 Policy Statement, far lower standards were applied. For instance, in 1927, the Supreme Court upheld the Commission's finding that offers for "free" encyclopedias tethered to an expensive subscription service were deceptive. The Court declared that "[t]here is no duty resting upon a citizen to suspect the honesty of those with whom he transacts business ... the rule of caveat emptor should not be relied upon to reward fraud and deception."[16]

Appellate courts have approved the FTC's determinations of customer deception. For example, the Second Circuit upheld the Commission's determination that consumers were deceived by a "rejuvenating" face cream, rejecting the company's argument that "since no straight-thinking person could believe that its cream would actually rejuvenate, there could be no deception." The court opined that the FTC Act was intended to protect the "public – that vast multitude which includes the ignorant, the unthinking and the credulous ..."[17] The same year, the Second Circuit deferred to the FTC's determination that Clairol's advertising for hair dyes

---

[16] *FTC v. Standard Education Society*, 302 US 112 (1937).

[17] *Charles of the Ritz Distributors Corp. v. FTC*, 143 F.2d 676 (2d Cir. 1944); *see also Giant Food, Inc. v. FTC*, 322 F.2d 977 (D.C. Cir. 1963), *cert. dismissed*, 376 US 967 (1964). ("The Act was not intended to protect 'sophisticates.' ")

was deceptive because the company claimed it was "permanent."[18] Courts have upheld commission findings that an advertisement was deceptive when small minorities of consumers were misled. For instance, in *Firestone Tire & Rubber Co.*, the Sixth Circuit found "it hard to overturn the deception findings of the Commission if the ad thus misled 15% (or 10%) of the buying public."[19] Indeed, the modern commission follows a "significant minority of consumers" test.[20]

There is also the problem that some consumer fraud occurs because ordinarily reasonable people make a mistake and act unreasonably for some time. In other words, they do not act reasonably under the circumstances. Many consumers are too busy for serious comparative shopping, and while *Consumer Reports* magazine has been available for decades, readers of the magazine tend to be better educated and resourced. In a way, it is the reasonable person who least needs help in the marketplace.[21]

Nonetheless, President Reagan administration's Transition Team wanted to cabin the scope of deceptive advertising enforcement. According to Professor Thomas O. McGarity, Reagan-appointed Chairman James Miller "told the staff to stop enforcing the Agency's truth-in-advertising requirements."[22] It endorsed a policy banning "only those advertising practices that deceive ordinary consumers and alter their purchase decisions accordingly."[23] This would appear to both introduce a reasonable consumer standard and require a causal link to materiality.

---

ON PUFFING

"Puffing," the expression of the seller's subjective opinion of a product – usually embellished with superlatives – is a kind of falsity considered not to

---

[18] *Gelb v. FTC*, 144 F.2d 580 (2d Cir.1944). This case is often cited as an example of the Commission protecting the too-gullible consumer, but, in fairness to the Commission, Clairol made a number of claims that its product constituted a new kind of technology. Clairol claimed that its coloring product was new and special, that it was "not a dye," and that "the trained technician will apply these corrective oils to your hair and scalp and as these nourishing unguents are deeply absorbed by the hair shaft and follicles the Clairol tints ... imparts color that is permanent." 33 F.T.C. 1450 (1941).

[19] 481 F.2d 246, 249 (6th Cir. 1973), *cert. denied*, 414 US 1112 (1973). Early cases supported single-digit percentage findings to support a commission finding, but in later cases the Commission's cases had higher percentages of deceived consumers. *See* Ivan L. Preston & Jef I. Richards, *Consumer Miscomprehension as a Challenge to FTC Prosecutions of Deceptive Advertising*, 19 JOHN MARSHALL L. REV. 605 (1985–1986).

[20] *POM Wonderful, LLC v. FTC*, 777 F.3d 478 (D.C. Cir. 2015) ("The Commission 'examines the overall net impression' left by an ad, and considers whether 'at least a significant minority of reasonable consumers' would 'likely' interpret the ad to assert the claim."); *Telebrands Corp. v. FTC*, 457 F.3d 354 (4th Cir. 2006).

[21] For a recent defense of the reasonable person standard, see Janis K. Pappalardo, *Product Literacy and the Economics of Consumer Protection Policy*, 46(2) J. CONSUMER AFF. 319 (2012).

[22] Thomas O. McGarity, FREEDOM TO HARM: THE LASTING LEGACY OF THE LAISSEZ FAIRE REVIVAL (2013).

[23] Federal Trade Commission Transition Team, Report submitted to the Reagan administration (1981).

be misleading in American law. Puffing is ubiquitous in advertising: consider such claims such as "The Ultimate Driving Machine." Puffing cannot include facts, and, as such, the law assumes that consumers do not incorporate information from puffing to make product decisions.

That raises a question: if we do not think consumers believe puffs and if we assume that it does not affect product decisions, why is there so much puffing? Professor Ivan L. Preston waged a decades-long battle against puffing, arguing that if puffing is "deceptive, [the advertiser] is acting illegally. If it's not, he's encouraging distrust and contributing to a credibility gap that may lead to rejection of his true factual claims as well as his puffs."[24]

Preston argued that caveat emptor has its roots in the 1534 work by Sir Anthony Fitzherbert on animal husbandry, describing the problem of warts on horses for sale.[25] According to Preston, the law's modern tolerance for puffing dates back to this common law precedent that makes the buyer responsible for problems in products that the buyer can inspect. The common law recognized two exceptions to the caveat emptor rule – even where the buyer could inspect a good, caveat emptor did not apply where the seller made a fraudulent misrepresentation or made a warranty (in modern law, a promise or statement about the quality of features of a good). Over time, the inspection rule evolved into a general proposition that certain claims are meaningless and ignored by the consumer.

Preston proposed that consumer protection law should not make puffing immune to false advertising claims, because consumers infer factual information from them. Thus, puffs should be considered deceptive if they include implied claims that are false.[26]

As the Edward Snowden affair raises concern about information security and causes companies to make more representations about security of products, lawyers will need to evaluate whether they are puffing or real claims about protection for data. More broadly, in its complaints, the Commission often quotes anodyne, pro-privacy language from privacy policies (material such as "We value our users' privacy first and foremost. Trust is the basis of everything we do, so we want you to be familiar and comfortable with the integrity and

---

[24] *Why Use False Puffery?, If Anyone Believes It, It's Got to Be Illegal*, THE NEW YORK TIMES, February 25, 1973.

[25] ANTHONY FITZHERBERT, THE BOOK OF HUSBANDRY (1882)("There is a defect in a horse, that is neither soreness, hurt, nor disease, and that is, if a horse has warts of the behind, beneath the place a horse has lameness, for then he is not marketable goods, if he is wild; but if the horse is tame and has been ridden upon, than let the buyer aware, for the buyer has both his eyes to see and his hands to handle the horse. It is a saying that if such a horse should die suddenly, when he has live as many years as the moon was days old, as such time as he was fouled.")

[26] IVAN L. PRESTON, THE GREAT AMERICAN BLOWUP: PUFFERY IN ADVERTISING AND SELLING (revised edition 1996).

> care we give your personal data.") Companies often want to include such
> language to assuage consumer fears about revealing data. Thus, we need to
> evaluate whether such statements are representations that can give rise to false
> advertising and Section 5 claims.

When the Deception Statement was adopted, the two dissenting commissioners
argued that the proper standard was that practices were unlawful if they had a
"tendency or capacity to deceive a substantial number of consumers."[27] commissioners Bailey and Pertschuk warned that the new test has the "potential to inhibit
the FTC's enforcement of the law to protect those most in need of protection. For
example, if this element were to require the Commission to find that consumers
acting 'reasonably' were misled ... it could undermine the Commission's ability to
protect vulnerable or unsophisticated consumers whose conduct was arguably not
reasonable."

### The totality of the practice

As with determining the meaning of a statement, the FTC also applies a totality of
the circumstances approach to determine how consumers are likely to respond to an
allegedly deceptive practice.[28] At the same time, the FTC will not accept gimmicks
that require the consumer to read all representations by the business. For instance, if
a business makes an express claim, it cannot disclaim it in the small print.

### Targeting specific groups

The perspective of the reasonable consumer standard suffers from a number of
problems, the most obvious being that unreasonable consumers are likely to be the
most in need of protection. The Deception Statement partially addresses this by
creating a different standard for targeted messages: "When representations or sales
practices are targeted to a specific audience, the Commission determines the effect
of the practice on a reasonable member of that group."

This standard goes both ways. When practices are targeted at sophisticated groups,
such as doctors, the standard is elevated. This elevated standard does not appear to
have been applied in the privacy cases.

### Small frauds deemphasized

The Reagan-era FTC sought a policy that reduced the Commission's focus on small
purchases. It stated, "when consumers can easily evaluate the product or service, it is
inexpensive, and it is frequently purchased, the Commission will examine the

---

[27] Patricia P. Bailey & Michael Pertschuk, *The Law of Deception: The Past as Prologue*, 33 AM. U. L. REV.
849 (Summer 1984).
[28] *See for instance FTC v. Commerce Planet, Inc.*, 878 F. Supp. 2d 1048 (C.D. Cal. 2012).

practice closely before issuing a complaint based on deception." The FTC thought that there was little incentive for sellers to abuse consumers because the seller of such small items would depend on repeat purchasers. The market would likely cure these small frauds, it was thought.

### Search and experience goods

Phillip Nelson, a well-known economist, highlighted the different attributes of "search goods" and "experience goods." Search goods are products that the consumer can inspect before purchase, such as the design and quality of furniture or clothes. Experience goods are more difficult to judge, because they require the individual to taste or otherwise consume the product in order to evaluate its merits. In addition, there are post-experience goods (also known as "credence" goods). These are products that are difficult for the consumer to evaluate even after they are consumed (e.g., a juice that proclaims health benefits).

The Deception Statement focuses commission attention away from search goods and toward experience and post-experience goods, on the theory that consumers should be able to evaluate quality of such goods themselves, and that if these goods are low-cost and frequently bought, the market will eliminate poor-quality search goods.

### The representation, omission, or practice must be material

Although not required by Section 5, the Deception Statement introduced a materiality factor.[29] The Deception Statement specified, "A 'material' misrepresentation or practice is one which is likely to affect a consumer's choice of or conduct regarding a product." Materiality was added as a factor in order to introduce a harm requirement. Under this logic, only material deceptions are important because those would lead a consumer to act differently and perhaps purchase an alternative product: "Injury exists if consumers would have chosen differently but for the deception."

Express claims and representations are material, as are representations or omissions involving health, safety, cost, or "other areas with which the reasonable consumer would be concerned." Where the act or practice does not involve presumptively material issues, the FTC determines its importance by analyzing credible testimony of consumers, surveys, or whether it involves a feature that alters the price of the product. Nonetheless, the statutory law and case law is clear: The FTC does not need to establish consumer injury, pecuniary loss, harm, or detriment to win a deception case.[30]

---

[29] The FTC Act's prohibition on false advertising at 15 U.S.C. § 55 does include a materiality requirement, but this is absent in 15 U.S.C. § 45.

[30] *Rothschild* v. *FTC*, 200 F.2d 39 (7th Cir. 1952), *cert. denied*, 345 US 941 (1953). ("It is not necessary that an unfair or deceptive act forbidden by the Trade Commission Act should cause a pecuniary loss. One

In their critique of the Deception Statement, former commissioners Bailey and Pertschuk helpfully described a wide array of representations found to be material. Their goal was to demonstrate that there was a low bar to agency action. Explicit material representations include claims that a product performs better or is safer than another, "bargain" prices, seals that attest to quality, and claims made in testimonials. Material omissions included a failure to disclose "that a product is used or reprocessed; that a book is abridged; that a product is manufactured in a foreign country . . ."[31]

UNFAIRNESS

Unfairness is a separate and independent legal theory that the Commission can use to prevent objectionable acts and practices.[32] The Commission brought its first internet-era privacy matter using unfairness in 2003, when a company reneged on a promise to not share personal information and required consumers to opt out of its new plan to sell data. Since 2003, unfairness has been increasingly used in both information privacy and security cases.

*History of the unfairness authority*

In 1964, in promulgating the cigarette rule, the FTC articulated factors for finding unfairness:

> (1) whether the practice, without necessarily having been previously considered unlawful, offends public policy as it has been established by statutes, the common law, or otherwise – whether, in other words, it is within at least the penumbra of some common-law, statutory, or other established concept of unfairness; (2) whether it is immoral, unethical, oppressive, or unscrupulous; (3) whether it causes substantial injury to consumers (or competitors or other businessmen).[33]

The FTC established a strong stance on cigarette warning labels. Indeed, the Agency thought the health hazards of smoking would furnish useful facts to articulate and defend the unfairness power. Later, the FTC was emboldened by its victory

---

of the purposes of the Act has been the protection of the public, and public interest may exist even though the practice deemed to be unfair does not violate any private right.")

[31] Patricia P. Bailey & Michael Pertschuk, *The Law of Deception: The Past as Prologue*, 33 AM. U.L. REV. 849 (Summer 1984).

[32] *FTC v. Sperry & Hutchinson Trading Stamp Co.*, 405 US 233 (1972). (The court considered: "does § 5 empower the Commission to define and proscribe an unfair competitive practice, even though the practice does not infringe either the letter or the spirit of the antitrust laws? Second, does § 5 empower the Commission to proscribe practices as unfair or deceptive in their effect upon consumers regardless of their nature or quality as competitive practices or their effect on competition? We think the statute, its legislative history, and prior cases compel an affirmative answer to both questions.")

[33] FTC, Statement of Basis and Purpose, Unfair or Deceptive Advertising and Labeling of Cigarettes in Relation to the Health Hazards of Smoking, 29 Fed. Reg. 8324, 8355 (1964).

in *FTC* v. *Sperry & Hutchinson Trading Stamp Co.*, where the court recognized the unfairness authority as an independent legal theory that the Commission was empowered to apply.[34] In that case, the court cited to the unfairness factors in a footnote, but did not comment upon them. The FTC saw this as an endorsement of the factors, while critics saw it as just a neutral listing or memorialization of the factors.

After the cigarette rule, the FTC began using unfairness in a number of rule-making efforts, against politically powerful businesses and in situations with more moral ambiguity than warning adults about the dire consequences of tobacco use. As a result of the zeal of the 1970s commission, Congress and the Agency itself began to limit the contours of unfair acts and practices. In 1980, the Commission adopted the FTC Policy Statement on Unfairness, and, in 1994, Congress codified the current limitation on the Agency's power to find an act or practice unfair. It reads:

> The Commission shall have no authority ... to declare unlawful an act or practice on the grounds that such act or practice is unfair unless the act or practice causes or is likely to cause substantial injury to consumers which is not reasonably avoidable by consumers themselves and not outweighed by countervailing benefits to consumers or to competition. In determining whether an act or practice is unfair, the Commission may consider established public policies as evidence to be considered with all other evidence. Such public policy considerations may not serve as a primary basis for such determination.[35]

### The Unfairness Statement

The 1980 Unfairness Statement is a more useful text for understanding the FTC's power than the Deception Statement. In part this is because it is a more balanced, consensus document. All five then commissioners signed the Unfairness Statement, which articulated the three factors that the Agency said it had used to support a finding of unfairness in consumer transactions: whether the practice injures consumers unjustifiably, whether it violates established public policy, and whether it is unethical or unscrupulous.[36]

In 1994, Congress codified the statement, but limited the public policy factor so that it could not independently support a claim of unfairness. In other words, practically this amendment means that there is only one factor in unfairness: unjustified consumer injury.

---

[34] *FTC* v. *Sperry & Hutchinson Trading Stamp Co.*, 405 US 233 (1972).

[35] 15 U.S.C. 45(n); added by the Federal Trade Commission Act Amendments of 1994, Pub. L. No. 103–312, August 26, 1994, 108 Stat 1691.

[36] Letter from Michael Pertschuk, FTC Chairman, and Paul Rand Dixon, FTC Commissioner, to Wendell H. Ford, Chairman, House Commerce Subcommittee on Commerce, Science, and Transportation (December 17, 1980).

The Agency today considers a three-prong test when pondering consumer injury. For a consumer injury to be unfair, it must be substantial, the injury must not be outweighed by countervailing benefits to competition or consumers produced by the practice, and it must be an injury that could not have been reasonably avoided.

### Substantial injury

Substantial injuries to consumers usually – but not always[37] – involve monetary harm, coercion into the purchase of unwanted goods or services, and health or safety risks. Substantial injury may also occur where a business practice causes a small harm to a large number of people. The subversion of some other law – even one not enforced by the FTC – can be the basis for substantial injury.[38] So-called "subjective harms," such as emotional injury, will not normally support a claim of unfairness. For instance, the Statement on Unfairness claims that the FTC "will not seek to ban an advertisement merely because it offends the tastes or social beliefs of some viewers ..."

The FTC has indicated that the unfairness theory could be successful in matters where children's privacy is violated. In 1997, the Agency warned websites targeted to children that "it is likely to be an unfair practice to collect personally identifiable information from children and sell or otherwise disclose that information to third parties without providing parents with adequate notice and an opportunity to control the collection and use of the information."[39] Congress later ratified this position in enacting the Children's Online Privacy Protection Act.

### The practice must not be outweighed by countervailing benefits

Injuries must not be outweighed by countervailing benefits to competition or consumers. The FTC notes that harm to customers must be "injurious in its net effects." When evaluating business practices, it will consider costs to the business and consumer, burdens on society from increased paperwork and regulation, burdens on the flow of information, and incentives for innovation.

### The practice must be practically unavoidable

The injury must not have been one that a customer could reasonably avoid. Noting that some sales techniques prevent customer choice, the FTC focuses on "seller behavior that unreasonably creates or takes advantage of an obstacle to the free exercise of consumer decisionmaking." For instance, unavoidable injury is more likely to be found where businesses withhold critical price or performance

---

[37] *In the Matter of DesignerWare, LLC*, FTC File No. 1123151 (April 15, 2013)(secret, invasive monitoring inside the home was unfair).

[38] *FTC v. Accusearch Inc.*, 570 F.3d 1187, 1195 (10th Cir. 2009) ("the FTC may proceed against unfair practices even if those practices violate some other statute that the FTC lacks authority to administer").

[39] FTC, *FTC Surfs Children's Web Sites to Review Privacy Practices* (December 15, 1997).

information, where the seller engages in coercion, or where the seller targets vulnerable populations.

## Public policy factor and unethical conduct

The 1980 articulation of unfairness included two other factors that guided the FTC in finding illegal practices: a violation of clearly established public policy and unethical or unscrupulous conduct. Public policy considerations can support a claim of unfairness, but cannot serve as the primary basis for agency action. For a policy to be clearly established, it must be widely followed, and embodied in statutes, judicial decisions, or the Constitution. For instance, the FTC found that it violated clearly established public policy where a company repossessed cars, sold them at auction, and kept surplus funds over the amount owed by the creditor. Since public policy cannot independently support an unfairness claim under the 1994 amendments to Section 5, it is usually employed only to evaluate consumer injury.

---

THE COMMUNICATIONS DECENCY ACT

Section 230 of the Communications Decency Act (CDA) broadly immunizes online services from defamation and other torts for the content posted by third parties. For instance, under the CDA, a website that allows user comments would not be liable if a user defamed another person. The law's provisions are so exceptional that few manage to beat a CDA defense. However, in *FTC v. Accusearch Inc.*, 570 F.3d 1187 (10th Cir. 2009), the FTC sued a website operator that connected third-party private investigators with consumers interested in buying confidential phone records of others. Accusearch claimed that it was entitled to immunity under the CDA because it "merely provided 'a forum in which people advertise and request' telephone records." However, the 10th Circuit held that Accusearch was involved in the creation of content: "Accusearch solicited requests for confidential information protected by law, paid researchers to find it, knew that the researchers were likely to use improper methods, and charged customers who wished the information to be disclosed. Accusearch's actions were not 'neutral' with respect to generating offensive content; on the contrary, its actions were intended to generate such content. Accusearch is not entitled to immunity under the CDA."

Many websites are used to pursue illegal ends, such as the solicitation of prostitution, the sale of counterfeit or copyright-protected goods, or the sale of drugs. The CDA is frequently used to argue that these behaviors, clearly illegal and subject to vicarious liability offline, should not trigger liability online.[40]

---

[40] *FTC v. LeanSpa, LLC*, 920 F. Supp. 2d 270 (D. Conn. 2013)

Finally, under the 1980 statement, unethical or unscrupulous conduct could constitute an unfair trade practice. However, the FTC declared that unethical conduct is "largely duplicative" of the public policy factor and is no longer used by the FTC to evaluate unfairness claims. Unethical conduct is not included in the statutory definition of unfairness; thus presumably it is no longer a factor.

## SUBSTANTIATION

In 1972, the Agency formally began its advertising substantiation program, which requires advertisers and advertising agencies to develop a reasonable basis for claims before they are made to consumers.[41] In effect, this approach switches the burden of proof of facts from the government to the private sector where companies make express or implied claims that make objective assertions about the item or service advertised.

Positive product claims are key to appealing to consumers. In his popular *Confessions of an Advertising Man*, David Ogilvy wrote, "The key to success is to promise the *consumer a benefit* – like better flavor, whiter wash, more miles per gallon, a better complexion."[42] Advertisers are deeply tempted to make such claims and for decades have engaged in research to uncover preferences that form the basis of advertising campaigns.[43] These claims are important and shape consumer choices, but they are also difficult to verify and sometimes highly difficult to disprove. Epistemic dilemmas are raised in cases against advertisers.

The Agency's first case calling for substantiation demonstrated these problems and resulted in the FTC placing the burden upon advertisers to prove their claims rather than on consumer protection officials to prove a negative. In it, the FTC found it unfair for Pfizer to make representations concerning a sunburn remedy where the company had no reasonable basis to support the claims. The Commission explained that substantiation was justified by a number of modern marketplace conditions that make it inefficient for consumers to bear the burden of evaluating claims.

The Commission's language mirrored the assumptions that privacy advocacy organizations use today in promoting consumer protection. Under Republican Chairman Miles Kirkpatrick, the FTC argued that consumers lack incentives to fully investigate claims, that products are too complex to investigate, that claims cannot be evaluated until after a product is purchased in many cases, and that there are power imbalances between consumer and seller that justify placing regulatory burdens on sellers.[44]

---

[41] The first substantiation case came in 1963, but limited the duty to health and safety claims. *See Kirchner v. FTC*, 337 F.2d 751 (9th Cir. 1964).

[42] David Ogilvy, CONFESSIONS OF AN ADVERTISING MAN 24 (1963) (emphasis added).

[43] *Id.* at 123.

[44] *In re Pfizer, Inc.*, 81 F.T.C. 23, 61–62 (1972). ("Generally, the individual consumer is at a distinct disadvantage compared to the producer or distributor of goods in reaching conclusions concerning the reliability of product claims. Very often the price of a consumer product is sufficiently low that the cost

In 1984, the FTC modified its substantiation requirements. Advertisers must have a "reasonable basis" for claims. Today, the FTC examines six factors to determine whether a reasonable basis exists: the type of claim, the product, the consequences of a false claim, the benefits of a truthful claim, the cost of developing substantiation for the claim, and the amount of substantiation experts in the field believe is reasonable for the claim.[45] Practically speaking, different products and different claims require different kinds of substantiation, and the advertiser has to determine what evidence is procedurally and substantively reliable enough to support product claims.[46] In 2015, in a high-stakes First Amendment challenge to substantiation, the FTC won a partial but important victory in the D.C. Circuit. The appellate court upheld the FTC's requirement that a seller perform a random, controlled clinical trial before making health claims about a product.[47]

While the Agency has targeted many advertising claims as both deceptive and unsubstantiated, substantiation has not been applied in privacy and security matters. Perhaps this is because the misrepresentations made by privacy-enhancing services were obviously just deceptive. Take, for instance, Snapchat, a service that claimed that messages sent to others would be automatically deleted, and thus that users could feel secure to send racy or sensitive messages without creating a permanent record. This was obviously wrong because popular applications were available to undo the protection, yet many of Snapchat's users believed its claims. The FTC charged the company with deception.[48]

As the Snowden revelations and state security breach notification rules have created markets for privacy-enhancing services, substantiation could become a powerful doctrine in privacy cases.

to the consumer of obtaining relevant product information exceeds the benefits resulting from the increased satisfaction achieved thereby. In other cases, the complexity of a consumer product, and accordingly the large amount of detailed product information necessary to an informed decision, makes the costs of obtaining product information prohibitive.

This problem is further magnified by the large number of competing products on the market. Thus, with the development and proliferation of highly complex and technical products, there is often no practical way for consumers to ascertain the truthfulness of affirmative product claims prior to buying and using the product. When faced with a vast selection of products to choose from, the typical family unit is not sufficiently large enough, and its requirements are too varied, to allow detailed investigation of the goods to be purchased. The consumer simply cannot make the necessary tests or investigations to determine whether the direct and affirmative claims made for a product are true.

Given the imbalance of knowledge and resources between a business enterprise and each of its customers, economically it is more rational, and imposes far less cost on society, to require a manufacturer to confirm his affirmative product claims rather than impose a burden upon each individual consumer to test, investigate, or experiment for himself. The manufacturer has the ability, the knowhow, the equipment, the time and the resources to undertake such information by testing or otherwise – the consumer usually does not.")

[45] Federal Trade Commission, FTC Policy Statement Regarding Advertising Substantiation (1984).
[46] *FTC v. Nat'l Urological Grp., Inc.*, 645 F. Supp. 2d 1167 (N.D. Ga. 2008) *aff'd*, 356 F. App'x 358 (11th Cir. 2009), *cert. denied*, 131 S. Ct. 505 (2010).
[47] *POM Wonderful, LLC v. FTC*, 777 F.3d 478 (D.C. Cir. 2015)
[48] *In re Snapchat, Inc.*, FTC File No. C-4501 (December 23, 2014).

### The substantiation controversy

Substantiation is one of the FTC's most controversial policies. Critiques surround several different areas: First, generating information is costly, and so substantiation results in more expensive advertising.

Second, some true claims are difficult to substantiate, and so these claims will not be presented, thus depriving the market of information. For instance, to rein in bunco, the FTC has required products that make disease-treating claims to be verified by random, controlled, clinical trials.[49] Substantiation opponents would rather have these claims tested in the marketplace. And under the worst-case scenario, a lean company with a miracle product, unable to advertise without scientific studies in hand, would lose out in the marketplace. Americans would lose health opportunities en masse; thus, substantiation would have very real costs and harms to the public.

For instance, the Kellogg Company began a high-profile campaign in 1984 to evangelize a high-fiber diet as effective in reducing colon cancer risk. While the FDA believed that fiber was key to lowering colon cancer risk, there were no large clinical trials to prove this true.[50] The Kellogg style of advertising was adopted by competitors, bathing the American public in advice about high-fiber diets. Over time, these ads were thought to have caused Americans to eat less fat.[51] The episode suggests that the advertising industry can mobilize health claims much more quickly and broadly than government and popular media, which were beating an anti-fat drum for decades with less effect.

The Kellogg example is a powerful anecdote in the anti-substantiation arsenal, but it is just one story. And in retrospect, it may be a bad anecdote – many foods that are low in something (fat, gluten, etc.) just use sugar to fill the void, raising the risk of obesity-related diseases. This becomes the problem of advertising's ability to quickly mobilize knowledge: false, misleading, and dangerous claims can be evangelized just as quickly and broadly as true ones.

If advertisers want to enjoy the credibility halo of scientific claims, they should be based on scientific proof. Otherwise, this behavior would likely have a corrosive effect on the market for pharmaceutical drugs, where products have to be proven both safe and effective. After all, why would one bother engaging in research innovation when one can just make marketing claims about fruit juice drinks and make hundreds of millions of dollars?

---

[49]  *POM Wonderful, LLC v. FTC*, 777 F.3d 478 (D.C. Cir. 2015) (upholding requirement of a randomized, controlled, human clinical trial study before a respondent could claim a causal relationship between consumption of a product and the treatment or prevention of any disease).

[50]  J. Howard Beales III, Timothy J. Muris, & Robert Pitofsky, In Defense of the Pfizer Factors (May 2012).

[51]  Pauline M. Ippolito & Alan D. Mathios, *Information and Advertising: The Case of Fat Consumption in the United States*, 85(2) Am. Econ. Rev. 91 (1995).

Third, if claims require substantiation, advertisers will just invest in low-information brand marketing. In the eyes of critics, substantiation serves big advertising agencies while reducing incentives for information-rich marketing.

Substantiation's roots can be found in the 1938 amendments, where Congress expressed concern about the government spending too many resources proving and disproving claims. Indeed, having advertisers generate information to substantiate claims may save consumers and the Commission time in trying to evaluate advertising.

---

### BRAND NAMES AND DECEPTION

In 1971, five law students from the George Washington University petitioned the FTC concerning objections to how branded products were marketed. The group, calling itself Students against Misleading Enterprises (SAME), argued that "[a]dvertising should inform consumers, but advertising that makes unsubstantiated claims or that implies superior qualities for products where none have been clinically found to exist denies consumer sovereignty and thwarts the operation of a free-market economy." The group urged the Commission to adopt a new trade regulation rule barring companies from using unsubstantiated claims or implications in advertising "chemically identical products" and require such products to display a label disclosing that all products in the industry are chemically identical (For example: "All liquid bleaches are chemically identical.").

Almost ten years later, the FTC settled a case concerning Bayer aspirin. Signaling skepticism of "uniqueness" claims, the Agency banned the advertisement of the aspirin without a disclosure of its ingredients and banned representations that it was more efficacious than alternatives with the same ingredients.[52]

---

Even before it became formal policy, sophisticated national advertisers were expending effort to substantiate claims.[53] A 1974 article in the *Journal of Marketing* noted widespread public distrust of advertising and recommended that

---

[52] *In re Dancer-Fitzgerald-Sample, Inc.*, 96 F.T.C. 1 (1980). The FTC has the power under 15 U.S.C. §1064 to petition to cancel a trademark if it becomes the generic name for goods or services.

[53] DAVID OGILVY, CONFESSIONS OF AN ADVERTISING MAN 158 (1963 edn). ("The lawyer at General Foods actually required that our copywriters prove that Open-Pit Barbecue Sauce has an 'old-fashioned flavor' before he would allow us to make this innocuous claim in advertisements.") A 1962 American Association of Advertising Agencies statement promised that members would not knowingly make "claims insufficiently supported, or which distort the true meaning or practical application of statements made by professional or scientific authority." John Samuel Healey, The Federal Trade Commission Advertising Substantiation Program and Changes in the Content of Advertising in Selected Industries (1978) (Ph.D. dissertation, University of California, Los Angeles, CA).

companies making claims subject them to rigorous and methodologically scientific testing and to a review committee.[54] While causing complaint at the time, substantiation was later cited as a part of a trio of policies (along with truth in mock-ups and corrective advertising) that cleaned up the flimflam "that prevailed in the 1960s." Writing in *Advertising Age* in 1982, Stanley Cohen credited these interventions, which he argued could not be pursued under a cost–benefit analysis approach, with raising standards for advertising nationally.[55]

But the embrace of substantiation fueled allegations that it was a "special interest" regulation that benefited large advertisers. Among some economists, an orthodoxy has arisen that substantiation is perverse. For instance, Professors Richard S. Higgins and Fred S. McChesney concluded that substantiation increased the wealth of large advertising firms because their stock prices increased after it was clear that substantiation was to become required.[56] A more credible and widely cited study by Sauer and Leffler appearing in the *American Economic Review* evaluated substantiation by looking for signals of advertising quality, including factors such as increased advertising of durable goods, and whether there was greater investment in television advertising, which was thought to be the primary beneficiary of truth-in-advertising campaigns. The pair concluded that substantiation did not increase barriers to entry for new firms, and that the policy promoted more credible advertising.[57]

However, perhaps the most careful study of substantiation comes in an unpublished Ph.D. thesis by John Samuel Healey, also finding mixed results from substantiation. The policy reduced advertisers' tendency to make ambiguous statements where the consumer was expected to fill in the details in favor of claims that "were either 'pure pap' or very factual in nature." Post-substantiation, ads had fewer claims and relied on inherently verifiable attributes. However, Healey found that substantiation did not cause the two classes of products studied to be advertised in a more informative way.[58]

[54]    Robert E. Wilkes & James B. Wilcox, *Recent FTC Actions: Implications for the Advertising Strategist*, 38 J. MKTG 55 (January 1974).

[55]    Stanley E. Cohen, *Consumer Safety Net Starting to Unravel*, 53(28) ADVERTISING AGE (March 8, 1982).

[56]    *Truth and consequences: The Federal Trade Commission's ad substantiation program*, 6 INT'L. REV. L. ECON. 151 (1986). This is a widely referenced article about substantiation but it has deep flaws in methods but also in assumptions. The findings are essentially based on the idea that once substantiation was mentioned in a news article, markets incorporated that knowledge and wealth was transferred to large firms that could handle the extra responsibilities of substantiation. Not only is this post hoc reasoning, but the propter hoc was misidentified – the time period the authors establish for the beginning of substantiation requirements is wrong, throwing off their entire method of measuring the effects of substantiation. Substantiation in tobacco was required in the Agency's 1955 *Cigarette Advertising Guide*, and required in other fields in the mid 1960s. As explained by Ogilvy, major advertisers had requested substantiation by the time he published his book in 1963.

[57]    Raymond D. Sauer & Keith B. Leffler, *Did the Federal Trade Commission's Advertising Substantiation Program Promote More Credible Advertising?*, 80(1) AM. ECON. REV. 191 (1990). J. Howard Beales III and Pablo T. Spiller provided commentary on these two papers *in* EMPIRICAL APPROACHES TO CONSUMER PROTECTION ECONOMICS (Pauline M. Ippolito & David T. Scheffman, eds.)(1986).

[58]    John Samuel Healey, The Federal Trade Commission Advertising Substantiation Program and Changes in the Content of Advertising in Selected Industries (1978)(Ph.D. dissertation, University of California, Los Angeles, CA).

## THE PUBLIC INTEREST REQUIREMENT

In order to bring an action, the Commission must act in the interest of the public. The FTC Act specifies that "if it shall appear to the Commission that a proceeding by it in respect thereof would be to the interest of the public," the Agency may issue a complaint.[59] Given the broad statutory language, courts afford great deference to the Agency's "public interest" determinations.[60] However, the Commission will not take action in private controversies.[61] Some private-interest false advertising claims can be brought by consumers under state law, or under the Lanham Act, which creates a federal course of action to competitors for challenging advertising claims.

---

### WHAT IS THE FTC'S MISSION?

Thomas K. McCraw observed in 1984 that "the FTC had many parents, but it captured the special attention of none. Troubled in its infancy, awkward in adolescence, clumsy in adulthood, the Agency never found a coherent mission for itself . . . The primary reason behind [its] dolorous history has been identified as the persistent confusion and ambiguity of the American public towards competition – the very problem the FTC Act was intended to solve."[62] Competition policy may seek several different goals, from the maintenance of desirable levels of growth from the economy as a whole, to the control of "big business," or to the encouragement of competition as an end in itself.

The lack of clear policy goals was a chief critique of commissioner Nelson Gaskill, who joined the Agency in 1920. He reflected: "Eagerly he (Chairman Victor Murdock, a progressive) asked me, 'What do you think unfair competition means?' I had never seen the animal, either roaming its native wilds or in a state of captivity . . . I had nothing to offer constructive." He continued, colorfully, "The truth of the matter is that in the beginning anybody's guess as to what unfair competition might mean was as good as anybody else's. Congress had strongly suspected that some predatory animal was robbing the henroost. It ordered that the animal be caught and killed. But it neglected to say whether the animal ran on two legs or four, sang, howled or grunted, was carnivorous or vegetarian, roosted in trees or slept on the ground . . ."[63]

---

[59] 15 U.S.C. §45(b).

[60] For an discussion of the limits of the public interest requirement, *see FTC* v. *Klesner*, 280 US 19 (1929) ("the mere fact that it is to the interest of the community that private rights shall be respected is not enough to support a finding of public interest. To justify filing a complaint, the public interest must be specific and substantial.").

[61] 16 C.F.R. § 2.3.

[62] Thomas K. McCraw, Prophets of Regulation 81 (1984).

[63] Nelson B. Gaskill, The Regulation of Competition: A Study of Futility as Exemplified by the Federal Trade Commission and National Industrial Recovery Act with Proposals for Its Remedy (1936).

> A recent articulation of the FTC's mission was "To prevent business practices that are anticompetitive or deceptive or unfair to consumers; to enhance informed consumer choice and public understanding of the competitive process; and to accomplish these missions without unduly burdening legitimate business activity."[64]

Some are trying to breathe more life into the "public interest" requirement. For instance, in 2009, commissioner Rosch argued that a settlement with Facebook failed to meet the public interest requirement because the company denied all the relevant facts in the complaint. Rosch reasoned that it could not be in the public interest to allow a company to deny everything it was accused of doing. Rosch's point gained traction with the Commission and staff, which promised to disfavor broad express denials of commission findings.

### STATE UNFAIR AND DECEPTIVE ACTS AND PRACTICES STATUTES

All states have their own versions of the FTC Act, commonly called Unfair and Deceptive Acts and Practices ("UDAP") statutes or "little FTC acts."[65] The FTC encouraged their adoption in an effort to reach local frauds that might not attract the attention of the federal government. Many are modeled on the FTC Act and follow the Agency's guidance on the definition of unfairness and deception. Some are broader than the FTC Act and provide for private rights of action.

States tend to adopt enforcement innovations developed by the FTC. For instance, corrective advertising has been applied in state courts, following the FTC lead.[66]

FTC actions have no formal effect on state enforcement efforts. Thus, when a company settles with the FTC, a state attorney general can bring an identical suit. In practice, this rarely happens, but when representing a company, it is important to note FTC actions have no estoppel effect on private or state litigants.

The FTC can apply its unfairness power against practices that are legal under state law. In *Spiegel, Inc. v. FTC*, 540 F.2d 287 (7th Cir. 1976), the Seventh Circuit upheld the FTC's determination that it was unfair for a mail-order retailer to bring

---

[64] For an in-depth discussion of the FTC's mission, see William E. Kovacic, *The Federal Trade Commission at 100: Into Our 2nd Century, the Continuing Pursuit of Better Practices* (January 2009).

[65] For a high-level summary of these laws, *see* Carolyn L. Carter, National Consumer Law Center, A 50-State Report on Unfair and Deceptive Acts and Practices Statutes (February 2009).

[66] H. Keith Hunt, *Second-Order Effects of the FTC Initiatives, in* MARKETING AND ADVERTISING REGULATION: THE FEDERAL TRADE COMMISSION IN THE 1990S (Patrick E. Murphy & William L. Wilkie, eds., 1990).

suit against customers in the retailer's home jurisdiction, far from the customers, even if the state's long-arm statute approved of such suits.

## CONCLUSION

The power to prevent unfair and deceptive trade practices is a remarkably broad one. The FTC's tools to act in this fashion were forged in decades of cases concerning false advertising and marketing. As a result, the FTC's privacy law is profoundly shaped by false advertising legal precedents, and by the FTC's experience in what constitutes false and misleading behavior in advertising. The FTC's tools are flexible enough to police privacy practices, but have not been used to their full extent in the privacy realm: that is, many, but not all, of the FTC's advertising law precedents and approaches have been applied in the privacy setting. The next part of this book turns to how Section 5 has been articulated in six contexts: online privacy, children's privacy, information security, to police direct marketing, financial privacy, and, finally, international privacy disputes.

# The FTC's regulation of privacy

# 6

## Online privacy

Part I of this book reviewed the history, procedures, and powers of the Commission. Part II now turns to how the Agency has brought its experience and tools to bear on the problem of consumer privacy.

In regulating privacy, the FTC has upset public choice theory predictions about how the Agency might act. Instead of becoming an inflexible institution, it changed as marketing changed. As marketing evolved from print to radio to television to the internet, the FTC retooled its investigative practices. It brought its first internet case in 1994, before most Americans were online, and when many thought that the internet was just a fad. The FTC started making policy statements on internet privacy in 1995, and began its enforcement strategy with children's privacy cases. Instead of becoming a tool of special interests, the FTC has brought cases against a variety of actors in internet commerce, including the largest, most important companies. In addition to being flexible in subject matter and in enforcement target selection, the FTC's approach has evolved. Early privacy matters focused on enforcing privacy representations, but companies learned quickly to not make specific promises, or to write vague privacy policies. As companies changed their strategy, the FTC shifted to an approach of enforcing consumer expectations. The FTC borrowed heavily from its expertise in recognizing and remedying false advertising. Just as it did a generation before when evaluating mass-media advertising, the Commission looked to website design, settings, and even informal remarks by employees as informing consumers' perceptions of privacy promises.

The FTC has been a key force for the protection of online privacy because it fills the gaps left by the US "sectoral" regulatory approach. In the United States, privacy is regulated sector by sector, meaning that certain kinds of businesses are subject to information privacy law statutes. As a result, different companies that possess the same information may be subject only to the Federal Trade Commission Act, or to the act and some sector-specific law, such as the Fair Credit Reporting Act.[1]

---

[1] Kenneth A. Bamberger & Deirdre K. Mulligan, *Privacy on the Books and on the Ground*, 63 STAN. L. REV. 247, 257 (2010).

When the FTC first signaled a commitment to policing consumer protection online, it relied on self-regulation of internet businesses combined with its deception power to police promises made to consumers. In recent years, the Agency's focus has shifted, reflecting a more nuanced understanding of consumer expectations and the influence of computer interfaces on consumer behavior. Use of the Commission's unfairness power has accompanied this shift. First used in 2003, the unfairness power is increasingly used for consumer protection online. The FTC has used case-by-case enforcement exclusively rather than of rule-making. The exception has been in children's privacy and fields such as telemarketing and credit reporting, where Congress has mandated that a rule apply.

The FTC uses many different inputs to guide its interpretation of the FTC Act. At core, the privacy cases flow from the Agency's decades-long experience and precedent in enforcing false advertising cases. In addition to building upon false advertising law, the FTC regularly borrows norms developed from the self-regulatory systems of industries and incorporates standards from statutory information privacy law to set standards under the FTC Act. This FTC approach means that even weak self-regulatory standards can be embraced by the Agency and tweaked into broader protections, and that stringent protections from certain sectoral laws, such as health care privacy statutes, can find their way into FTC Act theories and settlements with non-health-related companies.

The FTC's matter selection is creating an increasingly stringent set of requirements and expectations for online businesses. It is no longer the case that companies can simply point to a privacy policy and justify any kind of data practice. Thus, what started out as a law of disclosures had evolved into a law of unwelcome consumer surprise. The privacy practitioner must have a feel for consumer expectations and business practices that would contravene them in order to advise clients.

This chapter explains basic principles of privacy law, including fair information practices, which form the building blocks of most privacy protections. It describes the cases and the landscape of FTC law on online privacy. Then it shifts to present half a dozen controversies critical to the FTC's privacy stance: First, privacy debates have been dominated by the rational choice theory assumptions that individuals are the most important decision-makers, and that they are informed and empowered to take good decisions to protect privacy. These ideas underlie a notice-and-choice system where consumers receive privacy notices and make choices about which services to use. But growing psychological and economic research undermines the assertions of rational choice theory. Legal experts such as Lauren Willis point to a thicket of disclosures that have the effect of saddling the consumer with the blame for bad privacy choices. Yet, both industry and consumer groups push for greater transparency and individual choice options – hallmarks of rational choice approaches.

Second, notice-and-choice frameworks are deeply undermined by the "third-party problem," the fact that information brokers who have no relationship with the consumer are free to sell personal information. Information-selling companies make it impossible for consumers to exercise control over data, or to organize so that consumers can sell data themselves. Any notice and choice exercised by the consumer can simply be circumvented through purchases of personal information from third parties. Legislation to rein in these companies has been politically impossible to enact, in part because so many large businesses – and politicians themselves – use information brokers to amass data on people.

Self-regulation is the third topic taken up. The FTC begins its regulatory process by first encouraging industries to self-regulate. This is a strategically wise move, because it both sets norms for an industry and exposes companies to deception liability if they adopt self-regulatory rules and violate them. European, British, and Canadian scholars have outlined principles for effective self-regulation. These principles could help guide the FTC in assessing the success of self-regulatory initiatives in America, which have largely been hollow. In fact, at least two US-based self-regulatory privacy regimes have themselves been the target of FTC deception cases.

Fourth, the issue of default choices – whether opt-in or opt-out should govern uses of information – occupies much of the US privacy debate. Default choices allocate transaction costs, with opt-in imposing sales acquisition costs to businesses, and opt-out causing consumers to have to read notices and change privacy settings. The details of default choices are deceptively complex. It is also unsatisfying as an approach for protecting privacy, in part because businesses are not rigorous in their definition of opt-in, and because some define default choices to provide no choice at all. Ultimately, the issue is tied to rational choice assumptions about individual choice, and thus shifting lenses may provide approaches that are more suited to how consumers really act. Different assumptions about consumer decision-making may suggest data deletion rules and other interventions instead of focusing on choice.

Fifth, while content is said to be king, the internet is ruled by platforms, not content. Internet companies vie to achieve platform status, so that they have a monopoly over the user experience, and thus can monetize and control it. Traditionally, privacy concerns centered on third parties obtaining personal information, but with the rise of platforms that mediate users' internet experiences, first parties (the ones that the consumer has a direct relationship with) present significant privacy and autonomy risks. First-degree price discrimination is one manifestation of these risks. But privacy may not be the right tool to address the problem, because so much price discrimination can be accomplished without personal information.

Finally, the chapter concludes with a discussion of privacy by design, a promising and increasingly well-developed approach to incorporating pro-privacy values in design. But for it to be successful, companies have to embrace the underlying values that privacy attempts to protect. Since these values continue to be contested, companies are likely to continue to engage in surveillance by design–the tailoring of systems in order to collect as much data as possible.

## PRIVACY BASICS: GOALS, SCOPE, FAIR INFORMATION PRACTICES

Information privacy norms constantly evolve, and this change is reflected in the goals, conceptualization, and scope of privacy law. The protection of privacy is shaped by how it is conceived. But more broadly, our conceptions of privacy shed light on why we think it is important and worth protecting.

### Privacy control, contextual integrity, and privacy as autonomy

Many different interests animate privacy law, and the different worldviews of privacy thinkers elucidate conflicts over FTC policy. The US approach has long been influenced by "privacy control."[2] Under the privacy control approach, policy should empower individuals to make informed decisions about the collection and use of personal information. This takes the form of privacy notices issued by organizations and choices made by consumers to accept or reject such offers. With its roots in rational choice theory, privacy control rests on the assumption that individuals' choices will guide the marketplace to some acceptable balance between consumer and business interests.

One could envision weak or strong implementations of privacy control. For instance, the FTC could merely allow the market to order privacy norms, and only police privacy where a clear promise to a consumer has been broken and injury has occurred. On the other hand, the FTC could interpret privacy control as requiring default rules that placed the burden on businesses to obtain permission before using data, or even making some data inalienable, to protect the individual against coercive power by data collectors.

Privacy control's fundamental assumptions are similar to rational choice theory (RCT). Definitions of RCT vary, but its general contours include a focus on the individual as decision-maker and the idea that individuals are rational and act to maximize their utility in any given situation. RCT would predict that consumers would shop for privacy, if they had preferences for it. Somewhat circularly, some RCT adherents conclude that a weak market for privacy signals that consumers do not really care about privacy.

Privacy control has come under attack in recent years, primarily from behavioral economists.[3] These researchers argue that biases in consumer decision-making, knowledge gaps between individuals and businesses, and uncertainties surrounding the implications of sharing information make shopping for privacy impossible[4] and privacy control an illusion.[5] Other behavioral economic research has shown that

---

[2] Paul M. Schwartz, *Internet Privacy and the State*, 32 CONN. L. REV. 815 (2000).

[3] Alessandro Acquisti, Laura Brandimarte, & George Loewenstein, *Review: Privacy and Human Behavior in the Age of Information*, 347(6221) SCIENCE 509 (January 30, 2015).

[4] James P. Nehf, *Shopping for Privacy on the Internet*, 41 J. CONSUMER AFF. (2007).

[5] Alessandro Acquisti & Jens Grossklags, *What Can Behavioral Economics Teach Us about Privacy?*, in DIGITAL PRIVACY: THEORY, TECHNOLOGIES, AND PRACTICES (2007).

companies can shape user choices, even when default choices are assigned to require a business to obtain affirmative consent from the individual.[6]

---

PRIVACY DOES NOT SELL – NEITHER DID SAFETY

Why do consumers choose privacy-invasive services? Why are more privacy-protective services not available? One explanation is that "privacy does not sell." In fact, the marketplace is littered with failed companies that tried to sell privacy-protective services to consumers.

Ralph Nader, in his seminal *Unsafe at Any Speed*,[7] offers some parallels from the automobile industry to consider in the debate over whether the market will create privacy options. Nader's book concerned the safety characteristics of cars, and a chapter focuses on automobile companies' opposition to safety mandates, such as mandatory installation of seat belts (then known as "lap belts" because they only connected at the waist).

Representatives of General Motors led the charge against a belt mandate noting (1) that there was public apathy toward the problem – that consumers did not want seat belts; (2) that there was a lack of evidence available about the efficacy of seat belts; (3) that the seat belts tested were uncomfortable and rumpled clothing; (4) that drivers simply would not wear seat belts; (5) and that seat belts would not protect the driver any more than gripping the wheel strongly and positioning one's legs properly. There is some truth to all of these arguments (except the last), but, as Nader pointed out, they are circular – ignorance about the dangers of driving and the lack of safety options depressed demand for seat belts. Nader argued that fear of alienating drivers – by making them think of the dangers of driving every time they drove – was the underlying issue animating opposition to seat belts. Seat belts were a symbol of the horror of auto accidents.

Under then vice president Robert McNamara, the Ford Company had great success in selling seat belts as an option. The company reported selling more than 400,000 seat belts since their introduction, and that no other option "ever caught on so fast." So why didn't safety become a competitive advantage? According to Nader, Ford ended its safety campaign in 1956, after "an internal policy struggle won by those who agreed with the General Motors analysis of the probable unsettling consequences of a vehicle safety campaign." Selling safety, in the eyes of General Motors, was a threat to the entire industry.

Eventually New York State legislators threatened to require car companies to install mounts in new automobiles so that consumers could easily self-install

---

[6] Lauren E. Willis, *When Nudges Fail: Slippery Defaults*, 80 UNIV. CHI. L. REV. 1155 (2013).

[7] RALPH NADER, UNSAFE AT ANY SPEED: THE DESIGNED-IN DANGERS OF THE AMERICAN AUTOMOBILE (1965).

their own seat belts. The automotive industry's trade group relented, but proposed a compromise: belt mounts would only be installed in the front seats, since so few rear-seat passengers died in accidents. By 1964, federal law required seat belts as standard equipment.

Privacy may be experiencing a similar problem in the marketplace. The information industry has powerful incentives to direct consumer attention away from data practices and harms, to claim that the public is apathetic, and to frame privacy problems as the result of autonomous choices made by individuals. Consider that Google resisted placing a link to the company's privacy policy on Google.com – were Google executives concerned that users might think of privacy every time they clicked "search?"

Despite the undermining of RCT in the academy, privacy advocates and regulators still largely work within RCT assumptions when proposing new privacy laws and regulations, such as better disclosures and consumer education. Lucy Black Creighton went so far as to argue that the consumer movement has made consumers pawns of the economy – "pretenders to the throne" – rather than sovereigns, because of its adherence to RCT-based approaches.[8]

Behavioral economics may offer an alternative to the orthodox regulatory approaches specified by RCT. The limits of the "notice-and-choice" model have become clear as companies have formalized privacy policies and disclosed greater details about practices. Evidence has undermined the general assumption that consumers can and do negotiate privacy choices consistently with their preferences.[9] But notice and choice fails both consumers and the business community, because it does not handle post-transaction needs of consumers and businesses adequately. Post-transaction, a company may develop new uses of data that the consumer may or may not have wanted.

A proposed approach termed "contextual integrity" offers a way to address some of the deficits of privacy control by requiring an assessment of the "informational norms" at play in data systems.[10] Under this system, developed by Professor Helen Nissenbaum, privacy violations occur when information norms are not respected. As an example, contextual integrity would hold that search engine companies should not share search terms with third parties, because, in that context, companies are performing a librarian-like role. Contextual integrity has been embraced, although in a grotesque form, by some government officials

---

[8] Lucy Black Creighton, Pretenders to the Throne (1976).

[9] Alessandro Acquisti, Laura Brandimarte, & George Loewenstein, *Review: Privacy and human behavior in the age of information*, 347(6221) Science 509 (January 30, 2015).

[10] Helen Nissenbaum, Privacy in Context (2010).

as a way to regulate information based on how it is used, rather than how the data were collected.[11]

A progressive theory promoted by several academics including Professor Julie Cohen holds that privacy is an instrument for protecting autonomy. Without it, we are in danger of not being able to develop critical thinking and individuality.[12] Both government and private-sector information collection and decision-making may adversely affect individuals' autonomy. At its core, privacy-as-autonomy attempts to shape the power balance between individuals and institutions. It thus may be most aligned with the suspicious of bigness and concern about institutional power that animated the creation of the FTC.

Privacy-as-autonomy offers more than privacy control, because even de-identified data or decision-making not based on data at all could affect autonomy interests. But this approach has its problems too, which are acknowledged by its proponents. It requires us to consider what power balances are appropriate, and to accommodate some constraints on our private lives.[13] It also is amorphous, in that many aspects of our environment affect autonomy, including our personal and family relationships. As Evgeny Morozov argues, privacy's goal is to create boundaries on external influences that allow the self to emerge.[14]

## Privacy's scope

The scope of privacy law is changing. In the 1970s, its scope was limited to information concerning an individual. Today, with the computing and aggregation power of data companies, a much broader scope of data can affect individuals. Serious questions have been raised about the ability to make a database "anonymous," and thus even "de-identified" databases may be subject to privacy enforcement by the FTC. As contextual integrity suggests, there are privacy interests in data shared with third parties, and even informational norms in data that are publicly available.

---

### PRIVACY: NOT A MODERN CONCEPT

Policy arguments and analyses abound with ahistorical arguments concerning technology and privacy. In these arguments, privacy is often presented as a

---

[11] HELEN NISSENBAUM, "RESPECT FOR CONTEXT" – FULFILLING THE PROMISE OF THE WHITE HOUSE REPORT ON PRIVACY *in* PRIVACY THE MODERN AGE: THE SEARCH FOR SOLUTIONS (Marc Rotenberg & Jeramie Scott eds) (2015).

[12] JULIE E. COHEN, CONFIGURING THE NETWORKED SELF: LAW, CODE, AND THE PLAY OF EVERYDAY PRACTICE (2012); HERBERT MARCUSE, ONE-DIMENSIONAL MAN (1964). ("Can a society which is incapable of protecting individual privacy even within one's four walls rightfully claim that it respects the individual and that it is a free society?")

[13] *Id.*

[14] EVGENY MOROZOV, TO SAVE EVERYTHING, CLICK HERE (2013).

modern concept, one that came into focus with the rise of the commercial internet.

Privacy is not a modern concept; it is deeply embedded in the values of Western culture.[15] Nor are conflicts among technology, business practices, and privacy a new issue. Historians often point to the development of the United States Postal Service as an example. Prior to the creation of it, mail was carried privately, often collected and stored in taverns until travel to the next destination.[16] A number of factors eroded the confidentiality and integrity of these mails: letters were relatively rare, and aroused curiosity among those who routed them to their intended destination. The privacy-enhancing technology of the time – the wax seal – could fail because of tampering or rough handling. The paper envelope was not yet invented, and encryption schemes remained primitive.

To fill the gaps created by inadequate technology and practice, Ben Franklin, who was commissioned by the British to run the colonial mails, had carriers swear not to open the messages they carried.[17] This prohibition was eventually codified in federal law, and, today, First-Class Mail is secure against opening except where the government has a warrant.

Conflicts concerning technology are as old as civilization. Indeed, long before the internet, technological conflicts occupied debates among thinkers. The idea of technological knowledge, which was thought of as knowledge of craft as opposed to knowledge of life, was discussed by Plato.[18]

Our society has been struggling with the regulation of personal information for decades, dating back to the 1942 Federal Reports Clearance Act. A sustained attempt to address information privacy started in the 1970s, with the rise of computing and revelations of government spying on political opponents. In 1973, the Department of Health, Education, and Welfare released a report, *Records, Computers and the Rights of Citizens*, which set forth fair information practices (FIPs), a proposal for how institutions should handle information about individuals.[19] Over the years, several versions of FIPs have been proposed.[20] FIPs are the basis for virtually all

---

[15] Consider the five-volume treatise by Ariés and Duby, A HISTORY OF PRIVATE LIFE (Philippe Ariés and Georges Duby, eds., 1987), or Richard Sennett's discussion of the evolving and shifting ideas of "public" in RICHARD SENNETT, THE FALL OF PUBLIC MAN (1974).

[16] DAVID H. FLAHERTY, PRIVACY IN COLONIAL NEW ENGLAND (1967).

[17] ROBERT ELLIS SMITH, BEN FRANKLIN'S WEB SITE (2000).

[18] THE PHILOSOPHY OF TECHNOLOGY: THE TECHNOLOGICAL CONDITION (Robert C. Scharff & Val Dusek, eds., 2003).

[19] Department of Health, Education, and Welfare, Records, Computers and the Rights of Citizens, Report of the Secretary's Advisory Committee on Automated Personal Data Systems (July 1973).

[20] Robert Gellman, Fair Information Practices: A Basic History (March 2014).

information privacy regulation[21] and, in general, they specify procedural safeguards for data handling rather than substantive bans on practices. In 1998, the FTC embraced five practices:

Notice: data collectors must disclose their information practices before collecting personal information from consumers;

Choice: consumers must be given options with respect to whether and how personal information collected from them may be used for purposes beyond those for which the information was provided;

Access: consumers should be able to view and contest the accuracy and complete-ness of data collected about them; and

Security: data collectors must take reasonable steps to assure that information collected from consumers is accurate and secure from unauthorized use.

The FTC separately enumerated the following on enforcement: "the use of a reliable mechanism to impose sanctions for noncompliance with these fair informa-tion practices."

Throughout most of the FTC's history, it has endorsed self-regulatory approaches to promote these FIPs, while threatening the internet industry that it might endorse legislation. This threat is a credible one; the FTC has supported many proposals that are eventually enacted by Congress.

Prior to internet privacy debates, there were several notable public controversies concerning information use. For instance, in 1991, Lotus and Equifax canceled plans to sell a database about US households to small businesses. But the general strategy of US businesses seemed to be to avoid privacy matters. H. Jeff Smith explained that in the 1990s, companies were fearful of confronting privacy policies and only did so reactively. Smith found in his landmark survey of companies that executives went to "extensive lengths to avoid the topic's discussion and investiga-tion," leaving the problem to middle management. Then, "some external threat . . . shocks the corporation into an official response [then] the industry as a whole creates a policy to which individual firms then react."[22]

Studying this period before the FTC's online privacy campaign, Professor Priscilla Regan asked, "Why did the idea of privacy not serve as a lightning rod that sparked public support and timely legislation?"[23] Regan explained that while the idea of privacy is widely shared and latent among the public, it is a weak basis for the formation of public policy. Regan attributed the problem to several factors: Most importantly, the idea of privacy could be countered with the costs that it imposes on well-defined interests, such as law enforcement, employers, and national security. Groups representing these interests were able to shift the conversation away from the

[21] Marc Rotenberg, *Fair Information Practices and the Architecture of Privacy*, 2001 STAN. TECH. L. REV. 1 (2001).
[22] H. JEFF SMITH, MANAGING PRIVACY (1994).
[23] PRISCILLA M. REGAN, LEGISLATIVE PRIVACY: TECHNOLOGY, SOCIAL VALUES, AND PUBLIC POLICY (1995).

ideal of a privacy right, to the specifics of criminals being able to hide their past wrongs and the like. The diffuse definitions of "privacy" contributed to the problem, preventing Congress from coalescing around a clear goal to establish with law.

At a more conceptual level, Regan argued that the American legal understanding of privacy was too weak to be a major driver of legislative change. Legal concepts of privacy are based in theories of secrecy and replete with standards such as the "reasonable expectation of privacy." Our legal understanding was not rich enough to capture the kinds of problems posed to privacy by technology.

For a brief period, a case for legislation mounted. A 1998 study found that privacy notices were not widely implemented. A survey of 1,400 websites conducted by the FTC reported that 92 percent of commercial sites collected personal information but only 14 percent had privacy notices. Of the commercial sites, only 2 percent had a "comprehensive" privacy policy.[24] Many websites did adopt privacy notices after the FTC study,[25] but, in 2000, a 3–2 majority of commissioners formally recommended that Congress adopt legislation requiring compliance with FIPs among commercial websites and network advertising companies.[26] This recommendation proved short-lived, as the composition of the Commission shifted in 2000 with the election of George W. Bush as President. President Bush's Chairman, Timothy Muris, decided to focus the Commission's attention on enforcing existing laws rather than creating new legislative protections for online privacy.[27]

Professor Steven Hetcher has argued that the FTC acted as "norm entrepreneur" in the 1990s, making credible threats of endorsing legislation in a highly successful effort to motivate websites to adopt privacy policies. He argued, "promoting privacy policies allows the Agency to sink its jurisdictional hooks more firmly into the Internet privacy debate, and therefore the Internet."[28] Indeed, in a matter of a few years, almost all top websites had privacy policies that could be policed by the FTC.[29] As a result, understanding the law of online privacy requires a grasp of decisions under the FTC Act. But before there was even a commercial

---

[24] FTC, PRIVACY ONLINE: A REPORT TO CONGRESS, June 4, 1998.

[25] *See* FED. TRADE COMM'N, PRIVACY ONLINE: FAIR INFORMATION PRACTICES IN THE ELECTRONIC MARKETPLACE 10 (2000) (noting a "significant increase" in the percentage of websites posting privacy policies in the year following a Federal Trade Commission report on the subject).

[26] FTC, ONLINE PROFILING: A REPORT TO CONGRESS Part 2 RECOMMENDATIONS, July 2000.

[27] Timothy J. Muris, *Protecting Consumers' Privacy: 2002 and Beyond*, Remarks delivered at the Privacy 2001 Conference, October 4, 2001.

[28] Steven Hetcher, *The FTC as Internet Privacy Norm Entrepreneur*, 53 VANDERBILT L. REV. 2041 (2000). One problem with Hetcher's argument is that the FTC Act clearly gave the FTC jurisdiction over deception, unfairness, and false advertising online. As early as 1994, the FTC sued a credit repair business operating on American Online. *FTC v. Corzine*, CIV-S-94-1446 (E.D. Cal. 1994). By the time Hetcher published his article, the FTC had brought at least 200 internet fraud cases. See Paul H. Luehr, Commission Enforcement Actions Involving the Internet and Online Services, September 21, 1999.

[29] Allyson W. Haynes, *Online Privacy Policies: Contracting Away Control over Personal Information?*, 111 PENN ST. L. REV. 587 (2007).

internet, the FTC policed some privacy matters. The next sections turn to these enforcement actions.

## THE PRE-INTERNET PRIVACY MATTERS

Commercial espionage was among the turn-of-the-century problems that the FTC was created to address. The FTC brought several matters in the 1910s, including a 1918 matter where it issued a cease and desist order against a company that dealt with nosy competitors by crashing delivery trucks into them. The FTC ordered the company to stop "causing any of [its] trucks ... to collide with automobiles owned and operated by any competitor ... at times when the automobiles of such competitor may be following the trucks of ... The Brown Co."[30] In another matter, it ordered a company to cease the use of detectives in order to discover competitors' customer lists.[31] These efforts were limited to protecting companies from competitors' aggressive and illegal behavior.

It was not until 1951 that the FTC intervened to protect consumers from unfair collections of personal information. In the Gen-O-Pak matter, the FTC brought an administrative proceeding against a company that helped creditors locate debtors by sending debtors postcards promising a free gift in exchange for their personal information. One card read, "Dear Friend: We have on hand a package, which we will send to you if you will completely fill out the return card, giving sufficient identification to warrant our sending this package to you ... There are no charges whatsoever and the package will be sent to you all charges prepaid. Yours very truly, The Gen-O-Pak Co." The cards and surveys sent by the company solicited extensive personal information. The FTC found this practice both unfair and deceptive.[32]

In 1971, the FTC filed a complaint invoking both unfairness and deception against a company for generating direct mail lists from consumer questionnaires. The company wrote to consumers promising the chance to win prizes, and that there was "nothing to buy" and "no salesman will call on you."[33] To support its unfairness argument, the FTC stated in its complaint, "A substantial portion of the purchasing public has a preference that their names not appear on mailing lists. This preference arises out of various individual and personal reasons such as, but not limited to, the unauthorized invasion of personal privacy; being subjected to the repeated importuning of promoters, advertisers and sellers of merchandise, services and schemes; and being exploited by respondent and the users of said 'Metromail Elites' mailing list."

Later in the 1970s, the FTC brought a series of matters against tax preparation companies for using client information for marketing. In the 1972 matter concerning

[30] *FTC v. American Agricultural Chemical Co. and the Brown Co.*, 1 F.T.C. 226 (1918).
[31] *In the Matter of the Oakes Company*, 3 F.T.C. 36 (1920).
[32] *Lester Rothschild, Trading as Gen-O-Pak Co.*, 49 F.T.C. 1673 (1952); *Rothschild v. FTC*, 200 F.2d 39 (7th Cir. 1952).
[33] *In the Matter of Metromedia, Inc.*, 78 F.T.C. 331 (1971).

H&R Block, the company used information from client tax files to build lists, which in turn were used for marketing services of a joint venture and for selling these lists to third parties. H&R Block neither disclosed the practice nor attempted to obtain consent.

The Commission based its complaint on both deception and unfairness. H&R Block's customers were deceived because the relationship was impliedly and inherently confidential. The company misled "customers into the erroneous and mistaken belief that the information they provided [to H&R Block] will only be used for the purpose of preparation of their income tax returns and will remain confidential."[34] It was also unfair because secondary use of tax information without consent contravened the special relationship between the client and tax preparer.[35] H&R Block was ordered to obtain informed consent from clients at the initiation of the client relationship. It had to state exactly what information would be used, how it would be used, and a description of the entities that would acquire the data.[36]

The Commission's pre-internet matters suggested that in situations where there were implied norms of confidentiality, strong privacy rules would apply.[37] Its remedies were focused upon notice and opt-in consent, yet the orders appear to allow the companies to condition service on client consent to the information practices.

## THE FIRST INTERNET PRIVACY MATTERS

Policing the online marketplace presented a problem for the Commission. In the 1990s, FTC staff thought unfairness as a legal theory did not fit the privacy practices of online services.[38] Consumers could not identify a substantial injury from privacy

---

[34] *In the Matter of H&R Block, Inc.*, 80 F.T.C. 304 (1972). *See also In the Matter of Tax Corp. of Am. (Maryland), et al.*, 85 F.T.C. 512 (1975).

[35] A 1973 complaint examining similar practices at Beneficial Corporation more fully stated the Commission's privacy objections. Like H&R Block, Beneficial was using information from tax files for marketing, but doing so more aggressively. The administrative law judge found that Beneficial's information practices were "exploitative, unscrupulous, deceptive, and unfair." The FTC rested its unfairness theory on public policy grounds, pointing to the sensitivity of tax preparation information, the existence of statutes governing its privacy, ethical canons of confidentiality, the fiduciary role of the tax preparer, concluding, "the right of privacy has become a widely-valued public policy, with constitutional and statutory underpinning. Its violation in a commercial context would likely be unlawful under the Federal Trade Commission Act." Further, the Commission found the reuse of the information deceptive because customers were not told of its use for lending. *In re Beneficial Corp.*, 86 F.T.C. 119, 168 (1975)(internal citations omitted), *aff'd in Beneficial Corp. v. FTC*, 542 F.2d 611 (3rd Cir. 1976), *cert. denied*, 430 US 983 (1977).

[36] In 1982, after the enactment of tax privacy rules, H&R Block successfully petitioned to modify the consent order and eliminate this requirement. *In the Matter of H&R Block, Inc.*, 100 F.T.C. 523 (1982).

[37] The Commission later distinguished Beneficial from a case involving sale of lists of consumers who had purchased hearing aids. Beneficial involved the breach of a clear fiduciary duty, whereas no clear duty existed in hearing aid sales. *In the Matter of Beltone Elecs. Corp.*, 100 F.T.C. 68 (1982).

[38] *Interview with Joan Z. Bernstein*, Oral History Project, The Historical Society of the District of Columbia Circuit (2007). For an early opposing view holding that the FTC Act could address privacy

abuses, and such abuses could be avoided by simply not using the internet as a commercial channel. Deception requires a representation to the consumer about its practices, but many websites did not have privacy policies. Indeed, some lawyers recommended that sites not adopt a privacy policy to short-circuit claims that any privacy promises were made.

With legal uncertainty lingering, Congress and consumer groups urged the Agency to police privacy online. At this time, international pressure started to mount with the requirement that the EU Data Protection Directive 95/46/EC be transposed into law by 1998. This would require that the United States be deemed to have "adequate" privacy protections before Europeans' data could be transferred to America (see Chapter 11).[39] In 1995, the Agency held three events concerning privacy online. This initiative was led by commissioner Christine Varney, by Director of Consumer Protection Jodie Bernstein, and by attorneys David Medine and C. Lee Peeler.[40]

The Commission chose its early matters carefully. It only took enforcement actions where the facts were favorable, focusing on matters concerning children (see Chapter 7). It used deception rather than unfairness. It loudly signaled its position on privacy matters through the *KidsCom.com* matter.

In response to a request by the Center for Media Education (CME), the FTC investigated and released a public letter concerning KidsCom.com.[41] The site solicited personal information from children and gave them incentives to review products. The reviews exposed information to other users of the site and functioned as a social network of sorts, thus raising fears of adult predation on children. The FTC opined that it was deceptive for KidsCom.com to collect information from children and to reveal it to others without parental notice and consent.

A year after the KidsCom.com warning letter, the FTC settled a matter against GeoCities, an online service provider that shared children's information with third parties despite promising not to do so.[42] The other early matters were similar in that they involved a broken promise and generally concerned children or sensitive data. One site targeted children, broke promises, claimed to collect data anonymously, but linked it with contact information.[43] Another website promised to never sell

---

online, *see* Jeff Sovern, *Protecting Privacy with Deceptive Trade Practices Legislation*, 69 FORDHAM L. REV. 1305 (2001).

[39] Paul M. Schwartz, *European Data Protection Law and Restrictions on International Data Flows*, 80 *Iowa L. Rev.* 471 (1994); Colin J. Bennett, *Convergence Revisited: Toward a Global Policy for the Protection of Personal Data?*, *in* TECHNOLOGY AND PRIVACY: THE NEW LANDSCAPE (Philip E. Agre & Marc Rotenberg, eds., 1997).

[40] This effort concluded with the Agency's first major report on privacy. Federal Trade Commission, Staff Report on the Public Workshop on Consumer Privacy on the Global Information Infrastructure (December 1996).

[41] Letter from Jodie Bernstein, Director, FTC Bureau of Consumer Protection, to Kathryn C. Montgomery, President, Center for Media Education (July 15, 1997).

[42] *In the Matter of Geocities*, 127 F.T.C. 94 (February 5, 1999).

[43] *In the Matter of Liberty Fin. Companies, Inc.*, 128 F.T.C. 240 (1999).

personal information about children but then attempted to use it as an asset in bankruptcy.[44] Pharmacies servicing erectile dysfunction patients claimed to have Secure Sockets Layer (SSL) security and to do evaluations of patients in-house but lacked SSL and transferred the data to other pharmacies.[45]

Today, these early matters would be easy cases in privacy law. It is now well established that one should not violate the affirmative representations made in privacy policies and other communications to the consumer. Procedurally, these cases were important because they demonstrated how the FTC enters new areas of law: First come warnings in the form of letters, workshops, and other public pronouncements. Shortly thereafter, the FTC brings matters against particularly egregious transgressors. The thin edge of affirmative misrepresentations concerning children can pry open the door to matters involving omissions concerning adults' data.

## The political landscape in the early 2000s

As the FTC brought its early matters, privacy advocates pushed for federal baseline privacy legislation centered on FIPs. But calls for Congressional intervention agitated business groups and never gained real traction in Congress. General privacy legislation could potentially affect all businesses, which stimulated business lobbies to organize to shape or stop it. Privacy advocates faced an uphill battle, as it is easier to defeat legislation than to pass it. Also, the nature of privacy advocacy groups made them relatively easy to manipulate or marginalize. Generally, advocates had not been able to develop a unified agenda, and were prone to infighting and suspicion of others' motives. Thus, business privacy lobbyists could prevail with inertia. They did so by establishing relationships with lawmakers, gaining lawmakers' trust by appearing reasonable, and by trusting that privacy groups would fight each other over legislative compromises.

The most successful legislative effort, Senator Fritz Hollings' 2002 "Online Personal Privacy Act," found support in the Senate Commerce Committee but was blocked by then Minority Leader Senator Trent Lott, who invoked a rule to shut down the entire Senate. The extraordinary move, said to be requested by the financial services industry, signaled that the bill would fail on the Senate floor.

Still, it is not clear that privacy advocates could have had a positive outcome given the makeup of Congress at the time. Just a few years before the defeat of the Hollings bill, Congress passed the Financial Services Modernization Act (see Chapter 10), which explicitly allowed banks to sell personal and account information to third parties. This law weakened restraints on bank confidentiality and set a lower bar than the Commission's pre-internet matters concerning the alienation of financial information.

---

[44] *FTC v. Toysmart.com*, 00–11341-RGS, 2000 WL 34016434 (D. Mass. July 21, 2000).
[45] *FTC v. Rennert, Sandra L., et al.*, CV-S-00–0861-JBR (D. Nev. July 6, 2000).

## The harms-based approach

In the absence of federal privacy legislation, the FTC pursued a case-by-case enforcement strategy during the administration of President George W. Bush. These were the years of the "harms-based" approach. This was a politically smart maneuver by Chairman Muris: it signaled that the Agency would prioritize matters involving risk of physical harm and those that caused economic injury.[46] There clearly were benefits to this approach early in the Commission's activity because conservatives and liberals alike could not object to policing the practices targeted.

Telemarketing and spam were also targets of the harms-based approach (see Chapter 9). These were characterized by the industry as minor inconveniences of modern life and as a major driver of the economy. Nevertheless, the Agency used two strategies to bring "unwanted intrusions" into a harms framework: it linked telemarketing to privacy of the home, and it highlighted the aggregate costs of telemarketing and spam activities on consumers' lives.

### BLACK LETTER: PRIVACY UNFAIRNESS AND DECEPTION

Respondents in FTC proceedings settle almost all matters. Thus, FTC online privacy law is largely a body of complaints and consent decrees. Attorneys must read this sprawling material and try to give advice to clients about the contours of the FTC Act. Attorneys do this by writing case studies or circulating news articles about competitors and near-competitors that ran into trouble. In straightforward situations where a misrepresentation has been made, privacy officers can easily convince colleagues to change practices. But with time, the FTC advanced far beyond simple "broken promises" cases. The modern privacy officer has to convince others within the organization that consumer expectations matter and that companies cannot merely disclose their way out of unpleasant, unexpected data practices.

This practice of building law through settlement and consent decree has long been criticized in other contexts than information privacy.[47] But in enacting and strengthening the FTC Act, Congress wanted the Agency to quickly react to problematic business practices (see Chapter 1). It wanted an expert agency, one that could adjudicate complex matters without involving the federal courts.

Businesses offended by the FTC's approach could always appeal agency decisions to the federal courts, but few of them do. This is because of the FTC's careful matter selection and the deference that courts afford FTC determinations, and because, upon investigation, the FTC often discovers additional, latent deceptive practices at

---

[46] Timothy J. Muris, *Protecting Consumers' Privacy: 2002 and Beyond*, Remarks at the Privacy 2001 Conference, October 4, 2001.

[47] LOWELL MASON, THE LANGUAGE OF DISSENT 169 (1959). ("To the unwary practitioner defending a client, or to the average businessman searching for guidance as to what he can or cannot do, these uncontested orders in the printed volumes of the Federal Trade Commission reports give credence and a semblance of authority to rules that actually have no basis in law.")

companies. Reflecting favorably on the FTC's case-by-case approach, Professors Daniel Solove and Woodrow Hartzog have characterized it as the functional equivalent of common law.[48] In 2015, the Third Circuit Court of Appeals included a table in a decision that compared a respondent's practices with that of another company that had settled with the Commission. Although the respondent claimed that FTC settlements were adjudicated, the Third Circuit held that the respondent nevertheless had fair notice that its practices could violate the FTC Act.[49]

The next subsection gives the highlights of the "black letter" FTC rules under unfairness and deception.

### The contours of unfair privacy practices

The FTC primarily relies on deception rather than unfairness in its privacy matters. Starting in 2003, it started invoking unfairness as an independent theory for privacy violations. Since then, the FTC increasingly invokes unfairness.

For the business community, unfairness is a more controversial and troublesome legal theory than deception. This is because, practically speaking, it operates as a ban on certain practices. Unlike deceptive practices, which generally can be made non-misleading through better notice and consent procedures, unfair practices are more difficult to justify even when the consumer is told about them.

The history of unfair and deceptive practices was discussed in detail in Chapter 5. As a refresher, recall that an unfair practice is one that causes substantial consumer injury, the injury must not be outweighed by countervailing benefits to competition or consumers produced by the practice, and it must be an injury that could not have been reasonably avoided by the consumer. Unfairness matters are important because they signal when the FTC thinks substantial injury or harm has been caused. While in the Agency's early privacy days, it suspected privacy violations would not arise to unfairness, recent matters show a shift in outlook. Now, mere disclosure of personal information, concerning a large number of individuals to a third party, can create an aggregate harm in the Agency's eyes.

### A retroactive policy change

The FTC's first unfair practice matter, Gateway, concerned a company that promised not to sell data to third parties, but later changed its policy.[50] Companies change policy all the time, but Gateway's policy shift was unfair because the company required its customers to opt out from the data sale. From the FTC's perspective, this would require a consumer to monitor perhaps thousands of

---

[48] Daniel J. Solove & Woodrow Hartzog, *The FTC and the New Common Law of Privacy*, 144 COLUM. L. REV. 583 (2014).

[49] *FTC v. Wyndham Worldwide Corp.*, No. 14-3514, 2015 WL 4998121 (3d Cir. August 24, 2015).

[50] *In the Matter of Gateway Learning Corp.*, FTC File No. 042 3047 (September 17, 2004).

business relationships for detrimental policy changes and act to stop them. Similarly, in the FTC's matter against Facebook, retroactive policy changes that opened users' profiles to the public were considered unfair.[51]

In Gateway, the Commission noted that the matter involved data about children, and declared that the company's reversal caused substantial consumer injury. In the later Facebook case, the Agency went into greater detail, clearly indicating that it thought that exposure of previously restricted profile information arose to substantial injury. It emphasized that injury could come from unwelcome contacts from others: the exposure of controversial political views, business relationships, friends' lists, sexual orientation, and photos. This determination has very important implications for information-intensive firms: data that are shared, even widely, across the Web can become the basis of an unfairness action if they are mishandled. Small affronts to individual users become very large harms in the aggregate.

### Aggressive investigation

In the FTC's 1999 case against Touch Tone Information, Inc. (popularly known as the Rapp case), the Agency argued that "pretexting" was both deceptive and unfair. Pretexting is the practice of using various false pretenses in order to cause another business to disclose information about a customer. Touch Tone allegedly did this for clients in order to provide financial and contact information of individuals.[52] Following the 1999 case, the FTC conducted a sweep against private investigators who used pretexting to obtain phone records.[53] As part of this sweep, the 10th Circuit upheld an FTC unfairness claim against Abika.com, a website that connected consumers with investigators who would obtain others' information through pretexting.[54]

### Knowingly violating others' privacy commitments

The Commission found it unfair for a shopping cart provider, that is, a company that managed the payment function of third-party merchant websites, to rent information from transactions in violation of those merchants' privacy promises. In the matter, merchants had made unambiguous promises not to sell data to third parties. The shopping cart company knew this, yet collected information from the transactions and rented them for marketing purposes.[55] Thus, it is unfair to

---

[51] *In the Matter of Facebook, Inc.*, FTC File No. 092 3184 (July 27, 2012).

[52] *FTC v. Rapp d/b/a Touch Tone Information, Inc.*, No. 99-WM-783 (D. Colo. 1999).

[53] *See, for example, FTC v. 77 Investigations, Inc., and Reginald Kimbro*, No. EDCV06-0439 VAP (C.D. Cal. 2006).

[54] *FTC v. Accusearch Inc.*, 570 F.3d 1187 (10th Cir. 2009).

[55] *In the Matter of Vision I Properties, LLC*, FTC File No. 042–3068 (April 26, 2005).

knowingly violate the privacy commitments between a buyer and seller by virtue of one's relationship as service provider.

### Aiding and abetting – The "means and instrumentalities" of unfairness

Recall from Chapter 4 that the FTC, unlike state attorneys general, lacks explicit aiding and abetting authority in the FTC Act. To cure this deficit, the FTC sometimes invoked a "means and instrumentalities" of unfairness theory. In these matters, a company provides a technology and explicitly advertises it as a tool to invade others' privacy, or helps a company invade individuals' privacy, or gives advice on how to invade privacy with it. For instance, a software company that licensed computer-tracking software provided the means and instrumentalities of unfairness by collecting personal data on behalf of other businesses secretly, and by advising those businesses not to disclose the presence of the software, which was basically spyware (See Chapter 9).[56] Importantly, the consumers targeted by this software suffered no economic loss – the substantial injury was the invasion into their homes.

### Transferring data to unseemly businesses

One case found fault with data-selling companies for distributing information to other businesses that had publicly been charged with consumer fraud.[57] In another, the FTC found it unfair for a company to sell lists of consumers seeking payday loans to other businesses that did not offer loans of any type. One of the companies that purchased the data withdrew tens of millions of dollars from consumers' bank accounts who were on the list.[58]

### Unfair design

In the FTC's Frostwire case, the Agency sued a company in federal district court because it disseminated an application that was likely to cause users to unwittingly place their files on the internet. The application, by default on installation, marked many different kinds of files for sharing (all photos, all videos, etc.). The user had to uncheck each category to avoid sharing. Additionally, in order to share a single file, the user had to check a category box (such as videos) and then uncheck every video not to be shared on the network.[59] The Agency characterized these user interface functions as "unfair design." As with inadequate security (see below), the issue of unfair design is addressed in greater detail in Chapter 8.

---

[56] *In the Matter of DesignerWare, LLC*, FTC File No. 112 3151 (April 15, 2013).
[57] *US v. Direct Lending Source, Inc., et al.*, 12-CV-2441-DMS-BLM (S.D. Ca. October 10, 2012).
[58] *FTC v. Sitesearch Corp. d/b/a LeapLab*, FTC File No. 142 3192 (D. Ariz. December 23, 2014).
[59] *FTC v. Frostwire*, No. 111-CV-23643 (S.D.F.L. October 11, 2011).

## Inadequate security

As the Director of the Bureau of Consumer Protection, Howard Beales, and then Chairman Timothy Muris, made an economic case for applying unfair practices theory to businesses with inadequate security. This rather recent development has quickly gained momentum, leading to many novel FTC matters using unfair practices to find liability for data security problems. As a result of these decisions, entities that collect personal information are under an affirmative obligation to engage in a number of specific security procedures. This obligation exists independent of promises in a privacy policy.

## Contours of deceptive privacy practices

As described in Chapter 5, a deceptive practice is a representation, omission, or practice that is likely to mislead a consumer. The practice is considered from the perspective of a reasonable consumer, and the representation must be material.

## Material representations

As in non-privacy matters, the FTC broadly construes what constitutes a "representation." Any statement that is part of the consumer experience can become the basis of a deceptive practice. As explained in Chapter 5, the FTC need not prove intent, and even innocent misrepresentations can form the basis of an FTC matter. This approach has major implications for privacy practice. A privacy practitioner must read not only privacy policies, but also blog posts by employees relevant to privacy,[60] marketing materials, manuals,[61] certifications of compliance with self-regulatory agreements,[62] and the design of websites and apps (such as privacy settings,[63] information collection dialogue boxes,[64] and even whether systems are in technical compliance with representations).[65] Design choices and implementation of them can cause consumers to be misled. Deception can be found in situations where third parties are misled as well. For instance, in the Accusearch case, a website offered to obtain private telephone logs through pretexting: the practice of fooling customer

---

[60] *In the Matter of Facebook, Inc.*, FTC File No. 092 3184 (July 27, 2012).

[61] *In the Matter of HTC America Inc.*, FTC File No. 122 3049 (July 2, 2013)(statement in product manual that user would be notified of third-party sharing was a representation).

[62] *US v. Google, Inc.*, 512-cv-04177-HRL (N.D.Cal. November 12, 2012).

[63] *In the Matter of HTC America Inc.*, FTC File No. 122 3049 (July 2, 2013), *In re Facebook, Inc.*, FTC File No. 092 3184 (July 27, 2012).

[64] *US v. Artist Arena LLC*, 112-cv-07386-JGK (S.D.N.Y. October 4, 2012).

[65] *In the Matter of Facebook, Inc.*, FTC File No. 092 3184 (August 10, 2012) (representing that only "friends" of a user would receive information was false because data were passed onto third-party application providers used by "friends"); *In the Matter of Upromise, Inc.*, FTC File No. 102 3116 (April 3, 2012) (representation that data were encrypted in transit was material); *In the Matter of Chitika, Inc.*, FTC File. No. 102 3087 (June 17, 2011) (deceptive to code opt-out cookies to last only 10 days).

service representatives by lying about one's identity or circumstances in order to obtain information about a third person.

An omission can also form the basis of a deceptive practice. Omissions in privacy matters involve unexpected collection or uses of information. For instance, touting several beneficial activities in a privacy policy can be deceptive where important, less welcome collection and uses of information are not mentioned.

## Deception in information collection and handling

Making misrepresentations in order to obtain personal data can be unfair (see discussion of Rapp and Accusearch above), but it also can be deceptive, even in situations where a company is engaging in debt collection (see Chapter 8) or antifraud activities. For instance, when rent-to-own companies programmed computers to pop up messages requesting information from delinquent customers, the FTC considered it deceptive.[66] More generally speaking, making any material claim about privacy or security and failing to comply with it is deceptive.

## Omissions or inadequate notice of material practices can also be deceptive

Affirmatively lying about information collection is a clear wrong. But such clear wrongs become the thin edge of a larger privacy wedge. That larger wedge concerns important omissions in privacy policies and other communications. The FTC has taken a "surprise" approach: that is, if an information collection or use violates consumer expectations, it needs to be disclosed, sometimes prominently. Prominent or "clear and conspicuous" disclosures have long been a concern of the Commission. In 1970, for instance, the Commission released guidelines for what constituted a clear and conspicuous disclosure in the context of television advertising.[67]

The FTC has brought many matters alleging that a notice was inadequate for the depth of information collection or use involved. For instance, the department store Sears distributed a software program to monitor its customers consensually and paid them a fee. However, the full scope of the tracking involved was only disclosed in an end-user license agreement (EULA), a long legalistic document that few consumers read. Users would expect from the notice to have their "online browsing" tracked, but the software could also inspect secure browsing sessions, such as web mail communications and interactions with banks.[68] In this and more recent matters,

---

[66] *In the Matter of Aaron's, Inc.*, FTC File No. 122 3256 (October 22, 2013).
[67] FTC, Commission Enforcement Policy Statement in Regard to Clear and Conspicuous Disclosure in Television Advertising, October 21, 1970.
[68] *In the Matter of Sears Holdings Management Corporation*, FTC File No. 082 3099 (September 9, 2009). See also *In the Matter of Upromise, Inc.*, FTC File No. 102 3116 (April 3, 2012).

the FTC thought that such tracking was material and should have be prominently disclosed to the user.[69]

The category of "surprising" practices that need prominent disclosure includes sale of personal information to third parties;[70] collecting location (or other sensitive) information;[71] collecting information from a user's contact or address book;[72] transferring a unique identifier that leads to disclosure of personal information with third parties;[73] changing settings so that it degrades users' previous privacy protections;[74] settings that cause users to inadvertently make public files from their computer;[75] unexpected information collection, such as when software on music CDs phoned home to a central location;[76] and the use by a company of browser history sniffing to determine the websites a user has visited.[77]

## Trickery

Technology enables businesses to have the upper hand in many relationships, and those activities that mislead the consumer about the level of privacy they enjoy are deceptive. This is an old principle in FTC policy. As early as 1971, the Agency brought an administrative action against a mailing list company for tricking consumers into revealing information through a survey.[78] In 1975, the Agency was concerned that survey researchers were promising "anonymity" to data subjects, but using secret coding and other techniques to track responses to surveys. The Commission wrote that it was deceptive to induce "consumers to provide information about themselves by expressly or implicitly promising that such information is being provided anonymously, when, in fact, a secret or invisible code is used . . . that allows identification of the consumer who has provided the information." The Commission argued that such deception could also be unfair if used to obtain sensitive information, or if the information was used for some other purpose.[79] As for that matter, and generally speaking, companies should also not engage in "gotcha" techniques. For instance, telling the consumer that she will not be tracked

---

[69] *In the Matter of Compete, Inc.*, FTC File No. 102 3155 (February 25, 2013).

[70] *In the Matter of Goldenshores Technologies LLC & Erik M. Geidl*, FTC File No. C-4446 (F.T.C. April 9, 2014); *FTC v. Echometrix, Inc.*, CV10-5516 (E.D.N.Y. November 30, 2010).

[71] *In the Matter of Goldenshores Technologies LLC & Erik M. Geidl*, FTC Docket C-4446 (April 9, 2014).

[72] *US v. Path, Inc.*, No. C-13-0448 (N.D. Cal. January 31, 2013).

[73] *In the Matter of MySpace LLC*, FTC File No. 102 3058 (September 11, 2002); *In the Matter of Facebook, Inc.*, FTC File No. 092 3184 (July 27, 2012).

[74] *In the Matter of Facebook, Inc.*, FTC File No. 092 3184 (August 10, 2012).

[75] *FTC v. Frostwire*, No. 111-CV-23643 (S.D.F.L. October 11, 2011).

[76] *In the Matter of Sony BMG Music Entertainment*, FTC File No. 062 3019 (June 29, 2007).

[77] *In the Matter of Epic Marketplace, Inc., and Epic Media Group*, LLC, FTC File No. 112 3182 (March 19, 2013).

[78] *In the Matter of Metromedia, Inc.*, 78 F.T.C. 331 (1971).

[79] Use of Secret Coding in Marketing Research, 16 C.F.R. §14.12 (2014). It is also deceptive to use a "survey" to mask ordinary marketing activities. *In the Matter of International Publisher Services*, 49 F.T.C. 214 (1952).

by cookies but then using a similar technology to accomplish the same outcome can be deceptive.[80] Additionally, telling a user that they have a choice not to share information, but sharing it before they can make the choice is deceptive.[81]

Finally, implying that data will only be used for one purpose, and then using them for some other purpose unnecessary for service delivery is deceptive. For instance, a nonprofit that disseminated surveys broadly in public schools for "educational research" implied that the data were collected for college admission purposes. In fact, they were primarily collected for resale to marketers.[82] This matter and other signals from the Commission suggest that companies should disclose all material uses that would be important to the consumer, particularly third-party marketing uses of data.

### Copying social media profiles

In the Jerk.com matter, the FTC brought an administrative action against a company for creating a site where individuals could be labeled as a "jerk" or "not a jerk." Jerk.com claimed that the data were organic, user-generated content, but, in reality, they were copied from Facebook, and therefore users were deceived about the provenance of the data.[83] A similar set of facts was presented in ReverseAuction. com, an early commission privacy matter. In that enforcement action, there were two deceptions: the harvesting of data from another's site, and a subsequent e-mail message to eBay users that falsely stated that their account was going to expire.[84]

### FTC PRIVACY REMEDIES

Critics have often complained that without civil penalty authority, the FTC's remedies are weak. That argument overlooks the tremendous public relations cost of FTC enforcement actions. The FTC's targets frequently get "front-page" treatment in the *Wall Street Journal*. The label of privacy violator can also stick to a company's brand for years. As Peltzman found in studying FTC regulation of advertising, enforcement actions can have a dramatic effect on respondents.[85] The negative publicity and culture-changing effects of an enforcement action probably have a much more profound impact than would fining these companies a few or even tens of millions of dollars.

---

[80] *In the Matter of ScanScout, Inc.*, FTC Docket No. C-4344 (December 21, 2011) (flash cookies are small files that have similar properties to ordinary web cookies).

[81] *In the Matter of Goldenshores Technologies LLC & Erik M. Geidl*, FTC Docket No. C-4446 (April 9, 2014)

[82] *In the Matter of Educational Research Center of America, Inc.*, FTC File No. 022 3249 (May 9, 2003).

[83] *In the Matter of Jerk, LLC*, FTC File No. 122 3141 (January 12, 2015).

[84] *Id*

[85] Sam Peltzman, *The Effects of FTC Advertising Regulation*, 24(3) J. L. Econ. 403 (December 1981).

The FTC uses a standard form when resolving matters with respondents, and a familiar set of remedies are agreed to in privacy proceedings. All orders require the respondent company to refrain from similar misrepresentations. Typically, these consent orders last twenty years.[86] Violation of the orders can trigger civil penalties, which are currently set at $16,000/day per violation. Orders obtained in federal court presumably are permanent in effect.

The Commission custom-tailors other remedies, many of which constitute "fencing-in" relief that may go beyond the underlying violations of the FTC Act. In some privacy matters, the Commission has required respondents to establish a comprehensive privacy program. These require risk assessments, ongoing assessment of services, care in selecting service providers, review of design processes, and measures of accountability. This requirement comes at great expense to a company, because such a program requires significant staff resources devoted to identifying and remedying privacy risks across the enterprise. Microsoft, Google, and Facebook all have scores of employees who have some privacy function, and all three have implemented sophisticated systems to review products and services for privacy.

In some matters, companies have to self-report compliance with the order, but in others the FTC imposes a duty for a third-party assessment of compliance. Although many call this requirement an audit, it is not – it is an *assessment*. In the accounting world, an audit measures compliance against some predefined criteria, such as an International Organization for Standardization (ISO) standard. An assessment is a certification of compliance with a standard set by the respondent itself. In recent years, the FTC has ramped up the requirements of these assessments, for instance, by specifying that the assessor has to have years of experience or has to be approved by officials in the Division of Enforcement.

Public interest groups that have obtained copies of these third-party assessments have shown them to be less than rigorous, an exercise in compliance rather than privacy protection. For instance, the Electronic Privacy Information Center obtained the initial Google privacy assessment. The document was thirty pages long, but three of the pages were an appeal for confidential treatment and another five were the company's privacy policy. Moreover, the document was not signed by a specific individual at the assessor company. It is difficult to imagine how Google, a company with such a complicated role in modern information practices, could be evaluated in twenty-two pages.

Somewhat controversially, the consent decree in the Google matter required the company to obtain affirmative express consent for any new information sharing or use. Critics have argued that the FTC established an opt-in rule for new data uses by

---

[86] The author has heard various rationales for the twenty-year consent decree. Some say that it was commission custom, dating back to advertising matters, to use a twenty-year term. Others say that the Commission, by policy, shortened all decrees to twenty years in order to reduce the number of respondents it was overseeing.

settling the matter with that requirement. But it is unclear whether smaller companies and different kinds of firms will be subject to the opt-in requirement.

In some matters, the FTC has ordered respondents to delete data. In others, the FTC has obtained agreements for companies to change the technical design of their services. In the Frostwire case, a company disseminated an application that caused users to place their files, unwittingly, on peer-to-peer sharing networks. In that case, the Agency obtained an agreement that the company would only share files if the user affirmatively selected the file to be placed on the network. In the Sony matter, where the company installed software that endangered the security of users' computers, the FTC obtained remedies requiring the company to provide a tool to remove the software (see Chapter 9). Sony also agreed to buy keyword advertising so that people searching for how to remove the offending software would be directed to Sony's tool.

## THE FEDERAL COMMUNICATIONS COMMISSION AS COMPLEMENT TO THE FTC

The FTC was an early mover on internet privacy, but now other regulatory agencies are crowding the scene. The Federal Communications Commission is now vying for privacy policy relevance. The FCC's 2015 Open Internet Order reclassified broadband internet access providers as "telecommunication services," subject to Title II of the Telecommunications Act. It will take years to contemplate the full implications of the reclassification, but one immediate observation is that it subjects covered companies to new consumer protection[87] and privacy rules.[88] These rules set forth a normative goal (confidentiality of customer records) and require a notice and a consent experience before this information is used. Also, classified as "common carriers," as the FCC holds them to be, these companies will be exempt from the FTC's Section 5 authority. The FCC's authorities also give rise to private causes of action.[89]

The FCC's enforcement division is now led by Travis LeBlanc, a former special state attorney general from California with a reputation for action. In a year, LeBlanc had levied over $40 million in fines for privacy and security violations. Thus, the FCC will likely surpass the FTC's decade-long recovery efforts in just two years if trends continue. The FCC can move more quickly than the FTC because it delegates more power to staff to litigate.

The emergence of the FCC as privacy regulator raises a question – should privacy enforcement be tasked to a regulator with greater ability to levy fines? FCC action may be appropriate, because the companies involved are not policed by normal market mechanisms, such as brand reputation. Internet access providers are

---

[87]  47 U.S.C. §201(b).

[88]  47 U.S.C. §222.

[89]  47 U.S.C. §207.

essentially monopolies. These certainly are innovative companies, capable of important technical feats – ones that go unappreciated by those who work in software. However, changing one's broadband provider involves significant transaction costs, some of which are imposed by the provider itself. In such an environment, the FCC's enforcement alacrity and its large fines might be the best remedy for invasive privacy practices and insecurity.

This development could be a welcome complement to the FTC as a move that contributes to regulatory competition. For instance, in the FCC's order against Verizon for using customer data for marketing without appropriate permission, Verizon has agreed to deliver a monthly opt-out notice to all of its customers for three years. The FTC has not ordered similar relief, but could learn from the newest privacy enforcer on the block.

### ONGOING PRIVACY TUSSLES

In addition to modern matters, the FTC is constantly called upon by advocates to investigate new fields. This section details some of the more challenging policy issues the FTC has been called upon to resolve.

### *The limits of notice and (individual) choice*

The "privacy paradox" refers to the inconsistency between consumer attitudes and behavior. While consumers say in interviews and surveys that they want privacy, they often behave differently, exposing excessive personal information on social networks, signing up for free services that use personal information as payment, and so forth.[90] Businesses defend the status quo, arguing that what consumers do in the marketplace is more important than the kinds of complaints about privacy one sees in news reports and public opinion polls. The ability to freely alienate personal information is deeply engrained in the US privacy tradition.[91]

But at the same time, support for privacy control approaches is largely instrumental. On a policy level, some companies pursue a dignified, leave-it-to-consumer-choice posture, while, at the same time, they pursue a law of the jungle approach with profiling technology. For instance, after California prohibited retailers from asking customers their home addresses during credit card transactions, data brokers created tools that allowed retailers to infer this same information by merely asking for a

---

[90] PRIVACY ONLINE, PERSPECTIVES ON PRIVACY AND SELF-DISCLOSURE IN THE SOCIAL WEB (Trepte, Sabine, Reinecke, Leonard, eds. 2011).

[91] When Samuel Warren and Louis Brandeis published their influential *The Right to Privacy* in 1890, the duo argued that individuals could waive their privacy rights. Indeed, the right to sell or trade one's privacy is inherent in the idea of privacy control. *See* Samuel Warren & Louis Brandeis, *The Right to Privacy*, 4 HARV. L. R. 193 (1890). *See also* Paul M. Schwartz, *The EU–US Privacy Collision: A Turn to Institutions and Procedures*, 126 HARV. L. REV. 1966 (2013).

telephone number.[92] When requesting the phone number was prohibited, data brokers encouraged retailers to collect the ZIP code, which also could be used to identify the customer's home address.[93] These activities are entirely outside consumer control, and were designed in the words of one data broker to avoid "losing customers who feel that you're invading their privacy." Thus, businesses say that what consumers *do* matters more than what consumers say about privacy. Yet, even where consumers seek privacy or choose not to disclose data, businesses use systems to undo their efforts to protect personal information.

---

CONSUMER PROTECTION: EDUCATION VERSUS STRUCTURALISM

Should privacy be a matter of individual choice and individual responsibility, or an inherent part of products and services? Should public policy focus on educating the consumer, or on creating incentives to building attributes into the structure of products? Lessons from the 1950s and 1960s battle over car safety feature some of the same public debates as one sees in today's conflicts over protecting information privacy.

In the 1950s and 1960s, automakers strongly resisted safety mandates. Ralph Nader, in *Unsafe at Any Speed*,[94] recounted the opposition of the car industry to install seat belts (then lap belts). Nader argued that car companies feared that the seat belt would remind the driver of the risk of accident, and make them fearful of motoring.

The automobile industry tried to focus public policy on the driver – the "nut behind the wheel" instead of making major investments in car safety. In an oft-quoted portion of Nader's book, it was revealed that General Motors spent less than 1 percent of its $1.7 billion profit on studying safety. Meanwhile, huge numbers of individuals were dying in accidents – over 50,000 in 1966 alone (almost as many Americans died in the Vietnam War).

Today, just as in 1966, the driver is responsible for most accidents. However, the fatality rate per 100 million miles traveled today is only 1.1, versus 5.5 in 1966. What accounts for this difference?

A revolution in thinking about safety occurred. Cars are equipped with seat belts, air bags, and, importantly, accident avoidance technology such as automatic traction control. The importance of enforcing traffic safety laws, the advent of graduated licensing, as well as policing drunk driving have also contributed to lower mortality. Drivers do cause most accidents, but the

---

[92]  This practice is known as reverse enhancement. With a telephone number, e-mail address, or credit card number, the data broker can use other databases to match the consumer's home address to the telephone number, and then provide the home address to the retailer.

[93]  *Pineda v. Williams-Sonoma Stores, Inc.*, 246 P.3d 612 (SCT Ca. 2011).

[94]  RALPH NADER, UNSAFE AT ANY SPEED: THE DESIGNED-IN DANGERS OF THE AMERICAN AUTOMOBILE (1965).

conversation no longer ends by blaming the "nut behind the wheel." Hundreds of thousands of Americans are alive today because public policy has focused upon the structure and safety of the automobile instead of just blaming the driver.

If public policy discussions departed from blaming the consumer (he clicked "I agree" and shared the information) to a situation where we looked at the structure of the online marketplace, there would be a greater role for consumer protection in privacy.

Professor Gordon Hull explained this dynamic by arguing that privacy self-management regimes such as notice and choice are a "successful failure." Notice and choice forces the individual into a neoliberal framework where privacy is treated as an individual economic choice. Hull then paints notice and choice as a perverse policy, because it sets up the consumer for failure (as self-management of privacy is impractical): the "privacy self-management model obscures a social struggle, repackaging it as a well-functioning market."[95] For Hull and others,[96] bad privacy decisions are inevitable.

In their 2013 book, Professors Omri Ben-Shahar and Carl E. Schneider summarized a wealth of research on disclosure rules and argued that mandated disclosure – including privacy notices – simply does not work.[97] The notice model makes assumptions about human behavior and thinking that simply are not true in practice. The duo argue that consumers are decision-adverse, that consumers find it rational to ignore notices, that illiteracy and innumeracy problems plague understanding of notices, that notices help more affluent consumers rather than poorer ones, that people are overloaded with notice, that notice provides unneeded information, and that, even if understood, notices may not improve decision-making.

Regulators, businesses, and consumer groups nonetheless favor disclosure policies for a variety of reasons. To regulators and businesses, disclosure appears to be an inexpensive and market-preserving intervention. To consumer groups, it is the most politically obtainable intervention. The result is perverse: disclosure becomes a one-way ratchet, with more and more transparency washing the hands of businesses engaging in questionable tactics who claim "after all, the consumer was informed."

---

[95] Gordon Hull, Successful Failure: What Foucault Can Teach Us about Privacy Self-Management in a World of Facebook and Big Data, ETHICS & INFORMATION TECHNOLOGY (May 2015).

[96] Alessandro Acquisti, Laura Brandimarte, & George Loewenstein, *Review: Privacy and Human Behavior in the Age of Information*, 347(6221) SCIENCE 509 (January 30, 2015);Paul M. Schwartz, Internet Privacy and the State, 32 CONN. L. REV. 815 (2000).

[97] OMRI BEN-SHAHAR & CARL E. SCHNEIDER, MORE THAN YOU WANTED TO KNOW: THE FAILURE OF MANDATED DISCLOSURE (2014); *See also* MARGARET JANE RADIN, BOILERPLATE (2013).

More generally, policy-makers place much credence on notice as a tool for consumer protection, yet the goals of transparency are rarely examined in regulation.[98] For instance, is the goal of notice to serve users, or to appease regulators and privacy advocates? California legislators seemed to understand the difference when one proposed a law that would require all privacy policies to be 100 words or less. Technology companies and many academics were aghast, but that was largely because they see notice as an exercise in disclaiming liability rather than a means to educate users.

Professor Regan has argued that for privacy legislation to be enacted, privacy must be reframed as a social good, instead of as an individual right. Framed as an individual right, privacy invites interest-group competition, and individual privacy usually loses to social interests in efficiency and safety. Reframed as a social interest, however, privacy competes with and must be accommodated along with interests in efficiency and safety.

Regan argued that three aspects of privacy must be recognized to put it on a stronger footing so that it can drive public policy: First, the "common value" in privacy must be recognized. Regan argued that all individuals value privacy in their own way and have some common conceptions about what privacy is. Second, privacy has a "public value," in that it benefits democratic political systems. Third, privacy is a "collective value," because it is difficult for any given individual to enjoy privacy without a baseline level of the right being afforded to everyone.[99]

Declaring privacy a group right has consequences for individuals' freedom – it may restrict an individual's freedom to sell their data. Some lawmakers have dismissed this concern, and have created inalienable consumer privacy rights. The most prominent example is Article 1, Section 1, of the California constitution, which establishes privacy alongside the rights to safety and possession of property. Waivers of the extensive set of privacy rights against intrusions by businesses in California are unenforceable.[100]

Government prohibitions can have a freedom-protecting effect in aggregate. One example comes from littering. For any individual, littering may be rational, but, in the aggregate, littering diminishes the quality of public spaces. Thus, individual freedom and individually rational decisions can have a collectively negative outcome.[101] Similarly, if voluntary slavery or the use of highly addictive drugs were legal, one would have a certain kind of initial freedom to decide followed by a life of increasingly constrained choice.

---

[98] Natali Helberger, *Form Matters: Informing Consumers Effectively*, AMSTERDAM LAW SCHOOL RESEARCH PAPER NO. 2013–71 (November 2013).

[99] PRISCILLA M. REGAN, LEGISLATIVE PRIVACY: TECHNOLOGY, SOCIAL VALUES, AND PUBLIC POLICY (1995); *see also* James P. Nehf, *Recognizing the Societal Value in Information Privacy*, 78 WASH. L. REV. 1 (2003).

[100] Any waiver of a provision of this title is contrary to public policy and is void and unenforceable. Cal. Civ. Code §1798.84.

[101] TOM SLEE, NO ONE MAKES YOU SHOP AT WAL-MART: THE SURPRISING DECEPTIONS OF INDIVIDUAL CHOICE (2006).

In a 2011 book, Professor Anita Allen argued that because privacy is good for individuals and for society, in some contexts, it should be imposed on individuals. We force privacy in a number of realms, including in bans on nudity and in professional obligations to protect client and patient secrecy. The free alienability of privacy and the willingness of individuals to share may be denying ourselves opportunities individually and as a society to enjoy certain kinds of freedoms. She argues that the liberal ideal of choice "becomes an ironic joke in a society in which people freely choose to be always in others' lines of sight, much as it is a joke in a society in which they freely choose utter domination."[102]

Notice serves a pragmatic purpose of avoiding a real conversation about the normative aspects of data collection. As Evgeny Morozov put it, "A robust privacy debate should ask who needs our data and why, while proposing institutional arrangements for resisting the path offered by Silicon Valley. Instead of bickering over interpretations of Facebook's privacy policy as if it were the US Constitution, why not ask how our sense of who we are is shaped by algorithms, databases and apps . . .?"[103]

### The third-party problem

The privacy control underpinnings of the notice-and-choice system do not address third parties – information holders that have no direct relationship with the consumer. In particular, "data brokers" arose a century ago to collect personal information about individuals and sell it to businesses and governments. Data brokers are companies that amass information from many different sources and resell it, sometimes as files on individuals, as demographic information about individuals, or as lists of consumers who fit some criteria. Many data brokers have products that are comprehensively regulated by the Fair Credit Reporting Act (FCRA; see Chapter 10). However, many also sell products that fall outside the FCRA's protections. Those are discussed here.

Because of their dynamics, data brokers are immune from market incentives to promote privacy. First, data brokers have no direct consumer relationship with individuals. Second, they purchase information from thousands of sources (such as websites and retail stores) secretly, and thus consumers cannot avoid having information transferred to data brokers. Third, because much of their data acquisition is secret, there is no practical way for consumers to link privacy obligations made by data collectors to the data brokers that ultimately amass the information.[104]

---

[102] ANITA L. ALLEN, UNPOPULAR PRIVACY (2011).

[103] Evgeny Morozov, *Facebook Invades Your Personality, Not Your Privacy*, FINANCIAL TIMES, August 10, 2014.

[104] US Senate, Committee on Commerce, Science, and Transportation, Office of Oversight and Investigations Majority Staff, A Review of the Data Broker Industry: Collection, Use, and Sale of Consumer Data for Marketing Purposes, December 18, 2013 ("Data brokers typically amass data without direct interaction with consumers, and a number of the queried brokers perpetuate this

Fourth, when direct marketers (a major customer of data brokers) buy information, they are typically seeking only marginal gains in customer sales and acquisition. This search for small increases in sales means that they tolerate consumer lists that are wildly inaccurate. After all, a 1 percent increase in sales is considered a big success in direct marketing. As a result, data brokers have strong incentives to infer "facts" about individuals and to categorize them into various lists that can be sold to direct marketers.

The lack of market discipline for privacy means that data brokers engage in some of the most aggressive data uses, with little or no obligations to data subjects. Individuals have no right to notice of their activities, no right to access files, and no right to correct the data, although some data brokers voluntarily provide notice and limited access to consumers. The lack of rights and secrecy involved also means that data brokers can sell data to scam artists or other unseemly businesses. For instance, in the FCRA context, the FTC sued companies that sold credit data to companies that were targets of existing law enforcement investigations.[105] In another case, the FTC sued a data broker that collected data about financially vulnerable consumers and sold it to telemarketers, to other data brokers, and to a company that used the data to withdraw money without authorization from the consumers.[106] But some of data brokers' activities are scariest when employed by government. For instance, a data broker facilitated purging of the Florida voter rolls in advance of the 2000 presidential elections.[107]

Data brokers' technical abilities are impressive. Through complex data-matching capabilities, they can link individuals' online activities to their real identity, and to their offline purchasing behavior. This linkage is thought to be so privacy-invasive that a self-regulatory group representing online advertisers once promised to never do it without affirmative consent.

The third-party problem has also stunted the market for "privacy infomediaries." Starting in the 1990s, companies proposed to act as infomediaries, that is, services that would store and safeguard personal information in the consumer's interest.[108] Simply put, infomediaries are data brokers organized in a nonprofit or cooperative fashion, with limits on marketing and with profits from data use flowing back to the consumer (infomediaries are also discussed in Chapter 9). If one buys into the assumptions of personalization, these infomediaries would be the ultimate advertising targeting tool, because consumers would trust infomediaries with their most secret desires. Advertisers could pay into the cooperative and target individuals with

---

secrecy by contractually limiting customers from disclosing their data sources"); Woodrow Hartzog, *Chain-Link Confidentiality*, 46 Geo. L. Rev. 657 (2012).

[105] *US v. Direct Lending Source, Inc., et al.*, 12-CV-2441-DMS-BLM (S.D. Ca. October 10, 2012).

[106] *FTC v. Sitesearch Corp. d/b/a LeapLab*, FTC File No. 142–3192 (D. Ariz. December 23, 2014).

[107] Guy Stuart, *Databases, Felons, and Voting: Bias and Partisanship of the Florida Felons List in the 2000 Elections*, 119(3) Pol. Sci. Quarterly 453 (Fall 2004).

[108] Bethany L. Leickly, Intermediaries in Information Economies (2004)(Ph.D. dissertation, Georgetown University).

great insight. But for this model to work, the infomediary would have to have a monopoly on the most valuable personal data. And therein lies the problem. These business models all failed because buyers of personal data could always get "good enough" targeting information from other third parties. This good enough information was less expensive both in terms of monetary cost and in fewer privacy restrictions.

The political economy of data brokers makes them nearly impossible to regulate. Many kinds of businesses – including all lawmakers – purchase services from data brokers and they can do so secretly. In particular, the financial services industry has become reliant on data brokers and thus lobbies aggressively to keep data brokers free of privacy restrictions. Further complications come from the definition of data broker. They have a "I know it when I see it quality," but in writing legislative definitions of a data broker, many other businesses, including search engines, get swept in. Finally, companies that use data brokers can point to increased efficiencies and profitability. In competition with vague notions of "privacy," data brokers will always win in the legislative arena. Especially when their lobbyists can point to lawmakers' own use of these services and credibly claim that voter targeting and fund-raising would suffer from regulatory intervention.

### Self-regulation

In the United States, self-regulatory approaches dominate the discussion of policy rules. Self-regulation is a form of governance where businesses themselves define the rules and their scope, and are entrusted with their enforcement. Businesses themselves sometimes generate rules on their own initiative. However, in most situations, some external force, such as a threat of suit from the government or legislation, causes businesses to self-regulate.

Self-regulatory programs take many forms. Professors Colin Bennett and Charles Raab classify four: privacy commitments, privacy codes, privacy standards, and privacy seals.[109] The pair explain that the first self-regulatory statements tended to be privacy commitments, relatively bland and perhaps unfounded announcements that management was complying with the OECD privacy guidelines (see Chapter 11). Privacy codes represented a greater endeavor, in that they specified rules for the organization to follow. Examples include sectoral rules concerning telemarketing or behavioral advertising. Privacy standards have elements of a code, but also include some assessment mechanism to ensure compliance. A modern example is the American Institute of Certified Public Accountants' Generally Accepted Privacy Principles. Finally, privacy seals are attempts to create a generally recognized mark certifying that a company conforms to certain privacy rules.

---

[109] Colin J. Bennett & Charles D. Raab, The Governance of Privacy (2006).

From the FTC's perspective, all four types of self-regulatory programs are useful. Privacy commitments and seals are representations that the FTC can use to justify a deception claim. Privacy standards and codes also can be used to justify the Agency's interpretation of reasonable and unreasonable business practices.

Koops et al. have detailed many of the benefits and failings of self-regulation. The benefits include efficiency and flexibility, in that industries can come to the table more quickly to draft rules or to update them than a government can. In self-regulation, business experts on the subject matter help draft the rules. This collaboration means that if enough businesses with different interests participate, subtle issues and tensions in an industry that may not be apparent to nonexperts can be surfaced and addressed, rather than hidden from the regulator. Self-regulation may avoid the intense lobbying seen in legislative matters. Self-regulation can signal an internal commitment to rules, which is a powerful factor in gaining actual compliance. Self-regulation can transfer the costs of governance to the private sector. Finally, they argue that self-regulation may be more compatible with the architecture of the internet itself.[110]

On the other hand, self-regulation means that businesses themselves draft the rules and that they can change them. There may be transparency problems with the rules. Self-regulatory rules may be narrow and unwilling to accommodate conflicting societal values. They may even valorize the values of the strongest self-regulatory participants rather than the industry as a whole.

Koops et al. also set forth seven factors to identify appropriate situations for self-regulation. First, the rules should be fair, in that they protect social interests at stake. Additionally, if fundamental rights are at stake, or if certain groups will be discriminated against, rules should not be left to private actors. Second, the self-regulatory process should be inclusive, allowing weaker parties to participate. Third, actors should be able to be held accountable under the rules. Fourth, the rule and its drafting process need to be transparent. Fifth, the rules must be sufficiently clear that they provide legal certainty in the field. Sixth, the context must be right for self-regulation: "self-regulation is more suited to 'neutral' issues: issues that call for answers (what electronic signatures have sufficient legal validity) rather than policy choices ..." Finally, efficiency can weigh in favor of self-regulation, especially where it can be updated to address new circumstances more swiftly than the government can react.

Useful factors for exploring self-regulation were proposed by the UK-based National Consumer Council. That group recommended the following:

---

[110] Bert-Jaap Koops, Miriam Lips, Sjaak Nouwt, Corien Prins, & Maurice Schellekens, *Should Self-Regulation Be the Starting Point?*, in STARTING POINTS FOR ICT REGULATION (Bert-Jaap Koops, Mariam Lips, Corien Prins, & Maurice Schellekens, eds., 2006). *See also* Peter Swire, *Markets, Self-Regulation, and Government Enforcement in the Protection of Personal Information*, in PRIVACY AND SELF-REGULATION IN THE INFORMATION AGE BY THE US DEPARTMENT OF COMMERCE (1997).

1. A self-regulatory scheme must always have clear policy objectives.
2. Self-regulation should not inhibit the scope for competition to deliver benefits for consumers.
3. A strong independent element must be involved in the scheme's design and have a controlling influence on its governance.
4. A dedicated institutional structure must be set up, separate from the existing trade and professional organisations.
5. A pragmatic approach may be inevitable (meaning that self-regulation is the best bet where there is no practical chance of regulation).
6. There should be a presumption of scepticism towards self-regulation organised on a collective basis (this factor is aimed at Public Choice Theory criticisms that groups may organize to restrict competition or just to forestall legislation).
7. Effective self-regulation is usually best stimulated by a credible threat of statutory intervention.
8. Self-regulation works best within some form of legal framework.[111]

These frameworks are very useful for evaluating self-regulation, but alas they are not well known and rarely, if ever, applied by the FTC.

US self-regulation had an auspicious start. As early as 1988, using a privacy control framework, the Department of Commerce urged companies to provide consumers with a broad range of privacy rights, including notice of collection, notice of uses, notice of choices, a right to correct and amend, and a general security duty. It stated, "Effective self-regulation involves substantive rules, as well as the means to ensure that consumers know the rules, that companies comply with them, and that consumers have appropriate recourse when there is noncompliance."[112]

But in actual implementation, perhaps because of the special dynamics of information businesses, almost all of the failings of self-regulation mentioned by Koops et al. have been demonstrated. Moreover, few of the positive advantages have amounted to much. Consider the history of the Individual Reference Services Group (IRSG), which, at the FTC's nudging, proposed a self-regulatory code, the IRSG principles, for data brokers. These companies sold Social Security Numbers and other information to insurers, private investigators, law enforcement, and others.

Substantively, the code was weak. It allowed companies to sell any information they wanted to "qualified subscribers," which the companies were allowed to define. The code allowed individuals to opt out of the sale of information only to the "general public." In practice, this right was illusory because data brokers did not consider any of their customers to be members of the general public. One broker

---

[111] NATIONAL CONSUMER COUNCIL, MODELS OF SELF-REGULATION: AN OVERVIEW OF MODELS IN BUSINESS AND THE PROFESSIONS (2000).

[112] DEPARTMENT OF COMMERCE, THE EMERGING DIGITAL ECONOMY (1998).

stated that there was no need for it to create an opt-out mechanism because their customers were all qualified.

The IRSG was short-lived. The code seemed to be designed only to head off statutory financial privacy rules, and after these were passed in 1999, the IRSG lived on to challenge those provisions as unconstitutional.[113]

Another important self-regulatory group, the Network Advertising Initiative (NAI), presented a more mixed record. With involvement of the FTC and the Department of Commerce, the NAI proposed a code in 2000 to govern third-party advertisers. One principal element of its 2000 code was to limit the linkage of online and offline data, but the NAI quietly abandoned this rule with a 2008 update to its rules. The original 2000 code cannot even be found today on the NAI website.

Pam Dixon and Robert Gellman have detailed the NAI's history. They noted that once the FTC retreated from its recommendation for federal privacy legislation, the NAI's membership dropped to just two organizations. The authors observed, "Enforcement and audit activity lapsed as well. NAI did not fulfill its promises or keep its standards up to date with current technology until 2008, when FTC interest increased."[114] In recent years, the NAI has been reinvigorated. Nothing drives self-regulatory activities like the threat of government regulation.

Yet, despite the reinvigoration, the NAI's main privacy guarantee does not provide for any privacy, under any definition of the term. NAI's main guarantee to users now is that if they opt out of behavioral targeting, certain information will not be used to tailor ads to them. Other information can be used for this purpose, however, and advertising companies are free to track individuals, collect information about them, and use it for other purposes.

Privacy seal programs are the most successful self-regulatory initiatives, yet their record is checkered as well. Several seal programs, including the leading seal provider, TRUSTe, have been the target of FTC deception enforcement actions. In November 2014, TRUSTe settled charges with the FTC that it falsely represented its program compliance procedures and allowed websites to falsely hold out TRUSTe as nonprofit.[115] Similarly, Facebook's "Verified Apps" program was found to be deceptive because it implied that it took extra steps to verify participants but did not do so.[116]

Basic economic incentives make providing a seal difficult. On a basic level, the seal company must convince consumers that an independent third party has

---

[113] *Trans Union LLC v. FTC*, 295 F.3d 42 (D.C. Cir. 2002).

[114] Robert Gellman & Pam Dixon, Many Failures – A Brief History of Privacy Self-Regulation (2011).

[115] *In the Matter of True Ultimate Standards Everywhere, Inc., a corporation, doing business as TRUSTe, Inc.*, FTC File No. 132 3219 (November 17, 2014) (TRUSTe converted from a nonprofit to a for-profit in 2007; the author was once a paid advisor to the company); *see also* Chris Connolly, Graham Greenleaf, & Nigel Waters, *Privacy Self-Regulation in Crisis? – TRUSTe's "Deceptive" Practices*, 132 Privacy Laws & Bus. Int'l Rep., 13–17 (December 2014).

[116] *In the Matter of Facebook, Inc.*, FTC File No. 092 3184 (July 27, 2012). *See also FTC v. ControlScan, Inc.*, No. 1:10-cv-00532 (February 25, 2010).

evaluated and endorsed a website. At the same time, it must convince websites to pay for and buy into the evaluation. Despite these challenges, many companies entered the seal business in the 2000s.[117] In their 2006 review of privacy governance, Bennett and Raab concluded that no seal had achieved general recognition and credibility.[118] TRUSTe, however, transcended early challenges and outcompeted alternative seals, emerging as the leading seal later in the 2000s.

In addition to the chicken-and-egg problem of consumer and business buy-in, privacy seals have other economic problems. Most notably, less trustworthy sites have strong incentives to join the seal. Professor Benjamin Edelman reported in 2009 that "sites certified by ... TRUSTe ... are more than twice as likely to be untrustworthy as uncertified sites."[119] Conversely, highly trusted companies do not need privacy seals at all. As of this writing, for example, neither Google nor Facebook was TRUSTe certified.

In a scathing 2008 study of privacy seals, Chris Connolly surveyed the market of privacy seals and concluded that many were "worthless." One advertised that it would approve a site within 24 hours for just $200. Many seals were outright scams, or disappeared after a short time of business operation. Connolly referred to TRUSTe as the strongest of the seal programs, but nevertheless he found systemic problems in its operation.[120]

Even if a company can master the basic economics of seals, one still has to consider what consumers expect from seals. Basic facts about seals are difficult to verify. For instance, the Better Business Bureau (BBB) ended its online privacy seal in 2008. Confusingly, it still maintains a different, general membership seal, one element of which is to "safeguard privacy." After many clicks, a consumer can determine that BBB accreditation means that the business adheres to a high-level principles document that includes the promise to "[p]rotect any data collected against mishandling and fraud, collect personal information only as needed, and respect the preferences of consumers regarding the use of their information."

Many seals are just images on a website. A consumer cannot verify them. And sometimes it is confusing to determine what they even mean – some are trust seals, while others claim that the site is protected by transport encryption. The BBB seal simply means that the Better Business Bureau accredits the business.

In polls conducted by the author, large numbers of consumers appeared confused about the role of seals. In these studies, consumers were asked, "If a website has a TRUSTe privacy seal, it means that the site has the strongest privacy protections

---

[117] For an early, detailed comparison of competing web seals, *see* Ann Cavoukian and Malcolm Crompton, *Web Seals: A Review of Online Privacy Programs*, 22nd International Conference on Privacy and Personal Data Protection (Venice, September 2000).

[118] COLIN J. BENNETT & CHARLES D. RAAB, THE GOVERNANCE OF PRIVACY (2006).

[119] Benjamin Edelman, *Adverse Selection in Online "Trust" Certifications*, ICEC, August 12–15, 2009; Tom Van Goethem, Frank Piessens, Wouter Joosen, & Nick Nikiforakis, *Clubbing Seals: Exploring the Ecosystem of Third-Party Security Seals*, CCS'14, November 3–7, 2014.

[120] CHRIS CONNOLLY, GALEXIA, TRUSTMARK SCHEMES STRUGGLE TO PROTECT PRIVACY (2008).

possible." The correct answer to this question is false. However, in a 2013 Web-conducted study, 41 percent answered true, 11 percent false, and fourty-eight percent chose don't know. The 2013 sample performed worse than a 2009 group of internet users who were interviewed by telephone. In the 2009 study, 30 percent answered true, 20 percent false, and 50 percent said they did not know. Thus, large numbers of internet users still do not understand seals' actual level of protection.

The FTC has had some experience in policing self-regulatory seal programs in non-privacy contexts. For instance, in 1939, the FTC filed a complaint concerning *Good Housekeeping* magazine's various seals of approval for different kinds of products.[121] The magazine produced a wide variety of seals, with different conditions for earning them. Some products were tested, while others were only examined by *Good Housekeeping* staff. The FTC found several bases for violations of the FTC Act. In some situations, the testing was inadequate to substantiate claims made by advertisers. In other situations, the FTC found that material product claims were deceptive – the very claims the magazine "carefully investigates" before granting a seal.

The *Good Housekeeping* seal is a reminder that seal programs often suffer from a kind of solipsism – why should we believe that consumers are invested enough to investigate the meaning of seals, especially when there are several competing seals or various versions of seals for different web technologies? Seals are a form of representation that consumers rely upon and upon which they have great faith. Many consumers think that various seals guarantee protections that are actually not offered by any of them.[122]

Even if the procedural safeguards suggested by Koops et al. and the National Consumer Council are followed, self-regulation in privacy is bound to fail. The problem is more substantive and particular to privacy disputes. Unlike areas where self-regulation has been successful, for instance, in setting technical standards, privacy is a contested value.

Thus, while all reasonable people might agree that children should be shielded from certain advertising content, there is less consensus on what constitutes the right of privacy of adults, or even whether privacy is a particularly important right to protect. Adding to this problem, many self-regulatory participants categorically reject the proposition that their practices invade privacy. Self-regulatory groups in privacy probably spend more resources lobbying to prevent passage of privacy rules than policing their own members.

---

[121] *In re Hearst Magazines, Inc.*, 32 F.T.C. 1440 (1941). Taking up a long tradition, a Hearst executive claimed that the FTC's charges were motivated by a Communist plot. *See* INGER L. STOLE, ADVERTISING ON TRIAL: CONSUMER ACTIVISM AND CORPORATE PUBLIC RELATIONS IN THE 1930S (2006); Frank Jellinek, *Dies, Hearst and the Consumer*, 52(1) NEW REPUBLIC 10 (January 1, 1940).

[122] Thomas L. Parkinson, *The Role of Seals and Certifications of Approval in Consumer Decision-Making*, 9(1) J. CONSUMER AFF. 1 (1975). ("The data strongly support the conclusion that in general consumers attribute a great deal more meaning to the presence of these seals or certifications than is justified by the existing seal-granting programs.")

From the FTC's perspective, even weak self-regulatory regimes assist the Agency. These regimes derail possible First Amendment challenges to FTC action because a broken promise will not qualify as protected commercial speech. Violations of self-regulatory rules can be policed under deception, an easier legal theory for the Commission to employ than unfairness. Self-regulatory regimes take work off the Agency's plate and bind companies to promises that, even if weak, are likely to be broken. Self-regulatory regimes can also function as standards, giving the FTC traction in proceedings to argue that a consensus exists about a certain practice being unreasonable. Perhaps for these reasons, the FTC exhibits a kind of credulity when new groups appear claiming to represent entire industries and claiming a commitment to a set of rules. To privacy advocates, this activity is galling and empty, but to the Commission the industry has just rested its foot in a trap.

## Default choices

What default choices should govern privacy practices? Policy-makers often look to opt in and opt out.[123] In opt-in, the consumer must take some affirmative action to accept a collection or use of data. This places the burden on the business to get permission.[124] In opt-out, the consumer must take action to object to data collection or use, thus placing the burden on the consumer to act.[125]

There is significant confusion about the definition of opt-in and opt-out. Companies often describe opt-out practices as opt-in, by confounding the issues of product adoption and choice. That is, they claim so because they interpret the decision to use a certain product or service with giving the business an affirmative consent to collection or use of data unnecessary for the transaction.

---

### CHANGING PRIVACY POLICIES

In 2009, Facebook made major changes to privacy settings of its users that became part of the basis of FTC charges against the company. Prior to the 2009 changes, Facebook CEO Mark Zuckerberg announced that the service would radically change its privacy policies. Later, Zuckerberg explained, "People have really gotten comfortable not only sharing more information and different

---

[123] Daniel J. Solove, *Privacy Self-Management and the Consent Dilemma*, 126 HARV. L. REV. 1880 (2013); Jeff Sovern, *Opting In, Opting Out, or No Options at All: The Fight for Control of Personal Information*, 74 WASH. L. REV. 1033 (1999).

[124] PETER P. SWIRE & SOL BERMANN, INFORMATION PRIVACY: OFFICIAL REFERENCE FOR THE CERTIFIED INFORMATION PRIVACY PROFESSIONAL 9 (2007). ("Opt-in means an individual makes an affirmative indication of choice (e.g. an individual checks a box stating that she wants to share her information with third parties.")

[125] "Opt-out means that an individual's failure to object to a use or disclosure implies that a choice has been made . . . *Id.*

kinds, but more openly and with more people. That social norm is just something that has evolved over time. We view it as our role in the system to
constantly be innovating and be updating what our system is to reflect what
the current social norms are . . ."

Zuckerberg raised an important point: if societal norms change, shouldn't
services be able to change their policies to reflect or shape those changes? At
the same time, how comfortable should we be when a company with a
dominant network decides it wants to change social norms? Katherine Losse,
an assistant to Zuckerberg, recounts that within the company, there was little
dissent or even discussion about privacy issues and suggested that those who
flagged privacy issues were dismissed: "Forcing people to be more open
implied that we were all in some way closed, as though there was something
wrong in the way we conducted our personal lives. How was it a Web site's
place to say that we needed to reveal more about ourselves publicly?"[126]

FTC law surrounding policy changes is clearer today, as a result of the
matters against Gateway, Google, and Facebook. Retroactive changes that
affect data already collected require notice of the changes and affirmative
consent from the consumer. However, prospective changes can be accomplished through notice and opt-out.[127] Companies are free to cut off services to
those who refuse to agree to the prospective changes.

In a "clean" opt-in or opt-out model, decisions about data should be separate from
product adoption, except where the collection or use is technically required by the
service.[128] According to the International Association of Privacy Professionals, "It is
inappropriate to have a choice that says 'I opt in to this use' if the box is pre-checked.
Unless the individual checks the box personally, this is an opt-out offering."[129]

Opt-out is preferred by businesses and other institutions, because it is the most
convenient way to sign up large numbers of consumers for a service. The cost of
communicating with consumers is high; thus, simply contacting consumers with an
offer they want is difficult. If permission is required for information use, even
analysis that helps better target a solicitation becomes complicated. Viewed in this

---

[126] KATHERINE LOSSE, THE BOY KINGS (2012).

[127] Letter from Jessica L. Rich, Director of the Federal Trade Commission Bureau of Consumer
Protection, to Erin Egan, Chief Privacy Officer, Facebook, and to Anne Hoge, General Counsel,
WhatsApp Inc. (April 14, 2014).

[128] *See, for example*, FTC, PRIVACY ONLINE: A REPORT TO CONGRESS (June 4, 1998). ("choice relates to
secondary uses of information – i.e., uses beyond those necessary to complete the contemplated
transaction. Such secondary uses can be internal, such as placing the consumer on the collecting
company's mailing list in order to market additional products or promotions, or external, such as the
transfer of information to third parties.")

[129] PETER P. SWIRE & SOL BERMANN, INFORMATION PRIVACY: OFFICIAL REFERENCE FOR THE CERTIFIED
INFORMATION PRIVACY PROFESSIONAL 9 (2007)

light, opt-in leads to perverse results, as companies will just send more untargeted mail and telemarketing calls in order to get a consumer's attention and secure an opt-in.

As a result, Professor Fred Cate has argued that opt-in does not provide greater privacy protection. Instead, opt-in hampers open information flows and imposes transaction costs on marketers.[130] For instance, Cate explains that US West, a telecommunications company, estimated a cost of between $20 and $34 to contact consumers and to obtain a positive response from them. These costs are said to make the offering of some products, such as affiliate-marketed credit cards, simply uneconomical.[131] Cate also argued that consumers miss out on good deals, because they are unlikely to read opt-in notices, opt in, and enjoy the advertising. With coauthors, he argued, "according to the US Postal Service, 52 percent of unsolicited mail in this country is never read. If that figure translates to opt in requests, then more than half of all consumers in an opt in system would never learn of the opportunity to opt in and the consequences of not doing so."[132]

First Amendment concerns also inhibit opt-in regulations, as opt-in approaches can substantially limit how businesses communicate with people. At the same time, opt-in restrictions governing sensitive information probably can survive First Amendment scrutiny.[133]

But there are also problems with opt-out. While Cate objects to the costs to business from opt-in, opt-out externalizes those costs to consumers in several ways. First, opt-out gives companies incentives to hide the option and to impose transaction costs on opting out to dissuade its use.[134] In one non-privacy case, AT&T performed market research to design letters to consumers such that they would throw them away rather than read because the letters concerned how to opt out from binding arbitration.[135] Another anecdote comes from an early history of Google, where executives discussed the idea that their users probably wanted opt-in standards for cookies, but decided to just give users notice of them instead.[136] Yet another is

---

[130] Fred H. Cate, *Principles of Internet Privacy*, 32 CONN. L. REV. 877 (2000).

[131] Eric Goldman, *A Coasean Analysis of Marketing*, 2006 WISCONSIN L. REV. 1151 (2006); Michael E. Staten & Fred H. Cate, *The Impact of Opt-In Privacy Rules on Retail Credit Markets: A Case Study of MBNA*, 52 DUKE L. J. 745 (2003).

[132] Fred H. Cate, Robert E. Litan, Michael Staten, & Peter Wallison, Financial Privacy, Consumer Prosperity, and the Public Good (AEI-Brookings Joint Center for Regulatory Studies 2003).

[133] *See Nat'l Cable & Telecommunications Ass'n v. F.C.C.*, 555 F.3d 996 (D.C. Cir. 2009) (upholding opt-in restrictions on phone records data).

[134] Jeff Sovern, Opting In, Opting Out, or No Options at All: The Fight for Control of Personal Information, 74 WASH. L. REV. 1033 (1999); Paul Schwartz & Ted Janger, The Gramm–Leach–Bliley Act, Information Privacy, and the Limits of Default Rules, 86 MINN. L. REV. 1219 (2002).

[135] *Ting v. AT&T*, 182 F. Supp. 2d 902 (2002).

[136] DOUGLAS EDWARDS, I'M FEELING LUCKY: THE CONFESSIONS OF GOOGLE EMPLOYEE NUMBER 59 (2011). ("We would clearly want to set the default as 'accept Google's cookies.' If we fully explained what that meant to most users, however, they would probably prefer not to accept our cookie. So our default setting would go against users' wishes. Some people might call that evil, and evil made Marissa [then Google executive Marissa Mayer] uncomfortable. She was disturbed that our current cookie-setting

demonstrated by certain attempts to reduce transaction costs in opting out. Nonprofits such as Catalog Choice created platforms to allow consumers to quickly opt out of marketing, but marketing companies fought these requests vigorously. Some even demanded that Catalog Choice secure a formal power of attorney just to communicate the desire to opt out of a mailing list on behalf of each of its consumer members.

Second, the high expense of obtaining opt-in permissions from consumers could be reframed as a cost of doing business. It could be the case that consumers simply do not want to hear about US West's deals, no matter how good they are. Cate overlooked the idea that many companies are desperate to bombard people with similar deals, but for some consumers the total volume of these offers makes them equally worthless. Consider how many people who have rejected all telemarketing through the Do Not Call Registry – over 200 million numbers are registered, signaling a real disinterest in any kind of phone marketing. Viewed from this perspective, US West's expenses simply reflect normal consumer resistance to an unwanted offer. More broadly, the companies most prepared to direct mail – consider the 6 billion credit card offers mailed annually to Americans – may be the ones least interesting to hear from.

Third, the effects of opt-out may be unevenly distributed. A reader of this book is in a much better position to understand privacy options and to exercise them. While congratulations are in order to you, dear reader, average or economically disadvantaged consumers are not as well situated. A study of the FTC's case against Suntasia Marketing illustrates this problem. Suntasia Marketing was one of many scams that enticed consumers to reveal their checking account numbers in order to enroll in "free" trial offers. The goal of these companies was simply to obtain as much account information as possible in order to fraudulently charge small amounts from thousands of accounts. The court allowed Suntasia to continue business but, in the process, the court segmented Suntasia's consumers into two groups, thereby setting up a natural experiment. Some Suntasia customers had to opt in to stay subscribed, while others were retained unless the customer opted out. Almost all of the customers who were required to opt in let their subscriptions cancel. But only about forty-percent of those given opt-out notices canceled, and thus the remainder kept on being charged for "essentially worthless" products. Minorities from low-socioeconomic-status (SES) areas were 8 percent less likely to opt out than whites in high-SES areas.[137] The study illustrated that the power of default options is so great that they can cause many consumers to stay enrolled in an outright scam. The market can allow scams to flourish – Suntasia employed 1,000 people and collected $171 million in revenue.

practices made the argument a reasonable one. She agreed that at the very least we should have a page telling users how they could delete their cookies, whether set by Google or by some other website.")

[137] Robert Letzler, Ryan Sandler, Ania Jaroszewicz, Isaac T. Knowles, & Luke Olson, Knowing When to Quit: Default Choices, Demographics and Fraud, October 8, 2014.

At the same time, opt-in may not be a panacea. Professor Lauren Willis explains that default rules are not sticky, and that companies can influence consumers – particularly vulnerable ones – to give up protective default rules.[138] The language of opt-in is often illusory too. For instance, while it is popularly believed that individuals opt in to social networking sites, in fact, these sites build "shadow profiles" of nonmembers.[139] This means that many have no means to manage their online identity unless they choose to be a part of the online environment. In other contexts, companies "bundle" opt-in and use it to argue that the consumer gave consent to a much broader array of information uses than the consumer realized.

In light of this strategic behavior, opt-in and opt-out might impose similar costs, but allocate them differently among institutions and consumers. There may also be middle-way approaches. For instance, at least on the Web, sites can be programmed to require a response to a data-sharing question that has no default value.[140] Such a setup requires the consumer to take a choice. Data can be governed by other means as well, such as through ceilings on retention of information, or bright-line rules surrounding use.

### The power of the platform: user manipulation and discrimination

Because many internet companies do not charge consumers money for their services, they desperately try to achieve a "platform" status, so that they can broker interactions among users and third parties. With platform status, the company achieves a state of lock-in over users, and control over how third parties interact with them. Essentially, third parties are at the whim of the platform, which can make changes or shape how these third parties can interact with users at will.

Users too are at the whim of the platform. There is a long history of platforms switching users' privacy choices to push them toward "openness," such as the 2009 changes at Facebook. Shaping user behavior toward disclosure is one form of platform power. Others come from the power to engage in various kinds of service or price discrimination, to manipulate users to their disadvantage, or to subtly shape user behavior.[141] Consider these examples:

- In the 2010 midterm election, employees of Facebook displayed a "social message" to 60 million users, encouraging them to vote. The experiment had a limited but measurable effect – Facebook could credibly attribute an increase in voter turnout (to the tune of 300,000 votes) because of the intervention.[142]

---

[138] Lauren E. Willis, *When Nudges Fail: Slippery Defaults*, 80 UNIV. CHI. L. REV. 1155 (2013).
[139] KATHERINE LOSSE, THE BOY KINGS (2012).
[140] That is, the site can be programmed to not process a transaction until the consumer makes a decision concerning information sharing.
[141] Ryan Calo, *Digital Market Manipulation*, 82 GEO. WASH. L. REV. 995 (2014).
[142] Robert M. Bond et al., A 61-million-person experiment in social influence and political mobilization, 489 NATURE 295 (September 13, 2012).

- An executive from Uber, a company that created a highly successful platform for securing taxi and private car service, suggested that the company use its database to undermine critics. Specifically, it was reported that Uber could "prove a particular and very specific claim about [a critic's] personal life."[143]
- By carefully examining user purchase records, Target, a large department store, predicted that certain customers were likely pregnant, and sent them baby-related advertisements.
- An operator of a very popular dating website told users (falsely) that they were good "matches" for other people. The operator concluded, "When we *tell* people they are a good match, they act as if they are. Even when they should be wrong for each other."[144]

Historically, purchase and aggregation of data from many sources generated fears that companies could manipulate consumers. But in these examples, very large companies or platforms relied on *internal* data. Since this behavior did not involve third-party data and related consent rights, privacy law had little traction over the issues.

One can imagine pernicious uses of these platforms. Imagine if Facebook decided to support a particular certain candidate, and then only displayed prompts to vote to users who are likely to vote for the preferred candidate. Or imagine that the candidate paid for the prompts, or paid to have the prompts not displayed to likely hostile voters in order to drive down voter participation? Facebook is a for-profit company. If it indeed is a powerful platform for voting, it will be tempting to engage in such voter manipulations.[145]

---

### PRIVACY AS FOURTH-WAVE CONSUMER PROTECTION

Historians of consumerism have recognized three waves of consumer move-ments. The first surrounded the passage of the 1906 food and drug law. The second took hold after the Great Depression and reached its height with the passage of amendments to the FDA Act and the Wheeler–Lea Amendments to the FTC Act. The third was actuated by environmental and product safety

---

[143] Ben Smith, *Uber Executive Suggests Digging Up Dirt on Journalists*, BUZZFEED, n.d.
[144] Christian Rudder, *We Experiment on Human Beings!*, OKTRENDS (July 28, 2014) (emphasis in original).
[145] Bruce Schneier explains: "A truly sinister social networking platform could manipulate public opinion ... [b]y amplifying the voices of people it agrees with, and dampening those of people it disagrees with, it could profoundly distort public discourse. China does this with its 50 Cent Party: people hired by the government to post comments on social networking sites supporting, and challenge comments opposing, party positions." BRUCE SCHNEIER, DATA AND GOLIATH: THE HIDDEN BATTLES TO COLLECT YOUR DATA AND CONTROL YOUR WORLD (2015). *See also* Robert Epstein & Ronald E. Robertson, *The search engine manipulation effect (SEME) and its possible impact on the outcomes of elections*, 112 PROCEEDINGS OF THE NATIONAL ACADEMY OF SCIENCES (2015).

concerns and resulted in the institutionalization of consumerism at the FTC in the 1970s.

It seems that every thirty years or so, a new consumer protection movement takes hold. Online privacy would seem to fit the mold for such a movement, as defined by Robert O. Herrmann: "The movement has arisen as a reaction to three persisting problem areas: (1) ill-considered application of new technology which result in dangerous or unreliable products, (2) changing conceptions of the social responsibilities of business and (3) the operations of a dishonest fringe and the occasional lapses of others in the business community."[146]

The dating website's activities seem particularly problematic, as it deliberately manipulated individuals' intimate lives. Yet, the company's leader expressed an absolute right to experiment on users. In his view, this manipulation was a normal part of many kinds of business models.[147]

What responsibilities do large or dominant platforms owe to users concerning manipulation of results and advertisements? And what manipulations are part of acceptable business practices versus those that are deceptive or unfair?

Privacy advocates frequently invoke "first-degree" price discrimination as an unfair harm flowing from data collection. Price discrimination is common, legal (in most circumstances), and a generally accepted way to cross-subsidize customers. We readily accept business models that offer discounts to bulk purchasers, or that provide different classes of service, such as the business cabin versus coach on airlines. At the same time, price discrimination has long caused acrimony and suspicion in the United States. In 1887, Congress created the country's first federal consumer protection regulator, the Interstate Commerce Commission, in part because of concerns about price discrimination. Congress also passed the 1936 Robinson–Patman Act based on concerns that price discrimination enabled the capture of surplus not passed onto consumers.

"First-degree" discrimination, the object of consumer advocates' fears, involves a company knowing the maximum amount a consumer is willing to pay.[148] Perfectly executed, first-degree discrimination permits a company to extract surplus from consumers that it would not ordinarily capture without having the special information about them.[149] It uses hints at a return to nineteenth-century selling, where the retailer more strongly controlled consumers' buying options,[150] and haggling

---

[146] Robert O. Herrmann, *The Consumer Movement in Historical Perspective, in* Consumerism: Search for the Consumer Interest (Aaker and Day, eds., 2nd edn, 1974).
[147] *Id.*
[148] William W. Fisher III, *When Should We Permit Differential Pricing of Information?*, 55 UCLA L. REV. 1 (2007).
[149] Joseph Turow, The Daily You (2011).
[150] Joseph Turow, Niche Envy: Marketing Discrimination in the Digital Age (2006).

(complete with seller assessment of buyers' ability to pay) determined prices instead of the price tag.

Along these lines, one provocative book suggested that businesses divide their customer base into "angel customers," those who are profitable, and "demon customers," unprofitable customers who shop for discounts, return items, complain about service, and pay their credit card balances on time.[151] The authors argued that companies should segment the customer base, and find ways to nudge demon customers into buying more expensive items, or to discourage them from making returns. On its face, the book seems to recommend that companies use information to cause consumers to make uneconomical decisions. Shortly after the publication of the book, a discount retailer did ban two customers shopping with it.[152] The punishment was levied because the retailer felt that that the consumers had made excessive returns and complained about service.[153]

Price and search discrimination are difficult to study. Alternative explanations for differences in prices, for instance, more expensive distribution costs, may explain the phenomena. Nevertheless, studies suggest that price discrimination exists particularly related to geography.[154] The *Wall Street Journal* studied tens of thousands of ZIP codes for prices at an office supply store and found higher prices where there was a nearby physical store but no competitor in the immediate area.[155] Other researchers created different shopping profiles (budget and big spender) and found that users with a browsing history more indicative of luxury shopping were shown more expensive products.[156]

The closest that the FTC has come to addressing such business practices came in a credit card marketing context. In *FTC v. CompuCredit Corporation*, the Agency sued a credit card issuer for penalizing users of accounts based on their spending habits.[157] The FTC alleged that CompuCredit reduced credit lines to consumers based on a behavioral scoring model. Under it, CompuCredit inferred some credit risk if the customer made purchases at direct marketing merchants, marriage

---

[151] LARRY SELDEN & GEOFFREY COLVIN, ANGEL CUSTOMERS & DEMON CUSTOMERS: DISCOVER WHICH IS WHICH AND TURBO-CHARGE YOUR STOCK (2003).

[152] ASSOCIATED PRESS, SISTERS BANNED FROM FILENE'S BASEMENT STORES, July 14, 2003.

[153] Gary McWilliams, Analyzing Customers, Best Buy Decides Not All Are Welcome, Retailer Aims to Outsmart Dogged Bargain-Hunters, and Coddle Big Spenders, WALL ST. J., November 8, 2004.

[154] Aniko Hannak, Gary Soeller, David Lazer, Alan Mislove, & Christo Wilson, *Measuring Price Discrimination and Steering on E-Commerce Web Sites*, Proceedings of the 14th ACM/USENIX Internet Measurement Conference (IMC'14), Vancouver, Canada, November 2014. In the 1960s, the FTC performed a landmark study of "ghetto" retailing and found substantial differences in prices in poor neighborhoods. Much of the difference was ascribed to higher costs, but retailers were also taking advantage of innumeracy to raise prices through "easy credit" offers. FTC, ECONOMIC REPORT ON INSTALLMENT CREDIT AND RETAIL SALES PRACTICES OF DISTRICT OF COLUMBIA RETAILERS (1968).

[155] Jennifer Valentino-DeVries, Jeremy Singer-Vine, & Ashkan Soltani, *Websites Vary Prices, Deals Based on Users' Information*, WALL ST. J., December 24, 2012.

[156] Jakub Mikians, László Gyarmati, Vijay Erramilli, & Nikolaos Laoutaris, *Detecting price and search discrimination on the Internet*, Hotnets '12, October 29–30, 2012, Seattle, WA.

[157] *FTC v. Compucredit Corp.*, 1:08-CV-1976 (N.D. Ga. 2008).

counselors, personal counselors, automobile tire retreading and repair shops, bars and nightclubs, pool and billiard establishments, pawnshops, or massage parlors. If such purchases were observed, credit lines could be reduced. The key to the FTC's case was that these restrictions were disclosed only vaguely. CompuCredit promised customers the full use of their credit line, "Provided that your account has been used and maintained in a satisfactory manner." Thus, customers were deceived because they thought they had an ordinary, full-featured credit card. But given that this was a deception case, a company could engage in similar sorting so long as it was adequately disclosed.

The range of concerns from platform discrimination can trigger several FTC policy responses. Some businesses, such as the above-mentioned dating website, are generally in the leave-it-to-the-marketplace category. Such companies rest on their terms of use and consider the consumer's willingness to use the service as consent. But to pass FTC muster, the company would have to prominently disclose these activities even if they appeared somewhere in a license agreement or another contract. Material terms that are surprising and to the detriment of consumer interests are deceptive unless prominently disclosed. Recall from the Sears case that an initiative to monitor users and to compensate them for the privacy violation was deceptive because the specific terms were buried in a license agreement.

---

REINVIGORATING CONSUMER PROTECTION

Professor Mark Nadel suggests four core challenges to making consumer protection a widespread concern: First, consumer interests are diffuse; it is a collective value and must compete with other values. Second, individuals have varying levels of intensity of interest in consumer matters. Mostly, this is a low-level interest, and it can be satisfied with emotional or psychological appeals. Thus, individuals can be satisfied with symbolic consumer protection. But this is a double-edged sword. When symbolic protections are stripped away, individuals can react intensely.

Third, there is a gulf in consumer protection between objective and perceived needs. This leads to a focus on dramatic problems and a lack of attention to more structural, difficult problems.

Fourth, the "consumer interest" is difficult to define.[158]

---

Some have suggested that an "institutional review board" (IRB) should police companies' market research. IRBs are entities that evaluate and monitor experiments on humans, to ensure that they are not done needlessly and to protect research subjects from harm. Widely used in biomedical sciences, social sciences, and

---

[158] Mark V. Nadel, The Politics of Consumer Protection (1971).

university research, such boards are not required generally when private organizations do research on their own customers.[159]

Another approach is to simply prohibit differential pricing when it is based on certain factors. Puerto Rico lawmakers, sensitive to higher prices imposed by online retailers on shipping to the territory, prohibited merchants from excluding Puerto Rico from certain activities and from charging higher prices for shipping.[160]

Effective price discrimination requires some kind of information. But often discrimination can be done without personal information, for instance, from determining location based on IP address or by noting that a customer is using a high-end mobile device. There is reason to believe that price discrimination will continue to be done without personal information. After all, the individually targeted ads of dystopian films are, in reality, too costly to deliver. Targeting to broad segments and kinds of consumers, such as gender and age, is effective enough for many advertisers.

Is regulation of information – privacy law – the appropriate solution for price and service discrimination problems? Platform discrimination problems ultimately are about power. Privacy law can help balance that power, but information companies are natural monopolies: privacy rights are likely to be insufficient to address the problem. Consider the *Wall Street Journal* study that found that office supply stores without nearby competitors charged higher prices. That is an area where the FTC's prime mission – to ensure consumer protection through promoting competition – might be the best approach to the problem.[161]

## Privacy by design

To what extent should companies design their systems in order to protect user privacy? Former Information and Privacy Commissioner of Ontario, Dr. Ann Cavoukian,[162] has proposed privacy by design (PBD) as an approach to reduce privacy risks from information-intensive services. PBD is a series of procedural and substantive approaches to engineering and usability design. At core, PBD proposes to translate fair information practices into technological requirements. In its infancy, PBD was critiqued as a vague mandate, full of recursive definitions, but, subsequently, researchers have made serious attempts to more specifically define its elements.

At a high level of abstraction, PBD approaches seem sensible. PBD encourages system designers, who have previously thought that privacy issues were for

---

[159] See James Grimmelmann, *Illegal, Immoral, and Mood-Altering: How Facebook and OkCupid Broke the Law When They Experimented on Users*, MEDIUM, September 23, 2014.

[160] Nydia Galarza, *Launching Online Retail Services and Products in Puerto Rico*, BNA PRIVACY & SECURITY L. REP. (January 4, 2014).

[161] For a discussion of when the FTC's Bureau of Competition should police privacy, see Maureen K. Ohlhausen & Alexander P. Okuliar, *Competition, Consumer Protection, and The Right [Approach] to Privacy*, ___ ANTITRUST L. J. ___ (2015).

[162] ANN CAVOUKIAN, PRIVACY BY DESIGN: THE 7 FOUNDATIONAL PRINCIPLES (2012).

policy-makers to shape,[163] to think through ethical implications of their technologies from the beginning and to consider building privacy protections into products. Designers can make default choices to protect privacy and make these choices sticky, so that privacy is respected throughout the lifetime of a service. Professors Sarah Spiekermann and Lorrie Faith Cranor draw a distinction between PBD and privacy by policy. In PBD, system designers deliberate over how and whether they should collect less personally identifiable data and whether anonymization is possible, and potentially rely more strongly on client-side storage.[164] These interventions depart from the standard privacy-by-policy approach of making individuals aware of how data are used. They use an approach where the architecture itself skews services away the dead end of "privacy control."

The FTC is embracing PBD. In a 2010 report, the Agency declared that "Companies should promote consumer privacy throughout their organizations and at every stage of the development of their products and services." This theme has echoed in other policy documents, including a staff report on the "internet of things" that recommends comprehensive treatment of information security issues through design process. The FTC concluded that "Companies should incorporate substantive privacy protections into their practices, such as data security, reasonable collection limits, sound retention and disposal practices, and data accuracy."[165] Thus far, these principles are not part of any regulatory mandate.

In a 2013 article, two eminently qualified experts, one a former Microsoft lawyer and the other a well-known computer interface design expert, analyzed ten privacy gaffes by Google and Facebook. Professor Ira Rubinstein and Nathan Good concluded that if the companies had implemented PBD principles, all of these gaffes could have been avoided.[166] But as with self-regulatory schemes, PBD can only work where companies believe that consumers' concerns are legitimate. As the pair observed, Facebook has a strongly privacy control-based conception of privacy. Facebook's conception undercuts calls for data minimization. Similarly, they characterize Google's approach to privacy as esoteric, and suggest that it is flexible by design so as to accommodate the company's interest in reaching advertising revenue goals.

In sum, PBD is a promising approach, but one that needs more development. It will have limited success unless the companies implementing it recognize the importance of privacy interests and are willing to take on inconvenience and other implications of data minimization.

---

[163] Sarah Spiekermann & Lorrie Faith Cranor, *Engineering Privacy*, 35(1) IEEE Transactions on Software Engineering (2009).

[164] *Id.*

[165] FTC, Protecting Consumer Privacy in an Era of Rapid Change (2010).

[166] Ira S. Rubinstein & Nathaniel Good, *Privacy by Design: A Counterfactual Analysis of Google and Facebook Privacy Incidents*, 28 Berkeley Tech. L. J. 1333 (2013).

CONCLUSION

The Federal Trade Commission has emerged as the nation's top regulator of online privacy. It has done so carefully, often by translating the Agency's false advertising cases into the privacy context. The FTC brings matters incrementally and trumpets their arrival through blog posts and public events. While critics have described the FTC's work as policing broken promises, its proceedings – going back to the 1950s – signal that its lodestar is consumer expectations, just as it emphasized consumer expectations in false advertising cases. Under this approach, the excuse that "it's in the privacy policy" does not suffice to create consent, nor should it, even for those who want to leave privacy to the marketplace.

So many of the FTC's standard privacy tools rest on rational choice theory assumptions. An individualistic conception of the value of privacy causes both businesses and advocates to pursue notice-and-choice-style consumer protection. Thus, as companies hone their privacy disclosures so that all uses of information are disclosed and putatively consented to, the FTC will have to rely increasingly on its unfairness authority to police privacy online.

The next chapter turns to the privacy of children, an area where there is general societal agreement that privacy is a value worth protecting. A consensus in privacy's value goes a long way in empowering the Commission to act, and motivates businesses to design systems more thoughtfully.

# 7

## Privacy of children

The FTC has a long history of intervening in the marketplace to protect children. Recall from Chapter 1 that in the seminal case *FTC v. R. F. Keppel & Bro., Inc.*,[1] the Agency stopped a company from marketing candy to children with lottery-like inducements. In *Keppel*, some candies were packaged with a coin, so, once opened, the candy would technically be free, while non-winners would have to pay the price on the label. The FTC saw this as a form of gambling inappropriate for children.

With the advent of the commercial internet, similar, game-like tactics were used to entice children to reveal personal information online. Targeting of children online seemed to impinge on familial rights to privacy, and the right to privacy in the home. At the same time, the US privacy regime was viewed with skepticism by Europeans, who could point to the lack of protection for children in the US framework as a serious omission and signal of a generally weak commitment to privacy rights. After all, contracts are not enforceable against children in the United States, nor do we conceive of children as rational actors who can bargain for their privacy in the marketplace.[2] For Europeans, it was laissez-faire at its worst for children to be subject to the same privacy regime and roles as adults.

Widespread adoption of the internet also created a new risk landscape for children. High-profile stories circulated in the media about children using the internet with a technical skill that exceeded their judgment.[3] Law enforcement and state attorneys general invoked horrific anecdotes of child predation and luring made easier because of the internet.[4]

---

[1] 291 U.S. 304 (1934).
[2] Wouter M. P. Steijn & Anton Vedder, *Privacy under Construction: A Developmental Perspective on Privacy Perception*, Sci. Tech. Hum. Val. (2015).
[3] Brad Stone & Bronwyn Fryer, *The Keyboard Kids: Chatting on the Net Is Becoming the Social Activity of Choice for Techno-Savvy Early Teens*, Newsweek, June 8, 1998.
[4] Marlise Simons, *Dutch Say a Sex Ring Used Infants on Internet*, N.Y. Times, July 19, 1998; Elsa Brenner, *Child Abuse on Internet Heightens Vigilance*, N.Y. Times, April 19, 1998.

With these concerns in mind, Congress quickly enacted the Children's Online Privacy Protection Act of 1998 (COPPA). It was enacted in a matter of just months. As a result, COPPA had almost no legislative history to build upon, which led it to be used by different factions as both an information privacy law and an online safety measure.

Recall from Chapter 6 that Priscilla Regan described privacy as a topic that could start a public controversy, but often privacy could not marshal Congress to action. With COPPA, privacy concerns were sufficient to create legislative concern, but the law probably would not have been enacted without the added support of online safety advocates. This coalition between both privacy and safety advocates created an inherent weakness in the COPPA. Concerns about safety caused Congress to build a framework with scant regard to how children might want to use interactive services. Safety concerns also caused Congress to try to perfect the online environment against risks of child predation.

In the legal and business community, COPPA is seen as too burdensome, causing a bimodal response. Sites either fully embrace a child-oriented status that triggers COPPA, and then comply with the rules, or eschew it completely, sometimes by declaring that individuals under a certain age cannot use the site at all. Because of the all-or-nothing approach, children have only limited and sometimes unattractive options online. COPPA created incentives to develop services that are one-way, television-like broadcasting services. Designers do this because interactivity triggers legal duties under COPPA. Children also learn to lie about their age in order to join fun, highly interactive services that are supposedly only used by adults. In joining, children lose all the protections of COPPA. Yet, many of these protections are indeed sensible and could form the building blocks of a good law for adults' privacy.

Internet businesses see COPPA as difficult and burdensome, but, at the same time, COPPA has many effective protections. Among them are the allocation of privacy responsibilities for the behavior of vendors, such as third-party trackers, to the service; limitations on how data can be used; limitations on tracking; rules on how much data can be collected; a regulatory incentive for contextual advertising and against behavioral tracking; and ceilings on how long data can be retained. Congress enacted such significant protections because we as a society agree that children are worth protecting. Yet, COPPA protects only those who are under 13 years old. Many adolescents and many adults desire similar protections for their online activities.

This chapter outlines the history of children's privacy issues and shows that privacy is sometimes a proxy for still-unresolved tensions surrounding how companies should be able to advertise to children. It charts the FTC's incremental steps to regulating children's privacy, and then to the enactment and substance of the Children's Online Privacy Protection Act, a law motivated by both online privacy and safety concerns. Finally, this chapter assesses the act, noting that its emphasis on the high-transaction-cost and ultimately unverifiable requirement of parental consent causes companies to avoid the law if possible.

## CHILDREN'S PRIVACY

The privacy and security of children has been a third-rail issue for online businesses. Yet, kids' privacy issues are largely unregulated in the offline environment. The FTC's KidVid episode, where the FTC proposed banning television advertising to young children (see Chapter 2), cast a pall over government enthusiasm for similar initiatives. As a result, unresolved are issues raised by advertising to children, including an epidemic level of childhood obesity.[5] Because advertising itself is so difficult to regulate, child advocates have often used privacy to collaterally attack commercial attempts to influence children.

Until the 1990s, it was commonplace for database marketing companies to sell lists of children by age and their home addresses for advertising purposes. For instance, data brokers would sell lists of contact information for four- to six-year-old children. This practice came into scrutiny in 1996, when the longtime CNN reporter Kyra Phillips, then working for a Los Angeles television station, purchased personal information on 5,500 children from Metromail, a data broker.[6] To purchase the children's contact information, Phillips used the name of a notorious suspected child killer.[7] Phillips' stunt generated publicity but it did not result in new restrictions on children's information. Instead, data brokers avoided regulation by renaming their products. The same information was sold but labeled as databases of households with "presence of children." Such a database would be labeled the "Single Parents with Multiple Children Mailing List."

Shortly thereafter, a report by Professor Kathryn Montgomery and Shelley Pasnik showed that marketers had developed sophisticated and ethically troubling methods to interact with children online.[8] As with previous generations of marketing science – motivational research and subliminal advertising – Montgomery and Pasnik only needed to quote the advertisers themselves to show an ugly landscape of businesses planning to target children who were at an age susceptible to persuasive messaging. The duo also described the troubling information collection techniques of mainstream brands. Consider a website operated by D.C. Comics: "At the Batman Forever Web site, supplying personal information becomes a test of loyalty. 'Good citizens of the Web, help commissioner Gordon with the Gotham Census,' children are urged. Although the survey uses the guise of a virtual city's census, much of the information sought by this questionnaire pertains to purchasing habits and video

---

[5] Elizabeth S. Moore, *Should Marketers Be Persuading Our Children?*, *in* MARKETING AND THE COMMON GOOD (Patrick E. Murphy & John F. Sherry, Jr., eds., 2014).

[6] Gary Chapman, *Protecting Children Online Is Society's Herculean Mission*, L.A. TIMES, June 24, 1996, at D14.

[7] Largest Database Marketing Firm Sends Phone Numbers, Addresses of 5,000 Families with Kids to TV Reporter Using Name of Child Killer, BUS. WIRE (May 13, 1996).

[8] KATHRYN MONTGOMERY & SHELLEY PASNIK, WEB OF DECEPTION: THREATS TO CHILDREN FROM ONLINE MARKETING (June 1996).

preferences. For example, respondents are asked how likely they are to buy Batman Forever and Apollo 13 on video."[9]

---

### TELEVISION AND ONLINE ADVERTISING

In the 1950s and 1960s, television content began to attract public controversy, fed by the realization that game shows were rigged by commercial sponsors and concerns that the new medium was a powerful force for influence over consumers. Even laissez-faire commissioner Lowell Mason thought television advertising was unseemly, calling it the "pitchman in the parlor." Consumer advocates found the new medium immersive, that advertising on it exploited anxieties, that it had subliminal powers, and that it was harming viewers' well-being. The FTC started enforcement actions concerning activities such as false mock-ups and demonstrations on television that had been allowed for decades in magazines and newspapers.[10]

Could online advertising be triggering new objections because it is an unfamiliar medium? Just like television advertising, online advertising's advocates wildly overstate the power of their ads. A study by Google found that half of all digital ads are never seen by consumers. Added to this, in the study Google counted an ad as "viewable" if 50 percent of the ad was on the screen for a single second.[11] A miniscule percentage of consumers actually click on ads; in fact, "fat thumbs" and fraud probably contribute to more clicks than real traffic. Are advocates overreacting to a new, unfamiliar medium based on its hype? Will we soon learn that online advertising is not much more effective than other methods?

On the other hand, skilled advocates can recast online advertising as not a problem with marketing, but rather a problem of unrestrained surveillance of individuals. Viewed from a different lens, behavioral tracking, rather than ads, becomes a modern boogeyman.

---

By focusing on major advertisers, Montgomery and Pasnik showed that eliciting information from children using prizes and the like was a mainstream activity. Advertisers integrated pitches into the story content, obscuring the line between entertainment and marketing. These companies also used passive tracking

---

[9] *Id.*
[10] Peter Braton Turk, The Federal Trade Commission Hearings on Modern Advertising Practices: A Continuing Inquiry into Television Advertising (1977) (Ph.D. dissertation, University of Wisconsin, Madison, WI).
[11] Google, The Importance of Being Seen: Viewability Insights for Digital Marketers and Publishers (November 2014).

techniques, such as cookies, to follow children over time, raising the risk that interests and desires could be profiled and used to pitch more persuasive messages.

In May 1996, Montgomery's organization, the Center for Media Education (CME), petitioned the FTC to investigate KidsCom.com, one of the sites described in the report: "The KidsCom communications playground, aimed at children 4 to 15, uses a forceful approach. In order to enter the site, each child is required to disclose his/her name, age, sex and E-mail address. The mandatory questionnaire also requests his/her favorite TV show, commercial and musical groups, as well as the name of the child who referred him/her to KidsCom. Once children have entered the playground, they are encouraged to supply additional personal information in order to win 'KidsCash,' a form of virtual money that can be used to purchase conspicuously-placed products."[12]

Just over a year later, FTC staff released a public letter concerning the company.[13] The FTC opined that it would be deceptive for KidsCom.com to collect information from children and reveal it to others without parental notice and consent. If a disclosure to third parties occurred, it could rise to an unfair practice because of the risk of child predation. Yet the FTC chose not to take enforcement action, because KidsCom changed its practices, there was no evidence that it broadly released data to third parties, and an enforcement action could have had unintended policy effects on the emerging internet marketplace.

By 1998, the FTC and the White House[14] recommended legislation to protect privacy of children online. Upon Congressional request, the FTC studied the issue and the results were dismal – almost all child-oriented websites collected personal information from children while only about half had privacy policies.[15] In the physical world, such information collection was usually mediated by a parent or another responsible adult, but online, children were being encouraged to reveal personal information about themselves and others and frequently in troubling ways. For instance, some sites made information disclosure a kind of contest, where children were rewarded for revealing data useful to marketers, and the site then posted the information for anyone to see. Another site attempted to connect kids with "pen pals," listing children's ages and contact information. Such practices made it easy for the FTC to connect the dots between child-oriented websites and

---

[12] *Id.*

[13] Letter from Jodie Bernstein, Director, FTC Bureau of Consumer Protection, to Kathryn C. Montgomery, President, Center for Media Education (July 15, 1997).

[14] OFFICE OF THE VICE PRESIDENT, VICE PRESIDENT GORE ANNOUNCES NEW STEPS TOWARD AN ELECTRONIC BILL OF RIGHTS, July 31, 1998 ("Children's privacy: The Administration will seek legislation that would specify a set of fair information principles applicable to the collection of data from children, such as a prohibition on the collection of data from children under 13 without prior parental consent. The Federal Trade Commission would have the authority to issue rules to enforce these standards. Legislation is needed because children under 13 may not understand the consequences of giving out personally identifiable information.")

[15] FEDERAL TRADE COMMISSION, PRIVACY ONLINE: A REPORT TO CONGRESS (June 1998).

physical safety from child predators, strengthening the call for regulation by adding personal safety to personal privacy concerns.

The FTC began a case-by-case enforcement strategy concerning child-oriented websites. In 1999 (before COPPA was in effect), the FTC settled a matter against GeoCities, an online service provider that shared children's information with third parties despite promising not to.[16] Another pre-COPPA matter concerned sites that elicited personal information about children and their families' finances through contests and games.[17] The FTC also sued a company that promised to never sell children's personal information but then attempted to use its customer database as an asset in bankruptcy.[18]

These matters all involved deception. The FTC felt it was unable to act in situations, however, where children's information was collected but no affirmative deception was present. Because of this gap, the Agency formally supported enactment of the Children's Online Privacy Protection Act to strengthen its basis for legal action.

## THE CHILDREN'S ONLINE PRIVACY PROTECTION ACT OF 1998

Introduced by Senators Richard Bryan and John McCain as S. 2326 in July 1998,[19] Congress enacted the Children's Online Privacy Protection Act (COPPA) just months later, as a rider to an emergency appropriations bill.[20] Fulfilling an observation made by Professor Priscilla Regan, a privacy rationale (protecting children online) was sufficient to raise a public debate, but overcoming policy-maker inertia to enact legislation became possible only once online safety advocates joined the cause. The law thus had both privacy and online safety attributes.

In an introductory statement,[21] and later in committee testimony,[22] Senator Bryan identified the several concerns that animated the legislation:

- Websites collected personal financial and contact information about children, sometimes using cartoon characters and games to solicit the data.
- Websites could perform this collection without parental supervision or control.
- One could not identify the recipients of these data, and the solicitation of family members' financial data suggested less than above-board marketing.

---

[16] *In the Matter of GeoCities*, 127 F.T.C. 94 (February 5, 1999).
[17] *In the Matter of Liberty Fin. Companies, Inc.*, 128 F.T.C. 240 (1999).
[18] *FTC v. Toysmart.com*, 00–11341-RGS, 2000 WL 34016434 (D. Mass. July 21, 2000).
[19] Representative Edward Markey introduced companion legislation in the House that would also protect adults as 105 Cong. H.R. 4667, the Electronic Privacy Bill of Rights Act of 1998.
[20] Pub. L. 105–277, Div. C, Title XIII, §1302, October 21, 1998, 112 Stat. 2681–728. Codified at 15 U.S.C. §6501 et seq.
[21] 105 CONG. REC. S8482 (July 17, 1988).
[22] S. Hrg. 105–1069, 105 Cong. 2nd Sess. (September 23, 1988).

- Children can easily venture into inappropriate corners of the internet, attracting the attention of sexual predators and pedophiles.
- The internet is a spectacular tool for learning and for economic progress; children should not have to take the Hobson's choice of stopping internet use in order avoid commercial or sexual predation. This conundrum was highlighted in a hearing on COPPA, at which Bryan emphasized that the measure was pro-internet, adding: "proficiency with the Internet will be a necessary skill required to succeed in the 21st Century."[23]

According to Professor Deirdre Mulligan, early drafts of the legislation defined children as anyone under the age of eighteen. As introduced, the legislation applied to individuals under the age of sixteen. This was changed to under the age of thirteen in the final bill. Chairman Pitofsky argued against the extension of COPPA to teenagers, explaining that if it were applied, the parental consent requirement should be softened or dropped.[24]

The legislative history on COPPA is thin, and, as a result, COPPA is sometimes framed as a privacy law, sometimes as a measure to stop child predation, and sometimes as both. Additionally, there is no case law concerning COPPA, aside from consent decrees approved by district courts.

As Congress typically does in consumer law and other matters, it delegated the drafting of the actual regulations to the Commission. The rules were due by October 1999. The COPPA rule appears at 16 CFR §312 and it went into effect on April 21, 2000. The FTC was given Administrative Procedure Act rule-making power to promulgate the rule.[25] A rather uninspired 2007 report on the COPPA concluded that the law was working well and recommended no changes.[26] Just a few years later, however, the Commission promulgated major changes that became effective on July 1, 2013.[27]

### Scope

At a high level, COPPA regulates the collection of personal information from children on websites or other online services. A "child" is an individual under the age of thirteen.

---

[23] S. Hrg. 105–1069, 105 Cong. 2nd Sess. (September 23, 1988).

[24] *Id.*

[25] As opposed to its default rule-making powers under the Magnuson–Moss Act, which are popularly considered too burdensome to use. See Chapter 2.

[26] FTC, Implementing the Children's Online Privacy Protection Act: A Report to Congress (February 2007).

[27] FTC, Children's Online Privacy Protection Rule, Final Rule Amendments, 78(12) Fed. Reg. 3972, January 17, 2013.

Websites and other services are broadly construed, and can include mobile and desktop applications;[28] plug-ins on websites that capture data for metrics, social networking, or advertising purposes; advertising networks; location-based services; and services with voice over IP. COPPA does not apply to noncommercial services.

To trigger the COPPA obligations, a website or service must be directed at children, or have actual knowledge that it has collected information from children. The FTC uses a "totality of the circumstances" test to determine whether a site is child oriented. Factors include the subject matter of the site, use of animated characters, characteristics of music, whether the site uses child models or child celebrities, the use of childish fonts, and audience composition. Most of the FTC's cases thus far involve sites that are obviously child oriented, such as fan club sites for teenage celebrities,[29] and social networking services that explicitly serve children.[30] However, in the FTC's 2014 case against TinyCo, it labeled fantasy apps child oriented because they featured "brightly-colored, animated characters from little animals or zoo creatures to tiny monsters, and … involving subject matters such as a zoo, tree house, or resort inspired by a fairy tale."[31] TinyCo is the first COPPA case to rely so heavily on an app's appearance, and this may be problematic, as many general-audience apps have childish themes.

Actual knowledge of children on a site can occur in several ways, for instance, in coming across a comment posted by a user who self-identifies as a child. Several cases alleging actual knowledge concern services that had some age-screening mechanism that nonetheless allowed children to register.[32] In some situations, this appears just to be a technical error. For instance, Yelp.com excluded children from registering on its website, but its related app for cell phones would establish an account for a child.[33] Such technical mistakes do not prevent the FTC from finding a violation of the COPPA.

Actual knowledge issues can be a double whammy for companies: They both violate COPPA for registering children, but also violate the FTC Act because the companies have typically promised not to collect children's information at all.

---

[28] *US* v. *W3 Innovations, LLC*, CV-11–03958-PSG (N.D. Cal. 2011); *US* v. *Bonzi Software, Inc.*, CV-04–1048 RJK (C.D. Cal. 2004).

[29] *US* v. *UMG Recordings, Inc.*, CV-04–1050 JFW (C.D. Cal. 2004).

[30] *US* v. *Jones O. Godwin, doing business as skidekids.com*, 1:11-CV-3846 (JOF) (N.D. Ga. 2011)(promoted as the "Facebook and Myspace for kids.")

[31] *US* v. *TinyCo., Inc.*, 3:14-cv-04164 (N.D. Cal. 2014).

[32] *US* v. *Path, Inc.*, 3:13-cv-00448-RS (N.D. Cal. 2013); *US* v. *Artist Arena, LLC*, 112-cv-07386-JGK (S.D. N.Y. 2013); *US* v. *RockYou, Inc.*, 312-cv-01487-SI (N.D. Cal. 2012); (*US* v. *Iconix Brand Group, Inc.*, 09-CIV-8864 (S.D.N.Y. 2009); *US* v. *Sony BMG Music Entertainment*, 08 CV 10730 (LAK) (S.D.N.Y. 2008); *US* v. *Xanga.com, Inc.*, 06-CIV-6853 (SHS) (S.D. N.Y. 2006); *US* v. *UMG Recordings, Inc.*, CV-04–1050 JFW (C.D. Cal. 2004).

[33] *US* v. *Yelp Inc.*, 3:14-cv-04163 (N.D. Cal. 2014).

Sites that are directed at children cannot eliminate COPPA liability by simply declaring that those under thirteen should not register.[34]

The updated definition of collection of personal information in the rule was comprehensive and technology-neutral. Any type of persistent identifier tracking was covered – even when done passively – meaning that plug-ins and popular analytics and advertising services are subject to the rule. Information that allows contact with a child, such as usernames and identifiers for instant messaging, and other communications platforms, were considered personal information.

---

A SAMPLE OF MID-CENTURY CONSUMER PROTECTION REGULATIONS

It is difficult to imagine the scope of consumer hazards that have existed in the last century. For some time, a consumer shopping for shoes may have been presented with a fluoroscope (an x-ray machine) to ensure that the shoe fitted well.[35] Cars lacked seat belts. Sliding doors often lacked safety glass. Lawn mowers lacked automatic engine shutoff switches for the time when the operator lets go of the handle. Beginning in the 1950s, Congress enacted a number of statutes to address these hazards. Debates surrounding these issues rhyme with today's – To what extent can consumer education address these risks? What is the responsibility of the consumer to use products safely? Do structural interventions that prohibit certain technologies or mandate others, in order to protect consumers, inhibit innovation?

- In 1953, a rather edentulous Flammable Fabrics Act was enacted, with a stronger version passing in 1967 to address a rash of cases where children were seriously burned by flammable clothing.
- The 1956 Refrigerator Safety Act required refrigerators to have an internal latch opening mechanism (to prevent children from suffocating when trapped inside one).
- The 1960 Hazardous Substances Labeling Act required warnings on household chemicals.
- The 1962 National Traffic and Motor Vehicle Safety Act enabled the federal government to set safety standards for cars.
- The 1972 Consumer Product Safety Act established the Consumer Product Safety Commission, an independent agency tasked with protecting against unreasonable risks of injuries associated with consumer products.

---

[34] *US* v. *Bigmailbox.com*, 01–605-A (E.d. Va. 2001) (site declared, "You must be at least 13 years old or have your parent's permission to join this program.")

[35] *See* Paul Frame, Shoe-Fitting Fluoroscope (ca. 1930–1940) (2010).

> As consumer protection rules diffuse, some dangerous products disappear from the market, and others are redesigned to be safer. If consumer protection law is successful, it cures problematic products and practices, and memories of dangerous products fade. As a result, consumer protection is at risk of being taken for granted.

Critics have argued that the FTC exceeded the bounds of Congressional intent by defining collection to include the passive tracking of third-party services. However, these broad definitions of services and of personal information mirror Congress' dual concerns of safety and child marketing. COPPA's main thrusts concern information that allows strangers to contact children, thus justifying inclusion of usernames, as well as marketing techniques that could have a manipulative effect on children. The Agency concluded that even if a website could not name a particular user, if it could track that user over time, it could manipulate the child in ways that Congress found objectionable.

The COPPA has extraterritorial application, and thus child-directed sites hosted overseas must comply, as must sites hosted in the United States that serve children in other countries.[36]

### Protections

The COPPA has five major protections for services subject to the rule: first, services must post clear privacy notices that specifically identify all the parties receiving data from the service; second, services must obtain parental consent prior to collecting data from children; third, services must provide parents with the ability to review the information collected, to object to its further use, and to use the service without sharing data with third parties (if technically possible); fourth, services must limit the amount of data collected about children; and, finally, services must both limit the duration of data retention and reasonably secure data.

COPPA also requires services directed to children to vet vendors and third parties for compliance with these obligations. In this fashion, COPPA fills gaps that exist in other regimes, causing services to inspect third parties and creating incentives for vendors to make COPPA-compliant offerings. This requirement follows greater recent attention to vendors and services provider liability under other information privacy law, such as the Gramm–Leach–Bliley Act and the health privacy laws.

---

[36] 15 U.S.C. §6501(2); *US* v. *Playdom, Inc.*, SACV11-00724 (C.D. Cal. 2011) (defendant transferred accounts, including those of children, to a French company).

## Notice

COPPA's notice requirements include a duty to provide a general privacy notice as well as special, direct notices to parents before the service collects information from children. Notices cannot contain "confusing or contradictory" materials, by which the FTC means that there should not be marketing or fluff in the policy that would distract the decision-maker.[37]

The general privacy notice has three main requirements: First, it must list the identities of all "operators" associated with the service. Second, it must include a description of the kinds of data the operator collects, uses, and discloses. It must also state whether children can make personal information publicly available through the service. Finally, it must state that the parent can review, have deleted, and refuse to allow further collection or use of personal information.

Direct notices have four types, corresponding to four basic models of child-oriented services: first, a notice for sites that will disclose children's personal information (for instance, a child-directed social network service); second, a notice for sites that intend to contact the child repeatedly; third, a notice for sites that collect data only to protect the child; and fourth, a notice for sites that only collect contact information of parents and no data about children (this is a voluntary notice).

## Parental consent

In response to concerns that the internet allowed children to interact with marketers and others without parental supervision or control, COPPA imposed a parental consent requirement *before* a website can collect or use personal information of children. Under the Rule, the consent procedure must be "reasonably calculated, in light of available technology, to ensure that the person providing consent is the child's parent."[38] Thus, neither Congress nor the FTC thought that parental consent mechanisms would be foolproof.[39]

At the same time, the FTC recognized that more interactive services would require more parental involvement. Thus, social networking services and other services that disclose personal information publicly or to third parties must comply with the strongest consent mechanism. Services that only use information for internal purposes have a lower consent burden. And television-like sites with no interactivity and no information sharing need not obtain consent at all.

---

[37] Privacy provisions that were both in a privacy policy and in an end-user license agreement did not "document clearly, understandably, and completely disclosed its information practices, as required by the Rule." US v. *Bonzi Software, Inc.*, CV-04–1048 RJK (C.D. Cal. 2004).

[38] 16 C.F.R. §312.5(b).

[39] S. Hrg. 105–1069, 105 Cong. 2nd Sess. (September 23, 1988). (Chairman Pitofsky testified, "As I said once before, the FTC has vast authority, but controlling the behavior of 11-year-olds, for example, calling themselves 13-year-olds is beyond our reach.")

It is useful to think of COPPA sites as falling into three tiers ordered in high to low compliance risk. For the first tier, services that make disclosures to third parties, employ behavioral advertising, or allow children to publicly post information must obtain verified parental consent. The FTC has specified five methods to obtain parental permission: a consent form returned by mail, fax, or scan; a credit card number when used with a payment; operating a toll-free number for the parent to call; having the parent contact the company through video conference; and verifying parent consent through collecting government-issued identification.

For the middle tier, where a service only uses child data for internal purposes, it may use "e-mail plus" to gain consent. With this method, the site sends the parent an e-mail, and the parent responds giving consent and providing some other information, such as a contact phone number. Use of personal information for appropriate internal purposes includes that necessary to run and secure the site, but may also include contextual advertising.

In the lowest-risk tier, a service could be directed to children and simply not collect personal information at all (other than a persistent identifier for internal operation purposes). Such zero-interactivity sites need not obtain parental consent. Finally, consent must be obtained again whenever the site makes some material change to its privacy policy.

### Parental access

Consistent with the model of fair information practices (discussed in Chapter 6), parents can request a description of the specific types of personal information collected from their child and review the actual personal information collected.

The traditional concern about access concerns security: How can a service that only interacts with people online be certain that it is revealing personal information to the right parent? What if access requests are used to cause data breaches or identity theft? Here, sites must walk a tightrope: they have to create procedures that ensure the requestor is legitimate, but at the same time not create unreasonable burdens for the parent to authenticate identity.

### Excessive information collection

Businesses must allow children access to their services without conditioning it on the child "disclosing more personal information than is reasonably necessary to participate in such activity."[40] This provision is based on the concerns raised by advocates and by COPPA's sponsors about eliciting personal information from children using games and the like. The Commission takes the limitation seriously and is appearing to interpret it such that any information collection that is not

[40] 16 C.F.R. §312.7.

necessary to deliver a service is prohibited. For instance, in a case involving a company that operated a "Kids Club" that included a chance to win prizes, the company's collection of name, address, e-mail address, and day and month of birth was considered excessive. The practice was deemed excessive in light of the fact that the company collected data on 500 children yet only awarded 12 prizes.[41] Presumably, the club could have operated with just e-mail address and collected home addresses from the prize winners only.

As part of the access right described above, parents can object to specific information collection or sharing, demand that a site delete data, and yet still ask that the child be allowed to use the service.[42] The service provider can terminate the user if the information use is critical to the service. However, sharing with "third parties" for the kinds of business purposes typical on websites is not "critical" under the COPPA. Thus, a service cannot terminate a user just because it cannot collect as much advertising revenue on a child who objects.

## Security and deletion

COPPA requires that services have "reasonable procedures to protect the confidentiality, security, and integrity of information collected from children."[43] The service must also take "reasonable steps" to ensure that service providers and third parties have adequate security.

In addition, the rule imposes limits on how long data can be kept ("for only as long as reasonably necessary to fulfill the purpose for which the information was collected") and requires that it be deleted with "reasonable measures."[44] These provisions do not apply to data collected offline.

Only one commission case has dealt with deletion requirements. In it, a child-oriented social networking site tried to comply with the consent requirement by allowing children to create a profile but keeping it private until a parent approved the creation of the account. However, the site failed to delete information when the parent refused (or never got around to) approving the account.[45] This was found to violate the COPPA.

---

[41] *US* v. *American Pop Corn Company*, Co2-4008DEO (N.D. Iowa 2002). See also the "Girl's Life" case, where the FTC describes seven different website activities and follows the description with a blanket statement that the personal information collection was excessive. *US* v. *Monarch Services, Inc., et al.*, AMD 01 CV 1165 (D. Md. 2001).

[42] 16 C.F.R. §312.5(a)(2). ("An operator must give the parent the option to consent to the collection and use of the child's personal information without consenting to disclosure of his or her personal information to third parties.")

[43] 16 C.F.R. §312.8.

[44] 16 C.F.R. §312.10.

[45] *US* v. *Industrious Kid, Inc.*, CV-08-0639 (N.D. Cal. 2008).

*Enforcement*

There is no private right of action in COPPA. Actions can be brought by states, by the FTC, and by the regulators of specific industries (for instance, the financial regulators, the Department of Transportation, and even the Department of Agriculture have authority to enforce COPPA against companies they regulate).

The Children's Advertising Review Unit (CARU), a well-regarded self-regulatory organization, referred a number of COPPA actions to the FTC.

The FTC's internal matter tracking system classifies COPPA violations into six categories: first, where there is no privacy policy or where it is incomplete or not prominent; second, where the site misrepresents how data are used; third, where the site had no procedures for parental consent; fourth, where the parent is not given the opportunity to refuse consent to sharing of data to a third party; fifth, where the parent cannot see the child's information or where information is not deleted as requested; and, finally, where the service collects more information than necessary for an activity.

COPPA enforcement has generally concerned obvious violations of the rule, such as failing to post compliant privacy policies or failing to obtain verifiable parental consent. These cases have been uncontroversial as evidenced by unanimous commission votes to bring them. All COPPA cases have been brought in federal district court, rather than as administrative proceedings, signaling the Agency's confidence in its enforcement choices.

The FTC's first cases in any area tend to be conciliatory warnings to industry that become more punitive with time. From its first COPPA cases, the Agency included civil penalties and requirements that the sites delete the data they collected since the effective date of the COPPA rule.[46] These civil penalties averaged $30,000 in 2001 and 2002. In 2003, the FTC secured a $100,000 penalty in a settlement.[47] By 2004, it secured a $400,000 settlement against UMG Recordings.[48] The Agency's 2006 case and settlement against Xanga extracted a $1,000,000 penalty.[49] That company allowed over 1 million accounts to be created to users who indicated that they were under 13 and created profiles for them on the service. A 2011 case levied a $3,000,000 penalty.[50]

High penalties are applied in cases involving large numbers of children, where the service allowed children to post personal information, and where the

---

[46] See *US v. Ohio Art Company*, FTC File No. 022-3028 (N.D. Ohio 2002); *US v. American Pop Corn Company*, Co2-4008DEO (N.D. Iowa 2002); *US v. Lisa Frank, Inc.*, 01-1516-A (E.D. Va. 2001); *US v. Monarch Services, Inc., et al.*, AMD 01 CV 1165 (D. Md. 2001); *US v. Looksmart Ltd.*, 01-606-A (E.D. Va. 2001); *US v. Bigmailbox.com*, 01-605-A (E.d. Va. 2001).

[47] *US v. Mrs. Fields Famous Brands, Inc.*, 203 CV205 JTG (D. Utah 2003) ($100,000); *US v. Hershey Foods Corporation*, 4CV-03-350 (M.D. Pa. 2003) ($85,000).

[48] *US v. UMG Recordings, Inc.*, CV-04-1050 JFW (C.D. Cal. 2004).

[49] *US v. Xanga.com, Inc.*, 06-CIV-6853(SHS) (S.D. N.Y. 2006).

[50] *US v. Playdom, Inc.*, SACV11-00724 (C.D. Cal. 2011).

service collected information aggressively or excessively (GPS information, user address books).

Starting with the suit against Xanga, the FTC started naming company principals as defendants in COPPA suits. This is because those who own or control data are considered "operators" under COPPA and thus are jointly liable. By policy, the FTC has stated it will only name principals where they participate in, facilitate, or know of COPPA rule violations. Given that CARU cajoles companies to comply with COPPA first and then refers cases to the FTC, there can be ample evidence of knowing violation of the rule.

The FTC has not brought enforcement actions using the more recent changes to the COPPA rule that went into effect on July 1, 2013. However, the Agency has sent out scores of letters to mobile application developers and others, reminding them of the new definitions of the rule. One prominently announced letter was directed to a China-based app developer that was collecting precise GPS information from children and sharing the information with advertisers.[51] The letter caused Google to temporarily suspend the company's apps from its application marketplace.

### COPPA safe harbor

COPPA allows companies to apply and be certified as a "safe harbor" program. Services that meet the safe harbor's requirements are deemed compliant with COPPA.

In essence, COPPA safe harbor programs are self-regulatory bodies. However, because they must meet certain requirements and are overseen by the Commission, they do not suffer from the pathologies present in pure self-regulatory regimes (see discussion of self-regulation in Chapter 6).[52] Additionally, before passage of COPPA, the major trade groups had expressed some support for child privacy protections.[53] Thus, all participants could at least agree that the principle of protecting children was important. This consensus has made the COPPA self-regulatory effort more credible and more likely to achieve buy-in from participants.

COPPA safe harbor programs must have stated requirements for services that are at least as stringent as the COPPA rule. Safe harbor programs must assess services' compliance annually, and take disciplinary action for noncompliance with the requirements. The Commission reviews COPPA safe harbor programs. The review includes an opportunity for the public to comment, and programs must be given a

---

[51] Letter from Maneesha Mithal, Associate Director, Division of Privacy and Identity Protection, FTC, to BabyBus, December 17, 2014.

[52] See Ira S. Rubinstein, *Privacy and Regulatory Innovation: Moving beyond Voluntary Codes*, 6 I/S J. L. Pol. 355 (2011).

[53] S. Hrg. 105–1069, 105 Cong. 2nd Sess. (September 23, 1988) (testimony of Jull A. Lesser, Director, Law and Public Policy, America Online, Inc.).

determination within 6 months of application. The FTC has approved a handful of programs.

COPPA is widely criticized as a privacy measure. Its limitation to children below the age of thirteen, the burden of parental consent, its effects on anonymity, and how it balances parental versus website responsibility have attracted the most critique.

Yet, a more fundamental problem comes from what COPPA did to children's websites. Some advocates for children's privacy wanted a kind of PBS-like experience for children online. In particular, advocates were concerned about a blending of advertising and content. Others argued from a different viewpoint that the incentives created by COPPA risked turning child-directed sites into television-like, one-way media programs.

Yet, COPPA-compliant sites are probably worse than TV and even Saturday morning cartoon TV – they are fully immersive shopping experiences. For instance, one of the most popular COPPA sites allows children to customize a seabird with clothes and other accessories, such as a pet. The site seems entirely focused on training children to shop at a mall, and the seabirds, once decorated, have a Kardashianesque quality.

### Why thirteen?

As introduced, COPPA would have required parental consent until the age of sixteen. In fact, the high level of parental control over teens' internet use made the bill attractive to conservative groups, which saw COPPA and companion antipornography legislation, the Child Online Protection Act,[54] as levers to stop access to smut as well as other materials, such as information about sexual and reproductive health and abortion. Viewed in this light, parental consent becomes a tool to control children. Free speech advocates quickly realized this possibility and saw COPPA as detrimental to adolescents' freedom. They strongly opposed any precedent that created parental content requirements, for fear that they may spread into other contexts, such as learning about evolution or controversial literature.

---

[54] Creating fines and misdemeanor punishments for "[w]hoever knowingly and with knowledge of the character of the material, in interstate or foreign commerce by means of the World Wide Web, makes any communication for commercial purposes that is available to any minor and that includes any material that is harmful to minors ..." Pub. L. 105–277, 112 Stat. 2681–736. This law was invalidated on free speech grounds in Am. *Civil Liberties Union* v. *Mukasey*, 534 F.3d 181 (3d Cir. 2008).

CHAIRMAN PERTSCHUK'S LESSONS ON REGULATION

Chairman Michael Pertschuk was one of the most qualified FTC leaders ever. Educated at Yale Law School, he clerked for a federal district judge, practiced at a firm, and then spent fifteen years on Capitol Hill. His Hill experience brought him great expertise in consumer protection, as he was chief counsel to the Senate Commerce Committee during the expansion of consumer rights in the 1970s.

Pertschuk led the FTC during its most controversial years (see Chapter 2). In his 1982 book, *Revolt against Regulation*, he gave a personal account of lessons learned from the newfound skepticism of government regulation.[55] He offered consumer advocates seven lessons in consumer regulation. They should ask:

Is the rule consonant with market incentives to the maximum extent feasible?

Will the remedy work?

Will the chosen remedy minimize the cost burdens of compliance, consistent with achieving the objective?

Will the benefits flowing from the rule to consumer or to competition substantially exceed the costs?

Will the rule or remedy adversely affect competition?

Does the regulation preserve freedom of informed individual choice to the maximum extent consistent with consumer welfare?

To what extent is the problem appropriate for federal intervention and amendable to a centrally administered national standard?

Pertschuk's book is an anomaly for Washington memoirs, which typically involve some trope about "reforming Washington," with failures attributed to intractable "bureaucracies" and the like. Pertschuk wrestles with questions fundamental to whether consumer protection is effective, and declares that his experience taught him the (albeit limited) value of cost–benefit analysis.

Young adolescents experiment with intimacy. As Professor Sherry Turkle observed, some adolescents explore sexuality online, which could be a safer venue because there is no in-person contact.[56] Adolescents seek seclusion for such activities, but COPPA does not allow any secrecy from the parent. Designed as both privacy and online safety measure, COPPA does not recognize the parent as a potential invader of privacy.

---

[55] Michael Pertschuk, Revolt against Regulation (1982).
[56] Sherry Turkle, Life on the Screen (1995).

A teenager who seeks advice from an emergency online hotline for depression, such as a chat or instant messaging service, would have to undergo a delay in obtaining parental consent under COPPA. In addition, the parent could use the COPPA access rights to learn about how the child interacted with the service. Civil libertarians pointed out that children need privacy protections online, but they also need some level of privacy from their parental intrusiveness as well.[57]

Still, the civil libertarians' critique may be misplaced. This is because COPPA only covers commercial services. In most circumstances, a nonprofit can safely collect personal information from children and simply not be subject to COPPA,[58] or it could design its site so that it does not collect personal information and yet provides information about sexual health, depression, or abortion services.

### The bimodal compliance problem

To avoid the various duties imposed by COPPA, particularly the parental consent requirement, many services simply prohibit children from using them.[59] Congress did not provide any middle ground for compromise on parental consent. The Commission's tolerance for "e-mail plus," which allows for internal uses of personal information but not commercial ones, seems to be waning. Thus, sites tend to fully embrace COPPA, or pretend that children never visit their service.

COPPA applies to a very wide variety of services, including those that have nothing to do with social networking or otherwise posting personal information online. Thus, it prohibits offering e-mail or instant messaging services to children, tools that many families use to stay in touch.

This limitation is unfortunate for several reasons. First, parents may tell children to lie at enrollment about their age so that they can use the service.[60] Second, even without parental encouragement, children may lie because highly interactive services are so attractive. In addition to creating rewards for lying, these children are then as unprotected as adults online, sometimes with disastrous results. Consider the mobile flirting app Skout – it created a protected service for thirteen- to seventeen-year-olds and, despite its efforts, three children were attacked by older adults who were posing as teens.[61] *Consumer Reports* magazine estimated that "Of

---

[57] Bryce Clayton Newell, Cheryl Metoyer, & Adam D. Moore, Privacy in the Family, THE SOCIAL DIMENSIONS OF PRIVACY (Beate Roessler & Dorota Mokrosinska, eds., 2015); Benjamin Shmueli & Ayelet Blecher-Prigat, *Privacy for Children*, 42 COLUM. HUM. RTS. L. REV. 759 (2011).

[58] An exception would be where the nonprofit was functionally operating as a for-profit (*see* Chapter 4 and *FTC v. California Dental Association*, 526 US 756 (1999)).

[59] Jules Polonetsky & Omer Tene, *Who Is Reading Whom Now: Privacy in Education from Books to MOOCs*, VAN. J. ENT. TECH. L. (2014).

[60] Danah Boyd, Urs Gasser, & John Palfrey, *How the COPPA, as Implemented, Is Misinterpreted by the Public: A Research Perspective*, Berkman Center Research Pub. 2010-12 (April 29, 2010).

[61] Nicole Perlroth, *After Rapes Involving Children, Skout, a Flirting App, Bans Minors*, N.Y. TIMES, Jun 12, 2012.

the 20 million minors who actively used Facebook in the past year, 7.5 million – or more than one-third – were younger than 13 and not supposed to be able to use the site."[62]

Parental consent is both a burden for services and for parents, and it is ineffective, because consent does little to protect privacy or safety. For instance, parental consent would not have protected the older adolescents who used the Skout app from adults posing as children. In a way, COPPA might be more effective if efforts devoted to verifying parental consent were focused instead on keeping adults out of adolescent-oriented services. The social networking service Facebook realized this and has deployed extensive systems to flag suspicious activity. For instance, Facebook might flag an older man who is contacting several teenagers, because this could signal incipient child predation.[63]

COPPA's most efficacious protections come from limits on data collection and limits on commercial uses of data. While advertising is the often-invoked privacy interest, the bigger issue is the assemblage of profiles on children. Other protections, such as incentives for contextual rather than behavioral advertising, and requirements to delete data can reduce the profiling of children. Children might have much more actual privacy if all sites providing services to those under 18 had these duties and consent was reserved only for the minors using services that post profiles for others to see.

### Parental consent and anonymity

Privacy and free speech advocates have expressed concern that mechanisms for verifiable parental consent implicitly identify website users, and that this identity is very reliable. As consent mechanisms spread, identity will be hardened and well authenticated across the Web. These anonymous Web arguments had some validity back in 1999, but today users are much more identifiable by web services, because of the rise of behavioral advertising. Services such as Facebook and Google have a very large number of authenticated users, and can easily identify these users and then track them ubiquitously on the Web through their advertising delivery and metrics systems, even when these users are not logged into Facebook or Google.[64] Age verification may have a corrosive effect on anonymity, but other threats to anonymity have far surpassed the COPPA.

---

[62] CONSUMER REPORTS MAG., THAT FACEBOOK FRIEND MIGHT BE 10 YEARS OLD, AND OTHER TROUBLING NEWS (n.d. 2011).

[63] Joseph Menn, *Social Networks Scan for Sexual Predators, with Uneven Results*, REUTERS (July 12, 2012).

[64] For instance, a user who signs into a real-name-required service such as Facebook can be comprehensively tracked on the Web, in an identifiable manner, on any website with a Facebook "Like" button.

## The role of the parent and the state

As discussed in Chapter 2, the FTC caused widespread anger when it proposed to regulate television advertising to children. COPPA has raised some of the same concerns about government regulating family matters. Particularly in the Washington DC libertarian community, critics have pointed to the need for parental responsibility, the need for consumer education, and targeted enforcement as alternatives to COPPA. More generally, critics call for cost–benefit analyses of COPPA.

There are several problems with this nanny-state critique of the FTC. First, most parents probably welcome (or could use) help in policing children's internet use. Like television before it, internet-connected devices are often convenient babysitters, yet the internet is worse than TV because it presents a different, unpredictable risk landscape.

Some analysts cavalierly dismiss risks of child predation from online interactions. In fact, the best research suggests that such incidents are exceedingly rare.[65] The problem is that even if these incidents are rare, anecdotes about child predation are extremely powerful in the policy setting. Child safety advocates know that predators are resourceful, motivated, and even organized in their victimization of children.[66] Parents cannot supervise every moment of their children's lives: protections such as COPPA can help reduce the risk that children get into trouble online.

Second, the leave-it-to-parents and the market argument ignores the pre-COPPA history. The Center for Media Education report in 1996 illustrated that manipulative techniques were used not just by marginal actors, but that they were widespread even among reputable businesses. Advertisements of the good old days were anything but good for children.

Finally, cost–benefit analysis is often employed to argue that COPPA imposes excessive costs, and a system of user empowerment and education is more cost-effective. But how much does such empowerment and education cost? Calls for cost–benefit analysis of COPPA do not calculate these expenses, and so they are not particularly rigorous, no matter how much the term is repeated and promulgated by their advocates.

Advocates for cost–benefit analysis frame the issue improperly – counting costs that services incur in compliance, and ignoring the transaction costs and impossible burdens that a world without COPPA would impose upon parents. A world without COPPA would shift the burden of ensuring adequate privacy and security onto parents, who would have to read policy after policy to protect their

---

[65] DANAH BOYD, IT'S COMPLICATED: THE SOCIAL LIVES OF NETWORKED TEENS (2014).

[66] Consider *US* v. *Paul*, 274 F.3d 155 (5th Cir. 2001): "According to the government, Paul also used his e-mail to advise fellow consumers of child pornography how to 'scout' single, dysfunctional parents and gain access to their children and to solicit the participation of like-minded individuals in trips to 'visit' children in Mexico."

children.[67] There is little reason to believe that even such activity would promote privacy. Parents would have no ability to vet the activities of vendors and service providers on any given site.[68]

The argument that user education is a less costly alternative to a regulatory regime has not been verified. Education costs money: in fact, good education is expensive. Yet, these costs are never calculated by those putting forth cost–benefit critiques of COPPA.

Furthermore, education is imperfect. Education has many pitfalls. Education is often not delivered, or delivered poorly. When education fails, the user bears all the risk and the blame for making a bad privacy choice.

Thus, a proper cost–benefit analysis would view COPPA as transferring of cost from millions of parents, who are responsible for vetting different services, to the services themselves that propose to profit from using child data. These services are in a much better position to investigate and police their own activities and the actions of their vendors than parents. In other words, COPPA internalizes these costs to service providers.

### Educational technology companies and COPPA

Schools across the nation, both public and private, have adopted "cloud-based" services to enhance productivity and to enable students to interact with their teachers online. Yet, the very purpose of many cloud-based services is to advertise, to create profiles of individuals, and to scan the content they produce. These purposes do not nicely align with the horizon-expanding, liberal purposes of education.

These services have to comply with both the COPPA and the Federal Educational Rights and Privacy Act of 1974, among other laws.[69] To address the COPPA consent issue, the FTC allows schools to give consent on behalf of the parent. However, school-based consent only allows the company to use information for its internal purposes, and for school purposes. It cannot employ the data for some commercial purpose, including behavioral advertising or building commercial profiles on users, without gaining verified parental consent.[70]

---

[67] Aleecia M. McDonald & Lorrie Faith Cranor, *The Cost of Reading Privacy Policies*, 4 I/S J. L. Pol'y Info. Soc'y 543, 564 (2008); George R. Milne, Mary J. Culnan, & Henry Greene, A *Longitudinal Assessment of Online Privacy Notice Readability*, 25 J. Pub. Pol'y Marketing 238, 243 (2006) (based on the growing length and complexity of privacy policies, a user would have to read eight pages of text per competitor to evaluate their privacy choices).

[68] *See generally* James P. Nehf, *Shopping for Privacy on the Internet*, 41 J. Consumer Aff. 351 (2007).

[69] Jules Polonetsky & Omer Tene, *Who Is Reading Whom Now: Privacy in Education from Books to MOOCs*, Vand. J. Ent. Tech. L. (2014).

[70] California law explicitly prohibits amassing profiles on students through educational technologies. See Cal. Bus. & Prof. Code §22584.

A 2013 report by Fordham University's Center on Law and Information Policy found widespread noncompliance with the COPPA among schools employing cloud-based services.[71] That report, the implosion of a well-funded school data management system (InBloom) over privacy issues,[72] and growing interest in the educational technology market led the Future of Privacy Forum to develop a Student Privacy Pledge in October 2014. Just months later, President Obama endorsed the Pledge, along with over 200 leading companies in education technology. The Student Privacy Pledge has significant pro-privacy commitments, such as promises to never sell student data, to not use behavioral advertising, to limit retention of data, and to limit the purposes for which data are collected.[73] It will complement COPPA by causing much of the education technology industry to make promises that can be policed under Section 5.

### Missed research opportunities

The COPPA rule is now fifteen years old. Because it imposes so many requirements on websites, COPPA created a natural test bed for the performance of privacy laws. Yet, the academic literature on COPPA is as thin as its legislative history. This is a missed opportunity, as comparative studies of non-COPPA versus COPPA sights could yield insight into the efficacy of privacy law.[74] What is known about COPPA is that there appear to be many child-directed sites that are not in compliance with it. A 2015 sweep by the Global Privacy Enforcement Network found that only 31 percent of child-directed websites had "protective controls to limit collection of personal info" and 41 percent had policies that "left sweepers feeling uncomfortable."[75] A report released the same day on child-directed mobile applications found that 46 percent "had privacy policies that could be viewed from a direct link on the app store page."[76]

### CONCLUSION

Privacy advocates might view children's privacy as a wedge that could drive adoption of privacy regulation for older internet users, but this is unlikely, because COPPA

---

[71] Joel Reidenberg, N. Cameron, Jordon Kovnot, Thomas B. Norton, Ryan Cloutier, & Daniela Alvarado, *Privacy and Cloud Computing in Public Schools*, Center on Law and Information Policy (2013).

[72] Jules Polonetsky & Omer Tene, *The Ethics of Student Privacy: Building Trust for Ed Tech*, 21 INT'L REV. INFO. ETHICS 25 (July 2014).

[73] FUTURE OF PRIVACY FORUM, K–12 SCHOOL SERVICE PROVIDER PLEDGE TO SAFEGUARD STUDENT PRIVACY (2014).

[74] One early, and apparently one-time, study was performed by the Annenberg Public Policy Center. JOSEPH TUROW, ANNENBERG PUBLIC POLICY CENTER, PRIVACY POLICIES ON CHILDREN'S WEBSITES: DO THEY PLAY BY THE RULES? (2000).

[75] GLOBAL PRIVACY ENFORCEMENT NETWORK, RESULTS OF THE 2015 GLOBAL PRIVACY ENFORCEMENT NETWORK SWEEP (2015).

[76] Kristin Cohen & Christina Yeung, *Kids' Apps Disclosures Revisited* (2015).

is seen as too burdensome by service operators. Services tend to comply with the law by fully embracing child-directed status, or by attempting to ban children from services. This trains children to lie about their age in order to use highly attractive, interactive services, and leaves them protected in the same way adults are online.

COPPA's genesis as part privacy measure, part security measure drove Congress and later the FTC to create a rule that attempts to perfect children's online experience. But this is not possible. There will always be risks to children because of the persistence and guile of child predators.

Counterintuitively, the risk to children could be reduced with a *weaker* COPPA. The real privacy protection in COPPA comes from its non-consent-related provisions, such as limits on data collection, use, and retention. The responsibility of services to examine vendors and third parties for their practices and security protects privacy much more than a regime where consumers must guess about protections based on privacy policies.

Less attention to perfecting parental consent – or no parental consent at all – could result in a savings that makes COPPA's other sensible provisions in reach of sites that serve young adults. Unfortunately, however, the FTC seems to be moving toward tightening parental consent requirements. Perhaps this is because the FTC finds it easier to police consent mechanisms, which its staff can evaluate through testing, than more nuanced data issues such as how long data are retained.

# 8

## Information security

Information security is a challenging and costly problem for organizations. There are always financial incentives to cut corners on security or to displace the costs of insecurity onto others. Unless organizations self-disclose security incidents, regulators, consumers, and other competitors cannot assign responsibility for insecure practices.

Appeals to "security" also enjoy a special status in political debates, where many assume that it is an apolitical, value-neutral good. More properly viewed, invocations of security can mask underlying political or economic goals, such as controlling how consumers use a product, or locking them into a service.[1] Promoting security for certain individuals can create insecurity for others. This will come into full focus in Chapter 9, where we discuss how various companies install software on customers' computers in order to secure their own intellectual or physical property but, in so doing, reduce the security of the user.

To address the problems of insecurity in products and services, the FTC's information security enforcement actions create a series of responsibilities that companies assume when they handle personal information. The Agency analyzes an organization's entire security practices to determine whether "taken together" insecure elements are deceptive or unfair. With the addition of staff technologists, the FTC's information security actions have become technically complex and delve into details regarding how specific technologies are implemented within an organization.[2]

The FTC's deception power is not a perfect tool for policing information security problems, because privacy policies are often too vague to account for particular security lapses. Thus, early in its enforcement strategy, the FTC relied upon unfairness to police insecurity. By 2010, however, the Agency pivoted back to use of the deception theory, and interpreted any statement about security – even anodyne ones

---

[1] David D. Clark, John Wroclawski, Karen R. Sollins, & Robert Braden, *Tussle in Cyberspace: Defining Tomorrow's Internet*, 13(3) IEEE/ACM TRANS. NETW. 462 (June 2005).

[2] David C. Vladeck, *Charting the Course: The Federal Trade Commission's Second Hundred Years*, 83 GEO. WASH. L. REV. ___ (2015).

such as "[we are] proud of the innovations we have made to protect your data and personal identity" – as an assurance to the consumer of reasonable security practices. Thus, contemporary information security matters invoke deception, but often have characteristics of unfairness theory cases. The Agency can also use its false advertising authority against companies that misrepresent the security of products.

Information security matters, at least in the beginning, were an uncontroversial way for the FTC to police online privacy. Security enforcement was compatible with the "harms-based" approach promoted by then Chairman Muris. Most information security cases – and even security-related testimony of the Agency before Congress – were supported by unanimous votes of commission members. The FTC has brought over fifty security enforcement actions. Its actions related to financial services firms are discussed in Chapter 10.

Recently, however, information security matters have become more controversial, with respondents claiming that they were deprived of due process as a result of the lack of a formal data security rule. Critics also argue that data security breaches cause no harm to individuals, and that the FTC cannot use unfairness to police such breaches. Much of the controversy stems from FTC pursuit of companies that experienced security breaches. For some, suing companies for having a security breach appears to be a form of punishing a victim, because these companies have often been attacked by malicious hackers. Nevertheless, in 2015, the Third Circuit Court of Appeals upheld the Commission's use of its unfairness power in information security cases, reasoning that companies were put on fair notice of security requirements based on previous agency statements and settlements with other companies.[3]

In light of these critiques, the FTC voted 4–0 in 2014 to release a statement reaffirming its commitment to policing information security and stressing that the "touchstone" of the Agency's approach was reasonableness. Issued on the occasion of the Agency's 50th data security action, it stated: "a company's data security measures must be reasonable and appropriate in light of the sensitivity and volume of consumer information it holds, the size and complexity of its business, and the cost of available tools to improve security and reduce vulnerabilities."[4] The reasonableness approach finds its roots in an advisory committee report completed fourteen years earlier,[5] and is reflected in security safeguards rules for financial services institutions (see Chapter 10).

This chapter presents a framework for understanding information security as a public good. Companies and governments alike tend to underinvest in information security and pass off costs of insecurity to others. Security also suffers from collective action challenges, as important actors who run networks, write software, or otherwise provide services have conflicting business incentives, or sometimes stand to benefit

---

[3]  *FTC v. Wyndham Worldwide Corp.*, No. 14-3514, 2015 WL 4998121 (3d Cir. August 24, 2015).

[4]  FTC, Commission Statement Marking the FTC's 50th Data Security Settlement, January 31, 2014.

[5]  FTC, FINAL REPORT OF THE FTC ADVISORY COMMITTEE ON ONLINE ACCESS AND SECURITY, May 15, 2000.

from insecurity. The public good aspect of security is explained in the context of payment systems. From there, the chapter discusses the FTC's information security cases. The FTC has been ambitious and proactive in its information security agenda, affirmatively pursuing technological problems that could result in harm, such as websites with common vulnerabilities that allowed hackers to extract personal information.

## INCENTIVE CONFLICTS AND INFORMATION SECURITY

Why does the market produce insecure products, services, and relationships among actors in the economy? In a seminal 2001 article, Professor Ross Anderson observed that even in competitive markets, insecure products tended to drive out secure ones.[6] Anderson explained that companies seek first-mover advantage. Companies know that reaching the market first – even with a flawed product – is better than reaching it later with a secure one. For users, moreover, evaluation of security is difficult, because it requires expertise to judge and is not as important as is price or design to consumers. Insecurity is a latent safety defect, only found, if at all, when something goes wrong, or, in the case of the internet, when many people try to make it go wrong. In fact, defects can exist in systems widely assumed to be secure for decades before they are found and they are difficult to address.

Anderson argued that when companies build security into services and products, it is sometimes merely done to transfer risk to others, or to enable differential pricing, or to cause customer lock-in, such as through digital rights management technologies. Anderson concluded that neither technology nor law alone would solve security problems. Instead, "the management of information security is a much deeper and more political problem than is usually realized; solutions are likely to be subtle and partial, while many simplistic technical approaches are bound to fail. The time has come for engineers, economists, lawyers and policymakers to try to forge common approaches." Consistent with Anderson's argument, this text grounds security as a political and economic problem, in addition to a technical one. All of these forces are on display in debates about the security of card payments, a serious and enduring problem for internet commerce.

### *Systemic insecurity and externalization of costs in the payment field*

Modern credit card payment systems, a major focus of FTC information security matters, display many of the pathologies that Anderson describes. These payment systems almost always prioritize speed and convenience over security. Consumers naturally flock to the most convenient payment mechanism. Thus, competitors

---

[6]  Ross Anderson, *Why Information Security Is Hard – An Economic Perspective*, Proceedings of the Computer Security Applications Conference (2001).

that introduce responsible security measures lose the marketplace to others that are faster yet less secure.

### Insecure account establishment

Prophetically, the first effective credit card campaign was successful because of a bad security decision: in 1958, the BankAmericard was sent to thousands of consumers, unsolicited and activated, through the mail.[7] Almost immediately, fraud became an issue. This caused Congress to enact the Truth in Lending Act, which placed a $50 liability ceiling ($300 in today's dollars) on unauthorized purchases (major networks waive this $50 fee).[8] More importantly for the credit card company, however, was that the mass mailing of unsolicited cards worked. Soon thereafter, other issuers copied the method.

---

#### THE FTC AS LION OR LAMB

While some argue that the FTC is too stringent – a rogue agency attacking the American economy[9] – at times Congress has critiqued it for being too lenient on business. This cajoling has come from Democrats and Republicans alike. In fact, about every ten years, a commission or report concludes that the FTC needs to focus on more structural cases and to eliminate unnecessary procedure. These sensible recommendations turn out to be difficult to implement, in part because when the FTC does prospective, structural work, it upsets a different critic: Congress.

In a larger sense, the Commission is unlikely to become "antibusiness" because success of the country is tied to the flourishing of the private sector.[10] Commission leadership understands that the Agency should do its job well without strangling the economy. A typical example of this comes from Chairman Earl Kintner, who addressing a consumer conference in 1959 said, "We could . . . distribute Federal policemen so thickly that no merchant would dare even to think about skirting the law. The public would be completely protected. Nothing would be stolen except our system of government and our freedom."[11]

---

[7] JOSEPH NOCERA, A PIECE OF THE ACTION: HOW THE MIDDLE CLASS JOINED THE MONEY CLASS (1994).

[8] 15 U.S.C. §1643; *see also* JAMES B. RULE, PRIVATE LIVES AND PUBLIC SURVEILLANCE: SOCIAL CONTROL IN THE COMPUTER AGE (1974).

[9] Hasin argued that the FTC was captured in the 1970s not by business but by consumerist activists who were anticorporate and used the Agency to attack big business. She described an "iron triangle" linking the FTC, the Senate Commerce Committee, and consumerists. BERNICE ROTHMAN HASIN, CONSUMERS, COMMISSIONS, AND CONGRESS: LAW, THEORY, AND THE FEDERAL TRADE COMMISSION, 1968–1985 (1987).

[10] CHARLES E. LINDBLOM, POLITICS AND MARKETS: THE WORLD'S POLITICAL-ECONOMIC SYSTEMS (1977).

[11] FEDERAL TRADE COMMISSION, OPENING REMARKS OF CHAIRMAN EARL W. KINTNER AT THE FTC'S CONFERENCE ON PUBLIC DECEPTION, December 21, 1959.

Insecurity in card issuance continues because banks have found ways to externalize some of the costs of fraud, and because it is more economical for them to acquire new customers quickly rather than more carefully evaluate credit applications. For instance, the author performed a study of actual victims of identity theft, in order to learn how their identity was stolen, and found that "In analyzing 16 applications pertaining to 6 victims of identity theft, it is clear that the most basic anti-fraud tools would have spotted errors impostors made when masquerading as the victims. For instance, [study subject five's] impostor was using the wrong date of birth and an invalid drivers license number – one never issued by the state."[12]

### Structural insecurity in the payment system

An additional issue to establishing a new credit card account is the insecurity of the payment system itself. Today's payment system still relies on consumers using the same credit card number over and over at hundreds of different merchants. Instead of introducing more complex cryptologic approaches, such as one-time-use charge numbers or PINs, payment companies have imposed greater secrecy obligations on merchants through contract.

These contractual safeguards, known as the Payment Card Industry Data Security Standard (PCI DSS), are difficult to comply with and allow payment companies to avoid costly infrastructure improvements by shifting risk to card-accepting merchants. A leave-it-to-the-market approach might be appropriate for such purposes, but consider that most merchants are completely dependent on revenue from card acceptance. Additionally, the payment industry has in effect codified PCI-DSS in three states. State legislatures have enacted laws requiring compliance with rules similar to PCI-DSS.[13]

Structural weaknesses set up retailers for failure. These weaknesses resulted in some of the FTC's most controversial information security cases. Merchants struggle to comply with the safeguards, which create a Sisyphean task, that of keeping a widely shared number secret. Smart hackers find ways to learn these numbers despite the safeguards, because if the credit card number is ever in plaintext (even for an instant when the credit card is swiped), hackers can capture it. Once the data are obtained, the merchant must notify the public of a breach. Then, state attorneys general and sometimes the FTC pursue the merchant. Banks and payment companies have successfully framed the problem as one of merchant security. The result is to draw the FTC away from structural insecurity issues. A critical reevaluation would place the focus back on the structure of our payment systems, and the underlying incentives that have produced its insecurity.

---

[12] Chris Jay Hoofnagle, *Internalizing Identity Theft*, 13 UCLA J. L. TECH. 1 (Fall 2009); *see also* NICOLE SAMANTHA VAN DER MEULEN, FERTILE GROUNDS: THE FACILITATION OF FINANCIAL IDENTITY THEFT IN THE UNITED STATES AND THE NETHERLANDS (2010).

[13] Minn. Stat. §325E.64; Nev. Rev. Stat. §603A.215; Rev. Code Wash. §19.255.020.

Credit card systems were developed in the physical payment space, where one assumes that the purchaser would appear in person, carry a token (the credit card), and attest to their authority to use it with a signature and perhaps an identification card. But distance selling invalidated the model's security assumptions. As the assumptions were invalidated, payments still was largely a system where consumers gave the same, single number to hundreds or even thousands of businesses.

In recent decades, payment companies have tested more secure alternatives. But competitors with more convenient or faster alternatives end up winning in the market. For instance, both Visa and MasterCard implemented password systems to help secure Web transactions. The system was inelegant, and if the consumer forgot the password, he would be likely to just use a different, less secure card. Thus, both credit card issuers and merchants who did not use the more secure system would over time see more sales.

Another example comes from token security. In Europe and the United Kingdom, consumers are issued "chip and PIN" credit and debit cards. These cards are more secure and expensive tokens. Chip and PIN cars require the consumer to enter a short password to authorize each transaction. US payment companies resisted chip and PIN adoption until 2015, and then implemented them as "chip and signature," dropping the PIN requirement. The stated rationale for this was that payment terminals are costly to replace and most could not accommodate chip and PIN cards. The real rationale was speed. Chip and PIN transactions take longer, and run the risk that the consumer will forget the PIN. Market incentives drove an insecure implementation of an otherwise more secure technology.

## Consumer security decision-making

Insecurity is not only the product of business practices. Users have great difficulty securing their information and in making sensible security decisions. User behavior, including preferences for convenience over more secure systems, contributes to insecurity.

Focusing on user behavior that lends itself to insecurity, Cormac Herley explained in a 2009 paper that "users' rejection of the security advice they receive is entirely rational from an economic viewpoint. The advice offers to shield them from the direct costs of attacks, but burdens them with increased indirect costs, or externalities. Since the direct costs are generally small relative to the indirect ones, they reject this bargain. Since victimization is rare, and imposes a one-time cost, while security advice applies to everyone and is an ongoing cost, the burden ends up being larger than the problem it addresses."[14] Herley concludes that one cannot

[14] Cormac Herley, *So Long, and No Thanks for the Externalities: The Rational Rejection of Security Advice by Users*, NSPW Oxford (2009).

label users lazy or dumb. Rather, the costs of basic security efforts outweigh the benefit of avoiding a small risk of being a victim.

The FTC seems to recognize that users are a source of security problems, and even cites to the problem that consumers tend to reuse passwords across sites (violating key security advice). Thus, a website that leaks users' passwords causes harm because those passwords are likely to unlock many different services.

### Information security as a public good

Professors Deirdre Mulligan and Fred Schneider have offered a useful rationale for marshaling regulatory and economic resources to promote security: the duo argue that security, like public health, is a public good.[15] They employ the example of vaccination to illustrate how public health requires some mandates to overcome collective action problems, because individually rational behavior can have disastrous consequences for the general public.[16] Specifically, to enjoy the herd immunity from vaccination, almost everyone must be vaccinated. But individuals who decide to avoid vaccination undermine this herd immunity protection. For these individuals, avoidance of vaccines is rational, so long as they can still benefit from herd immunity.

Switching to security, one may rationally avoid some security precaution because it is expensive or inconvenient, with the harms accruing to others or the public. An early example came from weak credit card payment data protection – encryption and other secure payment procedures were expensive. Cutting corners made sense for merchants because there was no obligation to notify others of breaches, detection was unlikely, and, if the data were stolen, banks and other merchants would foot the bill.

Similar dynamics are present in distributed denial of service (DDOS) attacks. DDOS occurs when a hacker takes over many others' computers in order to make it impossible to access some other electronic service. With a DDOS attack, a malicious hacker could temporarily shut down some internet-connected service, potentially costing a business money, or a government the ability to operate a critical function.[17] Protection against DDOS requires all users to employ antivirus software and to keep it updated. These requirements can be expensive and inconvenient, and the costs of not following them are borne by third parties.

The public health conception of information security provides several benefits. First, a public health lens broadens the scope of cost–benefit analysis for security regulation and enforcement. It thus accommodates the many varied costs of

---

[15]  Deirdre K. Mulligan & Fred B. Schneider, *Doctrine for Cybersecurity*, 140(4) DÆDALUS 70 (2011).

[16]  TOM SLEE, NO ONE MAKES YOU SHOP AT WAL-MART: THE SURPRISING DECEPTIONS OF INDIVIDUAL CHOICE (2006) (giving the example of littering as an individually rational behavior that is perverse on a societal level).

[17]  John Markoff, *Before the Gunfire, Cyberattacks*, N.Y. TIMES, August 12, 2008.

insecurity and recognizes that those costs can accrue to other actors who are not part of the decision to secure or not secure a system. It also can frame insecurity as a collective action problem, one that needs intervention in order to align conflicting incentives. Second, a public health lens provides a rationale for variegated approaches to security, most of which are preventative and not punitive. For instance, public health prioritizes individual education and decision-making in most matters and reserves more punitive, compulsory mandates only when there is a clear risk to society from individual decisions. Third, the public health concept could provide the FTC with a rationale that supports intervention against collective harms, and permit private ordering to take place where powerful economic actors can redress security problems. In this view, payment data insecurity might be best left to the market, with interventions only occurring to right wrongs and expenses that consumers pay.

### Internet security risks are different from physical ones

Internet security problems are different from physical world risks. First, someone can cause a breach accidently and not be aware of it at all, while in the physical world such accidental harms are more obvious.

Second, internet security breaches are culturally different. Some are caused by people who are merely curious about systems security. These "hackers" may wish to see whether they can circumvent another's system or otherwise learn about how computer systems work without malevolent intent to steal data or cause harm. Other intruders are malicious because they want to steal data for profit. Still other intruders wish to break into systems and expose users' data "for the lulz," that is, for the fun of it. The problem is that regardless of subjective intent, computer intrusions cause harm. Even an innocent, "white hat" hacker who probes a computer to learn more about it creates a serious headache for the system owner. A company suffering from such an event cannot determine the subjective intent of an intruder and, regardless of intent, must assess what the intruder accessed and may have stolen.

Finally, regardless of attacker motivation, internet attacks can be automated on a very large scale and conducted with little risk of detection or interdiction. These qualities make them different from physical security risks. If one were to leave their car unlocked for a night, chances are that no one would notice. Moreover, attacks on unlocked doors do not scale. On the internet, in contrast, many people with many different motivations constantly scan networks looking for an unlocked door or a window left open a crack. The different dynamics of the internet mean that small and even transient vulnerabilities in websites are very likely to be found.[18]

---

[18] Peter Swire, *A Model for When Disclosure Helps Security: What Is Different about Computer and Network Security?*, 3 J. TELECOM. HIGH TECH. L. 163 (2004).

*Unfairness as remedy for insecurity*

Combined, these economic factors point to unfairness as a viable theory for addressing information security. As shown in Chapter 3, a small harm to a large number of individuals can constitute "substantial consumer injury." Consumers can and do experience injury from security breaches, including embarrassment, fraudulent charges,[19] and even stalking.

Those who claim that security breaches cause no injury ignore several costs that come from breaches. First, fraudulent charges are passed on to the consumer. Banks and merchants estimate these costs to be in the hundreds of billions. Second, consumers experience transaction costs in disputing such charges. Third, different breaches present varied kinds of risks. Access to a checking account or debit card can be more problematic for a consumer than when a credit card number is stolen. Consumers – not attorneys familiar with FTC or financial services laws – are the relevant individuals for consumer protection efforts. Ordinary consumers are unlikely to be familiar with financial chargeback regulations.

Victims of security breaches have to live with the idea that some unknown person with unknowable motivations has their personal information and may try to profit from it through fraud or extortion. Revelation of this information – even basic information about websites visited or products purchased – can also be deeply embarrassing. In the medical context, some people go untreated or treat themselves so as to avoid the possibility that, somehow, others will learn that they were once treated for a loathsome disease or have had mental health treatment. Revealing clickstream data of personal research on these topics can also be just as damaging as leaking medical record about them.

The injuries caused by security breaches are unjustified because the breaches do not benefit competition or consumers. Security cases are a classic example where the FTC can intervene to stop practices that are common among all competitors.

Finally, insecurity is unavoidable harm because consumers cannot evaluate firms' security practices and select more careful competitors. Consumers often cannot even tell which among the many companies they frequent were the subject of a security problem. Because many insecure practices are shared among all competitors, consumers are deprived of alternatives.

---

[19] Many consumers pay their bills without examining every line of it, and thus end up paying fraudulent charges. Evidence for this comes from the pre-acquired account number telemarketing cases and others, where scammers' business model was just to charge cards and see who ended up not objecting. *See, for example, FTC v. Ideal Financial Solutions, Inc. et al.*, 213-cv-00143-MMD-GWF (D. Nev. 2013) (company with no consumer relationship billed $25 million in small increments to individuals, and then erected a complicated dispute process to frustrate refunds).

## THE INFORMATION SECURITY CASES

The FTC's deception power does not neatly address security problems. As explained in Chapter 6, the first deception cases involved clear promises and obvious transgressions. Security promises are not as explicit, often taking the form of general guarantees of "reasonable" care. Furthermore, security wrongs are so varied that a company is unlikely to promise to specifically avoid them. Consider the FTC's early matter concerning Eli Lilly in 2002.[20] The pharmaceutical company operated a website and e-mail list about Prozac, a very popular antidepressant. In shutting down the service, it sent notice to about 600 users of the e-mail list, but, in doing so, put all the e-mail addresses in the "To:" line. Thus, all subscribers were sent the e-mail addresses of all other subscribers. The American Civil Liberties Union petitioned the FTC to address the problem, and just six months later the Agency voted unanimously to settle the matter with Eli Lilly.

The FTC faced some challenges in policing this problem. First, in 2001 when the e-mail addresses were exposed, it was not clear that e-mail addresses were personal information. Early e-mail addresses were strings of numbers, and were not personalized.

Second, Eli Lilly made vague promises about using Secure Sockets Layer technology to protect confidentiality of the website, but it never specifically promised to not put users' e-mail addresses in the "To:" line of an e-mail. Nevertheless, the FTC declared that Eli Lilly's vague privacy policy was a promise. It read that the company "employs measures and takes steps appropriate under the circumstances to maintain and protect the privacy and confidentiality of personal information obtained from or about consumers through its Prozac.com and Lilly.com Web sites."[21] The FTC declared that the disclosure resulted from several security lapses: the failure to maintain internal controls, a lack of training, a lack of employee oversight, and a lack of testing.

Thus, the FTC's first security case required the Agency to read a great deal into a privacy policy. The FTC found a duty implied by mere mention of a security technology, one that was unrelated to e-mail lists, and unrelated to confidentiality. The first information security cases invoked both unfairness and deception without specifying which theory was applied.

### Structured Query Language injection

Following the Eli Lilly matter, the Agency focused on a common security vulnerability that enabled hackers to steal credit card information easily: the Structured

---

[20] *In the Matter of Eli Lilly and Company*, FTC File No. 012 3214 (January 18, 2002).

[21] A third possible tension exists: Should the Food and Drug Administration (FDA) police Eli Lilly's disclosure? The answer appears to be no – FDA polices labeling of products while the FTC polices advertising of them. The Eli Lilly site appeared to be a promotional site created for advertising purposes.

Query Language (SQL) injection. In an SQL injection attack, one tricks a company's database to reveal all of its contents. SQL injection was a problem in the early 2000s, because malicious actors could test many websites to discover the vulnerability, and, once discovered, the actors could quickly obtain all the credit card numbers used at the website.

In a series of settlements starting in 2003, the FTC argued that since the SQL injection problem was so well known, it was unfair or deceptive for a site not to protect itself against it.[22] Because these cases came from the early years of web commerce, the FTC could often find statements in a privacy policy assuaging user fears of entering a credit card number for payment. For instance, in the Petco matter, a site stated, "you never have to worry about the safety of your credit card information."[23] This made it easier for the Commission to justify a deception theory where SQL injection was present.

### Security breach notification

State security breach notification laws shaped the FTC's next phase of information security cases. In 2002, California enacted legislation that required notice to consumers of certain security breaches.[24] This statute became effective in July 2003, but it was not until 2005 that California's law gained national attention.

In 2005, ChoicePoint, a data broker, suffered a security breach where criminals gained access to the company's service posing as business operators.[25] They allegedly used the ChoicePoint service to steal others' identities. ChoicePoint investigated the breach, but the company could not initially tell how many individuals were affected. This was troubling given that ChoicePoint was a leader in the information-selling industry, and an expert in business authentication. While ChoicePoint presented the incident as first of its kind, within weeks reporters discovered a previous company breach with similar facts.[26] ChoicePoint stumbled again from a press relations perspective when it announced that it would give notice of the more recent breach, but only to Californians because it was not legally required to notify others.

[22] *In the Matter of Genica Corporation (d/b/a Computer Geeks Discount Outlet and Geeks.com)*, FTC File No. 082 3113 (February 5, 2009); *In the Matter of Life is good, Inc.*, FTC File No. 072 3046 (January 17, 2008); *In the Matter of Guidance Software, Inc.*, FTC File No. 062 3057 (November 16, 2006); *In the Matter of CardSystems Solutions, Inc.*, FTC File No. 052 3148 (February 23, 2006); *In the Matter of Guess?, Inc.*, FTC File No. 022 3260 (August 5, 2003).

[23] *In the Matter of Petco Animal Supplies, Inc.*, FTC File No. 032 3221 (November 8, 2004).

[24] Joseph Simitian, *How a Bill Becomes a Law, Really*, 24(3) BERK. TECH. L. J. 1009 (2009).

[25] *US v. ChoicePoint Inc.*, 1:06-cv-00198-GET (N.D. Ga. 2006). ChoicePoint was later acquired as LexisNexis Risk Solutions.

[26] David Colker & Joseph Menn, *ChoicePoint CEO Had Denied Any Previous Breach of Database, Derek Smith described a recent leak as 'the First Time' Despite an Earlier Scam Case*, LOS ANGELES TIMES, March 3, 2005 ("A pair of fraud artists pleaded guilty in a 2002 case in which at least 7,000 ChoicePoint records were accessed, leading to what prosecutors said was at least $1 million in fraudulent purchases.")

ChoicePoint's ham-handed approach caused attorneys general and lawmakers in other states to ask why their citizens would not also receive notice. It also led to legislative copycatting, and now forty-seven states, along with the District of Columbia, Guam, Puerto Rico, and the Virgin Islands, have state security breach notification laws.[27]

Generally speaking, security breach notification laws require a company to disclose to its customers, and sometimes to regulators and/or the news media, unauthorized access to name combined with an enumerated list of trigger data: credit card numbers, Social Security numbers, and drivers' license numbers. Some states have broadened trigger data to include medical information, biometric identifiers, passwords, and even signature. If the stolen data were encrypted, the company is under no duty to give notification. Thus, security breach notification laws create strong incentives to collect less trigger information, to encrypt it, or to segment it technologically so that name was separate from other trigger information.

Security breach notification laws created a target-rich environment for commission enforcement. A series of massive data breaches occurred at retailers that were sending payment information over their wireless networks. This allowed hackers to eavesdrop on the transmissions and penetrate the networks, sometimes without even entering the store.

The FTC brought administrative matters against three companies targeted by the wireless network attacks: BJ's Wholesale;[28] DSW,[29] a discount shoe retailer; and the TJX retail chain.[30] These actions were important for several reasons: First, the companies were victims of an attack. Under tort law, individuals are generally not responsible for the criminal actions of third parties. But in these and later cases, the FTC found that the data holder had a responsibility to protect personal information from criminals. Just as banks must protect customers' money from bank robbers, the FTC has established a duty among companies to protect consumers from data theft or misuse. And this duty follows data wherever they are taken. For instance, in later cases, employees whose computers were stolen from locked cars violated Section 5 for keeping unencrypted data on movable media. Nevertheless, companies that were victims of security breaches felt twice victimized by FTC investigators.

Second, in the 2005 DSW matter, the FTC first employed language indicating that a series of bad security practices "taken together" failed to provide a reasonable level of security for personal information. This was the first of many security cases where a combination of practices explicitly justified the unfairness label. In later cases, the Agency would label insecure practices "taken together" as deceptive if the respondent made some claim, even a vague one, about its commitments to security.

---

[27] National Conference of State Legislatures, State Breach Notification Laws (January 12, 2015).
[28] *In the Matter of BJ's Wholesale Club, Inc.*, FTC File No. 042 3160 (September 23, 2005).
[29] *In the Matter of DSW Inc.*, FTC File No. 052 3096 (December 1, 2005).
[30] *In The Matter of The TJX Companies, Inc.*, FTC File No. 072 3055 (March 27, 2008).

Finally, in unfairness matters, the FTC must demonstrate substantial injury to *consumers* from security breaches, a factor that has frustrated attempts by private plaintiffs when bringing suit against companies for insecurity. Under the 15 U.S.C §45(n) limitation that unfairness only consider substantial injury to *consumers*, the Agency probably cannot invoke losses to banks from fraudulent charges. In its enforcement actions, the FTC has argued that substantial consumer injury flowed from the lost opportunity costs and small out-of-pocket costs from losing access to a checking account and from the inconvenience of having to have one's credit cards reissued,[31] and in TJX, the inconvenience associated with requesting new driver license or Social Security numbers.

### Security rules begin to emerge

The security breach cases also caused the FTC to make more rule-like statements for information systems. In the Reed Elsevier/Seisint matter, unauthorized individuals gained access to the company's data broker service because of a weak credentialing process. The complaint suggests attackers could guess the usernames and passwords of authorized users because Seisint did not use transport encryption (SSL), because it permitted usernames and passwords that were similar or the same, because clients did not have to change their password every ninety days, and because clients of Seisint were using shared login credentials, among other reasons. Taken together, the FTC concluded these practices to be unfair.

The matter was the first where the FTC's complaint looked as though it might be setting rules for security, such as a ninety-day password change requirement. A practitioner reading the Seisint matter might conclude that all of the password policies identified by the FTC were mandatory to avoid unfairness. However, it was the combination of bad practices that was ruled as unfair, rather than one single practice.

---

#### FREE MARKETS AND CONSUMER PROTECTION

For decades, the Commission has had critics that have argued that if the market were just allowed to operate freely, consumer problems would be solved without intervention by the government. Any given commission proceeding receives this critique – despite being invoked on different subjects, the argument always rhymes. Consider this historical one concerning cigarette safety:

> Competitive pressures should induce cigarette companies to search out
> ways of making their cigarettes less toxic and should evoke efforts to devise

---

[31] *In the Matter of CardSystems Solutions, Inc.*, FTC File No. 052 3148 (February 23, 2006).

a nontoxic substitute for cigarettes. Both forces have been at work. Cigarette companies have striven to reduce the tar and nicotine content of their tobaccos and to improve filtration, and ingenious people have invented cigarettes that contain lettuce or some other allegedly harmless tobacco substitute. In the ordinary course one would expect cigarette companies to advertise that a particular brand was safer than competitors' – thereby tipping the industry's hand, for such advertising unmistakably implies that there is a health hazard – and for the inventors of nontobacco cigarettes to advertise that their products, unlike tobacco cigarettes, are safe. Competition should thus cause the information barrier eventually to crumble. It is a profound irony that for years the FTC, encouraged by cigarette companies that feared the process I have described, forbade the disclosure in advertising of the tar or nicotine content of any cigarette brands.[32]

The critic is Judge Richard A. Posner (then University of Chicago professor). Evidence that cigarette smoking was dangerous began to emerge in the late 1930s, and the FTC brought its first cases against the industry in 1942.[33] Cigarette companies failed to make safer cigarettes, and the metrics tobacco companies used to imply safety, such as tar and "light" cigarettes, were specious, yet believed by Posner. In the public health battle surrounding smoking, the information-forcing interventions[34] favored by Posner and other market adherents have been less efficacious than structural changes, such as bans on smoking in the workplace, that make smoking inconvenient.

Perhaps the Seisint case demonstrates risks from creating rules through enforcement actions. Some of the FTC's guidance from the Seisint matter could result in reduced security in other enterprises. The recommendations to use complex passwords and to change them every ninety days could reduce security, because most individuals cannot remember their ever-changing passwords and might keep lists of them on sticky notes near their computer. And when they forget the password, they use password reset options that themselves cause security risks. For these reasons, enterprises should not follow these security pronouncements by rote, but select policies that, taken together, ultimately produce security rather than insecurity.

---

[32] Report of the ABA Commission to Study the Federal Trade Commission (September 15, 1969).
[33] NORMAN I. SILBER, TEST AND PROTEST: THE INFLUENCE OF CONSUMERS UNION (1983).
[34] Dennis Leary joked that it "[d]oesn't matter how big the warnings are. You could have cigarettes that were called the warnings. You could have cigarettes that come in a black pack, with a skull and a cross bone on the front, called tumors and smokers would be lined up around the block . . ."

*Sophisticated security analysis of physical data and devices*

The FTC's addition of staff technologists in 2010 changed the character of information security complaints. FTC complaints subsequently concerned practices that would have been outside the Agency's expertise in previous years. For instance, the Agency brought two cases faulting companies for how they *implemented* transport encryption (protection for data while they are being transmitted).

The FTC's understanding of information security threats is now more complex. Many conceive of "outsiders" – people not affiliated with the organization – as the main security threat. This assumption becomes coded into relationships, with implicit trust given to developers (even third-party developers) and employees.[35] However, security threats come from both inside and outside institutions, and some of the most damaging are those that combined corrupt employees with outsiders. The FTC's more recent cases focus on third-party vendors. These cases impose an obligation on companies with consumer relationships to obtain contractual and other guarantees that bind service providers to privacy and security constraints.

---

### THE PROMISES OF INNOVATION

Technology pundits argue forcefully that privacy is getting in the way of free-dom-enhancing technologies and making us less safe and less accountable to others. They argue that we are on the cusp of a new society with new, transcendent freedoms. Consider this argument:

> The democratizing impact of the Internet has been strikingly similar to the historic impact of printing. Even in this, the Internet's first half-century, we have seen its power to disband armies, to cashier presidents, to create a whole new democratic world – democratic in ways never before imagined, even in America. We cannot ignore the fact that the era when the Internet became a universal engrossing American experience, the first era when Americans everywhere could witness in living colors the Occupy Movements, the popularization of protests on an unprecedented scale, the new era for minority power, the newly potent public intervention in foreign policy ... The Arab Spring was the first war which was a Internet experience ...[36]

---

[35] KATHERINE LOSSE, THE BOY KINGS (2012) (Facebook "looked away from the fact that almost all of Facebook users' data was available to them [third-party developers] through the platform. Technically, they were supposed to scrub their servers of the data every twenty-four hours but, if they didn't, we had no way of knowing"); DAVID KIRKPATRICK, THE FACEBOOK EFFECT (2010).

[36] This quote is adapted from DANIEL BOORSTIN, THE REPUBLIC OF TECHNOLOGY (1978).

This was an exercise suggested by Evgeny Morozov in his book *The Net Delusion*.[37] The above quote was by Daniel Boorstin and described television, the Civil Rights Movement, and the Vietnam War. It is adapted here to show how comfortably broad, Pollyannaish claims about innovation can be made about any technology.

The FTC has also brought a series of cases to promote security even when data leave the premises of a company. For instance, a medical service provider experienced a breach when an employee's backpack was stolen from a car. The backpack contained physical media with unencrypted customer information.[38] The case also signaled that the FTC is interested in data throughout their life cycle, and sees excessively long retention periods (for instance, in backups) of personal information as a security risk that has to be protected by more stringent measures.

The addition of staff technologists shaped one of the most important matters in recent years: the case against the cell phone manufacturer HTC. Software developers have largely been given a legal pass for insecure products. The FTC's HTC matter showed that the Agency would hold *device makers* responsible for embedded software. This policy will become very important as the "internet of things" is deployed.

In the HTC matter, the phone maker installed "bundled software" on handsets that the user could not remove. This bundled software circumvented privacy and security controls that were present in the phones' Android operating systems, which, by default, restricted third-party applications from accessing a phone's microphone, functions (such as sending text messages), and diagnostic logging information. The FTC termed these oversights as both unfair, because they undermined the devices' privacy and security controls in a fundamental way, but also as deceptive because of statements in HTC's user manuals.[39] HTC's bundled software could be seen as malware – programs that enable profound privacy invasions.

### Information security duties

Taken together, the FTC's security matters imply a series of duties that all companies – from online service providers to device makers – assume when collecting personal information:

- *Appropriate internal controls.* Companies must have internal measures to protect sensitive personal information. These include designating employees

---

[37] EVGENY MOROZOV, THE NET DELUSION (2012).
[38] *In the Matter of CBR Systems, Inc.*, FTC File No. 112 3120 (January 28, 2013).
[39] *In the Matter of HTC America Inc.*, FTC File No. 122 3049 (February 22, 2013).

to be responsible for security; having an incident response plan to address security lapses;[40] establishing access controls that limits data to certain, authorized users;[41] securing corporate wireless networks;[42] requiring the use of strong passwords by employees;[43] and requiring the use of mechanisms to prevent outsiders on the internet to access corporate computers, such as firewalls.[44]

- *Controls on credit card data.* Credit card networks impose a duty on card-accepting merchants to properly[45] encrypt credit card data and to not retain them for longer than necessary for business purposes. Violating these duties can rise to an unfairness action[46] or a deception one where claims of protection are made.[47] Other credit card data protections that the FTC has suggested include IP address range specification,[48] data loss prevention technologies,[49] and isolation of credit card processing equipment from other networking infrastructure.[50] Additionally, the FTC has brought cases against pharmacies and financial institutions for failing to securely dispose of information.[51]
- *Controls on users, vendors, and service providers.* Companies have a duty to properly supervise vendors that receive customers' personal information.[52] Backup services that are holding data in an unencrypted format, or holding them for longer than necessary for business purposes, can breach information security obligations.[53] But, more generally, the FTC views companies as

---

[40] *In the Matter of Franklin's Budget Car Sales, Inc.*, FTC File No. 102 3094 (October 26, 2012); *In the Matter of EPN, Inc.*, FTC File No. 112 3143 (October 26, 2012).

[41] *In the Matter of DSW Inc.*, FTC File No. 052 3096 (December 1, 2005); *In the Matter of BJ's Wholesale Club, Inc.*, FTC File No. 042 3160 (September 23, 2005).

[42] *In the Matter of DSW Inc.*, FTC File No. 052 3096 (December 1, 2005); *In the Matter of BJ's Wholesale Club, Inc.*, FTC File No. 042 3160 (September 23, 2005).

[43] *In the Matter of Twitter, Inc.*, FTC File No. 092 3093 (June 24, 2010); *In The Matter of The TJX Companies, Inc.*, FTC File No. 072 3055 (March 27, 2008); *In the Matter of CardSystems Solutions, Inc.*, FTC File No. 052 3148 (February 23, 2006).

[44] *In The Matter of The TJX Companies, Inc.*, FTC File No. 072 3055 (March 27, 2008); *In the Matter of Life is good, Inc.*, FTC File No. 072 3046 (January 17, 2008); *In the Matter of CardSystems Solutions, Inc.*, FTC File No. 052 3148 (February 23, 2006).

[45] *US v. ValueClick, Inc., Hi-Speed Media, Inc., and E-Babylon, Inc.*, CV08-01711MMM (RZx) (C.D. Cal. 2008)(alphabetic substitution encryption was weaker than industry standard encryption).

[46] *In The Matter of The TJX Companies, Inc.*, FTC File No. 072 3055 (March 27, 2008); *In the Matter of DSW Inc.*, FTC File No. 052 3096 (December 1, 2005); *In the Matter of BJ's Wholesale Club, Inc.*, FTC File No. 0423160 (September 23, 2005).

[47] *In the Matter of Genica Corporation (d/b/a Computer Geeks Discount Outlet and Geeks.com)*, FTC File No. 082 3113 (February 5, 2009); *In the Matter of Life is good, Inc.*, FTC File No. 072 3046 (January 17, 2008).

[48] *In the Matter of Dave & Buster's, Inc.*, FTC File No. 082 3153 (March 25, 2010).

[49] *Id.*

[50] *Id.*

[51] *In the Matter of Rite Aid Corporation*, FTC File No. 072 3121 (July 27, 2010); *In the Matter of CVS Caremark Corporation*, FTC File No. 072 3119 (February 18, 2009); *In the Matter of Nations Title Agency, Inc., Nations Holding Company, and Christopher M. Likens*, FTC File No. 052 3117 (May 10, 2006)

[52] *In the Matter of CBR Systems, Inc.*, FTC File No. 112 3120 (January 28, 2013).

[53] *Id.*

having a responsibility to ensure that vendors have security policies.[54] In one case, the FTC faulted a company for transferring more sensitive customer data than necessary to service providers.[55]

- *Controls on sensitive personal data.* Companies that have sensitive data must implement special client protections. First, they must vet their clients' identities to ensure they are not criminals or otherwise using their access for malicious purposes.[56] Once accounts are established, other protections should be in place, including complex password requirements,[57] a requirement for users to have different log-ins (to differentiate among users of the service), and monitoring these accounts for password guessing, errors, and password resets requested by unauthorized individuals.[58] The FTC faulted Seisint for failing to require users to create new passwords every 90 days for accounts that could access sensitive data.[59]

- *Controls on specially regulated data.* The FTC deemed it unfair for Equifax to sell prescreening lists, which are regulated by the Fair Credit Reporting Act (see Chapter 10), to Direct Lending, a company that used the data for other purposes. Additionally, Equifax did not verify the identity of buyers of consumer reports or uses given to the data by other organizations working with Direct Lending.[60]

- *Risk assessment.* Companies must make efforts to identify reasonably foreseeable internal and external risks to the security, confidentiality, and integrity of personal information. They must also update these assessments.[61]

- *Prevent well-known attacks on confidentiality and avoid obvious security holes.* FTC attorneys look to the SANS Institute and Open Web Application Security Project (OWASP) lists of common security vulnerabilities to identify case priorities. These include Structured Query Language injection,[62] cross-site scripting attacks,[63] failure to ensure session control that allows one to look up

---

[54] *In the Matter of foru International Corporation formerly known as Genewize Life Sciences, Inc.,* FTC File No. 112 3095 (May 12, 2014).

[55] *Id.*

[56] *US* v. *ChoicePoint Inc.,* 1:06-cv-00198-GET (N.D. Ga. 2006); *see also In the Matter of Equifax Information Services LLC,* FTC File No. 102 3252 (October 10, 2012).

[57] *FTC* v. *LifeLock, Inc.,* 2:10cv00530 (D. Az. 2010).

[58] *In the Matter of Twitter, Inc.,* FTC File No. 0923093 (June 24, 2010); *FTC* v. *LifeLock, Inc.,* 2:10cv00530 (D. Az. 2010); *In the Matter of Reed Elsevier Inc. and Seisint, Inc.,* FTC File No. 0523094 (March 27, 2008).

[59] *In the Matter of Lookout Services, Inc.,* FTC File No. 102 3076 (May 3, 2011); *In the Matter of Reed Elsevier Inc. and Seisint, Inc.,* FTC File No. 052 3094 (March 27, 2008).

[60] *In the Matter of Equifax Information Services LLC,* FTC File No. 102 3252 (October 10, 2012); *see also US* v. *Rental Research Services, Inc.,* 0:09-cv-00524 (D. Minn. 2009).

[61] *In the Matter of Eli Lilly and Company,* FTC File No. 012 3214 (January 18, 2002).

[62] *In the Matter of Guess?, Inc.,* FTC File No. 022 3260 (August 5, 2003).

[63] *US* v. *RockYou, Inc.,* 312-cv-01487-SI (N.D. Cal. 2012).

the orders or information of other users,[64] storing passwords in unencrypted cookies,[65] failing to regularly apply security updates and patches,[66] failing to use antivirus software on employee computers,[67] storing passwords in unencrypted files,[68] running peer-to-peer sharing software on computers with customer records such that it exposes the records to others on the network,[69] failure to validate Security Sockets Layer certificates,[70] and storing sensitive personal information in unencrypted formats.[71]

- *Training.* Many of the FTC's matters fault companies for not training employees. It is clear that the FTC thinks that all companies that handle personal information should have reasonable data security training for employees.

- *Testing.* Companies must test or otherwise check controls for potential security problems.[72] Companies must have some means to know when security breaches have occurred.[73] For instance, in the 2008 matter concerning the data broker Seisint, the company allowed clients to use shared log-in accounts, thus making it difficult to track individual users who were making suspicious use of the service.[74] Other companies were faulted for not paying attention to security researchers who attempted to contact companies with vulnerabilities,[75] and one recent case suggested that a respondent should have had a dedicated way to communicate security vulnerabilities to the company, a kind of hotline to report security problems.[76] Thus, companies should think creatively to identify the kinds of incidents that would signal that their information security program is out of date, or has failed in some way.

- *Comply with security promises.* Companies that make specific technical promises must comply with them.[77] Furthermore, comparative claims that a

---

[64] *In the Matter of Lookout Services, Inc.*, FTC File No. 102 3076 (May 3, 2011); *In the Matter of MTS, Inc., doing business as Tower Records/Books/Video*, FTC File No. 032 3209 (June 2, 2004).

[65] *In the Matter of Reed Elsevier Inc. and Seisint, Inc.*, FTC File No. 052 3094 (March 27, 2008).

[66] *FTC v. LifeLock, Inc.*, 2:10cv00530 (D. Az. 2010); *In The Matter of The TJX Companies, Inc.*, FTC File No. 072 3055 (March 27, 2008).

[67] *FTC v. LifeLock, Inc.*, 2:10cv00530 (D. Az. 2010).

[68] *US v. RockYou, Inc.*, 312-cv-01487-SI (N.D. Cal. 2012).

[69] *In the Matter of Franklin's Budget Car Sales, Inc.*, FTC File No. 102 3094 (October 26, 2012); *In the Matter of EPN, Inc.*, FTC File No. 1123143 (October 26, 2012).

[70] *In the Matter of Credit Karma, Inc.*, FTC File No 1323091 (March 28, 2014).

[71] *In the Matter of foru International Corporation formerly known as Genewize Life Sciences, Inc.*, FTC File No. 112 3095 (May 12, 2014).

[72] *In the Matter of Eli Lilly and Company*, FTC File No. 012 3214 (January 18, 2002).

[73] *In the Matter of CVS Caremark Corporation*, FTC File No. 072 3119 (February 18, 2009); *In the Matter of CardSystems Solutions, Inc.*, FTC File No. 052 3148 (February 23, 2006); *In the Matter of DSW Inc.*, FTC File No. 052 3096 (December 1, 2005); *In the Matter of BJ's Wholesale Club, Inc.*, FTC File No. 042 3160 (September 23, 2005).

[74] *In the Matter of Reed Elsevier Inc. and Seisint, Inc.*, FTC File No. 0523094 (March 27, 2008).

[75] *In the Matter of HTC America Inc.*, FTC File No. 122 3049 (February 22, 2013).

[76] *In the Matter of Fandango, LLC*, FTC File No. 1323089 (March 28, 2014).

[77] *FTC v. ControlScan, Inc.*, 10-CV-0532 (N.D. Ga. 2010); *FTC v. Sandra L. Rennert et al.*, CV-S-00-0861-JBR (D. Nev. 2000).

service is more secure than another must not be misleading.[78] Even using "security" in the name of a product can be a misleading representation. For instance, in one matter, the FTC found a company's use of the trade name "SecurView" implied that its products were reasonably secure.[79]

## Online security remedies

The FTC's information security remedies are modeled on the Gramm–Leach–Bliley security rule, discussed in Chapter 10. These remedies typically require a respondent to have a security program with sufficient administrative, technical, and physical safeguards for the security, confidentiality, and integrity of personal information. These safeguards should be appropriate to the company's size and complexity.

From a distance, such security program seems simple. Close up, the details of a successful program are complex. Programs require employee training and management; assessments of network, software, and systems design; smart design of information systems, including how they store, transmit, and dispose of information; and even systems for detecting future security problems.

Credentials are important to the FTC as well. The Agency has long specified that security assessments should be conducted by persons with certifications in information security. Assessment periods can last for twenty years, and there are cases where lapses in compliance triggered fines. For instance, in 2009, ChoicePoint reported to the FTC that a monitoring system was not implemented for a short period of time, and that an unknown person accessed personal information of 13,000 individuals. ChoicePoint and the FTC stipulated a $275,000 penalty as a result of the lapse.

### CONCLUSION

Today the FTC reads any representation about security – even a trade name that suggests a secure product – as a promise to provide "reasonable" security. In a series of cases, it has developed general security standards that have become more rule-like over time. Some cases were the product of the FTC proactively investigating the claims or technology weaknesses of a company, while others come in response to security breaches. In security breach cases, some companies thus feel as though the FTC is punishing the victim of a crime. Chapter 12 will return to this issue and explain why the FTC Section 5 powers are a good fit for policing information security. The chapter will also make recommendations for focusing this power to address systemic problems with insecurity.

---

[78] *In the Matter of Microsoft Corp.*, FTC File No. 012 3240 (August 8, 2002).
[79] *In the Matter of TRENDnet, Inc.*, FTC File No. 122 3090 (January 16, 2014).

# 9

# Anti-marketing efforts: e-mail, telemarketing, and malware

Privacy protections can take many forms. These include rights to access and correction of false or incomplete data as well as limitations on how data are used. Privacy laws create rights and obligations concerning data. The "anti-marketing laws" are different: instead of regulating data use or collection, they limit how businesses *contact* individuals. Originally enacted to help protect against misuse of limited bandwidth resources, anti-marketing laws now are more important to shielding individuals' attention from overwhelming numbers of commercial offers and other distracting messages. As such, these are privacy problems that speak to seclusion and access to the self, rather than issues surrounding fair treatment of data.

Anti-marketing regulation has many complex attributes, including opt-in and opt-out restrictions, advertiser liability, bond requirements, labeling requirements, and even criminal sanctions for some kinds of activities. Anti-malware efforts, still governed by Section 5, are similar to the online privacy cases visited in Chapter 6.

In political debates, the value of "technology neutrality" is often touted. However, anti-marketing laws tend to be technology-specific.[1] That is, anti-marketing laws focus on how a company uses a specific method or technology to contact an individual. This approach reflects the reality that different marketing technologies present varied opportunities for regulation. For instance, an opt-out registry to avoid telemarketing was a fantastic success, while the FTC determined that such an approach to police e-mail would be perverse. Technical specificity also means that as technology produces new means to gain one's attention, existing rules may not capture new forms of annoyance.

First Amendment concerns also require technological specificity in marketing regulation. Historically, the Supreme Court has permitted different levels of government intervention based on the medium involved, such as broadcast, newspapers, and internet. Technologies such as the phone and e-mail impose different

---

[1] Paul Ohm, *The Argument against Technology Neutral Surveillance Laws*, 88 TEX. L. REV. 1685 (2010); Bert-Jaap Koops, Miriam Lips, Sjaak Nouwt, Corien Prins, & Maurice Schellekens, *Should ICT Regulation Be Technology-Neutral?*, in Starting Points for ICT Regulation (Bert-Jaap Koops, Mariam Lips, Corien Prins, & Maurice Schellekens, eds.).

costs on the speaker and recipient and afford different opportunities for preventing or shifting those costs. Thus, a technology-neutral marketing law could only be written in a vague way, perhaps mandating a right to block being contacted in principle, but without specifying the mechanism for such blocking.

Anti-marketing laws bring into contrast the regulatory approaches favored by the FTC and the market-based approaches favored by economists, including those at the FTC itself. The lawyer-driven tradition of the FTC militates in favor of intricate, seemingly impossible-to-circumvent restrictions on marketing. But, somehow, clever marketers find ways around the rules. Direct marketing is also a major vector for fraud, and committed fraudsters will seek to earn as much money as possible while evading detection.

Many economists and some lawyers see great waste in legalistic approaches to unwanted marketing. Instead of intricate legal rules, they favor technical approaches to better match consumers and marketers. For instance, Professor Eric Goldman, in his article "A Coasean Analysis of Marketing," makes a strong case against technology-specific marketing laws.[2] Goldman argues that anti-marketing regulations increase costs to senders, are insensitive to the costs borne by advertisers, and are ignore the desire of consumers to receive marketing.

Indeed, advertising has social utility, and, while consumers complain about advertising, they may have latent, unexpressed preferences for receiving more of it that is appropriate to their desires and needs. The tussle between advertisers and consumers is thus seen as wasted effort. Advertisers struggle to send marketing, while some consumers fight to block it and to litigate cases.

Goldman proposes a technological alternative to regulatory approaches that eliminates this advertiser–consumer tussle. In his thought experiment, he terms it the "Coasean filter." The Coasean filter would "monitor consumers to costlessly read their minds and effectuate their preferences by filtering unwanted content and soliciting wanted content. Coasean filters would improve consumer and social welfare by helping consumers get what they want without incurring significant costs to manifest their preferences."[3]

Entrepreneurs have sought to make real Goldman's vision. For instance, in the 1990s and early 2000s, companies proposed "infomediaries," services that would store personal data and license access to them on a trusted basis to advertisers.[4] Bethany Leickly published the most careful study of these companies, which essentially acted as data brokers organized in cooperative arrangements, with profits flowing to data subjects. Even Microsoft offered a version of such a service. Yet, in the end, all infomediaries failed in the marketplace because consumers did not trust

---

[2] Eric Goldman, *A Coasean Analysis of Marketing*, 2006 WIS. L. REV. 1151 (2006).
[3] *Id.*
[4] Bethany L. Leickly, Intermediaries in Information Economies (2004) (Ph.D. dissertation, Georgetown University).

them and because they did not provide value to businesses. Infomediaries never attracted a critical mass of adoption.

For infomediaries to work, there would have to be some strong economic or legal force to require marketers to use them and not to obtain information from substitutes such as data brokers. With Professor Jan Whittington, I have argued that infomediaries failed in part because of a lack of baseline privacy laws. We argue: "even if the economics of these models were sound, the models would fail precisely because the diffusion of personal information in the marketplace makes it possible for marketers to obtain personal information from other sources with fewer restrictions on its use. Because data are public – sometimes in the sense that the data are in public records – information buyers are free to go to lower cost (lower in price and in privacy restrictions) alternatives, such as data brokers, in order to obtain targeting information on consumers."[5]

On the political front, utopian schemes to perfect the matching of marketers and consumers have been viewed skeptically by the lawyers of the FTC. While there are earnest believers in such systems, companies opportunistically promote them in order to avoid having their marketing channels regulated. For instance, when the FTC was considering new telemarketing regulations, lobbyists for sales callers seemed willing to adopt a proposal where callers would pay consumers to listen to telemarketing. But the proposal was merely an instrument to ward off regulation. Telemarketers never adopted a pay-the-consumer model, nor did they make efforts to introduce it formally as a legal approach. Furthermore, without a legal framework to implement and enforce such a pay-per-call telemarketing system, such proposals lack credibility.

---

### DOES PRIVACY LAW WORK?

This provocative question was posed by Robert Gellman in a 1997 essay that explores the federal Privacy Act of 1974.[6] Gellman concluded that the Privacy Act largely failed to control the expansion of government personal information databases and matching of citizen data among agencies, but compared the act's failures to the wiretapping law, which he found to be successful.

The Privacy Act's failures are found in its vagueness, the social utility of computer matching, the intangible harms caused by government databases, and – crucially – its lack of a vigorous regulator. On the other hand, the wiretapping law regulates a much more specific and clearly harmful activity, it was backed by Fourth Amendment constitutional guarantees, wiretapping

---

[5]  Chris Jay Hoofnagle & Jan Whittington, *Unpacking Privacy's Price*, 90 N. CAROLINA L. REV. 1327 (2012).
[6]  Robert Gellman, *Does Privacy Law Work?*, in TECHNOLOGY AND PRIVACY: THE NEW LANDSCAPE (Philip E. Agre & Marc Rotenberg, eds., 1997).

takes place among a relatively small group of law enforcement, and, finally, it is overseen by federal judges and can be enforced by private plaintiffs.

Gellman's analysis militates strongly in favor of more narrow, technology- or industry-specific regulation, and in favor of stronger oversight of rules.[7]

Returning to Coasean filtering, the approach could be seen as a privacy-*protecting* alternative to online advertising. Current online advertising systems are akin to a one-way mirror. Goldman's Coasean filter would be a one-way filter. Implemented as software running on the user's computer, a Coasean filter could select advertising without ever revealing insights about the user to other parties. In fact, it could be engineered so that advertisers themselves never learn who the consumer is or even what ads they see.[8] The data in the filter, unlike online advertising data, would be protected by the Fourth Amendment because the data would never be transferred to a third party and avoid the "third-party doctrine" exception to constitutional protection.

Thus, while Goldman's proposal appears creepy at first, a careful look shows it to have substantial privacy benefits. Many consumers would happily jettison all the tracking and distraction inherent in behavioral advertising if they could limit marketing to just what appears from Goldman's one-way filter.

This chapter discusses the FTC's policing of anti-marketing laws, which are related to malware, spam, and telemarketing. Legal regulation of spam has failed, in part because Congress mistakenly thought it possible to use reputational and other standard market forces to bring e-mail marketers to heel. Almost all spam prevention today is technical, accomplished through extensive filtering by e-mail and internet service providers. More legal success has been had in the telemarketing area, where the FTC, FCC, and private litigants police callers. The agencies promulgated detailed, technology-specific rules, and anti-telemarketing activists, state attorneys general, and plaintiff litigators willing to sue callers bolstered their effect. Some of the FTC's most important work concerns malware, a kind of software that can enable profound privacy and security violations and contribute to attacks on others' computers. Malware is a term that encompasses spyware, ransomware, adware, and other software that operates maliciously. The FTC's interventions are creating a baseline of privacy protection that businesses cannot undo with elaborate consent mechanisms.

---

[7] *See* Robert Gellman, *A Better Way to Approach Privacy Policy in the United States: Establish a Non-Regulatory Privacy Protection Board*, 54 HASTINGS L. J. 1183 (2003).

[8] *See, for example,* Michael Backes, Aniket Kate, Matteo Maffei, & Kim Pecina, *ObliviAd: Provably Secure and Practical Online Behavioral Advertising*, IEE Symposium on Security and Privacy (2012); Mikhail Bilenko, Matthew Richardson, & Janice Tsai, *Targeted, Not Tracked: Client-Side Solutions for Privacy-Friendly Behavioral Advertising*, TPRC (2011); Vincent Toubiana, Arvind Narayanan, Dan Boneh, Helen Nissenbaum, & Solon Barocas, *Adnostic: Privacy Preserving Targeted Advertising*, NDSS (2010).

At the FTC, the Division of Marketing Practices polices anti-marketing laws. The Division of Privacy and Identity Protection covers other privacy issues.

SPAM

The early internet changed forever on April 12, 1994, when two attorneys posted an advertisement for their immigration services on Usenet:

> "Green Card Lottery 1994 May Be The Last One!
> The US Government deadline for participation in the program is the end of June. You must act now!
> The Green Card Lottery is a completely legal program giving away a certain annual allotment of Green Cards to persons born in particular countries. The lottery program was scheduled to continue on a permanent basis. However, recently, Senator Alan J Simpson introduced a bill into the US Congress which could end any future lotteries. THE 1994 LOTTERY, WHICH WILL END SOON, MAY BE THE VERY LAST ONE.
> . . .
> ONCE AGAIN, THERE IS A STRICT JUNE DEADLINE. THE TIME TO START IS NOW!!"

Thus began the modern problem of spam. The reaction was swift. Angry users sent large files to the spamming attorney, causing his internet service provider to cancel his account. Others complained to the state bar, which resulted in one of the senders being disbarred. Another developed a program to constantly call the attorneys and fill up their voice mail messages.[9] The internet of 1994 was small and cohesive enough to punish the senders for what was seen as an irrelevant and wasteful use of a limited resource. At the time, internet connections were so slow and expensive that most viewed spam as a grievous insult.

Today, the majority of e-mail is spam. Senders of marketing e-mails can leverage the technical and economic properties of the internet to send tens of billions of messages a day. Some miniscule number of recipients purchase items from these messages. Yet, that is enough to make spam profitable. For instance, a 2008 study from the University of California found that 350 million messages to promote online pharmaceutical companies resulted in twenty-eight sales, but it was still a profitable campaign.[10] The costs of the remaining 349 million messages are externalized to others through the need for antispam employees at internet service providers, in money spent on filtering technology, and in individuals' time.

Why do consumers purchase items marketed in spam? Brian Krebs sought to answer this question by focusing on records from a large online pharmaceutical sales network. He interviewed 400 purchasers from the network and found that many

---

[9] FINN BRUNTON, SPAM: A SHADOW HISTORY OF THE INTERNET (2013).
[10] Chris Kanich et al., *Spamalytics: An Empirical Analysis of Spam Marketing Conversion*, CCS08 (2008).

simply could not afford to buy pharmaceutical drugs in the United States because they are so expensive in the American market. Those with chronic conditions could save hundreds a month by buying from Russian-based pharmacy networks. The drugs shipped from India appeared to be the same one might obtain at the neighbor-hood pharmacy. Indeed, almost all pharmaceuticals used in the United States are made in India. Others bought from spammers because they were embarrassed to see a doctor, because they thought it was more convenient to self-diagnose and buy treatments online, or because they were dependent on the drugs and thus could not obtain a legal prescription.[11]

In 2003, the FTC hosted a workshop to begin efforts to regulate e-mail marketing. The FTC made national headlines by announcing that it wanted all the spam that it could get. It urged consumers to forward their spam messages to the Agency, where millions of messages were stored in a computer nicknamed the "refrigerator." The number of messages received was so high that within a year the FTC had to establish an entirely new domain to manage the onslaught (spam@uce.gov).

The economic cost of spam is high and is conservatively estimated at $20 billion annually. Despite this cost, illegal spammers are thought to collect only $200 million a year.[12] A paper written by two researchers, one from Google and the other from Microsoft Research, analyzed the "externality ratio" from illegal spam. This term refers to the difference between the private benefit from the activity and the social cost of the activity. The researchers concluded that the externality ratio from illegal spam was greater than that from automobile theft.[13]

---

### SPAM'S ENEMIES

As Professor Finn Brunton observes, spam evokes strong responses. Dan Balsam, a California lawyer, has made a career of suing spammers and main-tains one of the most comprehensive resources for small-claims antispam litigants.[14] Balsam and Timothy Walton brought the first consumer spam case that went to trial in California, against a spammer that raised eighteen affirmative defenses to the complaint. The trial court awarded Balsam $7,000 in damages and over $80,000 in attorneys fees. The case, which concerned eight e-mails, took three years to resolve and involved appeals to the US Supreme Court. Balsam and Walton have written a humorous history of the convoluted case.[15]

---

[11]  BRIAN KREBS, SPAM NATION: THE INSIDE STORY OF ORGANIZED CYBERCRIME – FROM GLOBAL EPIDEMIC TO YOUR FRONT DOOR (2014).

[12]  Justin M. Rao & David H. Reiley, *The Economics of Spam*, 26(3) J. ECON. PERSPECTIVES, 87 (2012).

[13]  *Id.*

[14]  Dan Hates Spam, www.danhatesspam.com/.

[15]  Dan Balsam & Timothy Walton, *Balsam v. Trancos Inc.*, TRIAL LAWYER 14 (Summer 2012).

The social cost of spam may be even higher. As Brian Krebs explained in *Spam Nation*, spam email is seen as a mere nuisance, yet it "has become the primary impetus for the development of malicious software."[16] In other words, the infrastructure created to support spamming can be used for a variety of computer crime. This ranges from sending phishing e-mails to hosting copyrighted content and child pornography.

The history and culture of spammers is bizarre, daring, and sometimes violent.[17] The early spammers were often flamboyant characters. They were also willing to use technology to harass their perceived enemies. For instance, when the FTC started a public inquiry into the spam problem, someone – presumably a spammer – published the e-mail address of then Chairman Timothy Muris and encouraged the community to inundate him with messages. Such stunts have created a widespread dislike of the leading spam kings. Some of these spammers live in hiding.

The early spammers were do-it-yourself types who had a relatively easy time taking advantage of the network to send messages. At that time, some mail-sending servers were "open relays" that would accept a message from any sender (much like a postal mailbox will allow any individual to deposit a letter and have it delivered – if it has postage). Eventually these open relays were closed, and mail servers incorporated authentication systems to limit the scope of senders.

As antispam technological measures increased, the market for sending spam matured and became more complex. The early spam marketers, a diffuse group of cowboy-like internet savants, evolved into a sophisticated network of specialists. Some of these specialists are cybercriminals who infect users' computers to create networks of machines ("botnets") that send enormous amounts of spam. Others break authentication "CAPTCHAs," establish affiliate selling networks, or process payments. This specialization and division of labor has driven down the cost of spam for its senders, and established a market for spam sending. Today, an advertiser who wants to send spam can simply buy spam-sending services at an extremely low price and avoid the do-it-yourself dirty work. Affiliate network arrangements allow buyers of spam services to stand at arm's length from illegal marketing activities.

Spammers need resources in order to send messages – reliable internet access, clean accounts to send from, e-mail addresses to target, and web pages with payment mechanisms to convert prospects into customers. These resources can be targeted by law enforcement or antispam services. Providers may dump a business for sending too much junk mail. Providers may also filter IP addresses used to originate messages and URLs mentioned in spam messages. The antispam community is so intense that they run "black holes" that automatically delete vast numbers of e-mails based on their provenance, metadata, or content. At the same time, "bulletproof" hosting

---

[16] Brian Krebs, Spam Nation: The Inside Story of Organized Cybercrime – From Global Epidemic to Your Front Door (2014).

[17] *Id*; Brett Forrest, *The Sleazy Life and Nasty Death of Russia's Spam King*, Wired (August 2006).

services have arisen that are willing to sell tools to spammers, to promise secrecy, and to ignore complaints – sometimes even from law enforcement.[18]

Meanwhile, spammers use legal and extralegal tactics to attack antispam activists. They sue the black-hole operators for defamation and interfere with collaborative filtering efforts. Entrepreneurism in antispam activities is dangerous, because of both physical and technical threats. For instance, Blue Security, an Israeli firm, found a promising way to automate opt-out requests and had some success in changing senders' behavior. However, its success attracted the wrath of a Russian spammer, who attacked the firm so vigorously that it ended its antispam activities.[19]

Still, technical interventions have great promise to reduce spam because the industry depends on sending billions of messages to make sales, and the infrastructure to make these sales appears to be highly concentrated. University of California researchers have found that servers used to effectuate sales are relatively few in number,[20] and that just a handful of companies process most sales for spammers.[21] The spam expert Professor Finn Brunton concludes, "A few carefully directed and executed interventions could make an enormous dent in the production of email spam. Filtering and laws did not stop it, by any means, but they have painted it into a developmental corner with severe bottlenecks: an almost totally centralized, consolidated business dependent on colossal volumes of mail to survive."[22] Brunton's analysis suggests that law can be combined with technical measures to address the spam problem.

Economic constraints and technical measures constitute essentially all of the antispam efforts in the United States today. This is because the law Congress passed to regulate spam, the Controlling the Assault of Non-Solicited Pornography and Marketing Act of 2003 (CAN-SPAM), explicitly allows the sending of spam. Its provisions are considered in the next subsection. Under this law, every e-mail marketer in the world can send commercial messages to every American without oversight or limitation. For this reason, the law has been derisively labeled the You-CAN-SPAM Act. At core, Congress recognized the power of e-mail as a marketing tool and the First Amendment rights of senders. Congress wished to make e-mail marketing safe for legitimate companies by enacting CAN-SPAM. Congress attempted to valorize e-mail marketing by subjecting it to basic market pressures,

[18] Brian Krebs, *Inside the Gozi Bulletproof Hosting Facility*, KrebsonSecurity, January 25, 2013.
[19] BRIAN KREBS, SPAM NATION: THE INSIDE STORY OF ORGANIZED CYBERCRIME – FROM GLOBAL EPIDEMIC TO YOUR FRONT DOOR (2014).
[20] David S. Anderson et al., *Spamscatter: Characterizing Internet Scam Hosting Infrastructure*, 16th US ENIX SECURITY SYMPOSIUM (2007). ("... although large numbers of hosts are used to advertise Internet scams using spam campaigns, individual scams themselves are typically hosted on only one machine.")
[21] Kirill Levchenko et al., *Click trajectories: End-to-end analysis of the spam value chain*, PROC. IEEE SYMP. SECURITY & PRIVACY (2011); Altaweel et al., *Hacking Your Way to the Top: Online Pharmacies in Highly-Ranked Organic Search Results* (2015).
[22] FINN BRUNTON, SPAM: A SHADOW HISTORY OF THE INTERNET (2013).

such as brand reputation. If a company sends too much e-mail, the consumer presumably would shop somewhere else.

Thus far, this chapter has used the term "spam" loosely. Brunton defines the term as "the use of information technology infrastructure to exploit existing aggregations of human attention."[23] Brunton was making the point that people use "spam" to refer to all kinds of unwanted messages, but also that spam appears everywhere people tend to congregate online (such as on blog comments, Twitter, Facebook, and other popular services), not just in e-mail. Technically, the CAN-SPAM Act concerns "commercial electronic mail messages," messages with a primary purpose of "the commercial advertisement or promotion of a commercial product or service." Such communications need not be sent in bulk – a manual or brief transmission is covered by CAN-SPAM. And even business-to-business messages are covered by the act.

### The Controlling the Assault of Non-Solicited Pornography and Marketing Act of 2003 (CAN-SPAM)

Enacted in 2003, the CAN-SPAM Act[24] was animated by a number of problems. As the discussion above illustrates, e-mail marketing could be a powerful tool, but scammers and pornographers were trashing the medium. Companies and consumers wanted marketing and relationship messages, but the volume of mail considered to be junk threatened e-mail's legitimacy as a marketing tool. Many consumers were frustrated by receiving unsolicited pornography, some of which had to be viewed in order to delete the message.

On a political level, the public placed pressure on Congress to act. Spam had become a massive annoyance, especially for those who had dial-up connections. These users could not receive phone calls while they used the internet and had to watch their computers slowly download messages that they did not want. Users also had small e-mail inboxes at the time, and so spam had a direct effect on how much e-mail they could keep.

Action was also necessary to head off state legislatures that had started to regulate spam.[25] In particular, California enacted legislation establishing an opt-in requirement for commercial messages with $1,000 damage provisions.[26] Businesses saw a tidal wave of antispam litigation approaching, and internet service providers, the longtime economic victims of spam, saw a new kind of unwanted message on the horizon – discovery requests from thousands of antispam litigants for the identities of e-mail senders. The situation was painful enough to inspire a broad coalition of support for a federal spam bill.

---

[23] *Id.*
[24] Pub. L. 108–187, §2, December 16, 2003, 117 Stat. 2699, 15 U.S.C. §§7701–13.
[25] David E. Sorkin, *Spam Legislation in the United States*, 22 J. MARSHALL J. COMPUTER INFO. L. 3 (2003).
[26] Cal. Bus. & Prof. Code §17529.

Sponsored by Senators Conrad Burns and Ron Wyden, the CAN-SPAM Act attempted to bring truthfulness to transmission practices of commercial messages. It did little to create rights over control of personal data. "Transactional" messages are exempt from the definition of commercial electronic messages, thus allowing a broad range of transmissions from sellers to buyers to complete a transaction. These include delivery information, terms, and warranty information.

The problems of the CAN-SPAM approach are now obvious: CAN-SPAM assumed that e-mail senders are similar to bricks-and-mortar retail stores that care about reputation. In spam marketing, too many senders do not care about reputation, because they are engaged in affiliate selling and are only compensated when a sale of a third party's product is made. Others are not in the United States and are unlikely to be policed here. Spam is also the conduit for many kinds of computer crimes and basic "Spanish Prisoner" fraud schemes.[27] These dynamics make e-mail marketing fundamentally different from advertising mail or other kinds of direct marketing. The CAN-SPAM approach also differs from the entire industrialized world. Almost all nations require commercial e-mail senders to use opt-in consent, or even double-opt-in consent mechanisms.

### Banning falsity

Even honest businesses have very strong incentives to falsify the provenance of messages. Because antispam activists operate spam "black holes" to block unwanted messages, companies that use their own domain name to initiate messages risk polluting their reputation, and thereby being blacklisted. When testing new marketing lists, companies often use different domain names that are similar to their main one in order to avoid blacklisting.

Honesty in provenance is also a compliance problem because CAN-SPAM's principal provisions prohibit false and misleading e-mail "header" information. Senders are required to use a working return address and to use a subject line that is not misleading,[28] and are barred from altering routing information in the header of the message to deceive.

### Disclosures

As with telemarketing, the CAN-SPAM Act requires that commercial electronic mail messages must disclose that they are advertisements. It must also disclose where the sender's business is physically located.

---

[27] The "Spanish Prisoner" is an ancient confidence trick where one is fooled into paying a fraudster a ransom in order to free some far-off, rich, imaginary prisoner. Once freed, this prisoner presumably will pay the victim a great sum. Modern "Nigerian 419" schemes, also known as "advance fee frauds," are updated versions of this old trick. *See* Arthur A. Leff, Swindling and Selling: The Spanish Prisoner and Other Bargains (1976).

[28] *US v. ValueClick* et al., CV08-0171 (C.D. Ca. March 17, 2008).

## Opt-out choice

CAN-SPAM allows the sending of commercial e-mail messages. Every marketer in the United States gets one bite at the apple with every consumer in the country under it.

Senders must offer an opt-out and honor opt-out requests within 10 days. Senders cannot charge an opt-out fee, but transaction costs in opting out are seemingly unregulated. Some senders make it very easy to opt out, with a one-click unsubscribe option. Others take the recipient to a landing page where they have to type in their e-mail address again, or choose from a menu of e-mail subscriptions.

The opt-out approach presents a dilemma for consumers: if one opts out, she confirms to the sender that her e-mail is an active account. If the sender is unscrupulous, the sender could ignore the opt-out, or sell the active e-mail address to others, although both of these activities violate CAN-SPAM. However, it would be exceedingly difficult for the consumer to address either problem on their own.

## Data rights

Although primarily an anti-marketing law, CAN-SPAM does have some elements regarding personal privacy. For instance, as mentioned above, once a recipient has opted out, the sender cannot sell or otherwise transfer the recipient's address to another company.

The law also treats address harvesting (the scraping of valid e-mail addresses off websites and the like) and dictionary attacks (using tools to generate e-mails to likely e-mail addresses) as "aggravated violations."

## Advertiser/vicarious liability

As with the FTC's advertising matters dating back to the 1960s, both advertising agencies and advertisers can be liable for CAN-SPAM violations. Thus, companies that are advertising products or services must supervise their contractors that send e-mail. Advertiser liability cannot be contracted away, and, in fact, the CAN-SPAM Act was drafted to make the procurement of e-mail sending services a trigger for vicarious liability.[29]

For advertiser liability to attach, the advertiser must know, or should have known, that its products were being promoted through messages that had misleading or false

---

[29] "The intent of this [procure] definition is to make a company responsible for e-mail messages that it hires a third party to send, unless that third party engages in renegade behavior that the hiring company did not know about. However, the hiring company cannot avoid responsibility by purposefully remaining ignorant of the third party's practices. The 'consciously avoids knowing' portion of this definition is meant to impose a responsibility on a company hiring an e-mail marketer to inquire and confirm that the marketer intends to comply with the requirements of this Act." S. REP. 108–102, 15, 2004 U.S.C.C.A.N. 2348, 2360.

header information. The advertiser has to expect to receive economic benefit from the illegal promotion, and to not have taken action to prevent its transmission or detect it and report it to the FTC.

## Criminal provisions

The CAN-SPAM Act amended Title 18 to specify that several hacking-related activities for spam violate federal criminal law and can be punished with up to a 5-year prison sentence.[30] For criminal liability to attach, these activities require the government to prove that the spammer had a subjective intent to mislead or deceive e-mail recipients. Proscribed behavior includes hacking into a computer to send messages, intentionally deceiving recipients of message provenance, falsifying headers, and taking over or registering e-mail accounts in order to send spam.

These activities are arguably all illegal already under the Computer Fraud and Abuse Act.[31] In order to reach the volumes of e-mail necessary to make sales, illegal spammers will violate these provisions. There are few reported cases, but, in them, the government fares well, in part because spamming activities are memorialized in logs that tend to substantiate the defendant's intent to deceive recipients.[32]

## Adult content labeling

Randomly sent, unwanted pornography was a major motivator for CAN-SPAM. Early e-mail programs caused some users to have to view e-mail in order to delete it, and thus unsolicited pornography could be quite annoying. CAN-SPAM requires pornography to carry a subject line of "SEXUALLY-EXPLICIT" and to have a "brown paper wrapper," meaning that no graphics should be displayed until the user scrolls down. The wrapper can come off once the recipient consents to receiving adult messages.

Such labeling is a modest and inexpensive regulatory requirement. However, server-level filtering and users are likely to automatically delete any message with a label.

## Preemption of state law

The CAN-SPAM Act is broadly preemptive of state and local laws, "except to the extent that any such statute, regulation, or rule prohibits falsity or deception in any portion of a commercial electronic mail message or information attached thereto." Thus, the landscape of state-level litigation surrounds the issue of what constitutes

---

[30]  15 U.S.C. §7703; 18 U.S.C. §1037.
[31]  18 U.S.C. §1030 et seq.
[32]  See *United States* v. *Kilbride*, 584 F.3d 1240 (9th Cir. 2009); *United States* v. *Twombly*, 475 F. Supp. 2d 1019 (S.D. Cal. 2007).

falsity. Antispam plaintiffs have brought many cases, desperately trying to characterize spammers' activities as false, because state antispam laws are strong and often offer liquidated damages.

### The do-not-e-mail registry

The fantastic success of the telemarketing Do Not Call Registry, which I will discuss below, inspired Congress to consider a similar system for e-mail. Congress ordered the FTC to make a report for establishing such a system and gave it authority to implement it. In a June 2004 report, the FTC recommended against an e-mail registry, however, because such a system would have perverse consequences.[33] The FTC was concerned that the registry would be used by marketers to send even more spam.

The Agency recommended that no action be taken to establish a registry until a tamperproof system for e-mail sender authentication was implemented. Now, 2 years later, almost all organizations use sender authentication (albeit not tamperproof), and rumor has it that the Agency is reevaluating the idea of a registry for spam.

### Enforcement

Congress specified that the FTC would be the principal enforcer of the act, along with state attorneys general. The FTC enforces CAN-SPAM as a violation of the FTC Act, and thus violations can trigger fines of $16,000 per message. Injunctive relief is also available.

One provision in the act gives a private right of action to providers of "internet access services" against senders. Congress defined the term broadly,[34] potentially giving standing to anyone who ran a website or provided e-mail accounts to others. Antispam activists realized that they could have standing and brought suit; however, courts looked to Congressional intent and read the provision more narrowly. The Ninth Circuit has held that plaintiffs must satisfy the definition of an internet access service provider and be adversely affected by the spam.[35] This adverse-effect requirement is a key limitation on private suits – the plaintiff must show a nexus between the harms and the prohibitions of CAN-SPAM, that the harm be something more than the general harm caused by commercial messages.

The FTC's internal coding for CAN-SPAM violations falls into six categories, and suggests the Agency's priorities and frequent topics of complaint. They are (1) "remove me" is missing, broken, or ignored; (2) spam shows pornographic

---

[33]  FTC, NATIONAL DO NOT EMAIL REGISTRY: A REPORT TO CONGRESS (June 2004).
[34]  47 U.S.C. §231(e)(4).
[35]  *Gordon v. Virtumundo*, 575 F.3d 1040 (9th Cir. 2009). Susuk Lim, *Death of the SPAM Wrangler: CAN-SPAM Private Plaintiffs Required to Show Actual Harm*, 6 WASH. J. L. TECH. ARTS 155 (2010).

image; (3) spam led to suspect information collection practices; (4) subject or from line is false or misleading; (5) spammer misuses computer resources; and (6) other/general annoyance.

## TELEMARKETING

As with spam, telemarketing first presented bandwidth problems, tying up phone lines unnecessarily and sometimes dangerously, for instance when sales callers rang lines of hospitals and emergency services. But by the 1990s, the problem shifted from one of overloaded technical bandwidth to an assault on everyone's attention and cognitive resources. At the time, unsolicited commercial sales calls became a massive annoyance. Telemarketers developed increasingly sophisticated and efficient ways to generate calls. New technologies allowed single companies to initiate millions of calls a day. These technologies resulted in "dead air" in many situations: a ringing phone with no telemarketer on the other end because the telemarketing systems dialed too many numbers at once in order to increase the efficiency of sales callers. As Professor Peter Swire explained, these calls externalized costs to consumers who were displeased with the calling, but also may have reduced the value of having a phone in general, because defensive techniques to avoid unwanted callers, such as call screening and not answering the phone, could get in the way of desirable calls.[36]

---

### IS TECHNOLOGY NEUTRAL?

A kind of paradox is presented by modern technophiles. In the same breath they declare that technology is neutral while touting technology as the actuator of pro-democratic political change.[37] In the academic community, many have argued that technology is not neutral but rather a profound "part of our very humanity."[38]

In *The Whale and the Reactor*, Langdon Winner invites the reader to consider the political dimensions of technologies that generate electricity. A society that adopts nuclear power must also have a military-like police force to protect spent rods and by-products of atomic power from misuse. It

---

[36] Peter P. Swire, *Efficient Confidentiality for Privacy, Security, and Confidential Business Information,* BROOKINGS-WHARTON PAPERS ON FINANCIAL SERVICES (2003).

[37] ERIC SCHMIDT AND JARED COHEN, THE NEW DIGITAL AGE: RESHAPING THE FUTURE OF PEOPLE, NATIONS AND BUSINESS (2013). (The authors say such things as "technology is neutral but people are not" and "Technology companies export their values along with their products, so it is absolutely vital who lays the foundation of connectivity infrastructure.")

[38] LANGDON WINNER, THE WHALE AND THE REACTOR (1986). *See also* Gary T. Marx, *Coming to Terms and Avoiding Information Techno-Fallacies, in* PRIVACY IN THE MODERN AGE: THE SEARCH FOR SOLUTIONS (Marc Rotenberg & Jermaine Scott eds., 2015).

must have extensive security to prevent a terrorist from flying a plane into the reactor or otherwise triggering a meltdown. Nuclear power distribution is centralized and owned by just a few people, so there are profound economic implications as well.

On the other hand, a society that adopted home solar power would have less of a need for a strong police force. Power generation and ownership would be decentralized and probably impossible to monitor. Simply put, nuclear energy requires a different set of political relationships, and thus Winner labeled it an inherently political technology. Winner suggests other examples of discrimination in design that "enhance the power, authority, and privilege of some over others," including the allegation that Robert Moses built low bridge overpasses to prevent city buses (and thus the urban poor) from visiting Jones Beach.

Understood in this way, claims that "technology is neutral" may be a technique to mask the political motives of technology companies: "All too often the design of technologies simply conceals the ideologies and political agendas of their creators."[39] Evgeny Morozov thus recommends that policy "clearly scrutinize both the logic of technology and the logic of society that adopts it . . ."[40]

Consumers had little ability to reduce the volume of calls. Some consumers used "Telezappers," a device that transmitted a signal to automated dialing systems, causing them to see the line as disconnected. But telemarketers then would disable the software that recognized the signal.[41] Phone companies profited from both sides of the dispute. On one hand, they sold expensive caller identification services to consumers to help them ignore sales calls, but on the other, they offered special high-volume calling lines to telemarketers that did not transmit caller identification information, thereby enabling sales calls that could not be detected with caller identification services. Legal protections were also difficult to use because consumers could only opt out on a per-company basis. This meant the consumer could opt out, and be called one minute later by the same telemarketing service calling on behalf of a different business. Telemarketers were also notorious for hanging up on consumers who tried to opt out.

Because the FTC is statutorily barred from regulating common carriers, and because telemarketing often involves highly technical uses of telecommunications equipment, Congress addressed it with two different consumer protection laws: the

[39] EVGENY MOROZOV, THE NET DELUSION (2011); Evgeny Morozov, *Don't Be Evil*, THE NEW REPUBLIC (August 4, 2011).
[40] EVGENY MOROZOV, THE NET DELUSION (2011).
[41] Scott Hovanyetz, *Call Center Mailer Touts TeleZapper Immunity*, DIRECT MARKETING NEWS (February 18, 2003).

Telemarketing and Consumer Fraud and Abuse Prevention Act of 1994[42] and the Telephone Consumer Protection Act of 1991 (TCPA).[43] The FTC is responsible for the first and issues the Telemarketing Sales Rule.[44] The FCC is responsible for the TCPA.

## The Telemarketing Sales Rule

Over the years, annoyance with telemarketing has caused the FTC to create a complex thicket of rules for telemarketing. These appear in the Telemarketing Sales Rule (TSR). The TSR uses a broad mix of regulatory requirements to protect privacy. They include disclosure requirements, performance standards, a safe harbor, data retention requirements, and flat bans on certain practices.

The TSR is extremely broad. Any plan to sell goods or services with interstate calls triggers it. However, most business-to-business calls are exempt. Despite the FTC's limited ability to pursue common carriers and financial institutions, the Agency applies the TSR to third-party call centers that make sales calls on behalf of entities that are themselves exempt from FTC oversight.

### Disclosure requirements

The disclosure requirements of the TSR attempt to help consumers identify telemarketing and the key terms of the bargain. Thus, telemarketers must transmit caller identification information at the initiation of the call. Once connected, the sales caller must identify herself and the goods or services sold. All material terms must be disclosed, and special rules are in place for prizes, promotions, and so-called negative-option offers (see below).

### Predictive dialers

Telemarketing companies use predictive dialers to initiate calls to many people at the same time. Telemarketing companies do this to reduce the downtime of sales callers. The dialers attempt to match caller and consumers precisely, by predicting when a call will end and how long it will take to get a listener on the line. Errors in the matching process create "dead air," a ringing phone with no sales caller on the line. Predictive dialing technology changed the landscape of telemarketing, making sales calling much more efficient, but in the process annoying consumers with more calls. The dead-air calls in particular concerned consumers. Some interpreted a call with no one on the line as a form of harassment.

---

[42]  15 U.S.C. §6101.
[43]  47 U.S.C. §227.
[44]  16 C.F.R. §310.

Under the TSR, callers using predictive dialers must connect the consumer with an agent within two seconds to prevent dead air. To address failures in meeting this standard, the FTC created a safe harbor allowing callers to play an automated message that identifies the caller. Also, to meet the safe harbor, no more than 3 percent of calls in a day can be abandoned.

### Pre-acquired account number telemarketing

Pre-acquired account number telemarketing represents the zenith of the FTC's deference for direct marketing business models. The practice involves a telemarketer who purchases the customer's credit card number or bank account number before the call even begins. Thus, the telemarketer can complete a sale without the customer providing a method of payment.

This practice lends itself to exploitation. Telemarketers would call consumers and offer them a free trial of some service, without mentioning that the caller already had the credit account information and could effectuate a charge. Some of the biggest consumer banks in the United States bought into this model, providing their customers' account numbers to telemarketers, who, predictably, made charges without authorization. Banks received a significant percentage of both the sales made and the fees for reversing charges. The Commissions that banks earned gave them a lucrative incentive to ignore fraudulent charges. In one case detailed by the Minnesota attorney general, "during a thirteen-month period, a national bank processed 95,573 cancellations of membership clubs and other products that were billed by preacquired account telemarketers without customers' authorization."[45]

The general deregulatory impulse emanating from the President George W. Bush administration caused the FTC to defend pre-acquired account number telemarketing. In one forum that the author participated in, an FTC attorney struggled to find a justification for the practice, and settled on the example that when a consumer receives a telemarketing call while driving, it would be convenient for her to be able to make a purchase without looking up a credit card number. Despite the weak rationale for this form of marketing, the risk of abuse, and the documented cases of fraud, the Bush-era FTC allowed pre-acquired account number telemarketing. Recognizing the risks of its approach, the Agency imposed the highest levels of documented consent for the practice. Free offers that ripen into for-pay services, "free-to-pay conversions," require explicit consent and for the seller to have the consumer read off the last four digits of the account that will be charged. The seller must audio-record the entire transaction. Congress later supplemented these protections in enacting the Restore Online Shoppers Confidence Act ("ROSCA").[46]

---

[45] Minnesota Attorney General, Supplemental Comments of the Minnesota Attorney General's Office, FTC File No. R411001 (2002).
[46] 15 U.S.C. §8401 *et seq.*

## National Do Not Call Registry

The National Do Not Call Registry (DNCR) was provoked by state adoption of do-not-call lists in the 1990s. These lists were very popular, but limited in efficaciousness because telemarketers often called from other states and simply did not comply with consumer preferences. Under the DNCR, consumers can easily enroll a phone number with minimal authentication – they need not do much to prove that they own the phone number. Telemarketers are required to regularly check the list and to scrub from their calling plans numbers that appear on it. The DNCR is paid for by telemarketers – they must subscribe to it individually, and these fees support its operation.

The DNCR was apparently developed by President Clinton-era leadership but shelved as a proposal. Thus, it was unexpected when the DNCR was taken up in 2002, because the Commission was then led by President George W. Bush appointee Chairman Timothy Muris. Chairman Muris surprised consumer advocates by framing telemarketing as something that could be policed under a "harms-based" approach, and by proposing the DNCR. The DNCR remains the most popular consumer intervention in recent decades at the federal level. Muris successfully defended the DNCR from a strong Congressional attack, when the then Chairman of the House Energy and Commerce Committee attempted to derail it. The Agency later successfully defended it from a First Amendment challenge.[47]

On the political front, the telemarketing industry opposed the creation of a universal opt-out through the DNCR. They wished to preserve a company-by-company opt-out approach.[48] They also wanted consumers to have to reenroll in the DNCR regularly, perhaps every 2 years. These policies would increase transaction costs for consumers and allow every telemarketer in the world to ring consumers' phones at least once.

In 2003, while the debate over the DNCR was raging, Professor Ian Ayers and Matthew Funk offered a provocative solution: require telemarketers (and perhaps other kinds of marketers) to pay consumers to listen to messages. The authors suggested that the pesky and detailed rules for telemarketing, such as calling time restrictions and the ban on prerecorded messages, could be eliminated, because consumers could set a price for the willingness to get inconvenient or prerecorded calls. Ayres and Funk concluded: "there is a real possibility that the telephone could become a major conduit for advertising. Have five minutes to spare waiting for your

---

[47] *Mainstream Mktg. Servs., Inc. v. FTC*, 358 F.3d 1228 (10th Cir. 2004)

[48] *See* Am. Teleservices Ass'n, Comments of the American Teleservices Association on the Review of the Telemarketing Sales Rule 10 (2000), *available at* www.ftc.gov/bcp/rulemaking/tsr/comments/ata.pdf. ("Additionally, the company specific 'Do-Not-Call' list is the best way to empower consumers to make the type of informed purchasing decisions that are necessary for a satisfactory sale. For consumers who do not want to receive calls, all they have to do is inform the caller at anytime during the call. However, for those consumers who want to receive calls or who only want to receive certain types of calls, the existing federal rule allows them the freedom to determine which calls they want to receive and prohibits those calls they don't.")

train? Why not turn on your cell phone and make some cool hard cash? Instead of asking the rhetorical question of how much we would be willing to pay to avoid these unsolicited solicitations, we should be able to ask ourselves the consequential question, How much do we want to be paid?"[49] For a short period of time, lobbyists for the marketing industry took up the idea and promoted it as an alternative to the DNCR. However, the telemarketing industry never took any steps to adopt the proposal. Instead, the Ayres and Funk proposal became a convenient tool to delay the FTC and Congress.

---

### SHOULD REGULATION BE TECHNOLOGY-NEUTRAL?

Both consumer and industry advocates argue that regulation should be "technology-neutral."

Bert-Jaap Koops has carefully explored the demand for technology-neutral regulation. He begins the inquiry by asking why technology law in particular should be technology-neutral. Koops uses the example of traffic law, where there are no calls for uniform technical rules for bicycles, cars, and heavy trucks.

Koops goes on to explain that "technical neutrality" carries three possible meanings, and these meanings can result in conflict:

> From the perspective of the goal of regulation, the statement stresses that, in principle, the effects of ICT should be regulated, but not technology itself; it may thus serve as a means to achieve equivalence between off-line and on-line regulation. From the perspective of technology development, the statement stresses that, in principle, regulation should not have a negative effect on the development of technology and should not unduly discriminate between technologies. From the perspective of legislative technique, [technology neutrality] stresses that legislation should abstract away from concrete technologies to the extent that it is sufficiently sustainable and at the same provides sufficient legal certainty.

Koops argues that the last justification is the most meritorious to promote sustainable lawmaking.[50]

Applied to US policy debates, these three meanings of technologically neutral regulation have very different outcomes. Consider Koops' first and third categories. These would militate for broad, preventative, principles-based legislation.

---

[49] Ian Ayers & Matthew Funk, *Marketing Privacy: A Solution for the Blight of Telemarketing (and Spam and Junk Mail)*, 20 Yale J. Reg. 77 (2003). For a detailed critique of this proposal *see* Paul M. Schwartz, *Property, Privacy, and Personal Data*, 117 Harv. L. Rev. 2055 (2004).

[50] Bert-Jaap Koops, *Should ICT Regulation Be Technology-Neutral?*, *in* STARTING POINTS FOR ICT REGULATION (Bert-Jaap Koops, Mariam Lips, Corien Prins, & Maurice Schellekens, eds., 2006).

Statutes such as the Fair Credit Reporting Act and the Video Privacy Protection Act, which define prohibited behaviors regardless of technology used, may qualify under this definition of technical neutrality. At the same time, laws such as the Communication Decency Act's immunity for online platforms would be suspect, because it creates radically different outcomes for online and offline intermediary liability.

Much US regulation, and virtually all self-regulation, violates the principles of Koops' second definition, which commands that technologies should not be discriminated against. In American parlance, this is often said as "regulation should not pick winners and losers."

However, almost all anti-marketing regulation is technology-specific, in the sense of picking winners and losers, as are most self-regulatory regimes in privacy. This is because of First Amendment constraints, which require the government to tailor regulation to the affordances of specific technologies. As a result, regulation tends to be reactive, rather than proactive, and target specific technologies. But it is also because of power dynamics. Automatic dialers, for instance, greatly enhanced the ability of telemarketers to call individuals, resulting in millions of "dead-air" hang-up calls. Regulation targets this technology for its power transfer to telemarketers. It is asymmetric as it greatly increases telemarketer efficiency while giving the consumer no tools (or even disabling their tools) to counter the interruption. Prerecorded voice marketing presents a similar, asymmetric threat to individuals. With minimal investment, a caller can cause massive interruption in individuals' daily lives.

Herbert Burkert argues that information communication technologies have fundamentally altered information handling. To maintain checks and balances in society, Burkert asserts that technology-specific "responses to such changes in the power structure is needed."[51] He points to the electronic data processing industry as one with practices more dangerous than paper file systems, and thus deserving of stronger regulation.

We might think about these lessons in coming decades, when marketing is likely to be delivered to us by robots or by automated systems that can recognize and confront us in real space. Such advertising is typically depicted in dystopian science fiction (the 2002 movie *Minority Report*, the 2011 series *Black Mirror*, and the 2013 work *The Zero Theorem*). We know that these technologies are coming, and we are likely to react to them in a non-neutral way, regulating each specifically as they arise, rather than prospectively, through principles-based neutral regulations.

---

[51] Herbert Burkert, *Four Myths about Regulating in the Information Society – A Comment, in* Starting Points for ICT Regulation (Bert-Jaap Koops, Mariam Lips, Corien Prins, & Maurice Schellekens, eds., 2006).

Professor Eric Goldman argued that the DNCR failed to "reflect consumer preferences granularly, personally, dynamically, and at low cost."[52] It was not granular, because the DNCR requires a binary, all-or-nothing choice about telemarketing. Perhaps consumers would welcome sales calls from certain companies but not others. It was not personal because it applies to the household, rather than to individual users of a phone line. It was not dynamic because registration lasts for so long, depriving the consumer of possible windows of wanted telemarketing.

When proposing the DNCR, the FTC anticipated that 60 million numbers would be enrolled in it. The program was successful far beyond that estimate. On its first day of operation, 7 million numbers were registered. By 2011, over 200 million numbers were listed in the registry.[53] Some perceive the DNCR as ineffective, because they still receive *some* sales calls, calls from charitable organizations, and calls from politicians. However, studies have shown that those who enroll receive fewer sales calls.[54] Our First Amendment makes it difficult to address calls from charities and politicians.

Completing the circle, AT&T, the company that did so much to profit from telemarketing and from consumers' anti-telemarketing preferences, was hired to implement the DNCR system at the FTC.

## Accountability measures

The TSR imposes a 24-month retention requirement on sales callers to keep advertising brochures, telemarketing scripts, and lists of customers who purchased goods.[55] These records are key in telemarketing enforcement actions. It is difficult to catch determined, dishonest telemarketers because technology enables them to set up "boiler rooms" for calling and to abandon them quickly when authorities detect the scheme. However, in order to achieve large-scale calling programs with many employees, in practice, dishonest telemarketers have to document and distribute their plans to illegally call or to misrepresent sales terms. Thus, authorities that obtain telemarketing scripts will often have direct evidence of intentional fraud.

## Investigating telemarketing fraud

In 1998, Congress simplified the process for obtaining business records concerning telemarketing.[56] Under the amended Stored Communications Act, any government

---

[52] Eric Goldman, *A Coasean Analysis of Marketing*, 2006 Wis. L. Rev. 1151 (2006).

[53] Fed. Trade Comm'n, Biennial Report to Congress: Under the Do Not Call Registry Fee Extension Act of 2007, FY 2010 and 2011 (2011).

[54] Press Release, Harris Interactive, National Do-Not-Call Registry: Seven in Ten Are Registered and All of Them Will Renew Their Registration, Large Majority Who Have Registered Report Receiving Far Fewer Telemarketing Calls 1 (October 31, 2007), *available at* www.harrisinteractive.com/vault/Harris-Interactive-Poll-Research-Do-Not-Call-2007–10.pdf.

[55] 16 C.F.R. §310.4.

[56] Pub. L. 105–184, §8, June 23, 1998, 112 Stat. 522.

agency – including state and local agencies – may require communication services to reveal the name, address, and place of business of a subscriber that is engaged in telemarketing. All that is needed is the submission of a "formal written request relevant to a law enforcement investigation concerning telemarketing fraud."[57] Civil investigative demands (CIDs; see Chapter 4) seem to be preferred in telemarketing investigations because CIDs offer the ability to obtain much more information about a subscriber.

### Advertiser vicarious liability

Advertisers can be vicariously liable for the activities of their sales callers. Under the "assisting and facilitating" standard, a company is liable when it gives "substantial assistance or support" to any sales caller when the company "knows or consciously avoids knowing" telemarketing rules.[58] The scope of rules subject to vicarious liability is quite broad and extends to any kind of abusive calling and failure to make basic disclosures about the sale.[59] As a practical matter, advertiser liability means that those who hire telemarketers must monitor sales calling activities. It is important to pay attention to telemarketing scripts, allegations of unauthorized charges, inquiries from law enforcement, and complaints that opt-out requests are not being honored.

### The Telephone Consumer Protection Act (TCPA)

Because telemarketing is such a hated practice among consumers, two federal agencies police it. In addition to the FTC's efforts on the TSR, the Federal Communications Commission regulates telemarketing and SMS marketing through the TCPA. The TCPA prohibits telemarketing and SMS to wireless phones without prior express written consent.[60] It flatly bans "prerecorded voice" telemarketing. It bans telemarketing calls to hospitals, homes for the elderly, and emergency phone numbers. The FCC has interpreted the consent provisions of the TCPA strictly so that consent has to be informed and explicit. For instance, to send marketing SMS, companies need to inform the individual that they will receive marketing messages from a specific sender, estimate the number of messages to be received, and have the consumer specify which number will receive the messages.

Notably, the TCPA grants jurisdiction to small-claims courts and establishes a liquidated damage standard of $500 for illegal telemarketing. This creates a very strong incentive for private plaintiffs to police telemarketing, and there exists a kind of TCPA litigator bar in America. To avoid these litigants, one company now

[57] 18 U.S.C. §2703(c)(1)(D).
[58] 16 C.F.R. §310.3(b).
[59] See *FTC v. Global Marketing Group, Inc.*, 594 F.Supp.2d 1281 (M.D. Fla. 2008).
[60] 47 U.S.C. §227(b)(1)(A)(iii).

offers a "LitigatorScrub" service to remove the phone numbers of known plaintiffs from marketing lists.[61]

## The Junk Fax Prevention Act

The TCPA also prohibits unsolicited commercial facsimile messages – "junk faxes."[62] Junk faxes were a plague upon fax machine owners, and they were a nettlesome form of marketing because the cost of the messages was transferred to the recipient. Indeed, before plain-paper fax machines, paper and ink could be quite expensive. When plaintiffs sued junk faxers, such as the notorious Fax.com, which reportedly sent over 500,000 faxes a week, defendants would claim that the recipient consented to the fax or that a previous owner of the phone number had consented to the fax.

Fed up with this litigation strategy, the FCC required senders to keep written documentation of recipient consent. Written consent was a major burden for small businesses, which quickly went to Congress for a fix – the Junk Fax Prevention Act.[63] The act reversed the FCC's written documentation mandate and added an established business relationship exemption to the ban on junk faxing. The FCC's pro-recipient regulation resulted in "blowback," with direct marketers reversing the mandate and gaining a new exemption to allow faxing.

## Advertising mail

The FTC can police unfair and deceptive practices effectuated through mails; however, the FTC has no authority to provide privacy or anti-marketing rights with regard to advertising mail. Commonly referred to as junk mail, advertising mail now comprises more than half of all mail pieces in the United States. The United States Postal Service has genuflected to direct mail companies, even creating "saturation mail" products that allow advertisements to be delivered to every home in a neighborhood without even requiring the advertiser to put an address on the mail piece. In other countries, such delivery is subject to opt-out rights (typically through placing a sticker on one's mailbox). But in the United States, there is no legally enforceable way to reduce the volume of advertising mail.[64] A self-regulatory system offered by the Direct Marketing Association (DMA) allows individuals to opt out of certain advertising mail sent by its members, but it is woefully ineffective

---

[61] Contact Center Compliance, Contact Center Compliance Announces LitigatorScrub, February 10, 2015.
[62] 47 U.S.C. §227(d).
[63] Pub L. No. 109–21, 119 Stat. 359 (2005).
[64] That is, aside from claiming that advertising mail is pandering pornography, and obtaining a prohibitory order against each sender under 39 U.S.C. §3008. The prohibitory order process is paper based and labor-intensive, requiring that the recipient open and send the mail piece to a specific U.S.P.S. office, and each order only applies to a single mailer.

because any company with an existing business relationship can still send mail, and because many marketers are not members of the DMA.

## MALWARE

Malware, short for malicious software, includes viruses, software that self-propagates; rootkits, software that gives another person access to the entire computer system; spyware, software that monitors the user; adware, software that displays ads to the user and is often installed through misleading procedures; ransomware, software that extorts the user into paying money; and other software that takes advantage of the user's computer for some malicious purpose. It is sometimes referred to as "badware."

The bounds of malware are difficult to define.[65] Sometimes consent is used to define its bounds, but quality of consent is an important factor to consider. The FTC brings enforcement actions against companies that use "constructive" consent to justify installation of malware. In fact, the FTC's cases point to an actual consent (affirmative consent paired with prominent notice) for certain kinds of adware.

It is also difficult to define malware by attention to functional capability. Consider antivirus software. Such software runs on one's computer constantly, scanning all files and communications for certain content. Antivirus software also is updated remotely to update its definitions of dangerous content. If these same activities were performed by a malicious actor, antivirus would be the computer equivalent of a wiretap – an extremely invasive program. Yet, antivirus programs are key to protecting privacy and security.

Some common functions of software classified as malware include stealing information from the computer, causing the computer to click on links that the user does not intend to, causing the computer to make purchases, sending spam, propagating more malware, and allowing the user's computer to become part of a "botnet." A botnet is a robot network: an organized group of computers under the control of some other actor. The creation of botnets, in particular, is a major point of malware. With a large number of computers, an individual can send an enormous amount of spam, or using the bandwidth of the botnet to attack other sites, in order to stop them from operating or to extort funds from the operator.

---

[65] Nathaniel Good, Jens Grossklags, David Thaw, Aaron Perzanowski, Deirdre K. Mulligan, & Joseph Konstan, *User Choices and Regret: Understanding Users' Decision Process about Consensually Acquired Spyware*, 2(2) I/S: A J. L. POL'Y INFO. SOC. 283 (2006). A broad consumer–industry coalition, the Anti-Spyware Working Group, defines spyware as "Technologies deployed without appropriate user consent and/or implemented in ways that impair user control over: Material changes that affect their user experience, privacy, or system security; Use of their system resources, including what programs are installed on their computers; and/or Collection, use, and distribution of their personal or other sensitive information." ANTI-SPYWARE WORKING GROUP, ANTI-SPYWARE COALITION DEFINITIONS DOCUMENT, November 12, 2007.

Thus, malware is a major factor in computer crime and larger issues of cybersecurity. In policing malware, the FTC has a role to play in cybersecurity, which it has exercised to a limited extent. In June 2009, the FTC sued and shut down 3FN, a major distributer of malware based in California, known in spam and computer crime circles as a "bulletproof" host.[66] Such hosts will tolerate or even foster illegal content and ignore requests from copyright holders, law enforcement, and others to remove it. The FTC used its unfairness authority to charge 3FN with distribution and hosting of malicious code and for computer intrusion. In effect, the FTC disconnected 3FN from the internet. The FTC found that 3FN was hosting child pornography, spyware, viruses, services for phishing, botnet command and control servers, and pornography featuring violence, bestiality, and incest. The FTC has not taken action against other bulletproof hosts, and agency inaction may be because such services left the United States in the 2000s for "New Europe" and China.[67]

The above-listed uses of others' computers are clearly malicious and unwanted. But a problem arises in clearly defining the boundaries of malware and advertising software. Recall Professor Goldman's Coasean filter. It foreshadows a key tension in malware cases: the best possible computer marketing system may be software that acts indistinguishably from malware. For this reason, and because of intensive lobbying by technology companies, Congress has considered several spyware bills but has not enacted any.

Users get malware in several ways. They might install it directly, for instance, when downloading some "free" utility such as a mouse pointer or screen saver. Malware can also be installed through drive-by downloads, where just visiting a website causes the software to be installed. Sometimes these drive-by downloads are spread through advertising banners.

One key point visited in Chapter 8 is the idea that internet security is a public good similar to public health. Not protecting oneself against malware can have subtle but, in the aggregate, harmful effects on network security. Users contribute to the malware problem and systemic insecurity by failing to update antivirus and other key software. Websites contribute to the problem by running insecure systems, and by using insecure advertising platforms. Software companies contribute to the problem by releasing code that is easily exploitable.

### When malware is illegal

The FTC has brought a handful of matters on malware, using theories of unfairness, deception, and "means and instrumentalities." The FTC uses the means and instrumentalities theory when a respondent aids or encourages some act of

---

[66] *FTC v. Pricewert LLC also d/b/a 3FN.net, Triple Fiber Network, APS Communications, and APS Communication*, 09-CV-2407 (N.D. Cal. 2009).
[67] Brian Krebs, Spam Nation: The Inside Story of Organized Cybercrime – From Global Epidemic to Your Front Door (2014).

deception or unfairness. The FTC does this because it lacks statutory aiding and abetting authority in most circumstances (see Chapter 4).

The malware matters highlight a few bright-line rules for application developers: constructive consent is inadequate for collection of sensitive data, companies that sell particularly invasive software must take steps to monitor both their marketing of and others' use of the software, it is never acceptable to change user settings so as to cause them to be more insecure, and deceptive marketing of software is illegal.

The FTC's actions in these matters often impose design mandates that warn users that the software can track them, and to prevent makers of the software from creating plausible deniability concerning how the software is marketed and used. Individuals can sue those who install spyware with state or federal computer crime violations, and malware vendors can also be charged criminally.

### Constructive consent is insufficient for certain forms of monitoring

Privacy law heavily relies on the consent of consumers to allow collection and uses of personal information. A full consideration of whether consent occurred would include whether the user had the competence to consent, whether there was adequate information about the bargain and its risks, whether consent was voluntary, and the terms of withdrawal of consent. But in many transactions, consent is simply implied or is constructive – critical terms are buried in a lengthy privacy policy or end-user license agreement that no one actually reads, or is given on a take-it-or-leave-it basis.

The FTC articulated the limits of constructive consent in its matter concerning Sears.[68] Sears wanted to gain more insight into how its customers shopped online, and so it offered some customers the opportunity to be paid $10 in exchange for installing software that functioned much like spyware. Selling one's privacy for cash money would seem to be an acceptable transaction in the United States.[69] However, the FTC found it deceptive, because the extent of tracking that Sears' application allowed was not sufficiently disclosed. While Sears did present the consumer with the basic details of the transaction – money in exchange for "confidential" tracking of online browsing – the complete details of this tracking, which included monitoring of secure sessions (such as internet purchasing and banking), only appeared in a lengthy end-user license agreement.

The Sears consent order required the company to obtain affirmative consent for tracking in the future, and this consent had to contain a clear and prominent disclosure, separate from the privacy policy, of the types of data monitored, the scope of the monitoring, whether data would be shared with third parties, whether

---

[68] *In re Sears Holdings Management Corporation*, FTC Matter 082 3099 (September 9, 2009).
[69] Even Warren and Brandeis supported the idea that one's privacy is alienable. Samuel Warren & Louis Brandeis, *The Right to Privacy*, 4 Harv. L. R. 193 (1890).

secure sessions might be monitored, and how data would be used. The description of Sears' notice obligations takes up nine lines in the settlement.

Under the FTC's order, Sears had to disclose so much, in such a prominent manner, that it became clear that gaining consent was practically impossible. A mobile screen would never accommodate the warning adequately. Even a desktop screen would be completely occupied with warnings. Thus, practically speaking, the Sears case showed how the FTC is beginning to narrow the kinds of data collection activities that can be subject to consent.

The Sears case puzzled some attorneys. It invokes deception as a theory, but it reads as if it were an unfairness case. Yet, to some, Sears' offer did not seem unfair at all, because Sears paid people to be tracked. Compensating the consumer for a privacy invasion seemed more legitimate than the adware schemes of the early 2000s. The common law imposed a duty to read disclosures, and contract law does not interpret non-readership as a defense. Consider this reaction by four D.C.-based privacy attorneys: "Given that the software in question was manifestly identified to consumers as an online tracking device, there would not appear to be any principle of contract law, industry practice, or previous FTC order requiring that the detailed explanation of the tracking be placed in a disclosure outside the [license agreement] ... The proposed Sears settlement is at odds with established industry and regulatory practice allowing consumers to opt in to contracts of their choice. It has the potential to create substantial uncertainty for online commerce, and could undercut the expectations that have helped the Internet become a robust engine of economic growth and consumer choice."[70]

But just how far should contract allow companies to push consumers to disclose data? One fundamental purpose in prohibit unfair practices is to promote fair ones. Viewed in this light, the FTC is remedying the systemic weakening of contract norms online. At the beginning of the Web economy, some thought that the internet would bring a contract utopia, where each person could obtain tailored terms.[71] Instead, we have a Web full of standard, adhesive contracts offered on a take-it-or-leave-it basis. Indeed, Professor Jane Winn argues that courts' inattention to formation elements of contract law makes contract as a doctrine inefficacious against unwanted spyware.[72] She concludes that piecemeal reform to contract doctrine would not address the spyware problem and has pointed to the European Union Unfair Contract Terms Directive as an alternative.

---

[70] Alan Charles Raul, Edward McNicholas, Colleen Theresa Rutledge, & Adam Rusnak, *End of the Notice Paradigm?: FTC's Proposed Sears Settlement Casts Doubt on the Sufficiency of Disclosures in Privacy Policies and User Agreements*, BNA PRIVACY SECURITY L. REP. (July 20, 2009).

[71] Esther Dyson, *Protect Internet privacy – privately*, WALL ST. J., June 17, 1997.

[72] Jane K. Winn, *Contracting Spyware by Contract*, 20 BERKELEY TECH. L. J. 1345 (2005).

## Software that spies versus software marketed to spy

Many software tools can be employed to spy upon on or "cyberstalk" another. For instance, basic software utilities, known as "packet sniffers," can monitor all communications on a network. Technicians also have valid uses for such sniffers, for instance, to diagnose problems and make the network more efficient. The FTC must distinguish this software from others that we view as tools meant to spy illegally.

The FTC and federal law enforcement agencies have addressed this problem by focusing on how software is marketed and implemented. Many technologies are advertised with a wink and a nod suggesting spying on others. The FTC's cases have focused on such business models, thus giving breathing space for makers of ordinary tools that could be put to illegal uses.

In *FTC* v. *CyberSpy Software*, the Commission brought suit to enjoin a company from selling software that would log users' keystrokes.[73] The company involved allegedly instructed buyers of the software how to deploy it secretly, even providing a configuration wizard and tutorial to disguise the program as an innocuous e-mail attachment. It also advertised the software as "100% undetectable." The FTC argued that CyberSpy's selling of the spyware was unfair, that it was unfair for CyberSpy to collect information from victims of the spyware, and that CyberSpy provided others the means and instrumentalities to both install software and engage in deception. The Commission obtained a temporary restraining order against CyberSpy, and, almost 2 years later, CyberSpy signed an order to settle the case.

In the settlement, CyberSpy agreed to remedies that set out the FTC's stance on highly intrusive software. The settlement crafted an imperfect compromise that allows users to surveil their own computers, while creating some protections for others. The company must cause the software to initiate a pop-up at installation, warning the user of the software; it must display a "tray icon" to indicate that the software is running. However, users who have full administrative privileges on the computer can install the software so that the notice and tray do not display. The company also has to warn users that it is illegal to install the software on others' computers, and it must also monitor licensure of the product to prevent the software from being installed on multiple computers.

The FTC could not simply shut down CyberSpy because there are legal uses of intrusive monitoring software. For instance, parents can use monitoring software to control kids' internet access, and employers can use filtering and monitoring extensively in the workplace. As a result, CyberSpy is still in business, offering RemoteSpy, "our highly rated remote computer monitoring software." The obvious references to secret spying are gone, but the overall tone set by the product name still suggests spying on others.

Owning a computer can give one authority to install spyware on it. But just as a landlord cannot place a listening device in a tenant's apartment, FTC actions make

[73] *FTC* v. *Cyberspy Software, LLC*, 6:08-CV-1872-ORL-31GJK (M.D. Fl. 2008).

it difficult to install monitoring software on leased or rented computers. One articulation of these efforts concerned "rent-to-own"[74] businesses. In one matter, the Commission (led by its Northwest Regional Office) brought an administration action against both the rental company and a software company for installing a program to monitor lessors.[75]

DesignerWare, LLC, marketed and supported "PC Rental Agent," a program that had enabled companies to track the physical location of leased computers. DesignerWare recommended, but did not require, rental companies to disclose the presence of the software. It was generally undetectable, and the user could not delete it.

The software also supported a "Detective Mode" to respond to the commercial problem of those who did not pay, as well as the problem of stolen and lost computers. It enabled keylogging and screen captures and could take pictures with the webcam. As in CyberSpy, the FTC noted DesignerWare's licensing practices, pointing out that it did not monitor how the software was used, and this could lead to abuse by licensees. The FTC alleged that it was unfair to install software and monitor users, and that DesignerWare provided the means and instrumentalities for rental companies to engage in unfairness. Crucial to DesignerWare's liability were its lack of involvement in monitoring licensees of the technology and its coaching of rental companies on how they should give notice of the monitoring. It also directly collected information on its own servers and generated a fake registration page to fool users into disclosing their credit card data.

DesignerWare and the rental company agreed to an order prohibiting direct monitoring or licensing software to monitor users. The FTC allowed DesignerWare to create systems that located user computers, so long as there was prominent notice of and consent to the tracking at rental, and notice each time the location beacon is activated. Companies continue to be free to condition rental on the user giving consent.

Rental companies used the software because of alarmingly high rates of renters reporting lost and stolen laptops. Some commentators thus argued that the case was unsound, because under the unfairness analysis, the software provided an important benefit to commerce that had to be balanced against the cost of the privacy invasion. Without monitoring, perhaps computers cannot be rented because of noncompliance with rental agreements. But these concerns should be allayed by the FTC's allowance of location-tracking software on rental computers so long as the rental agency obtains actual consent.

In these cases, the FTC was creating greater protections for communications privacy than provided for by federal statute. After all, even under the wiretapping laws, users can consent to having their computers comprehensively monitored, if

---

[74] Rent-to-own companies actually lease computers.
[75] *In the Matter of Watershed Development Corporation D/B/A Watershed and Aaron's Sales & Lease Ownership*, 155 F.T.C. 639 (2013); *In the Matter of DesignerWare, LLC*, 155 F.T.C. 421 (2013).

the consent is actual consent or fairly implied from the circumstances. Here, however, the FTC created a flat ban on surveillance, with an exception for GPS tracking after prominent notice is given to the user.

In physical spaces, companies are legally prohibited from some antifraud efforts, such as installing cameras in changing rooms and bathrooms to catch shoplifters. The FTC's efforts draw similar lines with respect to computing, much of which is personal, and much of which occurs in the home. Arguably, the FTC is extending the long-established principle that antifraud efforts have to be reasonable in the new realm of personal computing.

## Reducing user security

The FTC has brought cases concerning adware[76] and other practices that reduce users' privacy and security substantially. Professors Deirdre K. Mulligan and Aaron Perzanowski carefully detailed the facts that gave rise to the FTC's first reduced user security case.[77] The Sony BMG rootkit incident is the clearest example of misaligned incentives resulting an otherwise reputable company engaging in activities typical of malicious hackers. In order to secure its music CDs from piracy, Sony BMG deployed two different content protection programs, XCP and MediaMax. These programs were installed on users' computers when they tried to play the CDs on a computer. XCP introduced a "rootkit," a computer process that masked itself from the user's operating system. Rootkits can be used to mask malicious activity on a computer and make it possible for others to take over the computer. MediaMax created a folder on users' computers that could be commandeered by others and used for malicious purposes. Upon discovery of these problems, Sony stumbled, releasing poorly designed patches that intensified the insecurity. The FTC investigated Sony, finding that it engaged in both deception and unfair practices. The FTC found it unfair for Sony to install such an invasive program without more prominent notice. It also found that consumers suffered unjustified injury because it was difficult to find the programs and to uninstall them.[78]

In a matter similar to Sears, the FTC pursued Upromise.com, a company that urged consumers to install a "browser toolbar," that is, software in a web browser that has access to a record of websites a user visits, in exchange for credits that could be applied against college tuition.[79] Like Sears, it engaged in deceptive practices by not fully disclosing the scope of its data collection and by making overbroad promises about protecting the data it received from users' browsing. Critically, it reduced the

---

[76] Benjamin Edelman, *"Spyware": Research, Testing, Legislation, and Suits*, April 9, 2014.

[77] Deidre K. Mulligan & Aaron K. Perzanowski, *The Magnificence of the Disaster: Reconstructing the Sony BMG Rootkit Incident*, 22 Berkeley Tech. L. J. 1157 (2007).

[78] *In the Matter of Sony BMG Music Entertainment*, FTC File No. 062 3019 (January 30, 2007).

[79] *In the Matter of Upromise, Inc.*, FTC File No. 1023116 (January 5, 2012); *see also In the Matter of Compete, Inc.*, FTC File No. 1023155 (October 22, 2012).

security of users browsing, by relaying data from secure sessions over the internet in clear text. Thus, if a user had a secure session where a credit card number or the like were submitted, it could be rebroadcast for anyone to intercept. The FTC thought that this reduction in user security contravened promises it made to consumers about security and privacy.

In the HTC matter (discussed in Chapter 8), the FTC found that a cell phone manufacturer's inclusion of "bundled software" profoundly reduced the privacy and security measures built into the Android operating system. This allowed any third-party application to gain access to the phone's core functions, potentially making the device a form of mobile spyware. This creation of systemic insecurity was both unfair and deceptive to consumers.[80]

## Deceptive practices

The FTC has continued its century-long policing of deception in new contexts, including malware. For instance, Innovative Marketing, Inc., adapted an old selling technique to the Web: scaring people into buying a product. The company claimed that it scanned users' computers and detected "illegal" pornography, viruses, and spyware. In reality, no scan was done and it was all a ploy to make sales.[81] The Commission obtained a preliminary injunction against the company and orders for over $170 million in damages. The Commission has litigated other cases with similar facts.[82]

## Criminal prosecutions

Malware, especially when marketed as a spying tool, can lead to federal and state criminal charges. In September 2014, the Department of Justice charged an app developer with conspiracy and violations of federal wiretapping laws for creating and marketing StealthGenie. StealthGenie was an all-purpose spy application for cellular phones that could record conversations and phone calls without the knowledge of the user.[83] The developer planned to push liability onto whomever bought and installed the application. However, in marketing documents, the government alleged that the developer knew that most of their customers would not have the authority to install the app, and would be "people suspecting their partners to be checking on them." Such planning brought StealthGenie out of the realm of a tool that could be misused in a minority of cases to one that was deliberately designed to spy on others.

---

[80] *In the Matter of HTC America Inc.*, FTC File No. 1223049 (February 22, 2013).
[81] *FTC v. Innovative Marketing et al.*, 08-CV-3233-RDB (D. Md. 2010).
[82] *FTC v. Seismic Entertainment et al.*, 104-CV-00377-JD (D. NH 2004).
[83] *US v. Hammad Akbar*, 1:14-cr-276 (E.D. Va. 2014).

## CONCLUSION

The FTC's anti-marketing laws are technology-specific and highly detailed. They generally do not create rights in personal information, but instead focus on how companies can contact individuals. Technical neutrality is impossible, because these technologies are not neutral – they enable different kinds of privacy invasions that are more or less subject to technical and legal controls. The First Amendment also limits how the government can interfere with commercial speech activities, such that regulation has to be tailored to each technology. Most anti-marketing regulation is triggered by concerns about limited bandwidth of technological systems. But as connection speeds have increased and devices have proliferated, anti-marketing regulation takes on a different focus: protecting mental bandwidth from constant interruption. Some argue that privacy controls cause consumers to miss out on bargains, but, in aggregate, such communications become more costly than they are worth.

Evaluating CAN-SPAM and the telemarketing rules presents challenges. Gone are the days when users logged in with slow dial-up modems and had to watch their bandwidth occupied with downloading spam. Also gone are the days of the 1990s, where the only phone one had was shared with a family. When sales callers rang that phone a dozen times a day, the interruption was truly bothersome. Since we are now separated from these sources of annoyance, looking back, the stringency of these laws may seem unjustified. For instance, the ban on prerecorded voice telemarketing calls seems to invite First Amendment problems, yet this prohibition was upheld.[84] Perhaps that was a recognition that regardless of what we feel about technology neutrality, something about a robot calling an individual is offensive to the value of one's time and attention.

Spam continues to be treated as a minor annoyance, but if its full costs were considered in regulatory analysis, spam would emerge as a major consumer problem. Spam continues to be a leading vector for cyberattacks as well.

The FTC's anti-malware efforts provide a venue for the Agency to apply its unfairness power in relatively uncontroversial cases. As the Agency and the business community acclimate to the unfairness theory, it will be used in more matters. The FTC is likely to use unfairness to address bargaining power between companies and consumers, and to address the problems that have arisen from the practical automation of contract formation between the company and consumer.

---

[84] *Moser* v. *F.C.C.*, 46 F.3d 970 (9th Cir. 1995), *cert. denied* 515 US 1161 (1995).

# 10

# Financial privacy

Financial privacy has long been on the Federal Trade Commission's agenda. In the 1950s, the FTC used its unfairness power to stop a company from tricking debtors into revealing their personal information by mailing deceptive postcards that promised free prizes.[1] In the 1970s, the FTC brought matters against tax preparation companies for selling clients' data to third parties.[2] Congress also gave the FTC responsibility for overseeing consumer reporting in the 1970s. Later in the 1990s, the FTC pursued private investigators that used "pretexting" to trick banks and other companies into revealing personal information about customers.

In recent years, the FTC's financial privacy role has changed and become more complex because of the growth of federally chartered banks, the diversity of these banks' activities, and the rise of "FinTech," software and analytics companies that provide financial services. In addition, Congress' creation of the Consumer Financial Protection Bureau (CFPB) in 2011 has caused further jurisdictional line blurring.

Financial privacy is an important topic because of Americans' deep dependence on the credit system. As Americans, we have entrusted important determinations to a private industry that uses secret, proprietary methods – the credit score – to judge access to financial and other opportunities. We also treat scores as a kind of objective assessment of one's trustworthiness, and scores' use has spread outside the credit markets into other areas.[3] As will become clear, a marred consumer report or a low credit score can undermine economic mobility and mire the consumer in a credit dystopia. In such a dystopia, one may be bound to fail financially because of fees and because of the presence of bad bargains.

---

[1] *Lester Rothschild, Trading As Gen-O-Pak Co.*, 49 F.T.C. 1673 (1952); *Rothschild v. FTC*, 200 F.2d 39 (7th Cir. 1952).

[2] *In re Beneficial Corp.*, 86 F.T.C. 119, 168 (1975), aff'd in *Beneficial Corp. v. FTC*, 542 F.2d 611 (3rd Cir. 1976), cert. denied, 430 US 983 (1977); *In the Matter of Tax Corp. of Am. (Maryland), et al.*, 85 F.T.C. 512 (1975); *In the Matter of H&R Block, Inc.*, 80 F.T.C. 304 (1972).

[3] James B. Rule, Privacy in Peril: How We Are Sacrificing a Fundamental Right in Exchange for Security and Convenience (2009).

The goals of financial privacy also inform the Agency's other privacy efforts. Some of the FTC's current privacy attention is focused on a short-term challenge – the information collection and uses surrounding behavioral advertising. What most do not understand is that advertising is just a means to an end for technology companies. Their strategy is to use advertising as an instrument to develop technologies that can automate decisions or even have their own intelligence. When these longer-term goals come into focus, the FTC's history with financial privacy laws will be even more relevant. Financial privacy laws illuminate approaches to addressing issues of equity and inclusion and in giving incentives to fairly handle personal data.

Because of the jurisdictional constraints of the FTC, the Agency is handling many cases where the financially vulnerable are being targeted. More broadly, financial privacy rights are among the Agency's most important efforts, as access to credit and financial services on reasonable terms is critical for Americans. Information, after all, makes it possible to engage in phantom debt collection (to ask individuals to pay for discharged debts that they are not obligated to honor), to target predatory lending offers, and to engage in unauthorized credit card charging schemes.[4]

Financial practices is an area where there are sectoral privacy laws, and these laws enable the FTC to rely on a broader set of authorities and a firmer policy basis than just its discretion to interpret Section 5.

## CREATION OF THE CONSUMER FINANCIAL PROTECTION BUREAU

Historically, Congress vested the FTC with authority to enforce three financial privacy laws: the Fair Credit Reporting Act (FCRA), the Gramm–Leach–Bliley Act (GLBA), and the Fair Debt Collection Practices Act (FDCPA). Because the FTC's Division of Privacy and Identity Protection (DPIP) was created through a reorganization of the Division of Financial Practices (DFP), the Agency's privacy attorneys are deeply versed in dynamics of financial privacy protections. When DPIP was created in 2006, it was given responsibility to enforce the GLBA and FCRA, while the DFP kept the FDCPA.

Because of the housing bubble and ensuing economic crash, Congress created a new regulator in 2011, the Consumer Financial Protection Bureau (CFPB). In doing so, Congress created a confusing system of overlapping jurisdiction between the CFPB and FTC. There is also a fundamental difference between the two agencies: the CFPB has supervisory powers, meaning that it has authority to inspect the practices of companies even when there is no indication of wrongdoing. The FTC, although it has inquisitorial-like powers of investigation, is still primarily an enforcement agency. The FTC investigates companies when it perceives wrongdoing. Congress may have gotten it right in 2011. The incentives underlying

---

[4]   David C. Vladeck, *Charting the Course: The Federal Trade Commission's Second Hundred Years*, 83 GEO. WASH. L. REV. ___ (2015).

consumer reporting and other financial matters may be better regulated by the supervisory approach.

The CFPB was given the power to prescribe rules, issue guidelines, engage in supervision, and conduct studies or issue reports[5] of "enumerated consumer laws," which included the FCRA, GLBA, and FDCPA.[6] The FTC also retained some of these powers with respect to the FCRA and GLBA, as well as the power to enforce these two statutes.

In order to resolve disputes among the agencies, Congress charged the agencies to come to some kind of agreement on these authorities. In January 2012, the agencies did so at least to some extent, releasing a memorandum of understanding (MOU).[7] Much of the MOU is predictable and unremarkable. The agencies committed to information sharing, which in this context means that the FTC can obtain supervisory reports on entities the CFPB oversees.

Covered entities were most concerned about being double-teamed – from getting civil investigative demands (see Chapter 4) from both agencies, or conflicting signals from them. Thus, the agencies committed to regularly vetting investigations to see if the other is or has focused on the same target.

So far, the agencies have worked smoothly together, but, looking ahead, regulatory competition or conflicts between the agencies' priorities could cause one of the two to become more aggressive than the other. The creation of the CFPB may replicate the tensions that currently exist between the FTC's Bureau of Competition and the Department of Justice's Antitrust Division. The relationship between the bureau and the division is fraught, with the DOJ believing itself to be the superior organization. A similar dynamic could arise between the FTC's Bureau of Consumer Protection and the CFPB.

## THE FAIR CREDIT REPORTING ACT OF 1970

The Fair Credit Reporting Act of 1970 (FCRA)[8] is America's first federal consumer information privacy law and one of the first information privacy laws in the world.[9] Congress enacted it to comprehensively regulate consumer reporting and the practice of assembling files about consumers in order to evaluate them for credit, employment, tenancy, "consumer-initiated" transactions, or other opportunities.

---

5  12 U.S.C. §5581(b).
6  12 U.S.C. §5481(12).
7  Memorandum of Understanding between the Consumer Financial Protection Bureau and the Federal Trade Commission, January 20, 2012.
8  Pub. L. 91–508, Title VI, §601, October 26, 1970, 84 Stat. 1128. The FCRA is codified at 15 U.S.C. §1681.
9  Arguably, the 1942 Federal Reports Act was the nation's first privacy law. It required that government collection of information of over ten individuals be reviewed by the Office of Management and Budget.

Consumer reporting started in America just after the Civil War.[10] At the time, Americans had puritanical attitudes toward credit. But attitudes began to shift, and consumer debt began to increase dramatically in the 1950s.[11] For this credit to be safely allocated, some mechanism was needed to document consumers' reliability and credit commitments. Consumer reporting allows businesses to offer credit and other opportunities to complete strangers. As such, consumer reporting creates efficiencies for buyers and sellers. Consumer reporting is a key element of a modern economy. It enables social mobility and even physical mobility, as one can move from one region to the next and keep their credit reputation.

In a landmark 1973 work, Professor James B. Rule charted the development of consumer reporting. Rule presented consumer reporting as a form of public surveillance in the United States. Consumer reporting agencies (CRAs) operated locally at first, and then regionally in the 1950s and 1960s. Many CRAs were "specialty" operations, collecting information for a specific function, such as the creation of "investigative" reports. Investigative reports concerned habits and morals of individuals, and were based on interviews with neighbors and friends. Robert Ellis Smith recounts that CRAs collected information about sexual orientation, couples who lived out of wedlock, alcohol consumption habits, and rumors of encounters with the police.[12] Testifying before a Health, Education, and Welfare committee tasked to examine automated data processing, an aide to Senator William Proxmire, the sponsor of the FCRA, revealed that CRAs frequently provided credit files to law enforcement agencies. The aide continued to describe invasive investigations into the personal life of consumers by the automobile insurance industry: "We asked how is this related to driving ability and the witness said, it really isn't, but we are insuring these people against liability, so we may be compelled, some day to defend them in a legal action before a jury, and if they, in any way, have some deviant behavior characteristics, they wear pink shirts, or have long hair and a mustache, they read Karl Marx ... This is their rationale. If you admit that rationale, there is a certain spurious logic to it, there is no limitation to what they can collect. They can look in your library and see what books you read, what magazines you subscribe to ..."[13] This and other testimony demonstrated that consumer reporting agencies could justify amassing any fact about an individual, including personal lifestyle choices.

The American consumer reporting system has several important characteristics. First, the American consumer reporting system relies on positive and negative

[10] James B. Rule, Private Lives and Public Surveillance: Social Control in the Computer Age (1974). *See also* Evan Hendricks, Credit Scores & Credit Reports (2007 3rd edn).

[11] James B. Rule, David Caplovitz, & Pierce Barker, *The Dossier in Consumer Credit, in* On Record: Files and Dossiers in American Life (Stanton Wheeler, ed., 1969).

[12] Robert Ellis Smith, Ben Franklin's Web Site, Privacy and Curiosity from Plymouth Rock to the Internet (2004).

[13] Department of Health, Education, and Welfare (HEW) Secretary's Advisory Committee on Automated Personal Data Systems (SACAPDS)(testimony of Kenneth A. McLean, May 18, 1972).

information.[14] Negative information is known as "derogatory" information. In other countries, only derogatory information is reported. Thus, in other countries, not having a report is an indicator of good credit – the presence of a file means that collection items exist on the consumer. A derogatory-only information system could be considered much more private, in that it involves surveillance only when non-payment occurs. It also does not foreclose credit opportunities or a vibrant consumer culture. Professor Rule observed that in countries such as France and Australia, consumers enjoy a modern marketplace without having to have a credit report. The American system, on the other hand, relies on total surveillance. It gives individuals incentives to pay bills on time – and to have them monitored by CRAs – in order to have a report dominated by positive information.

Second, the consumer reporting system creates strong incentives to pay bills and debt. Consumer reporting is so effective at causing people to pay debts that companies buy up old debt at dramatic discounts, list it on consumers' reports, and trust that a sufficient number of consumers will pay the old debt, even if they are no longer legally required to do so. Some debt collectors leave obligations on reports even after they have been paid, resulting in consumers being pressured over and over by collectors. Consumers know that derogatory information placed on a report can harm their chances to get a new car, job, or place to live. Thus, threats to tarnish a consumer report are serious. As a result, both the FCRA and the FDCPA, discussed below, have prohibitions to address creditors who falsify information or omit the fact that a debt is contested in order to put derogatory information on a report.

Third, credit is no longer offered on a binary, grant or do not grant, basis. Today, almost anyone can get credit, even if they are improvident. The issue has switched from access to the terms of access to credit. In sum, consumer reports and credit scores determine the cost of credit.

Those with good reports and scores live in a kind of consumer utopia, where credit cards give them liberal, on-demand access to credit for whatever they want to purchase. Many consumers in the credit utopia even get "cash-back" incentives or airline loyalty points for use of credit cards. Credit access costs nothing[15] so long as the consumer is a "convenience" user of credit, meaning the consumer pays the balance every month in full. Credit "revolvers," those who carry a balance and pay interest and fees, end up subsidizing the convenience users, but also may end up in a vicious cycle. Over time, their credit scores will sink and limit their ability to enter into the consumer credit utopia. To stay in this utopia, some consumers closely monitor their credit scores, attempting to keep them as high as possible.

---

[14] James B. Rule, Privacy in Peril: How We Are Sacrificing a Fundamental Right in Exchange for Security and Convenience (2009).

[15] This overlooks the problem that the modern payment system imposes a 2–3 percent tax on all transactions, which is subsidized by cash users. Credit card fees are a fantastic tax on the consumer economy, and it appears to have regressive distributional effects. *See* Scott Schuh, Oz Shy, & Joanna Stavins, Federal Reserve Board of Boston, Who Gains and Who Loses from Credit Card Payments? Theory and Calibrations (2010).

A consumer report shows that negative information can translate into a lower score, miring the consumer in a credit dystopia. One's precise credit score does not matter so much as having one that remains in the "prime" range. Once this score falls below a certain range, the results are severe. The subprime market has much more costly credit, and sometimes these are plainly uneconomical deals. Subprime products are not only more costly, but their providers tend to prey on their own customers with unexpected rules, fees, and limitations that consumers in the credit utopia never experience.

Many, perhaps most, American consumers exist in a credit dystopia. A 2015 study found that over half of Americans have a subprime credit score.[16] There are two silver linings of this story. First, millions of these consumers have a low credit score because of errors on their consumer report.[17] If fixed, their scores might rise into the prime arena. Second, some financially disadvantaged consumers can still find economical financial services products. While big banks have a bad reputation, public scrutiny causes many larger financial institutions to offer advantageous services. For instance, Bank of America and a handful of other large banks will open accounts to undocumented immigrants, thus giving this population access to a mainstream institution. The bad news is that cultural barriers, the alluring convenience of credit cards, and other factors keep many low-socio-economic-status consumers using nonbanks and "storefront" financial services even when bargain alternatives are at hand. Fittingly, the focus of the FTC has been on these nonbank entities.

Fourth, credit scores are important, but they are poorly understood. The Fair Isaac Corporation score is the one most broadly used, but there is no definitive credit score. A lender may choose among dozens of different scoring systems offered by CRAs or other businesses. Consumers can now obtain access to their scores, but the decision making underlying scoring remains secret. Despite this secrecy of scoring, experts have a good idea of the important factors in developing scores.[18]

Fifth, most consumer and regulatory focus is on the "big three" nationwide CRAs: Experian Information Solutions, Inc.; Equifax Information Services, LLC; and TransUnion LLC. Historically, the FTC and the consumer litigation bar have thus focused on this exclusive group of large CRAs. Regulatory focus may change to smaller companies, however, as financial technology firms use personal information.

Sixth, consumer reporting is not only central to a modern economy; it can also support liberal norms. Consumer reporting can reduce credit discrimination. It can focus lenders' attention away from moral considerations or racial bias to more

---

[16] JENNIFER BROOKS, KASEY WIEDRICH, LEBARON SIMS, JR. & SOLANA RICE, CORPORATION FOR ENTERPRISE DEVELOPMENT, EXCLUDED FROM THE FINANCIAL MAINSTREAM (2015).

[17] See discussion below concerning the FTC's Section 319 report, which found that 13 percent of consumer reports had "material" errors, meaning that there was an error significant enough to alter a credit score.

[18] EVAN HENDRICKS, CREDIT SCORES & CREDIT REPORTS (2007 3rd edn).

objective financial risk factors. Consumer reporting reduces transaction costs for consumers, who can shop around for credit without having to establish a deep relationship with each potential creditor. Credit also plays a major role in social mobility in the United States. Because we have a national reporting system, one is no longer limited to having a consumer record in a single region or town.

At the same time, credit reporting must be carried out fairly for all to enjoy the benefits of credit. Prior to the passage of the FCRA, Congress recognized that absent a direct relationship with consumers, normal market pressures did not temper CRA activity. CRAs are business-to-business firms. Thus, CRAs have always lacked the reputational pressures that consumer-oriented, brand-name firms are subject to. Also, the kinds of fair procedures desired by Congress were costly, and so CRAs had little incentive to engage in them. CRAs had inadequate incentives to treat individuals fairly.

Robert Ellis Smith reported that the legislative record of the FCRA was peppered with allegations of CRA investigators falsifying information.[19] As Rule related, derogatory information was more important to CRAs than positive information, and CRAs rarely, if ever, deleted files or outdated information. At the time of Rule's study, individuals had no right of access to the file, and the trade association for CRAs, the Associated Credit Bureaus, told members that reports "must not be revealed to the subject reported on."[20] Even after passage of the original FCRA, consumers generally had to pay for access to their report.

The FTC had to bring many cases to cause CRAs to comply with the business-to-consumer requirements of the FCRA. For example, the FTC sued all three major CRAs in 2000 because they did not answer their phones, and when they did, some consumers were placed on unreasonably long holds. According to FTC complaints, over 1 million calls to Experian and TransUnion went unanswered; Equifax neglected "hundreds of thousands of calls."[21] The companies paid fines and agreed to supervision to ensure adequate call availability. A year later, Equifax paid additional fines for not answering phone calls. In another incident, a worker for TRW misinterpreted a list of taxpayers as one of tax delinquents, causing a large number of residents of a town from getting access to credit.[22]

Consumer reporting is so complex that even strategic use of truthful information can bias the system and disadvantage the consumer. For instance, one purpose of

---

[19] Robert Ellis Smith, Ben Franklin's Web Site, Privacy and Curiosity from Plymouth Rock to the Internet 317 (Privacy Journal 2004).

[20] James B. Rule, Private Lives and Public Surveillance: Social Control in the Computer Age (1974).

[21] *US v. Experian Information Solutions, Inc.*, 3-00CV0056-L (N.D. Tx. 2000)(citing complaint), available at www.ftc.gov/os/caselist/ca300cv0056l.shtm; *US v. Equifax Credit Information Services, Inc.*, 1:00-CV-0087 (N.D. Ga. 2000)(citing complaint); *US v. Trans Union LLC*, 00-C-0235 (ND Il. 2000) (citing complaint).

[22] David Dyer, TRW: Pioneering Technology and Innovation since 1900 (1988).

consumer reports is to assess how much "credit risk" that a consumer has. A consumer who has 10 credit cards, each with a $10,000 credit limit, has the potential to charge up $100,000 in debt in a matter of hours. Yet this same consumer may be a frugal, "convenience" user of credit cards who pays the bill in full every month. Such a consumer is placed at a disadvantage if card companies report the consumer's credit limit and not the credit balance. By reporting limits, the consumer appears overextended to creditors, as potentially owing $100,000 instead of nothing, and this could cause the consumer to not receive more competitive credit offers. A dozen other "facts" can be used strategically to disadvantage consumers or otherwise use the consumer reporting system to extract money from consumers.[23]

Before enactment of the FCRA, legislation was also needed to prevent gratuitous access to consumer reports. A 1969 study of the industry found that anyone with sufficient knowledge of the consumer reporting industry could obtain reports on other individuals.[24] Additionally, law enforcement frequently obtained reports, and so procedures were needed to ensure that such access was procedurally fair and substantively legitimate.

As the next subsection summarizing the FCRA will make it clear, the consumer reporting industry never embraced the various privacy and fairness mandates imposed by Congress. In numerous ways, it has acted to undermine the FCRA's consumer rights. CRAs did everything from creating confusing for-fee services to compete with the government-mandated free consumer report site to creating sham dispute procedures. CRAs are able to be wily because the industry is so technically and organizationally complex. As an example, to cabin misbehavior, Congress included broad prohibitions forbidding "corporate and technological circumvention" in the FCRA to prevent CRAs from skirting disclosure obligations. Things may change now, however, as the CFPB can supervise and examine companies for compliance with the FCRA. The CFPB may be able to detect more violations and interdict them earlier than is possible when using FTC-style, ex post enforcement powers.

## Substantive elements of the FCRA

The FCRA is a complex statute that has been amended multiple times. As originally enacted, its regulatory focus was on CRAs themselves and "users," that is, the purchasers of consumer reports. Major amendments in 1996 created obligations for companies that submit positive or derogative information to consumers' files. In

---

[23] *US v. Performance Capital Management, Inc.*, FTC File No. 982 3542 (C.D. Cal. 2000). (In the case, the FTC argued that the defendant "systematically reported accounts with delinquency dates that were more recent than the actual date of delinquency, resulting in negative information remaining on consumers' credit reports long beyond the seven-year period mandated by the FCRA.")

[24] James B. Rule, David Caplovitz, & Pierce Barker, *The Dossier in Consumer Credit*, in ON RECORD: FILES AND DOSSIERS IN AMERICAN LIFE (Stanton Wheeler, ed., 1969).

FCRA parlance, these are "furnishers," because they provide information to the consumer reporting system.

The 1996 amendments preempted state law until 2003, and, during this period, identity theft became a major consumer concern and topic of state legislation. The financial services industry convinced Congress to permanently extend this preemption, under the theory that states would create conflicting obligations that could harm a national consumer reporting system.

At the most basic level, the FCRA creates a bargain for companies engaged in consumer reporting. If CRAs follow a wide range of safeguards, some specified, some not, to promote "maximum possible accuracy"[25] and to limit disclosures, they enjoy limited immunity from state defamation, privacy, and negligence cases.[26] However, this bargain is beginning to fail. CRAs and other companies have attacked their obligations under the FCRA using the First Amendment.[27] If successful, these First Amendment challenges could cause CRAs to be free of their obligations of transparency, accuracy, and fairness and yet still enjoy statutory immunity from state tort suits.

### Scope: consumer reports and consumer reporting agencies

The definitions of the FCRA's main focus – consumer reports and consumer reporting agencies – are interdependent. Furthermore, these definitions focus on how information is used and the purposes for which it is collected. A consumer report is any communication "by a consumer reporting agency bearing on a consumer's credit worthiness, credit standing, credit capacity, character, general reputation, personal characteristics, or mode of living which is used or expected to be used or collected in whole or in part for the purpose of serving as a factor in establishing the consumer's eligibility for" credit, insurance, or employment purposes.[28]

A CRA is any entity that "regularly engages in whole or in part in the practice of assembling or evaluating consumer credit information or other information on consumers for the purpose of furnishing consumer reports to third parties, and which uses any means or facility of interstate commerce for the purpose of preparing or furnishing consumer reports."

The FCRA's focus on purpose of collection[29] and use often means that information about someone's reputation – even in a covered circumstance, such as employment – is nevertheless not a "consumer report." For instance, writing a

---

[25] 15 U.S.C. §1681e(b).
[26] 15 U.S.C. §1681h(e).
[27] *See, for example, Spokeo, Inc. v. Robins*, 135 S. Ct. 1892, 191 L. Ed. 2d 762 (2015).
[28] 15 U.S.C. §1681a(d)(1).
[29] *Ippolito v. WNS, Inc.*, 864 F.2d 440 (7th Cir. 1988). ("even if a report is used or expected to be used for a non-consumer purpose, it may still fall within the definition of a consumer report if it contains information that was originally collected by a consumer reporting agency with the expectation that it would be used for a consumer purpose.")

letter of recommendation is a statement of general character used for employment, yet it is not regulated (and should not be) by the FCRA.

At the same time, the interdependent definitions allow companies that would otherwise be CRAs skirt the FCRA, undermining the purpose and relevance of the act. For instance, a CRA could collect the same data twice, and use one copy of the data for FCRA-regulated purposes and the other for non-FCRA purposes. Data brokers are companies that act much like CRAs but sell data for unregulated purposes, such as for for marketing or identity verification purposes; these businesses are discussed in Chapter 6. If these companies merge non-FCRA information with FCRA data, it is all subject to the act.

Companies selling data that are aware that they are being used for credit, insurance, employment, or tenancy screening are CRAs, even if they bind data buyers to non-FCRA uses. Companies that advertise FCRA uses for data clearly are CRAs. For instance, a mobile application maker was a CRA despite prohibiting FCRA uses in its terms of service because it advertised the software for hiring purposes.[30] Additionally, deriving target marketing lists from consumer reports is regulated, and these lists can only be used for permissible purposes or for prescreening (discussed below).[31]

CRA status can also apply when the data seller engages in certain business practices. For instance, Spokeo, an aggregator of public records, engaged in a broad series of behaviors that the FTC believed conferred CRA status on it. These activities included selling high-volume access to companies in the background check and human resources industries, buying search engine advertising keywords related to pre-employment background screening, and creating an entire section of its website for job recruiters.[32] Spokeo settled the case for $800,000.

Credit header information forms an important subset of consumer reports. The credit "header" is information used to both identify and authenticate consumers: name, telephone number, mother's maiden name, address, ZIP code, year of birth, age, any generational designation, Social Security number, or "substantially similar identifiers or any combination thereof." Presumably, header information would be subject to the full FCRA regime, but in a 1993 settlement with a CRA, the FTC allowed this information to be used for target marketing, mailings to specific consumers based on the consumers' credit profile, under the rationale that header information does not inform creditworthiness.[33] It was "above the line," meaning it was not part of the consumer report.

The language creating the header distinction is found in the last paragraph of the settlement agreement. It appears to be gratuitous and was not needed to resolve

---

[30] *In the Matter of Filiquarian Publishing, LLC; Choice Level, LLC; and Joshua Linsk*, FTC File No. 112 3195 (2013).

[31] *US v. Teletrack, Inc.*, 111-CV-2060 (N.D. Ga. 2011).

[32] *US v. Spokeo, Inc.*, CV12-05001 (C.D. Cal. 2012).

[33] *In the Matter of Trans Union Corp.*, 116 F.T.C. 1334 (1993).

the underlying case, which involved marketing use of consumer reporting information. Nonetheless, the creation of the header distinction proved to be a disaster for privacy, by removing headers from the FCRA regime completely, allowing them to be sold to anyone. Other CRAs latched onto the header distinction and started selling header information promiscuously. Credit headers had tremendous utility for banks, debt collectors, and marketers, but from the mid 1990s until the passage of the Gramm–Leach–Bliley Act, anyone could obtain credit headers on complete strangers, which led to predictable problems with stalking and domestic violence.

### Investigative consumer reports

The FCRA imposes heightened duties for special reports on individuals' character that are collected through investigative interviews. These reports are typically used to screen a prospective employee. When an "investigative consumer report" is ordered, the person procuring the report must give notice to the individual.[34] If investigative information is used in a subsequent report, it must be verified again.[35]

### Transparency obligations

Consumers have a right to a free copy of their consumer report – but not the more crucial credit score – from each of the "nationwide" CRAs once a year. The major CRAs operate a site to request reports at www.annualcreditreport.com.

Yet, CRAs and others used a number of tactics to divert consumers from the free site when it was created. When this site was first created, CRAs used special code to prevent consumer and other organizations from directly linking to it on the Web. They engaged in upselling to convert the free site into a revenue-generating one. CRAs created numerous "free" sites for consumer reports (often with very similar names, such as freeannualreport.com), but many of these were actually for-fee subscription services. CRAs also bought search advertisements keyed to the terms "free credit report" such that if a consumer searched for the site on Google, ten ads appeared for the for-fee sites, and the free site did not even appear in the top ten search results. These series of technical measures intended to divert consumers and shape their behavior nicely illustrate how wily CRAs can be.

Consumers also receive notice when some adverse action is taken based on information in a consumer report and the identity of the CRA that supplied the report. The rule means that if the consumer report is relied upon *at all* to make an adverse decision, the consumer should be told. In employment situations, the employer is required to provide the copy of the consumer report used to make the determination and a statement of the applicant's rights under the FCRA. Hearing of an adverse action is a signal to the consumer to check her report to ensure errors are not hindering their opportunity.

---

[34]  15 U.S.C. 1681d.
[35]  15 U.S.C. 1681l.

## The file

Consumers have a right of access and correction to their "file." The FCRA defines this term broadly as, "all of the information on that consumer recorded and retained by a consumer reporting agency regardless of how the information is stored." The disclosure should also include sources of information and the identity of the parties that have requested consumer reports.

The idea of a file was straightforward in 1970, back when many CRAs literally kept paper folders and cards pertaining to single individuals. But as the industry has adopted standard database techniques, the definition of "file" has become problematic. In short, there is no "file" anymore. Today, information in the consumer reporting system is tagged with various identifiers, such as name and Social Security numbers. The "file" is the information produced when the database itself is queried, meaning that the query is critical to defining the file. A query for John Smith with the SSN 123-12-1234 results in a different file than a query for just John Smith, Johnny Smith, or the SSN alone. In fact, a search for just the SSN may turn up information about entirely different people who have used John's SSN. In other words, "file" is to be understood dynamically or as a process.

Consumer reporting experts have long argued that the obsolescence of the term "file" has resulted in a problem where the consumer does not receive the same information that is provided to a business. For instance, if a business could pull a report on a name alone, it would receive a broader "file" than would the consumer who is required to provide their name, SSN, and address. There is some evidence that credit grantors can query the credit system with less information than is required when consumers request their "file." For instance, in the FTC's Premier Capital Lending matter, a hacker gained access to a financial institution's CRA account. The hacker made up a series of sequential SSNs but used real names and addresses. Despite the mismatch between SSN and name, the hacker obtained over 300 credit files.[36]

## Permissible uses of consumer reports and prescreening

The FCRA enumerates permissible uses of consumer reports, including for new credit transactions and review of existing accounts, for employment purposes, for insurance underwriting purposes, for professional licensing, and for assessing child support obligations.[37] The FCRA also allows the sharing of consumer reports among affiliated entities.

While marketing is not a permissible use of consumer reports, an exception for "prescreening" allows creditors to buy marketing lists based on consumer reports. Prescreening can only be used to make "firm offers" of credit.[38] Marketers send billions of such offers to American consumers annually. The privacy scholar Dan

---

[36] *In the Matter of Premier Capital Lending, Inc.*, FTC File No. 072 3004 (November 6, 2008).
[37] 15 U.S.C. §1681b.
[38] 15 U.S.C. §1681b(c)(1).

Solove saved all of his offers and collected sixty-nine in a period of ten months. Twenty came from a single card marketing operation – Capital One. As explained below, this marketing increases the risk of identity theft to consumers.

### Data quality obligations

In preparing a consumer report, a CRA must "follow reasonable procedures to assure maximum possible accuracy of the information concerning the individual about whom the report relates."[39] As data collection and reporting systems improve, this standard becomes more stringent with time. CRAs must fix known systemic problems in their systems. The "maximum possible accuracy" duty is also supplemented with the duty of a CRA to verify disputed information, and in cases where data are "inaccurate or incomplete or cannot be verified," to promptly delete the disputed item.[40]

Critics have long argued that CRAs' verification investigations are pro forma at best. They allege that CRAs simply transmit an electronic code back to the creditor, which in turn instantly responds that the obligation is verified. A consumer who complains about inaccuracy gets no verification at all. In March 2015, New York attorney general Eric Schneiderman settled a matter requiring the nationwide CRAs to switch from an automated verification system to one that actually investigates disputes.[41] In perhaps the most significant development in the FCRA since the 2003 amendments, the settlement requires the big three CRAs to use humans to perform a manual review of disputes instead of automating the process.

In effect, the interplay between maximum possible accuracy and the duty to verify and delete is meant to impose a collection limitation rule in the FCRA. As noted above, prior to the passage of the FCRA, investigators fabricated embarrassing and irrelevant derogatory information. For instance, some investigators reported that consumers were homosexual, that they lived out of wedlock, or that they kept an untidy home. After passage of the FCRA, consumer reporting agencies were more restrained in collecting irrelevant information, because this information inherently cannot be verified. The requirement shifted the focus of consumer reporting agencies to verifiable credit-related information.[42]

Despite the statutory requirements of accuracy and verification, evidence exists of systemic inaccuracy in consumer reports. Part of the problem relates to the fuzzy matching logic of CRA systems. Because consumers make errors in credit applications (e.g., transposing SSNs), and because they sometimes use different names (nicknames, diminutives, maiden names, etc.), CRAs use complex decision-making

---

[39]  15 U.S.C. 1681e (2013).

[40]  15 U.S.C. 1681i (a)(5)(A) (2013).

[41]  In the Matter of the Investigation by Eric T. Schneiderman, Attorney General of the State of New York, of Experian Information Solutions, Inc.; Equifax Information Services, LLC; and TransUnion LLC, March 2015.

[42]  Mark Furletti, *An Overview and History of Credit Reporting*, Federal Reserve Bank of Philadelphia Payment Cards Center Discussion Paper No. 02-07, June 2002.

systems to match credit data to consumers. This can result in bizarre episodes of "mixed files," where data from two different people are amalgamated. One well-known anecdote concerns Judy Thomas, who sued TransUnion for regularly mixing her report with a Judith Upton. As the FCRA expert Evan Hendricks explained, "Upton's Social Security number was only one digit different than Thomas' SSN. That, combined with three common letters in the first name, was sufficient to cause a regular merging of the two women's credit histories."[43] How could a Judy Thomas be mixed with a Judith Upton? One hypothesis is that CRAs track women by their first names in order to address marital surname changes.

But the problem with errors is not just anecdotal: it has been shown to be structural. In a landmark and labor-intensive study, academics working in conjunction with the FTC studied almost 3,000 consumer reports belonging to 1,000 consumers and found that twenty-six percent identified an error on a report.[44] Thirteen percent experienced a change in their credit score as a result of correcting the error. Five percent of the study participants had errors that, once corrected, improved their credit score so that they could obtain credit at a lower price. The report suggests that over 10 million consumers are paying higher rates for credit as a result of report inaccuracies.

## Medical record privacy
Many Americans carry debt from medical procedures, and there is a risk that the appearance of such debt on a consumer report could identify the specific condition that a person has, and harm the consumer's credit and employment opportunities. Thus the FCRA requires that medical debt be coded to obscure a consumer's medical condition.

## Time limits on reporting adverse information
Most "adverse" information, such as records of civil judgments and arrests, cannot be reported by CRAs more than seven years after the event occurs.[45] Records of bankruptcy cannot be reported ten years after the event. Criminal convictions, as opposed to mere records of arrest, are not subject to any time limit and may always be reported. These rights are examples of a right to be forgotten in US law.

An important exemption exists for the FCRA's obsolescence requirements – CRAs cannot report these categories of outdated information, but they can keep it in their databases. Furthermore, they are permitted to ignore the time limitations when the underlying transaction is for $150,000 or more, or where someone is being considered for employment at a salary that is $75,000 or more. This means that for

[43] Evan Hendricks, *Oregon Jury, D.C. Circuit Continue Trans Union's Losing Streak*, 22 Privacy Times 15 (August 5, 2002), available at www.privacytimes.com/buttons/b3_FCRA.htm.

[44] FTC, REPORT TO CONGRESS UNDER SECTION 319 OF THE FAIR AND ACCURATE CREDIT TRANSACTIONS ACT OF 2003 (December 2012), available at www.ftc.gov/os/2013/02/130211factareport.pdf.

[45] 15 U.S.C. §1681c.

most home mortgages and for high-stakes job background checks, all adverse information can be included in the report.

In order to administer the seven- and ten-year limits for selling adverse data, CRAs must properly determine when adverse information first came into being. Under the FCRA, an adverse credit event starts at the time when the account first went delinquent. Creditors have attempted to game the time limits and extend the period that bad debts are reported by falsifying the date when the consumer failed to pay. For instance, the FTC sued a debt collector in 2000 for furnishing false date information in order to keep obligations on consumers' reports past the seven-year period.[46]

### Opt-out rights

The FCRA extends consumers two kinds of opt-out rights. First, companies are free to share consumer report information with affiliates, but they must allow consumers to opt out of marketing solicitations from affiliates.[47] Second, consumers can opt out of prescreened offers of credit.[48] One can opt out by calling 1-888-5OPTOUT or by visiting www.optoutprescreen.com. Written prescreened offers must contain notice of this opt-out right. Identity theft experts have long advocated that consumers do so, as prescreened offers can easily be stolen from one's mailbox and used to apply for a credit card.

Prescreening may also enable other kinds of fraud. In 2013, the FTC brought a matter against Equifax for selling prescreened lists to "Direct Lending," a company that in turn used the information to target "consumers in financial distress for loan modification, debt relief, and foreclosure relief services."[49]

Some do not opt out because the system requires consumers to submit their Social Security number to stop the offers. The Social Security number requirement apparently is in place to ensure that the correct person is opted out. But as discussed above, when selling reports, CRAs find it acceptable to allow business users to search on name alone. This dynamic is typical for opt-out schemes – opting out is subjected to higher security requirements than the much riskier act of delivering a full consumer report to a business (see Chapter 6 for a discussion of default choices and incentives).

A 2004 Federal Reserve study found that 6 percent of consumers with credit files had opted out of prescreening: "The large number of individuals who have opted out suggests that it is not especially difficult to do so if individuals are aware of this option. A consumer survey indicates that about one-fifth of consumers are aware of

---

[46] US v. *Performance Capital Management, Inc.*, FTC File No. 9823542 (C.D. Cal. 2000). Prior to the 1996 amendments, which added liability for furnishing false information, the FTC used its unfairness power to address the problem of forward-dating debt obligations. See *In the Matter of The May Department Stores Company*, 122 F.T.C. 1 (1996).

[47] 15 U.S.C. §1681s–3.

[48] 15 U.S.C. §1681e.

[49] *In the Matter of Equifax Information Services LLC*, FTC File No. 1023252 (October 10, 2012).

their right under federal law not to receive prescreened solicitations. If awareness of this right was more widespread, it is likely that more consumers would opt out."[50]

### Anti-identity theft provisions

CRAs are key intermediaries in the problem of identity theft. Generally speaking, in order for an impostor to open new credit, bank, or utilities accounts in a victim's name, the impostor must fool the targeted business into procuring a consumer report in the victim's name. Thus, the controls that businesses and CRAs place on new customer authentication can form a chokepoint to prevent fraud.

The problem is that such a chokepoint can squeeze the life out of legitimate credit applications. The vast majority of new applications for credit are not fraudulent. And any procedures implemented to catch fraud tend to cause delay and expense to honest consumers who are simply trying to get credit quickly. Identity thieves prey on this dynamic, knowing that creditors have incentives to process applications quickly and to address fraud, if it occurs, at a later time.

Consumers can erect different types of speed bumps to slow down the credit-granting process. On the most basic level, the FCRA allows consumers to place a 90-day fraud alert by simply calling a phone number. Once placed, creditors must employ "reasonable policies and procedures" to confirm the applicant's identity. This language unfortunately suggests that in the absence of a fraud alert, creditors need not even act reasonably when establishing accounts. Indeed, banks that have extended credit to impostors have argued that they owe no duty at all to the victim, despite the fact that they thought they were dealing with the victim.[51]

A different kind of speed bump is imposed when a consumer requests an "extended" fraud alert. This lasts for seven years and has the effect of suspending prescreening for five years. Extended alerts require the consumer to submit an identity theft report, but give the consumer the opportunity to specify contact information that must be used when creditors make lending decisions.

A virtual gate is imposed by "security freezes," an option that consumers can request under state laws that stops consumer reports from being issued at all. Security freezes are inconvenient for those who need credit frequently. But for those who do not foresee a need for transactions that trigger a consumer report, a freeze stops almost all risk of identity theft and lowers the risk of impulse purchases on credit.

Once identity theft has occurred, victims can instruct CRAs to block information from accounts alleged to be fraudulent.[52] Additionally, they can approach the business where their identity was stolen and request the materials the impostor

---

[50] BOARD OF GOVERNORS OF THE FEDERAL RESERVE SYSTEM, REPORT TO THE CONGRESS ON FURTHER RESTRICTIONS ON UNSOLICITED WRITTEN OFFERS OF CREDIT AND INSURANCE (2004).

[51] *Wolfe v. MBNA America Bank*, 485 F.Supp.2d 874 (2007).

[52] 15 U.S.C. §1681c-2.

used to establish the account. This gives victims the ability to investigate the case on their own.[53]

The 2003 amendments gave the FTC the authority to specify "red flags" for financial institutions and most creditors.[54] Under the red flag rule, covered entities must have a program to prevent identity theft. They must identify situations that might indicate identity theft and, when these situations arise, respond appropriately to prevent or mitigate fraud.

### Security of consumer reports

Recall that prior to the FCRA, anyone with knowledge of the workings of the consumer reporting system could obtain reports about others. Today, obtaining a report without a permissible purpose can expose an individual to both civil and criminal liability. Additionally, CRAs are required to have adequate physical and technical security for consumer reports. Security obligations include vetting the identity of buyers of consumer reports, ensuring that they are only using consumer reports for permissible purposes, and taking action when there are indications that buyers are sharing reports with others, or using them for impermissible purposes.[55]

Security obligations extend to users of consumer reports. Businesses that use consumer reports must dispose of them securely,[56] and the FTC has brought cases against companies that allow reports to be disposed of in ordinary trash cans.[57]

### Law enforcement access to consumer reports

Law enforcement agencies have several options to obtain consumer reports. They can use a court order or federal grand jury subpoena (although they may not use an attorney-issued or "unsupervised" subpoena).[58] Any governmental agency (presumably even a local police department) can obtain consumer reports for investigations related to international terrorism.[59] The FBI has its own provision to obtain consumer reports in counterintelligence or antiterrorism purposes by certifying its need in writing.[60]

### The FTC's current FCRA role

Congress never granted the FTC rule-making authority under the FCRA until 2003, and even then only allowed rule-making in specific areas. To help guide consumers

---

[53] 15 U.S.C. §1681g(e).
[54] 15 U.S.C. §1681m.
[55] *In the Matter of Equifax Information Services LLC*, FTC File No. 1023252 (October 10, 2012); *US v. Rental Research Services, Inc.*, 0:09-cv-00524 (D. Minn. 2009).
[56] 15 U.S.C. §1681w; 16 C.F.R. §682.
[57] *US v. PLS Financial Services, Inc., PLS Group, Inc., and The Payday Loan Store of Illinois, Inc.*, 112-cv-08334 (N.D. Il. 2012).
[58] 15 U.S.C. §1681b.
[59] 15 U.S.C. §1681v.
[60] 15 U.S.C. §1681u

and industry, the FTC issued a number of staff opinion letters, usually in response from business questions and concerns over the statute. The FTC stopped this practice in 2000 with the chairmanship of Timothy Muris. In July 2011, the FTC condensed this advice and produced a report summarizing its FCRA activities.[61]

The CFPB was given general rule-making authority under the FCRA, and most of the FTC's rule-making responsibilities were transferred to the CFPB.[62] The FTC retains authority over §1681m(e), which concerns red flags for identity theft, and §1681w, dealing with disposal of consumer report information.[63] The FTC retained its enforcement authorities under the FCRA.

### The FCRA's cracking foundations, and great potential

The FCRA was the first law that regulated "big data." In 1970, only the largest, most sophisticated companies could manage a "big" data set. Today, individual users can construct very large data sets and use them for automated decision-making. These dynamics have started to undermine the FCRA regulatory framework in several ways.

First, intermediaries with troves of information, such as search engines, can make automated determinations similar to those made by CRAs. For instance, some companies now make credit offers without a consumer report. They may do this by determining the websites that a person frequents – someone who visits luxury goods sites may get an advertisement for credit that another would not. In this, the line between pure target marketing and consumer reporting has been confused. While prescreening requires certain procedures and a "firm offer" of credit, websites that make direct credit offers to consumers without consulting a consumer report or prescreening list operate free of the FCRA. In the process, consumers may see ads for better or for worse credit terms than they would qualify for if the creditor had to obtain a report and score.

Second, a panoply of companies now offer scoring or identification services that are used for purposes almost identical to consumer reports yet fall outside the FCRA (see Chapter 6's discussion of data brokers). Sometimes these scores are used for purposes just as important as credit or employment, but the FCRA's transparency and accountability mechanisms do not apply.[64] The FCRA does not apply to marketing generally, but, at the same time, the line between marketing and credit offers is not entirely clear. A website might screen a consumer in its marketing efforts and show ads for different financial products. Woe to the consumer who is assessed

---

[61] FTC, 40 Years of Experience with the Fair Credit Reporting Act (2011).

[62] These concerned affiliate marketing, medical information, furnisher accuracy, disputes, opting out of prescreening, risk-based prices, address discrepancies, free credit reports, summaries of rights, negative information notice, and the nationwide status anti-circumvention rules.

[63] These are codified at 15 U.S.C. 1681m(e) and 1681w, respectively.

[64] Pam Dixon & Robert Gellman, World Privacy Forum, The Scoring of America: How Secret Consumer Scores Threaten Your Privacy and Your Future, April 2, 2014.

poorly in the marketing process – that consumer would receive an ad for a less economical credit card and pay more for credit, even if their file ultimately showed a more reliable payment history than the marketing screening did.

At the same time, the FCRA could be seen as a model law to address a new world of big data. The FCRA allows entities to collect almost any kind of data, and instead focuses on the remedies of fair decisions and transparency. The FCRA framework, if broadened, could be a workable framework to address tensions surrounding new data models.

Finally, technology may simply make the FCRA obsolete. The FCRA is built on the assumption that data collection, analysis, and modeling are too complex for most firms to handle. Thus, these processes must be outsourced to a third party. When these third parties aggregate information for others, they fit neatly into the definition of the CRA and are regulated.

But what if technology advances to the point where first parties can perform the same kinds of data analysis? With the widespread availability of personal information in public records, and with the rich transactional data available to companies from their interactions with consumers, companies may be able to do the data collection and analysis themselves. Already, there is evidence that employers are using search engines to screen employees.[65] Such activities would fall through the FCRA and not be subject to its transparency and fairness obligations.

## The FCRA and the First Amendment

Enacted before the broad expansion of free speech rights in the 1970s, the FCRA lies in tension with modern First Amendment jurisprudence. For instance, the First Amendment now recognizes an almost-unlimited right to report public record matters. Despite this constitutional right, the FCRA imposes *heightened* requirements on the use of public record information. For instance, under 15 U.S.C §1681k, CRAs must use "strict procedures" to ensure public record information is complete and up to date.

Like much of consumer protection law, provisions of the FCRA in effect compel or prohibit speech activities. For instance, the FCRA requires CRAs to indicate that a consumer has disputed or closed certain accounts. Other provisions mandate how long truthful public record information can be reported. If reporting data about a consumer is speech, perhaps the entire FCRA framework is suspect, because it inherently mandates limits on to whom data can be disclosed and the purposes of the disclosure.[66]

---

[65] Alessandro Acquisti & Christina M. Fong, *An Experiment in Hiring Discrimination via Online Social Networks*, NBER SUMMER SYMPOSIUM ON THE ECONOMICS OF DIGITIZATION (2013).

[66] *Trans Union LLC v. Federal Trade Commission*, 536 US 915 (2002) (J. Kennedy dissenting from denial of cert.).

The rationale for these various rules is complex and reflects the many compromises inherent in legislative bargains. One looming problem in the FCRA comes from courts that, in analyzing a challenge to a single fairness procedure, fail to understand its purpose and context in the larger legislative framework. Any single FCRA requirement can appear to be frivolous. Take the example of heightened procedures for public record information. That requirement is borne of the problem that public records often lack individual identifiers, so people with similar names can be confused. In a careful study of criminal records policy in the United States, Professor James Jacobs observes that data companies sometimes match arrest records and other derogatory information on name alone.[67] Public records also change over time, as final dispositions are added to matters. Finally, public records are sometimes wrong. If a consumer goes through the trouble of correcting a public record, the effort could be for naught if a CRA can still report the old version. A court looking at these procedures may see it as a simple, wrongheaded prohibition on activities instead of a balancing act crafted by Congress to address intricate problems in the use of public record information.

## FCRA preemption

The 1996 amendments to the FCRA preempted stronger state law in seven consumer reporting activities for seven years. These included bars on state regulation of prescreening, the sharing of consumer report information among affiliates, the duties of those who furnish information to CRAs, and time limits surrounding responding to inaccuracies. Thus, the 2003 amendments were strongly motivated by industry desires to retain preemption. CRAs feared that state and even local governments could interfere with their nationwide operations, and that plaintiffs' attorneys would bring crippling class actions based on state privacy laws.

Congress used floor, ceiling, and "conduct required" preemption in the 2003 amendments. In floor preemption, Congress sets a minimum "floor" of protections that can be enhanced by stronger state laws, so long as these protections do not dilute or interfere with the purpose of the federal law.[68]

Ceiling preemption imposes an upper limit on protections, thus barring state legislatures from creating new provisions. For instance, the 2003 amendments prohibited states from regulating prescreening offers in any way, because if Americans did not get as many credit card offers as they currently do, it would conflict with "the public good." The American Bankers Association successfully

---

[67] JAMES B. JACOBS, THE ETERNAL CRIMINAL RECORD (2015); *see also* Guy Stuart, *Databases, Felons, and Voting: Bias and Partisanship of the Florida Felons List in the* 2000 *Elections*, 119(3) POLIT. SCI. QUART. 453 (Fall 2004).

[68] For an extended discussion of preemption in privacy law, *see* Paul M. Schwartz, *Preemption and Privacy*, 118 YALE L. J. 902 (2008).

sued under the 2003 amendments to invalidate a portion of a California law that mandated opt-in protections for information sharing.[69]

"Conduct required" preemption exists between the two, acting as a ceiling in areas where the statute commands some specific performance. Many of the identity theft provisions are subject to conduct required preemption, meaning that states can enact laws such as credit freezes and other complementary privacy protections against fraud.

### *The many missed opportunities in the 2003 amendments to the FCRA*

The industry's need to amend the law created an awesome opportunity to fix well-known problems in consumer reporting, yet, during this period, the FTC's leadership used its muscle to lobby *for permanent* preemption of state law. Agency leaders styled the 2003 amendments as a "reauthorization" (it wasn't – the FCRA would continue to exist even if Congress took no action). In testimony to Congress, its first recommendation – discussed before identity theft provisions and free consumer report rights – was to permanently renew preemption.

While the FTC went to bat for the industry and successfully recommended improvements to the FCRA, including reforming rules surrounding investigations,[70] adding a series of rights for identity theft prevention and remediation, and establishing a right to free copies of consumer reports, there were too many missed opportunities: ones that are likely to never be revisited because the Agency supported permanent, rather than time-limited, preemption. The Agency could have lobbied to:

- Expand the scope of the FCRA from just credit, insurance, employment, and tenancy. Companies today are using automated decision methods to make many important decisions about people. The FTC could have explored whether, decades after the passage of the FCRA, new kinds of decisions should be subject to the act's fairness guidelines. Some prime candidates include systems that evaluate how willing someone is to comparison-shop (in order to assign them a score that could be used for dynamic pricing), systems that assess impulsivity,[71] systems that verify identity or engage in antifraud measures, systems to verify voting eligibility,[72] or algorithms used in college entrance acceptance. More generally, while the decisions made by FCRA-regulated systems are transparent, the methods they use are not. It was shortsighted of

---

[69] *Am. Bankers Ass'n v. Lockyer*, 541 F.3d 1214 (9th Cir. 2008).

[70] The FTC fixed the "Vail letter" problem that subjected employee misconduct investigations to the full scope of FCRA protections.

[71] Andrew Thompson, *Engineers of Addition, Slot Machines Perfected Addictive Gaming. Now, Tech Wants Their Tricks*, THE VERGE, May 6, 2015.

[72] Guy Stuart, *Databases, Felons, and Voting: Bias and Partisanship of the Florida Felons List in the 2000 Elections*, 119(3) POLIT. SCI. QUART. 453 (Fall 2004).

the Agency to not consider more carefully whether, for instance, credit scoring and similar methods of decision-making should remain in a "black box."

- Clarify the conception of "the file" problem so that consumers obtain a disclosure of all information that is being associated with them and reported to businesses.
- Lengthen the statute of limitations to address the problem that identity theft victims often take years to discover the crime.
- Fix the problem of perfunctory, automated dispute investigations.
- Rationalize civil penalties under the act, both to prevent annihilative liability and to encourage responsible actions by private litigants.
- Update the FCRA's various statutorily specified monetary awards and triggers so that they would keep up with inflation.[73]
- Address the problem that arrest information without a subsequent conviction or other disposition appears in consumer reports for 7 years. We know that arrests are focused on the poor and minority populations, and that an arrest alone does not indicate guilt.[74]
- Decouple the price of consumer reports from inflation measures. The cost of consumer reports is keyed to the consumer price index. As a result, the FCRA structurally ratchets up the price of reports while the cost of delivering reports has declined to nearly zero.
- Head off First Amendment challenges by CRAs by tying immunity from tort suits to the preservation of key FCRA rights. If CRAs are successful in invalidating the burdens of the FCRA, they should not enjoy the benefits of immunity from state privacy law.

## THE GRAMM–LEACH–BLILEY ACT

Following the 1929 stock market crash and the Great Depression, Congress enacted limits on how banks and investment firms could integrate. A 1933 law, the Glass–Steagall Act, created deposit insurance, limited the amount commercial banks could deal in securities, and strengthened the Federal Reserve. But by the 1980s, banks found ways to reintegrate investment banking as subsidiary entities. By the 1990s, there was more comfort with and demand for integrated financial institutions.

With the Financial Services Modernization Act of 1999 (commonly known as the Gramm–Leach–Bliley Act, "GLBA"), Congress formally repealed restrictions from Glass–Steagall and the Bank Holding Company Act to allow more integration among banks, investment, and insurance firms. As the GLBA proceeded through Congress,

---

[73] For instance, the FCRA in 1970 allowed creditors to look more deeply into the backgrounds of prospective employees for $20,000 salaries, and for credit applicants seeking $50,000 loans. To have kept up with inflation in 2003, these amounts would have to have been raised to $94,000 and $230,000, respectively (in 2015, they would have to be $120,000 and $302,000).

[74] James B. Jacobs, The Eternal Criminal Record (2015).

concerns were raised about privacy protections among behemoth financial services companies. Some of these companies had over 1,000 affiliates, raising the risk that transactional data relating to payment could find their way into insurance or lending operations. Furthermore, these affiliates often used different brand names; thus, the consumer would not expect that sharing information with a bank would authorize information to transfer to obscure, unheard-of companies. Congress added privacy provisions, known as Title V, to the GLBA to address these concerns.

---

### MARKETING MIASMA AND THE GLBA

In a June 1999 House Committee markup session of the bill that passed as the GLBA, financial service industry lobbyists expected Democrats to raise privacy issues, but thought that Republicans would successfully oppose adding privacy provisions to the bill. An earlier attempt by Democratic Representative Ed Markey of Massachusetts in May had failed on a 19–8 vote.[75]

But things changed between the May and June events. Right before the June markup, Minnesota attorney general Mike Hatch sued US Bancorp for selling customer records to a telemarketer. This suit opened a window onto ugly direct marketing being conducted by banks, where the institution would sell customer information to third-party telemarketers and receive some percentage of revenue. These and other practices encouraged banks to ignore fraudulent sales, because they made money from both the sale and the fees associated with reversing transactions.[76]

In the June markup session, Markey again introduced his privacy amendment, but this time he found support from Republicans. Representative Paul Gillmor of Ohio introduced his own privacy amendment, commenting that advances of technology and information gathering "carry with them unprecedented new threats to personal privacy."[77]

Others shared personal stories of perceived privacy invasion, including Representative Barton of Texas, who recently received a Victoria's Secret catalog at his Washington DC home. He had complained that his credit union must have sold his new address to Victoria's Secret. Barton feared that

---

[75] Dean Anason, In Focus: All of a Sudden, Customer Privacy Is Reform Bill Thorn, AMERICAN BANKER, June 14, 1999.

[76] Jessica Silver-Greenberg, *Banks Seen as Aid in Fraud against Older Consumers*, NEW YORK TIMES, June 10, 2013; Charles Duhigg, *Bilking the Elderly, with a Corporate Assist*, NEW YORK TIMES, May 20, 2007. The problem of financial institutions looking the other way when fraud is present has a long history. The FTC brought an administrative complaint against a company for ignoring high rates of chargebacks in 1993 and, in settlement, obligated the company to monitor merchants for evidence of fraudulent charges. *In the Matter of Citicorp Credit Service, Inc.*, 116 F.T.C. 87 (1993).

[77] Dawn Kopecki, *US Financial Industries Face Privacy Regs in Bank Bill*, DOW JONES NEWS SERVICE, June 11, 1999.

his spouse would see the catalog and conclude that he had impure thoughts while away from his home district. Barton believed that he should be able to stop financial institutions from selling personal information to third parties and supported the Markey amendment.[78]

The financial services lobbyists were distraught – one was anonymously quoted as being in "shell shock." After passage of the amendment, banking industry representatives threatened to oppose GLBA, but they were careful to not mention their opposition was based on privacy. Instead, they said the bill had "problems" and "negative changes."[79]

Ultimately, GLBA passed with privacy provisions intact.

In the minds of many consumers, banks are still the small-town, anchor business of the community. Many state courts have imposed an implied duty of confidentiality on these organizations.[80] But the modern bank is a business no different from any other retailer – in fact, some of the most successful banks are ones that adopted retail-like marketing strategies and high-risk credit-granting practices. This trend toward aggressive use of financial information for ordinary marketing activities dates back at least since the early 1990s. For instance, in a 1992 New York attorney general settlement, American Express agreed to disclose to the public that it sorted its cardholder base into various categories, such as "Rodeo Drive Chic" or "Fifth Avenue Sophisticated."[81]

Larger, federal banks are based on a premise that efficiencies result from size and from multiple product offerings. These efficiencies are often tied to the assumption that data from one's banking transactions could inform insurance, investment, and other products offered by the same institution. Large banks could only increase their revenue so much through new customer acquisition; they needed to deepen their offerings to their current customer base.

Although banks owe a common law duty of confidentiality to consumers, they have been notoriously blasé about accountholder privacy. Some in the financial sector share the Posnerian view that privacy is simply a tactic to hide derogatory information and to avoid financial obligations. These views may also be attributable to the discomfort that bank employees have with modern activities – which include

---

[78] Financial institutions regularly "furnish" data, including contact information, to consumer reporting agencies. That is probably what happened to Barton – his Washington address was likely furnished by his credit union to the CRA, which then sold the address as a "credit header." Recall from the FCRA section above that until the effective date of the GLBA, CRAs freely sold such headers for marketing purposes. GLBA treated headers, at least when they were sourced from financial institutions, as nonpublic personal information.

[79] Dean Anason, *In Focus: All of a Sudden, Customer Privacy Is Reform Bill Thorn*, AMERICAN BANKER, June 14, 1999.

[80] Woodrow Hartzog, *Reviving Implied Confidentiality*, 89 IND. L. J. 763 (2014).

[81] Denise Gallene, *Chalk One Up for Privacy American Express Will Inform Cardholders That It Sorts Them for Sales Pitches*, LOS ANGELES TIMES, May 14, 1992.

e-mailing spreadsheets of data about consumers to others for ordinary operations, detailed data mining of transactional data, and the marketing of financial products of dubious value.

In H. Jeff Smith's seminal 1994 study of privacy, he found that banks stood starkly opposed to the pro-privacy posture of healthcare organizations. One bank interviewee said, "We joke about it [privacy] all the time ... because we officially say that we don't reveal information and we treat it with the utmost respect. What a crock. I hear people laughing in the elevator about credit reports they've pulled!"

Things had not changed much later in the 1990s when banks faced serious threats of legislative action. In fact, banks argued that they had a First Amendment right to sell customer information, and that a customer right to opt-out would violate the banks' rights. Banks lobbied intensely to free themselves from privacy restrictions under the GLBA.

## The GLBA's provisions

Codified at 15 U.S.C §§6801 et seq., the GLBA is organized around notice and choice concerning financial institutions' information-sharing activities. Financial institutions are businesses "significantly engaged" in "financial activities," which are broadly defined by the Bank Holding Company Act.

### Scope

The GLBA only protects "nonpublic personal information" (NPI). NPI is personally identifiable financial information that is provided by the consumer to the institution, information generated by transactions with the consumer, or information otherwise obtained by the financial institution. Consumers are those who obtain a financial product from a financial institution. "Customers" are a class of consumers who have an ongoing relationship with a financial institution.

Importantly, the law exempts "publicly available information" from NPI. Publicly available information is broadly defined as data made available lawfully by governments or information that appears in widely distributed media (including phone books, newspapers, and websites). This would appear to narrow the scope of the GLBA, as many kinds of NPI may appear online or in a public record. However, the FTC interpreted the definitions to hinge on data provenance: if a consumer's date of birth appears in a public record somewhere, it is still NPI so long as the bank originally obtained it from the consumer.

### Information sharing

While the GLBA imposes a duty of confidentiality on banks,[82] its provisions conflict with traditional confidentiality obligations. For instance, physicians and lawyers

---

[82] 15 U.S.C. §6801(a).

generally cannot reveal their patients' and clients' secrets. These professionals certainly cannot use secrets for their own profit or advantage. However, in the banking context, the GLBA explicitly allows the sale of confidential account information to third parties, including facts such as how much an accountholder has and where money is spent.

Before sharing NPI, financial institutions must provide the consumer with a privacy notice and thirty days to opt out from the data transfer.[83] A consumer opt-out is presumed to last perpetually.

Consumers cannot opt out of "joint marketing" activities, and this forms a major loophole in the GLBA's privacy provisions. Small banks staked out joint marketing as an exception to allow smaller institutions to take advantage of information sharing and to create partnerships that large banks could effect without permission (because large institutions could share information among affiliates to cross-market services under GLBA). Joint marketing activities are only lightly regulated – all that is needed is a written contract among financial institutions that limits data use to marketing purposes.[84] Also, they are not limited to small banks – large banks can create an unlimited number of joint marketing agreements and circumvent the GLBA opt-out rights.

### Privacy notices

Financial institutions must deliver a description of information collection, use, and transfer practices. If the institution wishes to transfer data to a third party, it must also deliver an opt-out notice. The notice must be "clear and conspicuous," meaning that it is reasonably understandable and designed to call attention to information in the notice.

Financial institutions must disclose category information – the categories of information collected and disclosed and the categories of affiliates and third parties that receive the information. They must also contain an information security policy.

Finally, opt-out notices must describe a "reasonable means" for exercising choice. Some financial institutions actively discouraged opting out by warning customers that customer service would suffer and the like.

The FTC and other banking agencies spent an enormous amount of effort creating model opt-out notices for banks.[85] But the basic problem remains that regardless of clarity of notices, most Americans think their banks cannot sell personal information. They have no reason to pay attention to the notice. For this reason, the model notice is not called a "privacy notice" – testing showed that readership declined when it was labeled as such because it falsely suggested to the consumer that data could not be sold.[86]

---

[83] 15 U.S.C. §6802.
[84] 16 C.F.R. §313.13.
[85] 74 Fed. Reg. 62890 (2009).
[86] "What we learned in our testing was that consumers took something very specific from 'privacy policy,' those words 'privacy policy.' What they took that to mean is that the institution that is sending you this

## Information security

The GLBA security safeguards rule occupies only two pages in the Federal Register. Its core commandment is for financial institutions to have an information security program with administrative, technical, and physical safeguards. These safeguards can be tailored to the size of the institution and have the objective to (1) safeguard customer information, (2) protect against hazards to the security or integrity of the information, and (3) protect against access or use that could result in substantial harm or inconvenience to customers.

The security safeguards rule is slightly narrower than other protections in the GLBA – Congress specified that it should apply to "customer" (an individual with an ongoing relationship with the financial institution) rather than "consumer" information.

## Pretexting is prohibited

Chapter 6 introduced the 1999 Rapp "pretexting" case, where the FTC used its deception and unfairness authority to sue private investigators it alleged were using false information in order to trick institutions into revealing customer details.[87] Pretexting typically involves an investigator calling an institution for purposes of obtaining a third party's information without their consent. This is accomplished by pretending to be the third party, or through some other ruse. In enacting the GLBA, Congress formally prohibited pretexting performed against financial institutions.[88]

## Enforcement

Several courts have held that the GLBA did not create a private right of action.[89] The GLBA does not preempt state law;[90] however, federally chartered banks argue that state restrictions on information sharing do not apply to them.

The privacy rule specifies that a broad range of businesses are subject to the FTC's enforcement authority, including mortgage brokers/lenders, "payday" lenders, finance companies, account servicers, check cashers, wire transferors, travel agencies, collection agencies, credit and financial advisors, tax preparation firms, nonfederally insured credit unions, and some investment advisors.[91] At first glance, the FTC's enforcement efforts appear to be against small-fry operations, but this is because GLBA oversight of banks is entrusted to other agencies.

policy does not share your information, period, because it's a 'privacy' policy. Well, of course that's not the case or usually not the case, so we had to come up with another title that didn't create that implication." Conference on Behavioral Economics and Consumer Policy, April 20, 2007 (Comments of Joel Winston).
[87] *FTC v. Rapp d/b/a Touch Tone Information, Inc.*, No. 99-WM-783 (D. Colo. 1999).
[88] 15 U.S.C. §6821.
[89] *Newcomb v. Cambridge Home Loans, Inc.*, 861 F. Supp. 2d 1153 (D. Haw. 2012); *Enriquez v. Countrywide Home Loans, FSB*, 814 F. Supp. 2d 1042 (D. Haw. 2011); *In re Gjestvang*, 405 B.R. 316 (Bankr. E.D. Ark. 2009).
[90] 15 U.S.C. §6807.
[91] 16 C.F.R. §313.1(b).

The FTC's enforcement of the GLBA has been straightforward. The cases' most surprising attribute is the depravity of the defendants' conduct – the FTC's jurisdiction concerns some of the most marginal actors in the financial industry. If federal law enforcement were not otherwise occupied with antiterrorism efforts,[92] they could justifiably bring these cases, many of which focus on people who have swindled the most vulnerable members of society. For instance, recall that the GLBA prohibits pretexting. The FTC has brought a series of cases against investigators who pretexted.[93] It has also used the pretexting authority to police advance-fee credit card schemes, a swindle where a business offers a credit card that either never arrives or is actually a secured line of credit. These cases typically involve hundreds of dollars of charges debited from a consumer who is desperate to just get a regular credit card.[94]

The FTC has found great flexibility in the pretexting provisions. It uses them to police other misrepresentations, such as companies that claim to be "verifying" financial data in order to elicit data.[95] It uses pretexting authority to address phishing attacks, where the company tricks the consumer directly by pretending to be a financial institution[96] or another legitimate business.[97] The FTC also brought a series of cases under Section 5 for pretexting of phone records in 2006 (because the GLBA only concerns pretexting financial records).

The FTC has brought cases against companies that failed to issue privacy[98] and opt-out notices.[99]

The FTC has found violations of the security safeguards rule where companies failed to use access controls to limit the availability of NPI among employees,[100] where companies failed to monitor the business network for vulnerabilities, where companies failed to have training for employees, where companies failed to secure the workstations of remote employees,[101] where employees e-mailed NPI without

[92] Barry J. Cutler, *The Criminalization of Consumer Protection – A Brave New World for Defense Counsel*, 22(1) ANTITRUST 61 (Fall 2007).

[93] *FTC v. Victor L. Guzzetta, d/b/a Smart Data Systems*, No. 01-2335 (E.D.N.Y. 2002); *FTC v. Paula L. Garrett, d/b/a Discreet Data Systems*, No. H01-1255 (S.D. Tex. 2002); *FTC v. Corporate Marketing Solutions, Inc. et al.*, No. CIV-02 1256 PHX RCB (D. Az. 2002).

[94] *FTC v. Sun Spectrum Communications Organization, Inc.*, No. 03-8110 (S.D. Fl. 2005).

[95] *FTC v. Assail, Inc., et al.*, No. W03CA007 (W.D. Tex. 2003).

[96] *FTC v. Zachary Keith Hill*, No. 032-3102 (S.D. Tex. 2004); *FTC v. Global Mortgage Funding, Inc., et al.*, No. SACV 02-1026 DOC (C.D. Cal. 2002).

[97] *FTC v. A Minor*, No. 03-5275 (C.D. Cal. 2003).

[98] *US v. PLS Financial Services, Inc., PLS Group, Inc., and The Payday Loan Store of Illinois, Inc.*, 112-cv-08334 (N.D. Il. 2012); *In the Matter of Sunbelt Lending Services, Inc.*, FTC File No. 042 3153 (November 16, 2004); *In the Matter of Nationwide Mortgage Group, Inc., and John D. Eubank*, FTC File No. 042-3104 (November 9, 2004).

[99] *FTC v. 30 Minute Mortgage, Inc., Gregory P. Roth, and Peter W. Stolz*, No. 03-60021 (S.D. Fl. 2003).

[100] *In the Matter of Nationwide Mortgage Group, Inc., and John D. Eubank*, FTC File No. 042-3104 (November 9, 2004).

[101] *In the Matter of Premier Capital Lending, Inc.*, FTC File No. 0723004 (November 6, 2008); *In the Matter of Sunbelt Lending Services, Inc.*, FTC File No. 0423153 (November 16, 2004).

encrypting the data[102] (a practice common before the enactment of the GLBA), and where companies threw away NPI into unsecured trash bins.[103]

The FTC's internal GLBA violation codes are as follows: GLB1, company does not provide any opportunity for consumers to opt out of information sharing; GLB2, company fails to honor request to opt out/opt-out mechanism does not work; GLB3, company is violating its privacy policy; GLB4, privacy policy is misleading, unclear, or difficult to understand; GLB8, other GLB violation; GLB9, company does not have a privacy policy.

## Assessing GLBA

No one was happy with the privacy provisions of the GLBA. Banks found them wasteful and pointless, as the costs of producing annual notices were in the hundreds of millions and because so few people opted out. The highest estimate of opt-out rates was 5 percent, while others reported less than 1 percent opt-out rate. To the banking industry, the low opt-out rate was a demonstration that consumers did not care about privacy and that new privacy laws were unnecessary, as consumers were not exercising the rights they had. Meanwhile, the Commission reacted to low opt-out rates by turning the screws on disclosure requirements.

Consumer advocates thought the opt-out unacceptable and pointed to confusing notices and a likelihood that consumers failed to opt out because they thought their banks could not sell data. There were also transaction costs associated with opting out, and, in particular, when the GLBA first was implemented, few banks allowed consumers to opt out online.[104]

Consumer advocates are probably correct in their assessment that Congress chose a poor default rule in crafting GLBA. Studies have shown, as late as 2005, that almost three quarters of Americans falsely believe that banks are barred by laws from selling customer information. And most Americans probably do not want banks to sell data. The best evidence for this comes from North Dakota, where, in a voter referendum, 73 percent voted to reverse the legislature's swapping an opt-in standard with an opt-out.[105] Nevertheless, Congress was convinced that third-party information sharing would result in efficiencies that outweighed Americans' preferences.

---

[102] *In the Matter of Superior Mortgage Corp.*, FTC File No. 0523136 (September 28, 2005).

[103] *US v. PLS Financial Services, Inc., PLS Group, Inc., and The Payday Loan Store of Illinois, Inc.*, 112-cv-08334 (N.D. Il. 2012); *US v. American United Mortgage Company*, No. 07C 7064 (N.D. Il. 2007); *In the Matter of Nations Title Agency, Inc.*, FTC File No. 0523117 (May 10, 2006).

[104] A 2000 study by the Center for Democracy & Technology found that of 100 online banks, 34 said that they shared information with third parties, yet allowed opting out only through offline means. CENTER FOR DEMOCRACY & TECHNOLOGY, ONLINE BANKING PRIVACY: A SLOW CONFUSING START TO GIVING CUSTOMERS CONTROL OVER THEIR INFORMATION (2000).

[105] NORTH DAKOTA SECRETARY OF STATE, STATEWIDE ELECTION RESULTS, June 11, 2002.

The kinds of information sharing enabled by the GLBA were difficult to fathom. Some large banks had hundreds, or even over a thousand, affiliates. Under the plain terms of the GLBA, a bank could pass along the information that a customer paid a cancer clinic with a check for $10,000 to any affiliate – and to any joint marketer – regardless of consumer choice. These affiliates could include insurance or other companies that would grant, deny, or change the terms of an offer to an individual based on medical data. Congress seemed to realize this only after enactment of the GLBA. In proposing legislation to fix the problem, the American Bankers Association reacted swiftly, with a mostly empty statement that declared, "medical information will not be shared."[106]

The most sophisticated early assessment of the GLBA came from Professor Peter Swire, a deep expert in privacy law and counsel on financial services matters. Swire argued that the GLBA had unforeseen benefits, despite its rather weak privacy provisions. While not publishing specific examples, he found in discussions with banks that the GLBA's notice requirements had "reduced the risk of egregious privacy practices."[107] This is because in order to write the notice, banks had a hard look at some of their practices and felt that some were so problematic that even disclosing them would cause customer revolt. This improvement in practices was widely implemented, because the GLBA broadly defines "financial institution."

Swire did call attention to the "joint marketing" exception in the GLBA, pointing out that while the exception was enacted to put smaller banks on a level playing field with larger ones, the exception was being used by many large banks. Banks also appeared to be using it to circumvent the opt-out rights in the GLBA. The Center for Democracy & Technology found that a substantial number of banks did not offer any choice mechanisms to consumers, yet were reserving the right to share data with marketing partners.

Despite Swire's assessment, there is a fair argument that passage of the GLBA had a corrosive effect on other prospects for privacy law in other contexts. Financial institutions as an industry have at times been too big to fail, but also too big to regulate. They use their lobbying power aggressively against new privacy laws that are stronger than the GLBA, even when these laws regulate nonbank entities, such as data brokers. In other words, financial institutions want GLBA to be the ceiling for privacy protection. For instance, an earnest effort by technology companies and the Center for Democracy & Technology to pass online privacy legislation was scuttled by banks that joined the coalition but then adamantly opposed protections broader than the GLBA.

---

[106] AMERICAN BANKERS ASSOCIATION, TASK FORCE ON RESPONSIBLE USE AND PROTECTION OF CUSTOMER INFORMATION, VOLUNTARY GUIDELINES FOR RESPONSIBLE USE AND PROTECTION OF CUSTOMER INFORMATION, n.d. (The ten guidelines included "Preserving Trust is a Core Value" and "Responsible Use of Information Provides Customer Benefits.")

[107] Peter P. Swire, *The Surprising Virtues of the New Financial Privacy Law*, 86 MINN. L. REV. 1263 (2001).

## THE FAIR DEBT COLLECTION PRACTICES ACT OF 1978

At first glance, the Fair Debt Collection Practices Act of 1978 (FDCPA)[108] would not appear to be a privacy law. The statute was passed to address a series of abuses – characterized as abundant – in the debt collection field, such as threats and misrepresentations.[109] In passing it, Congress recognized that aggressive collection activities were privacy-invasive and led to marital discord and difficulty in holding a job.[110] Many of the law's provisions are similar to information privacy laws and some create anti-marketing-like protections against contacting the debtor.

Why would Congress pass a law to protect debtors, a group synonymous with "deadbeats" in many minds? First, in the mid 1970s, the *Chicago Tribune* ran a page-one series on illegal and abusive collection activities. Four reporters found that collectors falsified court documents, threatened to throw debtors in jail, pretended to be attorneys, added on additional fees to pad their profits, elicited information by impersonating Social Security Administration workers or policemen, and pocketed payments made by debtors instead of returning them to the creditor.[111] To expose these practices, the reporters obtained jobs at collection agencies. To sound scary to debtors, one reporter practiced by yelling at his wife on the phone: "It frightened the children, but I was finally able to come on strong enough in the job interviews to get hired."[112]

Second, the vast majority of people do plan to pay their debts, and so the debtor as deadbeat is a fiction. Very few people take out an obligation with no future intent to pay, and so those targeted by the tactics elucidated by reporters and Congress were ordinary people who found themselves in financial difficulty. Their difficulties were worsened by collection efforts that disturbed home and work life.

---

### A MASKED MAN TESTIFIES ON DEBT COLLECTION TACTICS

When a witness testifies before Congress using a pseudonym and wearing a mask, it might mean trouble for an industry. In a March 1976 hearing, a "James Clark" testified to his activities as a debt collector, practices he said were not condoned, yet widespread in the industry. Some choice quotes include:

---

[108] Pub. L. 95–109, 91 Stat 874, 15 U.S.C. §1692 et seq.

[109] 15 U.S.C. §1601 et seq.

[110] 15 U.S.C. §1692(a).

[111] Pamela Zekman, William Crawford, & William Gaines, *Bill collector's tactics: "Everything we do here is borderline illegal,"* CHICAGO TRIBUNE, April 8, 1974; Pamela Zekman, William Crawford, William Gaines, & Robert Under, *"Push them till they break": Bill collector terror tactics. Agencies operate by their own rules,* CHICAGO TRIBUNE, April 7, 1974.

[112] Hrg. On H.R. 29, the Debt Collection Practices Act, before the House Subcommittee on Consumer Affairs of the Committee on Banking, Finance and Urban Affairs, 95 Cong. 1st Sess., March 8, 1977.

- "The most common technique for collecting debts was known as beating. This is continuous calling of an individual."
- "You could call and threaten a debtor with any number of things. You could threaten him with suit; you could threaten him with losing his children and putting them in orphanages; you could threaten him with going to jail; you could threaten him physically."
- "[I asked a debtor] 'Ma'am, what size shoes do you wear?' And she told me, 'I wear a size 7.' And said, 'Fine, ma'am, I am going to have a pair made out of cement for you and we'll send them over.'"
- "[We had an arrangement with] a judge in the minor judiciary. And for a certain percentage, a certain dollar figure, this judge gave us blanks with his letterhead on it. And we were given a pad or two pads of these blanks in order to send them out to the debtors, to tell them that they owed the money, and that the account was now in his hands."
- "We in the office had a closet full of police and other law-enforcement-type uniforms. We had numerous badges of law-enforcement officers."
- "[W]e had a special line that answered 'Sheriff's Office' and this way we could call the debtor, and if he had not responded to the attorney, me, the sheriff could explain to him that he was going to jail or whatever."
- "The legitimate, strictly-by-the-law agencies are absolutely, definitely in the minority. They cannot operate effectively . . . we did not belong to any associations, clubs, whatever. It was a waste of time. They prescribed all kind of idealistic codes of conduct, and they were all a bunch of bull, because they themselves did not adhere to them. Why should we? They collected their membership fee, and that was all they did."[113]

Debt collection was an industry where self-regulation utterly failed. Abusive practices seemed to be ignored or even rewarded. As Representative Frank Annunzio related in a hearing for the act, the largest debt collection trade association had done nothing to police two agencies that had been sued by the FTC. In fact, the association's president-elect was under permanent injunction against engaging in illegal debt collection practices.[114]

More fundamentally, debt collection problems, similar to other information-intensive industry problems, are exacerbated by a lack of direct

[113] Hrg. on H.R. 11969, the Debt Collection Practices Act, before the Subcommittee on Consumer Affairs of the Committee on Banking, Currency and Housing, House of Representatives, 94th Cong. 2nd Sess., March 30, 1976.
[114] Hrg. on H.R. 29, the Debt Collection Practices Act, before the House Subcommittee on Consumer Affairs of the Committee on Banking, Finance and Urban Affairs, 95 Cong. 1st Sess., March 8, 1977.

business-to-consumer relationships. Such relationships temper business-to-consumer interactions, in hopes that the business can retain their customers and polish its reputation. But debt collection, by definition, gives a third party with no consumer relationship strong incentives to extract information and money from individuals.

The internet and new technologies have made debt collection information sharing and communications more efficient, but with these efficiencies have come predictable problems. Take the debt-buying industry, for instance. Some retailers and other companies sell their debt, sometimes for less than a penny on the dollar,[115] to debt buyers, which make money by recovering just a fraction of the original obligation. In the process of collection, the consumer debtor receives a call from someone they do not know[116] who demands money. If the consumer asks for documentation, the buyer is likely to have none, other than a spreadsheet or the like listing the basics of the amount owed and the original creditor. The consumer might have had a dispute with this creditor over the quality of services or products sold, but the debt buyer is unlikely to know this.[117] The calls from the debt buyer can be persistent, and if the buyer cannot squeeze money out of the debtor, the buyer might sell the obligation to another firm, starting the process over again.[118] Some collectors attempt to get consumers to acknowledge or pay just a nominal amount of a discharged or time-barred debt (a debt that under state law can no longer be collected because of the passage of time) to renew the debt status, thus restarting an obligation to pay. Such debt is known as "zombie debt."[119] Tens of millions of Americans at any given time have accounts in third-party collection, and so many could potentially benefit from the various protections provided by the FDCPA.

A number of other factors motivated the original passage of the FDCPA. Self-regulation did not work in the debt collection industry. Additionally, in an era when debt collection became an interstate business because of cheaper long-distance calling, not all states had debt collection laws, and some that did had weak laws. Congress was concerned that collectors hailing from a weakly regulated forum were targeting residents of other states.

---

[115] *US v. Whitewing Financial Group, Inc.*, 4:06–2102 (S.D. Tex. 2006). ("Defendants generally pay less than a third of a cent per dollar of the face value of the accounts to purchase these debts.")

[116] Sometimes the caller is just pretending to be a debt collector, and, as a result, the FTC has started an information campaign concerning "fake debt collectors."

[117] The FTC's holder in due course rule was developed in part to address this problem.

[118] Professor Dalié Jiménez has written a detailed account of the debt-buying industry and its pathologies. See Dalié Jiménez, *Dirty Debts Sold Dirt Cheap*, 52 HARV. J. LEGIS. 41 (2014).

[119] Neil L. Sobol, *Protecting Consumers from Zombie-Debt Collectors*, 44 NEW MEX. L. REV. 327 (2014); *US v. Whitewing Financial Group, Inc.*, 4:06-2102 (S.D. Tex. 2006). ("Defendants purchase very old debts and then attempt to collect on these debts. Most, if not all, of these debts are beyond the applicable statutes of limitations. Most are also beyond the time in which they may be reported on credit bureau reports. Many of the debts have been discharged in bankruptcy.")

## THE BLANKET SECURITY INTEREST

Imagine your family fell on hard times and that you could not satisfy a debt. A check box on the loan contract gave the creditor a "blanket security interest" in your household goods. Now, a debt collector stands at your door, eyeing your things, threatening to take them if you do not pay up.

In 1980, an FTC staff report highlighted the inequity of debt contracts that allowed creditors to seize household goods – even those that were not purchased with borrowed money. Based on interviews with lenders, the FTC found that household items often have little resale value, and thus the main point of seizing these items was to impose psychological discomfort on debtors. Instructions to debt collectors included commandments such as "work HHG (household goods) on wife," meaning that the debtor would be threatened with the taking of various things in their home. Imagine the fear instilled by the creditor who appears at a home and demands, "Give me $50 today or I'll have a truck at your door in the morning and take everything out of your house." Such threats could be used to force the debtor into even more disadvantageous repayment agreements.[120]

The debate between consumer protection lawyers and economists over blanket security debates has many of the contours of modern privacy debates. Consumer protection lawyers wanted to act to prohibit such agreements generally, and they determined blanket security interests to be unfair under Section 5. The stories of consumer debtors' plight (one was deprived of baby crib and refrigerator) were too awful to tolerate and were reminiscent of the debtors' prison or the selling of debtors into slavery. Consumers agreed to security interests through a check box on a model form contract. Thus, the consumer, attorneys reasoned, probably had no means in the market to secure better terms.

The Reagan-era commission leadership, however, thought that borrowers should be able to sign blanket security interests and observed that while such terms sounded iniquitous, they were rarely enforced. Blanket security interests provided a powerful psychological tool to address nonpayment, and their presence lowered the cost of credit. Then Bureau of Economics Director Wendy Gramm, spouse of then Congressman and coauthor of the GLBA Phil Gramm, argued that blanket security interests were an important expression of commitment to repay a loan that if absent, could result in no credit at all.[121] Consumers could shop around and find lenders who did not offer such terms. Finally, economists thought the lawyers' intervention to be perverse. In

---

[120] FTC, Credit Practices: Final Report to the Federal Trade Commission and Proposed Trade Regulation Rule (16 CFR Part 444) Bureau of Consumer Protection (August 1980).

[121] Michael deCourcy Hinds, *The Rift over Protecting Consumers in Debt*, N.Y. Times, May 8, 1983.

limiting blanket security agreements, some consumers would not be able to get credit at all. Thus, the cost of protecting debtors would ultimately limit their freedom to get credit.

Ultimately, the Commission adopted rules limiting the scope of security agreements and limiting the ability of creditors to attach wages, and banned provisions that waived debtors' rights to defend themselves in court.[122]

Prior to the passage of the act, the FTC brought matters against debt collectors under Section 5 theories, under the FCRA, and under the Truth in Lending Act.

### Provisions of the FDCPA

The confrontation between debt collectors and consumers is so fraught that Congress enacted consumer protections against collection. Debt collection efforts must be viewed through the lens of an unsophisticated[123] or, as some circuits have applied, "least" sophisticated consumer standard.[124] The protections only apply against personal debt, and only against debt collectors – people who collect obligations on behalf of others. Thus, corporate debtors are left uncovered, as are collection activities performed by the creditor itself.

### Controlling communications

As a general matter, debt collectors cannot call at odd times, such as nighttime or early morning. Collectors also are not to communicate with the consumer at the workplace if the consumer's employer bars such interactions.[125] Once a debtor is represented by counsel, the collector must cease contacting the consumer-debtor. Additionally, the consumer can instruct the collector to stop communicating[126] or to only communicate by writing. The consumer can stop collection efforts by disputing the debt, which requires the collector to verify the debt and to communicate the validated debt in writing to the debtor.

In the old days of debt collection, collectors would embarrass debtors by telling third parties about the obligation. Some would even post signs listing individuals by name and implicating they did not pay their obligations. The FDCPA prohibits these practices, making debts essentially a private matter. Debt collectors cannot

---

[122] 16 C.F.R. 444.2.
[123] *Chuway v. National Action Fin. Servs., Inc.*, 362 F.3d 944 (7th Cir. 2004).
[124] For a discussion of sophistication standards applied by the circuit courts, *see Sullivan v. Credit Control Servs., Inc.*, 745 F. Supp. 2d 2 (D. Mass. 2010).
[125] 15 U.S.C. §1692c.
[126] 15 U.S.C. §1692c(c).

communicate debt information to most third parties.[127] They also cannot communicate with postcards.[128]

Debt collectors may contact third parties to *locate* the consumer debtor; however, they must be discreet. Collectors must identify themselves and only state that they are trying to locate the consumer. Collectors are barred from telling the third party about the debt or from volunteering that they are from a debt collection agency.[129] In addition, collectors cannot use ruses, such as telling consumers that they have received a parcel and need an address to properly route it, in order to elicit the location of others.

### Harassment and abusive practices
Congress specifically prohibited several activities, such as threatening to harm the debtor or using profane language. Collectors are specifically prohibited from calling the debtor constantly or from threatening to publicize debts to embarrass the debtor.[130] The act also includes sixteen subsections of enumerated misleading practices (such as threatening jail time for nonpayment)[131] and eight unfair ones.[132]

### Enforcement of the FDCPA
The FDCPA does create a private right of action, which includes punitive damages; however, there is no liquidated damages provision. Thus, individual litigants must prove the losses they have suffered in order to recover monetary damages.[133] The FDCPA has "floor" preemption, meaning that states can pass more stringent rules.[134]

The FTC can enforce the FDCPA as a violation of Section 5.[135] Its cases have several characteristics: First, as was the case in the 1970s, enforcement is the key factor for reining in abusive collection practices. Many commission cases arise after hundreds or thousands of consumer complaints arrive at the Agency, and these complaints have exposed the same kinds of tactics used today as the *Chicago Tribune* pointed to in the 1970s. Among scofflaw collections operations, threats and false information remain effective ways to extract money from people.

In some ways, policing illegal debt collection is more challenging today than in the 1970s. The captions of the FTC's enforcement actions often feature a dozen or more companies that are somehow involved in the same collections effort. In many recent cases, lenders operate their own collections agencies because they expect that accounts will fail. Several have put fine print into their contracts allowing the

[127] 15 U.S.C. §1692c(b).
[128] 15 U.S.C. §1692f(7).
[129] 15 U.S.C. §1692b.
[130] 15 U.S.C. §1692d.
[131] 15 U.S.C. §1692e.
[132] 15 U.S.C. §1692f.
[133] 15 U.S.C. §1692k.
[134] 15 U.S.C. §1692n.
[135] 15 U.S.C. §1692l.

creditor to directly garnish debtors' wages without a court order. One agency even tried using a tribal court to enforce debts.

Second, FDCPA enforcement has picked up, with the FTC taking more cases to protect Spanish-speaking consumers and consumers in financial distress. Several cases have been referred to law enforcement, particularly where fraudsters pretend to be debt collectors in order to extract money from people.

Third, the FTC often pleads FCRA violations in addition to FDCPA claims, which is to be expected since consumer reporting and debt collection are so interrelated.

Fourth, as early as 1986, the FTC secured a six-figure penalty under the FDCPA,[136] and now there are regularly seven-figure penalties in debt collection cases. But these penalties are suspended often because of an inability to pay, and where there is an ability to pay, the fines nonetheless seem anemic. For instance, a $3.2 million penalty was levied against a collector with billion-dollar annual revenues.[137] The need to keep fines in new cases proportional to earlier cases has created a drag on penalty levels.

Fifth, the FTC often secures other forms of relief, such as lifetime bans on engaging in debt collection,[138] a requirement to contact CRAs and correct the false information that was furnished to them, prohibitions on reselling debt that cannot be verified,[139] and/or a duty to document collection activities by recording calls to ensure compliance. In an important victory against "zombie debt," the FTC required a collector to give debtors a time-barred debt "Miranda" warning. That company is required to tell debtors that they cannot be sued to recover time-barred debt, and that if the consumer pays some amount of time-barred debt, the debt will not be revived and become collectable again.[140] With this settlement, the Agency hopes to end the decades-old practice of getting consumers to pay debts they no longer legally owe by tricking them into making a small payment.

Of the twenty-one codes the FTC uses to classify FDCPA violations, nine deal with privacy issues: Debtor at Work Knowing Debtor Can't Take Calls; Calling Employer; Calls Debtor before 8AM or after 9PM or at Inconvenient Times; Calling Repeatedly; Third Party Communication; Calls Someone Repeatedly to Obtain Debtor's Location; Calls Debtor after Getting "Cease Communication" Notice; Tells Someone Other Than Debtor about Debt; Calls Any Person Repeatedly or Continuously.

---

[136] *US v. Cent. Adjustment Bureau, Inc.*, 667 F. Supp. 370 (N.D. Tex. 1986) *aff'd as modified*, 823 F.2d 880 (5th Cir. 1987).

[137] *US v. Expert Global Solutions, Inc.*, 3-13 CV 2611-M (N.D. Tex. 2013).

[138] *US v. DC Credit Services, Inc., and David Cohen*, 02-5115 MMM (C.D. Cal. 2002).

[139] *US v. Allied Interstate, Inc.*, 0:10-cv-04295-PJS (D. Minn. 2010).

[140] *US v. Asset Acceptance, LLC*, 812-cv-182-T-27EAJ (M.D. Fl. 2012).

CONCLUSION

The highly regulated area of financial privacy has left the FTC little room to be entrepreneurial. In the FCRA area, intricate definitions and specifications have contributed to the act's increasing irrelevance. As data brokers, scoring firms, and even websites are able to make predictions reliable enough to make credit offers, this decision-making leaves the ambit of the FCRA.

In the GLBA area, the FTC's jurisdictional limits relegate it to policing nonbank actors, a target-rich environment perhaps best policed by regular police. The Agency's policing of security safeguards is relatively straightforward and consistent with its other security cases discussed in Chapter 8.

In the FDCPA area, the FTC is bringing similar cases to those that motivated passage of the act. The FTC has ramped up fines to an eight-figure level, yet today's schemes to recover time-barred debt and to harass people into paying are no different from the wrongs that led to passage of the FDCPA. In the FDCPA area, however, the FTC has developed remedies to prevent future abuses, including lifetime bans on debt collection and the "Miranda" debt collection warning that informs consumers that they need not pay time-barred debt.

At the same time, information practices are closely linked to financial-world depredations against consumers. Particularly where marketing is targeted at vulnerable populations, the FTC will feel empowered to use its unfairness power. Already, the Agency is taking cases concerning how lead generators collect information and resell it to others. This creates the prospect of a general responsibility for how data are used after they are collected.

# 11

# International privacy efforts

The FTC has been active in international competition matters for almost a century,[1] and it devotes significant resources to international consumer protection efforts. The FTC's activities come in several forms. It both assists and receives assistance from international law enforcement authorities in order to address fraud. It guides other nations in developing competition and consumer protection regimes. It evangelizes the US approach to privacy protection, with the goal of assuring policy-makers, especially Europeans, that the United States is a safe place for personal data. And in this last function, it polices Europeans' privacy rights to a limited extent under the "Safe Harbor" agreement.

The challenge of evangelizing the US approach is difficult, because European privacy law, referred to as "data protection" law, is animated by different values and lessons from history about the power of information collection. The atrocities committed during the Holocaust were assisted through information technology, and private companies were complicit in Nazi activities.[2] Furthermore, the penetration of reliable census-taking activities is one explanation of why so many Dutch Jews were killed in the Holocaust while nearby countries with fewer information collection activities had higher rates of Jewish survival.[3] Stasi and Communist tracking of individuals and their social networks, and citizens "informing" on others reinforced the lesson that information can become a tool of oppression.

But it is too facile to invoke fear alone as the basis for international privacy rules. To foster a high level of respect for the individual, both the protection of private life

---

[1] One of the first topics the Agency turned to in 1915 concerned whether American companies were competitive against other exporters. Congress extended the power to police unfair methods of competition concerning acts occurring outside the United States. See 15 U.S.C. §61; see generally Marc Winerman, International Issues in the FTC's First Decade (1915–1925) – And Before, in WILLIAM E. KOVACIC LIBER AMERICORUM: AN ANTITRUST TRIBUTE, VOL. II (Nicolas Charbit & Elisa Ramundo, eds., 2014).

[2] EDWIN BLACK, IBM AND THE HOLOCAUST: THE STRATEGIC ALLIANCE BETWEEN NAZI GERMANY AND AMERICA'S MOST POWERFUL CORPORATION (2000) (arguing that IBM knowingly designed and optimized punch card technology to enhance German identification and classification of Holocaust victims).

[3] William Seltzer & Margo Anderson, The Dark Side of Numbers: The Role of Population Data Systems in Human Rights Abuses, 68(2) SOC. RES. 481 (Summer 2001).

and data protection are fundamental human rights in Europe.[4] Privacy is recognized as a condition for a certain quality of personal life. Europeans also say that the region's strong privacy protections will promote commerce.

Evangelizing the US approach is also a challenge as other nations adopt European models of privacy regulation.[5] Western Europe enjoys the highest living standards in history and is wealthier as a region than North America. This gives strong incentives for other nations to adopt European-style protections, so that they are eligible, or "adequate," regimes for Europeans' data. Other nations also find the European approach easier to adopt than the US sectoral model.

This chapter focuses on the FTC's international privacy efforts. To discuss these efforts, some background is needed concerning the European privacy regime. This background gives context for the FTC's most important international privacy activities: enforcement of the Safe Harbor Agreements, the development of competition and consumer protection law through technical assistance, and its increasing cooperation and involvement in international consumer protection investigations and matters.

| European Privacy Stakeholders | |
| --- | --- |
| Article 29 Working Party | An independent, advisory body consisting of members of the data protection authorities, the European Data Protection Supervisor, and a member of the European Commission. It advises the European Commission on questions of data protection, promotes uniformity, and offers opinions on many privacy matters, including whether non-EU countries have "adequate" privacy protection. The Working Party's opinions are influential, but not legally binding. |
| Council of Europe (CoE) | With forty-seven member states, the CoE is the Continent's most important human rights body. It is independent from the European Union. It enforces the European Convention on Human Rights (ECHR) through the European Court of Human Rights. In 1981, it proposed the Convention for the Protection of Individuals with regard to Automatic Processing of Personal Data. It is based in Strasbourg. |
| Council of the European Union | Under the auspices of Council of the European Union, government ministers from each member state meet to discuss and adopt law and policy. The council is the main decision-making body of the EU, along with the European Parliament. |

*(Continued)*

---

[4] Joel R. Reidenberg, *E-Commerce and Trans-Atlantic Privacy*, 38 Hous. L. Rev. 717 (2001).
[5] Graham Greenleaf, *The Influence of European Data Privacy Standards outside Europe: Implications for Globalisation of Convention* 108, 2(2) Int'l Data Priv. L. (2012).

(Continued)

| | European Privacy Stakeholders |
|---|---|
| European Council | The European Council is comprised of the heads of state of European Union nations. It serves a policy agenda-setting role, although it does not have formal powers. It nominates the president of the European Commission. |
| European Commission | The European Commission is the twenty-eight-member executive body of the European Union. With one commissioner per member nation, the Commission is tasked with proposing legislation and handling budget issues for the entire EU. |
| European Court of Human Rights | The European Court of Human Rights, the longest-standing international human rights court, rules on alleged violations of the rights in the European Convention on Human Rights. The court's judgments are binding on the countries concerned, and countries have adapted their national laws after such judgments. Individuals can bring matters before the court. Judgments are monitored and enforced by the CoE. |
| Court of Justice of the European Union (CJEU) | Also known as the European Court of Justice (ECJ), the CJEU is the EU's highest court, providing interpretation of EU law and its equal application across member states. Recently, the CJEU has delivered a number of important, pro-privacy decisions, including striking down the Data Retention Directive, striking down the US–EU Safe Harbor agreement, and granting people, under certain conditions, the right to have search results for their name delisted. |
| European Data Protection Supervisor (EDPS) | Created in 2001, the EDPS is tasked with "ensuring that the fundamental rights and freedoms of natural persons, and in particular their right to privacy, are respected by the Community institutions and bodies." The EDPS has broad powers to investigate and remedy unfair data handling among EU institutions, including powers to ban processing of data or even to erase data. |
| Organisation for Economic Co-Operation and Development (OECD) | The OECD is an economic forum for well-developed countries with commitments to democracy and a market economy. It adopts statements of policy that are influential in the treaty process, and forms benchmarks for practices. The 1980 OECD privacy guidelines form the basis for much of statutory privacy law. It is based in Paris, and thirty-four nations, including the United States, are members of it. Its Working Party on Information Security and Privacy (WPISP) convenes business and civil society groups for policy formation. |

## THE BASICS OF EUROPEAN PRIVACY LAW

Companies' Web efforts have international presence. By default, a local business with no intent to reach beyond its town's border could appear to a regulator in another country to be operating on a much broader level. Regulators may be concerned with a number of topics – from product safety, to standards or privacy. Many businesses address international regulatory risk by simply not granting accounts, charging credit cards, or making shipments to foreign customers.

But such "geo-fencing" is often impossible for information-intensive services, such as search engines and social networks. These companies have strong incentives to grant as many accounts as possible, wherever the user may be. But then such companies run the risk of a protracted battle with foreign regulators, who demand compliance with local laws. Web services often address these demands through a kind of regulatory arbitrage. Services argue that they are only subject to US laws, or that they adhere to a regime policed by a US-friendly foreign regulator. The current favorite is Ireland, because of tax advantages that appeal to other aspects of companies, language compatibility, and signaling from the nation that its policing efforts will be different than Continental regulators.

Companies in Europe operate in a different consumer protection landscape that operates alongside rules concerning privacy. The Charter of Fundamental Rights specifies, "[European] Union policies shall ensure a high level of consumer protection."[6] The European Union Consumer Rights Directive specifies details such as how a business must express that it is about to charge a consumer for a product or service, and prohibits pre-checked boxes for additional services that add to the transaction's cost. There are also EU-wide rules on subscription payment and requirements that digital downloads specify whether they are limited by digital rights management technologies, and the EU even provides a fourteen-day return period for distance sales.[7]

A separate directive on unfair commercial practices enumerates thirty-one practices that are categorically unfair, including the advertising of something as "free" if the consumer "has to pay anything other than the unavoidable cost of responding to the commercial practice and collecting or paying for delivery of the item."[8] More generally, however, contracts that are routinely used in the United States may be unenforceable in Europe. Another directive on consumer contracts specifies that terms that are not individually negotiated are unfair if they cause a significant imbalance in the parties' rights and obligations.[9] Thus, blanket disclaimers of warranties and limitations on liability may simply be unfair because they are

---

[6] Article 38, EU Charter on Human Rights (2000).

[7] Directive 2011/83/EU of the European Parliament and the Council on Consumer Rights, October 25, 2011.

[8] Directive 2005/29/EC of the European Parliament and of the Council of May 11, 2005 concerning unfair business-to-consumer commercial practices in the internal market.

[9] Council Directive 93/13/EEC of April 5, 1993 on unfair terms in consumer contracts.

not negotiated and may harm the consumer. While US companies routinely state that they can change their terms and conditions at any time, the consumer contract directive treats such disclaimers as unfair where "the seller or supplier [can] alter the terms of the contract unilaterally without a valid reason which is specified in the contract." It is unclear whether EU consumer law applies to privacy issues, but legal scholar Frederik Borgesius has made the case that it should.[10] In any case, European consumer law attention to power imbalances is also found in its regulation of privacy.

Many European rules become de facto practices in the United States, as multinational companies find it convenient to conform to the highest standard for consumer protection for all of their consumers.

Yet, conforming to a European standard for all users is not so easy with regard to privacy, because European privacy law approaches are fundamentally different from those of the United States, and several characteristics of international privacy norms sit in tension with American legal culture.[11]

## Sectoral versus omnibus approaches

The United States follows a sectoral model, with specific kinds of data collection or use being regulated. For instance, the United States has a specific law for credit reporting and another for financial services. Europe (and increasingly the rest of the world) follows an omnibus approach, where any handling of personal data implicates privacy rules. European rules apply to both public and private sectors, whereas in the United States, privacy rules typically focus either on public- or private-sector actors, but rarely both.

The American approach treats data handling as legal unless a specific rule prohibits it, while in Europe, for data handling to be legal, it must comport with several principles. On a high level, it must meet data quality guidelines: it must be fair, lawful, necessary, and not excessive. Fairness translates roughly to transparency, a norm embraced in America. But the rules on necessity and excessive processing are only present in a few statutory codes. Excessive processing, in particular, and an emphasis on "proportionality" of data handling shift European rules away from procedure to substance.

In addition to rules regarding data quality, European data protection law only allows personal data processing if a company has a legal basis for the processing. For the private sector, the most relevant legal bases are necessity for the performance of a

---

[10] Frederik J. Zuiderveen Borgesius, Improving Privacy Protection in the Area of Behavioural Targeting (2015).

[11] This chapter gives a high-level overview of differences between US and European privacy regulatory norms. For a deeper discussion of European rules, *see* Lee Andrew Bygrave, Data Privacy Law: An International Perspective (2014).

contract, necessity for the controller's legitimate interests that overrides the data subject's privacy rights, and the data subject's unambiguous consent.

The Data Protection Directive also imposes various duties. Data controllers, companies that possess personal information and determine the purposes and means of the personal data processing, must provide detailed information about how data are handled. This includes the categories of data held, and the purposes for which they are processed.

Data subjects have a right to access data, and to correct them in certain circumstances. Data subjects can also object to transfer of data to third parties. On paper, fully automated decision-making is prohibited in certain contexts and, in almost all cases, needs to be disclosed to a regulator before it is used. However, this last rule has rarely been applied.

### Specific rules versus high-level principles

A second area of tension surrounds cultures of legal compliance. US lawyers seek rules that will help bring clients into full legal compliance. But international rules are often stated as general, high-level principles for data handling. Read literally, these rules would be impossible to implement because they would regulate personal, inconsequential matters. Full compliance would be impossible, both because of the breadth of the law, and because the principles require a continuous reexamination of practices. Consider the legal requirement of "data minimization." This standard requires a consideration of how much data are needed to achieve some legitimate goal, and that controllers delete data after some period of time. In American law, only the COPPA (see Chapter 7) has similar requirements. These kinds of provisions inherently invite interpretation and directly conflict with the "collect everything and find a way to monetize it later" business models of Silicon Valley.

Full legal compliance is also daunting because of the variations of the implementation of the Data Protection Directive by European Union member states. The European Union Data Protection Directive requires member nations to "transpose" its high-level principles into national law. But some member states have chosen to embrace some provisions more firmly than others. In the United States, the Dormant Commerce Clause has squashed much of the state law regulating internet commerce.

| Sources of European Privacy Rights | |
|---|---|
| Universal Declaration of Human Rights (1948) | Article 12 states: "No one shall be subjected to arbitrary interference with his privacy, family, home or correspondence, nor to |

*(Continued)*

(Continued)

| Sources of European Privacy Rights | |
|---|---|
| | attacks upon his honour and reputation. Everyone has the right to the protection of the law against such interference or attacks." |
| Convention for the Protection of Human Rights and Fundamental Freedoms (1950) | Known as the European Convention on Human Rights (ECHR), the ECHR's Article 8 established in 1950 that "Everyone has the right to respect for his private and family life, his home and his correspondence." Individuals can petition the court to address states that provide insufficient privacy protection or that fail to prevent privacy invasions by non-state actors. |
| Organisation for Economic Co-Operation and Development (OECD) Privacy Principles (1980) | This formed the consensus view among European nations and America concerning the contours of data privacy law. The privacy guidelines are reflected in most data protection laws. They are mostly procedural, that is, based on the idea that a practice needs to be disclosed and consented to rather than blanket prohibitions on data practices. They were substantively updated in 2013. |
| Convention for the Protection of Individuals with regard to Automatic Processing of Personal Data (1981) | The CoE's Convention 108 sought to "secure in the territory of each Party for every individual, whatever his nationality or residence, respect for his rights and fundamental freedoms, and in particular his right to privacy, with regard to automatic processing of personal data relating to him." |
| Directive 95/46/Ce of the European Parliament and of the Council on the protection of individuals with regard to the processing of personal data and on the free movement of such data (1995) | This directive sought to ensure the ability to transfer data among member states, but also to "protect the fundamental rights and freedoms of natural persons, and in particular their right to privacy with respect to the processing of personal data." The directive is the basic legislative framework for privacy in Europe. An effort started in 2012 to replace the directive with a regulation, which would be binding and directly applicable in all EU nations. |

*(Continued)*

(Continued)

| Sources of European Privacy Rights | |
| --- | --- |
| Charter of Fundamental Rights of the European Union (2000) | A consolidated statement of political, social, and economic rights of the European Union. Proclaimed in 2000, it came into full force with the Treaty of Lisbon in 2009. Article 7 declares, "Everyone has the right to respect for his or her private and family life, home and communications," and Article 8 established data protection as a fundamental right. |
| Directive 2002/58/EC of the European Parliament and of the Council concerning the processing of personal data and the protection of privacy in the electronic communications sector (Directive on privacy and electronic communications)(2002) | Known as the E-Privacy Directive, it required member states to create opt-in protections against many kinds of direct marketing, and set strong norms surrounding confidentiality of communications. As amended in 2009, it required opt-in consent for the setting of cookies. |
| Directive 2006/24/EC of the European Parliament and of the Council on the retention of data and amending Directive 2002/58/EC (2006) | The "Data Retention Directive" broadly required communications service providers to retain traffic (not content) data about users "to ensure that the data are available for the purpose of the investigation, detection and prosecution of serious crime, as defined by each Member State in its national law." In 2014, the CJEU declared the directive invalid because it interfered too much with privacy and data protection rights. |

As of this writing, officials are making a major effort convert the 1995 directive into a "regulation." Directives require nation-states to "transpose" protections into state law. Regulations require no transposition as they are binding and directly applicable in the EU member states. Because transposition invites deviations from a uniform rule, the regulation is thought to have a unifying effect, and can result in massive savings to business.[12]

There are major disagreements over whether the United States or EU approach is more privacy protective. Privacy advocates generally attempt to enact more European-style, omnibus privacy laws. Critical assessments, although rarely conducted, point to merits in narrower legislation[13] and in the US approach. For

[12] Paul M. Schwartz, *The EU-US Privacy Collision: A Turn to Institutions and Procedures*, 126 HARV. L. REV. 1966 (2013).

[13] Robert Gellman, *Does Privacy Law Work?*, in TECHNOLOGY AND PRIVACY: THE NEW LANDSCAPE (Philip E. Agre & Marc Rotenberg, eds.) (1997).

instance, in an influential 2011 paper, Professors Kenneth Bamberger and Deirdre Mulligan argued that a revolution in the governance of privacy has occurred in American companies over the past decade.[14] The duo modeled their inquiry on Professor Jeff Smith's 1994 study of corporate privacy efforts. Smith concluded that firms avoided privacy leadership because obligations were unclear and costly, and thus privacy needed more comprehensive controls.[15]

Like Smith, Bamberger and Mulligan interviewed leading privacy officials at companies. But in the intervening period since Smith's inquiry, Bamberger and Mulligan found that (1) privacy officials understood privacy to include the satisfaction of consumer expectations, rather than the mere compliance with notice-and-choice or other legally imposed formalities; (2) the roving, broad authority of the FTC, along with security breach notification laws (which started to be promulgated in the 2000s; see Chapter 8), created significant incentives for companies to protect privacy or suffer reputational harm; and (3) pressure from advocates helped to set consumer norms around privacy and professionalization of privacy officers set expectations for responsible behavior across firms – a need for "company law."

In particular, this last factor seemed to change companies' posture on privacy. Chief privacy officers (CPOs) had entered the "C-suite," had become members of a profession, and networked and shared information among firms to solve privacy problems. Successful CPOs had pushed privacy responsibilities into different business units, causing a kind of privacy consciousness to be diffused into their institutions. In interviews, these CPOs argued that the European approach had imposed a regime of privacy compliance, while the US system gave more opportunities for privacy leadership. In particular, the ambiguity of legal requirements in the United States enabled CPOs to interpret obligations themselves, leading them to interpret obligations in a more privacy-protective manner. The ambiguity gave US CPOs strong incentives to share their strategies for addressing privacy (this occurs even among companies in sharp competition) and to feel responsibility for correcting irresponsible actions of competitors, as these could cast an entire industry in a bad light.

There are some limits to these observations. CPOs are likely to have a favorable view of their own activities. CPOs can also become a kind of cheerleading squad for their own practices and whitewash problematic privacy activities. For instance, some large technology companies' leaders are convinced that they have perfected privacy issues. But to come to this conclusion, they typically define privacy in a strained way, for instance by claiming that privacy is only about decisions to reveal

---

[14] Kenneth A. Bamberger & Deirdre K. Mulligan, Privacy on the Ground: Driving Corporate Behavior in the United States and Europe (2015); Kenneth A. Bamberger & Deirdre K. Mulligan, *Privacy on the Books and on the Ground*, 63 Stan. L. Rev. 247 (2011).

[15] H. Jeff Smith, Managing Privacy: Information Technology and Corporate America (1994).

data among friends while ignoring the problem that the platform itself still captures and uses the data.

Nevertheless, the Bamberger and Mulligan thesis has profound implications for the regulation of privacy. They suggest that a robust market for privacy reputation, enabled by the FTC's case-by-case development and by specific information-forcing laws, could better manage privacy instead of a comprehensive European-style regulatory regime. At the same time, the Bamberger/Mulligan evidence militates toward intervention when an industry lacks reputational pressure points on privacy. For instance, consumer reporting agencies (see Chapter 10) and behavioral advertising companies (see Chapter 6) lack direct consumer relationships, and often have incentives to act in a maximally privacy-invasive way.

### Sensitive data and public records

A third source of tension comes from European data protection law's treatment of "special categories of data," also called "sensitive data." The directive protects broad categories of sensitive personal information. Special categories of data under the directive include racial and ethic origin data, information about political opinions or membership in a trade union, medical data, sexual orientation information, and criminal records. Such data should not be processed unless required by some other law, or with express consent of the individual.

In the United States, companies are free to use many of these attributes in direct marketing and other commercial endeavors. In fact, these data often appear in public records, the treatment of which is another area of tension. American courts have even held that highly sensitive information, such as the name of a victim of a sex crime, can be reported upon if it appears in a public record. The rules are different in Europe, where public records ("public registers") are governed by a specific directive.[16] Under the European approach, even public information retains some privacy protection.

### Supervisory regulators

A fourth source of tension comes from regulatory oversight. Data protection authorities (DPAs) oversee international privacy rules, and these regulators have expertise and authority to address the many gaps left by high-level statements on privacy. This gives regulators flexibility that requires more attention from attorneys, and more continuous consultation with clients. DPAs also have the power to investigate and remedy individual cases, a power that the FTC possesses but in practice almost never uses.

---

[16] Directive 2013/37/EU of the European Parliament and of the Council of 26 June 2013 amending Directive 2003/98/EC on the reuse of public-sector information.

*Free speech rights versus interests*

Fifth, the value of free expression receives less weight in the European regime. It is not, as some say, that Europeans do not have free speech rights.[17] Instead, Europeans are willing to balance privacy with free expression rights. In the United States, the First Amendment has become a kind of corporate wrecking ball for privacy and other consumer protection[18] rules.

In Europe, individuals' right to private life, a right distinct from data protection, militates in favor of protections that simply would be unconstitutional in the United States. For instance, the European Court of Justice found that Europeans have, under certain conditions, the right to have information erased or delinked from the Web (if the data are inadequate, irrelevant or no longer relevant, or excessive in relation to the purposes for which they were processed).[19] A right to erasure may be formalized in the data protection regulation. In the United States, individuals have similar rights to erase information, but only in limited circumstances, and with respect to certain actors (see discussion of the Fair Credit Reporting Act in Chapter 10). Even these limited erasure rights seem vulnerable to First Amendment challenge, as they were enacted before the invention of the commercial free speech doctrine.

*Limits on "consent"*

Sixth, US lawyers deal with many consumer protection issues by getting "consent" from customers or waiver of consumer rights.[20] This is often done through contracts of adhesion that are enforceable simply because the user clicked "I agree."[21] European privacy law does not allow a data controller to cleanse their hands of obligations so simply; instead, consent must be freely given, specific, informed, and unambiguous, and one must be able to withdraw consent with the effect that further processing of collected data is stopped. Each of these requirements has real bite, at least in the opinion of the Article 29 Working Party.[22] The Working Party does not consider silence or inaction to be "consent." And even when consent is present, many data protection mandates, such as data minimization, security, and purpose limitation, remain mandatory.

[17] *See, for example*, Article 11 of the Charter of Fundamental Rights of the European Union (2010/C 83/02); Article 10 of the European Convention on Human Rights (1950); Article 19 of the Universal Declaration of Human Rights (1948).

[18] Tim Wu, *The Right to Evade Regulation: How Corporations Hijacked the First Amendment*, New Republic, June 3, 2013; Tamara R. Piety, Brandishing the First Amendment (2012).

[19] *Google Spain SL, Google Inc. v. Agencia Española de Protección de Datos, Mario Costeja González*, C-131/12 (Court of Justice of the European Union 2014).

[20] Lee A. Bygrave, Internet Governance by Contract (2015).

[21] Margaret Jane Radin, Boilerplate (2013).

[22] Article 29 Working Party, Opinion 15/2011 on the definition of consent, July 13, 2011.

## "Personal" data

Finally, the Data Protection Directive applies to any information "relating to an identified or identifiable natural person." Thus, unlike many US privacy laws that tie the definition of personal information to specific identifiers such as name or Social Security number, a broad set of data can be "personal."[23] In effect, by broadly construing covered data, European privacy regulators have carefully preserved their authority. This approach is reflected in the United States as well. The FTC uses a similar approach to defining personal information in its privacy consent decrees – for over ten years, it has broadly defined personal information in its orders.

## Dignity and liberty

The US–Europe clash invites broad cultural generalizations about whether privacy efforts in each region protect dignity or liberty from the state. Europeans are said to be more concerned about commercial collection of information and more tolerant of state activities, whereas Americans are said to be the opposite. The reality is much less clear. Contrary to popular libertarian narratives, most US privacy law concerns the private sector, and the most stringent federal privacy law is probably the Cable Communications Policy Act,[24] which regulates how cable TV providers can monitor Americans as they watch TV. Meta-reviews of survey research show that Americans are just as concerned about private-sector invasions of privacy as they are about government ones.[25]

Switching to privacy for protecting citizens from the state, the United States only lightly regulates government collection of information, and many states lack a statutory framework to govern how data are handled. American courts have read dozens of loopholes into the Fourth Amendment, including one that makes it possible for the government to obtain reams of data from private-sector companies about citizens. Congress essentially adopted a national identification card, and one must carry it to travel, except if on foot. The Snowden revelations elucidated a muscular and adept surveillance state in the United States, but little has been done to stop it. Americans have never developed a protest movement or means of effective resistance against government surveillance matters.

---

[23] Paul M. Schwartz & Daniel J. Solove, *Reconciling Personal Information in the United States and European Union*, 102 CAL. L. REV. 877 (2014).

[24] 47 U.S.C. §551.

[25] *See generally* Samuel J. Best et al., *Privacy in the Information Age*, 70 PUB. OPINION. Q., 375 (2006); James E. Katz & Annette R. Tassone, *Public Opinion Trends: Privacy and Information Technology*, 54 PUB. OPINION Q. 125 (1990).

---

### THE D-WORD: DIGNITY

Several months after joining the Commission as director of consumer protection, David Vladeck gave an interview to the *New York Times*, in which he invoked the d-word – dignity – four times. In describing his role at the Commission, he said, "I think there's a huge dignity interest wrapped up in having somebody looking at your financial records when they have no business doing that. I think there is a dignity interest that needs to be protected when someone's looking at, maybe, your prescription medications that you're getting online. I don't think the harm model that the Commission has used at times really captures those injuries."[26]

Supporters of the harm-based approach felt deeply threatened by the idea that the FTC would use dignity as a case selection factor. Harm supporters reacted hysterically, labeling Vladeck's views emotional, questionable, vague, nontraditional, and subjective. They warned of expanding liability, of influence from foreign legal interests, and so on. In critiquing Vladeck, harms-based supporters almost always put dignity in quotes, as if it were some Germanism. Even commission officials tried to soften the interpretation of Vladeck's use of the word "dignity."[27]

Maintaining dignity is a main reason why people seek privacy. Consider the lock on the bathroom or bedroom door as mechanisms that protect non-economic interests in shielding the naked body from observation. The Commission has taken action in several cases where business practices enabled spying into the home and the capture of images of people within their homes. Such spying does not cause an obvious economic harm to people, yet most people would support having the government defend against such intrusions.

Why would the idea of dignity be so alien to privacy? And if dignity means the idea of protecting a person's honor or worth, why would the business community be so threatened by it?

---

On the other hand, European law can be more protective of the citizen against government surveillance.[28] Law enforcement activities are arguably more constrained under the European system. Sometimes violent protests erupt in Europe concerning government data collection that would be considered routine in the United States, such as census-taking.

[26] New York Times, An Interview with David Vladeck, August 5, 2009.
[27] *Thumbs Down to Notice-and-Choice at FTC, But Firm Rules Not Planned*, 11(76) Warren's Washington Internet Daily, April 11, 2010.
[28] Paul M. Schwartz, *German and US Telecommunications Privacy Law: Legal Regulation of Domestic Law Enforcement Surveillance*, 54 Hastings L. Rev. 751 (2003); Francesca Bignami, *European versus American Liberty: A Comparative Privacy Analysis of Antiterrorism Data Mining*, 48 B. C. L. Rev. 609 (2007).

## THE SAFE HARBOR

A strong embrace of privacy meant that Europeans had to manage regulatory arbitrage and the creation of data havens – countries with weak privacy rules that could be used to circumvent data protection law. Much like governments attempt to control money flows to stop tax dodging and "offshoring" cash, Europeans had to find ways to prevent personal data, which is even easier to move than money, from leaving the sphere of European protections. It did so in the directive by requiring that transfers only occur to countries with "an adequate level of protection."

A handful of countries have been determined by the European Commission to be adequate – Andorra, Argentina, Canada, Isle of Man, Israel, New Zealand, and Uruguay are among them. While adequate does not mean equivalent, it is clear that the United States in the 1990s lacked safeguards comparable to the directive. Recall that the United States did not even have a children's privacy law until 1998, and no federal health privacy protections until 2000.

American businesses and policy-makers were in a near panic in 1998, with implementation of the directive looming. A Brookings Institution book, *None of Your Business*, carried two meanings: that Europeans thought that personal data should not be subject to processing for business purposes, but also that no business could operate under the directive's terms. The authors pointed out that, among other things, one's personal contacts book could be regulated under the directive. The authors predicted that Europe could levy a "data embargo" against other nations.[29]

The US Department of Commerce came to the rescue, negotiating the "US–EU Safe Harbor Privacy Principles." These are voluntary principles that companies can adhere to. All member states treat Safe Harbor companies as "adequate." The agreement also makes companies liable under the FTC Act for deviating from the principles. In exchange, companies limit their exposure to DPAs of foreign countries. Importantly, the Safe Harbor is a self-certification. There appears to be no vetting of self-certifying entities.

The Department of Commerce summarizes the seven Safe Harbor obligations as follows:

> Notice: Organizations must notify individuals about the purposes for which they collect and use information about them. They must provide information about how individuals can contact the organization with any inquiries or complaints, the types of third parties to which it discloses the information and the choices and means the organization offers for limiting its use and disclosure.
>
> Choice: Organizations must give individuals the opportunity to choose (opt out) whether their personal information will be disclosed to a third party or used for a purpose incompatible with the purpose for which it was originally collected or subsequently authorized by the individual. For sensitive information, affirmative or

---

[29] PETER P. SWIRE & ROBERT E. LITAN, NONE OF YOUR BUSINESS (1998).

explicit (opt in) choice must be given if the information is to be disclosed to a third party or used for a purpose other than its original purpose or the purpose authorized subsequently by the individual.

Onward Transfer (Transfers to Third Parties): To disclose information to a third party, organizations must apply the notice and choice principles. Where an organization wishes to transfer information to a third party that is acting as an agent, it may do so if it makes sure that the third party subscribes to the Safe Harbor Privacy Principles or is subject to the Directive or another adequacy finding. As an alternative, the organization can enter into a written agreement with such third party requiring that the third party provide at least the same level of privacy protection as is required by the relevant principles.

Access: Individuals must have access to personal information about them that an organization holds and be able to correct, amend, or delete that information where it is inaccurate, except where the burden or expense of providing access would be disproportionate to the risks to the individual's privacy in the case in question, or where the rights of persons other than the individual would be violated.

Security: Organizations must take reasonable precautions to protect personal information from loss, misuse and unauthorized access, disclosure, alteration and destruction.

Data integrity: Personal information must be relevant for the purposes for which it is to be used. An organization should take reasonable steps to ensure that data is reliable for its intended use, accurate, complete, and current.

Enforcement: In order to ensure compliance with the safe harbor principles, there must be (a) readily available and affordable independent recourse mechanisms so that each individual's complaints and disputes can be investigated and resolved and damages awarded where the applicable law or private sector initiatives so provide; (b) procedures for verifying that the commitments companies make to adhere to the safe harbor principles have been implemented; and (c) obligations to remedy problems arising out of a failure to comply with the principles. Sanctions must be sufficiently rigorous to ensure compliance by the organization. Organizations that fail to provide annual self certification letters will no longer appear in the list of participants and safe harbor benefits will no longer be assured.[30]

The Safe Harbor Privacy Principles had a chilly reception in the European Parliament, where a majority made a symbolic vote recommending that they be rejected as being too weak. But in July 2000, the European Commission approved the agreement such that it would come into force without member state ratification.

The Safe Harbor was a pragmatic approach, perhaps the only workable one, to satisfy European regulators. An array of factors prevented the United States from being "adequate" in the eyes of the European Union. First, Congress was unlikely to pass omnibus privacy legislation, and the sectoral bill it did enact at the time (the Gramm–Leach–Bliley Act; see Chapter 10) arguably diluted privacy norms in financial services law. Second, for political economy reasons, Congress was unlikely

---

[30] Department of Commerce, US–EU Safe Harbor Overview, December 18, 2013.

to enact an "adequate" framework. Because of Congress' structure, an omnibus privacy bill would be referred to dozens of committees. Each committee would have an opportunity to kill the effort, and because privacy laws affect so many industries, lawmakers would be under tremendous pressure to stop the legislation from progressing. Third, if enacted, omnibus privacy laws might be successfully challenged on First Amendment grounds. A voluntary certification like the Safe Harbor sidesteps commercial free speech arguments because it is seen as non-compulsory and thus not a government mandate. The Safe Harbor was the only approach that could neatly sidestep First Amendment and other substantive due process rights and avoid legislative impasse.

As of this writing, just over 5,000 entities had certified compliance with the Safe Harbor. However, over 900 had "not current" certifications.

### Enforcement of the Safe Harbor

The Safe Harbor was not warmly received at birth, nor did it attract praise as it aged. Initially, critics complained that few companies joined the Safe Harbor. But soon, thousands joined, and a different problem emerged: there was no vetting of self-certifying companies. A 2002 European Commission report found that the necessary elements for the Safe Harbor were in place, and that it was simplifying data transfers, but that many organizations had not posted adequate privacy policies.[31] An in-depth 2004 follow-up report found deficiencies in all of the privacy policies reviewed. They surmised that since enforcement by the FTC was predicated on promises made in privacy policies, Safe Harbor companies made vague or incomplete representations to avoid enforcement.[32]

A 2008 report by Chris Connolly pointed to major compliance problems. Hundreds of entities on the list were no longer certified or no longer existed. Only 348 of the 1,597 then-listed companies met the "most basic" elements of the Safe Harbor framework. These findings by Connolly appeared to be problematic, however, it was not clear how many of the listed companies were actually exchanging data, thus violating the Safe Harbor. Lawyers may have signed up their clients routinely just to prepare them for eventual international data transfers.

Connolly's report also found that seventy-three listed companies falsely claimed to be a member of a seal organization, and some companies characterized their membership as being a certification by the Department of Commerce (rather than a self-certification).[33] This last issue is aggravated by the Department of Commerce

---

[31] EUROPEAN COMMISSION, STAFF WORKING PAPER ON THE APPLICATION OF COMMISSION DECISION 520/ 2000/EC OF JULY 26, 2000 ON THE ADEQUATE PROTECTION OF PERSONAL DATA PROVIDED BY THE SAFE HARBOUR PRIVACY PRINCIPLES (February 13, 2002).

[32] Jan Dhont, María Verónica Pérez Asinari, & Prof. Dr. Yves Poullet, *Safe Harbour Decision Implementation Study* (April 19, 2004).

[33] Chris Connolly, The US Safe Harbor – Fact or Fiction? (2008).

itself, which has created a certification mark that does not indicate that the Safe Harbor is a self-certification.

Yet, apparently, no European DPA had ever made a complaint to the FTC concerning the Safe Harbor.[34] This in itself was problematic, as the Safe Harbor model assumed that European officials would refer cases to the FTC for enforcement.

The FTC brought its first Safe Harbor compliance case in 2009. It was against an American company that held itself out as operating in the UK. The company used ".co.uk" internet addresses, listed prices in pounds, and the like but was located in the United States and not complying with basic European rules on distance selling. The company also claimed that it had self-certified under the Safe Harbor, but it had not.[35] The FTC fined the company $500,000 for violations of the mail-order rule, yet it was suspended because the defendant could not pay. A stipulated agreement specified that the company would no longer misrepresent its participation in any privacy program.

Soon after, the FTC settled six matters concerning companies that once had a self-certification, but allowed it to lapse.[36] The six matters have sequential file numbers, suggesting an Agency initiative to start policing Safe Harbor registrations. Each matter had a three-page-long complaint, none had an allegation of data mishandling, and none was fined.

In 2014, the FTC again performed a Safe Harbor enforcement sweep, this time focused on companies that had allowed their certification to lapse for a single year in the US–EU Safe Harbor or a similar agreement between the United States and Switzerland. The fourteen companies chosen for the sweep were headline-grabbing respondents – several were football teams. Others targeted hailed from a broad array of different industries, as part of a strategy to give notice across business sectors of the importance of Safe Harbor compliance. As with the earlier sweep, the matter numbers were close in order, suggesting a coordinated effort in the Agency.[37]

---

[34] FTC, Privacy Enforcement and Safe Harbor: Comments of FTC Staff to European Commission Review of the US–EU Safe Harbor Framework (November 12, 2013).

[35] *FTC v. Javian Kamani, and Balls of Kryptonite, LLC, a California Limited Liability Company, all doing business as Bite Size Deals, LLC and Best Priced Brands, LLC*, 09-CV-5276 (C.D. Cal. 2009).

[36] *In the Matter of World Innovators, Inc.*, FTC File No. 092 3137 (2009); *In the Matter of ExpatEdge Partners, LLC*, FTC File No. 092 3138 (2009); *In the Matter of Onyx Graphics, Inc.*, FTC File No. 092 3139 (2009); *In the Matter of Directors Desk LLC*, FTC File No. 092 3140 (2009); *In the Matter of Progressive Gaitways LLC*, FTC File No. 092 3141 (2009); *In the Matter of Collectify LLC*, FTC File No. 092 3142 (2009).

[37] *In the Matter of Apperian, Inc.*, FTC File No. 142 3017 (2014); *In the Matter of Atlanta Falcons Football Club, LLC*, FTC File No. 142 3018 (2014); *In the Matter of Baker Tilly Virchow Krause, LLP*, FTC File No. 1423 019 (2014); *In the Matter of BitTorrent, Inc.*, FTC File No. 142 3020 (2014); *In the Matter of Charles River Laboratories, International*, FTC File No. 142 3022 (2014); *In the Matter of DataMotion, Inc.*, FTC File No. 142 3023 (2014); *In the Matter of DDC Laboratories, Inc.*, FTC File No. 142 3024 (2014); *In the Matter of PDB Sports, Ltd.*, FTC File No. 142 3025 (2014); *In the Matter of Fantage.com, Inc.*, FTC File No. 142 3026 (2014); *In the Matter of Level 3 Communications*, FTC File No. 142 3028

The Google "Buzz" matter was the FTC's first substantive enforcement action under Safe Harbor. "Buzz" was a desperate attempt by Google to launch a social network service competitive with Facebook. Google had designed an elegant and thoughtful platform, but Google also understood that network effects of Facebook's large membership base would make users resistant to joining a new service. In order to lower switching costs and to launch a service with millions of users already enrolled, Google pre-populated its social network using data from its popular e-mail service, Gmail.

This action proved to be a privacy disaster for Google, because, in doing so, Google unmasked users' address books and posted them publicly. Anyone with confidential relationships, or anyone at risk of harm from domestic violence or stalking would find their most frequent e-mail contacts listed online.

The FTC found Google's representations and enrollment dialogues deceptive, but also included Safe Harbor violations in the complaint. The FTC found Google to be in violation of both the notice-and-choice requirements of the Safe Harbor because the company's privacy policy specified that Gmail data would only be used for e-mail services. Users were not given a choice because Google's dialogue boxes announcing the service forced all users into elements of the Buzz system no matter what option they selected.[38] In the next year, the FTC also brought matters against Facebook[39] and MySpace[40] with similar Safe Harbor allegations.

Edward Snowden's disclosures surrounding the scope and power of US surveillance operations in June 2013 had great effects in Europe. In July 2013, Viviane Reding, then a Vice-President on the European Commission and responsible for data protection, announced a review of the Safe Harbor, citing the Snowden disclosures. Linking the review to Snowden reflects a key tension in the Safe Harbor debates – the agreement is supposed to police commercial transfers of personal information, and American policy-makers have thus argued that Snowden-like issues are not germane to Safe Harbor review. They have also argued that Europeans are engaging in a kind of protectionism through privacy, and that European governments are hypocritical, as they have embraced surveillance systems similar to the United States.

But Europeans see it differently. Yes, European governments surveil their citizen in similar ways, but in their view not with the power and expanse of the American spy agencies. Furthermore, there is a direct connection between private-sector regulation and nation-state spying. The power of American surveillance systems is dependent on commercial collection of data, and much of this collection is in

(2014); *In the Matter of Reynolds Consumer Products, Inc.*, FTC File No. 142 3030 (2014); *In the Matter of The Receivable Management Services Corporation*, FTC File No. 142 3031 (2014); *In the Matter of Tennessee Football, Inc.*, FTC File No. 142 3032 (2014); *In the Matter of American Apparel, Inc.*, FTC File No. 142 3036 (2014).

[38] *In the Matter of Google*, FTC File No. 102 3136 (2011).

[39] *In the Matter of Facebook*, FTC File No. 092 3184 (2011).

[40] *In the Matter of MySpace LLC*, FTC File No. 102 3058 (2012).

tension with European norms of minimization of data. Thus, US business models feed the National Security Agency's activities, and if such enterprises were policed by European norms, users would have more privacy as citizens and as individuals.

To allay concerns as Reding's team reviewed the Safe Harbor, the FTC defended its enforcement record of the Safe Harbor in a memo to the European Union.[41] The FTC revealed that it now includes a Safe Harbor analysis in all privacy and data security investigations. But it is important to note that "investigation" is a special term to the FTC. A staff attorney's many inquiries to various companies are not *investigations* and thus would not require a Safe Harbor assessment. See Chapter 4. The FTC declared that the Safe Harbor was a "top" enforcement priority.

Overall, the memo had a "doth protest too much" quality to it. The FTC could point to less than a dozen Safe Harbor cases. Most of these only dealt with certification. The small number of substantive Safe Harbor violations only addressed choice issues. It is inconceivable that among the thousands of Safe Harbor-certified companies, there are no problems with the other five principles.

Nor did the Agency frankly address the problem with Europeans' concerns. More vigorous investigation of the Safe Harbor compliance would require wasteful fishing expeditions. There are thousands of Safe Harbor-certified companies. The FTC can only do cursory investigations of these companies, to check whether they have a current certification and satisfactory policy. Doing more would require the FTC to act as supervisor, randomly checking certified companies for violations about which no one has complained. Such activity would be expensive, drive attention away from more pressing enforcement priorities, and alienate American businesses.

As of this writing, the Safe Harbor agreement is still up in the air, politically and legally. Just as this book went to press, the CEJ invalidated the Safe Harbor based on concerns about nation-state spying in the U.S. It is unclear how the U.S. and EU will resolve the conflict.

### Alternatives to the Safe Harbor

Several alternatives exist to the Safe Harbor to allow data to be transferred outside the European Union. First, a company can obtain unambiguous consent from the data subject. But companies tend to find this impractical, among other reasons because people can always withdraw their consent. Also, consent must be fairly obtained, and European norms surrounding freely given consent are different. For instance, power imbalances such as an employment relationship could cause consent to be invalid.

---

[41] FTC, PRIVACY ENFORCEMENT AND SAFE HARBOR: COMMENTS OF FTC STAFF TO EUROPEAN COMMISSION REVIEW OF THE US–EU SAFE HARBOR FRAMEWORK (November 12, 2013).

Second, a company could employ specially approved model contract clauses.

Third, a company could negotiate "binding corporate rules." These are tailored rules governing how a multinational corporation can transfer data within its organization internationally. Just a handful of large companies have completed the binding corporate rule process.

Finally, the Directive's Article 26 makes several exceptions for "necessary" transfers, but these transfers must genuinely be necessary for some legitimate purpose, such as for performing a contract in the interest of the data subject.

## OFFICE OF INTERNATIONAL AFFAIRS

The FTC's Office of International Affairs (OIA) is a critical part of the FTC's privacy and consumer protection mission. Created by Chairwoman Deborah Majoras, OIA consolidated separate international departments in the Consumer Protection and Competition bureaus, and in the Office of General Counsel.[42]

OIA is involved in both the Agency's competition and consumer protection mission. The OIA reports to the Chairman (rather than as an office of the Bureau of Consumer Protection). Two of OIA's functions are important for privacy practitioners: technical assistance to foreign countries, which in effect results in a evangelization of US approaches to consumer protection, and assistance in investigation.

## TECHNICAL ASSISTANCE

"Technical assistance" refers to outreach programs where, in effect, US approaches to competition and consumer protection law are evangelized overseas, primarily in developing countries. Most of the FTC's technical assistance efforts are in competition law; however, a significant amount is devoted to consumer protection. The FTC has short consultations with officials from other countries, it files comments on foreign governments' consumer protection initiative, it hosts formal events, and it even embeds employees in foreign government agencies.

Technical assistance is often mutually beneficial, in that the FTC can help a country with a problem that has spillover effects in the United States. One example comes from the FTC's counseling of Indian consumer protection authorities on telemarketing. Interstate telemarketing used to be a primary marketing conflict, but now that voice over IP has matured, much illegal telemarketing hails from overseas in Canada and India. But technical assistance is perhaps most effective when it meets the internal needs of the host country. In recent years, the FTC has assisted China with multilevel marketing schemes, the ASEAN (Association of Southeast

[42] Dina Kallay & Marc Winerman, *First in the World: The FTC International Program at* 100, 29(1) ANTITRUST 39 (2014).

Asian Nations) countries with credit reporting, and Latin American countries with data security.

## INVESTIGATIVE ASSISTANCE

The OIA is frequently consulted in the FTC's investigative efforts, as internet commerce – and particularly problematic commerce – hails from overseas. Early in an inquiry, an FTC attorney is likely to consult with OIA to learn about information-sharing and law enforcement cooperation dynamics in countries where the investigative target is located.

Many factors have to be considered in international investigations. In some cases, other federal agencies, such as the State Department, have to be notified. On a high level, OIA helps other staff attorneys consider whether an international action's costs outweigh potential benefits.

OIA assists in recommending how to receive and share information with foreign law enforcement authorities, whether the FTC can exercise jurisdiction, how to deliver effective service, how to conduct discovery, how to address evidentiary issues, how to identify and preserve assets outside the country, and whether a US judgment to seize such assets will be recognized abroad.

## THE US SAFE WEB ACT OF 2006

Consumer protection is now an international challenge. Voice over IP and other technologies that reduce costs in international communication make it much easier today for Americans to be targeted by complete strangers in faraway, impoverished places. These are the places where economic conditions can reward highly labor-intensive fraud schemes, bunco that is centuries old but still manages to find new victims.[43]

Conversely, Americans can target citizens of other countries for fraud, and thus US consumer protection authorities have some responsibility to prevent the country from becoming a safe haven for swindling. Because American companies own so many popular web services, foreign consumer protection authorities often need access to these companies' user information.

Internet frauds are difficult to investigate in some ways because it has become so much cheaper and convenient to send communications to others. Calls that would have cost dozens of dollars now are almost free to anyone with an internet connection, meaning that fraudsters can locate boiler rooms anywhere in the world. Websites can be hosted on "bulletproof" providers internationally, and moved in a matter of minutes if these providers decide to cancel a client's account.

---

[43] Most so-called 419 scams are modern variations of the "Spanish Prisoner." *See* Arthur A. Leff, Swindling and Selling: The Spanish Prisoner and Other Bargains (1976).

The increasing difficulty of tracking international fraudsters led the FTC to ask Congress for greater investigative authorities, which were granted in the "Undertaking Spam, Spyware, and Fraud Enforcement with Enforcers beyond Borders Act of 2006" (US SAFE WEB Act of 2006 or SAFE WEB).

The SAFE WEB Act fits within the narrative that while Congress often chastises the FTC in hearings, it has continually broadened its investigation and enforcement powers. SAFE WEB was enacted in December 2006 by a Republican President and Congress. Codified throughout the FTC Act, SAFE WEB has four important contours.

First, SAFE WEB allows the FTC to share information with foreign agencies tasked with consumer protection. The FTC can even act on behalf of these agencies and use its civil investigative demand power to obtain information for a foreign consumer protection agency. Thus, the FTC can both share information it already possesses, or acquire new information to pass on to foreign agencies.

The FTC's information-sharing power is broad. It can share data with any foreign agency "vested with law enforcement or investigative authority in civil, criminal, or administrative matters."[44] The matter being investigated must be "substantially similar" to practices prohibited by the FTC Act or other laws administered by the FTC.[45]

Second, the FTC can now obtain a delayed notice order from a federal court under the main law that governs access to user records (the Stored Communications Act) and the law that governs financial records (the Right to Financial Privacy Act). Law enforcement routinely obtains user data under these laws, and requires that the provider not tell the user. SAFE WEB extends this power to the FTC in all of its cases – not just international assistance efforts. In a 2009 report on SAFE WEB, the Agency claimed it had never used the delayed notice procedure because it could obtain commitments of confidentiality voluntarily.[46]

Third, SAFE WEB creates immunity for many different kinds of businesses (nonfederal financial institutions, courier services, commercial mail-receiving agencies, industry membership organizations, payment system providers, consumer reporting agencies, domain name registrars, and alternative dispute resolution services) that voluntarily share information with the government. If one of these businesses reasonably believes it is providing information relevant to an FTC Act violation, or for the purposes of asset recovery by the FTC, it will not be liable to any person under federal or state law.

Finally, SAFE WEB strengthens the Agency's international efforts by permitting staff exchanges with foreign governments.

A sunset provision originally terminating these powers was set for 2011, but President Obama extended SAFE WEB until September 30, 2020.

[44] 15 U.S.C. §44.
[45] 15 U.S.C. §46.
[46] FTC, THE US SAFE WEB ACT: THE FIRST THREE YEARS, A REPORT TO CONGRESS (December 2009).

## CONCLUSION

While much of the world adopts European-style, omnibus data protection regulation, the United States has retained a sectoral model, with the FTC filling in the large gaps left open by the sectoral approach. In recent years, the FTC has strained to defend the US model in international venues, and has attempted to increase Safe Harbor enforcement.

While defending the US approach, the FTC's case selection is causing American law to converge with some European norms. For instance, the FTC's matters concerning malware (see Chapter 9) reject traditional contract notions in favor of fairness principles that one would expect from European consumer protection efforts. Similarly, FTC actions against companies that collect information for one specified purpose and resell it for another reflect European ideals of purpose specification and limitation. Finally, the US–EU Safe Harbor Agreement itself, while only legally applicable to Europeans' data, causes some companies to extend Continental-style protections to American consumers.

# PART III

# Conclusion

# 12

# Strengthening the FTC and protecting privacy

This book has explored the FTC's consumer protection history, analyzed its powers, and examined how the Agency has regulated privacy in six different contexts. This exploration has focused on the FTC as an institution as much as it has canvassed privacy. This concluding chapter considers what the FTC must do in order to continue to police privacy credibly and effectively. It focuses on recommendations that both strengthen the Agency and help it address privacy. Congress envisioned the FTC to *prevent* unfair and deceptive practices. To meet this mandate, the FTC must understand the logic of the information industry and the urgency for quick action.

## THE FTC HAS TO SHARE THE RESPONSIBILITY TO PROTECT PRIVACY

This section gives an overview of the privacy challenge facing modern society and then turns to whether the FTC's jurisdiction, tools, and internal components are sufficient to police privacy rights.

### The privacy challenge

We stand at a technological precipice brought on by information-intensive firms. The transfer of power to information-intensive companies over the past twenty years is difficult to understand. Contemplate for a moment that we have, in a generation, transferred our communications from the mails and telephones, which were protected from snooping by statute and the Constitution, to privately owned and operated electronic systems. Electronic systems have privacy deficits in law. Some electronic service providers are dependent on the assumption that it is acceptable to read others' communications, in order to target advertisements or to improve other services offered by the company. Such monitoring was both illegal and impracticable with the mails and the telephone. Electronic systems also have serious technical faults, as most online communications are transferred in a format that is equivalent to a postcard and readable by anyone. With the weakening of legal and technical protections for communications, we have also seen a change in norms. Many enterprises have inculcated the idea that surveillance of once-impossible-to-monitor communications is necessary for these convenient technologies to work. But this is not always true.

The change from analog to digital enabled previously impracticable national security surveillance regimes and has enhanced the ability of all levels of law enforcement to monitor social activity. The change also shifted the dynamics of private-sector power and surveillance. A century ago, extortionists could fabricate stories of illegal behavior or snoop on people to blackmail others. Today, one's internet service provider, Google, and Facebook silently witness and record our sins. This record is complete, as some services can even discover the impertinent messages we compose but later decide to delete.

We all engage in legal behavior that nevertheless would be horrifying to have revealed to our employers, families, and friends. Professor Paul Ohm calls this the "Database of Ruin."[1] These facts about us are at the fingertips of for-profit companies with a history of "breaking things" and changing the rules to make the world more "open."

In an important 2015 essay, Professor Shoshana Zuboff argued that an era of "surveillance capitalism" has arisen. This market development presents new "possibilities of subjugation . . . as this innovative institutional logic thrives on unexpected and illegible mechanisms of extraction and control that exile persons from their own behavior." Zuboff argues that modern information practices are so new, so poorly understood – in fact, they depend on deception and on consumer ignorance – that we are entering a marketplace of more perfect control, altering social contract in ways we cannot anticipate.[2]

As examples of unexpected mechanisms, Zuboff points to Google's plans. The company's chief economist, Hal Varian, has sketched a future of complete monitoring and control through technological advances. Among them is the automation of the enforcement of contracts; perfect monitoring of workers to hold them accountable; services that can predict what people want before what they realize their own desires; and continuous experiments run on users. Companies that achieve a "platform" status can carry these activities out. Privacy law can do little to address these activities, because privacy law is still fixed on the problem of third parties, rather than first-party platforms, which collect data directly from the consumer.

Zuboff argues that platforms establish "a new form of power in which contract and the rule of law are supplanted by the rewards and punishments of a new kind of invisible hand."[3] Surveillance capitalism divorces individuals from human forms of

---

[1]  Paul Ohm, *Broken Promises of Privacy: Responding to the Surprising Failure of Anonymization*, 57 UCLA L. Rev. 1701 (2010).

[2]  Shoshana Zuboff, *Big Other: Surveillance Capitalism and the Prospects of an Information Civilization*, 30 J. Info. Tech. 75 (2015).

[3]  *Id.*

trust and mutual respect to a world of technical compliance. Understanding how surveillance norms have been built into these platforms helps us fathom the privacy challenge ahead.

Our regulatory regime, premised on quaint ideas of privacy control and sectoral privacy rules, is simply inadequate to address the kinds of decision-making and inferential powers that information-intensive industries now possess. This text has elucidated the work of several scholars who call into doubt the fundamentals of American privacy law. Recall that from a theoretical perspective, Paul Schwartz and Gordon Hull argued that our privacy control regime will not help consumers protect their own privacy. Schwartz and Hull are complemented by empiricists, such as Alessandro Acquisti, who can manipulate consumer disclosure based on framing, and Solon Barocas and Andrew Selbst, who can show that people cannot conceal facts through selective revelation because this information can be inferred based on observing consumers' behavior. Companies' inferential abilities mean that sectoral rules protecting bands of information, for instance those concerning medical records, will simply be inadequate, as companies will be able to detect medical conditions, and even predispositions toward medical problems, from publicly revealed data. Existing privacy and antidiscrimination regimes do not contemplate these problems.

We know from Langdon Winner that individuals are unlikely to perceive political values that are embedded in technology, and from Zuboff that the need to act is urgent, as technology provides the means for companies to both mask their decisions and instill a sense of inevitability about companies' design choices. The shift to surveillance platforms is robbing the public of the choice to take decisions about how they are monitored. When monitoring is built into services, and presented as necessary for provision of the service, it constrains the relevance and utility of the notice-and-choice regime.

### The FTC's jurisdiction, tools, and internal components

The challenge to privacy and freedom is grave. Is the FTC up to this challenge? That question is considered here in light of the FTC's tools: its jurisdiction, rule-making powers, enforcement powers, and internal organization.

Congress empowered the FTC with broad jurisdiction to investigate almost any business or person.[4] The FTC's jurisdictional breadth may explain why the Agency has not fallen victim to the pathologies described by public choice theorists – no single industry can capture it. Even partisan leadership changes have a limited effect on the Agency because consumer protection is a broadly

---

4   Recall from Chapter 4 that the FTC has narrow exceptions to its jurisdiction – for entities including common carriers and banks – but even these businesses can be policed by the Agency. In practice, common carriers and banks frequently use third parties and contractors to carry out unfair or deceptive trade practices. These third parties and contractors fall under FTC jurisdiction.

shared interest among Americans. Jurisdictionally, the FTC seems adequately prepared to address most information-age problems.

Turning to the FTC's powers, the landscape is more mixed. The Magnuson–Moss Warranty Act stripped the FTC of ordinary rule-making procedures, putting in its place a system for promulgating rules that is unwieldy and time consuming. While the architects of the FTC Act wanted the Agency to be nimble and able to respond to incipient problems in the economy, the Magnuson–Moss procedure impairs the FTC's agility. Under the FTC's current rule-making procedures, it must establish that a practice is prevalent in the economy, thus foreclosing the ability to *prevent* incipient noxious practices with a rule. Furthermore, commission rules can be overturned unless they are supported by a record with "substantial" evidence. The evidentiary requirements mean that routine litigation challenges to rules are more likely to be successful.

Because of the Magnuson–Moss limits on rule-making, the FTC now enforces on a case-by-case basis. In enforcement, the FTC has greater flexibility than in rule-making. The FTC can bring administrative cases or go to federal district court. The Agency selects a forum based on the remedies sought and to some extent on its confidence in the merits of a controversy. Strong cases go to the federal courts, while matters that are more challenging go to administrative adjudication. The FTC also attempts to make its enforcement actions rule-like by pursuing matters that are likely to have structural effect.

The FTC's ability to prevent unfair and deceptive trade practices is a remarkable power, but both unfairness and deception have limits. The Agency's unfairness power is politically controversial and tends to invoke howls of protest from critics. Because it requires "substantial consumer injury," those skeptical of the idea of privacy harms may categorically reject the use of unfairness in privacy cases.

Deception is increasingly difficult to use against online privacy problems because companies can write longer, more comprehensive, and more ambiguous privacy policies. Borrowing from its advertising cases, the FTC started basing its privacy cases on the overall impression and expectations set by companies, rather than the precise terms in the fine print of privacy policies. But how long this strategy can be employed is difficult to say. Zuboff and Varian note that consumer expectations can be shaped so that consumers expect capture and use of data. Moreover, services that achieve platform status can build in surveillance to systems and condition its use on monitoring. Businesses can say that privacy has to be sacrificed for convenience or efficiency, and that consumers should expect no privacy, even if this is not technically accurate.

The FTC's lack of usable civil penalty authority curtails both its unfairness and deception powers.[5] Congress restricted the FTC's civil penalty power because of

---

[5] Recall from Chapter 4 that the FTC can bring civil penalties in privacy cases if it follows certain procedures, and that it does have a general civil penalty authority to enforce some rules.

concerns about due process. At the inception of the Agency, and later when its consumer protection mandate was added, Congress felt that the Agency's broad jurisdiction combined with its ability to define unfair and deceptive practices could lead to deprivations of due process if it could also levy monetary fines.

The Agency is also limited in resources. The FTC's budget is only $300 million. Consider that the Food and Drug Administration's budget is over $4 billion and the newly created Consumer Financial Protection Bureau's is over $400 million. Almost half of the FTC's budget is devoted to competition matters. The FTC's Bureau of Consumer Protection is modest in size (about 638 employees), and just a fraction of its staff handle privacy matters (the FTC estimates 57 employees).

Unlike many of its sister agencies, the FTC has an active and independent arm devoted to economic analysis of its activities: the Bureau of Economics (BE). The BE is an important but poorly understood component of the FTC. The BE is a voice for balance and for taking a long view of consumer protection problems. The BE's presence tempers the FTC's activities and keeps the Agency out of Congress' cross-hairs. Yet, as explained in Chapter 4, BE appears to be skeptical of privacy claims. The BE's methods for determining damages drives them toward the sum of zero in privacy cases. In short, the BE appears to be a major institutional barrier to more aggressive privacy enforcement. Because of practical foreclosure of monetary relief, the FTC punishes companies by imposing long periods of oversight through third-party assessments. This remedy places the FTC, an enforcement agency, in the role of supervisor. Yet, this role is one that it cannot possibly excel at, given the growing number of respondents under 20-year consent decrees.

## The need to share privacy

In light of its jurisdiction, rule-making and enforcement powers, resources, and components, it is clear that the FTC cannot police the myriad privacy issues of a modern economy. The FTC's focus has been on Web-platform companies. As broad as the Web economy is, these enterprises are still a sliver of the overall privacy landscape. Many traditional industries now realize that they face complex privacy issues. As a recent example, consider the automobile industry, with its in-car computers that track drivers and can disable cars. As the "internet of things" develops, ordinary product manufacturers are wrestling with security and privacy issues. The FTC simply lacks the resources to cover the privacy and security issues for the entire twenty-first-century economy.

Privacy is such a politically popular topic that several other agencies have now entered the enforcement arena. The Federal Communications Commission (FCC) is the newest entrant. In the FCC's effort to impose "network neutrality" rules on broadband internet providers, it reclassified these providers as common carriers. This move has two effects: First, the initiative presumably removes broadband providers from FTC jurisdiction as common carriers. Second, the initiative places broadband providers under strict privacy rules that ordinarily apply to phone calling records. The new rules have a normative goal of protecting communications confidentiality, rather than the notice-and-choice model's goal of ensuring adequate disclosure of terms to the consumer and acceptance of those terms. Prior to the order, broadband providers' main regulation was a wiretapping law that explicitly allowed the sale of basic subscriber information and subscriber activity to almost anyone. Now, broadband companies will have to obtain affirmative consent before revealing users' activities.

The FCC has not only enlarged its jurisdiction, but also has shown an interest in penalizing companies more aggressively than the FTC. In a single year, the FCC levied $42 million in privacy fines. The FCC will soon eclipse the FTC's records of fines, which is approximately $60 million in the FTC's eighteen-year history of online privacy cases. Moreover, the FCC also developed a novel privacy intervention – it required one provider to place an opt-out notice in every bill sent to consumers for three years.

The challenge for the FCC is to strike a balance in its new pro-privacy activities. The FCC's enforcement activities may slow down. The FCC has never been known to be particularly pro-consumer and is often accused of being a victim of agency capture. At the same time, there is also the risk that without a substantial brake on its penalty authority, the FCC may become overzealous and find itself in Congress' crosshairs, as the FTC has so many times.

On many financial privacy matters, the Consumer Financial Protection Bureau (CFPB) now shares jurisdiction with the FTC. The CFPB can police a broader set of practices, as its statute prohibits unfair, deceptive, and *abusive* acts. Created partially in response to perceived deficits in the FTC approach after the credit and housing bubbles, the CFPB was given authority to pay its lawyers more. Many CFPB employees are former industry insiders, and experts in the regimes they oversee. The CFPB can *supervise* relevant actors, rather than just enforce the law after wrongdoing is apparent. Unlike the FCC, the CFPB has clear consumer bona fides, ones so strong that the CFPB is under constant attack from the financial sector.

Turning back to the FTC, it has done everything in its power to retain broad authority over policing privacy. Regulatory competition among these agencies thus far has been largely coordinated and has not created a thicket of conflicting rules for industry. So long as the competitive spirit remains cooperative, consumers will benefit from these new entrants to the privacy arena. The overlap among the FTC, FCC, and CFPB probably protects consumers against partisan changes in Washington. If a political faction disables one of the three agencies, the others can step up enforcement, just as the state attorneys general and private litigants did during the President Reagan-era FTC.

The FTC resisted incursions by the FCC and CFPB into privacy. But the FTC should welcome their presence. The FCC and CFPB are well suited for the roles they have staked out. The FCC, with its focus on broadband providers, is policing companies that for all practical purposes are monopolies, ones that are large and powerful. AT&T has existed longer than even the FTC, and it alone spends about as much on lobbying Congress as the FTC devotes to privacy. Broadband providers are unlikely to respond to the FTC's style of privacy interventions, which are mainly informational remedies. The FCC's proclivity for fining providers may be the only way to marshal the AT&Ts and Comcasts of the world.

Similarly, the FTC's tool set is simply inappropriate for much of the financial world. Consumer finance has become so complex that supervision in addition to enforcement is necessary to police the sector. As the discussion in Chapter 10 made clear, issues such as consumer reporting are not well policed by enforcement, because problems in the field arise from subtle changes in industry practices. It can take years to detect these changes and the harms to consumers. For instance, simply understanding the level of errors in consumer reports required an act of Congress and years of study.

This book is optimistic about the prospects of the FTC, but also realistic in the assessment that the FTC cannot police privacy on its own. Privacy is a big enough issue to need intervention from the FCC and CFPB, and these two agencies are well suited for the kinds of jurisdictional areas they have staked out.

## THE FTC NEEDS TO UPDATE ITS ECONOMIC UNDERSTANDING OF PRIVACY PROBLEMS AND REMEDIES

The Bureau of Economics (BE) is an important and valuable component of the FTC. Chapter 4 explains in detail the dynamics of this poorly understood entity and elucidates its value to the FTC and consumer protection. The BE grounds the Agency and helps the FTC temper the instinct to regulate all perceived wrongs to the consumer. At the same time, two issues developed in Chapter 4 surrounding the BE stand in the way of a more effective FTC on privacy. First, the BE's view that there is not an economic market for privacy features leads it to undervalue privacy wrongs, leading to many cases with no monetary remedy. Without some kind of penalty, companies may find it economically efficient to violate privacy. Second, the BE's focus on providing information to the consumer at service enrollment is antiquated and deficient for transactions based on personal information. The next sections explain these problems and how research and potential reframing of privacy issues could enhance the BE's understanding of the special context of personal information transactions.

### Monetary damages in a world with no privacy market

Recall from Chapter 3 that Chairman Leibowitz attempted to obtain a general civil penalty authority from Congress. Even if this venture had been successful, it is not clear that it would have resulted in fines that move the needle in privacy cases. The

FTC's civil penalties factors[6] paired with the BE's methods of evaluating relief drive monetary penalties to zero in most matters.

The BE, like the FTC's external critics, uses "harm" as a metric to recommend civil penalties and other monetary relief. In old-school frauds, such as a seller who lies about the purity of jewelry, the difference between the product promised and delivered is easily calculated. Today's deceptive and unfair practices can be much more subtle. Returning to the example of Google's tracking of Safari browser users is instructive here. In the matter, Google was fined $22.5 million, one of the largest privacy-related recoveries by the commission. Google's behavior was intentional, and the company was already under a consent decree for other privacy violations. Google clearly had the ability to pay a much larger fine, and it is difficult to see how such a relatively small fine could serve utilitarian or retributive goals. In a way, the fine created incentives for bad behavior by setting such a low penalty for intentional misbehavior. A rational executive might ask, why not violate our privacy promises if all we'll have to pay is the equivalent of a parking ticket?

To a BE analyst and under the Agency's civil penalty factors, the fine has its own logic. Consumers do not pay with money when they use search engines, and there is no option to pay extra to avoid the kind of tracking that Google used. While millions of consumers who use both Safari and Google would have been affected by the practice, perhaps few of them had ever read Google's privacy policy, knew of Google's statements on the matter, or even had chosen Safari because of its privacy features. Only a small number were actually deceived by the representation and subsequent tracking. In sum, the practice justified a relatively small fine because any price on the tracking would be speculative, and because many who were tracked probably did not care about it. The absence of any kind of monetary damages in other privacy cases, points to a general inability of the BE to assign a value to privacy.

### *Economic reasoning for physical-world products in the information age*

The BE's privacy work appears to still operate in a pre-information-industry era, with a fixation on price and on the information available to the user at enrollment in a service rather than on the complex interdependencies that develop between users and services as time goes on. For instance, a 2014 BE working paper modeled a market in which privacy policies were transparent and well understood by consumers – two key assumptions refuted by a wealth of research in consumer privacy. The authors concluded that under the two assumptions, a competitive marketplace would provide consumers privacy options.[7]

---

[6]  *United States v. Reader's Digest Ass'n, Inc.*, 662 F.2d 955, 967 (3d Cir. 1981) ("(1) the good or bad faith of the defendants; (2) the injury to the public; (3) the defendant's ability to pay; (4) the desire to eliminate the benefits derived by a violation; and (5) the necessity of vindicating the authority of the FTC.")

[7]  Daniel P. O'Brien & Doug Smith, *Privacy in Online Markets: A Welfare Analysis of Demand Rotations*, FTC BUREAU OF ECONOMICS WORKING PAPER NO. 323 (July 2014). This paper is deeply

Even apart from whether privacy policies are transparent and understood at enrollment, information products change over time.[8] Information-intensive industries change the bargain with the consumer through continuous transactions over time. A huge user base is built with promises of privacy, often ones that distinguish the company from competitors on privacy.[9] Once a large user base is obtained and competitors trumped, the company switches directions, adopting the very invasive practices protested against. There is an injury to competitors and to consumers from this strategy, but it is not reflected in price.

Network effects, lock-in, and the power of platforms to shift user expectations enable dramatic policy shifts. But the BE's tools, forged in the era of valuing jewelry, the sizes of television screens, and so on, cannot be readily applied to the problems posed by internet services. In fact, the BE approach militates against remedy, because of the bureau's method for analysis of marketplace effects of remedies. Because these policy changes occur over long periods of time and because competitors are shut out by the time the FTC gets involved, remedies come too late to improve privacy options in the marketplace.

## Measuring and fostering markets in privacy

There are tremendous opportunities for research that would assist the BE. Inherently, the BE's monetary relief calculations are impaired because it perceives there to be no market for pro-privacy practices. Academics could document the contours of the privacy market where it currently exists, most notably in the privacy differential between free, consumer-oriented services and for-pay, business-oriented services. Instead of levying civil penalties that raise due process concerns, the BE could recommend appropriate remedial monetary relief, such as disgorgement and restitution.

More importantly, the BE could explore ways to foster a market for privacy. Part of that effort should concern the FTC's traditional approach of ensuring effective disclosures to consumers. But the more difficult challenge comes in addressing industry players who do not have incentives to fairly use data. For instance, the data brokers discussed in Chapter 6 engage in practices, such as reverse data appends, that render consumers' attempts of selective revelation ineffective. That is, reverse appends make it impossible to avoid having a retailer learn personal information

---

problematic for other reasons. It cites information economics luminaries, but only their older work (Varian, 1996; Shapiro, 1980, etc.). The work of Alessandro Acquisti would seem especially relevant to the assumptions the paper proceeds from, but the only work the duo cite of Acquisti's voluminous work is a 2005 paper.

[8] Joseph Farrell, *Can Privacy Be Just Another Good?*, 10 J. Telecomm. High Tech. L. 251 (2012).

[9] Recall that Google presented its search services, which did not track users over time, as a privacy-friendly alternative to competitors. When Google changed strategies and used historical search data for targeting results, it did so secretly, and the shift was discovered by an outside analyst. Saul Hansell, *Google Tries Tighter Aim for Web Ads*, N.Y. Times, June 27, 2008.

about a consumer. The BE could use its empirical might to study how these information flows in the data broker market undermine alternatives that could result in better incentives and business practices more in line with consumer preferences.

Today, particularly among certain economists, there is a claim that consumers say they care about privacy, but their actions belie their stated preferences. For instance, it is sometimes said that if people cared about privacy, they would read privacy policies. Not only is there error in the underlying logic, but this statement also neglects the history of consumer protection. Consumer protection can radically change individuals' expectations and create markets where ones did not exist before. One example comes from auto safety, where automakers once claimed that consumers did not really care about safety, that consumers chose cars based on appearance, and that auto safety was the domain of a small group of malcontents. In the 1950s, there was no ability to express a preference for safety, but once seat belts became an option, they proved tremendously popular. The BE could be part of a movement to create the "seat belt" for internet commerce.

### Behavioral economics and empirical work in privacy

Another area for rethinking BE approaches comes from behavioral economics. As early as 1969, Professor Dorothy Cohen called for the creation of a "Bureau of Behavioral Studies," with the mission of gathering and analyzing data on "consumer buying behavior relevant to the regulation of advertising in the consumer interest."[10] The BE embraced this recommendation in several areas,[11] most visibly in false advertising. When analyzing what a person might understand from a marketing representation, the FTC is quite humanistic in its outlook. It eschews rational choice theories and the idea that the consumer reads the small print. The FTC focuses on the overall impression of an advertisement. It acknowledges that consumers are not perfectly informed, and that they have limited resources to investigate advertising claims. However, this expansive view of consumer behavior and the subtleties of information products do not appear to have informed the BE's own privacy work.

Academics could take several steps to bring the BE up to speed on better privacy literature. The author obtained training materials for BE and a literature review of privacy papers apparently used by the BE. Alessandro Acquisti, perhaps the most well-known scholar in the economics of privacy, makes no appearance in the paper list. Nor does Professor James Nehf's classic piece on consumer challenges in shopping for privacy, despite its publication in a journal that is familiar to

[10] Dorothy Cohen, *The Federal Trade Commission and the Regulation of Advertising in the Consumer Interest*, 33(1) J. MKTG 40 (1969).
[11] Consider the multidisciplinary approach taken in the FTC's tome on information remedies. FTC, CONSUMER INFORMATION REMEDIES: POLICY REVIEW SESSION (1979).

economists who work on consumer protection.[12] Instead, the first paper listed under the general topic of privacy is the product of an industry think tank supported by five- and six-figure donations from telecommunications companies and Silicon Valley firms.

Chapter 4 explains that the FTC is a staff-driven agency, yet most advocates attempt to engage the Agency through its commissioners. The BE's privacy literature list, although a few years out of date, serves as an example that engaging the staff, and, in particular, the BE, could be fruitful in preparing the Agency for future privacy cases and challenges. Simply broadening the ideological perspective of these training materials and updating them could provide a richer rationale for privacy interventions.

The BE clearly is capable of serious and valuable empirical work. A seminal example in privacy comes from BE's study of accuracy in consumer reports. The FTC's report was a difficult-to-execute endeavor. Yet it was so authoritative that despite its radical finding that 13 percent of consumer reports have a material error, it was not seriously challenged by industry.

The BE's empirical might, if enlisted to play a more constructive role in the consumer protection mission, could be very powerful for privacy. For instance, the BE could be a leader in developing theories of intangible harms from privacy violations. In valuing harms, the BE could learn from the plaintiff bar, which has developed methods for measuring how consumers conceive of the value of personal information. For instance, in one case involving illegal sale of driver record information, an economist polled citizens to explore what kind of discounts they would accept in renewing their driver's license in exchange for this information being sold to marketers. While the market valued the information at $0.01 per record, 60 percent of respondents said they would reject an offer of a $50 discount on their license in exchange for allowing the sale of their name and address to marketers.[13] This method represented a plausible, real-life, bounded expense: the discount one might accept in renewing a driver's license, which cost $50 at the time. The BE could also look to other markets, such as the remarkable expense and inconvenience of using a land trust to shield home address, the monthly charges paid by people who have unlisted phone numbers (this ranges from $1.25 to $5.50 a month, yet about 30 percent of Americans pay to un-list), the expenses associated with private mailboxes, etc.

The BE is key to effective enforcement of consumer privacy. The commissioners could launch an internal campaign to reframe how it perceives the market for privacy. A different framework could introduce disgorgement and restitution in matters currently settled with no monetary damages. The BE could also map an enforcement strategy that stimulates a market for privacy, one that helps consumers

---

[12] James P. Nehf, *Shopping for Privacy on the Internet*, 41 J. OF CONSUMER AFF. 351 (2007).
[13] *Richard Fresco v. Automotive Directions Inc., et al.*, 2004 WL 3671355 (S.D. Fla.) (expert affidavit of Henry Fishkind).

and policy-makers understand the value of the attention and data consumers pour into "free" online services.

## TEMPERING THE FTC'S SUPERVISORY ROLE

The FTC has been inconsistent semantically with the public in describing its oversight of companies as including an "audit." In fact, the standard FTC consent order calls for an outside "assessment," not an audit. The difference is not popularly understood. Assessments are a term of art in accounting. In an assessment, the client defines the basis for the evaluation, and the accounting firm certifies compliance (sometimes by just interviewing relevant employees) with the client-defined standard. Audits, on the other hand, are an evaluation against a defined, externally developed standard.

In assessments, the practitioner must only obtain "sufficient evidence to provide a reasonable basis for the conclusion that is expressed in the report."[14] Pursuant to assessment rules, an assessor can rely on statements from the company regarding its privacy practices, rather than testing. For instance, a company can claim that its scripts do not "respawn" cookies that are deleted by the user, and the assessor is permitted to accept that representation without further investigation.

The problem comes in focus when one confronts the standard that the FTC must prove in a contempt action to enforce a consent order settlement agreement. Courts construe agreements akin to contracts, requiring proof of substantial noncompliance with clear and convincing evidence. Winning a contempt proceeding is challenging when terms of a order are qualified with the word "reasonable." Because assessments are self-certifications of compliance, they are unlikely to document departures from the duties agreed to in an order. In fact, assessors are allowed to find departures from duties and still conclude that the program is in compliance.

In practice, one finds assessments to be empty. Accounting companies sometimes use confusing but impressive-sounding terminology to describe their activities. A company can claim that it engaged in a heightened version of assessment, known in industry terms as an "examination," with independent verification of facts, but this investigation can be as simple as having the accounting company visit the client's website to check for links to privacy policies. Assessments are short, sometimes less than two dozen pages, and are signed by an institution, rather than an individual responsible for the endeavor. Much of what is publicly revealed from these assessments is simply cut-and-paste boilerplate from forms.

How such a short document could, for instance in Google's case, in sixty pages account for all of the company's information collection and handling activities from its multiple product lines? PricewaterhouseCoopers claims it can, intoning, "Google's privacy controls were operating with sufficient effectiveness to provide

---

[14] AMERICAN INSTITUTE OF CERTIFIED PUBLIC ACCOUNTANTS, AT SECTION 101 ATTEST ENGAGEMENTS (2014).

reasonable assurance to protect the privacy of covered information and that the controls have so operated throughout the Assessment Period, in all material respects ..."

It is strange to use an assessment approach for a company that has been caught violating its own privacy policy. In a way, an FTC enforcement action results from a flawed assessment – the company declared its own privacy standards and its compliance with it, but the FTC found inadequacy in the company's policy or a lack of compliance.

But it is also problematic to place the FTC, an enforcement agency, in the role of supervisor, and that is exactly what these assessments do. The FTC is aware that it cannot effectively supervise all the companies under consent decree. Thus, in many cases, companies are required to perform an assessment but not required to submit it to the Agency. Doing so allows the FTC to avoid having knowledge of a problematic practice that is disclosed in an assessment, but not fully understood by the staff who review assessments.

Supervision requires subject matter expertise. The FTC does not have the resources to properly supervise all respondents. The assessment remedy is not only oversold as an "audit," but it also results in the Agency acting in a role of supervisor, a role it is not well positioned to fulfill.

## UNDERSTANDING THE FTC AS A COMMON LAW-STYLE BODY, FREED FROM MANY COMMON LAW RESTRICTIONS

The FTC was a radical creation. Never before had Congress created a body with such broad, inquisitorial powers of investigation along with some ability to police the market. The language of Section 5 itself departs from the common law requirements that were so difficult to satisfy in addressing turn-of-the-century competition problems. In 1938, with the addition of amendments to extend the FTC's ambit to consumer matters, again Congress omitted requirements of harm, causation, and specific intent that were a barrier to addressing products developed and circulating in a complex marketplace.

Yet, at any modern commission workshop, the discussion still surrounds common law elements not present in the statute. Lawyers representing information-industry companies argue for a return to the common law, but, in so doing, they cherry-pick from history. These lawyers do not, for instance, argue to reinvigorate the idea that difficult-to-detect frauds on the public should be criminally punished. Alas, if that common law principle were to resurface, it could result in criminal charges against companies that secretly violate privacy policies. Instead, they argue that Section 5 should include requirements of harm and intent.

Critics hewing to the common law have not confronted the realities of a modern marketplace and the failures of the common law to protect consumers. As we saw from Chapters 1 and 5, common law tort theories did not effectively address dangerous products (such as the patent medicine problem) nor did they address false advertising. Advertisers themselves abandoned the elements required to be proven in common law fraud cases by the 1910s. Advertisers endorsed modern, statutory regulation of marketing, with strict, criminal liability provisions.

Modern privacy problems arise from the complexity of our relationships and duties to each other. Privacy issues are problems of structure. They are too subtle to fit into common law rights of action, which often are framed around a single bad actor who directly injures another person. Privacy problems often arise of indirect conflicts and, although harmful, rarely create the kinds of injuries that the civil litigation system can accommodate. For these reasons, Congress has passed a series of statutory frameworks imposing safeguards for information handling, and freeing litigants from having to prove traditional elements in their cases.

The FTC best performs its mission in areas of failure for the common law, contract, and the market. The FTC actions against Facebook and Google illustrate this neatly: despite these companies giving permanent publicity to data of their users, it is unclear whether common law tort theories or contract actions would give consumers a remedy. Similarly, the Agency's action in Sears, where the company installed invasive spyware on users' computer, would likely fail as a contract dispute. This is because contract law imposes a duty to read agreements. The FTC's intervention gave life to a claim against Sears that would be unenforceable if left to the civil litigation system.

The FTC can recreate the dynamism that used to exist a century ago in the civil litigation system to a new regime based on Section 5. Thus, for the FTC to protect privacy in the future, it needs to embrace the subset of its cases that its critics are so quick to attack. These are the ones where the market and civil litigation dynamics cause a failure to provide remedies.

## RECOGNIZING THE HARMS-BASED APPROACH AS A POLICY INVENTION

Congress endowed the FTC with fantastic powers to investigate commercial wrongdoing and, over the century, enhanced the Agency's enforcement tools. Congress and the common law have both long policed activities that do not cause economic harm. In enacting the FTC Act, Congress gave the FTC the power to prevent practices that caused "detriment" and "injury." However, throughout FTC history, critics have tried to cabin the Agency's powers by introducing an element that does not even appear in Title 15: harm.

Chapter 6 described the advent of the "harms-based" approach, one where the FTC focuses on physical and economic injuries as a result of business practices. The harms-based approach is code for limiting commission action to pecuniary injuries. Defined in this way, the harms-based approach omits other kinds of injuries, such as affronts to dignity and violation of consumer expectations.

The harms-based approach has had political utility in periods where more conservative commissioners have led the Agency. While often heralded as "rigorous," the harms-based approach allowed the Commission to classify its priorities as harmful, without a serious inquiry into what harm means, or to how society decides what is harmful. The harms-based approach was broad enough that spam, telemarketing, and marketing uses of consumer reports were all included.[15]

There are many calls to bring back a harms-based approach in internet privacy. Calls for the harms approach implicitly plea for a reining in of privacy enforcement or for a refocusing of enforcement on smaller, more marginal actors rather than on large, dominant firms.

The lack of rigor of the harms-based approach is demonstrated by the Commission's aggressive stance on telemarketing as opposed to its leave-it-to-the-marketplace approach on internet privacy. Just as telemarketing involved intrusions into the home, internet tracking often occurs while people are using their home computers. Internet tracking is pervasive and often linked to individuals' identity. Thus, internet tracking raises both the access-to-the-self privacy interests common to telemarketing, as well as information control privacy interests. Web tracking occurs in the cloud, but if it were instead implemented on users' computers, it would be treated as spyware (see Chapter 9). Telemarketing is thought to be such a profound privacy invasion that its perpetrators are fined and consumers are provided with a good mechanism, the Do Not Call Registry, to prevent sales calls. Internet privacy is still largely a system of self-help and reading of lengthy privacy disclosures.

For the FTC to more effectively police privacy, it needs to start its discussions by emphasizing its true legal authority, and the intent of Congress for the Agency to police practices that cause detriment. "Harm," when limited to just economic injuries, is a policy invention without basis in the FTC Act. The harms-based approach was also not rigorous, as it was flexible enough to justify the FTC's priorities in telemarketing while ignoring more profound internet privacy problems. It is time to recognize the harms-based approach as a historical red herring. The harms-based approach was a tool used to substitute the determinations of Congress for the policy goals of the information industry.

## SHIFTING TO RELIANCE ON UNFAIRNESS

Deception forms the basis of most privacy matters. Deception is a legal principle shaped by decades of false advertising actions, the FTC's bread and butter. Contextual differences between advertising and privacy are important. Consider how advertising is developed. Even small firms spend tens or hundreds of thousands

---

[15] Fred H. Cate, Robert E. Litan, Michael Staten, & Peter Wallison, Financial Privacy, Consumer Prosperity and the Public Good (2003).

of dollars in developing an advertising message. Businesses agonize over the contours of advertising matters. Many people within the business review and even test the ads on consumers. Millions of consumers then see and even enjoy the advertisement.

The dynamics point to two legal issues. First, it is impossible to prove a subjective intent to mislead, because so many different people are involved in a message's formulation. This is one reason why Congress did not require the FTC to prove intent in its Section 5 actions. Second, advertisers are liable for almost any misleading representation. The law assumes that advertising is carefully crafted, carefully tested, and thus deliberate in its message.

These two assumptions do not hold when switching to the context of privacy policies. Yet, advertising enforcement profoundly shapes the FTC and its outlook on business behavior. Privacy policies may not be widely shared within a firm. They may be adopted long after services are designed, by outside counsel using a privacy form employed for a hundred other clients. Incentives run toward the drafting of vaguer privacy policies. Almost all companies have an advertising strategy reflecting serious thought but few have data strategies.

The perfection of notices through more comprehensive, but vague, disclosures causes the FTC to rely on increasingly theoretical deceptions in order to remedy a privacy problem. Consider the 2015 Jerk.com matter, where the FTC brought an administrative action against a company for scraping data from Facebook onto a new website that allowed users to rate people as "jerks." The FTC's basis for the matter was the false representation that the site was based on organic, user-generated content.[16] Similarly, Nomi, a company that tracks consumers by monitoring unique identifiers emitted from phones, violated Section 5 because it failed to live up to promises of providing notices of its activities.[17]

Why would anyone care about the provenance of data on Jerk.com or whether the tracking company posted a privacy notice? The privacy problem with these services comes from a lack of consumer relationship, predatory uses of data, and a desire to create online-world-like tracking in the offline world. Deception is not the problem: the problem is aggressive uses of personal information, regardless of disclosures.

Nonetheless, deception as a basis for legal action in these cases provides a remedy to contract-like disputes between consumers and businesses. But to achieve more parity and more reasonable privacy practices, consumers need rights that are more powerful than contract. Lock-in, the powerful network effects of information industries, the incentives of platforms to nudge consumers toward disclosure, and the lack of privacy-protective choices make bargaining and shopping for privacy difficult – and that is just for the companies with which

---

[16]  *In the Matter of Jerk, LLC*, FTC File No. 122 3141 (January 12, 2015).
[17]  *In the Matter of Nomi Technologies, Inc.*, FTC File No. 132 3251 (April 23, 2015).

consumers have relationships. Jerk.com and Nomi present even more difficult challenges for consumers because there is no direct consumer relationship.

Historically, the FTC has first entered new areas using its deception power and then selectively employed its unfairness authority. This transition is important because it signals where the FTC recognizes there is an inherent wrong in a business behavior. It moves the market from the empty formalism that online contracting has become to a market with consumer protection.

Consumer protection indeed means moving beyond contract law norms. We need to become more comfortable with the idea that the FTC should step in and affirmatively protect consumers even in the absence of misrepresentations. So far, the thin edge of the unfairness wedge has been used to police noxious problems such as cyber exploitation, also termed revenge pornography, and spyware.[18] The unfairness theory is key to balancing consumer privacy interests with information-intensive business models. Jerk.com and Nomi are unfairness cases dressed in a deception theory. The FTC needs to come to terms with this and develop a theory for why Jerk.com and Nomi caused consumers substantial unjustified injury.

### LIMITING ADVERTISING DATA TO ADVERTISING PURPOSES

Whether advertising is harmful has dominated the debate about privacy online. This is a misleading lens to view the problems presented by online advertising.

Online advertising has both enabled and justified a massive surveillance regime. Additionally, online advertising's logic assumes a world with individually targeted marketing. This logic provides no outer bound to surveillance activities, and, indeed, one plan of the Internet of Things is to embed devices into the home, such as "smart" televisions and thermostats, which monitor people for advertising purposes. Any kind of personal information, including medical information, and any kind of observable behavior are fodder for more perfectly targeted advertising. Consumer advocates can do little to push back against the demand for more monitoring. Pro-online advertising arguments of funding free content and the idea that advertising does not cause harm trump pro-privacy arguments.

The online advertising frame also misdirects the public and policy-makers from consideration of the more serious implications of surveillance. Commentators may quip, "what's the harm, it's only advertising?" In so doing, they miss the point that the surveillance systems being built for marketing have other, unforeseen uses. These surveillance systems may even have other purposes, as Shoshana Zuboff has explained. For companies such as Google, a company that rode to victory in search by critiquing the influence of advertising on search results, online tracking is just an instrument for grasping the yet-unrealized dream of artificial intelligence. In the

---

[18]   David C. Vladeck, *Charting the Course: The Federal Trade Commission's Second Hundred Years*, 83 GEO. WASH. L. REV. ___ (2015).

shorter run, advertising systems are training algorithmic decision-making systems, the very systems that are undermining existing consumer protections such as the FCRA.

In a way, online advertising has been a tremendous boon for consumers. Online advertising funds content creation, while currently being almost comically ineffective. Research shows that users quickly learn to ignore advertising by not looking at the banners and skyscraper ads on websites. Huge portions of the clicks on advertising come from fraudsters or from "fat thumbs." Both Google and comScore found that over half of display ads are never shown to the user.[19] The most popular browser add-on for years has been software that strips advertising from websites. Similar to dynamics present in the credit bubble, experts in advertising cannot explain how the online advertising marketplace works or even explain who clicks on ads, only that it generates money, somehow.

The FTC could take a simple step to reframe the online advertising debate. Perhaps surprisingly, the Direct Marketing Association (DMA) has suggested this step. Article 32 of the DMA's Guidelines for Ethical Business Practice has long specified, "Marketing data should be used only for marketing purposes."[20] Enforcing this long-ignored rule could have profound pro-privacy effects. Article 32 could stop online advertising surveillance systems from being repurposed into schemes to make credit or other decisions. The DMA rule could also force the debate out of its constrained and misleading framework of only being about online advertising. If Google wants to collect data in order to pitch advertisements that consumers do not see or ignore, that is one thing. If it wants its advertisement network to train systems to make decisions about people, to automate the enforcement of contracts, and so on, Article 32 could force a different debate to take place about the power of information systems.

### REFRAMING ONLINE ADVERTISING AND THIRD-PARTY TRACKING AS SECURITY THREAT

The FTC has treated online advertising and related issues of third-party tracking, such as monitoring for analytics purposes, as a privacy issue. It should broaden its frame to also acknowledge online advertising and third-party tracking as a security issue.

Recall from Chapter 8 that perverse incentives and collective action problems cause many information security problems. Third-party advertising and tracking is

---

[19] Suzanne Vranica, *Web Display Ads Often Not Visible*, WALL ST. J., June 11, 2013 (comScore found that glitches, fraud, and user behaviors caused 54 percent of online display ads to go unseen); DOUBLECLICK, HOW MANY ADS ARE ACTUALLY SEEN? NEW BENCHMARKS FOR VIEWABILITY, December 3, 2014 ("in a recent study of Active View data by Google, we found that 56.1% of all ads served were not measured viewable.")

[20] Direct Marketing Association, Guidelines for Ethical Business Practice (2014).

in tension with incentives for good security. Online advertising conflicts with security interests because Web advertising is inherently content that is sourced from a third party, because these third parties have incentives to deliver it quickly and not always to vet the content, and because the tracking for ad targeting and analytics encourage data collection.

Third-party content is not requested by the user, and ad networks that place it cannot always verify the integrity of the advertising material transmitted. As a result, network advertising is a very effective means of deploying computer attacks. Malicious hackers can put code into this advertising and deploy it through an advertising network to infect millions of computers with malware.[21] The user need not even click on the ad, as the malicious program can be self-executing in the form of a "drive-by download." To avoid this problem, security experts recommend "web filtering," a euphemism for blocking advertising.

Digital advertising's business model also has a corrosive effect on the security of the Web's infrastructure. For instance, Secure Sockets Layer (SSL) is a trusted privacy- and security-enhancing technology that reduces the ability of sites to track users and makes it more difficult to snoop on users' activity. SSL is not more widely deployed, in part because its privacy-enhancing features make tracking more difficult, but also because it is challenging to deliver ads on SSL-protected pages. When Google experimented with implementing SSL search in 2011, it learned that SSL blocked "referrer headers," information that operators and advertisers use to analyze the last website the user visited. After operators and advertisers complained, Google found a technical fix to cause this information to be transmitted again despite its negative impact on user privacy.

In order to serve advertising, companies also directly attack SSL implementations. For instance, Lenovo, a trusted manufacturer of the high-quality "ThinkPad" PC line, was discovered in 2015 to have installed software on a low-end line of computers that breaks into SSL.[22] Known as a "man-in-the-middle" attack, the technique is often used by malicious actors trying to steal credit card numbers and the like. But Lenovo was not interested in stealing information. Instead, it injected ads into sites secretly, making the ads look like native content on these third-party sites.

More broadly, advertising models cause reputable companies to behave like computer attackers. Professor Lorrie Cranor's team at Carnegie Mellon University documented that thousands of websites were using code to trick the Microsoft Internet Explorer browser, which by default rejects most advertising cookies, to accept advertising tracking.[23] Similarly, it was discovered that Google and other

---

[21] Aikaterinaki Niki, *Drive-By Download Attacks: Effects and Detection Methods*, IT Security Conference for the Next Generation (2009).

[22] Annalee Newitz, *Lenovo Joins the Malevolent Side of the Online Advertising Industry*, GIZMODO, February 20, 2015.

[23] Pedro Giovanni Leon et al., *Token Attempt: The Misrepresentation of Website Privacy Policies through the Misuse of P3P Compact Policy Tokens*, Workshop on Privacy in the Electronic Society (2010).

network advertisers circumvented cookie blocking in Apple's Safari browser. The method used by Google was particularly brazen. It opened a web page invisible to the user and used a program to simulate the user clicking on it.[24] It was as if a Google engineer grabbed the user's mouse and clicked on a "track me" button while the user was not watching.

Despite all of these security problems, the FTC has treated online advertising primarily as a privacy problem. If the Agency were to broaden its perspective, it would see that the business model causes many security pathologies. In cost–benefit and other considerations, the FTC should prevent these security pathologies of online advertising. In turn, this approach would lead to greater consumer privacy protections.

### MOVING FROM REMEDIATING FRAUD TO PROMOTING SECURITY

Chapter 8 introduced the idea that payment systems are fundamentally insecure, and that payment companies dealt with the problem through a kind of insecurity hot potato. Retailers hold risk of loss from the payment system unless they engage in procedures and precautions that toss the potato to the card-issuing bank. Instead of hardening mechanisms with better token security and PINs' prepayment, payment companies use contracts to shift risk, and post-transaction analysis to identify fraudulent purchasing behavior.

By relying on these post-transaction fraud efforts, payment companies have created a terrible outcome for both privacy and security. Payment networks use just-in-time analysis to see whether a charge is fraudulent. The analysis necessitates the creation of massive databases of credit card transaction information and comprehensive profiling of the customer. Many privacy costs flow from this arrangement – once these data are collected and analyzed for security purposes, they can easily be repurposed for marketing and profiling purposes. The data also become attractive to law enforcement and national security interests.

A post-transaction fraud system is also terrible for consumer protection. Because mere possession of account information makes it possible to effectuate charges, many scammers and even legitimate businesses have made it a goal to collect as many credit card numbers as possible for "negative option" and subscription charges. One company allegedly collected $25 million from vulnerable consumers without even having any relationship at all with them.[25] If the payment system had placed more emphasis on securing tokens, and provable techniques to show payment authorization, we may have had much more private and secure payment. The FTC has bought into the payment system worldview too, by ignoring its structure and bringing enforcement actions against retailers that failed to secure an

---

[24] Julia Angwin & Jennifer Valentino DeVries, *Google's iPhone Tracking*, WALL ST. J., February 17, 2012.
[25] *FTC v. Ideal Financial Solutions Inc., et al.*, No. 213-cv-00143-MMD-GWF (D. Nev. 2013).

inherently insecure system. TJX and other FTC security actions were important in making it clear that retailers must follow basic security precautions. But at the same time, retailers cannot seal all the cracks in the payment system dam. The FTC should refocus its security priorities to improve systemic security. It should identify practices that displace risk onto others, or use security justifications in order to impose other goals on consumers. It is time to leave credit card fraud to private ordering among payment companies, banks, and retailers. The FTC should focus on structural insecurity.

## THE NEED TO DEFEND THE FTC

The FTC is under constant attack from the business community, and it receives little praise from the consumer advocacy community. This continuous browbeating is a tactic to weaken the Agency and to blunt its efforts to protect consumers. It is also entirely an instrumental, opportunistic tactic by the business community. The FTC desperately needs an external community to defend it and explain its value as a tempering force on information-industry enthusiasm.

### The source of the "zombie ideas" about the FTC

The economist Paul Krugman used the term "zombie ideas" to describe bad arguments that resurface in the face of disconfirming evidence. In the FTC's case, zombie ideas about the Agency trace their lineage to the young Richard Posner. As discussed in Chapter 2, Richard Posner implicitly argued that the FTC was unnecessary. In his withering "Separate Statement" assessing the Agency in 1969, Posner argued that the market, combined with consumer skepticism, could police most frauds. Consumers and competitors had common law remedies for wrongs that did not require the FTC's intervention. For Posner, the FTC's information-forcing role was a waste, imposing costs on sellers to produce disclosures and on buyers to absorb the information. The Agency's bait-and-switch cases and other interventions for the poor were ill considered or unjustified. Posner recommended that Congress freeze the Agency's powers and responsibilities.

In an often-overlooked 2005 work, Posner reassessed the FTC considering the institutional changes triggered by the American Bar Association and Nader reports. Posner argued that the FTC had reformed itself in important aspects, becoming a champion of free markets, more bipartisan, and more incremental in its approach. While still skeptical of the FTC's contribution to antitrust innovations, Posner had a kinder view of its consumer protection activities, which he saw as important because no other agency was tasked to consumer law, and because of the FTC's role in actuating legislative change.[26]

---

[26] Richard A. Posner, *The Federal Trade Commission: A Retrospective*, 72(3) ANTITRUST L. J. 761 (2005).

Yet, all modern critiques of the FTC are a series of footnotes to the young Richard Posner. Still, even when written, Posner's assessments failed to appreciate challenges facing consumers in the marketplace. Today's critiques suffer from similar deficits.

### Bait-and-switch advertising, bait-and-switch privacy

Professor Ross Petty highlighted that some of Posner's objections reflected unstated assumptions and that recognizing these help us see the deficits of the Posner critique.[27] For instance, Posner dismissed the Agency's bait-and-switch advertising work without explaining his underlying objection to policing such marketing techniques. For Posner, bait advertising was merely a good-natured way to attract consumers to the store.[28] In recent years, bait-style advertising has become the main tool for information-intensive companies to pry personal information from customers.

When Posner wrote his critique, bait advertising was rightly a major concern of the Commission. By the 1950s, the Commission had developed a nuanced understanding of bait and misleading-discount issues. It distinguished between loss leaders, which are low-priced goods that are readily sold, and bait advertisements, for products that the seller would sell only reluctantly.

Posner also rejected the idea that companies would systematically abuse the poor, in part because of "the absence of theoretical reasons for expecting fraud to be rampant in sales to the poor."[29] While Posner in this early work characterized consumer poverty initiatives as based on anecdote and thin data, he overlooked the Commission's then-recent Washington DC initiative. In it, the FTC discovered that bait advertising was one of the principal deceptive tactics employed against poor consumers in the marketplace.[30] The FTC found that consumers would be told the product was sold out or was only available at another store branch. This was a major imposition for poor consumers without cars.

In Posner's dismissal of the bait advertising problem, we see the limits of his and derivative critiques of the FTC. To borrow Arthur Leff's phrase, Posner's critique suffered from a kind of tunnel vision.[31] A broader lens brings into focus problems of transaction costs, lock-in, collective action problems, and decision-making biases

---

[27] Ross D. Petty, *FTC Advertising Regulation: Survivor or Casualty of the Reagan Revolution?*, 30(1) AMERICAN BUSINESS L. J. 1 (1992).

[28] Compare Arthur Leff: "Once there you had already spent time, labor, and money to go there rather than elsewhere. That you got a 'fair' deal there means little; you were defrauded of the 'sunk cost' of going there rather than elsewhere the minute you went." ARTHUR ALLEN LEFF, SWINDLING AND SELLING (1976).

[29] Richard A. Posner, *The Federal Trade Commission*, 37(1) UNIV. CHI. L. REV. 47 (1969).

[30] FTC, REPORT ON DISTRICT OF COLUMBIA CONSUMER PROTECTION PROGRAM (June 1968).

[31] Arthur A. Leff, *Economic Analysis of Law: Some Realism about Nominalism*, 60 VIRGINIA L. REV. 451 (1974).

that lead consumers to uneconomical decisions. Moreover, the electronic market-place, although presented as a forum where "competition is a click away," has intensified these problems in some ways. Remarkably profitable fraud schemes rely on the basic premise that individuals are busy and may not be entirely focused on details. Thus, one can capture credit card numbers and make millions in charges for products that are never shipped,[32] or fake fees can be invented that the consumer assumes has to be paid.[33] Perhaps no rational person should pay these charges, yet consumers do.[34]

Bait and switch also provides a framework to think about information privacy problems. The website that lures consumers with various free services or other promises but that later switches and adopts privacy-invasive practices[35] is now a trope in our economy. The switch toward privacy invasion is made possible because of the kinds of consumer behaviors and information economics that exist outside some "tunnels." These behaviors include the reliance on brand instead of more objective factors in decision-making, the power of network effects, lock-in, and the absence of viable privacy-friendly alternatives.

Facebook provides a good example of digital bait. What was innovative about Facebook in 2004? Several other social networks existed with similar information-sharing features and profile linkages. The problem with social networking at the time came from MySpace's messy design, the ability of undesirable users to contact and troll others, and network outages that crippled rival network Friendster. Facebook's real innovation was its marketing, not its technology. The company created a social network based around trusted, existing social groups such as the students of a specific college. It initially was premised on exclusivity, leveraging the reputation of the Ivy League. But as users joined, it relaxed membership requirements, from top-tier private colleges to, eventually, anyone.

Facebook is an information-age bait and switch. Having lured users into its network, it substituted the advertised product for another. The company changed its disclosure settings, making user profiles dramatically more public over time, while masking its own economic motives[36] with claims that users wanted to be "more open." By the time Facebook made its major privacy changes in 2009, it had such a command of the market that users could not defect. Since then, thoughtful, well-designed alternatives to Facebook have been released. Yet these efforts always fail because of the power of Facebook's network and switching costs.

Google's history too could be seen as a policy bait-and-switch. Google entered the search engine market wearing its opposition to obtrusive advertising and to

---

[32] *FTC v. Sun Spectrum Communications Organization, Inc.*, No. 03-8110 (S.D. Fl. 2005).

[33] *FTC v. AmeriDebt, Inc. et al.*, No. PJM 03-3317 (D. Md. 2014).

[34] *FTC v. API Trade, LLC et al.*, No. 110-cv-01543 (N.D. Ill. 2010).

[35] Professor Paul Ohm has termed this the privacy "lurch." Paul Ohm, *Branding Privacy*, 97 MINN. L. REV. 907 (2013).

[36] PAOLA TUBARO, ANTONIO CASILLI, & YASAMAN SARABI, AGAINST THE HYPOTHESIS OF THE END-OF-PRIVACY. AN AGENT-BASED MODELLING APPROACH TO SOCIAL MEDIA (2014).

advertising-influenced search results on its sleeve. The company's founders promised a revolution in both search and advertising. Google even presented its search service as more privacy-protective than competitors because it did not take users' browsing history into account when delivering search results.

Today, it seems that Google's advertising policy is in a counterrevolutionary period. It quietly started using behavioral data in search without telling the public. It runs paid search ads prominently at the top of organic search results – mimicking the very thing it considered evil in the 1990s. Google even uses television-like commercials. But these are more invasive than those on television because Google's technology tracks the user and can tell whether the user is watching. Prior to the internet, one could always go to the restroom during the television commercial break. Someday soon, will Google watch users through their webcams and pause ads when the user visits the bathroom or averts their gaze?

Both Facebook and Google are a kind of privacy long con. The services roped users into a relationship that was promised to be different than competitors. Over time, both companies changed policies and mimicked their competitors. Just as the FTC developed expertise to address the bait-and-switch tactics of retailers in the 1950s, today's agency needs to focus on the modern version of this problem. Modern privacy bait-and-switches occur over longer periods of time and leverage network effects and lock-in.

### Common law theories, civil litigation, and consumer protection

Returning to Posner's views, he claimed that private litigation using common law theories addressed most of the wrongs policed by the FTC. Posner wrote in response to the trivial matters the FTC pursued in the 1950s and 1960s. Nonetheless, FTC critics still carry this torch, and claim our civil litigation system effectively addresses modern consumer law problems. At first blush, common law theories seem like a great tool to remedy privacy problems. The common law treated some "cheats" and frauds as public offenses. Business practices that affected the public and that common prudence would not guard against, such as false weights and measures, could simply be charged as crimes.

According to today's advocates of common law suits for privacy, individuals can right privacy problems by bringing litigation under the four privacy torts. These are invasion of privacy, appropriation, false light, and the private facts tort theories. Privacy suits brought by individuals using these theories have failed for a variety of reasons, including the problem that individual litigants often cannot convince a court to remedy small harms that are levied against a very large number of persons. Even mass fraud cases are unlikely to be policed by individual litigants because of collective action problems, and a lack of expertise and resources in pursuing scam artists, who do not behave like normal defendants and may be in distant locations, even outside the United States. The FTC's unfairness theory, along with its expertise in investigation, can address both of these deficits.

The FTC's most important privacy cases are those where our civil litigation system, using either common law privacy or contract theories, would not provide a remedy to an individual. But more generally, law today is driven by statutory and regulatory enhancements rather than judge-made common law. The privacy torts have become ossified.[37]

Class actions increasingly are not a viable option either, as procedural rules, arbitration clauses, and Article III standing requirements have become nearly insurmountable in privacy cases. Even where Congress has enacted a specific statute affording liquidated damages for an illegal information practice, some courts impose common law-like harm requirements in order to just get to discovery. The class actions that survive summary judgment often result in failure as well, as some conclude with settlements that do little to protect user privacy and are written off as a minor cost of doing business by the company.

### Why the FTC's 1910s mandate to protect the small from the big is relevant today

There is another, more subtle reason why individuals cannot remedy their rights by suing: they are afraid to do so. Exposing the plaintiff as hypocrite or money-grubber is the first strategy of some defense attorneys in consumer cases. In depositions, defense counsel interrogate plaintiffs about their online activities, suggesting that because they have an online profile or because they use the internet itself, they must not really care about privacy. Dominant platforms have another advantage: companies can use data about litigants' activity in order to embarrass them.

In creating the FTC, Congress intended it to help small entities police larger ones. Today, this has enabled the Agency to address the small, individual indignities pressed on users in the name of "innovation" or "openness."

The case against having an FTC, first fully articulated by Posner and frequently aped (sometimes unwittingly) by modern critics, is a dismissive, pat analysis of the kinds of problems consumers experience in the marketplace. A different lens elucidates a series of problems – well acknowledged even by economists – facing the consumer in the marketplace that can explain why rights go unenforced, why frauds persist, why companies with strong network effects can change the rules on consumers and yet not suffer in the marketplace, and why the consumer practically cannot shop for privacy on the internet.[38]

---

[37] Neil Richards & Daniel J. Solove, *Prosser's Privacy Law: A Mixed Legacy*, 98 Cal. L. Rev. 1887 (2010).
[38] Alessandro Acquisti, Curtis Taylor, & Liad Wagman, *The Economics of Privacy*, J. Econ. Lit. (forthcoming 2015); Alessandro Acquisti, Laura Brandimarte, & George Loewenstein, *Review: Privacy and Human Behavior in the Age of Information*, 347(6221) Science 509, January 30, 2015; James P. Nehf, *Shopping for Privacy on the Internet*, 41 J. Consumer Aff. (2007).

*Embrace legitimate cost–benefit analysis, recognize that*
*much of it is not legitimate*

The FTC is surrounded by critics who urge that Agency actions must be more "rigorous" or based in the "sound economic policy" of cost–benefit analysis. There is some merit to this argument. As Peter Schuck explains, cost–benefit analysis has much to offer policy-makers.[39] Consumer advocates remain wary of it for the wrong reasons – they tend to dismiss it categorically. If they took up the challenge, they would quickly find that so many analyses presented as "rigorous" to the Commission are anything but sound. Consider these examples.

### Cost–benefit analysis and telemarketing

Former Chairman James Miller, representing the "Consumer Choice Coalition," appeared at a commission roundtable to deliver a cost–benefit analysis of telemarketing regulations and the DNCR.[40] A major portion of the analysis concerned predictive dialers, a technology that allows telemarketers to ring many numbers at once, and then assign a telemarketer to whomever picks up first. This increases efficiencies for telemarketers – to the tune of billions according to Miller et al. Yet, there is also an externalized cost to predictive dialers: so-called "abandoned calls," the problem of a ringing telephone with no one on the other end, known as a "dead-air" call. Depending on how predictive dialers are configured, they could ring up to sixteen numbers at once, potentially interrupting fifteen people with abandoned calls. The FTC took an extensive record in the proceeding, including from small business owners who commented that a dead-air call cost them real money, because the calls interrupted work. Others felt harassed or even felt fear from the fact that their telephone rang so often with no caller on the line.

The Miller et al. analysis, however, omitted any examination of the costs of this interruption. Miller et al. should have included some miniscule amount to account for the costs of these calls to consumers. The problem was not that people's time could not be calculated. In the same analysis, Miller et al. looked at pre-acquired account number telemarketing, a practice where the telemarketer buys the consumer's credit card number in advance of the sale.[41] This practice saves consumers time at least when a purchase is made, as consumers do not need to reach for their wallet when making purchases. The analysis estimated that sharing billing information with telemarketers saves an average of seventy-five seconds per call. If the information were not shared, they argued, it would impose almost $1.5 billion in costs to telemarketers.

---

[39] Peter Schuck, Why Government Fails So Often: And How It Can Do Better (2014).
[40] James C. Miller III, Jonathan S. Bowater, Richard S. Higgins, & Robert Budd, *An Economic Assessment of Proposed Amendments to the Telemarketing Sales Rule*, June 5, 2002 (on file with author).
[41] *See* Chapter 9.

The myopia of Miller et al.'s analysis becomes clear when considering another, unaccounted-for but obvious cost of giving billing information to telemarketers: unauthorized charges. If telemarketers have consumers' billing information, they can make charges without obtaining consumer consent. Recall from Chapter 9 that a single bank had to process more than 95,000 refunds because of unauthorized pre-acquired account number charges. Because a call to a bank to reverse a charge can cost banks dozens of dollars in call support, fraudulent charges can impose massive costs on consumers and businesses.

Miller's cost–benefit analysis is typical of the quality of work often presented by academics at the Commission: it only counts costs and benefits that support a deregulatory agenda. Miller et al. could have calculated costs of the externalities of telemarketing practices defended. They chose not to.

### Fair Credit Reporting Act (FCRA) amendments

Recall from Chapter 10 that preemption of state law in the FCRA was set to expire in 2004. The financial services industry vigorously sought to renew the preemption, and the FTC obliged. The FTC endorsed the industry's request for *permanent* preemption rather than a sunset that would force Congress to revisit consumer reporting some time in the future. The FTC made permanent preemption its first policy recommendation rather than fix then-obvious problems in the FCRA. The FTC's fawning, uncritical assessment of the financial services industry with the subsequent credit bubble and crash is one of the reasons why Congress created a separate agency for financial consumer protection and stripped the FTC of some of its authority in the area.[42]

The AEI–Brookings Joint Center for Regulatory Studies produced an economic analysis typical of the era. The author participated in a workshop for the AEI–Brookings monograph, an event where financial services representatives were invited to share their thoughts about the benefits of information sharing. Written by Professors Fred Cate and Michael Staten, along with Robert Litan and Peter Wallison, the monograph valorized the policy goals of the bankers and discounted privacy concerns. Rising household and revolving debt presented "no evidence that they pose any major risk to the banking system." The quartet praised the rise of subprime lending and securitization. The very rise of credit markets serving the underserved, and the availability of personal information were proof themselves of its goodness and essential soundness.

At the time, privacy advocates wanted more controls over "prescreened" offers of credit, as discussed in Chapter 10. Readily available evidence showed that these offers made it easy to steal others' identities. Prescreened credit offer processing is often fully automated, meaning that the applications undergo no human review.

---

[42] Kirstin Downey, FTC at 100: The Agency in recent times to infinity and beyond!, 869 FTC:WATCH (March 13, 2015).

One prankster even ripped one up, reassembled it, and managed to get a bank to send him a card at a different address. To remediate this problem, the FTC had to create a "red flag" rule requiring the rather obvious precaution that creditors should exercise care when receiving an altered, forged, or destroyed and reassembled application. Identity theft experts even recommended that consumers opt out of all prescreened offers in order to avoid fraud.

The AEI–Brookings quartet dealt with the fraud problem by parroting the views of the financial services industry. At the time, the industry blamed identity theft on consumers: "it seems that most cases of identity theft involve a friend, family member, or coworker." What was their support for this position? The group cited a two-page-long statement reflecting the personal experiences of an official from a bank.[43] Even that statement, if fully read, undermined the AEI–Brookings position, as the same banker also testified that it is "extremely easy" to commit fraud and this could be done by going through another's mail. Security breach notification laws would later make the "blame it on the victim" strategy impossible to maintain, as credit card information is regularly stolen and sometimes pressed into the service of fraud. But the security breach laws, a state legislature innovation, came too late for Congress to rethink the FCRA. The FTC could have endorsed a sun-setting preemption, an approach Congress adopted in 1996.[44] Congress ultimately enshrined permanent preemption into the FCRA, making it unlikely that the law will be updated unless a major emergency arises.

### Public choice critiques

Public choice scholars have generated great insights into the pathologies of government, including the problem of agency capture. Public choice critique is often centered on agencies clearly in need of a shake-up. In the context of the FTC, however, these critiques generally miss the mark and are the products of the author's established ideological commitment. McCraw observed, "Even in some of the best scholarship on regulation, failure has often been applied not merely as a conclusion but also as a premise, a tacit assumption hidden behind apparently scholarly explanations presented in theoretical forms: the theories of capture, of public choice, of taxation by regulation, and several others."[45] Some public choice work lends insight into the FTC, but some of it borders on conspiracy theory[46] or, to put it more generously, simple naïveté.

---

[43] Identity Theft, Hearings before the House Subcommittees on Telecommunications; Commerce, Trade, and Consumer Protection; and on Environment and Hazardous Materials of the House Committee on Commerce, 106 Cong. 1 sess. (April 22, 1999) (Statement of Charles A. Albright, chief credit officer, Household International, Inc.).

[44] Paul M. Schwartz, *Preemption and Privacy*, 118(5) YALE L. J. 902 (2009).

[45] THOMAS K. McCRAW, PROPHETS OF REGULATION 308 (Belknap Press 1984).

[46] The author has encountered the following reasoning in researching this book: The FTC is the agent of large enterprises, creating regulations to help large businesses squash small ones; the FTC uses

A Hoover Institution volume published on the FTC from the public choice perspective alleges a long list of pathologies shared between Congress and the FTC. At one point, the editors conclude, "these four papers confirm the suspicions of those who have doubted that independent regulatory agencies such as the FTC are truly independent in formulating and executing regulatory policy."[47] The reality is that no institution is fully independent of its purse strings, and that, in any case, the FTC has rebuffed Congressional objections on many matters. Chapters 1–3 recounted many such examples of independence, including the meatpacking report, investigations into the insurance industry, and the rules surrounding cigarettes, flammable baby blankets,[48] funeral practices, telemarketing, and used-car sales.[49] When the FTC acts independently, public choice scholars are likely to switch tactics and characterize the Agency as unbalanced.

Methodologically, the Hoover volume, several papers from which are discussed in Chapter 5, relies upon post hoc reasoning;[50] ignores counterarguments; assumes that the FTC's mission is entirely economically motivated, rather than animated by concerns of fairness or small-business interests;[51] and otherwise suffers from general weaknesses in methods.[52]

---

small-business rhetoric to justify actions that help large businesses; the FTC Act was passed to benefit monopolies and help them control smaller, cutthroat firms; the FTC employees increase complexity of regulations so that they can command high prices when they leave the Agency for private practice, etc.

[47] Robert J. Mackay, James C. Miller III, & Bruce Yandle, *Public Choice and Regulation: An Overview*, in PUBLIC CHOICE & REGULATION: A VIEW FROM INSIDE THE FEDERAL TRADE COMMISSION (Robert J. MacKay, James C. Miller III, & Bruce Yandle eds., 1987).

[48] After the Flammable Fabrics Act was amended to strengthen it, a powerful Congressman (a member of the appropriations committee) threatened the Agency, urging it to make a determination that baby blankets are not clothes, and thus not subject to the act's requirements. Then-Chairman Paul Rand Dixon bent to the will of the member, concerned that the FTC's funding would dry up otherwise. Commissioner Philip Elman dissented from the Agency's position, and publicity surrounding it caused baby blankets to be considered clothing for purposes of the act. NORMAN I. SILBER, WITH ALL DELIBERATE SPEED, THE LIFE OF PHILIP ELMAN (2004).

[49] "At one time or another during the Commission's legislative travail, at least one congressional committee or house voted overwhelmingly to abort virtually every major FTC rule making, case or investigation that that had aroused the concern of affected industries or even individual companies." MICHAEL PERTSCHUK, REVOLT AGAINST REGULATION: THE RISE AND PAUSE OF THE CONSUMER MOVEMENT 73 (1982).

[50] An article in this volume concludes that advertising substantiation enriched large advertising firms by analyzing such companies' stock prices after mention of the substantiation doctrine in the *Wall Street Journal*. However, firms were engaging in substitution years before the study period, and other factors could explain why large advertising firms profited during the study period.

[51] An article in this volume alleges that large advertisers favor substantiation because it hurts smaller rivals. While for some that may be true, it could just as well be true that these advertisers are offended by false advertising and believe that it hurts the entire industry.

[52] An article in this volume concludes that FTC fines are regressive and anti-small business, but the study period ends in 1981 (when the coeditor of the volume James C. Miller takes the helm of the FTC), while the work was not published until 1984. The N is only 57, and the authors note that most cases in the study period were brought against large businesses. The cutoff date for the study is especially strange, given that the Miller FTC reversed course and sued far more smaller advertisers (thus targeting

There are many good reasons to be skeptical of public choice theory narratives of the FTC. Daniel A. Bring, analyzing the inception of the Agency, concluded that it is difficult to identify a prime private-sector beneficiary from the creation of the FTC.[53] This lack of primary beneficiary undermines public choice explanations for creation of the FTC. Considering more recent agency activity, over the course of many interviews with FTC staff, Robert A. Katzmann concluded that both popular public choice and liberal critiques of the Agency were too simplistic.

Katzmann focused his lens on the operating reality of the Commission and found that many factors led the Agency to not always act coherently on a policy front. For instance, while economists may think the FTC should bring a certain case, institutional concerns raised by lawyers about losing cases and creating bad precedent could override neatly prescribed economic policy ideals. Katzmann identified other considerations: the atmosphere of collegiality, which sometimes leads to compromise; different attitudes toward taking a reactive or proactive posture regarding problems in the economy; and disagreements between the Bureau of Economics and other arms of the Agency.

In fact, whether led by Republicans or Democratic Commissioners, the Agency has at times urged Congress not to expand its budget, staff, and mission. In not requesting more power, the FTC invites the vitriol of liberal groups.

The public choice notions concerning self-interested attempts to obtain power are also insensitive to the personal reasons why lawyers may forgo very high salaries in the private sector in order to work for a government agency, often for their entire career. Arguments concerning agency capture do not explain the vigorous rule-making the FTC has pursued in areas including cigarettes, the funeral rule, and telemarketing.

### The Beltway libertarians

The "marketplace of ideas" does not soften nor does it correct academic cost–benefit and other analyses for several reasons. Reports prepared for the Commission are sometimes "consulting work" and politely ignored by other faculty. Perhaps guided by lawyerly norms of confidentiality, authors of consulting work sometimes do not disclose corporate sponsorship of their research. Mainstream academics may see the work as policy entrepreneurship, and know not to touch it, because engaging with it is not considered serious. Consulting work sometimes is never published, academically or otherwise, and it disappears from the internet shortly after being delivered to the Commission. Consumer

---

smaller businesses). Ross Petty, in his 1992 study of the FTC, found that the Reagan-era leadership focused on national advertisers in only 10 percent of cases, but that, overall, case selection was much more rational and effective. *FTC Advertising Regulation: Survivor or Casualty of the Reagan Revolution?*, 30(1) AMER. BUS. L. J. 1 (1992).

[53] Danny A. Bring, The Origins of the Federal Trade Commission Act: A Public Choice Approach (1993) (Ph.D. dissertation, George Mason University).

groups lack the resources to counter it, in part because it often is presented in the moment, often on the same day of a public event.

The loud parroting of "rigorous" economic analysis by "Beltway libertarians" further skews the public debate. The Beltway libertarians are members of a business liberty movement, one that promotes a radical free-market agenda and equates any policing of business activity as a violation of fundamental freedoms.[54] These advocates want criminal procedure-like process for regulatory matters. Beltway libertarians are heavily funded by information-intensive companies, and these groups do the dirty rhetorical work that companies cannot without losing face in Washington.

Information policy debates suffer from the same dynamics as public controversies surrounding climate change. In their 2010 book, *Merchants of Doubt*, Professor Naomi Oreskes and Erik Conway connected the dots among different waves of libertarian-inspired regulatory attacks. The duo show that the same scientists were paid by industries to spread confusion and to oppose a variety of unrelated regulatory efforts concerning tobacco, climate change, and energy policy. The groups that Oreskes and Conway studied are active in information privacy as well. Technology companies, many of which are trying to create sustainably powered data centers and other environmentally responsible infrastructure, fund the same groups that denied any need to take action for the environment.

Beltway libertarians complain about specific FTC actions in hysterical terms, while devoting almost no ink to powers exercised by the state against individuals in their role as citizen. The Beltway libertarians are not civil libertarians; they are *commercial* libertarians.

As designed by Congress, the FTC was supposed to provide a quick and reliable alternative to litigation in the federal courts. It reflected a spirit from an earlier time in US history, where the FTC could take a less punitive posture, and businesses would swallow its medicine and move on.

Libertarians are able to leverage business frustration with the FTC. At the same time, it is not clear that business patrons of the libertarian movement share[55]

---

[54] Many Beltway libertarians are groomed by George Mason University's (GMU) School of Law. Professor Steven Teles frames GMU's law school as a project of activist conservative legal thinkers who found that placing scholars in top schools resulted in them becoming more moderate. GMU was a place where "libertarian professors could hone their ideas without the compromises associated with elite institutions." STEVEN M. TELES, THE RISE OF THE CONSERVATIVE LEGAL MOVEMENT (2008). GMU has been used as a kind of academic front for Google's activities. *See* Tom Hamburger & Matea Gold, *Google, Once Disdainful of Lobbying, Now a Master of Washington Influence*, WASH. POST, April 12, 2004. ("Facing a broad and potentially damaging FTC probe, Google found an eager and willing ally in George Mason University's Law & Economics Center.")

[55] The idea of an anything-goes, rugged-individualist California ignores the role of big government, railroads, and aerospace/defense companies in its creation; *see* JOAN DIDION, WHERE I WAS FROM (2003); GERALD NASH, THE FEDERAL LANDSCAPE: AN ECONOMIC HISTORY OF THE TWENTIETH-CENTURY WEST (1999). ("The size and scale of the new federal [military] establishments were unprecedented. Congress poured more than $100 billion into western installations between 1945 and 1973 ... The military-industrial complex was the West's biggest business in the cold war years.")

or understand its radicalism.[56] The true libertarian believers would go far beyond big businesses' agenda, smashing regulations and institutions that mainstream businesses' support. This happened in the 1980s, when even advertisers were surprised at and opposed the Reagan-administration FTC agenda against substantiation. And it is happening today in a challenge to the FTC's 2012 case against the hotel chain Wyndham Worldwide Corporation. In the case, the FTC sued the hotel chain after it suffered a series of security breaches. The FTC found that Wyndham was not following basic security precautions, and the FTC found this both deceptive and unfair. In the challenge, the Chamber of Commerce and other conservative legal activists have argued that Section 5 is unconstitutionally vague, that the FTC does not have standing to sue Wyndham under Article III, and that the FTC should have to plead its cases very specifically. Wyndham lost an interlocutory appeal at the Third Circuit on its constitutional claims,[57] and, as of this writing, the case continues on in district court.

As frustrated as some technology companies are with the FTC, few would find it wise to turn the regulatory clock back a century. If Wyndham's constitutional claims had been successful, it would have been a disaster for the business community and for consumers. Wyndham would have beaten an insignificant security case, while the libertarians would have struck at the heart of the regulatory state. All agencies that rely on some "unfairness" authority would be undermined. Their ability to act when Congress is silent, and how they act would all be called into question. Wyndham would be the first footnote in other challenges to tear down social regulations that clash with libertarian worldviews – things like clean air and water regulations, workplace safety rules, and efforts to ensure network neutrality.

Businesses would suffer because a Wyndham victory would require the Commission to engage in rule-making even on issues where there is broad social agreement, such as security of personal information. Problems that all participants acknowledge as actionable would fester in the marketplace, as the Agency struggled with its Magnuson–Moss rule-makings. The result of rule-making would be a security rule similar to the Gramm–Leach–Bliley Act – a two-page-long document that requires companies to have "reasonable" security measures. A Wyndham victory would even harm businesses internationally because it would mean that the FTC could no longer police privacy. Feeding EU frustration, a Wyndham victory would make it impossible for the FTC to enforce any successor to the US–EU Safe Harbor agreement.

---

[56] *See, for example,* Paulina Borsook's 2000 book in which she observed that the "technolibertarian" movement fundamentally rejects social contract. PAULINA BORSOOK, CYBERSELFISH: A CRITICAL ROMP THROUGH THE TERRIBLY LIBERTARIAN CULTURE OF HIGH-TECH (2000).

[57] *FTC v. Wyndham Worldwide Corp.*, No. 14-3514 (3d. Cir. Aug. 24, 2015).

## Solving the Beltway academic conundrum

The Beltway libertarians' intent is to slow down government action using a political pretense that has broad political appeal, at least in the abstract. The libertarians paint a patina of limited-government, free-market principle atop an agenda that is otherwise simply self-interested. Recognizing the Beltway libertarians as just an instrument of the business lobby is the first step to disarming them.

The second step is to start helping the FTC fend off the Beltway libertarians. Alone, the FTC cannot do it, in part because of its need to remain in the center during political debates. Practically speaking, the FTC needs consumer advocates and others, including academics, to analyze libertarian work, and give context to its deficits.

Finally, consumer advocates are generally unwilling to acknowledge the role of cost–benefit analysis in regulation, particularly where the right being evaluated is a fundamental or human right. Advocates are also suspicious that calls for cost–benefit analysis are attempts to slow down the Agency. But consumer advocates should overcome resistance to cost–benefit analysis. If consumer advocates only would take up these analyses and engage them seriously, the deficits of these "rigorous studies" would become clear quickly. Furthermore, if cost–benefit analysis took costs – particularly transaction costs – to consumers seriously, such analyses are likely to support consumer protection. As the discussion of telemarketing above showed, the only way the industry could justify its conclusions was to completely omit costs to the consumer in its cost–benefit analysis.

Cost–benefit analysis need not paralyze the Agency. As was shown in the 2015 Wyndham case, the Third Circuit did not require extensive economic analysis to come to the obvious conclusion that Wyndham should have invested in more security precautions.[58] Courts more generally will defer to the Agency's expertise and will not require it to engage in make-work.

### CONCLUSION

This work began with a description of *Man Controlling Trade*, the equine statuaries that stand on either side of the FTC. In one statue, the horse of industry will escape man's grasp and run wild. In the other, the beast is violently bridled and bent toward man's will. Both works evoke strongly held ideas about the role of government in regulating business. But while the two statues depict different approaches and results for FTC action, one outcome is the same: bridled or not, both horses remain untamed.

Neither consumers nor their advocates want a tamed industry in America. All of us desire information-industry innovations. But, at the same time, a stronger regulatory hand is needed today to bridle the information industry.

[58] *FTC v. Wyndham Worldwide Corp.*, No. 14-3514 (3d. Cir. Aug. 24, 2015).

FIGURE 12.1. The Bridled Horse. Photo credit: Rachel Lincoln.

The Federal Trade Commission has the potential to fairly address the balance between privacy rights and the needs of businesses to handle personal information in many contexts. The FTC is a nimble agency. It strives to build consensus. Congress imbued it with a moral backbone, such that economics can inform its deliberations without supplanting rule of law. The FTC is bipartisan. It takes its policy role seriously, deeply exploring topics before taking action. It is much more strategic than its critics give it credit for. In principle, the FTC is a common law-style agency, but stripped of the burdens of the civil litigation system. The FTC's common law-like style of addressing difficult, new information-age problems on a one-by-one basis is workable because the Agency's remedies are limited. The FTC can take action and experiment with its regulatory power without impairing the entire internet economy.

Yet the need for strengthening the FTC, and for the Agency to cooperate with sister regulatory bodies is great. All cultures share an interest in privacy. Theorists argue that privacy is a necessary condition to autonomy (to punish people, societies take away individuals' privacy). Psychological research shows that information-intensive companies can manipulate context to cause people to disclose information. As this book has argued, in both theory and demonstrated practice, the notice-and-consent regime is a rigged game, guaranteed to result in companies getting the data they want with no guarantees against transgressive uses of it. When companies do not get data voluntarily, some use technology to trick or force people into disclosing the information. Information-intensive companies are racing to embed their technologies into our daily lives, so that their politics are masked and assumptions unquestionable. These advances will undermine governance, consumer protection, and social contract in ways that are profound, and without public deliberation (or perhaps even awareness) of their adoption.

If we care about privacy as an instrument of fairness and of other liberal values, we need to take a much more aggressive stance with the information and technology industries. We will need an agency, and perhaps more, to meet the challenge. We also have to ask different questions about the stated and intended uses of personal information.

Issues such as targeted advertising will be seen as quaint – perhaps even a laughable – concern once the ambitious, technocratic policy goals of the information industry come into focus. For many companies, targeted advertising is just a means to a much more ambitious end of ubiquitous sorting and decision-making mechanisms. How the FTC chooses to – or whether it can – bridle this horse will determine whether we are the masters or the mere subjects of technology.

# Bibliography

## BOOKS, ARTICLES, AND REPORTS

David A. Aaker & George S. Day, A Guide to Consumerism, in CONSUMERISM: SEARCH FOR THE CONSUMER INTEREST (David A. Aaker & George S. Day eds., 1974).

DAVID A. AAKER & JOHN G. MYERS, ADVERTISING MANAGEMENT, pp. 43–44 (1975).

ABA, Report of the ABA Commission to Study the Federal Trade Commission (1969).

GABRIEL ABEND, THE MORAL BACKGROUND: AN INQUIRY INTO THE HISTORY OF BUSINESS ETHICS (2013).

ALESSANDRO ACQUISTI & CHRISTINA M. FONG, AN EXPERIMENT IN HIRING DISCRIMINATION VIA ONLINE SOCIAL NETWORKS (2013).

Alessandro Acquisti & Jens Grossklags, What Can Behavioral Economics Teach Us about Privacy?, in DIGITAL PRIVACY: THEORY, TECHNOLOGIES, AND PRACTICES (2007).

Alessandro Acquisti, et al., The Economics of Privacy, J. ECON. LIT (Forthcoming 2015).

Alessandro Acquisti, et al., Review: Privacy and Human Behavior in the Age of Information, 347 SCIENCE 509 (2015).

Samuel Hopkins Adams, The Patent Medicine Conspiracy Against the Freedom of the Press, COLLIER'S, Nov. 4, 1905.

ADMINISTRATIVE CONFERENCE OF THE UNITED STATES, HYBRID RULEMAKING PROCEDURES OF THE FEDERAL TRADE COMMISSION, RECOMMENDATION NUMBER 79–1 (1979).

Advertising Age, FTC Drops 70% of Its Cases to Untie Hands, 40 ADVERTISING AGE 126 (1969).

Advertising Age, FTC Tells FCC it Supports "Counter" Ads, ADVERTISING AGE, Jan. 10, 1972.

Charles A. Albright, Identity Theft, Hearings before the House Subcommittees on Telecommunications Commerce, Trade, and Consumer Protection and on Environment and Hazardous Materials of the House Committee on Commerce (1999).

GEORGE J. ALEXANDER, HONESTY AND COMPETITION: FALSE-ADVERTISING LAW AND POLICY UNDER FTC ADMINISTRATION (1967).

ANITA L. ALLEN, UNPOPULAR POLICY (2011).

ALTAWEEL, et al., HACKING YOUR WAY TO THE TOP: ONLINE PHARMACIES IN HIGHLY-RANKED ORGANIC SEARCH RESULTS (2015).

American Bankers Association, Task Force on Responsible Use and Protection of Customer Information, Voluntary Guidelines for Responsible Use and Protection of Customer Information (n.d.).

AMERICAN BAR ASSOCIATION, REPORT OF THE ABA COMMISSION TO STUDY THE FEDERAL TRADE COMMISSION (1969).

AMERICAN ENTERPRISE INSTITUTE, A CONVERSATION WITH MICHAEL PERTSCHUK (1979).

AMERICAN INSTITUTE OF CERTIFIED PUBLIC ACCOUNTANTS, AT SECTION 101 ATTEST ENGAGEMENTS (2014).

AMERICAN PSYCHOLOGICAL ASSOCIATION, REPORT OF THE APA TASK FORCE ON ADVERTISING AND CHILDREN (2004).

AMERICAN TELESERVICES ASSOCIATION, COMMENTS OF THE AMERICAN TELESERVICES ASSOCIATION ON THE REVIEW OF THE TELEMARKETING SALES RULE 10 (2000).

Dean Anason, *In Focus: All of a Sudden, Customer Privacy is Reform Bill Thorn*, AMERICAN BANKER, Jun. 14, 1999.

David A. Anderson & Jonathan Winer, *Corrective Advertising: The FTC's New Formula for Effective Relief*, 50 TEX. L. REV. 312 (1971).

David A. Anderson, et al., *Characterizing Internet Scam Hosting Infrastructure* (2007).

Ross Anderson, *Why Information Security is Hard – An Economic Perspective* (2001).

Julia Angwin & Jennifer Valentino DeVries, *Google's iPhone Tracking*, WALL ST. J., Feb. 17, 2012.

Anti-Spyware Working Group, *Anti-Spyware Coalition Definitions Document* (2007).

Antitrust Law Journal, *Interview of Lewis A. Engman*, 43 ANTITRUST L. J. 443 (1973–1974).

Judy Areen, et al., *The Consumer and the Federal Trade Commission (The Nader Report)*, 115 Cong. Rec., pt. 1539 (1969).

PHILIPPE ARIÉS & GEORGES DUBY, A HISTORY OF PRIVATE LIFE (Philippe Ariés & Georges Duby eds., 1987).

Article 29 Working Party, Article 29 Working Party, Opinion 15/2011 on the Definition of Consent (2011).

Associated Press, *Sisters Banned from Filenne's Basement Stores*, Jul. 14, 2003.

Association Management Magazine, *The Aggressive New Chairman at FTC*, Nov. 1973.

CARL A. AUERBACH, REPORT ON THE INTERNAL ORGANIZATION AND PROCEDURE OF THE FEDERAL TRADE COMMISSION (Administrative Conference of the United States, (1962).

Neil Averitt, *Viewing Consumer Abuses as Crimes*, FTC: WATCH, Jul. 30, 2015.

Ian Ayers & Matthew Funk, *Marketing Privacy: A Solution for the Blight of Telemarketing (and Spam and Junk Mail)*, 20 YALE J. on REG. 77 (2003).

Michael Backes, et al., *ObliviAd: Provably Secure and Practical Online Behavioral Advertising* (2012).

William J. Baer, *At the Turning Point: The Commission in 1978, in* MARKETING AND ADVERTISING REGULATION: THE FEDERAL TRADE COMMISSION IN THE 1990s (Patrick E. Murphy & William L. Wilkie eds., 1990).

Patricia P. Bailey & Michael Pertschuk, *The Law of Deception: The Past as Prologue*, 33 AM. U. L. REV. 849 (Summer 1984).

Eugene R. Baker & Daniel J. Baum, *Section 5 of the Federal Trade Commission Act: A Continuing Process of Redefinition*, 7 VILL. L. REV. 517 (1962).

Dan Balsam & Timothy Walton, *Balsam v. Trancos Inc.*, TRIAL LAWYER 14 Summer 2012.

Kenneth A. Bamberger & Deirdre K. Mulligan, *Privacy on the Books and on the Ground*, 63 STAN. L. REV. 247 (2011).

KENNETH A. BAMBERGER & DEIRDRE K. MULLIGAN, PRIVACY ON THE GROUND: DRIVING CORPORATE BEHAVIOR IN THE UNITED STATES AND EUROPE (2015).

J. Howard Beales, III, *Advertising to Kids & the FTC: A Regulatory Retrospective That Advises the Present* (2004).

J. Howard Beales, III, *The FTC in the 1980s, in* MARKETING AND ADVERTISING REGULATION: THE FEDERAL TRADE COMMISSION IN THE 1990s (Patrick E. Murphy & William L. Wilkie eds., 1990).

J. Howard Beales, III, et al., In Defense of the Pfizer Factors (2012).

J. Howard Beales, III, et al., *The Efficient Regulation of Consumer Information*, 24 J. L. & Econ. 491 (1981).

E. Beem & L. Isaacson, *Schizophrenia in Trading Stamp Analysis*, 41 The J. of Bus 340 (1968).

Carolyn Shaw Bell, *Liberty and Property, and No Stamps*, 40 The J. of Bus 194 (1967).

Omri Ben-Shahar & Carl E. Schneider, More Than You Wanted to Know: The Failure of Mandated Disclosure (2014).

Colin J. Bennett, *Convergence Revisited: Toward a Global Policy for the Protection of Personal Data?*, in Technology and Privacy: The New Landscape (Philip E. Agre & Marc Rotenberg eds., 1997).

Colin J. Bennett & Charles D. Raab, The Governance of Privacy (2006).

Louis D. Gerald Berk, Brandeis and the Making of Regulated Competition, 1900–1932 (2009).

Jodie Z. Bernstein, Letter from Jodie Bernstein, Director, FTC Bureau of Consumer Protection, to Kathryn C. Montgomery, President, Center for Media Education (1997).

Joan Z. Bernstein, *Oral History Project, the Historical Society of the District of Columbia Circuit* (2007).

Samuel J. Best, et al., *Privacy in the Information Age*, 70 Pub. Opinion Q. 375 (2006).

David O. Bickart, *Civil Penalties under Section 5(m) of the Federal Trade Commission Act*, 44 U. Chi. L. Rev. 761 (1977).

Francesca Bignami, *European Versus American Liberty: A Comparative Privacy Analysis of Antiterrorism Data Mining*, 48 B. C. L. Rev. 609 (2007).

Mikhail Bilenko, et al., *Targeted, Not Tracked: Client-Side Solutions for Privacy-Friendly Behavioral Advertising*, TPRC, Sept. 25 2011.

Edwin Black, IBM and the Holocaust: the Strategic Alliance between Nazi Germany and America's Most Powerful Corporation (2000).

Thomas Blaisdell, The Federal Trade Commission: An Experiment in the Control of Business, Vol. 261 (1932).

Board of Governors of the Federal Reserve System, Report to the Congress on Further Restrictions on Unsolicited Written Offers of Credit and Insurance (2004).

Thomas L. Bohen, *An Analysis of the Formal and Informal Enforcement Procedures of the Federal Trade Commission as Devices for Restraining Unfair Methods of Competition and Unfair and Deceptive Business Practices* (1971) (Ph.D. dissertation, University of Minnesota).

Robert M. Bond, et al., *A 61-Million-Person Experiment in Social Influence and Political Mobilization*, 489 Nature 295 (2012).

David Boorstin, The Republic of Technology (1978).

Paulina Borsook, Cyberselfish: A Critical Romp Through the Terribly Libertarian Culture of High-Tech (2000).

David M. Boush, et al., Deception in the Marketplace: The Psychology of Deceptive Persuasion and Consumer Self-Protection (2009).

Danah Boyd, It's Complicated: The Social Lives of Networked Teens (2014).

Danah Boyd, et al., How the COPPA, as Implemented, Is Misinterpreted by the Public: A Research Perspective (2010).

Barry B. Boyer, *Funding Public Participation in Agency Proceedings: The Federal Trade Commission Experience*, 70 Georgetown L. Rev. 51 (1981).

Louis D. Brandeis, *The Inefficiency of the Oligarchs*, Harper's Weekly Jan. 17, 1914.

Elsa Brenner, *Child Abuse on Internet Heightens Vigilance*, N. Y. Times, Apr. 19, 1998.

Danny A. Bring, *The Origins of the Federal Trade Commission Act: A Public Choice Approach* (1993) (Ph.D. dissertation, George Mason University).

Jennifer Brooks, et al., Corporation for Enterprise Development, Excluded from the Financial Mainstream (2015).

Finn Brunton, Spam: A Shadow History of the Internet (2013).

Herbert Burkert, *Four Myths about Regulating in the Information Society – A Comment, in* Starting Points for ICT Regulation (Bert-Jaap Koops, et al. eds., 2006).

Business Wire, *Largest Database Marketing Firm Sends Phone Numbers, Addresses of 5,000 Families with Kids to TV Reporter Using Name of Child Killer,* Bus. Wire, May 13, 1996.

Lee Andrew Bygrave, Data Privacy Law: An International Perspective (2014).

Lee A. Bygrave, *Internet Governance by Contract* (2015).

John H. Calfee, Fear of Persuasion (1997).

Stephen Calkins, *Kirkpatrick II: Counsel Responds, in* Marketing and Advertising Regulation: The Federal Trade Commission in the 1990s (Patrick E. Murphy & William L. Wilkie eds., 1990).

Ryan Calo, *Digital Market Manipulation,* 82 Geo. Wash. L. Rev. 995 (2014).

Fred H. Cate, *Principles of Internet Privacy,* 32 Conn. L. Rev. 877 (2000).

Fred H. Cate, et al., Financial Privacy, Consumer Prosperity, and the Public Good (AEI-Brookings Joint Center for Regulatory Studies, 2003).

David F. Cavers, *The Food, Drug, and Cosmetic Act of 1938: Its Legislative History and Its Substantive Provisions,* 6 Law & Contemp. Probs. 2 (1939).

Ann Cavoukian, Privacy by Design: The 7 Foundational Principles (2012).

Ann Cavoukian & Malcolm Crompton, Web Seals: A Review of Online Privacy Programs (2000).

Center for Democracy & Technology, Online Banking Privacy: A Slow Confusing Start to Giving Customers Control over Their Information (2000).

Gary Chapman, *Protecting Children Online Is Society's Herculean Mission,* L.A. Times, Jun. 24, 1996.

William R. Childs, *Measures of the Presidents: Hoover to Bush,* 21 Presidential Studies Quarterly 385–387 (1991).

Blake Clark, The Advertising Smoke Screen (1943).

David D. Clark, et al., *Tussle in Cyberspace: Defining Tomorrow's Internet,* 13 IEEE/ACM Trans. Netw. 462 (2000).

Kenneth W. Clarkson, *Executive Constraints, in* The Federal Trade Commission since 1970: Economic Regulation and Bureaucratic Behavior (Kenneth W. Clarkson & Timothy J. Muris eds., 1981).

Kenneth W. Clarkson, *Legislative Constraints, in* The Federal Trade Commission since 1970: Economic Regulation and Bureaucratic Behavior (Kenneth W. Clarkson & Timothy J. Muris eds., 1981).

Kenneth W. Clarkson & Timothy J. Muris, *Commission Performance, Incentives, and Behavior, in* The Federal Trade Commission since 1970: Economic Regulation and Bureaucratic Behavior (Kenneth W. Clarkson & Timothy J. Muris eds., 1981).

John Coffee, *Speech of the Honorable John M. Coffee,* 83 Cong. Rec. Appendix 1002 (1938).

Dorothy Cohen, *The Federal Trade Commission and the Regulation of Advertising in the Consumer Interest,* 33 J. of Mktg. 40 (1969).

Julie E. Cohen, Configuring the Networked Self: Law, Code, and the Play of Everyday Practice (2012).

Kristin Cohen & Christina Yeung, *Kids' Apps Disclosures Revisited* (2015).

Pieter A. Cohen, *Hazards of Hindsight – Monitoring the Safety of Nutritional Supplements*, 370 N. ENG. J. MED. 1277–1280 (2014).

Stanley E. Cohen, *Consumer Safety Net Starting to Unravel*, 53 ADVERTISING AGE (1982).

David Colker & Joseph Menn, *ChoicePoint CEO Had Denied Any Previous Breach of Database, Derek Smith Described a Recent Leak as "the First Time" Despite an Earlier Scam Case*, L. A. TIMES, Mar. 3, 2005.

Committee on Commerce US Senate, Science, and Transportation, Office of Oversight and Investigations Majority Staff, *A Review of the Data Broker Industry: Collection, Use, and Sale of Consumer Data for Marketing Purposes* (2013).

CHRIS CONNOLLY, THE US SAFE HARBOR – FACT OR FICTION? (2008).

CHRIS CONNOLLY, GALEXIA, TRUSTMARK SCHEMES STRUGGLE TO PROTECT PRIVACY (2008).

Chris Connolly, et al., *Privacy Self-Regulation in Crisis? – TRUSTe's "Deceptive" Practices*, 132 PRIVACY LAWS & BUS. INT'L REP. 13 (2014).

Consumer Reports Magazine, *That Facebook Friend Might Be 10 Years Old, and Other Troubling News*, 2011.

CONTACT CENTER COMPLIANCE, CONTACT CENTER COMPLIANCE ANNOUNCES LITIGATORSCRUB (2015).

Council of Europe, *Article 10 of the European Convention on Human Rights* (1950).

LUCY BLACK CREIGHTON, PRETENDERS TO THE THRONE (1976).

Barry J. Cutler, *The Criminalization of Consumer Protection – A Brave New World for Defense Counsel*, 22 ANTITRUST 61 (Fall 2007).

JOHN B. DAISH, THE FEDERAL TRADE COMMISSION LAW AND RELATED ACTS (1914).

Dan Hates Spam, available at www.danhatesspam.com/.

MICHAEL J. DAUGHERTY, THE DEVIL INSIDE THE BELTWAY (2013).

Michael deCourcy Hinds, *The Rift over Protecting Consumers in Debt*, N. Y. TIMES, May 8, 1983.

DEPARTMENT OF COMMERCE, THE EMERGING DIGITAL ECONOMY (1998).

DEPARTMENT OF COMMERCE, US–EU SAFE HARBOR OVERVIEW (2013).

Jan Dhont, *et al.*, *Safe Harbour Decision Implementation Study* (2004).

JOAN DIDION, WHERE I WAS FROM (2003).

DIRECT MARKETING ASSOCIATION, GUIDELINES FOR ETHICAL BUSINESS PRACTICE (2014).

PAM DIXON & ROBERT GELLMAN, WORLD PRIVACY FORUM, THE SCORING OF AMERICA: HOW SECRET CONSUMER SCORES THREATEN YOUR PRIVACY AND YOUR FUTURE (2014).

Paul Rand Dixon, *Statement of Chairman Paul Rand Dixon*, 115 CONG. REC. 1568 (1969).

DOUBLECLICK, HOW MANY ADS ARE ACTUALLY IN? NEW BENCHMARKS FOR VIEWABILITY (2014).

Kirstin Downey, *FTC at 100: The Agency in Recent Times to Infinity and Beyond!*, FTC: WATCH, Mar. 13, 2015.

Kirstin Downey, *Health Scare Leads to New Powers for the FTC, in* THE INSIDER'S GUIDE TO THE HISTORY OF THE FEDERAL TRADE COMMISSION (Kirstin Downey & Lesette Heath eds., 2015).

Kirstin Downey, *Robinson–Patman Act Devised to Save Main Street Shops, in* THE INSIDER'S GUIDE TO THE HISTORY OF THE FEDERAL TRADE COMMISSION (Kirsten Downey & Lesette Heath eds., 2015).

Charles Duhigg, *Bilking the Elderly, with a Corporate Assist*, N. Y. TIMES, May 20, 2007.

DAVID DYER, TRW: PIONEERING TECHNOLOGY AND INNOVATION SINCE 1900 (1988).

Esther Dyson, *Protect Internet Privacy – Privately*, WALL ST. J., Jun. 17, 1997.

Benjamin Edelman, *Adverse Selection in Online "Trust" Certifications* (2009).

BENJAMIN EDELMAN, "SPYWARE": RESEARCH, TESTING, LEGISLATION, AND SUITS (2014).

Education Department of Health, and Welfare, Records, Computers and the Rights of Citizens, *Report of the Secretary's Advisory Committee on Automated Personal Data Systems* (1973).

DOUGLAS EDWARDS, I'M FEELING LUCKY: THE CONFESSIONS OF GOOGLE EMPLOYEE NUMBER 59 (2011).

Andrea E. Eisenkraft, *Nutrition Advertising and Children: The Decisions and Events Leading Up to the 1978 Federal Trade Commission Proposal* (1978) (B.A. thesis, University of Texas).

Robert Epstein & Ronald E. Robertson, *The Search Engine Manipulation Effect (SEME) and Its Possible Impact on the Outcomes of Elections*, 112 PROCEEDINGS OF THE NATIONAL ACADEMY OF SCIENCES 4512(2015).

EUROPEAN COMMISSION, STAFF WORKING PAPER ON THE APPLICATION OF COMMISSION DECISION 520/2000/EC of 26 JULY 2000 ON THE ADEQUATE PROTECTION OF PERSONAL DATA PROVIDED BY THE SAFE HABOUR PRIVACY PRINCIPLES (2002).

European Convention, Article 11 of the Charter of Fundamental Rights of the European Union (2010/C 83/02) (2010).

European Parliament, Directive 2011/83/EU of the European Parliament and the Council on Consumer Rights (2011).

European Parliament, Directive 2013/37/EU of the European Parliament and of the Council of 26 June 2013 Amending Directive 2003/98/EC on the Re-Use of Public Sector Information (2013).

European Union, Article 38, EU Charter on Human Rights (2000).

Joseph Farrell, *Can Privacy Be Just Another Good?*, 10 J. TELECOMM & HIGH TECH. L. 251 (2012).

William W. Fisher, III, *When Should We Permit Differential Pricing of Information?*, 55 UCLA L. REV. 1 (2007).

ANTHONY FITZHERBERT, THE BOOK OF HUSBANDRY (1882).

DAVID H. FLAHERTY, PRIVACY IN COLONIAL NEW ENGLAND (1967).

Susan Bartlett Foote & Robert H. Mnookin, *The "Kid Vid"; Crusade*, 61 THE PUBLIC INTEREST 90 (Fall 1980).

Brett Forrest, *The Sleazy Life and Nasty Death of Russia's Spam King*, WIRED 2006.

PAUL FRAME, SHOE-FITTING FLUOROSCOPE (1930–1940) (2010).

FTC, ANNUAL REPORT OF THE FEDERAL TRADE COMMISSION 1970 (1970).

FTC, ANNUAL REPORT OF THE FEDERAL TRADE COMMISSION 1976 (1976).

FTC, ANNUAL REPORT ON THE FEDERAL TRADE COMMISSION FOR THE FISCAL YEAR ENDED JUNE 30, 1934 (1934).

FTC, ANNUAL REPORT OF THE FEDERAL TRADE COMMISSION FOR THE FISCAL YEAR ENDING JUNE 30, 1945 (1945).

FTC, *Biennial Report to Congress: Under the Do Not Call Registry Fee Extension Act of 2007, FY 2010 and 2011* (2011).

FTC, *Children's Advertising, Proposed Trade Regulation Rulemaking and Public Hearing*, 82 FED. REG. 17967 (1978).

FTC, *Children's Online Privacy Protection Rule, Final Rule Amendments*, 78 FED. REG. 3972 (2013).

FTC, *Commission Enforcement Policy Statement in Regard to Clear and Conspicuous Disclosure in Television Advertising* (1970).

FTC, *Commission Statement Marking the FTC's 50th Data Security Settlement* (2014).

FTC, CONSUMER INFORMATION REMEDIES: POLICY REVIEW SESSION (1979).

FTC, *Credit Practices: Final Report to the Federal Trade Commission and Proposed Trade Regulation Rule (16 CFR Part 444) Bureau of Consumer Protection* (1980).

FTC, Economic Report on Installment Credit and Retail Sales Practices of District of Columbia Retailers (1968).

FTC, The Federal Trade Commission during the Administration of President Lyndon B. Johnson, November 1963–January 1969 (1969).

FTC, Federal Trade Commission Staff Report on Television Advertising to Children (1978).

FTC, *Final Report of the FTC Advisory Committee on Online Access and Security* (2000).

FTC, FTC 1985 Annual Report 18 (1985).

FTC, FTC Surfs Children's Web Sites to Review Privacy Practices (1997).

FTC, *Implementing the Children's Online Privacy Protection Act: A Report to Congress* (2007).

FTC, National Do Not Email Registry: A Report to Congress (June 2004).

FTC, News Release: Advertising and Unfair Practices (Docket 8714) (1968).

FTC Office of Inspector General, *Evaluation of the Federal Trade Commission's Bureau of Consumer Protection Resources*, OIG Evaluation Report No. 14–003 (2014).

FTC Office of Inspector General, *Evaluation of the Federal Trade Commission's Bureau of Economics* (2015).

FTC, Online Profiling: A Report to Congress Part 2 Recommendations (2000).

FTC, *Opening Remarks of Chairman Earl W. Kintner at the FTC's Conference on Public Deception* (1959).

FTC, Oral History Interview: Mary Gardiner Jones (2003).

FTC, The Political Economy of Regulation: Private Interests in the Regulatory Process (1984).

FTC, Privacy Enforcement and Safe Harbor: Comments of FTC Staff to European Commission Review of the US–EU Safe Harbor Framework (2013).

FTC, Privacy Online: Fair Information Practices in the Electronic Marketplace 10 (2000).

FTC, Privacy Online: A Report to Congress (1998).

FTC, Protecting Consumer Privacy in an Era of Rapid Change (2010).

FTC, Report on District of Columbia Consumer Protection Program (1968).

FTC, *Report to Congress under Section 319 of the Fair and Accurate Credit Transactions Act of 2003* (2012).

FTC, *Section 319 of the Fair and Accurate Credit Transactions Act of 2003: Third Interim Federal Trade Commission Report to Congress Concerning the Accuracy of Information in Credit Reports* (2008).

FTC, Staff Memorandum on Television Advertising to Children (1970).

FTC, *Staff Report on the Public Workshop on Consumer Privacy on the Global Information Infrastructure* (1996).

FTC, *Statement of Basis and Purpose, Unfair or Deceptive Advertising and Labeling of Cigarettes in Relation to the Health Hazards of Smoking*, 29 Fed. Reg., pt. 8324, 8355 (1964).

FTC, The US Safe Web Act: The First Three Years a, Report to Congress (2009).

FTC, 40 Years Experience with the Fair Credit Reporting Act (2011).

FTC & CFPB, *Interagency Cooperation Agreement and MOU: Memorandum of Understanding between the Consumer Financial Protection Bureau and the Federal Trade Commission to Ensure Effective Cooperation to Protect Consumers, Prevent Duplication of Efforts, Provide Consistency, and Ensure a Vibrant Marketplace for Consumer Financial Products and Services* (2012).

Mark Furletti, *An Overview and History of Credit Reporting* Federal Reserve Bank of Philadelphia Payment Cards Center Discussion Paper No. 02–07, pt. (2002).

Y. Hugh Furuhashi & E. Jerome McCarthy, *Social Issues of Marketing in the American Economy*, in Marketing and the Common Good (Patrick E. Murphy & John F. Sherry, Jr. eds., 2014).

Future of Privacy Forum, K-12 School Service Provider Pledge to Safeguard Student Privacy (2014).

Nydia Galarza, *Launching Online Retail Services and Products in Puerto Rico*, BNA Privacy & Security L. Rep Jan. 4, 2014.

Denise Gallene, *Chalk One Up for Privacy American Express Will Inform Cardholders That It Sorts Them for Sales Pitches*, L. A. Times, May 14, 1992.

Nelson B. Gaskill, The Regulation Competition: A Study of Futility as Exemplified by The Federal Trade Commission and National Industrial Recovery Act with Proposals for Its Remedy (1936).

Robert Gellman, *A Better Way to Approach Privacy Policy in the United States: Establish a Non-Regulatory Privacy Protection Board*, 54 Hastings L. J. 1183 (2003).

Robert Gellman, *Does Privacy Law Work?*, in Technology and Privacy: The New Landscape (Philip E. Agre & Marc Rotenberg eds., 1997).

Robert Gellman, Fair Information Practices: A Basic History (2014).

Robert Gellman & Pam Dixon, Many Failures – A Brief History of Privacy Self-Regulation (2011).

Pedro Giovanni, et al., Token Attempt: The Misrepresentation of Website Privacy Policies Through the Misuse of P3P Compact Policy Tokens 1 (2010).

Global Privacy Enforcement Network, *Results of the 2015 Global Privacy Enforcement Network Sweep* (2015).

Eric Goldman, *A Coasean Analysis of Marketing*, 2006 L. Rev. 1151 (2006).

Nathaniel Good, et al., *User Choices and Regret: Understanding Users' Decision Process About Consensually Acquired Spyware*, 2 I/S: AJ. of L. & Pol'y for the Info. 283 (2006).

Google, *The Importance of Being Seen: Viewability Insights for Digital Marketers and Publishers* (2014).

James M. Graham, Appointments to the Regulatory Agencies the Federal Communications Commissions and the Federal Trade Commission, 1949–1974 (1976).

Harold E. Green, How Advertisers Are Helping Consumers in Their Buying, Printer's Ink (1946).

Graham Greenleaf, *The Influence of European Data Privacy Standards Outside Europe: Implications for Globalisation of Convention* 108, 2(2) Int'l Data Privacy Law 68 (2012).

Stephen H. Greyser, *Advertising: Attacks and Counters*, in Consumerism: Search for the Consumer Interest (David A. Aaker & George S. Day eds., 1974).

James Grimmelmann, *Illegal, Immoral, and Mood-Altering: How Facebook and OkCupid Broke the Law when They Experimented on Users*, Medium, Sept. 23, 2014.

Willis W. Hagen, *The State of the Collective Liver of the Federal Trade Commissioners*, 47 Marquette L. Rev. 342 (1963).

Tom Hamburger & Matea Gold, *Google, Once Disdainful of Lobbying, Now a Master of Washington Influence*, The Wash. Post, Apr. 12, 2004.

Aniko Hannak, et al., *Measuring Price Discrimination and Steering on E-commerce Web Sites* (2014).

Saul Hansell, *Google Tries Tighter Aim for Web Ads*, N. Y. Times, Jun. 27, 2008.

Pamela Jones Harbour & Tara Isa Koslov, *Section 2 in a Web 2.0 World*, 76 Antitrust L. J. 769 (2010).

John Maynard Harlan & Lewis M. Mccandless, The Federal Trade Commission: Its Nature and Powers (1916).

RICHARD A. HARRIS & SIDNEY M. MILKIS, THE POLITICS OF REGULATORY CHANGE: A TALE OF TWO AGENCIES (1989).

Harris Interactive, *National Do-Not-Call Registry: Seven in Ten Are Registered and All of Them Will Renew Their Registration, Large Majority Who Have Registered Report Receiving Far Fewer Telemarketing Calls* 1 (2007).

Woodrow Hartzog, *Chain-Link Confidentiality*, 46 GEO. L. REV. 657 (2012).

Woodrow Hartzog, *Reviving Implied Confidentiality*, 89 IND. L. J. 763 (2014).

BERNICE ROTHMAN HASIN, CONSUMERS, COMMISSIONS, & CONGRESS: LAW, THEORY, & THE FEDERAL TRADE COMMISSION, 1968–1985 (1987).

Allyson W. Haynes, *Online Privacy Policies: Contracting Away Control over Personal Information?*, 111 PENN. ST. L. REV. 587 (2007).

John Samuel Healey, *The Federal Trade Commission Advertising Substantiation Program and Changes in the Content of Advertising in Selected Industries* (1978) (Ph.D. dissertation, University of California, Los Angeles).

Natali Helberger, *Form Matters: Informing Consumers Effectively*, Amsterdam Law School Research. 2013–71 (2013).

Gerald C. Henderson, THE FEDERAL TRADE COMMISSION: A STUDY IN ADMINISTRATIVE LAW AND PROCEDURE, pp. 232–233 (1924).

EVAN HENDRICKS, CREDIT SCORES & CREDIT REPORTS (3rd ed., 2007).

Evan Hendricks, *Oregon Jury, D.C. Circuit Continue Trans Union's Losing Streak*, PRIVACY TIMES, Aug. 5, 2002.

Cormac Herley, *So Long, and No Thanks for the Externalities: The Rational Rejection of Security Advice by Users*, in NSPW '09 PROCEEDINGS OF THE 2009 WORKSHOP ON NEW SECURITY PARADIGMS WORKSHOP 133 (2009).

Pendleton Herring, *The Federal Trade Commissioners*, 8 GEO. WASH. L. REV. 339 (1939).

E. Pendleton Herring, *Politics, Personalities, and the Federal Trade Commission, I*, 28 AMER. POL. SCI. REV. 1016 (1934).

Robert O. Herrmann, *The Consumer Movement in Historical Perspective*, in CONSUMERISM: SEARCH FOR THE CONSUMER INTEREST (David A. Aaker & George S. Day eds., 1974).

Steven Hetcher, *The FTC as Internet Privacy Norm Entrepreneur*, 53 VANDERBILT L. REV. 2041 (2000).

Richard S. Higgins & Fred S. McChesney, *Truth and Consequences: The Federal Trade Commission's Ad Substantiation Program*, 6 INT'L REV. OF L. & ECON. 151 (1986).

PHILIP J. HILTS, PROTECTING AMERICA'S HEALTH: THE FDA, BUSINESS, AND ONE HUNDRED YEARS OF REGULATION (2003).

ALBERT O. HIRSCHMAN, EXIT, VOICE, AND LOYALTY, pp. 59–60 (1970).

DEBRA J. HOLT, et al., CHILDREN'S EXPOSURE TO TV ADVERTISING IN 1977 AND 2004 INFORMATION FOR THE OBESITY DEBATE (2007).

Chris Jay Hoofnagle, *Internalizing Identity Theft*, 13 UCLA J. OF L. & TECH. 1 (Fall 2009).

Chris Jay Hoofnagle & Jan Whittington, *Unpacking Privacy's Price*, 90 N. CAROLINA L. REV. 1327 (2012).

Hoover (First) Commission, *The Commission on Organization of the Executive Branch of the Government: The Independent Regulatory Commissions* (1949).

Hoover (Second) Commission, *Commission on the Organization of the Executive Branch of Government, Legal Services and Procedure* (1955).

Scott Hovanyetz, *Call Center Mailer Touts TeleZapper Immunity*, DIRECT MARKETING NEWS, Feb. 18, 2003.

Gordon Hull, *Successful Failure: What Foucault Can Teach Us About Privacy Self-Management in a World of Facebook and Big Data*, 17 ETHICS & INFORMATION TECHNOLOGY 89 (2015).

H. Keith Hunt, *Second-Order Effects of the FTC Initiatives, in* MARKETING AND ADVERTISING REGULATION: THE FEDERAL TRADE COMMISSION IN THE 1990s (Patrick E. Murphy & William L. Wilkie eds., 1990).

Pauline M. Ippolito & Alan D. Mathios, *Information and Advertising: The Case of Fat Consumption in the United States*, 85 THE AMER. ECON. REV. 91 (1995).

Pauline M. Ippolito & David T. Scheffman, *Empirical Approaches to Consumer Protection Economics* (1986).

JAMES B. JACOBS, THE ETERNAL CRIMINAL RECORD (2015).

Frank Jellinek, *Dies, Hearst and the Consumer*, 102 THE NEW REPUBLIC 10 (1940).

Dalié Jiménez, *Dirty Debts Sold Dirt Cheap*, 52 HARV. J. ON LEGIS. 41 (2014).

Mary Gardiner Jones, *The Federal Trade Commission in 1968: Times of Turmoil and Response*, 7 J. OF PUB. POL'Y & MKTG. 1 (1988).

Dina Kallay & Marc Winerman, *First in the World: The FTC International Program at 100*, 29 ANTITRUST 39 (2014).

ARTHUR KALLET & F.J. SCHLINK, 100,000,000 GUINEA PIGS: DANGERS IN EVERYDAY FOODS, DRUGS IN EVERYDAY FOODS, DRUGS, AND COSMETICS (1933).

Chris Kanich, et al., *Spamalytics: An Empirical Analysis of Spam Marketing Conversion*, CCS08 (2008).

James E. Katz & Annete R. Tassone, *Public Opinion Trends: Privacy and Information Technology*, 54 PUB. OPINION Q. 125 (1990).

Thomas C. Kinnear & Ann R. Root, *The FTC and Deceptive Advertising in the 1980s: Are Consumers Being Adequately Protected?*, 7 J. OF PUB. POL'Y & MKTG. 40 (1988).

DAVID KIRKPA TRICK, THE FACEBOOK EFFECT (2010).

LOUIS M. KOHLMEIER, THE REGULATORS: WATCHDOG AGENCIES AND THE PUBLIC INTEREST (1969).

GABRIEL KOLKO, THE TRIUMPH OF CONSERVATISM: A REINTERPRETATION OF AMERICAN HISTORY 1900–1916 (1963).

Bert-Jaap Koops, et al., *Should ICT Regulation be Technology-Neutral?*, in STARTING POINTS FOR ICT REGULATION (Bert-Jaap Koops, et al. eds., 2006).

Bert-Jaap Koops, et al., *Should Self-Regulation Be the Starting Point?*, in STARTING POINTS OF ICT REGULATION (Bert-Jaap Koops, et al. eds., 2006).

Dawn Kopecki, *US Financial Industries Face Privacy Regs in Bank Bill*, DOW JONES NEWS SERVICE, Jun. 11, 1999.

WILLIAM E. KOVACIC, AN ANTITRUST TRIBUTE: LIBER AMICORUM (Nicholas Charbit, et al. eds., 2012).

William E. Kovacic, *The Quality of Appointments and the Capability of the Federal Trade Commission*, 49 ADMIN. L. REV. 915 (1997).

WILLIAM E. KOVACIC & FTC, THE FEDERAL TRADE COMMISSION AT 100: INTO OUR 2nd CENTURY, CONTINUING PURSUIT OF BETTER PRACTICES (2009).

Brian Krebs, *Inside the Gozi Bulletproof Hosting Facility*, KREBSONSECURITY, 2013.

BRIAN KREBS, SPAM NATION: THE INSIDE STORY OF ORGANIZED CYBERCRIME – FROM GLOBAL EPIDEMIC TO YOUR FRONT DOOR (2014).

Dale Kunkel & Donald Roberts, *Young Minds and Marketplace Values: Issues in Children's Television Advertising*, 47 J. OF SOC. ISSUES 57 (1991).

PRICILLA LA BARBERA, CONSUMERS AND THE FEDERAL TRADE COMMISSION: AN EMPIRICAL INVESTIGATION (1977).

THE LANCET, *Selling to – and Selling out – Children*, Sept. 28, 2002.

James Landis, *Report on Regulatory Agencies to the President-Elect* (1960).

James C. Lang, *The Legislative History of the Federal Trade Commission Act*, 13 WASHBURN L. J. 6, 23 (1974).

Arthur A. Leff, *Economic Analysis of Law: Some Realism about Nominalism*, 60 VIRGINIA L. REV. 451 (1974).

ARTHUR A. LEFF, SWINDLING AND SELLING: THE SPANISH PRISONER AND OTHER BARGAINS (1976).

Bethany L. Leickly, *Intermediaries in Information Economies* (2004) (Ph.D. dissertation, Georgetown University).

ROBERT LETZLER, et al., KNOWING WHEN TO QUIT: DEFAULT CHOICES, DEMOGRAPHICS AND FRAUD (2014).

WILLIAM E. LEUCHTENBURG, THE SUPREME COURT REBORN: THE CONSTITUTIONAL REVOLUTION IN THE AGE OF ROOSEVELT 77 (1995).

Kirill Leychenko, et al., *Click Trajectories: End-to-End Analysis of the Spam Value Chain* (2011).

Susan Lim, *Death of the SPAM Wrangler: CAN-SPAM Private Plaintiffs Required to Show Actual Harm*, 6 WASH. J. L. TECH. & ARTS 155 (2010).

CHARLES LINDBLOM, POLITICS AND MARKETS: THE WORLD'S POLITICAL-ECONOMIC SYSTEMS (1977).

SUSAN LINN, CONSUMING KIDS: THE HOSTILE TAKEOVER OF CHILDHOOD (2004).

KATHERINE LOSSE, THE BOY KINGS (2012).

PAUL H. LUEHR, COMMISSION ENFORCEMENT ACTIONS INVOLVING THE INTERNET AND ONLINE SERVICES (1999).

Robert J. MacKay, et al., *Public Choice and Regulation: An Overview, in* PUBLIC CHOICE & REGULATION: A VIEW FROM INSIDE THE FEDERAL TRADE COMMISSION (Robert J. MacKay, et al. eds., 1987).

William C. MacLeod & Robert A. Rogowsky, *Consumer Protection at the FTC During the Reagan Administration, in* REGULATION AND THE REAGAN ERA: POLITICS, BUREAUCRACY AND THE PUBLIC INTEREST (Roger E. Meiners & Bruce Yandle eds., 1989).

WARREN G. MAGNUSON & JEAN CARPER, THE DARK SIDE OF THE MARKETPLACE: THE PLIGHT OF THE AMERICAN CONSUMER (1968).

HERBERT MARCUSE, ONE-DIMENSIONAL MAN (1964).

John Markoff, *Before the Gunfire, Cyberattacks*, N. Y. TIMES, Aug. 12, 2008.

Gary T. Marx, *Coming to Terms and Avoiding Information Techno-Fallacies, in* PRIVACY IN THE MODERN AGE: THE SEARCH FOR SOLUTIONS (Marc Rotenberg & Jermaine Scott eds., 2015).

LOWELL B. MASON, *A Funny Thing Happened on the Way to the Federal Trade Commission* (1964).

LOWELL B. MASON, THE LANGUAGE OF DISSENT (1959).

MARIANA MAZZUCATO, THE ENTREPRENEURIAL STATE: DEBUNKING PUBLIC VS. PRIVATE SECTOR MYTHS (2013).

MARC ERIC MCCLURE, THE LIFE AND PUBLIC WORK OF GEORGE RUBLEE (2003).

Andrew Jay McClurg, *A Thousand Words are Worth a Picture: A Privacy Tort Response to Consumer Data Profiling*, 98 NORTHWESTERN UNIV. L. REV. 63 (2003).

THOMAS K. MCCRAW, PROPHETS OF REGULATION (1984).

Aleecia M. McDonald & Lorrie Faith Cranor, *The Cost of Reading Privacy Policies*, 4 I/S: J. L. & POL'Y FOR INFO. SOC'Y. 543, 564 (2008).

THOMAS O. MCGARITY, FREEDOM TO HARM: THE LASTING LEGACY OF THE LAISSEZ-FAIRE REVIVAL (2013).

Kenneth A. McLean, *Department of Health, Education, and Welfare (HEW) Secretary's Advisory Committee on Automated Personal Data Systems (SACAPDS)* (1972).

Gary McWilliams, *Analyzing Customers, Best Buy Decides Not All Are Welcome, Retailer Aims to Outsmart Dogged Bargain-Hunters, and Coddle Big Spenders*, Wall St. J., Nov. 8, 2004.

Joseph Menn, *Social Networks Scan for Sexual Predators, with Uneven Results*, Reuters, Jul. 12, 2012.

Jakub Mikians, et al., *Detecting Price and Search Discrimination on the Internet, in* HotNets-XI Proceedings of the 11th ACM Workshop on Hot Topics in Networks(2012).

James C. Miller, iii, The Economist as Reformer: Revamping The FTC, 1981–1985 (1991).

James C. Miller, III, *Letter from James C. Miller III, FTC Chairman, to John D. Dingell, Chairman, House Comm. on Energy and Commerce* 5–6 (1984).

James C. Miller, iii, et al., An Economic Assessment of Proposed Amendments to the Telemarketing Sales Rule (2002).

James C. Miller, III, et al., *Industrial Policy: Reindustrialization through Competition or Coordinated Action?*, 2 Yale J. on Reg. 1 (1984).

Jeffrey Mills, *FTC Again Is Marking Time*, Washington Post, Jun. 3, 1980.

Ira M. Millstein, *The Federal Trade Commission and False Advertising*, 64 Col. L. Rev. 439, 440 (1964).

George R. Milne, et al., *A Longitudinal Assessment of Online Privacy Notice Readability*, 25 J. Pub. Pol'y & Marketing 238, 243 (2006).

Minnesota Attorney General, *Supplemental Comments of the Minnesota Attorney General's Office*, FTC File No. R411001 (2002).

Charles Louis Mitchell, *Federal Trade Commission Policy Making and Congress 1970–1983* (1984) (Ph.D. dissertation, University of Tennessee).

Maneesha Mithal, Letter from Maneesha Mithal, Associate Director, Division of Privacy and Identity Protection, FTC, to BabyBus (2014).

Maneesha Mithal, Letter from Maneesha Mithal, Associate Director, Division of Privacy and Identity Protection, FTC, to Dana Rosenfeld, Partner, Kelley Drye (2014).

Kathryn Montgomery & Shelley Pasnik, Web of Deception: Threats to Children from Online Marketing (June 1996).

Elizabeth S. Moore, *Should Marketers Be Persuading Our Children?*, in Marketing and the Common Good (Patrick E. Murphy & John F. Sherry, Jr. eds., 2014).

Evgeny Morozov, *Don't Be Evil*, The New Republic, Aug. 4, 2011.

Evgeny Morozov, *Facebook Invades Your Personality, Not Your Privacy*, Financial Times, Aug. 10, 2014.

Evgeny Morozov, The Net Delusion (2011).

Evgeny Morozov, To Save Everything, Click Here (2013).

Willard F. Mueller, *Advertising, Monopoly, and the FTC's Breakfast-Cereal Case: An "Attack on Advertising?*," 6 Antitrust L. & Econ. Rev. 59 (1972).

Deirdre K. Mulligan & Aaron Perzanowski, *The Magnificence of the Disaster: Reconstructing the Sony BMG Rootkit Incident*, 22 Berk. Tech. L. J. 1157 (2007).

Deirdre K. Mulligan & Fred B. Schneider, *Doctrine for Cybersecurity*, 140 Dædalus 70 (2011).

Timothy J. Muris, *Judicial Constraints, in* The Federal Trade Commission since 970: Economic Regulation and Bureaucratic Behavior (Kenneth W. Clarkson & Timothy J. Muris eds., 1981).

Timothy J. Muris, *What Can Be Done?*, *in* THE FEDERAL TRADE COMMISSION SINCE 1970: ECONOMIC REGULATION AND BUREAUCRATIC BEHAVIOR (Kenneth W. Clarkson & Timothy J. Muris eds., 1981).

Patrick E. Murphy, *Reflections on the Federal Trade Commission*, J. OF PUB. POL'Y & MKTG. 225 (2014).

MARK V. NADEL, THE POLITICS OF CONSUMER PROTECTION (1971).

RALPH NADER, UNSAFE AT ANY SPEED: THE DESIGNED-IN DANGERS OF AMERICAN AUTOMOBILE (1965).

GERALD NASH, THE FEDERAL LANDSCAPE: AN ECONOMIC HISTORY OF THE TWENTIETH-CENTURY WEST (1999).

NATIONAL CONFERENCE OF STATE LEGISLATURES, STATE BREACH NOTIFICATION LAWS (2015).

NATIONAL CONSUMER COUNCIL, MODELS OF SELF-REGULATION: AN OVERVIEW OF MODELS IN BUSINESS AND THE PROFESSIONS (2000).

National Industrial Conference Board, et al., *Public Regulation of Competitive Practices in Business Enterprise. New York City, pt.* (1940).

James P. Nehf, *Recognizing the Societal Value in Information Privacy*, 78 WASH. L. REV. 1 (2003).

James P. Nehf, *Shopping for Privacy on the Internet*, 41 J. OF CONSUMER AFF. 351 (2007).

Phillip Nelson, *Advertising as Information*, 82 J. OF POL. ECON. 729 (1974).

New England Journal of Medicine, *Wheeler-Lea Act* (1938).

The New Republic, *An Unseen Reversal*, Jan. 9, 1915.

New York Times, *F.T.C. Funds Bill is Signed*, May 29, 1980.

New York Times, *Trade Commission Aide Prods Movie Theaters on Commercials*, Nov. 6, 1977.

The New York Times, *Why Use False Puffery?, If Anyone Believes It, It's Got to Be Illegal*, Feb. 25, 1973.

Bryce Clayton Newell, et al., *Privacy in the Family*, *in* THE SOCIAL DIMENSIONS OF PRIVACY (Beate Roessler & Dorota Mokrosinska eds., 2015).

Annalee Newitz, *Lenovo Joins the Malevolent Side of the Online Advertising Industry*, GIZMODO, Feb. 20, 2015.

Newspaper Association of America, *Comments of the Newspaper Association of America, In the Matter of Rules and Regulations Implementing the Telephone Consumer Protection Act of 1991* (2002).

Aikaterinaki Niki, *Drive-By Download Attacks: Effects and Detection Methods* (2009).

Helen Nissembaum, PRIVACY IN CONTEXT (2010).

Helen Nissenbaum, *"Respect for Context" – Fulfilling the Promise of the White House Report*, *in* PRIVACY IN THE MODERN AGE: THE SEARCH FOR SOLUTIONS (Marc Rotenberg & Jermaine Scott eds., 2015).

JOSEPH NOCERA, A PIECE OF THE ACTION: HOW THE MIDDLE CLASS JOINED THE MONEY CLASS (1994).

North Dakota Secretary of State, *Statewide Election Results*.

Daniel P. O'Brien & Doug Smith, *Privacy in Online Markets: A Welfare Analysis of Demand Rotations*, *in* FTC BUREAU OF ECONOMICS WORKING PAPER NO. 323 Jul. 2014.

Office of the *Vice President, Vice President Al Gore Annouces New Steps Towards and Electronic Bill of Rights*, Jul. 31, 1998.

DAVID OGILVY, CONFESSIONS OF AN ADVERTISING MAN (1963).

David Ogilvy, *Should Advertising Be Abolished?*, *in* CONFESSIONS OF AN ADVERTISING MAN (1963).

Maureen K. Ohlhausen & Alexander P. Okuliar, *Competition, Consumer Protection, and The Right [Approach] to Privacy*, 80(1) ANTITRUST LAW JOURNAL (Forthcoming 2015).

Paul Ohm, *The Argument Against Technology Neutral Surveillance Laws*, 88 TEX. L. REV. 1685 (2010).

Paul Ohm, *Branding Privacy*, 97 MINN. L. REV. 907 (2013).

Paul Ohm, *Broken Promises of Privacy: Responding to the Surprising Failure of Anonymization*, 57 UCLA l. REV. 1701 (2010).

NAIOMI ORESKES & ERIK M. CONWAY, MERCHANTS OF DOUBT: HOW A HANDFUL OF SCIENTISTS OBSCURED THE TRUTH ON ISSUES FROM TOBACCO SMOKE TO GLOBAL WARMING (2010).

Alan L. Otten, *Politics and People: Final Rules*, WALL ST. J., Sept. 28, 1978.

Janis K. Pappalardo, *Product Literacy and the Economics of Consumer Protection Policy*, 46 J. OF CONSUMER AFF. 319 (2012).

Janis K. Pappalardo & William E. Kovacic, *Why Who Does What Matters: Governmental Design, Agency Performance, the CFPB and PPACA*, 82 GEO. WASH. L. REV. 1446 (2014).

Thomas L. Parkinson, *The Role of Seals and Certifications of Approval in Consumer Decision-Making*, 9 J. OF CONSUMER AFF. 1 (1975).

Molly Pauker, *The Case for FTC Regulation of Television Advertising Directed Toward Children*, 46 BROOK. L. REV. 513 (1979).

Paul A. Pautler, *A Brief History of the FTC's Bureau of Economics: Reports, Mergers, and Information Regulation*, 46 REV. IND. ORG. 59 (2015).

Sam Peltzman, *The Effects of FTC Advertising Regulation*, 24 J. L. & ECON. 403 (1981).

Nicole Perlroth, *After Rapes Involving Children, Skout, a Flirting App, Bans Minors*, N. Y. TIMES, Jun. 12, 2012.

MICHAEL PERTSCHUK, FTC Review (1977–1984) A REPORT PREPARED BY A MEMBER OF THE FEDERAL TRADE COMMISSION TOGETHER WITH COMMENTS FROM OTHER MEMBERS OF THE COMMISSION FOR THE USE OF THE SUBCOMMITTEE ON OVERSIGHT AND INVESTIGATIONS OF THE COMMITTEE ON ENERGY AND COMMERCE (1984).

MICHAEL PERTSCHUK, REVOLT AGAINST REGULATION: THE RISE AND PAUSE OF THE CONSUMER MOVEMENT (1982).

Michael Pertschuk & Paul Rand Dixon, Letter from Michael Pertschuk, FTC Chairman, and Paul Rand Dixon, FTC Commissioner, to Wendell H. Ford, Chairman, House Commerce Subcommittee on Commerce, Science, and Transportation (1980).

Ross D. Petty, *FTC Advertising Regulation: Survivor or Casualty of the Reagan Revolution?*, 30 AMER. BUS. LAW J. 1 (1992).

TAMARA R. PIETY, BRANDISHING THE FIRST AMENDMENT (2012).

Robert Pitofsky, *Beyond Nader: Consumer Protection and the Regulation of Advertising*, 90 HARV. L. REV. 661 (1977).

Jules Polonetsky & Omer Tene, *The Ethics of Student Privacy: Building Trust for Ed Tech*, 21 INT'L REV. OF INFO. ETHICS 25 (2014).

Jules Polonetsky & Omer Tene, *Who is Reading Whom Now: Privacy in Education from Books to MOOCs*, VAN. J. OF ENT. & TECH. L. (Forthcoming 2014).

Daniel Pope, *Advertising as a Consumer Issue*, 47 J. OF SOC. ISSUES 41 (1991).

Richard A. Posner, *The Federal Trade Commission*, 37 THE U. OF CHI. L. REV. 47 (1969).

Richard A. Posner, *The Federal Trade Commission: A Retrospective*, 72 ANTITRUST L. J. 761 (2005).

RICHARD A. POSNER, REGULATION OF ADVERTISING BY THE FTC (1973).

NEIL POSTMAN, CRAZY TALK, STUPID TALK (1976).

IVAN L. PRESTON, THE GREAT AMERICAN BLOWUP: PUFFERY IN ADVERTISING AND SELLING (rev. ed. 1996).

Ivan L. Preston & Jef I. Richards, *Consumer Miscomprehension as a Challenge to FTC Prosecutions of Deceptive Advertising*, 19 JOHN MARSHALL L. REV. 605 (1985–1986).

Printers' Ink, *Many States Still Lack Protection of "Printers Ink" Model Statute: National Vigilance Committee to Work for Its Adoption in States Where It Is Not Now a Law*, 121 PRINTERS' INK 101 (1922).

MARGARET JANE RADIN, BOILERPLATE (2013).

Justin M. Rao & David H. Reiley, *The Economics of Spam*, 26 J. OF ECON. PERSPECTIVES 87 (2012).

Alan Charles Raul, et al., *End of the Notice Paradigm?: FTC's Proposed Sears Settlement Casts Doubt on the Sufficiency of Disclosures in Privacy Policies and User Agreements*, 14(27) BNA Electronic Commerce & Law Report (2009).

PRISCILLA M. REGAN, LEGISLATIVE PRIVACY: TECHNOLOGY, SOCIAL VALUES, AND PUBLIC POLICY (1995).

Joel Reidenberg, et al., *Privacy and Cloud Computing in Public Schools*, in CENTER ON LAW AND INFORMATION POLICY (2013).

Joel R. Reidenberg, *E-Commerce and Trans-Atlantic Privacy*, 38 HOUS. L. REV. 717 (2001).

Jessica L. Rich, Letter from Jessica L. Rich, Director of the Federal Trade Commission Bureau of Consumer Protection, to Erin Egan, Chief Privacy Officer, Facebook, and to Anne Hoge, General Counsel, WhatsApp Inc. (2014).

JEF I. RICHARDS, DECEPTIVE ADVERTISING: BEHAVIORAL STUDY OF A LEGAL CONCEPT (1990).

Neil M. Richards & Daniel J. Solove, *Prosser's Privacy Law: A Mixed Legacy*, 98 CAL. L. REV. 1887 (2010).

Emily Rock, *Commerce and the Public Interest: James C. Miller at the Federal Trade Commission*, in STEERING THE ELEPHANT (Robert Rector & Michael Sanera eds., 1987).

John Irving Romer, *Legal Repression of Dishonest Advertising*, 77 PRINTER'S INK 66, 68 (1911).

Marc Rotenberg, *Fair Information Practices and the Architecture of Privacy*, 2001 STAN. TECH. L. REV. 1 (2001).

Ira S. Rubinstein, *Privacy and Regulatory Innovation: Moving Beyond Voluntary Codes*, 6I S J. OF L. & POL. 355 (2011).

Ira S. Rubinstein & Nathaniel Good, *Privacy by Design: A Counterfactual Analysis of Google and Facebook Privacy Incidents*, 28 BERKELEY TECH L. J. 1333 (2013).

Christian Rudder, *We Experiment on Human Beings!*, OKTRENDS, Jul. 28, 2014.

JAMES B. RULE, PRIVACY IN PERIL: HOW WE ARE SACRIFICING A FUNDAMENTAL RIGHT IN EXCHANGE FOR SECURITY AND CONVENIENCE (2009).

JAMES B. RULE, PRIVATE LIVES AND PUBLIC SURVEILLANCE: SOCIAL CONTROL IN THE COMPUTER AGE (1974).

James B. Rule, et al., *The Dossier in Consumer Credit*, in ON RECORD: FILES AND DOSSIERS IN AMERICAN LIFE (Stanton Wheeler ed., 1969).

Raymond D. Sauer & Keith B. Leffer, *Did the Federal Trade Commission's Advertising Substantiation Program Promote More Credible Advertising?*, 80 AMER. ECON. REV. 191 (1990).

ERIC SCHMIDT & JARED COHEN, THE NEW DIGITAL AGE: RESHAPING THE FUTURE OF PEOPLE, NATIONS AND BUSINESS (2013).

Eric Schnapper, *Consumer Legislation and the Poor*, 76 YALE L. J. 745 (1967).

BRUCE SCHNEIER, DATA AND GOLIATH: THE HIDDEN BATTLES TO COLLECT YOUR DATA AND CONTROL YOUR WORLD (2015).

PETER SCHUCK, WHY GOVERNMENT FAILS SO OFTEN: AND HOW IT CAN DO BETTER (2014).

SCOTT SCHUH, et al., FEDERAL RESERVE BOARD OF BOSTON, WHO GAINS AND WHO LOSES FROM CREDIT CARD PAYMENTS? THEORY AND CALIBRATIONS (2010).

Paul Schwartz & Ted Janger, *The Gramm-Leach-Bliley Act, Information Privacy, and the Limits of Default Rules*, 86 MINN. L. REV. 1219 (2002).

Paul M. Schwartz, *European Data Protection Law and Restrictions on International Data Flows*, 80 Iowa L. Rev. 471 (1994).

Paul M. Schwartz, *The EU-US Privacy Collision: A Turn to Institutions and Procedures*, 126 Harv. L. Rev. 1966 (2013).

Paul M. Schwartz, *German and US Telecommunications Privacy Law: Legal Regulation of Domestic Law Enforcement Surveillance*, 54 Hastings L. Rev. 751 (2003).

Paul M. Schwartz, *Privacy*, Internet Privacy and the State, 32 Conn. L. Rev. 815 (2000).

Paul M. Schwartz, *Preemption and Privacy*, 118 Yale L. J. 902 (2009).

Paul M. Schwartz, *Property, Privacy, and Personal Data*, 117 Harv. L. Rev. 2055 (2004).

Paul M. Schwartz & Daniel J. Solove, *The PII Problem: Privacy and a New Concept of Personally Identifiable Information*, 86 N.Y.U. L.Q. Rev. 1814 (2011).

Paul M. Schwartz & Daniel J. Solove, *Reconciling Personal Information in the United States and European Union*, 102 Cal. L. Rev. 877 (2014).

Teresa Moran Schwartz & Alice Saker Hrdy, *FTC Rulemaking: Three Bold Initiatives & Their Legal Impact* (2004).

Larry Selden & Geoffrey Colvin, Angel Customers & Demon Customers: Discover Which is Which and Turbo-Charge Your Stock (2003).

William Seltzer & Margo Anderson, *The Dark Side of Numbers: The Role of Population Data Systems in Human Rights Abuses*, 68 Soc. Res. 481 (Summer 2001).

Richard Sennett, The Fall of Public Man (1974).

Benjamin Shmueli & Ayelet Blecher-Prigat, *Privacy for Children*, 42 Colum. Human Rights L. Rev. 759 (2011).

Norman I. Silber, Test and Protest: The Influence of Consumers Union (1983).

Norman I. Silber, With All the Deliberate Speed: The Life of Philip Elman (2004).

Jessica Silver-Greenberg, *Banks as Aid in Fraud Against Older Consumers*, N. Y. Times, Jun. 10, 2013.

Joseph Simitian, *How a Bill Becomes a Law, Really*, 24 Berk. Tech. L. J. 1009 (2009).

William Simon, *The Case Against the Federal Trade Commission*, 19 The U. of Chi. L. Rev. 297 (1952).

Marlise Simons, *Dutch Say a Sex Ring Used Infants on Internet*, N. Y. Times, Jul. 19, 1998.

Glenn Simpson, *Consumer-Privacy Issue Turns a Retired Professor into a Hot Item*, Wall St. J., Jun. 25, 2001.

Tom Slee, No One Makes You Shop at Wal-Mart: The Surprising Deceptions of Individual Choice (2006).

Ben Smith, *Uber Executive Suggests Digging Up Dirt on Journalists*, BUZZFEED (n.d.).

H. Jeff Smith, Managing Privacy: Information Technology and Corporate America (1994).

Robert Ellis Smith, Ben Franklin's Web Site, Privacy and Curiosity from Plymouth Rock to the Internet (2004).

Neil L. Sobol, *Protecting Consumers from Zombie-Debt Collectors*, 44 New Mex. L. Rev. 327 (2014).

Daniel J. Solove, *Privacy Self-Management and the Consent Dilemma*, 126 Harv. L. R. 1880 (2013).

Daniel J. Solove & Woodrow Hartzog, *The FTC and the New Common Law of Privacy*, 144 Colum. L. Rev. 583 (2014).

David E. Sorkin, *Spam Legislation in the United States*, 22 J. Marshall J. Computer & Info. 3 (2003).

Jeff Sovern, *Opting In, Opting Out, or No Options at All: The Fight for Control of Personal Information*, 74 Wash. L. Rev. 1033 (1999).

Jeff Sovern, *Protecting Privacy with Deceptive Trade Practices Legislation*, 69 FORDHAM L. REV. 1305 (2001).

Sarah Spiekermann & Lorrie Faith Cranor, *Engineering Privacy*, 35 IEEE T. SOFTWARE ENG. 67 (2009).

Thomas H. Stanton, *Comments on the Commission in 1978*, in MARKETING AND ADVERTISING REGULATION: THE FEDERAL TRADE COMMISSION IN THE 1990s (Patrick E. Murphy & William L. Wilkie eds., 1990).

Michael E. Staten & Fred H. Cate, *The Impact of Opt-in Privacy Rules on Retail Credit Markets: A Case Study of MBNA*, 52 DUKE L. J. 745 (2003).

Wouter M. P. Steijn & Anton Vedder, *Privacy under Construction: A Developmental Perspective on Privacy Perception*, 40(4) SCI. TECH., & HUMAN VALUES 615 (2015).

Louis W. Stern, *The Federal Trade Commission: Going, Going …*, in MARKETING AND ADVERTISING REGULATION: THE FEDERAL TRADE COMMISSION IN THE 1990s (Patrick E. Murphy & William L. Wilkie eds., 1990).

INGER L. STOLE, ADVERTISING AT WAR (2012).

INGER L. STOLE, ADVERTISING ON TRIAL: CONSUMER ACTIVISM AND CORPORATE PUBLIC RELATIONS IN THE 1930s (2006).

R.L. Stole, *Consumer Protection in the Historical Perspective: The Five-Year Battle over Federal Regulation of Advertising, 1933–1938*, 3 MASS COMMUNICATION AND SOCIETY 351 (2000).

Brad Stone & Bronwyn Fryer, *The Keyboard Kids: Chatting on the Net is Becoming the Social Activity of Choice for Techno-Savvy Early Teens*, NEWSWEEK, Jun. 8, 1998.

Guy Stuart, *Databases, Felons, and Voting: Bias and Partisanship of the Florida Felons List in the 2000 Elections*, 119 POL. SCI. QUARTERLY 453 (Fall 2004).

PAMELA STUART, THE FEDERAL TRADE COMMISSION (1991).

FREDERICK D. STURDIVANT, THE GHETTO MARKETPLACE (1969).

Peter P. Swire, *Markets, Self-Regulation, and Government Enforcement in the Protection of Personal Information*, in PRIVACY AND SELF-REGULATION IN THE INFORMATION AGE BY THE US DEPARTMENT OF COMMERCE (1997).

Peter P. Swire, *A Model for When Disclosure Helps Security: What is Different about Computer and Network Security?*, 3 J. ON TELECOM & HIGH TECH. L. 163 (2004).

PETER P. SWIRE, PROTECTING CONSUMERS: PRIVACY MATTERS IN ANTITRUST ANALYSIS (2007).

Peter P. Swire, *Efficient Confidentiality for Privacy, Security, and Confidential Business Information*, in BROOKINGS-WHARTON PAPERS ON FINANCIAL SERVICES (2003).

Peter P. Swire, *The Surprising Virtues of the New Financial Privacy Law*, 86 MINN. L. REV. 1263 (2001).

PETER P. SWIRE & SOL BERMANN, INFORMATION PRIVACY: OFFICIAL REFERENCE FOR THE CERTIFIED INFORMATION PRIVACY PROFESSIONAL 9 (2007).

PETER P. SWIRE & ROBERT E. LITAN, NONE of YOUR BUSINESS (1998).

STEVEN M. TELES, THE RISE OF THE CONSERVATIVE LEGAL MOVEMENT (2008).

*Tell the Truth and Run: George Seldes and the American Press* (New Day Films, 1996).

Gerald J. Thain, *Television Advertising to Children & The Federal Trade Commission: A Review of the History & Some Personal Observations*, in UNIVERSITY OF ILLINOIS ADVERTISING WORKING PAPER NO. 9 (1981).

Andrew Thompson, *Engineers of Addition, Slot Machines Perfected Addictive Gaming. Now, Tech Wants Their Tricks*, THE VERGE May 6, 2015.

Mayo Thompson, *Memorandum from F.T.C. Commissioner Mayo J. Thompson to the Commission*, 7 ANTITRUST L. & ECON. REV. (1974–1975).

Marcy J.K. Tiffany, *Consumer Protection: The Nuts and Bolts of an FTC Investigation*, 60 ANTITRUST L. J. 139 (1991).

Vincent Toubiana, et al., *Adnostic: Privacy Preserving Targeted Advertising, in* NDSS (2010).

PAOLA TUBARO, et al., AGAINST THE HYPOTHESIS OF THE END-OF-PRIVACY. AN AGENT-BASED MODELLING APPROACH TO SOCIAL MEDIA (2014).

Peter Braton Turk, *The Federal Trade Commission Hearings on Modern Advertising Practices: A Continuing Inquiry into Television Advertising* (1977) (Ph.D. dissertation, University of Wisconsin, Madison).

SHERRY TURKLE, LIFE ON THE SCREEN (1995).

JOSEPH TUROW, ANNENBERG PUBLIC POLICY CENTER, PRIVACY POLICIES ON CHILDREN'S WEBSITES: DO THEY PLAY BY THE RULES? (2000).

JOSEPH TUROW, THE DAILY YOU (2011).

JOSEPH TUROW, NICHE ENVY: MARKETING DISCRIMINATION IN THE DIGITAL AGE (2006).

United Nations, *Article 19 of the Universal Declaration of Human Rights* (1948).

US Senate, *Conference Report Agreed to by Senate* § 83 (1938).

Jennifer Valentino-DeVries, et al., *Websites Vary Prices, Deals Based on Users' Information*, WALL ST. J., Dec. 24, 2012.

NICOLE SAMANTHA VAN DER MUELEN, FERTILE GROUNDS: THE FACILITATION OF FINANCIAL IDENTITY THEFT IN THE UNITED STATES AND THE NETHERLANDS (2010).

Tom Van Goethem, et al., *Clubbing Seals: Exploring the Ecosystem of Third-Party Security Seals* (2014).

Kirk Victor, *Michael Pertschuk's Turbulent Years as FTC Chairman, in* THE INSIDER'S GUIDE TO THE HISTORY OF THE FEDERAL TRADE COMMISSION (Kirstin Downey & Lesette Heath eds., 2015).

David C. Vladeck, *Charting the Course: The Federal Trade Commission's Second Hundred Years*, 83 GEO. WASH. L. REV. (Forthcoming 2015).

Suzanne Vranica, *Web Display Ads Often Not Visible*, WALL ST. J., Jun. 11, 2013.

SUSAN WAGNER, THE FEDERAL TRADE COMMISSION (1971).

Samuel Warren & Louis D. Brandeis, *The Right to Privacy*, 4 HARV. L. R. 193 (1890).

*The Washington Post, The FTC as National Nanny*, Mar. 1, 1978.

Robert Weisman, *Academics' "PR" Work Raises Eyebrows Ethicists Questioning Efforts for Greenberg Maurice R. "Hank"; Greenberg, Resigned in 2005*, THE BOSTON GLOBE, Apr. 5, 2005.

Tracy Westen, *Government Regulation of Food Marketing to Children: The Federal Trade Commission and the Kid-Vid Controversy*, 39 LOY. L. A. L. REV. 79 (2006).

Janet Whitman, *Newspapers Press to Keep Subscribers*, WALL ST. J., Feb. 4, 2004.

Joshua L. Wiener, *Federal Trade Commission: Time of Transition*, 33 J. OF PUB. POL'Y & MKTG. 217 (2014).

Robert E. Wilkes & James B. Wilcox, *Recent FTC Actions: Implications for the Advertising Strategist*, 38 J. OF MKTG. 55 (1974).

William L. Wilkie, *Affirmative Disclosure at the FTC: Objectives for the Remedy and Outcomes of Past Orders*, 4 J. OF PUB. POL'Y & MKTG. 91 (1985).

William L. Wilkie, *My Memorable Experiences as a Marketing Academic at the Federal Trade Commission*, 33 J. OF PUB. POL'Y & MKTG. 194 (2014).

William L. Wilkie & Elizabeth S. Moore, A Larger View of Marketing: *Marketing's Contributions to Society, in* MARKETING AND THE COMMON GOOD (Patrick E. Murphy & John F. Sherry, Jr. eds., 2014).

Lauren E. Willis, *When Nudges Fail: Slippery Defaults*, 80 UNI. OF CHI. L. REV. 1155 (2013).

Marc Winerman, *International Issues in the FTC's First Decade (1915–1925) – And Before, in* WILLIAM E. KOVACIC LIBER AMERICORUM: AN ANTITRUST TRIBUTE, Vol. II (Nicholas Charbit & Elisa Ramundo eds., 2014).

Jane K. Winn, *Contracting Spyware by Contract*, 20 BERK. TECH. L. J. 1345 (2005).

LANGDON WINNER, THE WHALE AND THE REACTOR (1986).

Ralph K. Winter, *The Consumer Advocate Versus the Consumer, in* CONSUMERISM: SEARCH FOR THE CONSUMER INTEREST (David A. Aaker & George S. Day eds., 1974).

Edward Mott Woolley, *What the Federal Trade Commission Will Do for You*, COLLIER'S WEEKLY, Nov. 18, 1916.

Joshua D. Wright, *Statement of Commissioner Joshua D. Wright on the FTC's Bureau of Economics, Independence, and Agency Performance* (2015).

Tim Wu, *The Right to Evade Regulation: How Corporations Hijacked the First Amendment*, THE NEW REPUBLIC, Jun. 3, 2013.

Guang-Xin Xie & David M. Boush, *How Susceptible Are Consumers to Deceptive Advertising Claims? A Retrospective Look at the Experimental Research Literature*, 11 THE MARKETING REV. 293 (2011).

Pamela Zekman, et al., *Bill Collector's Tactics: "Everything We Do Here is Borderline Illegal"*, CHICAGO TRIBUNE, Apr. 8, 1974.

Pamela Zekman, et al., *"Push Them Till They Break": Bill Collector Terror Tactics Agencies Operate by Their Own Rules*, CHICAGO TRIBUNE, Apr. 7, 1974.

Shoshana Zuboff, *Big Other: Surveillance Capitalism and the Prospects of an Information Civilization*, 30 J. OF INFO. TECH. 75 (2015).

FREDERIK J. ZUIDERVEEN BORGESIUS, IMPROVING PRIVACY PROTECTION IN THE AREA OF BEHAVIOURAL TARGETING (2015).

## CASES AND OTHER MATERIALS

*Am. Bankers Ass'n v. Lockyer*, 541 F.3d 1214 (9th Cir. 2008).

*Am. Civil Liberties Union v. Mukasey*, 534 F.3d 181 (3d Cir. 2008).

*Am. Med. Ass'n v. FTC*, 638 F.2d 443 (2d Cir. 1980).

*Ass'n of Nat. Advertisers, Inc. v. FTC*, 627 F.2d 1151 (D.C. Cir. 1979).

*Bear Mill Mfg. Co. v. FTC*, 98 F.2d 67 (2d Cir. 1938).

*California Dental Ass'n v. FTC*, 526 US 756 (1999).

*Carlson v. Coca-Cola Co.*, 483 F.2d 279 (9th Cir. 1973).

*Carter Products, Inc. v. FTC*, 392 F.2d 921 (5th Cir. 1963).

*Charles of the Ritz Distributors Corp. v. FTC*, 143 F.2d 676 (2d Cir. 1944).

*Chuway v. National Action Fin. Servs., Inc.*, 362 F.3d 944 (7th Cir. 2004).

*Cliffdale Associates, Inc.*, 103 F.T.C. 110 (1984).

*Community Blood Bank v. FTC*, 405 F.2d 1011 (8th Cir. 1969).

*Ctr. for Auto Safety v. FTC*, 586 F. Supp. 1245 (D.D.C. 1984).

*Deer v. FTC*, 152 F.2d 65 (1945).

*Doherty, Clifford, Steers & Shenfield, Inc. v. FTC*, 392 F.2d 921 (6th Cir. 1988).

*Dwyer v. American Express*, 341 N.E.2d 1351 (Ill. App. 1995).

*Dyer v. Nw. Airlines*, 334 Supp. 2d 1196 (D.N.D. 2004).

*Enriquez v. Countrywide Home Loans, FSB*, 814 F. Supp. 2d 1042 (D. Haw. 2011).

*Federal Trade Commission v. AmeriDebt, Inc., et al.*, No. PJM 03–3317 (D. Md. 2014).

*Federal Trade Commission v. API Trade, LLC, et al.*, No. 110-cv-01543 (N.D. Ill. 2010).

*FTC v. 30 Minute Mortgage, Inc., Gregory P. Roth, and Peter W. Stolz*, No. 03–60021 (S.D. Fl. 2003).

*FTC* v. *77 Investigations, Inc., and Reginald Kimbro*, No. EDCV06-0439 VAP (C.D. Cal. 2006).

*FTC* v. *Accusearch Inc.*, 570 F.3d 1187 (10th Cir. 2009).

*FTC* v. *Algoma Lumber Co.*, 291 US 67 (1934).

*FTC* v. *Am. Tobacco Co.*, 264 US 298 (1924).

*FTC* v. *American Agricultural Chemical Co. and the Brown Co.*, 1 F.T.C. 226 (1918).

*FTC* v. *AmeriDebt, Inc.*, 343 F. Supp. 2d 451 (D. Md. 2004).

*FTC* v. *AMREP Corp.*, 705F. Supp. 119 (S.D.N.Y. 1988).

*FTC* v. *Amy Travel Serv., Inc.*, 875 F.2d 564 (7th Cir.).

*FTC* v. *Assail, Inc., et al.*, No. W03CA007 (W.D. Tex. 2003).

*FTC* v. *Balme*, 23 F.2d 615 (2d Cir. 1928).

*FTC* v. *California Dental Association*, 526 US 756.

*FTC* v. *Carter*, 464 F. Supp. 633 (D.D.C. 1979).

*FTC* v. *Colgate-Palmolive Co.*, 380 US 374 (1965).

*FTC* v. *Commerce Planet, Inc.*, 878 F. Supp. 2d 1048 (C.D.C. Cal. 2012).

*FTC* v. *Compucredit Corp.*, No. 1:08-CV-1976 (N.D. Ga. 2008).

*FTC* v. *ControlScan, Inc.*, No. 1:10-cv-00532 (N.D. Ga. Feb. 25, 2010).

*FTC* v. *Corporate Marketing Solutions, Inc., et al.*, No. CIV-02 1256 PHX RCB (D. Az. 2002).

*FTC* v. *Corzine*, No. CIV-S-94-1446 (E.D. Cal. 1994).

*FTC* v. *Cyberspy Software, LLC*, No. 6:08-CV-1872-ORL-316JK (M.D. Fl. 2008).

*FTC* v. *Echometrix, Inc.*, CV10-5516 (E.D.N.Y. Nov. 30, 2010).

*FTC* v. *Figgie Int'l, Inc.*, 994 F.2d 595 (9th Cir. 1993).

*FTC* v. *Freecom Commc'ns, Inc.*, 401 F.3d 1192 (10th Cir. 2005).

*FTC* v. *Frostwire*, No. 111-CV-23643 (S.D.F.L. Oct. 11, 2011).

*FTC* v. *Global Marketing Group, Inc.*, 594 F. Supp. 2d 1281 (M.D. Fla. 2008).

*FTC* v. *Global Mortgage Funding, Inc., et al.*, No. SACV 02–1026 DOC (C.D. Cal. 2002).

*FTC* v. *Ideal Financial Solutions Inc., et al.*, No. 213-cv-00143-MMD-GWF (D. Nev. 2013).

*FTC* v. *Innovative Marketing, et al.*, 08-CV-3233-RDB (D. Md. 2010).

*FTC* v. *Javian Karnani, and Balls of Kryptonite, LLC, a California Limited Liability Company, All Doing Business as Bite Size Deals, LLC and Best Priced Brands, LLC*, No. 09-CV-5276 (C.D. Cal. 2009).

*FTC* v. *Klesner*, 280 US 19 (1929).

*FTC* v. *LeanSpa, LLC*, 920 F. Supp. 2d 270 (D. Conn. 2013).

*FTC* v. *LifeLock, Inc.*, 2:10cv00530 (D. Az. 2010).

*FTC* v. *Lights of Am. Inc.*, SACV 10–1333 JVS, 2012 WL 695008 (C.D. Cal. Jan. 20, 2012).

*FTC* v. *A Minor*, No. 03–5275 (C.D. Cal. 2003).

*FTC* v. *Nat'l Urological Grp., Inc.*, 645 F. Supp. 2d 1167 (N.D. Ga. 2008).

*FTC* v. *Paula L. Garrett, d/b/a Discreet Data Systems*, No. H01-1255 (S.D. Tex. 2002).

*FTC* v. *Pricewert LLC also d/b/a 3FN.net, Triple Fiber Network, APS Communications, and APS Communication*, No. 09-CV-2407 (N.D. Cal. 2009).

*FTC* v. *Raladam*, 283 US 643 (1931).

*FTC* v. *Raladam*, 316 US 149 (1942).

*FTC* v. *Rapp d/b/a Touch Tone Information, Inc.*, No. 99-WM-783 (D. Colo. 1999).

*FTC* v. *Rennert, Sandra L., et al.*, CV-S-00–0861-JBR (D. Nev. Jul. 6, 2000).

*FTC* v. *Sears, Roebuck & Co.*, No. 81-A-503, 1983 WL 1889 (D. Colo. Oct. 18, 1983).

*FTC* v. *Seismic Entertainment, et al.*, No. 104-CV-00377-JD (D. NH 2004).

*FTC* v. *Sitesearch Corp. d/b/a LeapLab*, FTC File No. 142–3192 (D. Ariz. Dec. 23, 2014).

*FTC* v. *Sperry & Hutchinson*, 432 F.2d 146 (5th Cir. 1970).

*FTC* v. *Sperry & Hutchinson.*, 405 US 233 (1972).

*FTC* v. *Standard Educ. Soc.*, 86 F.2d 692 (2d Cir. 1936).

*FTC* v. *Standard Educ. Soc.*, 302 US 112 (1937).

*FTC* v. *Sun Spectrum Communications Organization, Inc.*, No. 03–8110 (S.D. Fl. 2005).

*FTC* v. *Toysmart.com*, 2000 WL 34016434 (D. Mass. July 21, 2000).

*FTC* v. *Trudeau*, 579 F.3d 754 (7th Cir. 2009).

*FTC* v. *Turner*, 1982 WL 1947 (M.D. Fla. Dec. 29, 1982).

*FTC* v. *Victor L. Guzzetta, d/b/a Smart Data Systems*, No. 01–2335 (E.D.N.Y. 2002).

*FTC* v. *Winsted Hosiery Co.*, 258 US 483 (1922).

*FTC* v. *Wyndham Worldwide Corp.*, No. 14–3514 (3d. Cir. Aug. 24, 2015).

*FTC* v. *Zachary Keith Hill*, No. 032–3102 (S.D. Tex. 2004).

*Gelb* v. *FTC*, 144 F.2d 580 (2d Cir. 1944).

*Ger-Ro-Mar, Inc.* v. *FTC*, 518 F.2d 33 (2d Cir. 1975).

*Giant Food, Inc.* v. *FTC*, 322 F.2d 977 (D.C. Cir. 1963).

*Google Spain SL, Google Inc.* v. *Agencia Española de Protección de Datos, Mario Costeja González*, C–131/12 (Court of Justice of the European Union 2014).

*Gordon* v. *Virtumundo*, 575 F.3d 1040 (9th Cir. 2009).

*Haskelite Mfg. Corp.* v. *FTC*, 127 F.2d 884 (7th Cir. 1942).

*Humphrey's Executor* v. *US*, 295 US 602 (1935).

*In the Matter of Aaron's, Inc.*, FTC File No. 122 3256 (Oct. 22, 2013).

*In the Matter of American Apparel, Inc.*, FTC File No. 142 3036 (2014).

*In the Matter of Apperian, Inc.*, FTC File No. 142 3017 (2014).

*In the Matter of Atlanta Falcons Football Club, LLC*, FTC File No. 142 3018 (2014).

*In the Matter of Baker Tilly Virchow Krause, LLP*, FTC File No. 1423 019 (2014).

*In the Matter of Beltone Elecs. Corp.*, 100 F.T.C. 68 (1982).

*In the Matter of BitTorrent, Inc.*, FTC File No. 142 3020 (2014).

*In the Matter of BJ's Wholesale Club, Inc.*, FTC File No. 042 3160 (Sept. 23, 2005).

*In the Matter of CardSystems Solutions, Inc.*, FTC File No. 052 3148 (Feb. 23, 2006).

*In the Matter of CBR Systems, Inc.*, FTC File No. 112 3120 (Jan. 28, 2013).

*In the Matter of Charles River Laboratories, International*, FTC File No. 142 3022 (2014).

*In the Matter of Chitika, Inc.*, FTC File. No. 102 3087 (Jun. 17, 2011).

*In the Matter of Collectify LLC*, FTC File No. 092 3142 (2009).

*In the Matter of Compete, Inc.*, FTC File No. 102 3155 (Feb. 25, 2013).

*In the Matter of Credit Karma, Inc.*, FTC File No 1323091 (Mar. 28, 2014).

*In the Matter of CVS Caremark Corporation*, FTC File No. 072 3119 (Feb. 18, 2009).

*In the Matter of Daniel Chapter One, A Corp., & James Feijo*, 2010 WL 387917 (Jan. 25, 2010).

*In the Matter of DataMotion, Inc.*, FTC File No. 142 3023 (2014).

*In the Matter of Dave & Buster's, Inc.*, FTC File No. 082 3153 (Mar. 25, 2010).

*In the Matter of DDC Laboratories, Inc.*, FTC File No. 142 3024 (2014).

*In the Matter of DesignerWare, LLC*, 155 F.T.C. 421 (2013).

*In the Matter of Directors Desk LLC*, FTC File No. 092 3140 (2009).

*In the Matter of DSW Inc.*, FTC File No. 052 3096 (Dec. 1, 2005).

*In the Matter of Educational Research Center of America, Inc.*, FTC File No. 022 3249 (May 9, 2003).

*In the Matter of Eli Lilly and Company*, FTC File No. 012 3214 (Jan. 18, 2002).

*In the Matter of Epic Marketplace, Inc., and Epic Media Group, LLC*, FTC File No. 112 3182 (Mar. 19, 2013).

*In the Matter of EPN, Inc.*, FTC File No. 112 3143 (Oct. 26, 2012).

*In the Matter of Equifax Information Services LLC*, FTC File No. 102 3252 (Oct. 10, 2012).

*In the Matter of ExpatEdge Partners, LLC*, FTC File No. 092 3138 (2009).

*In the Matter of Facebook*, FTC File No. 092 3184 (2011).

*In the Matter of Facebook, Inc.*, FTC File No. 092 3184 (July 27, 2012).

*In the Matter of Fandango, LLC*, FTC File No. 1323089 (Mar. 28, 2014).

*In the Matter of Fantage.com, Inc.*, FTC File No. 142 3026 (2014).

*In the Matter of Filiquarian Publishing, LLC, Choice Level, LLC and Joshua Linsk*, FTC File No. 112 3195 (2013).

*In the Matter of Foru International Corporation Formerly Known as Genewize Life Sciences, Inc.*, FTC File No. 112 3095 (May 12, 2014).

*In the Matter of Franklin's Budget Car Sales, Inc.*, FTC File No. 102 3094 (Oct. 26, 2012).

*In the Matter of Gateway Learning Corp.*, FTC File No. 042 3047 (Sept. 17, 2004).

*In the Matter of Genica Corporation* (d/b/a Computer Geeks Discount Outlet and Geeks. com), FTC File No. 082 3113 (Feb. 5, 2009).

*In the Matter of Geocities*, 127 F.T.C. 94 (Feb. 5, 1999).

*In the Matter of Goldenshores Technologies LLC & Erik M. Geidl*, FTC Docket No. C-4446 (Apr. 9, 2014).

*In the Matter of Google*, FTC File No. 102 3136 (2011).

*In the Matter of Guess?, Inc.*, FTC File No. 022 3260 (Aug. 5, 2003).

*In the Matter of Guidance Software, Inc.*, FTC File No. 062 3057 (Nov. 16, 2006).

*In the Matter of H&R Block, Inc.*, 80 F.T.C. 304 (1972).

*In the Matter of H&R Block, Inc.*, 100 F.T.C. 523 (1982).

*In the Matter of HTC America Inc.*, FTC File No. 122 3049 (July 2, 2013).

*In the Matter of International Publisher Services*, 49 F.T.C. 214 (1952).

*In the Matter of Jerk, LLC*, FTC File No. 122 3141 (Jan. 12, 2015).

*In the Matter of JS&A Group*, 111 F.T.C. 522 (1989).

*In the Matter of Level 3 Communications*, FTC File No. 142 3028 (2014).

*In the Matter of Liberty Fin. Companies, Inc.*, 128 F.T.C. 240 (1999).

*In the Matter of Life is Good, Inc.*, FTC File No. 072 3046 (Jan. 17, 2008).

*In the Matter of Lookout Services, Inc.*, FTC File No. 102 3076 (May 3, 2011).

*In the Matter of The May Department Stores Company*, 122 F.T.C. 1 (1996).

*In the Matter of Metromedia, Inc.*, 78 F.T.C. 331 (1971).

*In the Matter of Microsoft Corp.*, FTC File No. 012 3240 (Aug. 8, 2002).

*In the Matter of MTS, Inc., Doing Business as Tower Records/Books/Video*, FTC File No. 032 3209 (Jun. 2, 2004).

*In the Matter of MySpace LLC*, FTC File No. 102 3058 (Sept. 11, 2002).

*In the Matter of Nations Title Agency, Inc., Nations Holding Company, and Christopher M. Likens*, FTC File No. 052 3117 (May 10, 2006).

*In the Matter of Nationwide Mortgage Group, Inc., and John D. Eubank*, FTC File No. 042–3104 (Nov. 9, 2004).

*In the Matter of Nomi Technologies, Inc.*, FTC File No. 132 3251 (Apr. 23, 2015).

*In the Matter of Novartis Corp., et al.*, 127 F.T.C. 580 (1999).

*In the Matter of the Oakes Company*, 3 F.T.C. 36 (1920).

*In the Matter of Onyx Graphics, Inc.*, FTC File No. 092 3139 (2009).

*In the Matter of PDB Sports, Ltd.*, FTC File No. 142 3025 (2014).

*In the Matter of Petco Animal Supplies, Inc.*, FTC File No. 032 3221 (Nov. 8, 2004).

*In the Matter of Premier Capital Lending, Inc.*, FTC File No. 072 3004 (Nov. 6, 2008).

*In the Matter of Progressive Gaitways LLC*, FTC File No. 092 3141 (2009).

*In the Matter of The Receivable Management Services Corporation*, FTC File No. 142 3031 (2014).

*In the Matter of Reed Elsevier Inc., and Seisint, Inc.*, FTC File No. 0523094 (Mar. 27, 2008).

*In the Matter of Reynolds Consumer Products, Inc.*, FTC File No. 142 3030 (2014).

*In the Matter of Rite Aid Corporation*, FTC File No. 072 3121 (July 27, 2010).
*In the Matter of ScanScout, Inc.*, FTC Docket No. C-4344 (Dec. 21, 2011).
*In the Matter of Sears Holdings Management Corporation*, FTC File No. 082 3099 (Sept. 9, 2009).
*In the Matter of Sony BMG Music Entertainment*, FTC File No. 062 3019 (Jun. 29, 2007).
*In the Matter of Sunbelt Lending Services, Inc.*, FTC File No. 042 3153 (Nov. 16, 2004).
*In the Matter of Superior Mortgage Corp.*, FTC File No. 052 3136 (Sept. 28, 2005).
*In the Matter of Tax Corp. of Am.* (Maryland), *et al.*, 85 F.T.C. 512 (1975).
*In the Matter of Tennes Football, Inc.*, FTC File No. 142 3032 (2014).
*In The Matter of The TJX Companies, Inc.*, FTC File No. 072 3055 (Mar. 27, 2008).
*In the Matter of Touch Tone Information, Inc.*, File No. 982 3619 (1999).
*In the Matter of Trans Union Corp.*, 116 F.T.C. 1334 (1993).
*In the Matter of TRENDnet, Inc.*, FTC File No. 122 3090 (Jan. 16, 2014).
*In the Matter of True Ultimate Standards Everywhere, Inc., a corporation, doing business as TRU.S.Te, Inc.*, FTC File No. 132 3219 (Nov. 17, 2014).
*In the Matter of Twitter, Inc.*, FTC File No. 092 3093 (Jun. 24, 2010).
*In the Matter of Upromise, Inc.*, FTC File No. 102 3116 (Apr. 3, 2012).
*In the Matter of Vision I Properties, LLC*, FTC File No. 042 3068 (Apr. 26, 2005).
*In the Matter of Watershed Development Corporation D/B/A Watershed and Aaron's Sales & Lease Ownership*, 155 F.T.C. 639 (2013).
*In the Matter of World Innovators, Inc.*, FTC File No. 092 3137.
*In re Beneficial Corp.*, 86 F.T.C. 119 (1975).
*In re Dancer-Fitzgerald-Sample, Inc.*, 96 F.T.C. 1 (1980).
*In re Facebook, Inc.*, FTC File No. 092 3184 (July 27, 2012).
*In re Gjestvang*, 405 B.R. 316 (Bankr. E.D. Ark. 2009).
*In re Hearst Magazines, Inc.*, 32 F.T.C. 1440 (1941).
*In re Holland Furnace Co.*, 341 F.2d 548 (7th Cir. 1965).
*In re ITT Continental Baking Co*, 83 F.T.C. 942 (1973–1974).
*In re JetBlue Airways Corp. Privacy Litig.*, 379 F. Supp. 2d 299 (E.D.N.Y. 2005).
*In re Pfizer, Inc.*, 81 F.T.C. 23 61–62 (1972).
*In re Pharmatrak, Inc.*, 329 F.3d 9 (1st Cir. 2003).
*In re Sears Holdings Management Corporation*, FTC Matter 082 3099 (Sept. 9, 2009).
*In re Snapchat, Inc.*, FTC File No. C-4501 (Dec. 23, 2014).
*Indiana Quartered Oak Co. v. FTC*, 26 F.2d 340 (2d Cir. 1928).
*Ippolito v. WNS, Inc.*, 864 F.2d 440 (7th Cir. 1988).
*J. B. Williams Co. v. FTC*, 381 F.2d 884 (6th Cir. 1967).
*Johnson Products Co. v. FTC*, 549 F.2d 35 (7th Cir. 1977).
*Kirchner v. FTC*, 337 F.2d 751 (9th Cir. 1964).
*LaPeyre v. FTC*, 366 F.2d 117 (5th Cir. 1966).
*Lester Rothschild, Trading As Gen-O-Pak Co.*, 49 F.T.C. 1673 (1952).
*Mainstream Mktg. Servs., Inc. v. FTC*, 358 F.3d 1228 (10th Cir. 2004).
*Moser v. F. C.C.*, 46 F.3d 970 (9th Cir. 1995).
*Nader v. Gen. Motors Corp.*, 25 N.Y.2d 560 (1970).
*Nat'l Cable & Telecommunications Ass'n v. F. C.C.*, 555 F.3d 996 (D.C. Cir. 2009).
*Nat'l Harness Mfrs.' Ass'n v. FTC*, 268 F. 705 (6th Cir. 1920).
*Nat'l Petroleum Refiners Ass'n v. FTC*, 482 F.2d 672 (D.C. Cir. 1973).
*Newcomb v. Cambridge Home Loans, Inc.*, 861 F. Supp. 2d 1153 (D. Haw. 2012).
*Ostler Candy Co. v. FTC*, 106 F.2d 962 (10th Cir. 1939).
*P.F. Collier & Son Corp. v. FTC*, 427 F.2d 261 (6th Cir.).

*Pineda* v. *Williams-Sonoma Stores, Inc.*, 246 P.3d 612 (SCT Ca. 2011).

*POM Wonderful, LLC* v. *FTC*, 777 F.3d 478 (D.C. Cir. 2015).

Privacy Online, *Perspectives on Privacy and Self-Disclosure in the Social Web* (Trepte, et al. eds., 2011).

*Resort Car Rental System, Inc.* v. *FTC*, 518 F.2d 962 (9th Cir. 1975).

*Richard Fresco* v. *Automotive Directions Inc., et al.*, 03 No. 03-CIV-61063 61063 (S.D. Fla. 2009).

*Rothschild* v. *FTC*, 200 F.2d 39 (7th Cir. 1952).

*S.E.C.* v. *Apuzzo*, 689 F.3d 204 (2d Cir. 2012).

*Shibley* v. *Time, Inc.*, 341 N.E.2d 337 (Ohio Ct. App.).

*Spiegel, Inc.* v. *FTC*, 494 F.2d 59 (7th Cir.).

*Spokeo, Inc.* v. *Robins*, 135 S. Ct. 1892 (US 2015).

*St. Regis Paper Co.* v. *US*, 368 US 208 (1961).

*Sullivan* v. *Credit Control Servs., Inc.*, 745 F. Supp. 2d 2 (D. Mass. 2010).

*Telebrands Corp.* v. *FTC*, 457 F.3d 354 (4th Cir. 2006).

*Ting* v. *AT&T*, 192 F. Supp. 2d 902 (2002).

*Trans Union LLC* v. *FTC*, 295 F.3d 42 (D.C. Cir. 2002).

*Trans World Accounts, Inc.* v. *FTC*, 594 F.2d 212 (9th Cir. 1979).

*US* v. *Allied Interstate, Inc.*, 0:10-cv-04295-PJS (D. Minn. 2010).

*US* v. *American Pop Corn Company*, No. C02-4008DEO (N.D. Iowa 2002).

*US* v. *American United Mortgage Company*, No. 07C 7064 (N.D. Il 2007).

*US* v. *Artist Arena, LLC*, 112-cv-07386-JGK (S.D.N.Y. Oct. 4, 2012).

*US* v. *Asset Acceptance, LLC*, 812-cv-182-T-27EAJ (M.D. Fl. 2012).

*US* v. *Bigmailbox.com*, No. 01–605-A (E.d. Va. 2001).

*US* v. *Bonzi Software, Inc.*, CV-04–1048 RJK (C.D. Cal. 2004).

*US* v. *Cent. Adjustment Bureau, Inc.*, 667 F. Supp. 370 (N.D. Tex. 1986).

*US* v. *ChoicePoint Inc.*, No. 1:06-cv-00198-GET (N.D. Ga. 2006).

*US* v. *DC Credit Services, Inc., and David Cohen*, No. 02–5115 MMM (C.D. Cal. 2002).

*US* v. *Direct Lending Source, Inc., et al.*, 12-CV-2441-DMS-BLM (S.D. Ca. Oct. 10, 2012).

*US* v. *Equifax Credit Information Services, Inc.*, No. 1:00-CV-0087 (N.D. Ga. 2000).

*US* v. *Experian Information Solutions, Inc.*, No. 3-00CV0056-L (N.D. Tx. 2000).

*US* v. *Expert Global Solutions, Inc.*, 3–13 CV 2611-M (N.D. Tex. 2013).

*US* v. *Google, Inc.*, 512-cv-04177-HRL (N.D. Cal. Nov. 12, 2012).

*US* v. *Hammad Akbar*, 1:14-cr-276 (E.D. Va. 2014).

*US* v. *Hershey Foods Corporation*, No. 4CV-03–350 (M.D. Pa. 2003).

*US* v. *Iconix Brand Group, Inc.*, 09-CIV-8864 (S.D.N.Y. 2009).

*US* v. *Industrious Kid, Inc.*, No. CV-08–0639 (N.D. Cal. 2008).

*US* v. *Jones O. Godwin, Doing Business as skidekids.com*, 1:11-CV-3846 (JOF) (N.D. Ga. 2011).

*US* v. *Lisa Frank, Inc.*, No. 01–1516-A (E.D. Va. 2001).

*US* v. *Looksmart Ltd.*, No. 01–606-A (E.d. Va. 2001).

*US* v. *Monarch Services, Inc., et al.*, No. AMD 01 CV 1165 (D. Md. 2001).

*US* v. *Mrs. Fields Famous Brands, Inc.*, No. 203 CV205 JTG (D. Utah 2003).

*US* v. *Ohio Art Company*, FTC File No. 022–3028 (N.D. Ohio 2002).

*US* v. *Path, Inc.*, No. C-13–0448 (N.D. Cal. Jan. 31, 2013).

*US* v. *Paul*, 274 F.3d 155 (5th Cir. 2001).

*US* v. *Performance Capital Management, Inc.*, FTC File No. 982 3542 (C.D. Cal. 2000).

*US* v. *Playdom, Inc.*, SACV11-00724 (C.D. Ca. 2011).

*US* v. *PLS Financial Services, Inc., PLS Group, Inc., and The Payday Loan Store of Illinois, Inc.*, 112-cv-08334 (N.D. Il 2012).

*US* v. *Rental Research Services, Inc.*, 0:09-cv-00524 (D. Minn. 2009).

*US* v. *RockYou, Inc.*, 312-cv-01487-SI (N.D. Cal. 2012).

*US* v. *Sony BMG Music Entertainment*, No. 08 CV 10730 (LAK) (2008).

*US* v. *Spokeo, Inc.*, CV12-05001 (C.D. Cal. 2012).

*US* v. *Teletrack, Inc.*, 111-CV-2060 (N.D. Ga. 2011).

*US* v. *TinyCo., Inc.*, 3:14-cv-04164 (N.D. Cal. 2014).

*US* v. *Trans Union LLC*, No. 00-C-0235 (ND Il 2000).

*US* v. *UMG Recordings, Inc.*, CV-04-1050 JFW (C.D. Cal. 2004).

*US* v. *ValueClick Inc., Hi-Speed Media, Inc., and E-Babylon, Inc.*, No. CV08-01711MMM (RZx) (C.D., Cal. 2008).

*US* v. *ValueClick, et al.*, No. CV08-0171 (C.D. Ca. Mar. 17, 2008).

*US* v. *W3 Innovations, LLC*, CV-11–03958-PSG (N.D. Cal. 2011).

*US* v. *Whitewing Financial Group, Inc.*, No. 4:06–2102 (S.D. Tex. 2006).

*US* v. *Xanga.com, Inc.*, No. 06-CIV-6853(SHS) (S.D.N.Y. 2006).

*US* v. *Yelp Inc.*, 3:14-cv-04163 (N.D. Cal. 2014).

*US* v. *Johnson*, 541 F.2d 710 (8th Cir. 1976).

*US* v. *JS & A Grp., Inc.*, 716 F.2d 451 (7th Cir. 1983).

*US* v. *Kilbride*, 584 F.3d 1240 (9th Cir. 2009).

*US* v. *Reader's Digest Ass'n, Inc.*, 662 F.2d 955 (3d Cir. 1981).

*US* v. *Twombly*, 475 F. Supp. 2d 1019 (S.D. Cal. 2007).

*Waltham Watch Co.* v. *FTC*, 318 F.2d 28 (7th Cir. 1963).

*Warner Lambert Co.* v. *FTC*, 562 F.2d 749 (D.C. Cir. 1977).

*Wolfe* v. *MBNA America Bank*, 485 F. Supp. 2d 874 (2007).

# Index